J.K. LASSER'S™

SMALL BUSINESS TAXES 2015

Your Complete Guide to a Better Bottom Line

Barbara Weltman

WILEY

*This book is dedicated with love to my
understanding husband, Malcolm Katt.*

For general information on our other products and services or for technical support,
please contact our Customer Care Department within the United States at (800) 762-2974,
outside the United States at (317) 572-3993 or fax (317) 572-4002.

Wiley also publishes its books in a variety of electronic formats. Some content that appears in
print may not be available in electronic books. For more information about Wiley products,
visit our web site at www.wiley.com.

ISBN 978-1-118-92203-3; 978-1-119-02613-6 (ebk);
978-1-119-02611-2 (ebk)

Printed in the United States of America

10 9 8 7 6 5 4 3 2 1

Contents

Preface

According to the National Small Business Association (NSBA), 86% of small businesses use paid tax preparers to file their returns. So why do you need to read up on taxes? The answer is simple: You, not your accountant or other financial adviser and not software, run the business, so you can't rely on someone else to make decisions critical to your activities. NSBA found that 73% of small businesses say that federal taxes have a significant impact on their day-to-day operation of their businesses. You need to be informed about tax-saving opportunities that continually arise so you can strategically plan to take advantage of them. Being knowledgeable about tax matters also saves you money; the more you know, the better able you are to ask your accountant key tax and financial questions that can advance your business, as well as to meet your tax responsibilities.

This is still a great time to be a small business. Not only is small business a major force in our economy but it also is the benefactor of numerous tax rules that make it easier to write off expenses and minimize the taxes you owe. This edition of the book has been revised to include all of the new rules taking effect for 2014 returns. Your business needs to use every tax-saving opportunity to survive and thrive at this time. The book also provides information about future changes scheduled to take effect in order to give you an overall view of business tax planning. Most importantly, it addresses the many tax questions I have received from readers as well as visitors to my web site, www.barbaraweltman.com.

This book focuses primarily on federal income taxes. Businesses may be required to pay and report many other taxes, including state income taxes, employment taxes, sales and use taxes, and excise taxes. Some information about these taxes is included in this book to alert you to your possible obligations so that you can then obtain further assistance if necessary. However, the book takes a holistic approach to taxes, showing you where applicable the ramifications that tax decisions can have on your business activities and your bottom line. Statistics, resources, and other materials are provided to help you better run your business by making good tax decisions and implementing sound business practices.

It is important to stay alert to future tax changes. Uncertainty has been labeled an impediment to business growth. Pending or possible changes are noted in this book, including the expiration of more than 4 dozen tax rules at the end of 2013 that had not yet been extended for 2014 despite expectations that they would. Be sure to check on any final action before you complete your tax return or take any steps that could be affected by these changes.

For a free supplement on tax developments affecting small businesses (available in February 2015), go to www.jklasser.com or www .barbaraweltman.com.

How to Use This Book

The purpose of this book is to make you acutely aware of how your actions in business can affect your bottom line from a tax perspective. The way you organize your business, the accounting method you select, and the types of payments you make all have an impact on when you report income and the extent to which you can take deductions. This book is not designed to make you a tax expert. It is strongly suggested that you consult with a tax adviser before making certain important decisions that will affect your ability to minimize your taxes. I hope that the insight you gain from this book will allow you to ask your adviser key questions to benefit your business.

In Part 1, you will find topics of interest to all businesses. First, there is an overview of the various forms of business organization and an explanation of how these forms of organization affect reporting of income and claiming tax deductions. The most common forms of business organization include independent contractors, sole proprietors, and sole practitioners—individuals who work for themselves and do not have any partners. If self-employed individuals join with others to form a business, they become partners in a partnership. Sometimes businesses incorporate. A business can be incorporated with only one owner or with many owners. A corporation can be a regular corporation (*C corporation*), or it can be a small business corporation (*S corporation*). The difference between the C and S corporations is the way in which income of the business is taxed to the owner (which is explained in detail in Part 1). There is another form of business organization called a *limited liability company* (LLC). Limited liability companies with 2 or more owners generally are taxed like partnerships even though their owners enjoy protection from personal liability. The important thing to note is that each form of business organization will affect what deductions can be claimed and where to claim them. Part 1 also explains tax years and accounting methods that businesses can select.

Part 1 contains another topic of general interest to all businesses. It covers important recordkeeping requirements and suggestions to help you audit-proof your return to the extent possible and protect your deductions and tax credits. In the course of business you may incur certain expenses, but unless you have specific proof of those expenses, you may not be able to claim a deduction or credit. Learn how to keep the necessary records to back up your write-offs in the event your return is questioned by the IRS.

Part 2 details how to report various types of income your business may receive. In addition to fees and sales receipts—the bread-and-butter of your business—you may receive other types of ordinary income such as interest income, royalties, and rents. You may have capital gain transactions as well as sales of business assets. But you may also have losses—from operations or the sale of assets. Special rules govern the tax treatment of these losses. The first part of each chapter discusses the types of income to report and special rules that affect them. Then scan the second part of each chapter, which explains where on the tax return to report the income or claim the loss.

Part 3 focuses on specific deductions and tax credits. It provides you with guidance on the various types of deductions you can use to reduce your business income. Each type of deduction is explained in detail. Related tax credits are also explained in each deduction chapter. In the first part of each chapter, you will learn what the deduction is all about and any dollar limits or other special requirements that may apply. As with the income chapters, the second part of each deduction chapter explains where on the tax return you can claim the write-off. The answer depends on your form of business organization. You simply look for your form of business organization to learn where on the return to claim the deduction. The portion of the appropriate tax form or schedule is highlighted in certain instances. For your convenience, key tax forms for claiming these deductions have been included. While the forms and schedules are designed for the 2014 returns, they serve as an example for future years. Also, in Chapter 22, Miscellaneous Business Deductions, you will find checklists that serve as handy reference guides on all business deductions. The checklists are organized according to your status: self-employed, employee, or small corporation. You will also find a checklist of deductions that have not been allowed.

Part 4 contains planning ideas for your business. You will learn about strategies for deferring income, boosting deductions, starting up or winding down a business, running a sideline business, running multiple businesses, and avoiding audits. It also highlights the most common mistakes that business owners make in their returns. This information will help you avoid making the same mistakes and losing out on tax-saving opportunities. You will also find helpful information about electronic filing of business tax forms and how to use the Internet for tax assistance and planning purposes. And you will find information about other taxes on your business, including state income taxes, employment taxes, sales and use taxes, and excise taxes.

In Appendix A, you will see a listing of information returns you may be required to file with the IRS or other government agencies in conjunction with your tax obligations. These returns enable the federal government to crosscheck tax reporting and other financial information. Appendix B contains a checklist of tax-related corporate resolutions to help you keep your corporate minutes book up to date. Appendix C is a list of dollar limits and amounts in certain tax rules that are adjusted annually for inflation to help you plan ahead.

Several forms and schedules as well as excerpts from them have been included throughout the book to illustrate reporting rules. These forms are not to be used to file your return. (In many cases, the appropriate forms were not available when this book was published, and older or draft versions of the forms were included.) You can obtain the forms you need from the IRS's web site at www.irs.gov or where otherwise indicated.

Another way to stay abreast of tax and other small business developments that can affect your business throughout the year is by subscribing to *Barbara Weltman's Big Ideas for Small Business*®, a free online newsletter geared for small business owners and their professional advisers, and my "Small Business Idea of the Day®" (via email) at www.barbaraweltman.com. For more information on the tax implications of your small business and any developments on the Alerts throughout the book, visit www.jklasser.com. Here you will also find a supplement to this book (available in February 2015), with updated information as it develops; the supplement is also posted on my site.

I would like to thank Sidney Kess, Esq. and CPA, for his valuable suggestions in the preparation of the original tax deduction book and Elliott Eiss, Esq., for his expertise and constant assistance with this and other projects.

Barbara Weltman
September 2014

Introduction

Small businesses are vital to the U.S. economy. They employ half of the country's private sector workforce and contribute more than half of the nation's gross national product. Historically, small businesses created 65% of all new jobs over the past 15 years.

For the 2012 tax year (the most recent year for statistics), there were 23 million sole proprietorships in the United States. More than 1 in 6 Form 1040 filers had a sole proprietorship that year. Another 7.3 million filers reported income from partnerships and S corporations. And the numbers of small businesses are growing.

Small businesses fall under the purview of the Internal Revenue Service's (IRS) Small Business and Self-Employed Division (SB/SE). This division services approximately 57 million tax filers, including 9 million small businesses (partnerships and corporations with assets of $10 million or less) and more than 41 million of whom are full-time or partially self-employed. The SB/SE division accounts for about 40% of the total federal tax revenues collected. The goal of this IRS division is customer assistance to help small businesses comply with the tax laws.

Toward this end, the Small Business Administration (SBA) has teamed up with the IRS to provide small business owners with help on tax issues. The SBA provides tax information for start-ups at www.sba.gov and search "taxes."

There is also an IRS Tax Center devoted exclusively to small business and self-employed persons at www.irs.gov/Businesses/Small-Businesses-&-Self-Employed. Here you will find special information for your industry—agriculture, automotive, child care, construction, entertainment, gaming, manufacturing, real estate, restaurants, retailers, veterinarians, and even tax professionals are already covered, and additional industries are set to follow. You can see the hot tax issues for your industry, find special audit guides that explain what the IRS looks for in your industry when examining returns, and links to other tax information.

As a small business owner, you work, try to grow your business, and hope to make a profit. What you can keep from that profit depends in part on the income tax you pay. The income tax applies to your net income rather than to your gross income or gross receipts. You are not taxed on all the income you bring in by way of sales, fees, commissions, or other payments. Instead, you are essentially taxed on what you keep after paying off the expenses of providing the services or making the sales that are the crux of your business. Deductions for these expenses operate to fix the amount of income that will be subject to tax. So deductions, in effect, help to determine the tax you pay and the profits you keep. And tax credits, the number of which has been expanded in recent years, can offset your tax to reduce the amount you ultimately pay.

Special Rules for Small Businesses

Sometimes it pays to be small. The tax laws contain a number of special rules exclusively for small businesses. But what is a small business? The Small Business Administration (SBA) usually defines small business by the number of employees—size standards range from 500 employees to 1,500 employees, depending on the industry or the SBA program. The SBA also uses revenue for certain business size standards. Size matters because only "small businesses" can qualify for SBA-guaranteed loans and for special consideration with federal contracting.

For tax purposes, however, the answer varies from rule to rule, as explained throughout the book. Sometimes it depends on your revenues, the number of employees, or total assets. In Table I.1 are various definitions from the Internal Revenue Code on what constitutes a small business.

Reporting Income

While taxes are figured on your bottom line—your income less certain expenses—you still must report your income on your tax return. Generally all of the income your business receives is taxable unless there is a specific tax rule that allows you to exclude the income permanently or defer it to a future time.

When you report income depends on your method of accounting. *How* and *where* you report income depends on the nature of the income and your type of business organization. Over the next several years, the declining tax rates for owners of pass-through entities—sole proprietorships, partnerships, limited liability companies (LLCs), and S corporations—require greater sensitivity to the timing of business income as these rates decline.

TABLE I.1 Examples of Tax Definitions of Small Business

Tax Rule*	Definition
Accrual method exception for small inventory-based businesses (Chapter 2)	Average annual gross receipts of no more than $10 million in the 3 prior years (or number of years in business if less)
Bad debts deducted on the nonaccrual-experience method (Chapter 11)	Average annual gross receipts for the 3 prior years of no more than $5 million
Building improvements safe harbor (Chapter 10)	Average annual gross receipts for the 3 prior years of no more than $10 million *and* building's unadjusted basis no greater than $1 million
Corporate alternative minimum tax (AMT) exemption for small C corporations (Chapter 22)	Average annual gross receipts of no more than $7 million ($5 million for the first 3-year period)
DbK retirement plan (Chapter 16)	500 or fewer employees
Disabled access credit (Chapter 10)	Gross receipts of no more than $1 million in the preceding year or no more than 30 full-time employees
Exemption from reporting health coverage on employees' W-2s	Fewer than 250 W-2s filed for the previous year
Employer mandate exemption from providing affordable health coverage*	More than 50 full-time employees
Employer wage differential credit for activated reservists (Chapter 7)	Fewer than 50 employees
First-year expensing election (Chapter 14)	Equipment purchases for 2014 of no more than $2.5 million if the rule is extended as expected ($225,000 if not extended)
Independent contractor versus employee determination—shifting burden of proof to IRS (Chapter 7)	Net worth of business does not exceed $7 million
Late filing penalty for failure to file information return—cap (Appendix)	Average annual gross receipts of no more than $5 million for a 3-year period
Reasonable compensation—shifting the burden of proof to the IRS (Chapter 7)	Net worth of business not in excess of $7 million
Retirement plan start-up credit (Chapter 16)	No more than 100 employees with compensation over $5,000 in the preceding year
Savings Incentive Match Plans for Employees (SIMPLE) plans (Chapter 16)	Self-employed or businesses with 100 or fewer employees who received at least $5,000 in compensation in the preceding year
Simple cafeteria plans (Chapter 7)	100 or fewer employees on business days during either of the 2 preceding years
Small employer health care credit (Chapter 19)	No more than 25 full-time equivalent employees
Small business stock—deferral or exclusion of gain on sale (Chapter 5)	Gross assets of no more than $50 million when the stock is issued and immediately after
UNICAP small reseller exception (Chapter 2)	Average annual gross receipts of no more than $10 million for a 3-year period
UNICAP simplified dollar value last-in, first-out (LIFO) method (Chapter 2)	Average annual gross receipts of no more than $5 million for a 3-year period

*Those with 50 or fewer employees are exempt; those with 50–99 employers are subject to the mandate beginning in 2016 (larger employers in 2015).

The IRS reported a "tax gap" (the spread between revenues that should be collected and what actually is collected) of $450 billion a year and that $122 billion of this can be traced to entrepreneurs who underreport or don't report their income, or overstate their deductions. In order to close the tax gap, the IRS is stepping up its audit activities for self-employed individuals, and increased reporting to the IRS and other measures may be adopted.

Claiming Deductions

You pay tax only on your profits, not on what you take in (gross receipts). In order to arrive at your profits, you are allowed to subtract certain expenses from your income. These expenses are called "deductions."

The law says what you can and cannot deduct (see below). Within this framework, the nature and amount of the deductions you have often vary with the size of your business, the industry you are in, where you are based in the country, and other factors. The most common deductions for businesses include car and truck expenses, utilities, supplies, legal and professional services, insurance, depreciation, taxes, meals and entertainment, advertising, repairs, travel, rent for business property and equipment, and in some cases, a home office.

Are your deductions typical? The Government Accountability Office (formerly the General Accounting Office) in January 2004 compiled statistics on deductions claimed by sole proprietors for 2001 (no data more current is available). These numbers show the dollars spent on various types of deductions, the percentage of sole proprietors who claimed the deductions, and what percentage of total deductions each expense represented. For example, 25% of sole proprietors with business gross receipts under $25,000 claimed a deduction for advertising costs. This percentage rose to 65% when gross receipts exceeded $100,000. You can view these old statistics at www.gao.gov/new.items/d04304.pdf.

What Is the Legal Authority for Claiming Deductions?

Deductions are a legal way to reduce the amount of your business income subject to tax. But there is no constitutional right to tax deductions. Instead, deductions are a matter of legislative grace; if Congress chooses to allow a particular deduction, so be it. Therefore, deductions are carefully spelled out in the Internal Revenue Code (the Code).

The language of the Code in many instances is rather general. It may describe a category of deductions without getting into specifics. For example, the Code contains a general deduction for all *ordinary and necessary* business expenses, without explaining what constitutes these expenses. Over the years, the IRS and the courts have worked to flesh out what business expenses are ordinary and necessary. "Ordinary" means common or accepted in business and "necessary" means appropriate and helpful in developing and maintaining a business. Often the IRS and the courts reach different conclusions about whether an item meets this definition and is deductible, leaving the taxpayer in a somewhat difficult position. If the taxpayer uses a more favorable court position to claim a deduction, the IRS may very well attack the deduction in the event that the return is examined. This puts the taxpayer in the position of having to incur legal expenses to bring the matter to court. However, if the taxpayer simply follows the IRS approach, a good opportunity to reduce business income by means of a deduction will have been missed. Throughout this book, whenever unresolved questions remain about a particular deduction, both sides have been explained. The choice is up to you and your tax adviser.

Sometimes the Code is very specific about a deduction, such as an employer's right to deduct employment taxes. Still, even where the Code is specific and there is less need for clarification, disputes about applicability or terminology may still arise. Again, the IRS and the courts may differ on the proper conclusion. It will remain for you and your tax adviser to review the different authorities for the positions stated and to reach your own conclusions based on the strength of the different positions and the amount of tax savings at stake.

A word about authorities for the deductions discussed in this book: There are a number of sources for these write-offs in addition to the Internal Revenue Code. These sources include court decisions from the U.S. Tax Court, the U.S. district courts and courts of appeal, the U.S. Court of Federal Claims, and the U.S. Supreme Court. There are also regulations issued by the Treasury Department to explain sections of the Internal Revenue Code. The IRS issues a number of pronouncements, including Revenue Rulings, Revenue Procedures, Notices, Announcements, and News Releases. The IRS also issues private letter rulings, determination letters, field service advice, and technical advice memoranda. While these private types of pronouncements cannot be cited as authority by a taxpayer other than the one for whom the pronouncement was made, they are important nonetheless. They serve as an indication of IRS thinking on a particular topic, and it is often the case that private letter rulings on topics of general interest later get restated in revenue rulings.

What Is a Tax Deduction Worth to You?

The answer depends on your tax bracket. The tax bracket is dependent on the way you organize your business. If you are self-employed and in the top tax bracket of 39.6% in 2014, then each $100 deduction will save you $39.60. Had you not claimed this deduction, you would have had to pay $39.60 of tax on that $100 of income that was offset by the deduction. If you have a personal service corporation, a special type of corporation for most professionals, the corporation pays tax at a flat rate of 35%. This means that the corporation is in the 35% tax bracket. Thus, each $100 deduction claimed saves $35 of tax on the corporation's income. Deductions are even more valuable if your business is in a state that imposes income tax. The impact of state income tax and special rules for state income taxes are not discussed in this book. However, you should explore the tax rules in your state and ascertain their impact on your business income.

When Do You Claim Deductions?

Like the timing of income, the timing of deductions—when to claim them—is determined by your tax year and method of accounting. Your form of business organization affects your choice of tax year and your accounting method.

Even when expenses are deductible, there may be limits on the timing of those deductions. Most common expenses are currently deductible in full. However, some expenses must be capitalized or amortized, or you must choose between current deductibility and capitalization. Capitalization generally means that expenses can be written off ratably as amortized expenses or depreciated over a period of time. Amortized expenses include, for example, fees to incorporate a business and expenses to organize a new business. Certain capitalized costs may not be deductible at all, but are treated as an additional cost of an asset *(basis)*.

Credits versus Deductions

Not all write-offs of business expenses are treated as deductions. Some can be claimed as tax credits. A tax credit is worth more than a deduction since it reduces your taxes dollar for dollar. Like deductions, tax credits are available only to the extent that Congress allows. In a couple of instances, you have a choice between treating certain expenses as a deduction or a credit. In most cases, however, tax credits can be claimed for certain expenses for which no tax deduction is provided. Business-related tax credits, as well as personal credits related to working or running a business, are included in this book.

Tax Responsibilities

As a small business owner, your obligations taxwise are broad. Not only do you have to pay income taxes and file income tax returns, but you also must manage payroll taxes if you have any employees. You may also have to collect and report on state and local sales taxes. Finally, you may have to notify the IRS of certain activities on information returns.

It is very helpful to keep an eye on the tax calendar so you will not miss out on any payment or filing deadlines, which can result in interest and penalties. You might want to view IRS Publication 1518A, *Small Business Tax Calendar* (go to www.irs.gov/pub/irs-pdf/p1518a.pdf).

You can obtain most federal tax forms online at www.irs.gov. Nonscannable forms, which cannot be downloaded from the IRS, can be ordered by calling toll free at 800-829-4933.

Organization

Business Organization

Alert

At the time this book was printed, Congress had not extended numerous breaks for 2014 that had expired at the end of 2013. Check the online supplement in February 2015 at www.jklasser.com or www.barbaraweltman.com to see whether these breaks apply for 2014 returns.

If you have a great idea for a product or a business and are eager to get started, do not let your enthusiasm be the reason you get off on the wrong foot. Take a while to consider how you will organize your business. The form of organization your business takes controls how income and deductions are reported to the government on a tax return. Sometimes you have a choice of the type of business organization; other times circumstances limit your choice. If you have not yet set up your business and do have a choice, this discussion will influence your decision on business organization. If you have already set up your business, you may want to consider changing to another form of organization.

According to the Tax Foundation, more than 90% of all businesses are organized as sole proprietorships, partnerships, limited liability companies (LLCs), or S corporations, all of which are "pass-through" entities. This means that the owners, rather than the businesses, pay tax on business income. Nearly 50% of the private sector workforce is employed by these pass-through entities. The way in which you set up your business impacts the effective tax rate you pay on your profits (after factoring income taxes and employment taxes). Taxes, however, are only one factor in deciding what type of entity to use for your business.

As you organize your business, consider which type of entity to use after factoring in taxes and other consequences. Also consider whether to change from your current form of business entity to a new one and what it means from a tax perspective. Finally, be sure to obtain your business's federal tax identity number (or a new one when making certain entity changes).

For a further discussion on worker classification, see IRS Publication 15-A, *Employer's Supplemental Tax Guide*.

Sole Proprietorships

If you go into business for yourself and do not have any partners (with the exception of a spouse, as explained shortly), you are considered a *sole proprietor*, and your business is called a *sole proprietorship*. You may think that the term *proprietor* connotes a storekeeper. For purposes of tax treatment, however, proprietor means any unincorporated business owned entirely by one person. Thus, the category includes individuals in professional practice, such as doctors, lawyers, accountants, and architects. Those who are experts in an area, such as engineering, public relations, or computers, may set up their own consulting businesses and fall under the category of sole proprietor. The designation also applies to independent contractors.

Sole proprietorships are the most common form of business. The IRS reports that one in 6 Form 1040s contains a Schedule C or C-EZ (the forms used by sole proprietorships). Most sideline businesses are run as sole proprietorships, and many start-ups commence in this business form.

There are no formalities required to become a sole proprietor; you simply conduct business. You may have to register your business with your city, town, or county government by filing a simple form stating that you are doing business as the "Quality Dry Cleaners" or some other business name other than your own (a fictitious business name, or FBN). This is sometimes referred to as a DBA, which stands for "doing business as."

From a legal standpoint, as a sole proprietor, you are personally liable for any debts your business incurs. For example, if you borrow money and default on a loan, the lender can look not only to your business equipment and other business property but also to your personal stocks, bonds, and other property. Some states may give your house homestead protection; state or federal law may protect your pensions and even Individual Retirement Accounts (IRAs). Your only protection for your personal assets is adequate insurance against accidents for your business and other liabilities and paying your debts in full.

Simplicity is the advantage to this form of business. It is the reason why over 70% of all U.S. firms operate as sole proprietorships. This form of business is commonly used for sideline ventures, as evidenced by the fact that half of all sole proprietors earn salaries and wages along with their business income. For 2012 (the most recent year for statistics), more than 23 million taxpayers filed returns as sole proprietors.

Independent Contractors

One type of sole proprietor is the *independent contractor*. To illustrate, suppose you used to work for Corporation X. You have retired, but X gives you a consulting contract under which you provide occasional services to X. In your retirement, you decide to provide consulting services not only to X, but to other customers as well. You are now a consultant. You are an independent contractor to each of the companies for which you provide services.

More precisely, an independent contractor is an individual who provides services to others outside an employment context. The providing of services becomes a business, an independent calling. In terms of claiming business deductions, classification as an independent contractor is generally more favorable than classification as an employee. (See "Tax Treatment of Income and Deductions in General," later in this chapter.) Therefore, many individuals whose employment status is not clear may wish to claim independent contractor status. Also, from the employer's perspective, hiring independent contractors is more favorable because the employer is not liable for employment taxes and need not provide employee benefits. (It costs about 30% more for an employee than an independent contractor after factoring in employment taxes, insurance, and benefits.) Federal employment taxes include Social Security and Medicare taxes under the Federal Insurance Contribution Act (FICA) as well as unemployment taxes under the Federal Unemployment Tax Act (FUTA).

You should be aware that the Internal Revenue Service (IRS) aggressively tries to reclassify workers as employees in order to collect employment taxes from employers. A discussion about worker classification can be found in Chapter 7.

There is a distinction that needs to be made between the classification of a worker for income tax purposes and the classification of a worker for employment tax purposes. By statute, certain employees are treated as independent contractors for employment taxes even though they continue to be treated as employees for income taxes. Other employees are treated as employees for employment taxes even though they are independent contractors for income taxes.

There are 2 categories of employees that are, by statute, treated as non-employees for purposes of federal employment taxes. These 2 categories are real estate salespersons and direct sellers of consumer goods. These employees are considered independent contractors (the ramifications of which are discussed later in this chapter). Such workers are deemed independent contractors if at least 90% of the employees' compensation is determined by their output. In other words, they are independent contractors if they are paid by commission and not a fixed salary. They must also perform their services under a written contract that specifies they will not be treated as employees for federal employment tax purposes.

Statutory Employees

Some individuals who consider themselves to be in business for themselves—reporting their income and expenses as sole proprietors—may still be treated as employees for purposes of employment taxes. As such, Social Security and Medicare taxes are withheld from their compensation. These individuals include:

- Corporate officers
- Agent-drivers or commission-drivers engaged in the distribution of meat products, bakery products, produce, beverages other than milk, laundry, or dry-cleaning services
- Full-time life insurance salespersons
- Homeworkers who personally perform services according to specifications provided by the service recipient
- Traveling or city salespersons engaged on a full-time basis in the solicitation of orders from wholesalers, retailers, contractors, or operators of hotels, restaurants, or other similar businesses

Full-time life insurance salespersons, homeworkers, and traveling or city salespersons are exempt from FICA if they have made a substantial investment in the facilities used in connection with the performance of services.

Day Traders

Traders in securities may be viewed as being engaged in a trade or business in securities if they seek profit from daily market movements in the prices of securities (rather than from dividends, interest, and long-term appreciation) and these activities are substantial, continuous, and regular. Calling yourself a day trader does not make it so; your activities must speak for themselves.

Being a trader means you report your trading expenses on Schedule C, such as subscriptions to publications and online services used in this securities business. Investment interest can be reported on Schedule C (it is not subject to the net investment income limitation that otherwise applies to individuals).

Being a trader means income is reported in a unique way—income from trading is *not* reported on Schedule C. Gains and losses are reported on Schedule D unless you make a mark-to-market election. If so, then income and losses are reported on Form 4797. The mark-to-market election is explained in Chapter 2.

Gains and losses from trading activities are not subject to self-employment tax (with or without the mark-to-market election).

Husband-Wife Joint Ventures

Usually when 2 or more people co-own a business, they are in partnership. However, husbands and wives who file jointly and conduct a joint venture can opt *not* to be treated as a partnership, which requires filing a partnership return (Form 1065) and reporting 2 Schedule K-1s (as explained later in this chapter). Instead, these "couplepreneurs" each report their share of income on Schedule C of Form 1040. To qualify for this election, each must materially participate in the business (neither can be a silent partner), and there can be no other co-owners. Making this election simplifies reporting while ensuring that each spouse receives credit for paying Social Security and Medicare taxes.

One-Member Limited Liability Companies

Every state allows a single owner to form a limited liability company (LLC) under state law. From a legal standpoint, an LLC gives the owner protection from personal liability (only business assets are at risk from the claims of creditors) as explained later in this chapter. But from a tax standpoint, a single-member LLC is treated as a "disregarded entity." (The owner can elect to have the LLC taxed as a corporation, but this is not typical. An election may be made to be taxed as a corporation, followed by an S election, so that the owner can easily make tax payments through wage withholding rather than making estimated tax payments, as well as minimize Social Security and Medicare taxes.) If the owner is an individual (and not a corporation), all of the income and expenses of the LLC are reported on Schedule C of the owner's Form 1040. In other words, for federal income tax purposes, the LLC is treated just like a sole proprietorship.

Tax Treatment of Income and Deductions in General

Sole proprietors, including independent contractors and statutory employees, report their income and deductions on Schedule C, see *Profit or Loss From*

Business (Figure 1.1). The net amount (profit or loss after offsetting income with deductions) is then reported as part of the income section on page 1 of your Form 1040. Such individuals may be able to use a simplified form for reporting business income and deductions: Schedule C-EZ, *Net Profit From Business* (see Figure 1.2). Individuals engaged in farming activities report

SCHEDULE C (Form 1040)	Profit or Loss From Business (Sole Proprietorship)	OMB No. 1545-0074
Department of the Treasury Internal Revenue Service (99)	▶ Information about Schedule C and its separate instructions is at *www.irs.gov/schedulec*. ▶ Attach to Form 1040, 1040NR, or 1041; partnerships generally must file Form 1065.	20**14** Attachment Sequence No. **09**

Name of proprietor	Social security number (SSN)

A	Principal business or profession, including product or service (see instructions)	B Enter code from instructions ▶
C	Business name. If no separate business name, leave blank.	D Employer ID number (EIN), (see instr.)

E   Business address (including suite or room no.) ▶
City, town or post office, state, and ZIP code

F   Accounting method: **(1)** ☐ Cash   **(2)** ☐ Accrual   **(3)** ☐ Other (specify) ▶

G   Did you "materially participate" in the operation of this business during 2014? If "No," see instructions for limit on losses ☐ Yes ☐ No

H   If you started or acquired this business during 2014, check here . . . . ▶ ☐

I   Did you make any payments in 2014 that would require you to file Form(s) 1099? (see instructions) . . . . ☐ Yes ☐ No

J   If "Yes," did you or will you file required Forms 1099? . . . . ☐ Yes ☐ No

Part I **Income**

1	Gross receipts or sales. See instructions for line 1 and check the box if this income was reported to you on Form W-2 and the "Statutory employee" box on that form was checked . . . . . . ▶ ☐	1	
2	Returns and allowances	2	
3	Subtract line 2 from line 1	3	
4	Cost of goods sold (from line 42)	4	
5	**Gross profit.** Subtract line 4 from line 3	5	
6	Other income, including federal and state gasoline or fuel tax credit or refund (see instructions) . . .	6	
7	**Gross income.** Add lines 5 and 6 . . . ▶	7	

Part II **Expenses.** Enter expenses for business use of your home **only** on line 30.

8	Advertising	8		18	Office expense (see instructions)	18	
9	Car and truck expenses (see instructions). . . .	9		19	Pension and profit-sharing plans .	19	
10	Commissions and fees .	10		20	Rent or lease (see instructions):		
11	Contract labor (see instructions)	11		a	Vehicles, machinery, and equipment	20a	
12	Depletion	12		b	Other business property . . .	20b	
13	Depreciation and section 179 expense deduction (not included in Part III) (see instructions). . . .	13		21	Repairs and maintenance . . .	21	
				22	Supplies (not included in Part III) .	22	
				23	Taxes and licenses	23	
				24	Travel, meals, and entertainment:		
14	Employee benefit programs (other than on line 19) . .	14		a	Travel	24a	
15	Insurance (other than health)	15		b	Deductible meals and entertainment (see instructions) .	24b	
16	Interest:			25	Utilities	25	
a	Mortgage (paid to banks, etc.)	16a		26	Wages (less employment credits) .	26	
b	Other	16b		27a	Other expenses (from line 48) . .	27a	
17	Legal and professional services	17		b	Reserved for future use . . .	27b	

28	**Total expenses** before expenses for business use of home. Add lines 8 through 27a . . . . ▶	28	
29	Tentative profit or (loss). Subtract line 28 from line 7	29	
30	Expenses for business use of your home. Do not report these expenses elsewhere. Attach Form 8829 unless using the simplified method (see instructions). **Simplified method filers only:** enter the total square footage of: (a) your home: _____ and (b) the part of your home used for business: _____. Use the Simplified Method Worksheet in the instructions to figure the amount to enter on line 30 . . .	30	
31	**Net profit or (loss).** Subtract line 30 from line 29. • If a profit, enter on both **Form 1040, line 12** (or **Form 1040NR, line 13**) and on **Schedule SE, line 2.** (If you checked the box on line 1, see instructions). Estates and trusts, enter on **Form 1041, line 3.** • If a loss, you **must** go to line 32.	31	
32	If you have a loss, check the box that describes your investment in this activity (see instructions). • If you checked 32a, enter the loss on both **Form 1040, line 12,** (or **Form 1040NR, line 13**) and on **Schedule SE, line 2.** (If you checked the box on line 1, see the line 31 instructions). Estates and trusts, enter on **Form 1041, line 3.** • If you checked 32b, you **must** attach **Form 6198.** Your loss may be limited.	32a ☐ All investment is at risk. 32b ☐ Some investment is not at risk.

For Paperwork Reduction Act Notice, see the separate instructions.   Cat. No. 11334P   Schedule C (Form 1040) 2014

FIGURE 1.1 Schedule C, Profit or Loss From Business

Schedule C (Form 1040) 2014　　　　　　　　　　　　　　　　　　　　　　　　　Page **2**

Part III　**Cost of Goods Sold** (see instructions)

33　Method(s) used to
　　value closing inventory:　**a** ☐ Cost　**b** ☐ Lower of cost or market　**c** ☐ Other (attach explanation)

34　Was there any change in determining quantities, costs, or valuations between opening and closing inventory?
　　If "Yes," attach explanation . . . . ☐ Yes　☐ No

35	Inventory at beginning of year. If different from last year's closing inventory, attach explanation	**35**
36	Purchases less cost of items withdrawn for personal use	**36**
37	Cost of labor. Do not include any amounts paid to yourself	**37**
38	Materials and supplies	**38**
39	Other costs	**39**
40	Add lines 35 through 39	**40**
41	Inventory at end of year	**41**
42	**Cost of goods sold.** Subtract line 41 from line 40. Enter the result here and on line 4	**42**

Part IV　**Information on Your Vehicle.** Complete this part **only** if you are claiming car or truck expenses on line 9 and are not required to file Form 4562 for this business. See the instructions for line 13 to find out if you must file Form 4562.

43　When did you place your vehicle in service for business purposes? (month, day, year) ▶ ___ / ___ / _____

44　Of the total number of miles you drove your vehicle during 2014, enter the number of miles you used your vehicle for:

a Business _____ **b** Commuting (see instructions) _____ **c** Other _____

45　Was your vehicle available for personal use during off-duty hours? . . . . ☐ Yes　☐ No

46　Do you (or your spouse) have another vehicle available for personal use? . . . . ☐ Yes　☐ No

47a　Do you have evidence to support your deduction? . . . . ☐ Yes　☐ No

　b　If "Yes," is the evidence written? . . . . ☐ Yes　☐ No

Part V　**Other Expenses.** List below business expenses not included on lines 8–26 or line 30.

48	**Total other expenses.** Enter here and on line 27a **48**

Schedule C (Form 1040) 2014

FIGURE 1.1 *(Continued)*

business income and deductions on Schedule F, the net amount of which is then reported in the income section on page 1 of Form 1040. Individuals who are considered employees cannot use Schedule C to report their income and claim deductions. See page 28 for the tax treatment of income and deductions by employees.

SCHEDULE C-EZ (Form 1040)	**Net Profit From Business** (Sole Proprietorship)	OMB No. 1545-0074
Department of the Treasury Internal Revenue Service (99)	▶ Partnerships, joint ventures, etc., generally must file Form 1065 or 1065-B. ▶ Attach to Form 1040, 1040NR, or 1041. ▶ See instructions on page 2.	20**14** Attachment Sequence No. **09A**

Name of proprietor	Social security number (SSN)

Part I   **General Information**

You May Use Schedule C-EZ Instead of Schedule C Only If You:

- Had business expenses of $5,000 or less.
- Use the cash method of accounting.
- Did not have an inventory at any time during the year.
- Did not have a net loss from your business.
- Had only one business as either a sole proprietor, qualified joint venture, or statutory employee.

And You:

- Had no employees during the year.
- Are not required to file **Form 4562,** Depreciation and Amortization, for this business. See the instructions for Schedule C, line 13, to find out if you must file.
- Do not deduct expenses for business use of your home.
- Do not have prior year unallowed passive activity losses from this business.

A	Principal business or profession, including product or service	B	Enter business code (see page 2) ▶
C	Business name. If no separate business name, leave blank.	D	Enter your EIN (see page 2)
E	Business address (including suite or room no.). Address not required if same as on page 1 of your tax return.		
	City, town or post office, state, and ZIP code		

F   Did you make any payments in 2014 that would require you to file Form(s) 1099? (see the Schedule C instructions) . . . .   ☐ Yes   ☐ No

G   If "Yes," did you or will you file required Forms 1099? . . . .   ☐ Yes   ☐ No

Part II   **Figure Your Net Profit**

1   **Gross receipts. Caution.** If this income was reported to you on Form W-2 and the "Statutory employee" box on that form was checked, see *Statutory employees* in the instructions for Schedule C, line 1, and check here . . . . ▶ ☐ | **1** |

2   **Total expenses** (see page 2). If more than $5,000, you **must** use Schedule C . . . . | **2** |

3   **Net profit.** Subtract line 2 from line 1. If less than zero, you **must** use Schedule C. Enter on both **Form 1040, line 12,** and **Schedule SE, line 2,** or on **Form 1040NR, line 13** and **Schedule SE, line 2** (see instructions). (Statutory employees **do not** report this amount on Schedule SE, line 2.) Estates and trusts, enter on **Form 1041, line 3** . . . . | **3** |

Part III   **Information on Your Vehicle.** Complete this part **only** if you are claiming car or truck expenses on line 2.

4   When did you place your vehicle in service for business purposes? (month, day, year) ▶ _____ .

5   Of the total number of miles you drove your vehicle during 2014, enter the number of miles you used your vehicle for:

a   Business _____   b   Commuting (see page 2) _____   c   Other _____

6   Was your vehicle available for personal use during off-duty hours? . . . .   ☐ Yes   ☐ No

7   Do you (or your spouse) have another vehicle available for personal use? . . . .   ☐ Yes   ☐ No

8a   Do you have evidence to support your deduction? . . . .   ☐ Yes   ☐ No

b   If "Yes," is the evidence written? . . . .   ☐ Yes   ☐ No

For Paperwork Reduction Act Notice, see the separate instructions for Schedule C (Form 1040).   Cat. No. 14374D   Schedule C-EZ (Form 1040) 2014

FIGURE 1.2 Schedule C-EZ, Net Profit From Business

Partnerships and Limited Liability Companies

If you go into business with others, then you cannot be a sole proprietor (with the exception of a husband-wife joint venture, explained earlier). You are automatically in a *partnership* if you join together with one or more people to share the profits of the business and take no formal action. Owners of a partnership are called *partners*.

There are 2 types of partnerships: *general partnerships* and *limited partnerships*. In general partnerships, all of the partners are personally liable for the debts of the business. Creditors can go after the personal assets of any and all of the partners to satisfy partnership debts. In limited partnerships (LPs), only the general partners are personally liable for the debts of the business. Limited partners are liable only to the extent of their investments in the business plus their share of recourse debts and obligations to make future investments. Some states allow LPs to become limited liability limited partnerships (LLLPs) to give general partners personal liability protection with respect to the debts of the partnership.

Example

If a partnership incurs debts of $10,000 (none of which are recourse), a general partner is liable for the full $10,000. A limited partner who initially contributed $1,000 to the limited partnership is liable only to that extent. He or she can lose the $1,000 investment, but creditors cannot go after personal assets.

General partners are jointly and severally liable for the business's debts. A creditor can go after any one partner for the full amount of the debt. That partner can seek to recoup a proportional share of the debt from other partner(s).

Partnerships can be informal agreements to share profits and losses of a business venture. More typically, however, they are organized with formal partnership agreements. These agreements detail how income, deductions, gains, losses, and credits are to be split (if there are any special allocations to be made) and what happens on the retirement, disability, bankruptcy, or death of a partner. A limited partnership must have a partnership agreement that complies with state law requirements.

Another form of organization that can be used by those joining together for business is a limited liability company (LLC). This type of business organization is formed under state law in which all owners are given limited liability. Owners of LLCs are called *members*. These companies are relatively new but have attracted great interest across the country. Every state now has LLC statutes to permit the formation of an LLC within its boundaries. Most states also permit limited liability partnerships (LLPs)—LLCs for accountants, attorneys, doctors, and other professionals—which are easily formed by existing partnerships filing an LLP election with the state. A partner in an LLP has personal liability protection with respect to the firm's debts, but remains personally liable for his or her professional actions. And Delaware, District of Columbia, Illinois, Iowa, Kansas, Missouri, Montana, Nevada, Oklahoma, Tennessee, Utah, Texas, and Wisconsin (to a limited extent) permit multiple LLCs to operate under a single LLC umbrella called a "series LLC" (each LLC is called a "cell"). The debts and liabilities of each LLC remain separate from those of the other LLCs, something that is ideal for those owning several pieces of real estate—each can be owned by a separate LLC under the master LLC as long as each LLC maintains separate bank accounts and financial records. At present, state law is evolving to determine the treatment of LLCs formed in one state but doing business in another.

As the name suggests, the creditors of LLCs can look only to the assets of the company to satisfy debts; creditors cannot go after members and hope to recover their personal assets.

Tax Treatment of Income and Deductions in General

Partnerships are *pass-through* entities. They are not separate taxpaying entities; instead, they pass income, deductions, gains, losses, and tax credits through to their owners. More than 24 million partners file over 3.6 million partnership returns each year. Of these, 64.3% are limited liability companies, representing the most prevalent type of entity filing a partnership return; more common than general partnerships or limited partnerships. The owners report these amounts on their individual returns. While the entity does not pay taxes, it must file an information return with IRS Form 1065, *U.S. Return of Partnership Income*, to report the total pass-through amounts. Even though the return is called a *partnership return*, it is the same return filed by LLCs with 2 or more owners who do not elect to be taxed as a corporation. The entity also completes Schedule K-1 of Form 1065 (Figure 1.3), a copy of which is given to each owner. The K-1 tells the owner his or her allocable share of partnership/LLC amounts. Like W-2 forms used by the IRS to match employees' reporting of their compensation, the IRS employs computer matching of Schedules K-1 to ensure that owners are properly reporting their share of their business's income.

> **NOTE**
>
> K-1s can be distributed to partners electronically if the partnership has the partners' consent. Obtain consent by sending instructions to partners on how to obtain, complete, and submit a consent form to the partnership.

For federal income tax purposes, LLCs are treated like partnerships unless the members elect to have the LLCs taxed as corporations. This is done on IRS Form 8832, *Entity Classification Election*. See Figure 1.4. For purposes of our discussion throughout the book, it will be assumed that LLCs have not chosen corporate tax treatment and so are taxed the same way as partnerships.

651113

Schedule K-1
(Form 1065)

20**14**

OMB No. 1545-0123

☐ Final K-1   ☐ Amended K-1

Department of the Treasury
Internal Revenue Service

For calendar year 2014, or tax
year beginning _____ , 2014
ending _____ , 20 _____

Partner's Share of Income, Deductions,
Credits, etc.   ▶ See back of form and separate instructions.

Part III	**Partner's Share of Current Year Income, Deductions, Credits, and Other Items**

1	Ordinary business income (loss)	15	Credits
2	Net rental real estate income (loss)		
3	Other net rental income (loss)	16	Foreign transactions
4	Guaranteed payments		
5	Interest income		
6a	Ordinary dividends		
6b	Qualified dividends		
7	Royalties		
8	Net short-term capital gain (loss)		
9a	Net long-term capital gain (loss)	17	Alternative minimum tax (AMT) items
9b	Collectibles (28%) gain (loss)		
9c	Unrecaptured section 1250 gain		
10	Net section 1231 gain (loss)	18	Tax-exempt income and nondeductible expenses
11	Other income (loss)		

Part I	**Information About the Partnership**

A Partnership's employer identification number

B Partnership's name, address, city, state, and ZIP code

C IRS Center where partnership filed return

D ☐ Check if this is a publicly traded partnership (PTP)

Part II	**Information About the Partner**

E Partner's identifying number

F Partner's name, address, city, state, and ZIP code

G ☐ General partner or LLC member-manager   ☐ Limited partner or other LLC member

H ☐ Domestic partner   ☐ Foreign partner

I1 What type of entity is this partner? _____

I2 If this partner is a retirement plan (IRA/SEP/Keogh/etc.), check here . . . . ☐

12	Section 179 deduction	19	Distributions
13	Other deductions	20	Other information

J Partner's share of profit, loss, and capital (see instructions):

	Beginning	Ending
Profit	%	%
Loss	%	%
Capital	%	%

K Partner's share of liabilities at year end:

Nonrecourse . . . . . . $ _____
Qualified nonrecourse financing . $ _____
Recourse . . . . $ _____

14	Self-employment earnings (loss)

L Partner's capital account analysis:

Beginning capital account . . . $ _____
Capital contributed during the year $ _____
Current year increase (decrease) . $ _____
Withdrawals & distributions . . $ (_____)
Ending capital account . . . . $ _____

☐ Tax basis   ☐ GAAP   ☐ Section 704(b) book
☐ Other (explain)

M Did the partner contribute property with a built-in gain or loss?
☐ Yes   ☐ No
If "Yes," attach statement (see instructions)

*See attached statement for additional information.

For IRS Use Only

For Paperwork Reduction Act Notice, see Instructions for Form 1065.   IRS.gov/form1065   Cat. No. 11394R   Schedule K-1 (Form 1065) 2014

FIGURE 1.3 Schedule K-1, Partner's Share of Income, Deductions, Credits, etc.

Form **8832**		OMB No. 1545-1516
(Rev. December 2013) Department of the Treasury Internal Revenue Service	**Entity Classification Election** ▶ Information about Form 8832 and its instructions is at *www.irs.gov/form8832*.	20**14**

Type or Print	Name of eligible entity making election	Employer identification number
	Number, street, and room or suite no. If a P.O. box, see instructions.	
	City or town, state, and ZIP code. If a foreign address, enter city, province or state, postal code and country. Follow the country's practice for entering the postal code.	

▶ Check if: ☐ Address change   ☐ Late classification relief sought under Revenue Procedure 2009-41
☐ Relief for a late change of entity classification election sought under Revenue Procedure 2010-32

Part I   Election Information

1   Type of election (see instructions):

a ☐ Initial classification by a newly-formed entity. Skip lines 2a and 2b and go to line 3.
b ☐ Change in current classification. Go to line 2a.

2a Has the eligible entity previously filed an entity election that had an effective date within the last 60 months?

☐ **Yes.** Go to line 2b.
☐ **No.** Skip line 2b and go to line 3.

2b Was the eligible entity's prior election an initial classification election by a newly formed entity that was effective on the date of formation?

☐ **Yes.** Go to line 3.
☐ **No.** Stop here. You generally are not currently eligible to make the election (see instructions).

3 Does the eligible entity have more than one owner?

☐ **Yes.** You can elect to be classified as a partnership or an association taxable as a corporation. Skip line 4 and go to line 5.
☐ **No.** You can elect to be classified as an association taxable as a corporation or to be disregarded as a separate entity. Go to line 4.

4 If the eligible entity has only one owner, provide the following information:

a Name of owner ▶ ....
b Identifying number of owner ▶ ....

5 If the eligible entity is owned by one or more affiliated corporations that file a consolidated return, provide the name and employer identification number of the parent corporation:

a Name of parent corporation ▶ ....
b Employer identification number ▶ ....

For Paperwork Reduction Act Notice, see instructions.   Cat. No. 22598R   Form **8832** (Rev. 12-2013)

FIGURE 1.4 Form 8832, Entity Classification Election

Form 8832 (Rev. 12-2013)

Page **2**

| Part I | Election Information (Continued) |

6   Type of entity (see instructions):

a ☐ A domestic eligible entity electing to be classified as an association taxable as a corporation.
b ☐ A domestic eligible entity electing to be classified as a partnership.
c ☐ A domestic eligible entity with a single owner electing to be disregarded as a separate entity.
d ☐ A foreign eligible entity electing to be classified as an association taxable as a corporation.
e ☐ A foreign eligible entity electing to be classified as a partnership.
f ☐ A foreign eligible entity with a single owner electing to be disregarded as a separate entity.

7   If the eligible entity is created or organized in a foreign jurisdiction, provide the foreign country of organization ▶ --

8   Election is to be effective beginning (month, day, year) (see instructions)   .   .   .   . ▶ _____

9   Name and title of contact person whom the IRS may call for more information | **10** Contact person's telephone number

Consent Statement and Signature(s) (see instructions)

Under penalties of perjury, I (we) declare that I (we) consent to the election of the above-named entity to be classified as indicated above, and that I (we) have examined this election and consent statement, and to the best of my (our) knowledge and belief, this election and consent statement are true, correct, and complete. If I am an officer, manager, or member signing for the entity, I further declare under penalties of perjury that I am authorized to make the election on its behalf.

Signature(s)	Date	Title

Form **8832** (Rev. 12-2013)

FIGURE 1.4 *(Continued)*

Part II Income or Loss From Partnerships and S Corporations Note. If you report a loss from an at-risk activity for which any amount is **not** at risk, you **must** check the box in column **(e)** on line 28 and attach **Form 6198.** See instructions.

27	Are you reporting any loss not allowed in a prior year due to the at-risk, excess farm loss, or basis limitations, a prior year unallowed loss from a passive activity (if that loss was not reported on Form 8582), or unreimbursed partnership expenses? If you answered "Yes," see instructions before completing this section.			☐ Yes ☐ No

28	(a) Name	(b) Enter P for partnership; S for S corporation	(c) Check if foreign partnership	(d) Employer identification number	(e) Check if any amount is not at risk
A			☐		☐
B			☐		☐
C			☐		☐
D			☐		☐

	Passive Income and Loss		Nonpassive Income and Loss		
	(f) Passive loss allowed (attach Form 8582 if required)	(g) Passive income from Schedule K-1	(h) Nonpassive loss from Schedule K-1	(i) Section 179 expense deduction from Form 4562	(j) Nonpassive income from Schedule K-1
A					
B					
C					
D					
29a	Totals				
b	Totals				

30	Add columns (g) and (j) of line 29a	30	
31	Add columns (f), (h), and (i) of line 29b	31	( )
32	Total partnership and S corporation income or (loss). Combine lines 30 and 31. Enter the result here and include in the total on line 41 below	32	

FIGURE 1.5 Schedule E, Part II, Income or Loss From Partnerships and S Corporations

A single-member LLC is treated for tax purposes like a sole proprietor if it is owned by an individual who reports the company's income and expenses on his or her Schedule C. Under proposed regulations, for federal tax purposes a series LLC is treated as an entity formed under local law, whether or not local law treats the series as a separate legal entity. The tax treatment of the series is then governed by the check-the-box rules.

There are 2 types of items that pass through to an owner: trade or business income or loss and separately stated items. A partner's or member's share is called the *distributive share*. Trade or business income or loss takes into account most ordinary deductions of the business—compensation, rent, taxes, interest, and so forth. Guaranteed payments to an owner are also taken into account when determining ordinary income or loss. From an owner's perspective, deductions net out against income from the business, and the owner's allocable share of the net amount is then reported on the owner's Schedule E of Form 1040. Figure 1.5 shows a sample portion of Schedule E on which a partner's or member's distributive share is reported.

Separately stated items are stand-alone items that pass through to owners apart from the net amount of trade or business income. These are items that are subject to limitations on an individual's tax return and must be segregated from the net amount of trade or business income. They are reported along with similar items on the owner's own tax return.

Example

A charitable contribution deduction made by a partnership passes through separately as a charitable contribution. The partner adds the amount of the pass-through charitable contribution to his or her other charitable contributions. Since an individual's cash contributions are deductible only to the extent of 50% of adjusted gross income, the partner's allocable share of the partnership's charitable contribution is subject to his or her individual adjusted gross income limit.

Other items that pass through separately to owners include capital gains and losses, Section 179 (first-year expensing) deductions, investment interest deductions, and tax credits.

When a partnership or LLC has substantial expenses that exceed its operating income, a loss is passed through to the owner. A number of different rules operate to limit a loss deduction. The owner may not be able to claim the entire loss. The loss is limited by the owner's *basis*, or the amount of cash and property contributed to the partnership, in the interest in the partnership.

Example

You contributed $2,000 to the AB Partnership. In 2014 the partnership had sizable expenses and only a small amount of revenue. Your allocable share of partnership loss is $3,000. You may deduct only $2,000 in 2014, which is the amount of your basis in your partnership interest. You may deduct that additional $1,000 of loss when you have additional basis to offset it.

There may be additional limits on your write-offs from partnerships and LLCs. If you are a passive investor—a silent partner—in these businesses, your loss deduction is further limited by the passive activity loss rules. In general, these rules limit a current deduction for losses from passive activities to the extent of income from passive activities. Additionally, losses are limited by the individual's economic risk in the business. This limit is called the *at-risk rule*. The passive activity loss and at-risk rules are discussed in Chapter 4. For a further discussion of the passive activity loss rules, see IRS Publication 925, *Passive Activity and At-Risk Rules*.

S Corporations and Their Shareholder-Employees

There are about 4.5 million S corporations, making these entities the most prevalent type of corporation. About 67% of all corporations file a Form 1120S, the return for S corporations. About 78% of S corporations have only 1, 2, or 3 shareholders.

S corporations are like regular corporations (called *C corporations*) for business law purposes. They are separate entities in the eyes of the law and exist independently from their owners. For example, if an owner dies, the S corporation's existence continues. S corporations are formed under state law in the same way as other corporations. The only difference between S corporations and other corporations is their tax treatment for federal income tax purposes.

For the most part, S corporations are treated as pass-through entities for federal income tax purposes. This means that, as with partnerships and LLCs, the income and loss pass through to owners, and their allocable share is reported by S corporation shareholders on their individual income tax returns. The tax treatment of S corporations is discussed more fully later in this chapter.

S corporation status is not automatic. A corporation must elect S status in a timely manner. This election is made on Form 2553, *Election by Small Business Corporations to Tax Corporate Income Directly to Shareholders*. It must be filed with the IRS no later than the fifteenth day of the third month of the corporation's tax year.

Example

A corporation (on a calendar year) that has been in existence for a number of years wants to elect S status. It has to file an election no later than March 17, 2014, to be effective for its 2014 tax year. If a corporation is formed on August 1, 2014, and wants an S election to be effective for its first tax year, the S election must be filed no later than November 17, 2014.

If an S election is filed after the deadline, it is automatically effective for the following year. A corporation can simply decide to make a prospective election by filing at any time during the year prior to that for which the election is to be effective.

Example

A corporation (on a calendar year) that has been in existence for a number of years wants to elect S status for its 2015 tax year. It can file an election at any time during 2014.

To be eligible for an S election, the corporation must meet certain shareholder requirements. There can be no more than 100 shareholders. For this purpose, all family members (up to 6 generations) are treated as a single share-holder. Only certain types of trusts are permitted to be shareholders. There can be no nonresident alien shareholders.

An election cannot be made before the corporation is formed. The board of directors of the corporation must agree to the election and should indicate this assent in the minutes of a board of directors meeting.

Remember, if state law also allows S status, a separate election may have to be filed with the state. Check with all state law requirements.

Tax Treatment of Income and Deductions in General

For the most part, S corporations, like partnerships and LLCs, are pass-through entities. They are generally not separate taxpaying entities. Instead, they pass through to their shareholders' income, deductions, gains, losses, and tax credits. The shareholders report these amounts on their individual returns. The S corporation files a return with the IRS—Form 1120S, *U.S. Income Tax Return for an S Corporation*—to report the total pass-through amounts. The S corporation also completes Schedule K-1 of Form 1120S, a copy of which is given to each shareholder. The K-1 tells the shareholder his or her allocable share of S corporation amounts. The K-1 for S corporation shareholders is similar to the K-1 for partners and LLC members.

Unlike partnerships and LLCs, however, S corporations may become taxpayers if they have certain types of income. There are only 3 types of income that result in a tax on the S corporation. These 3 items cannot be reduced by any deductions:

1. **Built-in gains.** These are gains related to appreciation of assets held by a C corporation that converts to S status. Thus, if a corporation is formed and immediately elects S status, there will never be any built-in gains to worry about.

2. **Passive investment income.** This is income of a corporation that has earnings and profits from a time when it was a C corporation. A tax on the S corporation results only when this passive investment income exceeds 25% of gross receipts. Again, if a corporation is formed and immediately elects S status, or if a corporation that converted to S status does not have any earnings and profits at the time of conversion, then there will never be any tax from this source.

3. **LIFO recapture.** When a C corporation using last-in, first-out or LIFO to report inventory converts to S status, there may be recapture income that is taken into account partly on the C corporation's final return, but also on the S corporation's return. Again, if a corporation is formed and immediately elects S status, there will not be any recapture income on which the S corporation must pay tax.

To sum up, if a corporation is formed and immediately elects S status, the corporation will always be solely a pass-through entity and there will never be any tax at the corporate level. If the S corporation was, at one time, a C corporation, there may be some tax at the corporate level.

C Corporations and Their Shareholder-Employees

A *C corporation* is an entity separate and apart from its owners; it has its own legal existence. Though formed under state law, it need not be formed in the state in which the business operates. Many corporations, for example, are formed in Delaware or Nevada because the laws in these states favor the corporation, as opposed to the investors (shareholders). However, state law for the state in which the business operates may still require the corporation to make some formal notification of doing business in the state. The corporation may also be subject to tax on income generated in that state.

According to IRS data, there are about 2.3 million C corporations, more than 98% of which are small or midsize companies (with assets of $10 million or less).

For federal tax purposes, a C corporation is a separate taxpaying entity. It files its own return (Form 1120, *U.S. Corporation Income Tax Return*) to report its income or losses. Shareholders do not report their share of the corporation's income. The tax treatment of C corporations is explained more fully later in this chapter.

Personal Service Corporations

Professionals who incorporate their practices are a special type of C corporation called **personal service corporations (PSCs)**.

Personal service corporation (PSC)   A C corporation that performs personal services in the fields of health, law, accounting, engineering, architecture, actuarial science, performing arts, or consulting and meets certain ownership and service tests.

Personal service corporations are subject to special rules in the tax law. Some of these rules are beneficial; others are not. Personal service corporations:

- Cannot use graduated corporate tax rates; they are subject to a flat tax rate of 35%.
- Are generally required to use the same tax year as that of their owners. Typically, individuals report their income on a calendar year basis (explained more fully in Chapter 2), so their PSCs must also use a calendar year. However, there is a special election that can be made to use a fiscal year.

- Can use the cash method of accounting. Other C corporations cannot use the cash method and instead must use the accrual method (explained more fully in Chapter 2).

- Are subject to the passive loss limitation rules (explained in Chapter 4).

- Can have their income and deductions reallocated by the IRS between the corporation and the shareholders if it more correctly reflects the economics of the situation.

- Have a smaller exemption from the accumulated earnings penalty than other C corporations. This penalty imposes an additional tax on corporations that accumulate their income above and beyond the reasonable needs of the business instead of distributing income to shareholders.

Tax Treatment of Income and Deductions in General

The C corporation reports its own income and claims its own deductions on Form 1120, *U.S. Corporation Income Tax Return.* Shareholders in C corporations do not have to report any income of the corporation (and cannot claim any deductions of the corporation). Figure 1.6 shows a sample copy of page 1 of Form 1120.

C corporations pay taxes according to corporate tax rates that run from 15% on taxable income up to $50,000, to 35% on taxable income over $15 million (with very large corporations subject to a higher marginal rate that has the effect of eliminating the graduated rates so that they are eventually taxed at a flat 35%) (see Table 1.1). These brackets are not adjusted annually for inflation as are the tax brackets for individuals.

There has been sentiment in Congress to reduce the top corporate rate in order to make U.S. corporations more competitive with foreign corporations. For example, in Singapore the rate is 17%, in South Korea, 24%, in Canada 26%, and in Germany, 30%. Japan reduced its rate from 40% (the highest in industrialized countries) to 38%, leaving the United States with the highest rate (an effective rate of 40% after averaging in state corporate tax rates).

Distributions from the C corporation to its shareholders are personal items for the shareholders. For example, if a shareholder works for his or her C corporation and receives a salary, the corporation deducts that salary against corporate income. The shareholder reports the salary as income on his or her individual income tax return. If the corporation distributes a dividend to the shareholder, again, the shareholder reports the dividend as income on his or her individual income tax return. In the case of dividends, however, the corporation cannot claim a deduction. This, then, creates a 2-tier tax system, commonly referred to as *double taxation*. First, earnings are taxed at the corporate level. Then, when they are distributed to shareholders as dividends, they are taxed again, this time at the shareholder level. There has been sentiment in Congress over the years to eliminate the double taxation, but as of yet there has been

Form **1120**	**U.S. Corporation Income Tax Return**		OMB No. 1545-0123
Department of the Treasury Internal Revenue Service	For calendar year 2014 or tax year beginning _____ , 2014, ending _____ , 20 ____ ▶ Information about Form 1120 and its separate instructions is at *www.irs.gov/form1120.*		20**14**

A Check if:		Name		B Employer identification number
1a Consolidated return (attach Form 851) ☐	TYPE OR PRINT			
b Life/nonlife consolidated return . . ☐		Number, street, and room or suite no. If a P.O. box, see instructions.		C Date incorporated
2 Personal holding co. (attach Sch. PH) . ☐				
3 Personal service corp. (see instructions) ☐		City or town, state, or province, country and ZIP or foreign postal code		D Total assets (see instructions) $
4 Schedule M-3 attached ☐	E Check if: **(1)** ☐ Initial return **(2)** ☐ Final return **(3)** ☐ Name change **(4)** ☐ Address change			

Income	1a	Gross receipts or sales	1a		
	b	Returns and allowances	1b		
	c	Balance. Subtract line 1b from line 1a		1c	
	2	Cost of goods sold (attach Form 1125-A)		2	
	3	Gross profit. Subtract line 2 from line 1c		3	
	4	Dividends (Schedule C, line 19)		4	
	5	Interest		5	
	6	Gross rents		6	
	7	Gross royalties		7	
	8	Capital gain net income (attach Schedule D (Form 1120))		8	
	9	Net gain or (loss) from Form 4797, Part II, line 17 (attach Form 4797)		9	
	10	Other income (see instructions—attach statement) . . . . ▶		10	
	11	**Total income.** Add lines 3 through 10 . . . . ▶		11	

Deductions (See instructions for limitations on deductions.)	12	Compensation of officers (see instructions—attach Form 1125-E) . . . . ▶		12	
	13	Salaries and wages (less employment credits)		13	
	14	Repairs and maintenance		14	
	15	Bad debts		15	
	16	Rents		16	
	17	Taxes and licenses		17	
	18	Interest		18	
	19	Charitable contributions		19	
	20	Depreciation from Form 4562 not claimed on Form 1125-A or elsewhere on return (attach Form 4562) .		20	
	21	Depletion		21	
	22	Advertising		22	
	23	Pension, profit-sharing, etc., plans		23	
	24	Employee benefit programs		24	
	25	Domestic production activities deduction (attach Form 8903)		25	
	26	Other deductions (attach statement)		26	
	27	**Total deductions.** Add lines 12 through 26 . . . . ▶		27	
	28	Taxable income before net operating loss deduction and special deductions. Subtract line 27 from line 11.		28	
	29a	Net operating loss deduction (see instructions)	29a		
	b	Special deductions (Schedule C, line 20)	29b		
	c	Add lines 29a and 29b		29c	

Tax, Refundable Credits, and Payments	30	**Taxable income.** Subtract line 29c from line 28 (see instructions)		30	
	31	Total tax (Schedule J, Part I, line 11)		31	
	32	Total payments and refundable credits (Schedule J, Part II, line 21)		32	
	33	Estimated tax penalty (see instructions). Check if Form 2220 is attached . . . . . ▶ ☐		33	
	34	**Amount owed.** If line 32 is smaller than the total of lines 31 and 33, enter amount owed . . .		34	
	35	**Overpayment.** If line 32 is larger than the total of lines 31 and 33, enter amount overpaid		35	
	36	Enter amount from line 35 you want: **Credited to 2015 estimated tax** ▶	Refunded ▶	36	

Sign Here	Under penalties of perjury, I declare that I have examined this return, including accompanying schedules and statements, and to the best of my knowledge and belief, it is true, correct, and complete. Declaration of preparer (other than taxpayer) is based on all information of which preparer has any knowledge.		May the IRS discuss this return with the preparer shown below (see instructions)? ☐ Yes ☐ No
	▶ Signature of officer Date	▶ Title	

Paid Preparer Use Only	Print/Type preparer's name	Preparer's signature	Date	Check ☐ if self-employed	PTIN
	Firm's name ▶			Firm's EIN ▶	
	Firm's address ▶			Phone no.	

For Paperwork Reduction Act Notice, see separate instructions.   Cat. No. 11450Q   Form **1120** (2014)

FIGURE 1.6 Form 1120, U.S. Corporation Income Tax Return

Form 1120 (2014)   Page **2**

Schedule C	Dividends and Special Deductions (see instructions)	(a) Dividends received	(b) %	(c) Special deductions (a) × (b)
1	Dividends from less-than-20%-owned domestic corporations (other than debt-financed stock)		70	
2	Dividends from 20%-or-more-owned domestic corporations (other than debt-financed stock)		80	
3	Dividends on debt-financed stock of domestic and foreign corporations		see instructions	
4	Dividends on certain preferred stock of less-than-20%-owned public utilities . . .		42	
5	Dividends on certain preferred stock of 20%-or-more-owned public utilities		48	
6	Dividends from less-than-20%-owned foreign corporations and certain FSCs . . .		70	
7	Dividends from 20%-or-more-owned foreign corporations and certain FSCs . . .		80	
8	Dividends from wholly owned foreign subsidiaries		100	
9	**Total.** Add lines 1 through 8. See instructions for limitation			
10	Dividends from domestic corporations received by a small business investment company operating under the Small Business Investment Act of 1958		100	
11	Dividends from affiliated group members		100	
12	Dividends from certain FSCs		100	
13	Dividends from foreign corporations not included on lines 3, 6, 7, 8, 11, or 12 . . .			
14	Income from controlled foreign corporations under subpart F (attach Form(s) 5471) .			
15	Foreign dividend gross-up			
16	IC-DISC and former DISC dividends not included on lines 1, 2, or 3			
17	Other dividends			
18	Deduction for dividends paid on certain preferred stock of public utilities			
19	**Total dividends.** Add lines 1 through 17. Enter here and on page 1, line 4 . . . ▶			
20	**Total special deductions.** Add lines 9, 10, 11, 12, and 18. Enter here and on page 1, line 29b . . . . ▶			

Form **1120** (2014)

FIGURE 1.6 *(Continued)*

Form 1120 (2014)   Page **3**

Schedule J	**Tax Computation and Payment** (see instructions)		

Part I–Tax Computation

1	Check if the corporation is a member of a controlled group (attach Schedule O (Form 1120)) . . . . ▶ ☐		
2	Income tax. Check if a qualified personal service corporation (see instructions) . . . . ▶ ☐	**2**	
3	Alternative minimum tax (attach Form 4626)	**3**	
4	Add lines 2 and 3	**4**	
5a	Foreign tax credit (attach Form 1118)	**5a**	
b	Credit from Form 8834 (see instructions)	**5b**	
c	General business credit (attach Form 3800)	**5c**	
d	Credit for prior year minimum tax (attach Form 8827)	**5d**	
e	Bond credits from Form 8912	**5e**	
6	**Total credits.** Add lines 5a through 5e	**6**	
7	Subtract line 6 from line 4	**7**	
8	Personal holding company tax (attach Schedule PH (Form 1120))	**8**	
9a	Recapture of investment credit (attach Form 4255)	**9a**	
b	Recapture of low-income housing credit (attach Form 8611) . .	**9b**	
c	Interest due under the look-back method—completed long-term contracts (attach Form 8697)	**9c**	
d	Interest due under the look-back method—income forecast method (attach Form 8866)	**9d**	
e	Alternative tax on qualifying shipping activities (attach Form 8902) . .	**9e**	
f	Other (see instructions—attach statement)	**9f**	
10	**Total.** Add lines 9a through 9f	**10**	
11	**Total tax.** Add lines 7, 8, and 10. Enter here and on page 1, line 31	**11**	

Part II–Payments and Refundable Credits

12	2013 overpayment credited to 2014	**12**		
13	2014 estimated tax payments	**13**		
14	2014 refund applied for on Form 4466	**14** (		)
15	Combine lines 12, 13, and 14	**15**		
16	Tax deposited with Form 7004	**16**		
17	Withholding (see instructions)	**17**		
18	**Total payments.** Add lines 15, 16, and 17	**18**		
19	Refundable credits from:			
a	Form 2439	**19a**		
b	Form 4136	**19b**		
c	Form 8827, line 8c	**19c**		
d	Other (attach statement—see instructions). . . .	**19d**		
20	**Total credits.** Add lines 19a through 19d	**20**		
21	**Total payments and credits.** Add lines 18 and 20. Enter here and on page 1, line 32	**21**		

Schedule K	**Other Information** (see instructions)		

		Yes	No
1	Check accounting method: **a** ☐ Cash **b** ☐ Accrual **c** ☐ Other (specify) ▶ _____		
2	See the instructions and enter the:		
a	Business activity code no. ▶ _____		
b	Business activity ▶ _____		
c	Product or service ▶ _____		
3	Is the corporation a subsidiary in an affiliated group or a parent-subsidiary controlled group?		
	If "Yes," enter name and EIN of the parent corporation ▶ _____		
4	At the end of the tax year:		
a	Did any foreign or domestic corporation, partnership (including any entity treated as a partnership), trust, or tax-exempt organization own directly 20% or more, or own, directly or indirectly, 50% or more of the total voting power of all classes of the corporation's stock entitled to vote? If "Yes," complete Part I of Schedule G (Form 1120) (attach Schedule G)		
b	Did any individual or estate own directly 20% or more, or own, directly or indirectly, 50% or more of the total voting power of all classes of the corporation's stock entitled to vote? If "Yes," complete Part II of Schedule G (Form 1120) (attach Schedule G) .		

Form **1120** (2014)

FIGURE 1.6 *(Continued)*

Form 1120 (2014)   Page **4**

| Schedule K | Other Information *continued* (see instructions) | | | | Yes | No |

5   At the end of the tax year, did the corporation:

a   Own directly 20% or more, or own, directly or indirectly, 50% or more of the total voting power of all classes of stock entitled to vote of any foreign or domestic corporation not included on **Form 851,** Affiliations Schedule? For rules of constructive ownership, see instructions. If "Yes," complete (i) through (iv) below.

(i) Name of Corporation	(ii) Employer Identification Number (if any)	(iii) Country of Incorporation	(iv) Percentage Owned in Voting Stock

b   Own directly an interest of 20% or more, or own, directly or indirectly, an interest of 50% or more in any foreign or domestic partnership (including an entity treated as a partnership) or in the beneficial interest of a trust? For rules of constructive ownership, see instructions. If "Yes," complete (i) through (iv) below.

(i) Name of Entity	(ii) Employer Identification Number (if any)	(iii) Country of Organization	(iv) Maximum Percentage Owned in Profit, Loss, or Capital

6   During this tax year, did the corporation pay dividends (other than stock dividends and distributions in exchange for stock) in excess of the corporation's current and accumulated earnings and profits? (See sections 301 and 316.) . . . .
     If "Yes," file **Form 5452,** Corporate Report of Nondividend Distributions.
     If this is a consolidated return, answer here for the parent corporation and on Form 851 for each subsidiary.

7   At any time during the tax year, did one foreign person own, directly or indirectly, at least 25% of **(a)** the total voting power of all classes of the corporation's stock entitled to vote or **(b)** the total value of all classes of the corporation's stock? . . . .
     For rules of attribution, see section 318. If "Yes," enter:
     (i) Percentage owned ▶ _____ and **(ii)** Owner's country ▶ _____
     (c) The corporation may have to file **Form 5472,** Information Return of a 25% Foreign-Owned U.S. Corporation or a Foreign Corporation Engaged in a U.S. Trade or Business. Enter the number of Forms 5472 attached ▶ _____

8   Check this box if the corporation issued publicly offered debt instruments with original issue discount . . . . . ▶ ☐
     If checked, the corporation may have to file **Form 8281,** Information Return for Publicly Offered Original Issue Discount Instruments.

9   Enter the amount of tax-exempt interest received or accrued during the tax year ▶ $ _____

10   Enter the number of shareholders at the end of the tax year (if 100 or fewer) ▶

11   If the corporation has an NOL for the tax year and is electing to forego the carryback period, check here . . . . . ▶ ☐
     If the corporation is filing a consolidated return, the statement required by Regulations section 1.1502-21(b)(3) must be attached or the election will not be valid.

12   Enter the available NOL carryover from prior tax years (do not reduce it by any deduction on line 29a.) ▶ $ _____

13   Are the corporation's total receipts (page 1, line 1a, plus lines 4 through 10) for the tax year **and** its total assets at the end of the tax year less than $250,000? . . . .
     If "Yes," the corporation is not required to complete Schedules L, M-1, and M-2. Instead, enter the total amount of cash distributions and the book value of property distributions (other than cash) made during the tax year ▶ $ _____

14   Is the corporation required to file Schedule UTP (Form 1120), Uncertain Tax Position Statement (see instructions)? . . . .
     If "Yes," complete and attach Schedule UTP.

15a Did the corporation make any payments in 2014 that would require it to file Form(s) 1099? . . . .

b   If "Yes," did or will the corporation file required Forms 1099? . . . .

16   During this tax year, did the corporation have an 80% or more change in ownership, including a change due to redemption of its own stock? . . . .

17   During or subsequent to this tax year, but before the filing of this return, did the corporation dispose of more than 65% (by value) of its assets in a taxable, non-taxable, or tax deferred transaction? . . . .

18   Did the corporation receive assets in a section 351 transfer in which any of the transferred assets had a fair market basis or fair market value of more than $1 million? . . . .

Form **1120** (2014)

FIGURE 1.6 *(Continued)*

Form 1120 (2014) Page **5**

Schedule L — Balance Sheets per Books

	Assets	Beginning of tax year		End of tax year	
		(a)	(b)	(c)	(d)
1	Cash				
2a	Trade notes and accounts receivable				
b	Less allowance for bad debts	( )		( )	
3	Inventories				
4	U.S. government obligations				
5	Tax-exempt securities (see instructions)				
6	Other current assets (attach statement)				
7	Loans to shareholders				
8	Mortgage and real estate loans				
9	Other investments (attach statement)				
10a	Buildings and other depreciable assets				
b	Less accumulated depreciation	( )		( )	
11a	Depletable assets				
b	Less accumulated depletion	( )		( )	
12	Land (net of any amortization)				
13a	Intangible assets (amortizable only)				
b	Less accumulated amortization	( )		( )	
14	Other assets (attach statement)				
15	Total assets				
	Liabilities and Shareholders' Equity				
16	Accounts payable				
17	Mortgages, notes, bonds payable in less than 1 year				
18	Other current liabilities (attach statement)				
19	Loans from shareholders				
20	Mortgages, notes, bonds payable in 1 year or more				
21	Other liabilities (attach statement)				
22	Capital stock: a Preferred stock				
	b Common stock				
23	Additional paid-in capital				
24	Retained earnings—Appropriated (attach statement)				
25	Retained earnings—Unappropriated				
26	Adjustments to shareholders' equity (attach statement)				
27	Less cost of treasury stock		( )		( )
28	Total liabilities and shareholders' equity				

Schedule M-1 — Reconciliation of Income (Loss) per Books With Income per Return

Note: The corporation may be required to file Schedule M-3 (see instructions).

1	Net income (loss) per books		7	Income recorded on books this year not included on this return (itemize):	
2	Federal income tax per books			Tax-exempt interest $ _____	
3	Excess of capital losses over capital gains				
4	Income subject to tax not recorded on books this year (itemize): _____				
			8	Deductions on this return not charged against book income this year (itemize):	
5	Expenses recorded on books this year not deducted on this return (itemize):		a	Depreciation $ _____	
a	Depreciation $ _____		b	Charitable contributions $ _____	
b	Charitable contributions $ _____				
c	Travel and entertainment $ _____				
			9	Add lines 7 and 8	
6	Add lines 1 through 5		10	Income (page 1, line 28)—line 6 less line 9	

Schedule M-2 — Analysis of Unappropriated Retained Earnings per Books (Line 25, Schedule L)

1	Balance at beginning of year		5	Distributions: a Cash	
2	Net income (loss) per books			b Stock	
3	Other increases (itemize): _____			c Property	
			6	Other decreases (itemize):	
			7	Add lines 5 and 6	
4	Add lines 1, 2, and 3		8	Balance at end of year (line 4 less line 7)	

Form **1120** (2014)

FIGURE 1.6 *(Continued)*

TABLE 1.1 Federal Corporate Tax Rate Schedule

If taxable income is:

Over	But Not Over	Tax Is	Of the Amount Over
$ 0	$ 50,000	15%	$ 0
50,000	75,000	$ 7,500 + 25%	50,000
75,000	100,000	$ 13,750 + 34%	75,000
100,000	335,000	$ 22,250 + 39%	100,000
335,000	10,000,000	$ 113,900 + 34%	335,000
10,000,000	15,000,000	$ 3,400,000 + 35%	10,000,000
15,000,000	18,333,333	$ 5,150,000 + 38%	15,000,000
18,333,333		35%	0

no legislation to accomplish this end other than the relief provided by capping the rate on dividends (zero for individuals in the 10% or 15% tax bracket; 15% for those in the 25%, 28%, 33%, or 35% brackets; 20% for those in the 39.6% bracket).

Other Tax Issues for C Corporations

In view of the favorable corporate rate tax structure (compared with the individual tax rates), certain tax penalties prevent businesses from using this form of business organization to optimum advantage.

- **Personal holding company penalty.** Corporations that function as a shareholder investment portfolio rather than as an operating company may fall subject to the personal holding corporation (PHC) penalty tax of 20% on certain undistributed corporate income. The tax rules strictly define a PHC according to stock ownership and adjusted gross income. The penalty may be avoided by *not* triggering the definition of PHC or by paying out certain dividends.

- **Accumulated earnings tax.** Corporations may seek to keep money in corporate accounts rather than distribute it as dividends to shareholders with the view that an eventual sale of the business will enable shareholders to extract those funds at capital gain rates. Unfortunately, the tax law imposes a penalty on excess accumulations at 20%. Excess accumulations are those above an exemption amount ($250,000 for most businesses, but only $150,000 for PSCs) *plus* amounts for the reasonable needs of the business. Thus, for example, amounts retained to finance planned construction costs, to pay for a possible legal liability, or to buy out a retiring owner are reasonable needs not subject to penalty regardless of amount.

Employees

If you do not own any interest in a business but are employed by one, you may still have to account for business expenses. Your salary or other compensation is reported as wages in the income section as seen on page 1 of your Form 1040. Your deductions (with a few exceptions), however, can be claimed only as miscellaneous itemized deductions on Schedule A. These deductions are subject to 2 limitations. The total is deductible only if it exceeds 2% of adjusted gross income and, if your income exceeds a threshold amount that depends on your filing status, the otherwise deductible portion of miscellaneous itemized deductions reduced by a phase-out. For 2014, the threshold amount at which itemized deductions (including miscellaneous itemized deductions) begins to phase out is $254,200 for singles; $279,650 for heads of households; $305,050 for joint filers; and $152,525 for married persons filing separately.

Under the 2% rule, only the portion of total miscellaneous deductions in excess of 2% of adjusted gross income is deductible on Schedule A. *Adjusted gross income* is the tax term for your total income subject to tax (gross income) minus business expenses (other than employee business expenses), capital losses, and certain other expenses that are deductible even if you do not claim itemized deductions, such as qualifying IRA contributions or alimony. You arrive at your adjusted gross income by completing the Income and Adjusted Gross Income sections on page 1 of Form 1040.

Example

You have business travel expenses that your employer does not pay for and other miscellaneous expenses (such as tax preparation fees) totaling $2,000. Your adjusted gross income is $80,000. The amount up to the 2% floor, or $1,600 (2% of $80,000), is disallowed. Only $400 of the $2,000 expenses is deductible on Schedule A.

If you fall into a special category of employees called *statutory employees*, you can deduct your business expenses on Schedule C instead of Schedule A. Statutory employees were discussed earlier in this chapter.

Factors in Choosing Your Form of Business Organization

Throughout this chapter, the differences of how income and deductions are reported have been explained for different entities, but these differences are not the only reasons for choosing a form of business organization. When you are deciding on which form of business organization to choose, tax, financial, and many other factors come into play, including:

- Personal liability
- Access to capital
- Lack of profitability
- Fringe benefits
- Nature and number of owners
- Tax rates
- Social Security and Medicare taxes
- Restrictions on accounting periods and account methods
- Owner's payment of company expenses
- Multistate operations
- Audit changes
- Filing deadlines and extensions
- Exit strategy

Each of these factors is discussed below.

Personal Liability

If your business owes money to another party, are your personal assets—home, car, investment—at risk? The answer depends on your form of business organization. You have personal liability—your personal assets are at risk—if you are a sole proprietor or a general partner in a partnership. In all other cases, you do not have personal liability. Thus, for example, if you are a shareholder in an S corporation, you do not have personal liability for the debts of your corporation.

Of course, you can protect yourself against personal liability for some types of occurrences by having adequate insurance coverage. For example, if you are a sole proprietor who runs a store, be sure that you have adequate liability coverage in the event someone is injured on your premises and sues you.

Even if your form of business organization provides personal liability protection, you can become personally liable if you agree to it in a contract. For example, some banks may not be willing to lend money to a small corporation unless you, as a principal shareholder, agree to guarantee the corporation's debt. For example, SBA loans usually require the personal guarantee of any owner with a 20% or more ownership interest in the business. In this case, you are personally liable to the extent of the loan to the corporation. If the corporation does not or cannot repay the loan, then the bank can look to you, and your personal assets, for repayment.

There is another instance in which corporate or LLC status will not provide you with personal protection. Even if you have a corporation or LLC, you can be personally liable for failing to withhold and deposit payroll taxes, which are called trust fund taxes (employees' income tax withholding and their share of

FICA taxes, which are held in trust for them) to the IRS. This liability is explained in Chapter 29.

Access to Capital

Most small businesses start up using an owner's personal resources or by turning to family and friends. However, some businesses need outside capital—equity and/or debt—to get started properly. A C corporation may make it easier to raise money, especially now. For example, access to equity crowdfunding, which allows businesses to raise small amounts from numerous investors, is effectively limited to C corporations (S corporations cannot have more than 100 investors; partnerships and LLCs would have difficulty in divvying up ownership among an ever-changing number of owners). Equity crowdfunding was not operational at the time of publication so check the Supplement for any update.

Lack of Profitability

All businesses hope to make money. But many sustain losses, especially in the start-up years and during tough economic times. The way in which a business is organized affects how losses are treated.

Pass-through entities allow owners to deduct their share of the company's losses on their personal returns (subject to limits discussed in Chapter 4). If a business is set up as a C corporation, only the corporation can deduct losses. Thus, when losses are anticipated, for example in the start-up phase, a pass-through entity generally is a preferable form of business organization. However, once the business becomes profitable, the tables turn. In that situation, C corporations can offer more tax opportunities, such as fringe benefits. Companies that suffer severe losses may be forced into bankruptcy. The bankruptcy rules for corporations (C or S) are very different from the rules for other entities (see Chapter 25).

Fringe Benefits

The tax law gives employees of corporations the opportunity to enjoy special fringe benefits on a tax-free basis. They can receive employer-provided group term life insurance up to $50,000, health insurance coverage, dependent care assistance up to $5,000, education assistance up to $5,250, adoption assistance, and more. They can also be covered by medical reimbursement plans. This same opportunity is not extended to sole proprietors. Remember that sole proprietors are not employees, so they cannot get the benefits given only to employees. Similarly, partners, LLC members, and even S corporation shareholders who own more than 2% of the stock in their corporations are not considered employees and thus not eligible for fringe benefits.

If the business can afford to provide these benefits, the form of business becomes important. All forms of business can offer tax-favored retirement plans. Corporations make it possible to give ownership opportunities to employees. Corporations—both C and S—can offer employee stock ownership plans (ESOPs) in which employees receive ownership interests through a plan that is much like a qualified retirement plan (see Chapter 16). Certain C corporations can offer employees an income tax exclusion opportunity for stock they buy or receive as compensation. For 2014, 50% or 75% of the gain on qualified small business stock (explained in Chapter 7) is excludable from gross income as long as the stock has been held for more than five years. C corporations can also offer incentive stock option (ISO) plans and nonqualified stock option (NSO) plans (see Chapter 7). The tax law does not bar S corporations from offering stock option plans, but because of the 100-shareholder limit (discussed earlier in this chapter), it becomes difficult to do so.

Nature and Number of Owners

With whom you go into business affects your choice of business organization. For example, if you have any foreign investors, you cannot use an S corporation, because foreign individuals are not permitted to own S corporation stock directly (resident aliens are permitted to own S corporation stock). An S corporation also cannot be used if investors are partnerships or corporations. In other words, in order to use an S corporation, all shareholders must be individuals who are not nonresident aliens (there are exceptions for estates, certain trusts, and certain exempt organizations).

The number of owners also presents limits on your choice of business organization. If you are the only owner, then your choices are limited to a sole proprietorship or a corporation (either C or S). All states allow single-member LLCs. If you have more than one owner, you can set up the business in just about any way you choose. S corporations cannot have more than 100 shareholders, but this number provides great leeway for small businesses.

If you have a business already formed as a C corporation and want to start another corporation, you must take into consideration the impact of special tax rules for multiple corporations. These rules apply regardless of the size of the business, the number of employees you have, and the profit the businesses make. Multiple corporations are corporations under common control, meaning they are essentially owned by the same parties. The tax law limits the number of tax breaks in the case of multiple corporations. Instead of each corporation enjoying a full tax benefit, the benefit must be shared among all of the corporations in the group. For example, the tax brackets for corporations are graduated. In the case of certain multiple corporations, however, the benefit of the graduated rates must be shared. In effect, each corporation pays a slightly higher tax because it is part of a group of multiple corporations. If you want to avoid restrictions on multiple corporations, you may want to look to LLCs or some other form of business organization.

Tax Rates

Both individuals and C corporations (other than PSCs) can enjoy graduated income tax rates. The top tax rate paid by sole proprietors and owners of other pass-through businesses is 39.6%. The top corporate tax rate imposed on C corporations is 35%. (There is some political support for reducing the top corporate tax rate.) Personal service corporations are subject to a flat tax rate of 35%. (The domestic production activities deduction in Chapter 21 effectively lowers the top rate to less than 32% for corporations that are eligible to claim it.) But remember, even though the C corporation has a lower top tax rate, there is a 2-tier tax structure with which to contend if earnings are paid out to you as dividends—tax at the corporate level and again at the shareholder level.

While the so-called double taxation for C corporations has been eased by lowering the tax rate on dividends, there is still some double tax because dividends remain nondeductible at the corporate level. The rate on qualified dividends for most taxpayers is 15% (zero for taxpayers who are in the 10% or 15% tax bracket; 20% for those in the 39.6% tax bracket).

The tax rates on capital gains also differ between C corporations and other taxpayers. This is because capital gains of C corporations are not subject to special tax rates (they are taxed the same as ordinary business income), while owners of other types of businesses may pay tax on the business's capital gains at no more than 15% (zero if they are in the 10% or 15% tax bracket; 20% if they are in the 39.6% tax bracket). Of course, tax rates alone should not be the determining factor in selecting your form of business organization.

Social Security and Medicare Taxes

Owners of businesses organized any way other than as a corporation (C or S) are not employees of their businesses. As such, they are personally responsible for paying Social Security and Medicare taxes (called *self-employment* taxes for owners of unincorporated businesses). This tax is made up of the employer and employee shares of Social Security and Medicare taxes. The deduction for one-half of self-employment taxes is explained in Chapter 13.

However, owners of corporations have these taxes applied only against their salary and taxable benefits. Owners of unincorporated businesses pay self-employment tax on net earnings from self-employment. This essentially means profits, whether they are distributed to the owners or reinvested in the business. The result: Owners of unincorporated businesses can wind up paying higher Social Security and Medicare taxes than comparable owners who work for their corporations. On the other hand, in unprofitable businesses, owners of unincorporated businesses may not be able to earn any Social Security credits, while corporate owners can have salary paid to them on which Social Security credits can be generated.

There have been proposals to treat certain S corporation owner-employees like partners for purposes of self-employment tax. To date, these proposals have failed, but could be revived in the future.

The additional Medicare surtaxes on earned income and net investment income (NII) are yet another factor to consider. The 0.9% surtax on earned income applies to taxable compensation (e.g., wages, bonuses, commissions, and taxable fringe benefits) of shareholders in S or C corporations; it applies to all net earnings from self-employment for sole proprietors, partners, and limited liability company members. The 3.8% NII tax applies to business income passed through from an entity in which the owner does not materially participate (i.e., one in which the owner is effectively a silent investor).

Restrictions on Accounting Periods and Accounting Methods

As you will see in Chapter 2, the tax law limits the use of fiscal years and the cash method of accounting for certain types of business organizations. For example, partnerships and S corporations in general are required to use a calendar year to report income.

Also, C corporations generally are required to use the accrual method of accounting to report income. There are exceptions to both of these rules. However, as you can see, accounting periods and accounting methods are important considerations in choosing your form of business organization.

Owner's Payment of Company Expenses

In small businesses it is common practice for owners to pay certain business expenses out of their own pockets—either as a matter of convenience or because the company is short of cash. The type of entity dictates where owners can deduct these payments.

A partner who is not reimbursed for paying partnership expenses can deduct his or her payments of these expenses as an above-the-line deduction (on a separate line on Schedule E of the partner's Form 1040, which should be marked as "UPE"), as long as the partnership agreement requires the partner to pay specified expenses personally and includes language that no reimbursement will be made.

A shareholder in a corporation (S or C) is an employee, so that unreimbursed expenses paid on behalf of the corporation are treated as unreimbursed employee business expenses reported on Form 2106 and deducted as a miscellaneous itemized deduction on Schedule A of the shareholder's Form 1040. Only total miscellaneous itemized deductions in excess of 2% of the shareholder's adjusted gross income are allowable; if the shareholder is subject to the alternative minimum tax, the benefit from this deduction is lost.

However, shareholders can avoid this deduction problem by having the corporation adopt an accountable plan to reimburse their out-of-pocket expenses.

An accountable plan allows the corporation to deduct the expenses, while the shareholders do not report income from the reimbursement (see Chapter 8).

Multistate Operations

Each state has its own way of taxing businesses subject to its jurisdiction. The way in which a business is organized for federal income tax purposes may not necessarily control for state income tax purposes. For example, some states do not recognize S corporation elections and tax such entities as regular corporations.

A company must file a return in each state in which it does business and pay income tax on the portion of its profits earned in that state. Income tax liability is based on having a *nexus*, or connection, to a state. This is not always an easy matter to settle. Where there is a physical presence—for example, a company maintains an office—then there is a clear nexus. But when a company merely makes sales to customers within a state or offers goods for sale from a website, there is generally no nexus. (However, a growing number of states are liberalizing the definition of nexus in order to get more businesses to pay state taxes so they can increase revenue; some states are moving toward "a significant economic presence," meaning taking advantage of a state's economy to produce income, as a basis for taxation.)

Assuming that a company does conduct multistate business, then its form of organization becomes important. Most multistate businesses are C corporations because only one corporate income tax return needs to be filed in each state where they do business. Doing business as a pass-through entity means that each owner would have to file a tax return in each state the company does business.

Audit Chances

Each year the IRS publishes statistics on the number and type of audits it conducts. The rates for the government's fiscal year 2013, the most recent year for which statistics are available, show a slight decrease in overall audit activity of business returns (with no change for partnerships and S corporations).

The chances of being audited vary with the type of business organization, the amount of income generated by the business, and the geographic location of the business. While the chance of an audit is not a significant reason for choosing one form of business organization over another, it is helpful to keep these statistics in mind.

Table 1.2 sheds some light on your chances of being audited, based on the most recently available statistics.

Not only does entity choice impact your chances of an audit (a sole proprietor with high gross receipts is nearly 10 times as likely to be audited as an S corporation, even one that has a single owner); your location also makes a difference.

TABLE 1.2 Percentage of Returns Audited

	FY 2012*	FY 2013*
Sole proprietors (Schedule C) (based on gross receipts)		
Under $25,000	1.2%	1.0%
$25,000 to under $100,000	2.4	2.3
$100,000 to under $200,000	3.6	3.0
$200,000 or more	3.4	2.7
Farming (Schedule F) (based on gross receipts)		
All farm returns	0.4	0.4
Partnerships	0.5	0.4
S corporations	0.5	0.4
C corporations (based on assets)		
Under $250,000	0.9	0.8
$250,000 to under $1 million	1.7	1.3
$1 million to under $5 million	2.1	1.4
$5 million to under $10 million	2.6	2.0

*Fiscal year from October 1 to September 30.
Source: IRS Data Book.

High audit zones include Los Angeles, California; Houston, Texas; and Brooklyn and Manhattan, New York.

Past audit rates are no guarantee of the likelihood of future IRS examinations. The $450 billion tax gap for 2006 (the most recent year for statistics), which represents the spread between what the government is owed and what it collects, has been blamed in part on those sole proprietors/independent contractors who underreport income or overstate deductions. In June 2008, an IRS official said publicly that the Small Business/Self-Employed (SB/SE) division would increase audits of sole proprietors with an adjusted gross income over $200,000 as well as partnerships and S corporations; audits of sole proprietors have slightly increased while audits of partnerships and S corporations have not. However, due to budgetary constraints, the number of audits are on the decline.

Filing Deadlines and Extensions

How your business is organized dictates when its tax return must be filed, the form to use, and the additional time that can be obtained for filing the return. For instance, calendar-year S corporations must file their income tax returns by March 15 and can obtain a 6-month filing extension to September 15. In contrast, calendar-year limited liability companies must file their income tax returns by April 15 but can only obtain a 5-month filing extension to September 15. The September 15 extended due date gives S corporations, limited liability companies, and partnerships time to provide Schedule K-1 to owners so they can file their personal returns by their extended due date of October 15.

TABLE 1.3 Filing Deadlines, Extensions, and Forms

Type of Entity	Return Due Date	Income Tax Return	Automatic Filing Extension	Form to Request Filing Extension
Sole proprietorship	April 15	Schedule C of Form 1040	October 15	Form 4868
Partnership/LLC	April 15	Form 1065	September 15	Form 7004
S corporation	March 15*	Form 1120S	September 15	Form 7004
C corporation	March 15*	Form 1120	September 15	Form 7004

*The scheduled due date is March 16, 2015, because March 15 falls on a Sunday.

Table 1.3 lists the filing deadlines for calendar-year businesses, the available automatic extensions, and the forms to use in filing the return or requesting a filing extension. Note that these dates are extended to the next business day when a deadline falls on a Saturday, Sunday, or legal holiday.

Exit Strategy

The tax treatment on the termination of a business is another factor to consider. While the choice of entity is made when the business starts out, you cannot ignore the tax consequences that this choice will have when the business terminates, is sold, or goes public. The liquidation of a C corporation usually produces a double tax—at the entity and owner levels. The liquidation of an S corporation produces a double tax *only* if there is a built-in gains tax issue—created by having appreciated assets in the business when an S election is made. However, the built-in gains tax problem disappears a certain number of years after the S election, so termination after that time does not result in a double tax.

If you plan to sell the business some time in the future, again your choice of entity may have an impact on the tax consequences of the sale. The sale of a sole proprietorship is viewed as a sale of the underlying assets of the business; some may produce ordinary income while others trigger capital gains. In contrast, the sale of qualified small business stock, which is stock in a C corporation, may result in tax-free treatment under certain conditions. Sales of business interests are discussed in Chapter 5.

If the termination of the business results in a loss, different tax rules come into play. Losses from partnerships and LLCs are treated as capital losses (explained in Chapter 5). A shareholder's losses from the termination of a C or S corporation may qualify as a Section 1244 loss—treated as an ordinary loss within limits (explained in Chapter 5).

If the business goes bankrupt, the entity type influences the type of bankruptcy filing to be used and whether the owners can escape personal liability for the debts of the business. Bankruptcy is discussed in Chapter 25.

Forms of Business Organization Compared

So far, you have learned about the various forms of business organization. Which form is right for your business? The answer is really a judgment call based on all the factors previously discussed. You can, of course, use different forms of business organization for your different business activities. For example, you may have a C corporation and personally own the building in which it operates—directly or through an LLC. Or you may be in partnership for your professional activities, while running a sideline business as an S corporation.

Table 1.4 summarizes 2 important considerations: how the type of business organization is formed and what effect the form of business organization has on where income and deductions are reported.

Changing Your Form of Business

Suppose you have a business that you have been running as a sole proprietorship. Now you want to make a change. Your new choice of business organization is dictated by the reason for the change. If you are taking in a partner, you would consider these alternatives: partnership, LLC, S corporation, or C corporation. If you are not taking in a partner, but want to obtain limited personal liability, you would consider an LLC (if your state permits a one-person LLC), an S corporation, or a C corporation. If you are looking to take advantage of certain fringe benefits, such as medical reimbursement plans, you would consider only a C corporation.

Whatever your reason, changing from a sole proprietorship to another type of business organization generally does not entail tax costs on making the changeover. You can set up a partnership or corporation, transfer your business assets to it, obtain an ownership interest in the new entity, and do all this on a tax-free basis. You may, however, have some tax consequences if you transfer your business liabilities to the new entity.

But what if you now have a corporation or partnership and want to change your form of business organization? This change may not be so simple. Suppose you have an S corporation or a C corporation. If you liquidate the corporation to change to another form of business organization, you may have to report gains on the liquidation. In fact, gains may have to be reported both by the business and by you as owner.

Partnerships can become corporations and elect S corporation status for their first taxable year without having any intervening short taxable year as a C corporation if corporate formation is made under a state law formless conversion statute or under the check-the-box regulations mentioned earlier in this chapter.

Before changing your form of business organization it is important to review your particular situation with a tax professional. In making any change in business, consider the legal and accounting costs involved.

TABLE 1.4 Comparison of Forms of Business Organization

Type of Business	How It Is Formed	Where Income and Deductions Are Reported
Sole proprietorship	No special requirements	On owner's Schedule C or C-EZ (Schedule F for farming)
Partnership	No special requirements	Some items taken into account in figuring trade or business income directly on Form 1065 (allocable amount claimed on partner's Schedule E); separately stated items are passed through to partners and claimed in various places on partner's tax return.
Limited special partnership	Some items taken into account in figuring partnership under state law	Trade or business income directly on Form 1065 (allocable amount claimed on partner's Schedule E); separately stated items passed through to partners and claimed in various places on partner's tax return
Limited liability company	Organized as such under state law	Some items taken into account in figuring trade or business income directly on Form 1065 (allocable amount claimed on member's Schedule E); separately stated items passed through to members and claimed in various places on member's tax return
Limited liability partnership	Organized as such under state law	Some items taken into account in figuring trade or business income directly on Form 1065 (allocable amount claimed on member's Schedule E); separately stated items passed through to members and claimed in various places on member's tax return
S corporation	Formed as corporation under state law; tax status elected by filing with IRS	Some items taken into account in figuring trade or business income directly on Form 1120S (allocable amount claimed on shareholder's Schedule E); separately stated items passed through to shareholders and claimed in various places on shareholder's tax return
C corporation	Formed under state law	Claimed by corporation in figuring its trade or business income on Form 1120
Employee	No ownership interest	Income reported as wages; deductions as itemized deductions on Schedule A (certain expenses first figured on Form 2106)
Independent contractor	No ownership interest in a business	Claimed on individual's Schedule C

Tax Identification Number

For individuals on personal returns, the federal tax identification number is the taxpayer's Social Security number. For businesses, the federal tax identification number is the employer identification number (EIN). The EIN is a 9-digit number assigned to each business. Usually, the federal EIN is used for state income tax purposes. Depending on the state, there may be a separate state tax identification number.

If you are just starting your business and do not have an EIN, you can obtain one instantaneously online using an interview-style application at www.irs.gov (search "EIN online") or by filing Form SS-4, *Application for Employer Identification Number*, with the IRS service center in the area in which your business is located. Application by mail takes several weeks. An SS-4 can be obtained from the IRS web site at www.irs.gov or by calling a special business phone number (1-800-829-4933) or the special Tele-TIN phone number. The number for your service center is listed in the instructions to Form SS-4. If you call for a number, it is assigned immediately, after which you must send or fax a signed SS-4 within 24 hours.

If you change your business entity (e.g., from a sole proprietorship to an S corporation), you usually need to obtain a new EIN. You can determine whether you need a new EIN at www.irs.gov (search "do you need a new EIN?").

SPECIAL RULES FOR SOLE PROPRIETORS

Because sole proprietors report their business income and expenses on their personal returns, they may not be required to use an EIN. Instead, they simply use their Social Security number for federal income tax reporting.

A sole proprietor *must* use an EIN if the business has any employees or maintains a qualified retirement plan. A sole proprietor *may* need an EIN to open a business bank account (it depends on the institution). An EIN can also be used in place of a Social Security number by an independent contractor for purposes of Form 1099-MISC reporting (a consideration today with concerns about identity theft). A sole proprietor *should* use an EIN as a way in which to build a business credit profile in order to qualify for credit without relying entirely on the owner's credit history and personal guarantee.

A single-member limited liability company, which is a disregarded entity taxed as a sole proprietorship (unless an election is made to be taxed as a corporation) for income tax purposes, must obtain an employer identification number if it has *any* employees. This is because the LLC, and not the member, is liable for employment taxes.

Tax Year and Accounting Methods

Alert

At the time this book was printed, Congress had not extended numerous breaks for 2014 that had expired at the end of 2013. Check the online supplement in February 2015 at www.jklasser.com or www.barbaraweltman.com to see whether these breaks apply for 2014 returns.

Once you select your form of business organization, you must decide how you will report your income. There are 2 key decisions you must make: What is the time frame for calculating your income and deductions (called the tax year or accounting period), and what are the rules that you will follow to calculate your income and deductions (called the accounting method). In some cases, as you will see, your form of business organization restricts you to an accounting period or accounting method. In other cases, however, you can choose which method is best for your business. Depending upon circumstances, you may want to need to change your accounting method. Sometimes making a change is easy, with automatic procedures; other situations require IRS consent, as you will see later in this chapter.

For a further discussion on tax years and accounting methods, see IRS Publication 538, *Accounting Periods and Methods*. Inventory rules are discussed in Chapter 4.

Accounting Periods

You account for your income and expenses on an annual basis. This period is called your *tax year*. There are 2 methods for fixing your tax year: *calendar* and *fiscal*. Under the calendar year, you use a 12-month period ending on December 31. Under the fiscal year, you use a 12-month period ending at the end of any month other than December.

You select your tax year when you first begin your business. You do not need IRS approval for your tax year; you simply use it to govern when you must file your first return. You use the same tax year thereafter. If you commence your business in the middle of the tax year you have selected, your first tax year will be short.

Example

You start your S corporation in May 2014. It uses a calendar year to report expenses. The corporation will have a short tax year ending December 31, 2014, for its first tax year. Then, for 2015, it will have a full 12-month tax year.

A short tax year may occur in the first or final year of business. For example, if you closed the doors to your business on May 1, 2014, even though you operated on a calendar year. Your final tax year is a short year because it is only 4 months. You do not have to apportion or prorate deductions for this short year because the business was not in existence for the entire year. Different rules apply if a short year results from a change in accounting period.

Seasonal Businesses

Seasonal businesses should use special care when selecting their tax year. It is often advisable to select a tax year that will include both the period in which most of the expenses as well as most of the income is realized. For example, if a business expects to sell its products primarily in the spring and incurs most of its expenses for these sales in the preceding fall, it may be best to select a fiscal year ending just after the selling season, such as July or August. In this way, the expenses and the income that are related to each other will be reported on the same return.

Limits on Use of the Fiscal Year

C corporations, other than personal service corporations (PSCs), can choose a calendar year or a fiscal year, whichever is more advantageous. Other entities, however, cannot simply choose a fiscal year, even though it offers tax advantages to its owners. In general, partnerships, limited liability companies (LLCs), S corporations, and PSCs must use a **required year**. Since individuals typically use a calendar year, their partnership or LLC must also use a calendar year.

Required year   For S corporations, this is a calendar year; for partnerships and LLCs, it is the same year as the tax year of the entity's owners. When owners have different tax years, special rules determine which owner's tax year governs.

Business Purpose for Fiscal Year

The entity can use a fiscal year even though its owners use a calendar year if it can be established to the satisfaction of the IRS that there is a business purpose for the fiscal year. The fact that the use of a fiscal year defers income for its owners is not considered to be a valid **business purpose** warranting a tax year other than a required tax year.

Business purpose   This is shown if the fiscal year is the natural business year of the entity. For a PSC, for example, a fiscal year is treated as a natural business year if 25% or more of its gross receipts for the 12-month period ending on the last month of the requested tax year are received within the last 2 months of that year.

Certain companies may use a fiscal year because it is the natural year of the type of business they are in (see examples in Table 2.1). The end of the fiscal year coincides with the close of the business cycle. They do not have to use this fiscal year, however, and many such businesses use a calendar year.

Section 444 Election for Fiscal Year

If an entity wants to use a fiscal year that is not its natural business year, it can do so by making a Section 444 election. The only acceptable tax years under this election are those ending September 30, October 31, and November 30. Use of these fiscal years means that at most there can be a 3-month deferral for the owners. The election is made by filing Form 8716, *Election to Have a Tax Year Other Than a Required Tax Year*, by the earlier of the due date of the return

TABLE 2.1 Examples of Fiscal Years of Certain Businesses

Year-End	Business Type
January	Auto accessories (wholesale)
	Department stores (retail)
	Hardware stores (retail)
February	Building contractors (services)
	Plumbing supplies (wholesale)
March	Warehouses (services)
June	Appliances (retail)
	Books (retail)
	Building supplies (manufacturing)
	Furniture (retail)
	Groceries (wholesale)
	Office equipment (manufacturing)
	Paper (wholesale)
	Ski shops (retail)
September	Electrical equipment (manufacturing)
	Garages (services)
	Real estate agencies (services)

for the new tax year (without regard to extensions) or the fifteenth day of the sixth month of the tax year for which the election will be effective.

If the election is made, then partnerships, LLCs, and S corporations must make certain *required payments*. These essentially are designed to give to the federal government the tax that has been deferred by reason of the special tax year. This payment can be thought of as simply a deposit, since it does not serve to increase the tax that is otherwise due. The payment is calculated using the highest individual income tax rate plus one percentage point. Therefore, the rate for 2014 is 40.6%. The required payment is made by filing Form 8752, *Required Payment or Refund Under Section 7519 for Partnerships and S Corporations*, by May 15 of the calendar year following the calendar year in which the election begins. For example, if the election begins on October 1, 2014, the required payment must be made no later than May 15, 2015. In view of the high required payment and the complications involved in making and maintaining a Section 444 election, most of these entities use a calendar year.

Personal service corporations that make a Section 444 election need not make a required payment. Instead, these corporations must make *required distributions*. They must distribute certain amounts of compensation to employee-owners by December 31 of each year for which an election is in effect. The reason for the required elections is to ensure that amounts will be taxed to owner-employees as soon as possible and will not be deferred simply because the corporation uses a fiscal year. Required distributions are figured on Part I of Schedule H of Form 1120, *Section 280H Limitations for a Personal Service Corporation*.

Pass-Through Business on a Fiscal Year

Owners in pass-through entities who are on a calendar year report their share of the business's income, deductions, gains, losses, and credits from the entity's tax year that ends in the owners' tax year.

Example

You are in a partnership that uses a fiscal year ending October 31. The partnership's items for its 2014 fiscal year ending October 31, 2014, are reported on your 2014 return. The portion of the partnership's income and deductions from the period November 1, 2014, through December 31, 2014, are part of its 2015 fiscal year, which will be reported on your 2015 return.

Short Tax Years

You may have a year that is less than a full tax year. This results most commonly in the year you start or end a business.

Example

You start an LLC on August 1, 2014, and use a calendar year to report your income and expenses. The LLC's first tax year is a short tax year, running from August 1, 2014, through December 31, 2015.

A short tax year can also result when a C corporation that had been reporting on a fiscal year elects S status and adopts a calendar year. The tax year of the C corporation ends on the date the S election becomes effective.

Alternatively, if an S election is terminated within the year or there is a substantial change in ownership (50% or more), then the corporation can have 2 short tax years in this case.

Example

A C corporation with a fiscal year ending on June 30 elects to become an S corporation and adopts a calendar year. The election is effective on January 1, 2015. The C corporation has a short tax year starting on July 1, 2014, and ending on December 31, 2014.

Example

An S corporation reporting on a calendar year has its election involuntarily terminated on July 31, 2014, when another corporation becomes a shareholder.

The corporation has 2 short tax years: the S tax year running from January 1, 2014, through July 31, 2014, and the C tax year running from August 1, 2014, through December 31, 2014.

The IRS says that an unincorporated entity converting to a corporation under a state law formless conversion statute or check-the-box rules and which is eligible for S corporation status as of the first day of its first year does *not* have any short tax year for the momentary period it was a C corporation.

Change in Tax Year

If your business has been using a particular tax year and you want to change to a different one, you must obtain IRS approval to do so. Depending on the reason for the change, approval may be automatic or discretionary. You can request a change in your tax year by filing Form 1128, *Application to Adopt, Change, or Retain a Tax Year*. There is a user fee (an amount set by the IRS) for this request.

Accounting Methods

An accounting method is a set of rules used to determine when and how to record income and expenses on your books and for tax-reporting purposes.

There are 2 principal methods of accounting: *cash basis* and *accrual basis*. Use of a particular method determines when a deduction can be claimed. However, restrictions apply for both methods of accounting. Also, the form of business organization may preclude the use of the cash method of accounting even though it may be the method of choice.

Cash Method

Cash method is the simpler accounting method. Income is reported when it is actually or constructively received, and a deduction can be claimed when and to the extent the expense is paid.

Example

You are a consultant. You perform services and send a bill. You report the income when you receive payment. Similarly, you buy business cards and stationery. You can deduct this expense when you pay for the supplies.

Actual receipt is the time when income is in your hands. Constructive receipt occurs when you have control over the income and can reduce it to an actual receipt.

You earn a fee for services rendered but ask your customer not to pay you immediately. Since the customer was ready and able to pay immediately, you are in constructive receipt of the fee at that time.

Payments received by check are income when the check is received even though you may deposit it some time later. However, if the check bounces, then no income results at the time the check was received. You only report income when the check is later honored.

Sole proprietors and independent contractors on the cash method (and reporting on a calendar year basis) can run into a problem with respect to Form 1099-MISC for year-end payments. A company may send a payment late in December 2014 and include it on Form 1099-MISC for 2014; the contractor may receive the payment in January 2015. While this income is not taxable to the contractor until 2015, he or she must report the income on the return as it is reported by the company (because of IRS computer matching of information returns with income reported by recipients on their returns) and then make a subtraction to eliminate this amount from income. The payment is included in income in 2015 even though it is not reflected on a Form 1099-MISC for 2015.

Expenses usually are fully deductible when paid. Payments by a general credit card, such as MasterCard or Visa, are deductible in the year they are charged, even if you pay the credit card bill in the following year. Payments using "pay by phone" with your bank are deductible when the bank sends the payment (check your bank account statement). There has been no IRS guidance on deductibility when using PayPal, Bitcoin, or other electronic payment methods, but it appears that payments are deductible when you instruct PayPal or other provider to make them because that is when the funds are taken from your account.

You may not be able to deduct all expenses when they are paid because there are some limitations that come into play. Generally, you cannot deduct advance payments (so-called prepaid expenses) that relate to periods beyond the current tax year.

You take out a 3-year subscription to a business journal and pay the 3-year subscription price this year. You can deduct only $\frac{1}{3}$ of the payment—the amount that relates to the current year. You can deduct another $\frac{1}{3}$ next year, and the final $\frac{1}{3}$ the following year.

Prepayments may occur for a number of expenses. You may prepay rent, insurance premiums, or subscriptions. Generally, prepayments that do not extend beyond 12 months are currently deductible.

In the case of interest, no deduction is allowed for prepayments by businesses. For example, if you are required to pay points to obtain a mortgage on your office building, these points are considered to be prepaid interest. You must deduct the points ratably over the term of the loan.

Example

If the mortgage on the office building runs for 30 years (or 360 months) and you pay the points on July 1, you can deduct 6/360 of the points in the first year. In each succeeding year you would deduct 12/360 of the points. In the final year, you would again deduct 6/360.

Deposits may be called advances. If they are refundable, then they cannot be deducted when paid. If they are nonrefundable, they can be deducted when made.

If you pay off the mortgage before the end of the term (you sell the property or refinance the loan), you can then write off any points you still have not deducted.

RESTRICTIONS ON THE USE OF THE CASH METHOD

You cannot use the cash method of accounting if you maintain inventory unless you qualify for a small business exception. If you are barred from using the cash method, you must use the accrual method or another method of accounting.

Corporate Exceptions. While farming corporations and farming partnerships in which a corporation is a partner usually must use the accrual method, the business is exempt from this rule if it is an S corporation, a family farming corporation with annual **gross receipts** not exceeding $25 million, and any corporation (other than a family farming corporation) with gross receipts not exceeding $1 million. A farming business includes any business that operates a nursery or sod farm or that raises or harvests trees bearing fruit, nuts, or other crops and ornamental trees.

Gross receipts All the income taken in by the business without offsets for expenses. For example, if a consultant receives fees of $25,000 for the year and has expenses of $10,000, gross receipts are $25,000.

PSC Exception. A **qualified personal service corporation** (PSC) can use the cash method of accounting.

> ***Qualified personal service corporation*** A corporation (other than an S corporation) with a substantial number of activities involving the performance of personal services in the fields of medicine, law, accounting, architecture, actuarial sciences, performing arts, or consulting by someone who owns stock in the corporation (or who is retired or the executor of the estate of a deceased former employee).

Small Business Exception. Corporations other than S corporations and partnerships that have a corporation (other than an S corporation) as a partner can use the cash method of accounting if they are considered to be *small businesses* even if they do not qualify for the inventory-based exception below. A small business for this purpose is one that has average annual gross receipts of $5 million or less in at least one of 3 prior taxable years. In view of the gross receipt rule, you can see that a business may be able to use the cash method for one year but be precluded from using it in the following year. As a practical matter, if a business gets big enough to approach $5 million in gross receipts, it may have outgrown the cash method and may prefer to change permanently to the accrual method to avoid changes dependent upon gross receipts.

Small Inventory-Based Business Exception. Even though you maintain inventory, you are permitted to use the cash method if your average annual gross receipts for the 3 prior years do not exceed $10 million and you are not otherwise prohibited from using the cash method (see Small Business Exception above). More specifically, you can use the cash method if your average annual gross receipts for the 3 tax years (or the years in which you are in business if less than 3 years) do not exceed $10 million. In effect, in order to qualify for the cash method under this exception in 2014, your average annual gross receipts must not exceed $10 million in each 3-year period starting in 1998 (or when the corporation was formed, if later).

You can use the cash method of accounting even though you use the accrual method for financial accounting purposes (for example, on profit and loss statements). However, you do not qualify for this exception if your principal business activity is retailing, wholesaling, manufacturing (other than custom manufacturing), mining, publishing, or sound recording. (Principal business activity is based on the largest percentage of your gross receipts using the North American Industry Classification System [NAICS], published by the U.S. Department of Commerce and which can be found in instructions to Schedule C of Form 1040.) NAICS codes are also used for government contracting purposes, so be sure that you use the correct code if you want to work with the government. You can get help determining which NAICS code is most appropriate for your business by using an online tool at www.naics.com/search.htm.

Alternatively, you can contact the U.S. Census Bureau for help by calling 888-75NAICS.

In addition to the inventory limitation, certain types of business organizations generally cannot use the cash method of accounting. These include:

- Corporations other than S corporations
- Partnerships that have a corporation (other than an S corporation) as a partner
- Tax shelters

However, there are exceptions under which some of these businesses can still use the cash method of accounting.

If you are a small inventory-based business that has been using the accrual method but is qualified to change to the cash method, you can make the change under an automatic change of accounting rule. For more information about qualifying for the cash method and changing to it, see Revenue Procedure 2002-28.

Accrual Method of Accounting

Under the accrual method, you report income when it is earned rather than when it is received, and you deduct expenses when they are incurred rather than when they are paid. There are 2 tests to determine whether there is a fixed right to receive income so that it must be accrued and whether an expense is treated as having been incurred for tax purposes.

ALL EVENTS TEST

All events that fix the income and set the liability must have occurred. Also, you must be able to determine the amount of the income or expense with reasonable accuracy.

ECONOMIC PERFORMANCE TEST

In order to report income or deduct an expense, economic performance must occur. In most cases, this is rather obvious. If you provide goods and services, economic performance occurs when you provide the goods or services. By the same token if goods or services are provided to you, economic performance occurs when the goods or services are provided to you. Thus, for example, if you buy office supplies, economic performance occurs when the purchase is made and the bill is tendered. You can accrue the expense at that date even though you do not pay the bill until a later date.

If you sell *gift cards* to customers, do not report the income until the cards are redeemed. For example, if you sell a gift card to a customer in December 2014 and the customer gives the card to a friend who redeems it in January 2015, under the all events test the income from the sale of the gift card is not fixed until 2015. If you give gift cards to customers in exchange for returns of merchandise, you can now treat the card as a payment of a cash refund and a sale of a gift card, allowing you to defer the income to be received through the gift cards. This is treated as a change in accounting method for which automatic consent is provided, but you must file for a change in accounting method as explained later in this chapter.

There is an exception to the economic performance test for certain *recurring items* (items that are repeated on a regular basis). A deduction for these items can be accrued even though economic performance has not occurred.

There is a special rule for *real estate taxes*. An election can be made to ratably accrue real property taxes that are related to a definite period of time over that period of time.

Example

You own a building in which you conduct your business. Real property taxes for the property tax year ending June 30 are $12,000. You are an accrual method taxpayer on a calendar year of reporting. You can elect to ratably accrue the taxes. If the election is made, you deduct $6,000 in the current year, the amount of taxes that relates to the period for your tax year. The balance of the taxes is deductible next year.

Any real property taxes that would normally be deductible for the tax year that apply to periods prior to your election are deductible in the year of the election.

The election must be made for the first tax year in which real property taxes are incurred. It is made simply by attaching a statement to the return for that tax year. The return must be filed on time (including any extensions) in order for the election to be valid. Include on the statement the businesses to which the election applies and their methods of accounting, the period of time to which the taxes relate, and the computation of the real property tax deduction for the first year of the election.

Once you make this election, it continues indefinitely unless you revoke it. To revoke your election you must obtain the consent of the IRS. However, there is an automatic procedure rule that allows you to elect or revoke an election by attaching a statement to your return. Under this method, you may assume you have IRS consent; you do not have to request it and wait for a reply.

If you have been accruing real property taxes under the general rule for accrual, you must file for a change in accounting method, which is explained later in this chapter.

You can make an election to ratably accrue real property taxes over the period to which they relate for each separate business you own.

TWO-AND-A-HALF-MONTH RULE

If you pay salary, interest, or other expenses to an unrelated party, you can accrue the expense only if it is paid within 2½ months after the close of the tax year.

Example

You declare a year-end bonus for your manager (who is not related to you under the rules discussed). You are on the calendar year. You can accrue the bonus in the year in which you declare it if you actually pay it no later than March 15.

Related Parties. If expenses are paid to related parties, a special rule applies. This rule, in effect, puts an accrual taxpayer on the cash basis so that payments are not deductible until actually paid. Related parties include:

- Members of an immediate family (spouses, children, brothers and sisters of whole or half blood, grandchildren, and grandparents).

- An individual and a C corporation (other than a PSC) in which he or she owns more than 50% of the corporation's outstanding stock (based on the stock's value). Stock ownership may be *direct* or *indirect*. Direct means that the individual holds the stock in his or her name. Indirect ownership means the stock is owned by a member of the individual's immediate family (listed above) or by a corporation, partnership, estate, or trust owned in full or in part by the individual. If the individual has only a partial ownership interest, that same proportion of stock owned by the entity is treated as owned by the individual. For example, if an individual owns 75% of stock in Corporation X and X owns 100% of the stock in Corporation Y, the individual is treated as owning 75% of the stock in Y for purposes of this accrual method limitation.

- An individual and an S corporation in which he or she owns any of the corporation's outstanding stock.

- A PSC and any owner-employee (regardless of the amount of stock ownership). Thus, if an individual owns 10% of the stock in Corporation X (a PSC), and X owns 100% of the stock in Y, the individual is treated as owning 100% of the stock in Y.

- Other categories of related parties (e.g., 2 corporations that are members of a controlled group—they have certain owners in common).

If you fall under this related party rule, you cannot deduct the expense until payment is actually made and the related party includes the payment in his or her income.

Example

You have an accrual business in which your child is an employee. Your business is on the calendar year. On December 31, 2014, you declare a year-end bonus of $5,000 for your child. You may not accrue the bonus until you pay the $5,000 to your child and your child includes the payment as income. Therefore, if you write a check on January 15, 2015, for the bonus and your child cashes it that day, you can accrue the expense in 2015.

Accounting Methods for Long-Term Contracts

For businesses involved in building, constructing, installing, or manufacturing property where the work cannot be completed within 1 year, special accounting rules exist. These rules do not affect the amount of income or expenses to be reported—they merely dictate the timing of the income or expenses.

Generally, you must use the percentage-of-completion method to report income and expenses from these long-term contracts. Under this method, you must estimate your income and expenses while the contract is in progress and report a percentage of these items relative to the portion of the contract that has been completed. However, income and expenses are not fully accounted for until the earlier of either the completion of the job and acceptance of the work or the buyer starts to use the item and 5% or less of the total contract costs remain to be completed.

You may also have to use a *look-back method* (discussed later) to compensate for any inaccuracies in your estimates for income or expenses.

EXCEPTIONS FROM THE PERCENTAGE-OF-COMPLETION METHOD

Under this method you account for your income and expenses when, as the name implies, the contract has been completed. You can account for income and expenses using the completed-contract method if:

1. The contracts are small construction contracts that will be completed within 2 years and average annual gross receipts for the 3 preceding years from the start of the contract do not exceed $10 million.
2. The contracts are for the construction of homes containing 4 or fewer dwelling units. Eighty percent or more of the estimated total costs of the contract must be for these homes plus any related land improvements.
3. The contracts are for the construction of residential apartments (80% or more of the total contract costs are attributable to these buildings).

You can account for your income and expenses using the completed-contract method if you meet either of the first 2 exceptions. If you meet the third exception, you account for your income and expenses under a special method called the percentage-of-completion/capitalized-cost method. Under this hybrid method, 70% of income and expenses are reported under the percentage-of-completion method while 30% of income and expenses are reported under the completed-contract method.

Manufacturing contracts are treated as long-term contracts only if they involve the manufacture of unique items that cannot be completed within a 12-month period. Thus, income and expenses relating to most manufacturing contracts are reported under the company's usual method of accounting.

LOOK-BACK METHOD

At the end of the contract period, you must look back to each year that the contract was in progress and recalculate the income using the correct contract price and costs. These revised numbers determine whether the business owes additional interest on the taxes it should have paid or it is entitled to receive interest on the taxes already paid. Interest for this purpose is hypothetical interest on the overpayment and underpayment for each of the years in issue. This interest is calculated on Form 8697, *Interest Computation Under the Look-Back Method for Completed Long-Term Contracts*.

Small business owners, however, may escape the application of the look-back method. This method is *not* required if the contract is completed within a 2-year period and the contract's gross sale price does not exceed the lesser of $1 million or 1% of the business' average annual gross receipts for the 3 years preceding the tax year in which the contract is completed.

Even if the exception for small businesses cannot be met, it is still possible to avoid the look-back method and its complications. You can elect not to use the look-back method if the estimated income and expenses are within 10% of the actual income and expenses. Once this election is made, it applies to all future contracts. In order to make the election, you must make the recalculations of the actual income and expenses for the prior years to see if the 10% threshold has been satisfied.

Other Accounting Methods

The cash and accrual methods of accounting are the most commonly used methods. There are, however, other accounting methods.

INSTALLMENT METHOD ACCOUNTING

If you sell property and receive payments over time, you generally can account for your gain on the *installment method*. More specifically, the installment method applies if one or more payments are received after the year of the sale. *Gain* is reported when payments are received. The capital gain rate applicable to the gain on the installment received in the current year is the rate to which the taxpayer is now subject. For example, say a sole proprietor makes an installment sale in 2010. In 2014, the sole proprietor is considered to be a

high-income taxpayer whose capital gain rate is 20%. This is the rate imposed on the gain from the installment received in 2014, even though this taxpayer had a 15% capital gain tax rate in the year of the sale. This method can be used by taxpayers who report other income and expenses on the cash or accrual method.

Example

You sell business property and figure your gain to be $10,000. Under the terms of sale you receive $5,000 in 2014, the year of sale, and $5,000 in 2015. You report one-half of your gain, or $5,000, in 2014 and the other half of your gain, $5,000, in 2015.

However, if the sale involves depreciable property, the recapture rules trigger the immediate reporting of this portion of the gain—without regard to payments received. Recapture rules are discussed in Chapter 6.

The installment method applies only to gains on certain sales; it generally cannot be used for inventory sales even though payment is received over time. The installment method does not apply to losses. It cannot be used by dealers in personal property or for real estate held for resale to customers.

You can elect *not* to report on the installment basis and instead report all of the gain in the year of sale. The election is made simply by reporting all of the gain on the appropriate tax form or schedule. Once made, however, this election generally is irrevocable. The election out of installment reporting may make sense, for example, if an owner is subject to the 15% capital gains rate in the year of the installment sale but expects to be a high-income taxpayer subject to the 20% capital gains rate in one or more of the years in which installment payments will be received.

MARK-TO-MARKET ACCOUNTING

Traders in securities (often referred to as "day traders") can use a special accounting method that enables them to report paper transactions rather than waiting for actualized gains and losses, and losses no longer are limited to the extent of capital gains and up to $3,000 of ordinary income. Under mark-to-market accounting, gains and losses are reported on Form 4797 (rather than on Schedule D). These include completed trades throughout the year as well as paper gains and losses in securities held at the end of the year (these are treated as if they had been sold on December 31).

A trader is someone who seeks to profit from daily market swings rather than long-term appreciation, interest, or dividends. The trader's activities must be substantial and carried on with continuity and regularity.

Make the mark-to-market election by filing a statement attached to your return for the prior year, stating you are making the election under Code Sec.

475(f) and the year for which it is effective. For example, if you want the election to start in 2015, you must attach this statement to your 2014 income tax return. Those who are not required to file a return for 2014 should place such statement in their books and records no later than March 16, 2015, and then attach a copy to the 2015 return. The election is treated as a change in accounting method (see filing Form 3115 earlier in this chapter) and is irrevocable without obtaining IRS permission to revoke it.

OTHER ACCOUNTING METHODS

These include, for example: Special Accounting for Multi-Year Service Warranty Contracts and Special Rules for Farmers.

Accounting for Discounts

DISCOUNTS YOU RECEIVE

When vendors or other sellers give you cash discounts for prompt payment, there are 2 ways to account for this discount, regardless of your method of accounting. They are:

- Deduct the discount as a purchase in figuring the cost of goods sold.
- Credit the discount to a special discount income account you set up in your records. Any balance in this account at the end of the year is reported as other income on your return.

Trade discounts are not reflected on your books or tax returns. These discounts are reductions from list price or catalog prices for merchandise you purchase. Once you make the choice, you must continue to use it in future years to account for all cash discounts.

DISCOUNTS YOU GIVE

When you reduce the price of your goods and services, you cannot deduct the price reduction. Your gross receipts are reduced accordingly, so you simply report less income.

Uniform Capitalization Rules

Regardless of your method of accounting, special tax rules limit your ability to claim a current deduction for certain expenses. These are called the *uniform capitalization rules*, referred to as the UNICAP rules for short. The uniform capitalization rules are a form of accounting method that operates in coordination with the accrual method, but overrides it. In essence, these rules require you to add to the cost of property certain expenses—instead of currently deducting them. The cost of these expenses, in effect, are recovered through depreciation or amortization, or as part of the costs of goods sold when you use, sell, or otherwise dispose of the property. The uniform capitalization rules are complex. Important things to recognize are whether you may be subject to them and that expenses discussed throughout this book may not be currently deductible because of the application of the uniform capitalization rules.

Capitalization Required

Unless one of the exceptions is applicable, you must use the uniform capitalization rules and add certain expenses to the basis of property if you:

- Produce real property or tangible personal property for use in your business or for sale to customers (producers), or
- Acquire property for resale (resellers).

EXCEPTIONS TO THE UNICAP RULES

There are many exceptions to the uniform capitalization rules. Small businesses may be able to escape application of the uniform capitalization rules by relying on one of these exceptions.

- You do not have to capitalize costs if the property you produce is for your personal or nonbusiness use.
- You do not have to capitalize costs if you acquire property for resale and your average annual gross receipts do not exceed $10 million (small reseller exception). If a reseller has been in business for less than 3 years, application of the exception is determined by annual gross receipts for the shorter period.
- Creative expenses incurred by freelance authors, photographers, and artists are not subject to the uniform capitalization rules. According to the IRS, this exception does not apply to a musician's demo tape or other sound recording.
- There is a de minimis exception for certain producers who use a simplified method and whose total indirect costs are $200,000 or less.
- There are other exceptions not detailed here, for certain farming businesses and other types of businesses.

CAPITALIZED COSTS

If you are subject to the uniform capitalization rules, you capitalize all direct costs of your production or resale activities. Direct costs for producers include direct material costs and direct labor costs. Direct costs for resellers mean acquisition costs.

You also capitalize a portion of indirect costs. Indirect costs for producers and resellers include costs of purchasing, handling, and storage, as well as taxes, interest, rent, insurance, utilities, repairs, engineering and design costs, quality control, tools and equipment, licensing, and more.

Change in Accounting Method

If you want to change your method of accounting (for example, from the accrual method to the cash method), you must file Form 3115, *Application for Change in Accounting Method*, during the year for which the change is to be effective. (Instructions on how and where to file this form are included in instructions to the form.) Some changes are automatic—just by filing you are ensured that your change is recognized; other changes require the consent of the IRS.

Periodically the IRS modifies its list of automatic changes (for example, see Revenue Procedure 2012–19, modified by Revenue Procedure 2014–16). These include changing to a required accounting method from an incorrect one, switching to the cash method by an eligible small inventory-based business, implementing depreciation changes pursuant to a cost segregation study, changing the treatment of repair and maintenance costs from capitalized to currently deductible, deducting the cost of "smallwares" (such as dishes and glassware) in the year they are first put to use by restaurants, and applying the de minimis rule for certain repairs.

CHAPTER 3

Recordkeeping for Business Income and Deductions

Alert

At the time this book was printed, Congress had not extended numerous breaks for 2014 that had expired at the end of 2013. Check the online supplement in February 2015 at www.jklasser.com or www.barbaraweltman.com to see whether these breaks apply for 2014 returns.

Recordkeeping is a tiresome and time-consuming task. Still, you have little choice but to do it. Records show whether your business is producing a profit or a loss. The information in your records can enable you to prepare financial statements, such as profit and loss statements and balance sheets, which may be required by your lenders or investors. From a tax perspective, you need records to determine your gain or loss when you sell property. And as a general rule, you must be able to back up your deductions with certain clear proof, such as receipts, canceled checks, and other documentation. If you do not have this proof, your deductions may be disallowed or force you to litigate in order to win your position (a costly and time-consuming activity). Certain deductions require specific evidence. Other deductions are based on more general means of proof.

For further information on recordkeeping, see IRS Publication 334, *Tax Guide for Small Business (for Individuals Who File Schedule C or C-EZ)*; IRS Publication 552, *Recordkeeping for Individuals*; and IRS Publication 583, *Starting a Business and Keeping Records*.

General Recordkeeping

The tax law does not require you to maintain books and records in any particular way. It does, however, require you to keep an accurate and complete set of books for each business you operate. Statistics show that this can be an awesome task averaging 10 hours each week (that amounts to about 520 hours each year) for small business owners.

Set up your books when you begin your business. Your books are based on your choice of tax year and accounting method, as explained in Chapter 2. In the past, when you kept your books in paper ledgers, you needed to choose a bookkeeping method—single-entry or double-entry. If you are a service business, single-entry bookkeeping may be sufficient. Today, with software and online accounting solutions, you don't need to know about bookkeeping methods; you merely input income and expense items, and the program does the rest.

Your books should be set up with various accounts in order to group your income and expenses. The broad categories of accounts include income, expenses, assets, liabilities, and equity (or net worth). Within these accounts you can keep various subaccounts. For example, in an account called Expenses you can have subaccounts for advertising, bad debts, interest expense, taxes, rents, repairs, and more. In fact, your subaccounts should reflect the various income and deduction topics discussed throughout this book.

Technology for Recordkeeping

More and more businesses are using computers, tablets, and smartphones to maintain books and records rather than having bookkeepers make handwritten entries. Computer-generated records save time—an important commodity for the small business owner—and generally are more accurate than handwritten entries.

The IRS accepts computer-generated records if they are legible and provide all the necessary information. You are required to keep a description of the computerized portion of your accounting system. You must keep this documentation as long as you keep the records themselves. Your document should show:

- Applications being performed
- Procedures used in each application

- Controls used to ensure accurate and reliable processing
- Controls used to prevent the unauthorized addition, alteration, or deletion of retained records

Use recordkeeping software that facilitates recordkeeping both for tax purposes as well as for financial matters. Using software and cloud-based versions of programs such as Intuit's Quickbooks Online, Online Simple Start, Quickbooks Pro; Sage Peachtree Accounting; Simply Accounting; Bookkeeper FreshBooks; Kashoo; Outright; Xero; or AccountEdge enables you to forward data to your tax professional as well as transfer information into tax return preparation programs at tax time, saving you both time and money. As your business grows (and the number of users for your accounting solution exceeds your current licensing limit), you likely will move to more a sophisticated accounting product that can accommodate your needs.

An increasing number of accounting products are now accompanied by apps for tablets and smartphones to enable you to record information on the fly. For example, if you are a QuickBooks user, you can view your company's data, such as receivables and bank account balance, on your iPhone with QuickBooks Online app. FreshBooks, a cloud-based accounting solution, offers MiniBooks app for the iPhone; it enables you to send an invoice from your mobile device.

Your books alone do not entitle you to deductions; you need supporting evidence. This evidence includes sales slips, invoices, canceled checks, paid bills, time sheets for part-time help, duplicate deposit slips, brokerage statements on stock purchases and sales, and other documents that help to explain a particular entry in your books. Certain deductions—travel and entertainment expenses and charitable contributions—require specific types of supporting evidence, as explained later in this chapter. The IRS considers your own memoranda or sketchy records to be inadequate when claiming deductions. Keep these records and documentation in an orderly fashion. Use files or other storage facilities to retain receipts and other evidence.

Keep your files in a safe place. For example, keep a copy of computer files off premises, and store paper files in a fireproof safe. If you lose files with receipts because they were not stored safely, you may lose deductions and face penalties as well. If you "lose" records before or during an audit, you may be charged with a hefty negligence or accuracy-related penalty. If, despite your best efforts, files and records are lost or destroyed by a casualty (such as a fire, storm, earthquake, or flood), you may be permitted to reconstruct records if you can prove those records existed before the casualty. Of course, reconstruction takes considerable time, and it is probably impossible to reconstruct all of your expenses. Therefore, take special care to safeguard your records.

Electronic Imaging Systems

Storage of receipts and other records in paper form makes retrieval of wanted items difficult. This is especially so for large companies, but it can be problematic for smaller businesses as well. Recognizing the problem, the IRS now allows books and records to be maintained by **electronic imaging systems**.

Electronic imaging system   A system that prepares, records, transfers, indexes, stores, preserves, retrieves, and reproduces books and records by electronically imaging hard copy to an electronic storage media or transferring computerized books and records to an electronic storage media using a technique such as COLD (computer output to laser disk). This technique allows books and records to be viewed or reproduced without the use of the original program.

If an electronic imaging system is used, it must ensure accurate and complete transfer of the hard copy or the computerized books and records. It must include:

- Reasonable controls to ensure the integrity, accuracy, and reliability of the system
- Reasonable controls to prevent and detect the unauthorized creation of, addition to, alteration of, deletion of, or deterioration of records
- An inspection and quality assurance program evidenced by regular evaluations of the electronic storage system
- A retrieval system that includes an indexing system
- The ability to reproduce legible hard copies of electronically stored books and records

In the past, most small businesses could not undertake the expense of using an electronic imaging system for their books and records with the technology that was available. However, today's technology allows you to use an alternative imaging method that is acceptable to the IRS. You can transfer data to a DVD—you burn the information onto the disk and cannot alter it thereafter. You can scan the information to be transferred into your computer and then transfer it to the disk.

Specific Substantiation Requirements for Certain Expenses

The law requires businesses to maintain books and records, and to provide special substantiation for certain deductions. There is a negligence penalty that can be imposed for 20% of an underpayment resulting from the failure to keep adequate books and records or to substantiate items properly.

Travel and Entertainment Expenses

The tax law imposes special substantiation requirements for claiming travel and entertainment expenses. If you fail to satisfy these requirements, your deduction for these business expenses may be disallowed. There are 2 types of records you need in order to claim deductions for your travel and entertainment expenses:

- *Written* substantiation in a diary, log book, or other notation system containing certain specific information, and
- *Documentary evidence* (receipts, canceled checks, or bills) to prove the amount of the expense.

The IRS accepts certain electronic or faxed information to be treated as documentary evidence (e.g., a faxed statement attesting to a "ticketless" airline ticket is considered documentary evidence). Sites such as Shoeboxed.com can be used to scan receipts and create electronic records. Smartphones and other mobile devices may be used for written substantiation in lieu of a logbook. You may even be able to use an app for your iPhone or Android, such as Pocket Quicken or Quicken Online Mobile (an iPhone app), to track travel and entertainment costs and transfer data to your PC. There are other apps, such as ProOnGo, that can be used to keep records and send them to QuickBooks Online edition. There are a number of apps for tracking business car mileage.

There are a number of elements to substantiate for each business expense. In general, to substantiate each item you must show the amount, time, place, and business purpose for the travel or entertainment expense or the business relationship with the person or persons you entertain or provide gifts to and, in some cases, a description of the item. The exact substantiation requirements depend on the type of business expense.

In all cases, you are strongly advised to use a written or electronic daily log or diary to record expenses. As you will see, you need written proof of your expenses (or an electronic log that can be turned into written proof), and this proof must be recorded "contemporaneously" with the expenses—generally meaning at the time you incur the expense or as soon as is practical thereafter to record it. Use a separate credit card for business expenses. The monthly statement from the credit card company is also useful in substantiating these expenses.

TRAVEL

You must show the amount of each separate expense for travel, lodging, meals, and incidental expenses. You can total these items in any reasonable category. For example, you can simply keep track of meals in a category called Daily Meals. You must also note the dates you left for the trip and returned, as well as the days spent on the trip for business purposes. You must list the name of the city or other designation of the place of the travel, along with the reason for the trip or the business benefit gained or expected to be gained from it.

While this may sound like a great deal of recordkeeping, as a practical matter, hotel receipts may provide you with much of the information necessary. For example, a hotel receipt typically shows the dates you arrived and departed, the name and location of the hotel, and separate charges for lodging, meals, telephone calls, and other items. A sample log for travel expenses can be found in Chapter 8.

ENTERTAINMENT

Again, you must list each separate expense. Incidental expenses, such as taxis and telephone calls, may be totaled on a daily basis. You must list the date of the entertainment. For meals or entertainment directly before or after a business discussion, list the date and duration of the business discussion. Include the name and address or location of the place of entertainment, as well as the type of entertainment if it is not apparent from the name of the place. Also list the place where a business discussion was held if entertainment took place directly before or after the discussion. Again, state the business reason or the business benefit gained or anticipated and the nature of the business discussion. Include the names of the persons entertained, including their occupations or other identifying information, and the names of those who took part in the business discussion. If the deduction is for a business meal, you must note that you or your employer were present at the meal.

Again, a restaurant receipt typically supplies much of the information required. It shows the name and location of the restaurant, the number of people served, and the date and amount of the expense. Be sure to retain these slips as your proof. A sample log for entertainment expenses can be found in Chapter 8.

GIFTS

Show the cost of the gift, the date it was given, and a description of the gift. Also show the business reason for the gift or the business benefit gained or expected to be gained from providing it. Include the name of the person receiving the gift, his or her occupation or other identifying information, and his or her business relationship to you.

A canceled check, along with a bill, generally establishes the cost of a business item. However, the check alone does not prove a business expense without other evidence of its business purpose.

If you do not have adequate records and your return is questioned, you may still be able to deduct an item if you can prove by your own statement or other supporting evidence an element of substantiation. Where receipts are destroyed, you may be able to reconstruct your expenses. You must, of course, show that you actually maintained records and how the records were destroyed (for example, in a fire, storm, or flood). The IRS may require additional information to prove the accuracy or reliability of the information contained in your records.

CAR EXPENSES

Show the number of miles driven for business purposes (starting and ending odometer readings), the destination, the purpose of the trip, and the name of the party visited (if relevant). Simply jot down the odometer reading on January 1 to start a good recordkeeping habit. Or use an app that simplifies recordkeeping for your car mileage. Include notations of expenses for gas, oil, parking, tolls, and other expenses. Recordkeeping shortcuts and tips, and a sample log for keeping track of car expenses, can be found in Chapter 9.

RECORDKEEPING RELIEF

You do not need receipts, canceled checks, bills, or other proof of the cost of a travel or entertainment expense in the following situations:

- You use a standard rate (such as a standard mileage rate for car use or a per diem rate for meals and lodging). Per diem rates are explained in Chapter 8; the standard mileage rate is explained in Chapter 9.
- The expense is less than $75. However, you cannot use this exception for lodging (you must have documentary evidence for lodging regardless of amount).
- You have a transportation expense (such as a taxi fare) for which a receipt is not readily available.

THE COHAN RULE

While the IRS says that deductions will be disallowed if you do not have adequate substantiation, you may be able to rely on a special rule developed by the courts. The *Cohan rule*, named after noted songwriter/showman George M. Cohan, is based on approximation. A court may agree to approximate your expenses if your records are inadequate to establish actual expenses and you have some way to show your approximate expenses. A court cannot be compelled to use the Cohan rule; it must be persuaded to do so because of special circumstances. The Cohan rule is only a last resort for claiming unsubstantiated travel and entertainment expenses. The Cohan rule has been used for some expenses other than travel and entertainment expenses (e.g., research expenses, licensing fees, and building sign replacements).

Charitable Contributions

Cash contributions of any amount must be substantiated by a written acknowledgment from the charity, a bank statement, or other permissible method (which depends on the amount of the donation). Presumably, a credit card statement showing the date of a contribution and the amount is also acceptable proof. Cash contributions of $250 or more require a written acknowledgment from the charity (the bank statement is not sufficient).

If a property donation is valued at over $5,000, you may also be required to obtain an appraisal by a certified appraiser and keep a record of this appraisal.

Records for Depreciation, Basis, Carryovers, and Prepaid Expenses

For some tax items you must keep a running account, because deductions will be claimed not only in the current year but also in years to come.

Depreciation

Depreciation allows you to recover the cost of property over the life of that property by deducting a portion of the cost each year. In order to claim your annual deductions, you must keep certain records:

- Costs and other information necessary to calculate your depreciation
- Capital improvements to depreciable assets
- Depreciation deductions already claimed
- Adjustments to basis as a result of depreciation deductions

This information not only is necessary for depreciation purposes but will also be needed to calculate gain or loss and any depreciation recapture on the sale or other disposition of a depreciable asset. For full details on claiming depreciation, see Chapter 14.

The same recordkeeping rules apply not only to depreciation but also to amortization and depletion deductions.

Basis

Basis is the cost of property or some other value assigned to property. Basis is used for several purposes: It is the amount on which depreciation deductions are based, as well as the amount used to determine gain or loss on the sale or other disposition of property.

The basis of property can vary from its basis upon acquisition. Some items increase basis; others decrease it. Keep track of changes in basis. These can result from:

- Depreciation deductions or first-year expensing
- Casualty deductions relating to the property
- Certain tax credits
- Capitalized costs

- One court has said that proof of capital improvements to increase basis includes such items as written records, canceled checks, construction permits, and before-and-after pictures.

S Corporation Shareholder's Basis

One of the most important records that must be kept for shareholders is their basis in corporate stock and loans they made to the corporation. This basis limits the amount of losses passed through to them that they can deduct. How items of income, loss, loan repayment, and other amounts impact this basis is explained in Chapter 4.

Carryovers

A number of deductions may be limited in a current year, but you may be able to carry over any unused portion to other years. In order to take advantage of carryover opportunities, you must keep records of deductions you have already taken and the years in which they were taken. What is more, you must maintain relevant records for the carryover periods. The following list details the types of carryovers for which records should be maintained and limits on the carryover period, if any:

- *At-risk losses*. Losses disallowed because of the application of the at-risk rules (see Chapter 4) can be carried over indefinitely.
- *Capital losses*. There is no limit on the carryover period for individuals. There is a 5-year limit on carryover losses for corporations.
- *Charitable contributions*. Individuals who cannot fully use current charitable contributions because of adjusted gross income limits can carry over the unused deductions for a period of 5 years. C corporations that cannot fully use current charitable contributions because of the 10%-of-taxable-income limit can carry over the unused deductions for a period of 5 years. If the deductions cannot be used within that 5-year period (there is insufficient taxable income to offset the deduction in the carryover years), the deductions are lost forever.
- *Home office deductions*. Individuals who maintain an office in their home and whose actual home office deductions are limited in the current year by gross income earned in the home office can carry forward unused deductions indefinitely. The unused deductions can be used in a future year if there is gross income from the home office activity to offset it. (There is no carryover if the simplified method is used to figure the home office deduction.)
- *Investment interest*. Individuals (including partners, LLC members, and S corporation shareholders) may be limited in their current deduction for

investment interest by the amount of their net investment income. Excess investment interest can be carried forward indefinitely. There is no limitation on corporations, so there is no carryover.

- *Net operating losses.* When operating losses cannot be used in full in the current year, they may be applied against income in certain other years. The carryover period depends on the year in which the net operating loss arises. For example, a carryback for a small business arising in 2009 could have been 3, 4, or 5 years, while NOLs arising in 2014 usually have a 2-year carryback. Good recordkeeping is necessary to track these carrybacks and apply them in the correct order (see Chapter 4).

- *Passive activity losses.* Losses disallowed because of the application of the passive activity loss rules (*suspended losses*) can be carried forward indefinitely. The same rules apply to credits from passive activities.

- *Cash basis and prepayment.* Depreciation and carryovers are not the only tax items that may run beyond the current tax year. If you are on the cash basis and prepay certain expenses, you may not be allowed a current deduction for your outlays. You may be required to deduct the expenses ratably over the period of time to which they relate. Some examples of commonly prepaid expenses that may have to be deducted ratably include:

  Insurance premiums. If your insurance premiums cover a period of more than 12 months, you may be required to deduct them over the term covered by the policy.

  Prepaid interest. If you pay points or other amounts treated as prepaid interest to obtain financing to acquire real estate for your business, you deduct the prepaid interest ratably over the term of the loan. If you dispose of the property or refinance the loan before the end of the term, you can then deduct any unused portion of the prepaid interest in that final year.

  Rents. If you prepay rents for a period of more than 12 months, you may be required to deduct the rents over the term of the lease.

  Subscriptions. If you pay for subscriptions running more than 12 months, you generally have to deduct the cost over the term of the subscriptions. For example, if you pay in full the cost of a 3-year subscription to a business journal, you generally must deduct the cost over the same 3-year period.

You need to keep a running record of Section 1231 losses—losses on the sale of certain business assets. This is because of a special recapture rule that applies to net ordinary losses from Section 1231 property. A net Section 1231 gain is treated as ordinary income to the extent it does not exceed nonrecaptured net Section 1231 losses taken in prior years. *Nonrecaptured losses* are the total of net Section 1231 losses for the 5 most recent years that have not yet been applied (recaptured) against any net Section 1231 gains in those same years. In order to determine this recapture, you must retain information on Section 1231 gains and losses. Section 1231 losses are explained in more detail in Chapter 6.

Finally, you need to keep track of tax credits that are not completely used in the current year. Tax credits that are part of the general business credit (such as the work opportunity credit, employer Social Security credit, and the disabled access credit) are subject to a carryback and carryforward period depending on the year in which the excess credits result. For credits arising in years beginning before January 1, 1998, the excess credits are carried back 3 years and forward for up to 15 years. For credits arising in years beginning after December 31, 1997 (except for 2010), the excess credits are carried back one year and forward for up to 20 years. For credits of small businesses (average annual gross receipts under $50 million) arising in 2010 only, the carryback period was 5 years; the carryforward period remained 20 years. No election can be made to forgo this carryback period.

How Long You Should Maintain Records

Your books and records must be available at all times for inspection by the IRS. You should keep these books and records at least until the time when the IRS's ability to question your deductions runs out. This time is called the *statute of limitations*. In general, the statute of limitations is either 3 years after the due date of your return or 2 years after the date the tax was paid—whichever is later. Some records must be kept even longer. You need to keep records to support the basis in property owned by the business. You also need to keep records for depreciation and carryovers, as discussed earlier.

Tax Returns

Keep copies of tax returns to help you prepare future returns, as well as to help you if your return is questioned by the IRS. While you can obtain old returns from the IRS, this entails unnecessary time and expense. Although you may only need information on an old return for 3 additional years, it is a good idea to keep old tax returns indefinitely. If the IRS claims you never filed a return it has an unlimited number of years in which to audit you. But if you have your old return along with proof that you filed it (for example, a certified receipt or an acknowledgment of efiling from the IRS), the IRS only has 3 years, in most cases, to start an audit.

Keep a record of the basis of property used in your business for as long as you own the property, plus the statute of limitations on filing the return for the year in which property is sold or otherwise disposed of. For example, if in 2014 you buy equipment that you will sell in 2015, keep records on the basis of the property at least until 2019 (3 years from the due date of the return for the year in which the property was sold).

Employer Records

If you have employees, special recordkeeping rules apply. For tax purposes, you are required to keep records on employment taxes for at least 4 years after the due date of the return or after the tax is paid, whichever is later. Keep copies of all returns you have filed and the dates and amount of tax deposits you have made. Your records should also show your employer identification number (EIN). Every business type of, sole (sole proprietorship, partnership, and corporation) must have one if wages are paid (see Chapter 1).

Income Tax Withholding

You must keep records of each employee's name, address, and Social Security number, the amount of each wage payment, the amount of each payment subject to income tax withholding, and the amount of income tax withheld. You must also keep copies of all employees' withholding allowance certificates (Form W-4). Similarly, you must keep any earned income credit advance payment certificates (Form W-5) filed with you by low-income wage earners who want to receive an advance on their earned income credit.

Other Employment Taxes

Similar records must be kept for each employee for Social Security and Medicare taxes, as well as for federal unemployment taxes (FUTA).

Other Tax Records

Certain documents should be retained indefinitely. These include IRS letters and private rulings you've obtained. For corporations, retain all corporation resolutions related to taxes and other matters. And, of course, retain all accounting records, annual financial statements, and audit reports forever.

> **NOTE**
> The IRS is not the only government agency to require record retention related to employees. Be sure to check on recordkeeping requirements of the Equal Employment Opportunity Commission (EEOC), the Occupational Safety and Health Administration (OSHA), as well as other federal and state agencies.

How to Dispose of Tax Records

Gone are the days when you could simply toss your old files in the garbage. Today, because of the potential for identity theft affecting both individuals and businesses, proper disposal is essential. Shredding documents on paper or CDs and DVDs is a good way to prevent unwanted eyes from viewing confidential information. Use special technology to wipe tax and other confidential information off computers being disposed of.

Business Income and Losses

Income or Loss from Business Operations

Alert

At the time this book was printed, Congress had not extended numerous breaks for 2014 that had expired at the end of 2013. Check the online supplement in February 2015 at www.jklasser.com or www.barbaraweltman.com to see whether these breaks apply for 2014 returns.

The fees you earn for your services or the receipts you collect from the sale of goods are the bread-and-butter income of your business. Hopefully your pricing policies are realistic and you have a strong customer or client base so that you can make a profit.

Even if sales are healthy, expenses can outrun receipts, resulting in a loss for the business. You will not know whether you have a net income or loss until all of the expenses discussed throughout the book have been taken into account. Income and loss for accounting purposes, which reflects the actual money in and out of the business, may not be the same as income and loss for tax purposes. The reason: some income may be treated as tax free or tax deferred so it is not counted currently, while some expenses may not be fully or even partially deductible. For example, the business pays a $1,000 governmental fine, which reduces its profits for accounting purposes by $1,000; for tax purposes, the fine is not deductible (see Chapter 22), so it cannot be used to offset income on a tax return. For tax purposes, if there is a net loss, then limitations may come into play on when and the extent to which business losses can be deducted.

It is now harder for businesses to hide income (not report it) because of reporting requirements for transactions made on credit and debit cards. The processors must report to the IRS and to merchants the annual transactions, although there is an exception for small merchants (see Appendix A).

Special limits on losses from sideline businesses ("hobby loss rules") are discussed in Chapter 26.

For further information about business income and losses, see IRS Publication 225, *Farmer's Tax Guide*; IRS Publication 334, *Tax Guide for Small Business*; IRS Publication 536, *Net Operating Losses—Individuals, Trusts & Estates*. IRS Publication 541, *Partnerships*; and IRS Publication 542, *Corporations*. A further discussion of the hobby loss rules may be found in IRS Publication 535, *Business Expenses*. For information on the at-risk rules and passive activity loss limitations, see IRS Publication 925, *Passive Activity and At-Risk Rules*.

Business Income

Whether you work full-time or part-time, income received for your business activity is part of your business income. How you report it depends on your accounting method (explained in Chapter 4).

Where you report it depends on how your business is organized. For example, self-employed individuals report income on Schedule C or Schedule C-EZ or on Schedule F if the business is farming. Partnerships and LLCs report income on Form 1065, S corporations use Form 1120S, and C corporations report income on Form 1120. Where to report income is explained at the end of this chapter.

Payment Methods

Most business transactions are in cash. For tax purposes the term *cash* includes checks, credit card charges, PayPal, and smart cards. However, in some cases, payments may take a different form.

PAYMENTS IN KIND

If you exchange your goods or services for property, you must include the fair market value of the property you received in income. Bartering does not avoid the requirement to report income. This is true whether you barter directly—one-on-one—or receive property through a barter exchange that gives you credit for the goods or services you provide. Bartering through a barter exchange is reported to the IRS on Form 1099-B, *Proceeds from Broker and Barter Exchange Transactions*.

> **CAUTION**
>
> Bartering does not avoid sales taxes. For example, if you barter your goods to dispose of excess inventory, be sure to follow the same sales tax rules that you would if you had been paid in cash. See Chapter 29.

If you are paid in virtual or digital currency, such as Bitcoin, it's treated like property, not currency. It is income when received based on the fair market value of the Bitcoin, which may be determined by an exchange on which it is traded.

PAYMENTS IN SERVICES

If you exchange your goods or services for someone else's services, you are also taxed on the value of the services you receive. If services are exchanged for services, you both can agree to the value of the services you report as income.

> ### Example
>
> You are a house painter who paints the offices of an attorney who handles a legal matter for you in exchange for your work. You must include the value of the attorney's services in your income. You may value this according to what the attorney would have charged you if you had paid cash for the work. Or you can both agree to the value of the services, assuming that value is reasonable.

CONSIGNMENTS

If items owned by others are consigned to you for sale, do not include these items in your inventory. Instead, report income from any commissions or profits you are entitled to upon sale.

If you consign your goods to others, do not report this arrangement as a sale. You report income from the sale of consigned goods when they are sold by the consignee. Do not remove the items from your inventory until a sale by the consignee.

KICKBACKS

Amounts you receive as kickbacks are included in income. However, do not include them as a separate income item if you properly treat these amounts as a reduction to the cost of goods sold, a capital expenditure, or an expense item.

LOANS

If you obtain business loans, do not include the proceeds in income. They are merely loans that must be repaid according to the terms of the loan agreement.

LOCATION TAX INCENTIVES

If you receive a state or local location tax incentive, in the form of an abatement, credit, deduction, rate reduction, or exemption, in order to attract your company to a particular area, the incentive is not taxable income. Of course, only the amount of state and local tax you are liable for, after reduction by any location tax incentives, is deductible (you can't deduct what you aren't required to pay) (see Chapter 13).

Income for Service Businesses

If your main business activity is providing services to customers and clients, you are in a service business. As such, reporting business income is generally a simple matter. You report as income all of your revenues from performing services according to your method of accounting. Since most service businesses are on the cash basis, income usually is reported when fees are collected.

1099 Income

If you are an independent contractor, your clients or customers who are in business are required to report income paid to you on Form 1099-MISC, *Miscellaneous Income*. This informs the IRS of income you have received. Income is required to be reported on Form 1099 if annual payments are at least $600, but you are required to report on your tax return *all* income you receive (even if no Form 1099 has been issued). Form 1099-MISC must also be given by businesses to incorporated attorneys and law firms for payments of $600 or more.

Advances and Prepayments

If you receive income for services to be performed in the future, you usually report the income if you have free and unrestricted use of the money.

However, if you use the accrual method and receive an advance payment for services to be performed by the end of the next year, you can elect to postpone, including the advance payment in income, until the next year. Postponement cannot extend beyond that next year.

Example

You own a dance studio and on November 1, 2014, receive payment for a 1-year contract for 48 1-hour lessons beginning on that date. You give 8 lessons in 2014. You include only one-sixth (8/48) of the advance payment in income in 2014. All of the remaining 5/6s (40/48) must be included in income in 2015, even if all lessons have not been given by the end of 2015. If the advance payment has been for a 2-year contract, then *all* of the advance would be included in income for 2014 since part of the services may be postponed after the following year.

You can postpone reporting income from an advance payment for a service agreement on property you sell, lease, build, install, or contract, provided that you offer the property without a service agreement in the normal course of business. You cannot postpone income if you are to perform any part of the service after the end of the tax year immediately following the year you receive the advance payment or you are to perform any part of the service at an unspecified future date that may be after the end of the year immediately following the year you receive advance payment. You usually cannot postpone reporting income received under a guarantee or warranty contract.

Example

You sell computers that you refurbish. You also sell 1-year service contracts on these computers. You can postpone the income from the service contracts as long as you also sell computers without such contracts.

Income from the Sale of Goods

Reporting income from the sale of goods involves a 2-step process. First you must figure your *gross receipts*—amounts received from sales (determined by your method of accounting). Then you must subtract from gross receipts your **cost of goods sold**.

Cost of goods sold The cost of buying raw materials and producing finished goods. Essentially it is the cost of buying inventory or manufacturing inventory.

Cost of Goods Sold

Cost of goods sold (COGS) is determined each year by adjusting beginning inventory for changes made during the year. For Forms 1065, 1120, and 1120S, the cost of goods sold is figured on Form 1025-A (rather than on a schedule on the return).

Inventory at the beginning of the year (generally your closing inventory reported on last year's return) is increased by adding any inventory purchases or manufactured items purchased that year. Include not only purchases but also the cost of labor and other costs required to be included under the uniform capitalization (UNICAP) rules explained in Chapter 4. Decrease this figure by sales from inventory.

To know what your opening inventory and closing inventory is, you need to take a physical inventory. A physical inventory must be taken at reasonable intervals, and the actual count must be used to adjust the inventory figures you have been maintaining all along. Generally, a physical inventory is taken at year-end. You are permitted to estimate year-end inventory by factoring in a reasonable allowance for shrinkage (for example, loss due to theft that you failed to detect). If you make such an estimate, then you must take a physical count on a consistent basis and adjust—upward or downward—the actual inventory count.

There are 4 methods for reporting inventory. They are:

1. Cost
2. Lower of cost or market method
3. Write-down of subnormal goods
4. Other inventory methods

Retailers can use a retail inventory method (see Rev. Proc. 2014-48 for instructions on how to change to this method if the business is currently using a different method).

Resellers—those who buy items for sale to others—use certain rules and methods to assign the cost of these items to those sold during the year:

- *First-in, First-out (FIFO).* An item sold is deemed to be the first item booked into inventory. For example, if you bought 10 widgets on 3 occasions at a cost of 10¢ each, 15¢ each, and 20¢ each and you sell 15, under FIFO you have sold 10 at 10¢ each and 5 at 15¢ each.
- *Last-in, First-out (LIFO).* An item sold is deemed to be the last item booked into inventory. In the widge example, you have sold 10 at 20¢ each and 5 at 15¢ each.
  Note: There have been proposals to repeal LIFO, but at the time of publication, there has been no legislation to do this; check the Supplement.
- *Specific identification method.* The actual cost of the items is used. This method generally is used when a business owns large or unique items (for example, an antique store would use this method for its objects since items are not identical and cannot be commingled).

Small businesses are allowed to use a simplified value LIFO method that makes it easier to determine the value of inventory. If you elect FIFO, you must use the lower of cost or market method to report inventory. If you elect LIFO, you must use cost to report inventory.

Gross Profits

Gross profits from the sale of goods is the difference between the gross receipts (sales revenues) and the cost of goods sold (as well as other allowances). If you remove items from inventory for your personal use, be sure to adjust your figures accordingly.

You generally cannot use the installment method of accounting to report the sale of inventory items—even if you receive payment on an installment plan. You report the sale according to your usual method of accounting so that on the accrual basis you pick up the income in full in the year of sale even though the full payment will not be received at that time.

Other Income for Direct Sellers

In addition to income from sales of products to customers, direct sellers may receive income in other ways:

- Commissions, bonuses, or percentages you receive for sales and the sales of others who work under you.
- Prizes, awards, and gifts resulting from your sales activities.

Income from Farming

When a business earns its income from sales of livestock and produce, payments from agricultural programs and farm rents and other similar sources, it is considered a farming business. Since most small farms use the cash method of accounting to report income and expenses, the following discussion is limited to this method of accounting. However, if items regularly produced in the farming business or used in the farming business are sold on an installment basis, the sale can be reported on the installment method, deferring income until payment is received.

While many income items of farms are similar to nonfarm businesses, there are a number of income items unique to farming. These include:

- *Agricultural payments* (cash, materials, services, or commodity certificates) from government programs generally are included in income. If you later refund or repay a portion of the payments, you can deduct these amounts at that time. For details on how to treat specific government payments, see IRS Publication 225, *Farmer's Tax Guide*.
- *Conservation Reserve Program (CRP) payments.* If you own or operate highly erodible or other specified cropland and have entered into a long-term contract with the USDA, agreeing to convert to a less intensive use of that cropland, include the annual rental payments and any onetime

incentive payment you receive under the program as ordinary income (there is a special line on Schedule F for reporting Agricultural Program Payments). Cost-share payments may qualify for the cost-sharing exclusion.

- *Crop insurance and crop disaster payments* received as a result of crop damage. This type of income is generally included in income in the year received. Farmers can request federal income tax withholding at the rate of 7%, 10%, 15%, or 25% by filing Form W-4V, *Voluntary Withholding Request.*

- *Feed assistance and payments.* If you receive partial reimbursement for the cost of purchased feed, certain transportation expenses, and/or the donation or sale at a below-market price of feed owned by the Commodity Credit Corporation, include in income (1) the market value of the donated feed, (2) the difference between the market value and the price you paid for feed you buy at below-market prices, and (3) any cost reimbursement you receive.

- *Forest health protection payments.* Payments to landowners who voluntarily participate in the FHPP are tax free.

- *National Tobacco Settlement payments* to landowners, producers, and tobacco quota owners in Alabama, Florida, Georgia, Indiana, Kentucky, Maryland, Missouri, North Carolina, Ohio, Pennsylvania, South Carolina, Tennessee, Virginia, and West Virginia. Amounts reported to owners of tobacco quotas in termination of the quota can be reported under the installment method (see Chapter 6). Payouts should have been completed by 2011, but some recipients may still be reporting payments under the installment method.

- *Patronage dividends* from farm cooperatives through which you purchase farm supplies and sell your farm products are included in income.

- *Rents, including crop shares.* Generally, rents are not treated as farm income but as rental income, and these rents are not part of your net income or loss from farming. However, rents are treated as farm income if you materially participate in the management or operations of the farm (material participation is explained later in this chapter).

- *Sales of livestock caused by drought, flood, or other weather conditions.* While such sales are generally reported in the current year, you can opt to report them in the following year if you can show that you would not have sold the livestock this year but for the weather conditions *and* you are eligible for federal assistance because of the weather conditions. You must file a separate election with your tax return for the year of the weather conditions for each class of animals (e.g., cattle, sheep). Alternatively, deferral is indefinite, if proceeds are reinvested in similar livestock, until the end of the first tax year ending after the first "drought-free year" (assuming the drought-free year ends in or after the last year of a 4-year replacement period). The IRS lists affected counties (e.g., counties for

2013 were listed in Notice 2013-62; check the IRS website for affected counties in 2014).

- *Sales of livestock (including poultry) and produce.* The sale of livestock classified as Section 1231 property may result in Section 1231 gain or loss (explained in Chapter 6). If crops are sold on a deferred payment contract, you report the income when payment is received.

- *Sales of timber.* Outright sales of timber qualify for capital gain treatment if the timber was held for more than one year before the date of disposal. Similar treatment applies to sales of timber under a contract with a retained economic interest. However, for purposes of outright sales, the date of disposal is not deemed to be the date timber is cut; you can elect to treat the payment date as the date of disposal.

Commodity Credit Corporation loans

Loan proceeds generally are not income. However, farmers who pledge part or all of their production to secure a Commodity Credit Corporation (CCC) loan can make a special election to treat the loan proceeds as income in the year received and obtain a basis in the commodity for the amount reported as income. The election is made by including the loan proceeds as income on Schedule F and attaching a statement to the return showing the details of the loan. Then the amount you report as income becomes your basis in the commodity, so that when you later repay the loan, redeem the pledged commodity, and sell it, you report as income the sale proceeds minus the basis in the commodity. A forfeiture of pledged crops is treated as a sale for this purpose. Farmers who do not make this election must report market gain as income.

The repayment amount generally is based on the lower of the loan rate or the prevailing world market price of the commodity on the date of repayment. If the world price is lower when the loan is repaid, the difference between the repayment amount and the original loan amount is market gain. Whether cash or CCC certificates are used to repay the loan, Form 1099-CCC is issued to show the market gain. Market gain is included in income in the year of repayment if the CCC loan was not included in income in the year received.

Not all income received by farmers and ranchers is includable in gross income. Income from federal or state cost-sharing conservation, reclamation, and restoration programs can be excluded in whole or in part (depending on the program and other factors). Qualifying programs include, but are not limited to, small watershed programs as well as the water bank program under the Water Bank Act, emergency conservation measures program under Title IV of the Agricultural Credit Act of 1978, and the Great Plains conservation program authorized by the Soil Conservation and Domestic Policy Act.

Farm Income Averaging

You can choose to figure the tax on your farming income (*elected farm income*) by averaging it over the past 3 years. If you make this election, it will lower the tax on this year's income if income was substantially lower in the 3 prior years. However, it does not always save taxes to average your farming income—it is a good idea to figure your tax in both ways (the usual way and averaging) to determine which method is more favorable to you.

The same averaging option applies to commercial fishermen.

Investment-Type Income

Operating income from a business may include certain investment-type income, such as interest on business bank accounts and rents from leasing property. Pass-through entities segregate investment-type income and, in most cases, report these separately to owners. How to report this income can be found later in this chapter. Capital gains are discussed in Chapter 5, and other gains from the sale of business property are discussed in Chapter 6.

Interest Income

Interest received on business bank accounts and on accounts or notes receivable in the ordinary course of business is a common type of ordinary business income. If the business lends money, interest received on business loans is business income. Deductions for business loans that go sour are explained in Chapter 22.

Businesses that make below-market or interest-free loans may be deemed to receive interest, called *imputed interest*. Below-market loan rules from the deduction perspective are discussed in Chapter 13.

Dividends

Businesses that own stock in a corporation may receive dividends. C corporations report the dividends as ordinary income. Pass-through entities report the dividends as separately stated items to enable owners to apply favorable tax rates on their personal returns. For example, if the dividends are "qualified," owners may pay tax at no more than 15% on their share of the dividends (those in the 39.6% tax bracket would pay no more than 20% on their share of dividends).

DIVIDENDS-RECEIVED DEDUCTION

C corporations that receive dividends from domestic (U.S.) corporations can effectively exclude some or all of these dividends by claiming a special dividends-received deduction. The amount of the dividends-received deduction depends on the percentage of ownership in the corporation paying the dividend. This special write-off for C corporations is discussed in Chapter 22.

Rents

Rents can be generated from leasing personal property items such as equipment, formal wear, or vehicles. Rents can also be generated from leasing out real property.

REAL ESTATE RENTS

A business that provides services in conjunction with rentals reports rents as business income. For example, if you own a motel, you report your rentals as business income because you provide maid service and other services to your business guests.

If your tenant pays expenses on your behalf in lieu of making rental payments to you, these payments to third parties are part of your business income. For example, if your tenant pays your property taxes, you report the payment of taxes as rental income.

PREPAID RENT

Advances, including security deposits, must be reported as income if you have unrestricted right to them. If you are required by law or contract to segregate these payments, you do not have to report them as income until you are entitled to enjoy them (the restrictions no longer apply).

LEASE BONUS OR CANCELLATION PAYMENTS

Amounts your tenant pays to secure a lease (lease bonus payments) or to get out of a lease early (cancellation payments) are income to you.

Cancellation of Debt

If you owe money and some or all of your debt is forgiven by the lender, you generally must include this debt forgiveness in income. However, you do not have to include debt forgiveness in income if any of the following conditions apply:

- You file for bankruptcy under Title 11 of the U.S. Code.
- You are insolvent at the time of the cancellation. Your exclusion is limited to the extent of your insolvency.
- The canceled debt is a qualified farm debt. This is a debt incurred by a business that received at least 50% of its gross receipts in the prior 3 years from farming activities. This debt must be owed to one who is regularly engaged in lending money, including the U.S. Department of Agriculture.
- The canceled debt is qualified real property business debt—secured by the property and incurred before January 1, 1993, or after December 31, 1992, if incurred or assumed to acquire, construct, or substantially improve real property used in the business. You must elect this exclusion for the

year in which the cancellation occurs. The exclusion cannot exceed certain amounts.

Instead of recognizing income from the cancellation or discharge of indebtedness (referred to as DOI income), you can choose to reduce certain **tax attributes**. This has the effect of limiting your future write-offs with respect to these tax attributes. Generally the amount excluded from income reduces the tax attributes (in a certain order) on a dollar-for-dollar or $33^1/_3$ cents basis. As follows:

- Net operating loss (NOL) for the year of the DOI (dollar-for-dollar)
- General business credit carryover to or from the year of DOI ($33^1/_3$ ¢ per dollar)
- Minimum tax credit as of the beginning of the tax year immediately after the year of DOI ($33^1/_3$ ¢ per dollar)
- Net capital loss for the year of DOI (dollar-for-dollar)
- Basis of property (dollar-for-dollar)
- Passive activity loss (dollar-for-dollar) and credit ($33^1/_3$ ¢ per dollar) carryovers from the year of DOI
- Foreign tax credit carryover to or from the year of DOI

However, a corporation can elect to adjust the basis of property in a manner that is different from the general rule described in Reg. §1.1082-3(b).

Tax attributes   These are tax aspects that provide a tax benefit in the current year or future years. They include the basis of depreciable real property, the basis of other depreciable property, net operating losses and loss carryovers, general business credit carryovers, minimum tax credit, capital losses and loss carryovers, passive activity loss and credit carryovers, and foreign tax credit carryovers.

The election to reduce tax attributes instead of recognizing DOI income is made on Form 982, *Reduction of Tax Attributes Due to Discharge of Indebtedness*.

Note: C corporations that had DOI income from the reacquisition of debt after December 31, 2008, and before January 1, 2011, could have elected to defer recognition for 5 years (e.g., until 2014 for 2009 DOI income) and then report the income ratably over 5 years.

Cancellation of debt income for S corporations. When corporate debt is forgiven and the S corporation opts not to report the cancellation of debt income but rather to reduce tax attributes, special rules apply. Any disallowed losses or deductions, including those of a shareholder who transferred all stock during the year, are included in an S corporation's deemed NOL (it is "deemed" because technically NOLs are reported only at the shareholder level, but adjustments to the NOL are made at the corporate level). If the deemed NOL exceeds the discharged cancellation of debt income, the excess deemed NOL is allowed to the shareholders as disallowed losses and deductions that shareholders can later take into account.

The character of the excess deemed NOL that is allocated to shareholders will consist of a proportionate amount of each item of the shareholder's loss or deduction that is disallowed for the year of the debt discharge. The corporations are required to provide information to shareholders regarding these suspended losses.

Damages and Other Recoveries

If you receive damages for patent, copyright or trademark infringement, breach of contract, or other business-related injuries, you report the damages as business income.

Miscellaneous Business Income

Almost any type of income earned by a business is considered to be business income. In addition to the types of income already discussed, the following are other examples of business income you must report:

- Credit for alcohol used as fuel (for details see the instructions to Form 6478, *Credit for Alcohol Used as Fuel*)
- Credit for federal tax paid on gasoline or other fuels claimed on the prior year return
- Finance reserve income
- Income adjustments resulting from a change in accounting method
- Income under the tax benefit rule of Section 111 (recoveries of previously deducted items)
- Prizes and awards for the business
- Recapture of the deduction for clean-fuel vehicles used in the business and clean-fuel refueling property (for details see IRS Publication 535, *Business Expenses*)
- Recapture of first-year expensing deduction (first-year expensing is explained in Chapter 14)
- Recapture of depreciation for so-called luxury cars if business use drops below 50% (figure recapture amount on Form 4797 in Chapter 4)
- Recovery of bad debts previously deducted under the specific charge-off method

- Scrap sales
- State gasoline or fuel tax refunds received in the current year
- State grants to businesses whose property is damaged or destroyed in a disaster (but gain on the resulting income may be postponed under the rules for involuntary conversions discussed in Chapter 6)
- Taxable income from insurance proceeds (such as key person insurance)
- World Trade Center grants made to businesses

Trade discounts provided to a retailer by a manufacturer or wholesaler are *not* taken into income; they are subtracted from the invoice price to figure inventory cost.

Small businesses that borrow under the America's Recovery Capital (ARC) Loan Program are not taxed on the interest paid by the Small Business Administration. The ARC Loan Program ran only through September 2010, but loans under that program may still be outstanding.

Special Income Items for S Corporations

If a corporation operated as a C corporation and then converted to S status, certain unique income items may result. These items are taxed to the S corporation; they are not pass-through items taxed to the shareholders:

- *Last-in, first-out inventory recapture on the conversion from C status to S status.* It can also result from the transfer of LIFO inventory by a C corporation to the S corporation in a transaction in which no income was recognized. Recapture results in an income adjustment payable in 4 equal installments, one reported on the final return of the C corporation (or the year of the transfer), and one-fourth each in the first, second, and third years of the S corporation's life (or the year of the transfer and the 2 successive years).
- *Excess net passive income.* If there were accumulated earnings and profits (E&P) from the time when the corporation was a C corporation *and* it has passive income for the year in excess of 25% of gross receipts, then tax is due at the rate of 35%. The S corporation must have taxable income for the year to be subject to this special tax.
- *Built-in capital gains.* If the corporation has appreciated property when it converts, the appreciation to the date of conversion is reported as built-in gains if the property is sold or otherwise disposed of within 5 years of conversion (7 years in 2009; 10 years before 2009 and after 2013 unless the 5-year period is extended to 2014, which will be updated in the Supplement). The tax on the net recognized built-in gains is 35%.

If a corporation elects S status for its first year of existence it need not be concerned with any of these income items; they will never arise.

Special Income Items for C Corporations

If a C corporation converts to S status and reports inventory using LIFO, it must recapture one-fourth of the resulting income adjustment, reporting it as income on its final return (the year of conversion).

If the corporation receives a tax refund of taxes deducted in a prior year, the refund must be reported as income to the extent that it produced a tax benefit for the corporation.

State Income Taxes on Business Income

Federal income taxes on your business income may not be your only concern. You may also be subject to state income taxes. This liability depends on whether you do business within the state. Generally, this means having a nexus (connection) to the state. This is based on having a physical presence there, which may be evidenced by maintaining an office or sending a sales force into the state; merely shipping goods into the state without some additional connection is not enough to prove a business presence within the state. You may have a nexus to more than 1 state, no matter how small your business is.

If there is a business connection, the business income is apportioned among the states in which you do business. Apportionment is based on a sales factor, a payroll factor, and a property factor (the states have different apportionment rules). The rules are highly complex, but there is considerable wiggle room to shift income into the state with the lowest taxes.

For more information about state income taxes, contact the tax or revenue departments of each state in which you do business.

Net Operating Losses

If deductions and losses from your business exceed your business income, you may be able to use the losses to offset income in other years. Net losses from the conduct of your business are *net operating losses (NOLs)*. In 2011 (the last year for which statistics are available), NOLs claimed on individual returns was almost $490 billion.

Net operating losses are not an additional loss deduction. Rather, they are the result of your deductions exceeding the income from your business. The excess deductions are not lost; they are simply used in certain other years.

You have an NOL if you have deductions from a trade or business, deductions from your work as an employee, or deductions from casualty and theft losses.

Only individuals and C corporations can claim NOLs. Partnerships, limited liability companies (LLCs), and S corporations cannot have NOLs, since their income and losses pass through to owners. However, partners, LLC members, and S corporation shareholders can have NOLs on their individual returns. These NOLs are created by their share of the business's operating losses.

Calculating NOLs

After you have completed your tax return for the year, you may find that you have an NOL. If you are an individual, you may have an NOL if your adjusted gross income, reduced by itemized deductions or the standard deduction (but before personal exemptions), is a negative figure. C corporations may have an NOL if taxable income is a negative figure. This negative figure merely indicates a possibility of an NOL; then you must determine whether, in fact, there actually is one. This is due to the fact that certain adjustments must be made to that negative figure in arriving at an NOL. Individuals and corporations calculate NOLs in a slightly different manner.

INDIVIDUALS

An NOL does not include personal exemptions, net capital losses, nonbusiness losses, or nonbusiness deductions. The NOL can be computed on Schedule A of Form 1045. This form adds back to taxable income any of these items claimed on the return and makes other adjustments required to compute the NOL. For example, individuals must add back to taxable income any deductions for Individual Retirement Account (IRA) contributions, alimony, the standard deduction, and charitable contributions. More specifically, nonbusiness deductions in excess of nonbusiness income get added back. Do not add back business-related deductions for:

- One-half of self-employment tax
- Moving expenses
- State income tax on business profits
- Interest and litigation expenses on state or federal income taxes related to business
- Payments by a federal employee to buy sick leave
- Loss on rental property
- Loss on the sale or exchange of business real estate or depreciable business property
- Loss on the sale of accounts receivable if you are on the accrual method
- Loss on the sale or exchange of stock in a small business company or small business investment company if the loss is treated as an ordinary loss (such as loss on Section 1244)

CORPORATIONS

The NOL for corporations generally is calculated by reducing gross income by deductions. Special rules then apply to adjust the NOL. They are:

- A full dividends-received deduction is taken into account in calculating the NOL. For example, the 70% or 80% limit is ignored.
- NOLs from other years are not taken into account in calculating a current NOL.
- Losses that fall under the passive activity rules cannot be used to calculate an NOL.

If a corporation's ownership changes hands, limits apply on the use of NOL carryforwards. The tax law does not want one corporation to acquire another for the purpose of using NOLs of the target corporation to offset the income of the acquiring corporation. These rules are highly complex.

S corporations do not have net operating losses. Instead, losses are passed through to owners who figure their NOLs on their individual returns. NOL carryovers of a C corporation cannot be claimed after the conversion to S corporation status (they remain in limbo and can be used by the corporation if it terminates its S status and returns to being a C corporation). However, the S corporation can use the C corporation's NOL carryover as a deduction to offset any net recognized built-in gain (built-in gain is explained earlier in this chapter).

Carrybacks and Carryovers

Net operating losses may be carried back and, if not used up, carried forward for a certain number of years. The carryback and carryforward periods depend on the year in which the NOL arose.

For NOLs arising in tax years beginning before August 6, 1997, the carryback period was 3 years and the carryforward period continues to be 15 years.

For NOLs arising in tax years beginning after August 5, 1997, generally there is a 2-year carryback and a 20-year carryforward period. However, for small businesses (those with average annual gross receipts of $5 million or less during a 3-year period), a 3-year carryback applies to NOLs arising from government-declared disasters, and for farmers and ranchers and certain specified disaster victims, there is a 5-year carryback for all NOLs. There is a 10-year carryback for NOLs arising from product liability.

Special (longer) carrybacks apply for small businesses in 2008 and 2009. The same carryforward period of 20 years applies to NOLs from 2008 and 2009.

Note: For partnerships, limited liability companies, and S corporations, the election of the longer carryback period was made at the entity level even though the carryback was claimed by owners on their personal returns.

If you have an NOL in 2014, the basic 2-year carryback period again applies. You first carry the loss back to a year that is 2 years before the year in which the

NOL arose (the NOL year), which is 2012. If it is not used up in that year, carry it to the year before the NOL year, which is 2013. If the NOL is still not used up, you can begin to carry it forward (with modifications explained below). However, if it is not used up after carrying it forward for 20 years, it is lost forever.

Be sure to keep track of each category of NOL. For example, do not lump your pre-August 6, 1997, carryforwards together with your post-August 5, 1997, carryforwards.

Personal service corporations (PSCs) are not allowed to carry back an NOL to any year in which there is a Section 444 election in effect to use a tax year other than a required tax year.

If your marital status in the carryback or carryover years differs from your status in the NOL year, only the spouse who has the NOL can claim it. If you file a joint return, the NOL deduction is limited to the income of the spouse who had the NOL. Special rules apply for carrybacks to a year involving a different marital status from the status in the year the NOL arises.

Example

In 2013, you divorce after many years of marriage. In 2014, you have an NOL. If you do not forgo the 2-year carryback, the NOL carryback is applied only against your income on the 2012 return, which was a joint return (in 2013 you were divorced by the end of the year, and your filing status was single). After you deduct the NOL calculated with reference to your taxable income, you then apply the tax rates for married filing jointly.

If your NOL is greater than the taxable income for the year to which you carried it, you must make certain modifications to taxable income to see how much of the NOL is used up in that carryback/carryover year and how much is still available as a *carryover*. The carryover is the excess of the NOL deduction over modified taxable income for the carryback/carryforward year. *Modified taxable income* is taxable income without regard to the NOL and with no deduction for net capital losses or personal exemptions. Also, you must recalculate items affected by a change in adjusted gross income. Your modified taxable income cannot be less than zero. You can determine your modified taxable income using Schedule B of Form 1045 for any carryback years and for carryovers from those years. If you have carryovers from more than one year, you use the carryovers in the order in which they were incurred. Thus, if you have a carryforward from 2010 and 2011, first use the amounts from 2010; if income is not fully offset, then use the 2011 carryforward.

While the NOL carryforward reduces income in the carryforward years for income tax purposes, it does *not* affect income for self-employment tax purposes in the carryforward years.

ELECTION TO FORGO CARRYBACK

Instead of carrying a 2014 NOL back 2 years and then forward, you can elect to forgo the carryback and just carry forward the loss for 20 years. You make this election in the NOL year by attaching a statement to your return if you are an individual, or by checking the appropriate box on the corporate return for C corporations. Once the election is made, it cannot be changed. If you incur another NOL in a subsequent year, you must make a separate election if you also want to forgo the carryback.

Some taxpayers prefer to forgo the carryback because they are afraid of calling attention to prior tax years and risking an audit. While this is certainly a possibility, claiming a carryback will not necessarily result in an audit of a prior year.

The election to forgo the NOL carryback applies not only to regular income tax purposes but also to alternative minimum tax purposes.

QUICK REFUNDS FROM CARRYBACKS

If your business is struggling, you can use an NOL carryback to generate quick cash flow. The carryback will offset income in the carryback years, and you will receive a refund of taxes paid in those years.

Individuals can file Form 1045, *Application for Tentative Refund*, to obtain a relatively quick refund. The IRS generally will act on the refund within 90 days of the filing of the form. When you carry back an NOL, you may have to recalculate certain deductions, credits, and other items in the carryback years. These are items figured with respect to adjusted gross income. For example, the NOL will lower your adjusted gross income in the carryback years and therefore allow for greater itemized deductions that have an adjusted-gross-income floor. You may also have to recalculate alternative minimum tax.

C corporations can expedite a refund from an NOL carryback by using a special form, Form 1139, *Corporation Application for Tentative Refund*, to obtain a quick refund. This form cannot be filed before the income tax return for the NOL year is filed, and it must be filed no later than 1 year after the NOL year. What is more, if a corporation expects to have an NOL in the current year, it can delay filing the income tax return for the prior year with the knowledge that the tax on the prior year's return will be fully or partially offset by the NOL.

A corporation that expects an NOL for the current year may extend the time for payment of tax for the immediately preceding tax year by filing Form 1138, *Extension of Time for the Payment of Taxes by a Corporation Expecting a Net Operating Loss Carryback*. This form is filed *after* the start of the year in which the NOL is expected but *before* the tax for the preceding year is required to be paid. Such corporations can also further extend the time for payment by filing Form 1139, explained earlier. Doing so extends the time for payment of tax for the immediately preceding tax year until the IRS has informed the corporation that it has allowed or disallowed its application in whole or in part.

You can also claim an NOL on an amended return, Form 1040X or Form 1120X. Individuals who carry back NOLs cannot recalculate self-employment tax and get a refund of this tax. The NOL applies for income tax purposes only.

Limitations on Business Losses

Once you figure whether your business has sustained operating losses, you must then determine the extent to which you can deduct these losses. A number of limits apply that restrict full and immediate write-offs of business losses. For example, the hobby loss rules may limit deductions from certain business activities, as explained in Chapter 26. Not all of the rules that follow apply to all types of businesses, so only review those rules applicable to your company.

Basis

If you own a pass-through entity, business losses claimed on your personal return cannot exceed your tax basis in the company. Losses in excess of basis can be carried forward and used in future years to the extent of basis at that time. There is no time limit on these carryforwards.

PARTNERSHIPS AND LLCS

Basis is determined, in part, by the way in which a partner or member acquires his interest in the entity.

- If the interest is acquired by contributing directly to the entity (typically in the start-up of the business), then basis is the cash and owner's basis of the property contributed to the entity.
- If the interest is purchased from an owner (for example, a retiring partner), then basis is the cash and value of the property paid.
- If the interest is acquired by performing services for the business, then basis is the amount of compensation reported. However, the receipt of an interest in the profits of the business (and not a capital interest) is not taxable under certain conditions and so does not give rise to any basis.
- If the interest is inherited from a deceased owner, then basis is the value of the interest for estate tax purposes (typically the value of the interest on the date of the owner's death).

If property transferred to the entity is subject to liabilities, owners increase their basis by their share of the liabilities.

After the initial determination of basis, it may be increased or decreased annually. Basis is increased by the following items (determined on a per-share, per-day basis):

- The owner's distributive share of entity income
- The owner's share of tax-exempt income (such as life insurance proceeds)
- Excess of depletion deductions over the basis of depletable property
- Additional capital contributions
- Share of new partnership liabilities (Limited partners in limited partnerships do not increase their basis by a share of liabilities assumed by the general partners.)

Basis is decreased (on a per-share, per-day basis), but not below zero, by:

- The owner's distributive share of entity losses (including capital losses)
- The owner's share of expenses that are not deductible in figuring entity income
- Distributions to the owner by the entity

S CORPORATIONS

Basis for the purpose of deducting pass-through losses means your basis in your S corporation stock—what you contributed to the corporation to acquire your shares—plus the amount of any money you loaned to the corporation. If S corporation stock is acquired by inheritance, the basis, which is generally the value of the stock on the date of the owner's death, is reduced by the portion of the value attributable to income in respect of a decedent. This is income earned by the owner prior to death that is received by and reported by the person who inherits the stock.

Guaranteeing corporate debt, which is a common practice for bank loans to S corporations, does *not* give rise to basis. However, if you are called on to make good on your guarantee, then you can increase your basis by the amount you pay to the bank on the corporation's behalf. A better strategy: Talk to third party lenders so that outstanding loans are reworked to make you primarily liable on the debt, which allows you to increase your basis. It's as if the third party loaned money to you and then you loaned it to your S corporation. Be sure that the corporation repays you, and then you repay the third party lender.

A shareholder's basis is not affected by the corporation's liabilities. Unlike a partner who can increase his basis by his share of partnership liabilities, an S corporation shareholder may not increase his basis by his share of corporate liabilities.

After the initial determination of basis, it may be increased or decreased annually. Basis is increased by:

- The shareholder's share of the corporation's ordinary income
- The shareholder's share of separately stated items reported on the Schedule K-1 (including tax-exempt income)
- Excess of depletion deductions over the basis of depletable property
- Additional capital contributions

Basis is decreased (but not below zero) by:

- The shareholder's share of the corporation's losses
- The shareholder's share of expenses and losses that are not deductible in figuring ordinary income
- Noncapital and nondeductible corporate expenses reported on the Schedule K-1 (e.g., 50% of meal and entertainment costs and nondeductible penalties)
- Distributions not includible in the shareholder's income (e.g., dividends in excess of basis)

If an S corporation donated appreciated property to charity in 2014, the shareholder reduced his or her basis by the allocable share of the corporation's basis in the property (not the corporation's charitable contribution, which is based on the property's fair market value). (This is assuming that the 2013 rule is extended for 2014 as expected; see the Supplement for details).

At-Risk Rules

In the past it was not uncommon for someone to invest in a business by contributing a small sum of cash and a large note on which there was no personal liability. The note increased the investor's basis against which tax write-offs could be claimed. If the business prospered, all was well and good. If the business failed, the individual lost only the small amount of cash invested. Congress felt this arrangement was unreasonably beneficial to investors and created *at-risk rules*. At-risk rules operate to limit your losses to the extent of your at-risk amounts in the activity. Your at-risk amounts are, in effect, your economic investment in the activity. This is the cash you put into a business. It also includes the adjusted basis of other property you contribute and any debts secured by your property or for which you are personally liable for repayment.

You are not considered at risk if you have an agreement or arrangement that limits your risk. As a practical matter, if you set up and conduct an active business operation, you probably do not have to be concerned with the at-risk rules. First, you may qualify for an exception to the at-risk rules for closely held C corporations (discussed later). Also, in all probability your investment is what has started and sustained the business. But, if you are an investor, your contribution may be limited, and your losses may be limited as well.

Example

You invest in a partnership to distribute a motion picture. You invest $1,000 cash and sign a promissory note for $9,000. The note is nonrecourse (you are not personally liable for the debt). Your at-risk amount is $1,000, the cash you invested. You cannot deduct losses from this activity in excess of $1,000.

If you are subject to the at-risk rules, you do not lose your deductions to the extent they exceed your at-risk amounts; you simply cannot claim them currently. The losses can be carried forward and used in subsequent years if your at-risk amount increases. There is no limit on the carryover period. If the activity is sold, your gain from the disposition of property is treated as income from the activity, and you can then offset the gain by the amount of your carried-over losses.

At-risk rules do not apply to investments in closely held C corporations that meet active business tests and that do not engage in equipment leasing or any business involving master sound recording, films, videotapes, or other artistic, literary, or musical property.

CALCULATING YOUR AT-RISK LIMITATION

Your at-risk amounts—cash, adjusted basis of property contributed to the activity, and recourse loans—form your *at-risk basis*. It is this basis that is used to limit your losses. Your at-risk basis is calculated at the end of the year. Losses allowed reduce your at-risk basis. Thus, once you have offset your entire at-risk basis, you cannot claim further losses from the activity until you increase your at-risk basis.

Partners and LLC members are treated as at risk to the extent that basis in the entity is increased by their share of the entity's income. If the partnership or LLC makes distributions of income, the amount distributed reduces the partner's or LLC member's at-risk amount.

If you are subject to the at-risk rules, you must file Form 6198, *At-Risk Limitations*, to determine the amount of loss you can claim in the current year. You file a separate form for each activity. If you have an interest in a partnership, LLC, or S corporation that has more than 1 investment in any of the 4 categories listed, you can aggregate these activities. The 4 categories subject to these aggregation rules are:

1. Holding, producing, or distributing motion picture films or videotapes
2. Exploring for or exploiting oil and gas properties

3. Exploring for or exploiting geothermal deposits

4. Farming (but not forestry)

For example, if your S corporation distributes films and videotapes, you can aggregate these activities and treat them as one activity. In addition, all leased depreciable business equipment is treated as one activity for purposes of the at-risk rules.

You may also aggregate activities that you actively manage. This allows you to use losses from one activity as long as there is sufficient at-risk basis from another. If you invest in a partnership, LLC, or S corporation, the activities of the entity can be aggregated if 65% or more of the losses for the year are allocable to persons who actively participate in the management of the entity.

SPECIAL RULE FOR REAL ESTATE FINANCING

You can treat nonrecourse financing from commercial lenders or government agencies as being at risk if the financing is secured by the real estate. This special rule does not apply to financing from related parties, seller financing, or financing from promoters. It does apply to real property placed in service after 1986. However, if you acquire an interest in a partnership, LLC, or S corporation after 1986, you can use this special rule regardless of when the entity placed the realty in service.

Passive Activity Loss Rules

If you work for your business full-time, you need not be concerned with the *passive activity loss (PAL) rules*. These rules apply only to a business in which you have an ownership interest but do not work in the day-to-day operations or management (i.e., **materially participate**) as well as rental real estate activities. If an owner is subject to the PAL rules, then deductions from the activity for the year are limits (see under How the Passive Activity Loss Rules Limit Deductions for Expenses). If the owner falls under the PAL rules, he or she may also be subject to the 3.8% additional Medicare tax on net investment income (NII).

Limited partners can never materially participate because they are barred by their status from making day-to-day operating decisions in their business. However, some courts have decided that LLC members are not treated the same as limited partners because they can participate in daily activities; their material participation determines whether they are subject to the PAL rules. The IRS has acquiesced in these cases.

Passive activity   Any activity involving the conduct of a business in which you do not materially participate and all rental activities. These rules operate to limit a current deduction for losses from these activities unless certain exceptions, discussed later in this chapter, apply.

Material participation   Participation in a passive activity that satisfies 1 of 7 tests set forth in the tax law. The basic test requires a minimum of 500 hours of participation during the year. Material participation may be allowed for as little as 100 hours of participation during the year if no other owner in the activity participates more.

The 7 tests for proving material participation include:

1. You participate in the activity for more than 500 hours during the year. You need only participate for a mere 10 hours a week for 50 weeks in the year to satisfy this test.
2. Your participation is substantially all of the participation in the activity of all individuals for the year, including the participation of individuals who did not own any interest in the activity. This means that if you are a sole proprietor and do not hire someone else to run the business, you meet this participation test, even if you work only 5 hours each week.
3. You participate in the activity for more than 100 hours during the tax year, and you participate at least as much as any other individual (including individuals who do not own any interest in the activity) for the year.
4. The activity is a *significant participation activity*, and you participate in all significant participation activities for more than 500 hours. A significant participation activity is any business in which you participate for more than 100 hours during the year and in which you did not materially participate under any of the other material participation tests.
5. You materially participated in the activity for any 5 (whether or not consecutive) of the 10 preceding tax years. This rule can be useful to someone who retires from the business while continuing to own an interest but who materially participated prior to retirement.
6. The activity is a personal service activity in which you materially participated for any 3 (whether or not consecutive) preceding tax years.
7. Based on all the facts and circumstances, you participate in the activity on a regular, continuous, and substantial basis. At a minimum, you must have participated during more than 100 hours. Managing the activity is not treated as participation if any person other than you received compensation for managing it or any individual spent more hours during the year managing the activity than you (regardless of whether such individual was compensated).

Limited partners are automatically treated as subject to the passive activity loss rules because they are prohibited from participating in the business activities. Under regulations proposed, limited liability company (LLC) members would be treated like limited partners only if:

- The LLC is treated like a partnership, and
- The member does not have rights to manage the LLC at all times during the LLC's tax year under the law of the jurisdiction in which the LLC was organized and under the LLC governing agreement. Rights to manage include the power to bind the entity to a contract.

RENTAL REAL ESTATE EXCEPTIONS

There are 2 special rules for rental real estate activities that may allow you to claim losses in excess of rental income. Rule 1 allows a limited amount of loss in excess of income to be deducted if participation is considered to be active (**active participation**). This limited loss deduction is called the $25,000 allowance and can be claimed by individuals whose adjusted gross income does not exceed $100,000. The allowance is phased out for those with adjusted gross income over $100,000 and is entirely eliminated when adjusted gross income is $150,000 or more. Married couples must file jointly to claim this allowance unless they lived apart for the entire year. In this case, up to $12,500 in losses can be deducted on a separate return (with a phase-out of the allowance for adjusted gross income over $50,000).

Active participation   Participation in a rental real estate activity that is less than the material participation standard. Participation in decision making may be sufficient. For example, if you set the rents, screen tenants, and review expenses, you may satisfy the active participation test. Having a managing agent to collect rents and see to property repairs does not prevent active participation by an owner.

Rule 2 allows real estate professionals to escape the PAL limitations altogether for purposes of deducting losses from their rental real estate activities. Individuals can be considered real estate professionals if they meet certain tests regarding their participation in real estate activities in general, including real estate construction, conversion, management, or brokerage activities, as well as rental real estate. If a qualifying real estate professional then meets material participation tests with respect to the rental real estate, losses from the rental real estate activity escape PAL restrictions. (Details of these rules are in the instructions to Form 8582.)

The PAL rules are very complicated. Determine whether you may be subject to the rules or whether you can ignore them. If you are subject to the rules, be sure you understand the potential impact that they can have on deducting expenses of an activity.

If you run a business or work full time, you need not be concerned with the PAL rules. You will certainly meet the tests for material participation. If you are a silent partner in a partnership, LLC, or S corporation, you should be concerned that you may be subject to the PAL rules. However, you may fall within an exception to the PAL rules in order to deduct losses in excess of income from the activity (for example, you may be able to eke out enough participation to be considered a material participant). Keep a diary or log book noting the time you put into the business and the types of activities you perform for the business.

HOW THE PASSIVE ACTIVITY LOSS RULES LIMIT DEDUCTIONS FOR EXPENSES

If the rules apply, your losses from passive activities that exceed income from all other passive activities cannot be deducted in the current year. You can carry over your unused deductions to future years. These are called *suspended losses*, for which there is no limit on the carryover period.

You can claim all carryover deductions from an activity in the year in which you dispose of your entire interest in the activity. A disposition includes a sale to an unrelated party, abandonment of the business, or the business becoming completely worthless. Simply giving away your interest does not amount to a disposition that allows you to deduct your suspended losses.

The PAL limitation for noncorporate taxpayers is computed on Form 8582, *Passive Activity Loss Limitations*. Closely held C corporations subject to the PAL rules must file Form 8810, *Corporate Passive Activity Loss and Credit Limitations*. Similar rules apply to tax credits from passive activities. The limitation on tax credits from passive activities for noncorporate taxpayers is computed on Form 8582-CR, *Passive Activity Credit Limitations*.

COORDINATION WITH AT-RISK RULES

At-risk rules are applied first. Any amounts that are deductible after applying your at-risk loss limitation are then subject to the passive activity loss rules. Complete Form 6198 first; then complete Form 8582.

Limits on Farm Losses

Farming losses cannot be used as a tax shelter. Farming losses by those receiving certain subsidies are limited in how much can be used to offset nonfarm income on Schedule F. The limit is the greater of $300,000 ($150,000 for married persons filing separately) or the net farm income received over the past 5 years.

Losses limited by this rule are not lost forever; they can be carried forward and used in future years to the extent allowed by this rule. The limit applies to farmers (other than those operating as C corporations) who receive any direct or countercyclical payments under Title I of the Food, Conservation, and Energy Act of 2008, or Commodity Credit loans. For partnerships and S corporations, the limit applies at the partner or shareholder level, based on the year in which the entity's tax year ends.

Where to Report Business Income

Self-Employed (Including Independent Contractors)

Business income generally is reported on Schedule C, *Profit or Loss from Business*. The results from this schedule are part of your personal income tax return, Form 1040. You may be able to use a simplified return to report your business income—Schedule C-EZ, *Net Profit from Business*. You can use the simplified return if you meet *all* of the following requirements:

- You are on the cash method of accounting.
- You do not maintain inventory.
- You do not have any employees.
- Your business expenses do not exceed $5,000.
- You do not place in service any depreciable property during the year.
- You do not claim a home office deduction.
- You show a profit for the year.
- You do not have any other sole proprietorship.
- You do not have any passive activity loss carryovers for this business.

If you maintain inventory, you must complete Part III of Schedule C to figure your cost of goods sold.

In reporting the business's investment-type income, the specific items are not listed on Schedule C. Instead attach a schedule detailing these items and report only the total amount on Schedule C. Be sure to distinguish between your business and personal investment-type income. For example, if you own stock, dividends received on the stock generally are reported as personal, not business income, unless you are a dealer in securities.

Net operating losses are computed on Form 1045, *Application for Tentative Refund*. Use this form or Form 1040X to claim a net operating loss (NOL) carryback. If you are carrying forward an NOL, you claim the loss as a negative amount entered on Form 1040 as other income.

Farmers

If you are a sole proprietor operating a farming business, instead of using Schedule C (or C-EZ) to report your income, you use Schedule F, Profit or Loss from Farming. The section of the schedule used to report your farm income depends on your method of accounting. Cash basis farmers use Part I of Schedule F to report income. Accrual basis farmers use Part III of Schedule F to report farm income.

If you received rental income based on farm production or crop shares and you did not materially participate in the management or operation of the farm, use Form 4835, *Farm Rental Income and Expenses*, to report this rental income. Since you did not materially participate, this income is not part of your farming income on which self-employment tax is assessed. If you elect to income-average your farm income, you must file Schedule J, *Farm Income Averaging*.

Net operating losses are computed on Form 1045, *Application for Tentative Refund*. You use this form or Form 1040X to claim an NOL carryback. If you are carrying forward an NOL, you claim the loss as a negative amount entered on Form 1040 as other income.

Partnerships and LLCs

Operating income of a partnership or LLC, called *total income* (loss), is reported on Form 1065, *U.S. Return of Partnership Income*. For inventory-based partnerships and LLCs, the cost of goods sold is figured on Schedule A of Form 1065.

Miscellaneous income items discussed in this chapter are reported separately from the gross profit, fees, and sales. Miscellaneous items are detailed on a separate schedule attached to the return. Partners and members in LLCs then report their share of net income or loss from the business on Schedule E, *Supplemental Income and Loss*, as part of their personal return.

Other income items are separately stated items that pass through to partners and members apart from the business' total income, and are reported on Schedule K-1, *Partner's Share of Income, Credits, Deductions, Etc.* Owners then report these separate items on the appropriate place on their personal returns. For example, items considered to be portfolio income—income other than that derived in the ordinary course of business—are separately stated items.

If the partnership or LLC passes through losses to the partners and members, they may be able to claim an NOL deduction on their personal returns. Refer to the earlier discussion of "Self-Employed."

S Corporations

Operating income of an S corporation is reported on Form 1120S, *U.S. Income Tax Return for an S Corporation*. For inventory-based S corporations, the cost of goods sold is figured on Schedule A of Form 1120S.

Miscellaneous income items discussed in this chapter are reported separately from the gross profit from fees and sales. These miscellaneous items are detailed on a separate schedule attached to the return. Shareholders then report their share of net income or loss from the business on Schedule E, *Supplemental Income and Loss*.

Income taxed to the S corporation for LIFO recapture, excessive passive income, or built-in gains is explained on a separate schedule. The tax on this income is then reported on Form 1120S.

Other income items are separately stated items that pass through to shareholders apart from the corporation's total income and are reported on Schedule K-1, *Shareholder's Share of Income, Credits, Deductions, Etc.* Shareholders then report these separate items on the appropriate place on their personal returns. For example, items considered to be portfolio income—income other than income derived in the ordinary course of business—are separately stated items.

If the S corporation passes through losses to the shareholders, it may be able to claim an NOL deduction. Refer to the earlier discussion of "Self-Employed."

C Corporations

C corporations report their income on Form 1120, *U.S. Corporation Income Tax Return*. For inventory-based corporations, the cost of goods sold is figured on Schedule A of Form 1120. Dividends are reported on Schedule C of Form 1120 to enable the corporation to figure its dividends-received deduction. Tax-exempt interest received or accrued is reported on Schedule K of Form 1120.

Miscellaneous income items, such as recoveries of bad debts deducted in prior years or recapture of the first-year expense deduction, are detailed on a separate schedule attached to the return.

Net operating losses carried from other years to the current year are deducted on the specific line provided for this item on Form 1120. If a corporation has an NOL for the current year, it can obtain a quick refund by filing Form 1139, *Corporation Application for Tentative Refund*. If it expects to have an NOL in the current year and it will be able to offset tax in the prior year, it can delay the filing of the prior year's return by filing Form 1138, *Extension of Time for Payment of Taxes by a Corporation Expecting a Net Operating Loss Carryback*. On this form you explain why a loss is expected. The extension is in effect until the end of the month in which the return for the NOL year is due, including extensions. If a corporation wants to forgo the carryback, it must indicate this election by checking the appropriate box in Schedule K, *Other Information*, of Form 1120.

All Taxpayers

Merchant card and third-party payment providers must report transactions on Form 1099-K that total more than $20,000 for at least 200 transactions. Include the income from these transactions along with other gross receipts. Adjust the income reported by any returns, refunds, allowances, cash-backs, or other amounts that reduced the revenue from these transactions. No reconciliation with 1099-K amounts is required.

COST OF GOODS SOLD.   Taxpayers other than Schedule C filers with inventory who must figure cost of goods sold do so on Form 1125-A, *Cost of Goods Sold*.

AT-RISK LOSS LIMITS AND PASSIVE LOSS RULES.   Taxpayers subject to the PAL rules and the at-risk rules must figure any limitations on business losses on specific tax forms. Figure the at-risk loss limits first. Then compute the PAL limits.

Only individuals and pass-through entities must figure the at-risk loss limits (closely held C corporations that are active companies are exempt from these rules). The limits are figured on Form 6198, *At-Risk Limitations*.

Noncorporate taxpayers compute their PAL limits on Form 8582, *Passive Activity Loss Limitations*. Closely held C corporations subject to the PAL rules must file Form 8810, *Corporate Passive Activity Loss and Credit Limitations*.

Capital Gains and Losses

Alert

At the time this book was printed, Congress had not extended numerous breaks for 2014 that had expired at the end of 2013. Check the online supplement in February 2015 at www.jklasser.com or www.barbaraweltman.com to see whether these breaks apply for 2014 returns.

Companies may sell assets other than inventory items. These sales may result in gains or losses that are classified as *capital gains or losses*. Similarly, companies may exchange assets, also producing capital gains or losses unless tax-free exchange rules apply. Further, owners may sell their interests in the business for gain or loss.

Capital gains generally are treated more favorably than other types of income. However, C corporations do not realize any significant tax benefit from capital gains. What's more, capital losses may be subject to special limitations.

The treatment of gains and losses from Section 1231 property and income resulting from depreciation recapture are discussed in Chapter 6.

For further information about capital gains and losses, see IRS Publication 537, *Installment Sales*; IRS Publication 544, *Sales and Other Dispositions of Assets*; and IRS Publication 550, *Investment Interest and Expenses*.

What Are Capital Gains and Losses?

The tax law generally looks more favorably on income classified as capital gains than on other types of income—at least for pass-through entities. On the flip side, the tax law provides special treatment for capital losses. To understand how capital gains and losses affect your business income, you need to know what items are subject to capital gain or loss treatment and how to determine gains and losses.

Capital Assets

If you own property used in or owned by your business (other than Section 1231 property discussed in Chapter 6, or Section 1244 stock discussed later in this chapter), gain or loss on the disposition of the property generally is treated as capital gain or loss. *Capital gains and losses* are gains and losses taken on **capital assets**.

Capital assets   **Property held for investment and other property not otherwise excluded from capital asset treatment. For example, your interest in a partnership or stocks and securities is treated as a capital asset.**

Most property is treated as capital assets. Excluded from the definition of capital assets are:

- Property held for sale to customers or property that will physically become part of merchandise for sale to customers (inventory)
- Accounts or notes receivable generated by your business (e.g., accounts receivable from the sale of inventory)
- Depreciable property used in your business, even if already fully depreciated (e.g., telephones)
- Real property used in your business (e.g., your factory)
- A copyright; literary or artistic composition; a letter or memorandum; or other similar property (e.g., photographs, tapes, manuscripts) created by your personal efforts or acquired from the creator by gift or in another transaction entitling you to use the creator's basis
- U.S. government publications

Under a special rule, self-created musical works qualify for capital asset treatment, if the musician so elects.

Determining the Amount of Your Gain or Loss

The difference between the **amount received** for your property on a sale, exchange, or other disposition, and your **adjusted basis** in the property is your gain or loss.

Amount received The cash, fair market value of property, and relief of liability you get when you dispose of your property. For example, if you own a computer system for your business and you upgrade with a new system and sell your old system to another business, any cash you receive is considered an amount received. Upon the sale, you receive $5,000 cash, plus the buyer agrees to pay the remaining balance of $2,000 on a bank loan you took to buy the system; your amount received is $7,000 ($5,000 cash, plus $2,000 liability relieved).

Adjusted basis This is your basis in the property, adjusted for certain items. Start with the original cost if you bought the property (the cash and other property you paid to acquire it). Even if the cash did not come out of your pocket—for example, if you took a loan—the cash you turn over to the seller is part of your basis. Adjust the basis by reducing it for any depreciation claimed (or that could have been claimed) and any casualty loss you claimed with respect to the property. For example, if your original computer system cost you $10,000, and you claimed $2,000 depreciation, your adjusted basis is $8,000.

You adjust basis—upward or downward—for certain items occurring in the acquisition of the asset or during the time you hold it. Amounts that *increase* basis include:

- Improvements or additions to property.
- Legal fees to acquire property or defend title to it.
- Selling expenses (e.g., a real estate broker's fee or advertising costs).
- Unharvested crops sold with the land.

Amounts that *decrease* basis include:

- Amortized bond premiums.
- Cancellation of income adjustments (e.g., debt forgiveness because of bankruptcy or insolvency or on farm or business real property).
- Casualty losses that have been deducted (e.g., insurance awards and other settlements).
- Deductions for energy-efficient commercial buildings.
- Depletion allowances with respect to certain natural resources.

- Depreciation, amortization, first-year expensing, and obsolescence. (You must reduce the basis of property by the amount of depreciation that you were entitled to take even if you failed to take it.)
- Investment credit claimed with respect to the property. (The full credit decreases basis but one-half of the credit claimed after 1982 is added back for a net reduction of one-half of the credit.)
- Return of capital. (Dividends on stock are paid out of capital or out of a depletion reserve instead of earnings and profits or surplus.)
- Tax credit for alternative fuel vehicles and plug-in electric vehicles.

You do not adjust basis for selling expenses and related costs. These amounts are factored into the amount received (they reduce the amount received on the transaction).

Note: Overstating (inflating) the adjusted basis to minimize gain can result in tax penalties.

DETERMINING BASIS ON ASSETS TRANSFERRED BETWEEN YOU AND YOUR ENTITY

The entity takes over your basis in any assets you contribute in a nontaxable transaction. Thus, if you contribute property to your partnership, the partnership assumes your basis in the property. Similarly, if you contribute property to your corporation as part of a tax-free incorporation, the corporation takes over your basis in the property. The rules for determining the basis in interests in pass-through entities are explained in Chapter 4.

FIGURING GAIN OR LOSS

When the amount received exceeds the adjusted basis of the property, you have a gain. When the adjusted basis exceeds the amount received, you have a loss.

Sale or Exchange Requirement

In order to obtain capital gain or loss treatment on the disposition of a capital asset, you generally must sell or exchange property. Typically, you sell your property, but other transactions may qualify for sale or exchange treatment. For example, if your corporation redeems some or all of your stock, you may be able to treat the redemption as a sale or exchange. Capital losses are subject to limitation on current deductibility as explained later in this chapter.

If you dispose of property in some way other than a sale or exchange, gain or loss generally is treated as ordinary gain or loss. For example, if you abandon business property, your loss is treated as ordinary loss, even though the property is a capital asset. However, if the property is foreclosed on or repossessed, your loss may be a capital loss. If stock becomes worthless, this is treated as a capital loss. Ordinary losses are deductible without regard to the results from other transactions and can be used to offset various types of income (such as interest income).

Holding Period

Whether gains and losses are short-term or long-term depends on how long the asset disposed of has been held. If the holding period is more than 1 year, then gain or loss is long-term. If the holding period is 1 year or less, then the gain or loss is short-term.

If the business buys an asset, the holding period commences at that time (technically on the day after the acquisition date). If you transfer property to your business and the transfer is viewed as a nonrecognition transaction (for example, a tax-free incorporation), the company's holding period includes your holding period.

Example

You form a corporation and transfer ownership of your truck and other items to the corporation in exchange for all of its stock. You acquired your truck on June 1, 2013, and transfer it to the corporation on July 1, 2014. On November 1, 2014, the corporation sells the truck. Its gain or loss on the sale of the truck is long-term because the holding period for the truck is more than one year—measured from the time you acquired it.

If a partnership makes an in-kind (property) distribution to you, include the partnership's holding period in your holding period. However, if the distribution is from the partnership's inventory, then you cannot add the partnership's holding period to yours if you sell the property within 5 years.

TRANSFERS TO A PARTNERSHIP OR LIMITED LIABILITY COMPANY

If you transfer an asset to your company, the company takes on your holding period since this is a nontaxable transaction. If you sell an asset to your company, the company starts its own holding period since the sale generally is a taxable transaction (the company obtains a stepped-up basis for the property).

Tax-Free Exchanges

Gain need not be immediately reported as income if the transaction qualifies as a tax-free exchange. The term *tax-free* is not an entirely apt description because the tax rules for these transactions merely *postpone* the reporting of gain rather than make gain permanently tax free. You reduce the basis of the property you acquire in the exchange by the gain you realized on the trade but did not have to report. Then, when you later sell the replacement property in a taxable transaction, you will report the gain on both initial exchange and the later disposition (if any). There has been a proposal to eliminate tax-free exchange treatment, but nothing concrete has developed; check the Supplement for any update.

> **Example**
>
> You exchange one office building for another of equal value. Your building is worth $175,000, but has a basis of $100,000. The value of the new building is $175,000. You have a gain of $75,000, which may be postponed because of the tax-free exchange rules. The basis in the new building is $100,000 ($175,000 minus $75,000 gain not recognized). If you sell the new building in the future for $225,000, you will recognize gain of $125,000 ($75,000 deferred from the initial exchange, plus $50,000 from the appreciation of the replacement building).

To qualify for the tax-free exchange treatment, both the old property (the property you are giving up) and the new property (the property you are acquiring, called *replacement property*) must be business or investment property (certain property cannot be exchanged tax free). And both of the properties must be of *like kind*. This means they must be of the same class of property. Depreciable tangible personal property can be either like kind or *like class* (the same General Asset Class or Product Class based on the 4-digit codes in the Industrial Classification Manual of the U.S. Department of Commerce). Examples of like-kind property include:

- Vacant lot for a factory building
- Factory building for an office complex
- City property for farmland
- Real estate owned outright for real estate subject to a lease of 30 years or more
- Pickup truck for a panel truck used in the business
- Telephone equipment for computer equipment used in the business
- Stock rights in water rights

The IRS has determined that intangibles, such as trademarks, trade names, newspaper mastheads, and customer-based intangibles, can be treated as like kind if they can be separately described and valued apart from goodwill.

If non-like-kind property is also received in the exchange, you must recognize gain to the extent of this other property, called *boot*.

> **Example**
>
> Use the example of the building, except that the replacement building is only valued at $150,000 and you receive $25,000 cash to make the exchange of equal value. You must recognize gain of $25,000, the extent of the boot

received. The basis of the replacement building in this case is reduced by only $50,000, and the gain is not recognized.

TIMING

Like-kind exchanges must be completed within set time limits. The new property must be identified within 45 days after you transfer the old property. This identification applies to up to 3 properties (or any number where the value of the properties is not more than double the value of the property given up). To identify the property, a good description of it must be put in writing. *Incidental property*, property valued at not more than 15% of the total value of the other property, is disregarded; it need not be identified. Then, the exchange must be completed (you must receive the new property) within 180 days after you transfer the old property or the due date of your return (including extensions) for the year you gave up the old property if this is earlier than 180 days after the transfer.

Since it is not always easy to locate appropriate exchange property, you may work with a qualified intermediary to locate the property, acquire it, and then exchange it with you. A *qualified intermediary* is someone (other than your attorney, accountant, broker, employee, or a related person) who makes a written agreement to acquire the property you are giving up and to transfer replacement property to you. The agreement must limit your rights to receive, pledge, borrow, or otherwise obtain the benefits of money or other property held by the qualified intermediary.

Installment Sales

Gain need not be reported all at once if the sale is structured as an installment sale. This generally allows you to report gain as payments are received. An *installment sale* occurs when at least one payment is received after the year of sale.

Under the installment method, a portion of each payment received represents a return of your investment (part of your adjusted basis), and another part represents your profit (gain). You figure the amount of gain reported each year by a ratio:

$$\text{Gross profit percentage (reportable gain)} = \frac{\text{Gross profit}}{\text{Selling price (contract price)}}$$

ELECTION OUT OF INSTALLMENT REPORTING

You can opt out of installment reporting and elect to report the entire gain in the year of sale (even though payments will be received at a later time). The election does not require any special forms. You simply report your entire gain in the year of sale. But once you do so, you generally cannot change your mind later on, even if your choice proved to be the wrong one taxwise.

> **Example**
>
> You sell property worth $100,000 for 5 annual installments of $20,000, plus 8% interest. Your adjusted basis in the property is $60,000 so your gross profit is $40,000 ($100,000 − $60,000). Your gross profit percentage is 40% ($40,000 ÷ $100,000). This means that 40% of each installment represents your gain while 60% is a return of your investment. Thus, in the first year, $8,000 of the $20,000 payment is gain while $12,000 is a return of your investment.

Why would you want to report all of your gain in one year when you can spread it out over a number of years? Reporting the entire gain in the year of sale may be wise, for example, if you have a net operating loss carryforward that can be used to offset the gain.

INTEREST ON DEFERRED PAYMENTS

Payments must bear a reasonable rate of interest. If you fail to fix a reasonable rate of interest, then a portion of each payment is deemed to represent interest rather than capital gain. *Reasonable rate of interest* usually is the applicable federal rate (AFR) of interest for the term of the installment sale. (Applicable federal rate is explained in Chapter 7.)

If the seller finances the purchase, the required minimum interest rate is the lower of 9% ("safe harbor rate") compounded semiannually or the AFR, provided the financed amount does not exceed $5,557,200 in 2014. With interest rates running below the 9% safe harbor rate, charging the AFR will produce a lower allowable interest rate. If the deferred amount exceeds $5,557,200, then the required minimum interest rate is 100% of the AFR.

DEPRECIABLE PROPERTY

If you sell depreciable property on the installment basis, any depreciation recapture must be reported in full in the year of sale regardless of when payments are actually received. In other words, gain resulting from depreciation recapture may exceed the cash payments received in the year of the installment sale but must be reported as income anyway. Installment sales are also discussed in Chapter 2.

Tax Treatment of Capital Gains and Losses for Pass-Through Entities

Capital gains and losses are separately stated items that pass through separately to owners. They are not taken into account in figuring the entity's total income (or loss). The reason for this distinction is to allow individual owners to apply the capital gain and loss rules on individual tax returns.

The impact of pass-through treatment of capital gains and losses is that owners may have favorable capital gains rates applied to their share of the business's capital gains. Similarly, they may offset pass-through gains and losses from their business against their personal gains and losses.

> ### Example
>
> In 2014, a shareholder in an S corporation has pass-through capital loss from his corporation of $10,000. He also has a $10,000 capital gain distribution from a mutual fund he owns in his personal investment account. He can offset the business loss by his personal gain on his individual income tax return.

Tax Rates on Capital Gains

Owners who are individuals pay tax on their share of capital gains as they would on their gains from personal investments. Thus, long-term capital gains generally are subject to a basic capital gains rate of 15%. However, owners in the 10% and 15% tax brackets pay no tax on their share of capital gains; those in the 39.6% tax bracket pay a 20% rate. Owners who are "high income taxpayers" may also pay the 3.8% additional Medicare tax on net investment income (although gains from the sale of business property may not be treated as investment income). These rates apply to sales and exchanges in 2014 as well as to payments received in 2014 on installment sales made in prior years.

SHORT-TERM GAIN

This type of gain is subject to the same tax rates as ordinary income. Owners in a pass-through entity may pay different tax rates on the same share of short-term capital gain.

> ### Example
>
> An LLC with 2 equal owners sells at a profit a capital asset held for 6 months. In 2014, one owner may be in the 36.9% tax bracket while another is in the 25% tax bracket. Even though each owner receives an equal share of the gain, one owner pays a greater amount of tax on that gain than the other according to each owner's own tax bracket.

UNRECAPTURED GAIN

Gain from the sale of real property on which straight line depreciation was taken results in unrecaptured gain (the amount of straight line depreciation). This portion of capital gain is taxed at the rate of 25% if the owner is in a tax bracket higher than the 15% tax bracket.

If property with unrecaptured gain is sold on the installment basis (discussed later in this chapter), then the first payment is deemed to reflect unrecaptured gain. When this amount has been fully reported, all additional amounts are capital gains subject to the lower rates detailed above.

SECTION 1202 GAIN

Gain on the sale of Section 1202 stock (referred to as "small business stock"), which is stock in a C corporation that meets certain requirements, is partly or fully excludable. The exclusion depends on when the sale takes place. Later in this chapter there is more on the sale of small business stock.

CAPITAL LOSSES

Special rules determine how capital losses of individuals may be used. These rules are discussed later in this chapter.

Tax Treatment of Capital Gains and Losses for C Corporations

C corporations must follow the rules discussed throughout this chapter on reporting capital gains and losses separately from their other income. These gains and losses are detailed on the corporation's Schedule D. However, C corporations at present realize no benefit from capital gains. *Net gains*, capital gains in excess of capital losses, are simply added to other business income. In effect, capital gains are taxed at the same rate as the corporation's other income. In the past, C corporations enjoyed a favorable tax rate on their capital gains and it may be possible that this treatment will be restored in the future.

While there are no benefits from capital gains, capital losses of C corporations are subject to special limitations discussed later in this chapter.

Loss Limitations

In some cases, even if you sell or exchange property at a loss, you may not be permitted to deduct your loss. If you sell, exchange, or even abandon a Section 197 intangible (see Chapter 14 for a complete discussion of the amortization of Section 197 intangibles), you cannot deduct your loss if you still hold other Section 197 intangibles that you acquired in the same transaction. Instead, you increase the basis of the Section 197 intangibles that you still own. This means that instead of deducting your loss in the year you dispose of one Section 197 intangible, you will deduct a portion of the loss over the remaining recovery period for the Section 197 intangibles you still hold.

Similarly, you cannot deduct losses on sales or exchanges of property between related parties (defined later). This related party rule prevents you from deducting a loss if you sell a piece of equipment to your spouse. However, the party acquiring the property from you (the original transferee, or in this case, your spouse) can add to the basis the amount of loss you were not allowed to deduct in determining gain or loss on a subsequent disposition of the property.

Example

You sell your partnership interest to your daughter for $7,500. Your basis in the interest is $10,000. You cannot deduct your $2,500 loss. However, if your daughter then sells the partnership interest for $12,000, her gain is minimized to the extent of your nondeductible loss. Her tentative gain is $4,500 ($12,000 amount received less basis of $7,500). The amount of gain she must report is $2,000 ($4,500 tentative gain less $2,500 nondeductible loss).

Related Parties

The tax law defines who is considered a *related party*. This includes not only certain close relatives (spouses, siblings, parents, children, grandparents, and grandchildren), but also certain businesses you control. A *controlled entity* is a corporation in which you own, directly or indirectly, more than 50% of the value of all outstanding stock, or a partnership in which you own, directly or indirectly, more than 50% of the capital interest or profits interest.

Businesses may be treated as related parties. These relationships include:

- A corporation and partnership if the same persons own more than 50% in the value of the outstanding stock of the corporation and more than 50% of the capital interest or profits interest in the partnership.
- Two corporations that are members of the same controlled group (one corporation owns a certain percentage of the other, or owners own a certain percentage of each corporation).
- Two S corporations if the same persons own more than 50% in value of the outstanding stock in each corporation.
- Two corporations, one of which is an S corporation, if the same person owns more than 50% in value of the outstanding stock of each corporation.
- Special rules are used to determine control. These rules not only look at actual ownership but also take into account certain constructive ownership (ownership that is not actual but has the same effect in the eyes of the tax law). For example, for purposes of the related party rule, you are treated as constructively owning any stock owned by your spouse.

Special rules also apply to transactions between partners and their partnerships. It is important to note that what you may view as a related party may not be treated as such for tax purposes. Thus, for example, your in-laws and cousins are not treated as related parties. If you sell property to an in-law or cousin at a loss, you are not prevented from deducting the loss.

Loss Limits on Individuals

You can deduct capital losses against capital gains without limit. Short-term losses from sales of assets held 1 year or less are first used to offset short-term gains otherwise taxed up to 39.6%. Similarly, long-term losses from sales of assets held more than one year offset long-term gains otherwise taxed as low as 15% (zero for those in the 10% and 15% tax brackets; 20% for those in the 39.6% tax bracket), depending on when the transaction occurred. Losses in excess of their category are then used to offset gains starting with those taxed at the highest rates. For example, short-term losses in excess of short-term capital gains can be used to offset long-term capital gains from the sale of qualified small business stock acquired before February 18, 2009, and held more than 5 years, 50% of such gain of which is otherwise taxed at up to 28% (for an effective tax rate of 14%). However, if your capital losses exceed your capital gains, you can deduct only $3,000 of losses against your other income (such as salaries, dividends, and interest income).

If married persons file separate returns, the capital loss offset to other income is limited to $1,500. If you do not use up all of your capital losses, you can carry over any unused amount and claim it in future years. There is no limit on the carryover period for individuals.

Loss Limits on Corporations

If your corporation realizes capital losses, they are deductible only against capital gains. Any capital losses in excess of capital gains can be carried back for 3 years and then, if not used up, carried forward for up to 5 years. If they are not used within the 5-year carryover period, they are lost forever.

The carryback may entitle your corporation to a refund of taxes from the carryback years. The corporation can apply for this refund by filing Form 1120X, *Amended U.S. Corporation Income Tax Return*. A corporation cannot choose to forgo the carryback in order to simply carry forward the unused capital losses.

Special rules apply in calculating the corporation's carryback and carryforward. You do not use any capital loss carried from another year when determining the corporation's capital loss deduction for the current year. If you have losses from more than one year carried to another year, you use the losses as follows: First, deduct the loss from the earliest year. After that is fully deducted, deduct the loss from the next earliest year. You cannot use a capital loss carried from another year to produce or increase a net operating loss (NOL) in the year to which you carry it.

Sales of Business Interests

The type of interest you own governs the tax treatment accorded to the sale of your interest.

Sole Proprietorship

If you sell your incorporated sole proprietorship, you are viewed as selling the assets of the business. The sale of all the assets of a business is discussed in Chapter 6.

Partnerships and LLCs

PARTNERSHIPS

Gain or loss on the sale of your partnership interest is treated as capital gain *except* to the extent any gain relates to **unrealized receivables** and inventory items. Gain in this case is ordinary income.

Unrealized receivables   These are amounts not previously included in income that represent a right to payments for noncapital assets, which include inventory, services rendered, and services to be rendered.

If you receive items that were inventory to the partnership, they may be treated as capital assets to you. However, if you dispose of the items within 5 years, then any gain with respect to these items is ordinary income, not capital gain.

LLCs

Generally, the rules governing the sale of a partnership interest apply with equal force to the sale of an interest in an LLC. However, there are 2 special situations to consider:

1. *Sale of multiple-owner LLC to a single buyer*. The entity is treated as hypothetically making a liquidating distribution of all of its assets to the sellers, followed by a deemed purchase by the single buyer of all the assets now hypothetically held by the sellers. The sellers then recognize gain or loss (depending on their basis in the LLC interests).

2. *Sale of a single-member LLC to multiple buyers*. This entity is treated as hypothetically selling its assets and then contributing them to the new entity comprised of multiple buyers (treated as a partnership). You recognize gain or loss on the deemed sale of your interest to the buyers. There is no gain or loss recognition upon the contribution of the assets to the new entity.

S and C Corporations

When you sell your stock in a corporation, you recognize capital gain or loss. The amount of your gain or loss is the difference between your adjusted basis in the stock and the amount received in exchange.

If another corporation acquires 80% or more of the stock in your corporation within a 12-month period, it can elect to treat the stock purchase as if it had purchased the underlying asset. If so, your corporation must recognize gain or loss as if it had sold its assets for fair market value. From the buyer's perspective, this enables the corporation to step up the basis of its assets as if it were a new corporation. The purchase price is allocated to the assets as explained in Chapter 6.

Special Situations

Sale of Qualified Business Stock

Tax laws encourage investments in small businesses by offering unique tax incentives. If you own stock in a corporation treated as a **small business**, you may be able to defer your gain or exclude it entirely.

Small business For purposes of deferring or excluding gain on the sale of stock, a small business is a C corporation with gross assets of no more than $50 million when the stock is issued. The small business must be an active business and not a mere holding company. The stock must have been issued after August 10,1993.

There are many conditions surrounding this exclusion:

- It applies only to stock issued by a small business after August 10, 1993.
- As of the date the stock was issued, the corporation was a qualified small business (see definition).
- The company must be a C corporation (not an S corporation).
- You must have acquired the stock at its original issue, either in exchange for money or other property, or as pay for services.
- During substantially all of the time you held the stock:

  - The corporation was a C corporation.
  - At least 80% of the value of the corporation's assets were used in the active conduct of one or more qualified businesses.
  - The corporation was engaged in any business *other than*: the performance of services in the fields of health, law, engineering, architecture,

accounting, actuarial science, performing arts, consulting, athletics, financial services, brokerage services, or any trade or business where the principal asset of such trade or business is the reputation or skill of one or more of its employees; banking, insurance, financing, leasing, investing, or similar business; farming business (including the business of raising or harvesting trees); mining; or operating a hotel, motel, restaurant, or similar business. Which types of businesses *do* qualify? Manufacturing, retail and wholesale, and technology companies are the types of companies that can qualify as a small business for purposes of the exclusion.

○ The corporation was not a foreign corporation, domestic international sales corporation (DISC), former DISC, regulated investment company, real estate investment trust, real estate mortgage investment conduit (REMIC), financial asset securitization investment trust (FASIT), cooperative, or a corporation that has made a Section 936 election.

DEFERRING GAIN

If you own Section 1202 stock in a small business for more than 6 months and sell it, you can defer any tax on the gain—called Section 1202 gain after the section in the Internal Revenue Code—by acquiring other small business stock within 60 days of the sale. If you reinvest only part of your proceeds, you can defer gain to the extent of your reinvestment.

By making this rollover (called a Section 1045 rollover), the basis of the newly acquired stock is reduced by the gain that was not recognized on the initial sale. Reducing basis means that the unrecognized gain will be recognized when the replacement stock is sold in a taxable transaction.

CAUTION

The excluded gain is a tax preference for the alternative minimum tax (AMT). This means that individuals subject to the AMT lose part of the exclusion, unless the 100% exclusion applies. See Chapter 28.

EXCLUDING GAIN

If you own stock in a small business for more than 5 years and sell it, you can usually exclude some or all of your gain.

The amount of the exclusion depends on *when* the stock is acquired, and to some extent *where* the corporation is located.

- *50% exclusion.* Stock acquired before February 18, 2009, and after December 31, 2013 (unless the 100% exclusion that applied for 2013 is extended to acquisitions of qualified small business stock in 2014).

Example

In 2014, an individual sells small business stock that she acquired in 2007 for $10,000; it is now worth $100,000. Of her $90,000 gain ($100,000 – $10,000), 50%, or $45,000, is excludable. If she acquired the stock after February 17, 2009, and sold it after February 18, 2014, the exclusion would be $67,500, or 75% of her gain; only $22,500 would be includible in income. It is the date that the stock was acquired, not the date it is sold, that governs the exclusion amount.

- *60% exclusion*. Stock acquired in a corporation in an empowerment zone business through December 31, 2018. Empowerment zone businesses are explained in Chapter 7 with respect to the empowerment zone employment credit; the same definitions apply here. Of course, even if the stock is in an empowerment zone business, the higher exclusions that follow may apply instead of the 60% exclusion.
- *75% exclusion.* Stock acquired after February 17, 2009, and before September 29, 2010.
- *100% exclusion.* Stock acquired after September 28, 2010, and before January 1, 2014, unless the 100% exclusion is extended (see the Supplement for details).

The amount of the exclusion related to stock from a particular company is limited to the greater of 10 times your basis in the stock or $10 million ($5 million if married filing separately) minus any gain on stock from the same company excluded in a prior year.

DEFERRING GAIN FROM PUBLICLY TRADED SECURITIES BY INVESTING IN A SPECIALIZED SMALL BUSINESS INVESTMENT COMPANY

If you own publicly traded securities, gain from their sale can be deferred by rolling over the proceeds into qualified small business stock. In this case, qualified small business stock is stock or a partnership interest in a specialized small business investment company (SSBIC). The rollover must be completed within 60 days. The amount of the gain deferred under this option reduces the basis in the stock or partnership interest you acquire.

This deferral option is limited annually to $50,000 ($25,000 if married filing separately). This deferral option has a lifetime limit of $500,000 ($250,000 if married filing separately).

Zero Percent Gain from Community Renewal Property

If you own a business that invested in business assets within a specially designated renewal community before January 1, 2010, and hold the assets for more than 5 years, you do not have to pay *any* tax on your gain (40 authorized community renewal areas were designated by the Secretaries of Housing and Urban Development and Agriculture). However, any portion of the gain attributable to periods before January 1, 2002, is ineligible for this special treatment and is taxed in the usual way.

Section 1244 Losses

If you own stock in a company considered to be a small business (whether it is a C or an S corporation) and you realize a loss on this stock, you may be able to treat the loss as an ordinary loss (within set limits). This loss is referred to as a *Section 1244 loss* because it is this section in the Internal Revenue Code.

Ordinary loss treatment applies to both common stock issued at any time and preferred stock issued after July 18, 1984. You can claim an ordinary loss if you sell or exchange the stock or if it becomes worthless. This special tax rule for small business stock presents another win-win situation for owners. If the company does well and a disposition of the stock produces a gain, it is treated as capital gain. If the company does not do well and the disposition of the stock results in a loss, the loss is treated as ordinary loss, which is fully deductible against your other income (such as salary, dividends, and interest income).

QUALIFYING FOR ORDINARY LOSS TREATMENT

The corporation issuing the stock must be a small business. This means that it can have equity of no more than $1 million at the time the stock is issued. This equity is the amount of cash or other property invested in the company in exchange for the stock. The stock must be issued for cash and property other than stock and securities. This definition of small business stock applies only to the loss deduction under Section 1244. Other definitions of small business stock apply for other purposes under the tax law.

You must acquire the stock by purchase. The ordinary loss deduction is allowed only to the original purchaser of the stock. If you inherit stock in a small business, receive it as a gift, or buy it from someone who was the original purchaser of the stock, you do not qualify for ordinary loss treatment.

Most important, the corporation must have derived over half its gross receipts during the 5 years preceding the year of your loss from business operations, and not from passive income. If the corporation is in business for less than 5 years, then only the years in which it is in business are considered. If the corporation's deductions (other than for dividends received and NOL) exceed gross income, the 5-year requirement is waived.

LIMIT ON ORDINARY LOSS DEDUCTION

You can treat only the first $50,000 of your loss on small business stock as an ordinary loss. The limit is raised to $100,000 on a joint return, even if only one spouse owned the stock. However, losses in excess of these dollar limits can be treated as capital losses, as discussed earlier in this chapter.

The ordinary loss deduction can be claimed only by individuals. If a partnership owns Section 1244 stock and sustains a loss, an ordinary loss deduction can be claimed by individuals who were partners when the stock was issued. If the partnership distributes stock to partners and the partners then realize a loss on the stock, they cannot treat the loss as an ordinary loss.

If an S corporation owns Section 1244 stock and sustains a loss, it cannot pass the loss through to its shareholders in the same way that partnerships can pass the loss through to their partners. Even though S corporation shareholders receive tax treatment similar to that of partners, one court that has considered this question concluded that the language of the tax law results in a difference in this instance. The denial of an ordinary loss deduction for Section 1244 stock is 1 important way in which the tax treatment differs between partnerships and S corporations.

Worthless Securities

If you buy stock or bonds (collectively called *securities*) in a corporation and they become worthless, special tax rules apply. In general, loss on a security that becomes worthless is treated as a capital loss. If the stock is Section 1244 stock, you can claim an ordinary loss deduction, as explained earlier.

To claim a deduction, you must be able to show that the securities are completely worthless. If they still have some value, you cannot claim the loss. You must show that there is no reasonable possibility of receiving repayment on a bond or any value for your stock. Insolvency of the corporation issuing the security is certainly indicative of worthlessness. However, even if a corporation is insolvent, there may still be some value to your securities. The corporation may be in a bankruptcy restructuring arrangement designed to make the corporation solvent again someday. In this instance, the securities are not considered to be worthless.

A deduction for worthless securities is also allowed if the securities are "abandoned" (the owner permanently relinquishes all rights without receiving any payment; gives up ownership).

You can claim a deduction for worthless securities only in the year in which worthlessness occurs. Since it is difficult to pinpoint when worthlessness occurs, you have some flexibility. The tax law allows you 7 years to go back and amend a prior return to claim a deduction for worthless securities.

Example

In 2015 you learn that stock you owned in a business became worthless in 2011. In general, you have 7 years from the due date of your 2011 return, or April 15, 2019, to amend your 2011 return to claim the loss deduction.

If you own stock in a publicly held corporation, it is advisable to check with a securities broker to see whether there has been some definite event to fix the time of worthlessness. If you are unsure whether a security actually became worthless in a particular year, consider claiming it anyway. You can renew your claim in a subsequent year if the facts show worthlessness did, in fact, occur in that subsequent year. If you fail to claim the loss in the earlier year and that year proves to be the year of worthlessness, your claim may be lost forever.

If you own stock in an S corporation that becomes worthless, you must first adjust the basis in the stock for your share of corporate items of income, loss, and deductions. If there is any excess basis remaining, you can then claim the excess as a loss on worthless securities.

Where to Report Capital Gains and Losses

Employees

Employees may buy stock in their employer (or acquire it through stock options or as compensation). When this stock is disposed of at a loss (or it becomes worthless), the loss may be a capital loss or an ordinary loss on Section 1244 stock. Capital losses are reported on Form 8949 and then on Schedule D and are carried over to page 1 of Form 1040. An ordinary loss on Section 1244 stock is reported in Part II of Form 4797. The results of Form 4797 are then reported on page 1 of Form 1040. If you need to amend a tax return to claim a deduction for worthless securities, file Form 1040X, *Amended U.S. Individual Income Tax Return*.

Self-Employed

Self-employed individuals report any capital gains and losses on their personal Form 8949 and then on Schedule D—there is no special reporting for the business since these assets are viewed as personal assets, not business assets, even if acquired with business profits.

Partnerships and LLCs

Capital gains and losses are separately stated items that are not taken into account in calculating ordinary business income or loss. However, the entity figures the net amount of capital gains or losses on its own Schedule D. The net amount is then entered on Schedule K, and the partners' or members' allocable share of the capital gains or losses is reported to them on Schedule K-1.

Gain on the sale of qualified small business stock is passed through as such. Partners and members must have held their interest in the entity on the date that the pass-through entity acquired the qualified small business stock *and* at all times until the stock was sold in order to qualify for the exclusion.

S Corporations

Capital gains and losses are separately stated items that are not taken into account in figuring the S corporation's ordinary income or loss. However, the corporation figures its net amount of capital gain or loss on its own Schedule D. The net amount is entered on Schedule K, and the shareholder's allocable share of the gain or loss is reported to them on Schedule K-1.

Gain on the sale of qualified small business stock is passed through as such. Shareholders must have held their interest in the corporation on the date that it acquired the qualified small business stock *and* at all times until the stock was sold in order to qualify for the exclusion.

Built-in capital gains of the S corporation, however, are *not* passed through to shareholders since they are taxed to the corporation. They are reported on a separate part of Schedule D. The computation of built-in gains is made on a separate attachment (of your own making). If there is an excess of recognized built-in gain over recognized built-in losses for the year and this net amount exceeds taxable income (figured without regard to this net gain), the tax is figured on the net amount. It can be reduced by the general business credit and minimum tax credit carryforwards from years in which the corporation was a C corporation. The tax is then entered on Form 1120S. The amount of the built-in gains tax is treated as a loss sustained by the corporation (so that shareholders can report their share of this loss on their personal returns). Deduct the tax attributable to an ordinary gain as a deduction for taxes on page 1 of Form 1120S; for tax attributable to short-term or long-term capital gain, report the loss as a short-term or long-term capital loss on Schedule D.

C Corporations

Capital gains and losses are reported on the corporation's Schedule D. The net amount of gain or loss is entered on Form 1120 on the line provided for capital gain net income. If there is a net loss, then the corporation must apply its own limitations on capital losses, as explained in this chapter. If the corporation discovers that it suffered a loss from worthless securities in a prior year and wants to file an amended return, use Form 1120X, *Amended U.S. Corporation Income Tax Return*.

Tax-Free Exchanges

Regardless of your form of business organization, all tax-free exchanges are reported on Form 8824, *Tax-Free Exchanges*. Any gain resulting from the exchange is then carried to the appropriate tax schedule or form for the entity. For example, if your C corporation makes a tax-free exchange of capital gain property (other than Section 1231) that results in a gain, the gain is then reported on the corporation's Schedule D. Tax-free exchanges involving Section 1231 property are reported on Form 4797, *Sales of Business Property*, discussed in Chapter 6.

Installment Sales

Regardless of your form of business organization, all installment sales are reported on Form 6252, *Installment Sales*. The gain reported in the current year is then carried to the appropriate tax schedule or form for the entity. For example, if your C corporation makes an installment sale of capital gain property (other than Section 1231) that results in a gain, the gain is then reported on the corporation's Schedule D. Installment sales involving Section 1231 property are reported on Form 4797, *Sales of Business Property*, discussed further in Chapter 6.

CHAPTER 6

Gains and Losses from Sales of Business Property

CHAPTER 6

Gains and Losses from Sales of Business Property

Complex rules govern the overall treatment of these transactions. (The treatment of capital gains and losses from other property is also discussed in Chapter 5.) The purpose of this chapter is to alert you to the basic rules governing certain sales of business property. If any transaction applies to your business, you may wish to delve deeper with the assistance of a tax professional.

For further information about capital gains and losses, see IRS Publication 537, *Installment Sales*, and IRS Publication 544, *Sales and Other Dispositions of Assets*.

Section 1231 Gains and Losses

Certain assets used in business are granted special tax treatment. This treatment seeks to provide a win-win situation for a business. If a sale or other disposition of these assets (called **Section 1231 property**) results in a net gain, the gain can be treated as capital gain. If a net loss results, the loss is an ordinary loss.

Section 1231 property   **Property held for more than one year and used in a business or held for the production of rents or royalties.**

Examples of Section 1231 property include:

- Real property and depreciable personal property (such as equipment)
- Leaseholds
- Timber, coal, and iron ore
- Certain livestock and unharvested crops

Gains or losses due to casualty, theft, or condemnation may also be treated as Section 1231 gains or losses if the property was held for more than one year. Also, the payment from a manufacturer to a distributor to cancel the distributor agreement is treated as a long-term capital gain, provided the distributor made a substantial capital investment in the distributorship and the investment is reflected in physical assets.

Section 1231 property does *not* include:

- Inventory or other property held for sale to customers
- Copyrights; literary, musical, or artistic compositions; letters or memoranda; or similar property created by your efforts
- Government publications

Determining Section 1231 Gains or Losses

You must use a *netting process* to determine your Section 1231 gains or losses. This means combining all gains and losses from the sale or other disposition of Section 1231 property. If your Section 1231 gains exceed your Section 1231 losses, then all of your gains and losses are treated as capital gains and losses. In contrast, if your Section 1231 losses equal or exceed your Section 1231 gains, all of your gains and losses are treated as ordinary gains and losses.

If you sell appreciated Section 1231 property to a *related party*, gain that would otherwise be capital gain is recharacterized as ordinary income if the property is depreciable property in the hands of the buyer. Related parties for this purpose means a person and all entities that are controlled entities. A *controlled entity* is:

- A corporation with more than 50% of the value of the outstanding stock that is owned, directly or indirectly, by you.
- A partnership with more than 50% of the capital interest or profits interest that is owned, directly or indirectly, by you.
- Two corporations that are members of a controlled group.
- A corporation and a partnership if the same person owns more than 50% of the value of the stock and more than 50% of the capital interest or profit interest in the partnership.
- An S corporation and another S corporation where the same person owns more than 50% of each.

LOSSES

The fact that your Section 1231 losses for the year equal or exceed Section 1231 gains does not automatically ensure ordinary loss treatment. You must check to see whether a special recapture rule applies. Under the recapture rule, net Section 1231 gain is treated as ordinary income to the extent it does not exceed **nonrecaptured** net Section 1231 **losses** taken in prior years.

Nonrecaptured losses   Total of net Section 1231 losses for the 5 most recent preceding tax years that have not been applied (recaptured) against any net Section 1231 gains in those years.

The recapture rules for Section 1231 gains and losses are extremely complex. They are designed to prevent you from being able to time gains and losses from year to year so that you take your gains as capital gains and your losses as ordinary losses. (Do not confuse these recapture rules with those that apply to depreciation, which are discussed later in this chapter.) The recapture rules, in effect, treat your gains and losses as occurring in the same year so that what would ordinarily have been treated as capital gains is partially or fully treated as ordinary income.

Losses are recaptured beginning with the earliest year subject to recapture.

Installment Sales

If you sell property and receive at least one payment after the year of sale, you have automatically transacted an installment sale. You report your gain over the period in which you receive payment *unless* you elect to report all of the gain in the year of sale. Installment reporting does not apply to losses. This is called the installment method. You can use it regardless of your other accounting method for reporting income. Installment reporting does not affect the amount of gain you report, nor the characterization of that gain. It merely affects the timing of reporting the gain.

Under the Fair and Equitable Tobacco Reform Act of 2004, tobacco growers were able to receive annual payments beginning in 2005 and ending September 20, 2014; they report in 2014 only payments received for 2014.

Installment reporting is explained in greater detail in Chapter 2.

Recapture

If part of the gain on an installment sale relates to depreciation recapture, this gain must be reported up front, regardless of the payments received.

Recapture

Certain write-offs you may take can come back to haunt you. The benefit you enjoy now may have to be repaid at a later time. For instance, if you claim certain *depreciation* on business assets (explained in Chapter 14)—a write-off of the cost of the assets over a set time—you must *recapture* the benefit when you dispose of the assets. Recapture in some instances is merely a matter of recharacterizing gain—instead of capital gain, the recapture amount is treated as ordinary income. However, in other instances, recapture means reporting income that would not otherwise be due.

Most of the following discussion about recapture applies only to businesses other than C corporations. The reason: C corporations do not have favorable tax rates on capital gains. There is, however, one recapture rule specifically for C corporations, which is explained later in this chapter.

Recaptured Depreciation

If you claim accelerated depreciation on realty (generally this applies to realty placed in service before 1987), then you must recapture (report as ordinary income) the portion of gain relating to the excess of accelerated depreciation.

- For equipment and other personal property, recapture all of depreciation claimed (to the extent of gain).

- For nonresidential realty depreciated under the Accelerated Cost Recovery System (ACRS) (placed in service after 1981 and before 1987), recapture the excess of ACRS depreciation in excess of straight-line depreciation. Different rules apply to pre-ACRS property.

Unrecaptured Depreciation

If you claim a home office deduction for business use of a portion of your home (these rules are explained in Chapter 18), you do *not* have to apportion your gain; in effect, you can apply the home sale exclusion to your entire gain. However, all depreciation claimed on a home office after May 6, 1997, is unrecaptured depreciation—it must all be reported as gain upon the sale of the home. This gain is taxed at a maximum of 25%.

Recapture on Installment Reporting

When to report recapture on an installment sale depends on the type of recapture involved:

- *For recaptured depreciation*—All of the depreciation must be reported in full in the year of sale. This recapture is reported without regard to the proceeds received in the year of sale.
- *For unrecaptured depreciation*—The gain, with respect to each installment payment received, is reported first at the 25% rate. Once unrecaptured depreciation has been fully reported, the balance of any gain is reported at the basic capital gains rate (generally 15% for owners of pass-through entities, but 20% for owners who are in the 39.6% tax bracket).

Example

You purchased realty for $100,000 that you depreciated by $20,000 (for a basis of $80,000). In July 2014, you then sell the property for $130,000, payable in 5 equal annual installments. Of these installments, $10,000 of gain must be reported each year. (*Gain* is the difference between $130,000 received for the property and $80,000 basis.) Thus, gain on the first 2 installments is taxed at 25%. Gain on the 3 remaining installments will be taxed at 15% (if you're not in the top income tax bracket).

Involuntary Conversions

Special Recapture by C Corporations

When a C corporation sells depreciable realty, such as a factory or office building, 20% of the gain (referred to in tax parlance as unrecaptured gain) is characterized as ordinary income rather than capital gain. While this does not impact the regular income tax of a C corporation because it pays the same tax rate on ordinary income and capital gain, it can impact the corporation's alternative minimum tax (AMT) if the business is subject to this tax. As a practical matter, since small C corporations are exempt from the corporate AMT, this recapture rule is not likely to impact a small business set up as a C corporation.

If business property is destroyed or stolen, condemned or disposed of through threat of condemnation and you receive insurance proceeds or other funds to compensate you for your loss, you have suffered an *involuntary conversion*. *Condemnations* are the taking of your property for public purposes, such as building roads or putting up utility poles—in effect a forced sale. Threat of condemnation occurs when you learn from a government official or other authorized person that the government intends to take your property. If you do not sell it to the government, it will be condemned.

If the funds you receive for the involuntary conversion of your property exceed your **adjusted basis** in the involuntarily converted property, you have a gain that is currently taxable unless you qualify to postpone your gain (explained later). If the funds you receive are less than your adjusted basis in the involuntarily converted property, you have a loss that is currently deductible (subject to usual loss limitation rules discussed in this chapter and in Chapter 5).

Adjusted basis   This is your basis in the property, adjusted for certain items. Start with your original cost if you bought the property (the cash and other property you paid to acquire it). Even if the cash did not come out of your pocket, for example, if you took a loan, the cash you turn over to the seller is part of your basis. Then, adjust the basis by reducing it for any depreciation claimed (or that could have been claimed) and any casualty loss you claimed with respect to the property. For example, if your original computer system cost you $10,000 and you claimed $2,000 depreciation, your adjusted basis is $8,000. (Other basis adjustments are explained in Chapter 5.)

In reporting condemnation awards, you can reduce your receipts by any legal fees or other expenses you incurred to obtain the payment as well as any special assessments levied against the part of the property if only a portion of the property was condemned. If amounts are withheld from the award to pay off your mortgage or outstanding taxes, you treat these amounts as payment you receive. Also add to the amount any severance payments you receive for the decrease in the value of the property you retain if only a portion of the property was condemned. The portion of gain relating to severance damages can be postponed in the same way as direct payments for the condemned property.

In figuring your gain or loss from an involuntary conversion, certain payments related to the event are not taken into account (they are treated separately):

- *Relocation payments from the federal government or an assistance program*. If you are displaced from your business (including a home in which you maintain a home office) or farm, you may be eligible for these funds. These amounts are tax-free payments.
- *Interest on a condemnation award*. The municipality may pay you out over time, plus interest. This interest is reported separately as interest income (see Chapter 4).

Election to Postpone Gain

You make the election to postpone gain by acquiring replacement property within set time limits. In deciding whether or not to postpone gain, keep in mind that you do not have to use the insurance proceeds or other funds to acquire the replacement property—you need only invest a similar amount. You can, for example, spend the proceeds and take a loan to buy the replacement property. First, consider the advantage and disadvantage to help you decide whether or not you want to postpone gain.

- *Advantage*—Postponing gain allows you to use the proceeds undiminished by taxes on your gain.
- *Disadvantage*—You must reduce the basis of the replacement property by the amount of gain not immediately recognized. This results in a lower basis for purposes of figuring depreciation on the replacement property as well as for determining gain or loss on the disposition of the property.

REPLACEMENT PROPERTY

Replacement property is property that is similar or related in service or use to the involuntarily converted property. *Similar or related* means that the functions of the old and replacement properties are related. For example, if 1 piece of machinery is destroyed in a storm and you buy a new machine to perform the same work in your business, the new machine is clearly replacement property.

You need not buy the property directly. You are treated as acquiring replacement property if you buy at least an 80% interest in a corporation that owns property similar or related in service or use to the involuntarily converted property. However, you cannot buy replacement property from a *related party*—a business you control or a close relative—if the gain is more than $100,000. You can buy replacement property from a related party if the gain is $100,000 or less.

If your business property is destroyed in a disaster within an area qualifying for federal disaster relief, acquiring *any* tangible property for your business is treated as similar or related, even if the functions of the old and new property are entirely different.

REPLACEMENT TIME LIMITS

You must decide whether or not to postpone gain by acting with set time limits to place replacement property in service for your business. Generally, you have until the end of the 2 years following the close of the year in which gain from the involuntary conversion was realized to acquire replacement property. For property involuntarily converted after certain major catastrophes (such as Hurricane Katrina), the replacement period may be extended to 5 years. Similar extensions can be granted for other disasters; check the IRS' Tax Relief in Disaster Situations at www.irs.gov/uac/Tax-Relief-in-Disaster-Situations.

If business property has been condemned (or sold under threat of condemnation), the replacement period is 3 years from the close of the year in which the gain from condemnation (or threat of condemnation) was realized. However, if you buy replacement property by acquiring a controlling interest in a corporation, then the 2-year replacement period applies.

Example

In February 2014, a machine is destroyed by a storm, and the insurance proceeds you receive produce a gain. You can postpone the reporting of this gain by obtaining replacement property no later than December 2016.

If you decide you want to postpone gain but time is running out on buying replacement property, you can request an extension. For example, if you have already found property but have yet to close on the sale, ask for more time to do so. Address your request to the local district director of the IRS. Do not let the replacement period expire without submitting your extension request—it may be almost impossible to obtain an extension at this late date.

Abandonment, Foreclosure, and Repossession of Property

Disposing of business property by abandonment, foreclosure, or repossession generally produces taxable results.

Abandonment

If you abandon business property, you *automatically* have a loss that is treated as an ordinary loss. The amount of your loss is the adjusted basis of the abandoned property. However, if you effectively abandon inventory that has become unsalable because it is obsolete or defective, you do not report it as a loss. Instead, you adjust your inventory valuation to reflect the actual value of the items, which may be merely their scrap value.

If the property you are abandoning is subject to a debt for which you are personally liable and the debt is canceled, you have ordinary income to the extent of this debt cancellation. Report this income separately from the abandonment loss—do not net one against the other. (Income from the cancellation of debt is also discussed in Chapter 4.)

Foreclosure or Repossession

If you cannot pay a loan or the mortgage on your business property, the lender will recoup this amount by *foreclosing* on the property or *repossessing* it. Fore-closure and repossession are treated as a sale or exchange for tax purposes, producing a gain or loss on the transaction. This is the case even if you volun-tarily transfer the property back. The amount realized usually is the debt you no longer have to pay. The difference between this amount and the adjusted basis in the property is the amount of your gain or loss.

- *If the debt is recourse debt* (you are personally liable for it)—do not in-clude the debt cancellation in the amount realized (you report the debt cancellation separately as income as explained in Chapter 4). *Exception:* If the value of the property is less than the canceled debt, then the amount realized includes the debt cancellation to the extent of the value of the property.
- *If the debt is nonrecourse debt* (you are not personally liable for it)—include the full debt cancellation in the amount realized, regardless of the property's value.

Example

The business bought a car for $30,000, financing $25,000 of the purchase price. The business stops paying the loan when there is still $20,000 outstanding and the adjusted basis of the car is $22,040. The lender repossesses the car and walks away from the remaining debt. If the debt is nonrecourse, report $2,040 as a loss (the difference between the amount realized of $20,000 and the adjusted basis of the car, $22,040).

Example

Continuing with the car example, except that the debt is recourse. The value of the car at the time of the repossession is $19,000. In this instance, report a loss of $3,040 (the difference between the amount realized of $19,000 less $22,040). But you must also report income of $1,000 (the amount of the canceled debt in excess of the value of the car).

Lender's Perspective

If you are the lender and foreclose or repossess property because of non-payment, you recognize gain or loss on the transaction. This is so whether or not the debtor cooperates and voluntarily transfers the property back to you.

REAL PROPERTY

Generally, your gain is the difference between the total payments you have already received for the property and the gain you already reported as income. However, your reportable gain on a foreclosure or repossession is limited to the gross profit on your original gain minus any gain already reported. Reduce your profit by any costs related to the foreclosure or repossession, such as legal fees, court costs, and costs of recording or clearing title to the property.

Example

You foreclose on an office building for nonpayment of the mortgage you hold on the property you sold. You figure your basis in the building as follows:

Original basis	$200,000
Plus: Gain reported on principal received	+18,000
Plus: Gain on foreclosure	+27,000
Less: Principal received	(−90,000)
New basis	$155,000

Your basis in the reacquired property is your original basis in the property, increased by any gain recognized on the receipt of principal and foreclosure/repossession, and decreased by any principal payments received.

EQUIPMENT AND OTHER PERSONAL PROPERTY

If you sold property on the installment method and repossess it for nonpayment, report gain or loss on the transaction. In review, gain or loss is the difference between your basis in the installment obligations and the value of the property you repossess. Reduce the basis in the installment obligations by any costs for the repossession. Increase the value of the property by anything you receive from the debtor upon the repossession, such as a partial payment.

What is your basis in the installment obligations? This depends on how you originally opted to report the sale. If you used the installment method, your basis in the installment obligations is the unpaid balance of the installment obligations divided by your gross profit percentage.

Sale of All the Assets of the Business

If you sell your business, such as a sole proprietorship, by selling all of its assets, the rules for reporting gain or loss are really no different from a single-asset sale. You allocate the purchase price of the sale to each of the assets, including goodwill or going concern value, in order to determine your gain or loss. You usually arrive at this allocation through negotiations between you and the buyer.

Asset classes reported on Form 8594, *Asset Acquisition Under Section 1060,* include the following:

- *Class I assets*—Cash, and savings and checking accounts.
- *Class II assets*—Certificates of deposit, government securities, publicly traded stock or securities, and foreign currency.
- *Class III assets*—Mark-to-market assets.
- *Class IV assets*—Stock in trade and inventory.
- *Class V assets*—All assets that do not fall within another class. Furniture and fixtures, buildings, land, vehicles, and equipment generally fall within this class.
- *Class VI assets*—Section 197 assets (other than goodwill and going concern value) such as patents, copyrights, licenses, permits, franchises, trademarks, and covenants not to compete. (Section 197 assets are discussed in Chapter 14.)
- *Class VII assets*—Goodwill and going concern value.

The sale price is allocated in descending order—first to Class I assets, then Class II assets, and so on. There is no debate on allocating part of the purchase price to assets in the first 2 classes since the value of the assets is not in dispute. But as a seller, you generally want to allocate as much of the remaining purchase price to assets that will produce the most favorable tax results to you. For example, if you can allocate an amount to goodwill, you will achieve capital gain treatment.

In contrast, if such an amount is allocated to inventory, you have ordinary income. However, the buyer has competing interests and wants to allocate as much as possible to depreciable assets. That would give him or her the opportunity to maximize depreciation deductions. Ultimately, the price you receive for the assets will reflect negotiations that include the allocation process.

Corporations that acquire stock in another corporation may, under certain circumstances, elect to treat the stock purchase as an asset sale (see Chapter 5).

Where to Report Gains and Losses on Business Property

For All Taxpayers

Section 1231 gains and losses are reported on Form 4797, *Sales of Business Property,* regardless of the type of entity. The results from Form 4797 are carried over and reported on the business's tax return. For individuals, Form 4797 gains and losses are reported directly on Form 1040.

Installment sales are figured on Form 6252, *Installment Sale Income*. The results are carried over to Form 4797 (or Form 8949 and Schedule D as explained in Chapter 5). Use a separate Form 6252 for each installment sale you transact. Do not complete the form if you elect out of installment reporting—instead simply report your entire gain on Form 4797 (or Form 8949 and Schedule D).

A sale of all the assets of the business is reported on Form 8594, *Asset Acquisition Statement*. This form is used to allocate the purchase price to specific assets.

Self-Employed

Gains and losses on Section 1231 property are reported on Form 4797. The results are carried over to page 1 of Form 1040. Do not enter the results on Schedule C (or on Schedule F in the case of farming operations).

If you elect to postpone gain on a casualty, theft, or condemnation, make your election on the return for the year in which you realized gain. If you acquired replacement property before filing your return, attach a statement to the return showing the amount realized, how you computed your gain, and any gain reported. If you have not yet acquired replacement property by the time you must file your return, simply attach a statement to your return showing the circumstances of the casualty, theft, or condemnation giving rise to the gain, how you calculated your gain, and that you intend to acquire replacement property within the replacement period. Then, when you do buy replacement property, attach another statement to the return for the year of the replacement purchase explaining the replacement.

If the replacement period expires before you acquire replacement property (and you do not obtain an extension for the replacement period), you must file an amended return for the year in which you realized gain. You report your full gain on this amended return. You must also file an amended return if you buy replacement property and the cost is not sufficient to postpone the reporting of all of your gain. You report the portion of the gain not covered by the replacement property on this amended return.

Once you have designated certain property as your replacement property, you cannot later substitute other property for it. However, if your replacement property is found to be unsuitable, you can then substitute other qualified property, provided the replacement period has not expired.

Partnerships and LLCs

Section 1231 gains and losses are calculated on Form 4797 and then entered on Schedule K and allocated to partners on Schedule K-1.

If there is a gain as a result of a casualty or theft to business property, the partnership or LLC must elect to defer the recognition of gain and buy the replacement property. The individual partners or LLC members cannot make a separate election. Each partner or LLC member reports his or her distributive share of business income or loss on his or her personal income tax return.

S Corporations

Section 1231 gains and losses are computed on Form 4797 and then entered on Schedule K and allocated to shareholders on Schedule K-1.

If there is a gain as a result of a casualty or theft to business property, the S corporation must elect to defer the recognition of gain and buy the replacement property. The individual shareholders cannot make a separate election. Each shareholder reports his or her distributive share of S corporation income or loss on his or her personal income tax return.

C Corporations

Section 1231 gains and losses are computed on Form 4797 and then entered on Form 1120. Both capital losses and Section 1231 losses are part of the corporation's taxable income.

If the corporation discovers that it suffered a loss from worthless securities in a prior year and wants to file an amended return, use Form 1120X, *Amended U.S. Corporation Income Tax Return*.

PART 3

Business Deductions and Credits

CHAPTER 7

Employee Compensation

Salary, Wages, and Employee Benefits

Alert

At the time this book was printed, Congress had not extended numerous breaks for 2014 that had expired at the end of 2013. Check the online supplement in February 2015 at www.jklasser.com or www.barbaraweltman.com to see whether these breaks apply for 2014 returns.

If you are an employee of someone else's business, you do not pay compensation to another individual. You can skip most of this chapter and go on to look at deductible expenses. However, you might want to review the areas covered to understand your employer's burdens and responsibilities for the wages and benefits paid to you. You may also be interested in 2 tax credits to which you may be entitled by virtue of working.

If you are the owner of a sole proprietorship, partnership, or limited liability company, you are not an employee and cannot receive employee compensation. Money you take out of your business is a "draw," but it is not a deductible expense for the business (you already pay tax on your share of business income, whether or not it is distributed to you). However, your business may have employees, and payments to them are deductible according to the rules discussed in this chapter. According to the Summer 2013 Statistics of Income Bulletin, wages and compensation was the largest deduction category for sole proprietorships (other than cost of goods sold and depreciation).

As a business owner, you need to understand a number of matters related to compensation: how to properly classify workers, the rules for deducting compensation to employees, the rules for claiming employment-related tax credits, and payroll obligations for employers.

Also discussed in this chapter are the *earned income credit* and the *dependent care credit*. These are not business credits; rather, they are personal credits that arise by virtue of employment. The earned income credit is a refundable credit for low-income householders, and the dependent care credit is designed to offset the costs of babysitting and other dependent-related expenses incurred to allow parents to work.

Employment taxes on compensation you pay to your employees, including federal income tax withholding, FICA (Social Security and Medicare taxes), FUTA (federal unemployment tax), and state taxes (income, unemployment, and disability), are discussed in Chapter 29.

Medical coverage is an important facet of employee compensation. It is also a necessary item for self-employed individuals. Medical coverage for you and your employees is explained in Chapter 19.

For further information about employee compensation, see IRS Publication 334, *Tax Guide for Small Business*; IRS Publication 15, *Circular E, Employer's Tax Guide*; IRS Publication 15-A; *Employer's Supplemental Tax Guide*; and IRS Publication 15-B, *Employer's Guide to Fringe Benefits*.

Worker Classification

In order to know whether payments to workers are wages, you must first determine whether the workers are employees or independent contractors. This is a hot issue for the IRS because there are substantial tax dollars at stake. The IRS believes that as many as 30% of workers are erroneously treated as independent contractors, which costs the government $7 billion in revenue. The issue, however, goes beyond the IRS and concerns the Department of Labor (because wage and hour laws apply to employees but not to independent contractors) and the National Labor Relations Board (because only employees can be unionized).

State labor departments are also concerned with correct worker classification because only employees can claim unemployment benefits and workers' compensation.

A worker is treated as an employee if your company exercises sufficient control over when, where, and how the work gets done. If you control only the final results, the worker may be an independent contractor. The IRS agents are provided with a special audit manual designed to help the agents reclassify a worker as an employee if appropriate (view this manual at www.irs.gov/pub/irs-utl/emporind.pdf). The key to worker classification is control. In order to prove independent contractor status, you, as the employee, must show that you do not have the right to control the details and means by which the work is to be accomplished. You may also want to show that the worker has an economic stake in the work (that the worker stands to make a profit or loss depending on how the work turns out). It is helpful in this regard for the worker to supply tools and place of work, although working from home, using his or her own computer, and even setting hours (flex time) are not conclusive factors that preclude an employee classification. Various behavioral, financial, and other factors can be brought to bear on the issue of whether a worker is under your control. You can learn more about worker classification in IRS Publication 15-A, *Employer's Supplemental Tax Guide*.

Misclassifying Workers

It is critical to note that the consequences for misclassifying workers can be dire for an employer. If you fail to treat a worker as an employee when you should do so, you are penalized for not withholding income taxes on wages and paying employment taxes. Penalties and interest in this regard can, in some instances, be enough to bankrupt your company. Misclassification can also wreak havoc with employee benefit plans, including retirement plans. If the IRS successfully reclassifies workers as employees, you will be required to provide back benefits (medical, retirement plan contributions, and other benefits you provided to your correctly classified employees).

You may be able to rely on a "safe harbor" rule (called Section 530 relief) to avoid employment tax penalties. (This relief provision is not in the Internal Revenue Code; it's from the Revenue Act of 1978.) At a minimum, if you want to treat workers as independent contractors, make sure you do so consistently and that you have a reasonable basis for doing so. The tax law considers these situations to be a reasonable basis:

- You relied on a court case about federal taxes or a ruling issued to you by the IRS.
- You have already gone through an IRS audit in which the issue of worker classification was raised and your workers were not reclassified.

- A significant segment of your industry (at least 25%) treats such workers as independent contractors.

Require your independent contractors to complete Form W-9, *Request for Taxpayer Identification Number and Certification*, a form on which they accept responsibility for paying their required taxes.

Also make sure you file the required information return for independent contractors (Form 1099-MISC) if the worker earned at least $600 (see Appendix A for details).

If the IRS questions your worker classification and you cannot prove your position on audit or resolve it through the classification settlement program, you can now bring your case to Tax Court for a determination. This means you do not have to pay the taxes up front to have your case reviewed in court.

VCSP. The IRS has a Voluntary Classification Settlement Program (VCSP) that allows companies to reclassify workers as employees with nominal penalties. As of March 2012, fewer than 1,000 applications had been made to the program (and no additional statistics are available). To qualify, you must not be under an audit by the IRS, must have issued required 1099s (although temporary relief with a higher penalty cost could have been used through June 30, 2013, even if the 1099s were not issued), and must meet other qualifications. You can choose to reclassify one group of workers while not reclassifying another. Before you request participation in this program, be sure to talk with a tax advisor. Participation protects you only from IRS audit on worker classification; it provides no protection from challenges by other government agencies, third parties, or workers.

Temporary Workers and Outsourced HR

There are other ways to obtain workers who are not independent contractors and also are not your employees:

- *Temporary workers.* If you engage someone through a temporary agency, such as Kelly Services or Manpower, the worker is the employee of the agency. The agency, and not you, is responsible for all employer obligations. You merely pay the agency a fee for the services (the deduction for this fee is explained in Chapter 22).

- *Outsourced HR.* You may continue using existing employees, but shift employer obligations to an outside source. For example, a professional employer organization (PEO) effectively creates a co-employer situation. You have the right to hire and fire, but the PEO is responsible for all HR functions, including payroll taxes and insurance. Again, the PEO fee is deductible (see Chapter 22).

Deductible Employee Compensation

Compensation you pay to your employees can take many forms. In general, most types of compensation are fully deductible by you. *Deductible compensation* includes the more common forms, such as salary, wages, bonuses for services performed, vacation pay, sick pay (not otherwise paid by insurance), and fringe benefits, whether or not they are tax-free to your employee. In setting compensation, determine what you can afford and what your competitors are paying their workers. Understand that the law does not require you to offer paid leave for federal or state holidays, vacation, sick days, personal days, or other time off. As a rule of thumb, the average number of paid holidays is only 5 per year at firms with under 100 employees (it is 7 per year at larger companies).

The deduction for these items must be reduced, however, by any employment tax credits claimed. These tax credits are discussed later in this chapter. The timing of when to deduct year-end bonuses paid after the end of the year is discussed in Chapter 2.

General Rules for Deductibility of Compensation

To be deductible, compensation must meet 5 tests. Test 1 requires that the compensation be an *ordinary and necessary business expense*. The payments must be directly connected to the conduct of your business, and they also must be necessary for you to carry on your business.

Ordinary and necessary business expense An *ordinary expense* is one that is common and accepted in your business. A *necessary expense* is one that is helpful and appropriate to your business.

For test 2, the compensation must be reasonable. For most employees, this issue never comes up; it is assumed that pay to rank-and-file employees is reasonable. The question of reasonableness typically arises in connection with pay to owners and top executives. There are no absolute guidelines for determining what is reasonable—it depends on the individual facts and circumstances. Ask yourself: "Would another business pay the same compensation under your circumstances?" If you are confident that the answer is yes, most likely the compensation is reasonable. To get an idea of what other companies are paying for comparable work, go to monster.com (www.monster.com) or Salary.com (www.salary.com).

The IRS uses a number of factors to determine whether compensation is reasonable. These factors include:

- *The job description of the employee*. What duties must the employee perform? How much responsibility does the employee shoulder? How much time is required to perform the job? How much business is handled by the employee?

- *The nature of the business.* What are the complexities of your business? What has been your pay policy for all employees? What is the pay to a particular employee as compared with the gross and net profit of the business and distributions to shareholders?
- *The general cost of living in your locality.* Formula-based compensation (such as a percentage of sales or some other fixed arrangement) may be reasonable if it is an industrywide practice to use these formulas.

Courts have also used a hypothetical independent investor standard to test reasonableness. Under this test, courts decide whether a disinterested investor would approve the compensation level in light of the dividends and return on equity. In determining reasonableness, you must look at the total compensation package and not merely the base salary. Also, each employee's pay package must be reasonable by itself. The fact that your total payroll is reasonable is not sufficient.

Remember, if compensation paid to an employee who is also an owner of the corporation is not reasonable, then it may be viewed as a constructive dividend to such an owner-employee. As such, it is not deductible by the corporation even though it is fully taxable to the owner. However, the owner-employee and corporation can enter into a disallowance repayment agreement to preserve deductibility. Such agreements are discussed later in this chapter.

Generally, it is up to you to prove the reasonableness of compensation. However, if the issue goes to court, the burden of proof shifts to the IRS once you have presented credible evidence of reasonableness. Only small businesses (corporations and partnerships whose net worth does not exceed $7 million) can shift the burden of proof to the IRS.

Test 3 requires that the payment be for services actually performed. This issue does not generally arise for ordinary employees. However, in a family situation, the IRS may pay closer attention to see that work has actually been performed for the compensation paid. Thus, for example, if you employ your spouse, children, or parent, be sure to document their work hours and duties should your return be questioned. In one case, a parent was able to deduct salary paid to his 7-year-old son because he showed that the child performed meaningful tasks for his business. In another case, a parent who had her 3 children perform services in her home office, including photocopying, stuffing envelopes, and shredding, could not deduct their wages because she never actually paid them; merely buying things they wanted did not establish that they were paid. In several cases, a deduction for equal pay to both spouses was denied where one spouse was a professional (e.g., an engineer or a doctor) and the other performed only administrative and secretarial duties. The compensation to the professional might have been reasonable, but the same pay to the spouse clearly was not.

Guaranteed annual wages may be deductible as salary even though work is not performed. The deduction is limited to full-time guaranteed wages paid under a collective bargaining agreement.

Test 4 is that you must actually have paid the compensation if you are on the cash basis, or incurred the expense if you are on the accrual basis. Incurring the expense means that economic performance has occurred. For a complete discussion on economic performance, see Chapter 2.

Test 5 applies to year-end bonuses and other payments by accrual basis businesses. Bonuses accrued before year-end cannot be deducted unless they are actually paid within a certain time. The time limit depends upon who is receiving the payment.

- *Rank-and-file employees*—payment must be completed within 2½ months after the close of the year. For example, a bonus declared on December 24, 2014, by an accrual basis corporation for an employee who is not a shareholder must be paid by March 15, 2015, in order to be deductible in 2014. If you create a pot for bonuses to be divvied up among employees, you can deduct the lump sum as long as bonuses are paid within the 2½ month rule. However, if you reserve the right to alter bonus amounts or which employees are eligible to receive them, you cannot deduct the bonuses until actually paid.

- *Shareholders in C corporations*—payments to those owning more than 50% of the stock cannot be deducted until actual payment is made. Shareholders who own 50% or less are considered rank-and-file employees for purposes of this rule.

- *Owners of pass-through entities*—payments cannot be deducted until actual payment is made, regardless of the percentage of ownership. For example, a year-end bonus paid to an S corporation shareholder by an accrual basis corporation is not deductible until the bonus is actually paid.

Other Types of Deductible Compensation

Here are some less common, but equally deductible, compensation items:

- *Outplacement services provided to workers you have laid off.* The types of outplacement services that are deductible include career counseling, resume assistance, skills assessment, and even the cost of renting equipment to facilitate these services.

- *Black Lung benefit trust contributions made by coal mine operators*, provided the contributions are paid no later than the filing of the return (including extensions). The contribution must be made in cash (check) or property; a promissory note is not currently deductible.

- *Interest-free or below-market loans to employees.* The amount of interest not charged that is less than the applicable federal interest rate (a rate that changes monthly and depends on whether the loan is short-term, mid-term, or long-term) is treated as compensation. The employer includes that same amount as taxable interest.

- *Severance pay.* If you are forced to downsize your work force or otherwise let employees go, you may offer them some benefits package. The IRS has acknowledged that severance pay generally is deductible as an ordinary and necessary business expense even though an argument could be made that it provides some future benefit (which would suggest capitalizing the cost). However, if severance pay is part of a plan, method, or arrangement deferring the receipt of income, then it is deductible only when it is included in the worker's income (whether or not the employer is on the cash or accrual method of reporting).

- *Salary continuation.* If you want to continue paying wages to an owner-employee who becomes disabled and to claim a deduction for such payments, do so under a salary continuation plan that you set up for this purpose. Without such a plan in place, you risk having the IRS label the payments as dividends or withdrawals of capital, neither of which are deductible by the company.

- *Director's fees.* A corporation's payment of fees to its directors is deductible, but such fees are not treated as compensation even if the director is also an officer or other employee of the corporation. The fees are deductible as other business expenses (see Chapter 22).

- *Employment agency fees.* If you pay a fee to an employment agency or headhunter to hire an employee, you may deduct the cost as another business expense.

- *Incentives for special vehicle purchases.* If you offer employees a cash payment or other incentive so they buy a hybrid or electric vehicle rather than a standard vehicle, the amount is treated as additional compensation; it is deductible by you and taxable to the employee.

Other Limits on Deducting Compensation

Besides the reasonable compensation and other tests discussed earlier, there are several limitations on deducting compensation.

- *Deferred compensation.* If your employee agrees to defer compensation to some future date, such as retirement, you cannot claim a deduction until such time as the employee includes the compensation in his or her income. This is true for accrual method businesses as well as cash basis businesses.

- *Prizes and awards.* You can deduct prizes and awards you pay to employees, but only certain ones are tax free to them. An *employee achievement award* is tangible personal property given for an employee's length of service or safety achievement, which is awarded as part of a meaningful presentation and under conditions and circumstances that do not create a significant likelihood of disguising the award as compensation. An award is not considered a length-of-service award if made within the first 5 years of employment. An award is not considered a safety achievement award if it is given to a manager, administrator, clerical employees, or other professional employee, or if it is given to more than 10% of employees (other than those just listed). Awards can be qualified or nonqualified; the difference impacts what is tax free to employees. A *qualified achievement award* is one given under a written plan that does not discriminate in favor of highly compensated employees as to eligibility or benefits; it is fully tax free. A *nonqualified achievement award,* which does not meet the definition of a qualified achievement award, is tax free to an employee as long as it does not exceed $400 per year and total awards (qualified and nonqualified) made to any one employee do not exceed $1,600.

- *Vacation pay by accrual basis employers.* Vacation pay earned by an employee is deductible in the current year only if you actually pay it out by the close of the year or within 2½ months of the close of the year. If you fail to pay it out within this time frame, it becomes deductible in the year it is actually paid out. Of course, for cash basis employers, vacation pay is deductible as wages when it is paid to an employee.

Noncash Payments

In some cases, you may pay your employees with property instead of cash. What is the amount you deduct? Your cost for the property (*basis*), or its value at the time it is paid to employees? You can deduct only your basis in the property, even though its value is included in the employee's income as compensation and employment taxes are based on this value.

Example

You own a car with a basis (after depreciation deductions) of $8,000. The car is worth $12,000. You give the car to your top salesperson as a bonus. You may deduct $8,000, the basis of the car. On the employee's W-2 form you include $12,000 as compensation.

Payments in virtual currency (e.g., bitcoin) are treated as payments in property, not cash. You have to determine the value of the bitcoin payment in order to claim a deduction for making the payment.

Restricted Property

If you transfer stock or other property that is subject to restrictions to an employee in payment for services, you generally cannot deduct the expense until such time as the stock or other property is no longer subject to restrictions. Restrictions include limits on transferring the stock or property. The term also covers property that is not **substantially vested** in the employee.

Substantially vested   A person can transfer the property and is not subject to a risk of forfeiture (is not likely to be forced to give up rights in the future).

When and how much you can deduct for this type of compensation depends on a number of factors, such as the kind of property transferred and when the property is included in the employee's gross income. In the past, an employer could deduct restricted property only when such property was subject to withholding. Sometimes this was impossible, because a worker was no longer in the employer's employment. The IRS has eased its position and has dropped the withholding requirement. The property must still be included in the worker's income in order for the employer to claim a deduction. According to the IRS, the worker will be deemed to have included the amount in income in the year for which an employer complies with W-2 reporting requirements.

Compensation to Owners

How much should you pay yourself? What are the tax ramifications? The answers depend on your business's financial situation, your personal needs, how the business is organized, and more.

Employee versus Self-Employed

If your business is a corporation, whether C or S, you are an employee if you provide services for the corporation. Compensation is deductible by the corporation and taxable to you. Compensation is subject to Social Security and Medicare (FICA) taxes, and the additional Medicare tax of 0.9% if compensation exceeds a threshold amount for your filing status ($200,000 for singles; $250,000 for joint filers; $125,000 for married persons filing separately).

In contrast, if you are a self-employed person because your business is a sole proprietorship, partnership, or limited liability company, you do not receive compensation. Instead, you can take a *draw*, which can be fixed to appear like a salary. The draw is not deductible by the company; it is not separately taxable to you (it is part of the net earnings from the business on which you are taxed). The draw is not separately subject to self-employment tax (which is effectively the employer and employee share of Social Security and Medicare taxes). Instead, self-employment tax is paid on all of the net earnings allocated to the owner (with some modifications), regardless of whether earnings are paid out (as draw or otherwise) or retained by the business. Net earnings from self-employment over your applicable threshold amount (the same threshold that applies to employees described earlier) is subject to the 0.9% additional Medicare tax; the amount of your draw has no impact on whether and to what extent this tax applies to you.

Guaranteed payments to partners are different from a draw. These payments are made for services without regard to the income of the partnership. The payments are deductible by the partnership (before determining partnership profit or loss), are treated as ordinary income to the recipient-partner, and generally are subject to self-employment tax.

Audit Strategies

The compensation payment strategy varies for C and S corporations.

- *C corporations.* The general approach is to maximize compensation to create large tax deductions for the business. Deductible compensation cannot exceed what is reasonable under the circumstances; what is reasonable is a highly litigated issue in tax law. Whereas public corporations can deduct compensation to certain employees only up to $1 million ($500,000 for the top 5 executives in medical insurance companies and companies directly assisted by the government under the Emergency Economic Stabilization Act) (provided this is reasonable), privately held corporations do not have any dollar limit on deductible compensation.

- *S corporations.* The general approach is to minimize compensation to reduce FICA taxes for the corporation and owner. The owner pays income tax on all of the net earnings allocated to him or her, but FICA tax applies only to amounts distributed as compensation. Some owners have opted to take *no* compensation in order to avoid any FICA tax, but courts have said that owners must receive at least some compensation for work performed (essentially what the corporation would have to pay a third party to do the same work). The IRS has identified the lack of compensation to S corporation owner-employees as a key audit target.

Stock Options and Restricted Stock

If your business is incorporated, you can give or sell to employees (including owner-employees) the right to buy shares in the corporation. They can be a useful form of compensation when the business does not have cash on hand. Of course, when the options are exercised and employees obtain stock, this dilutes the ownership interests of previously existing shareholders.

There are 2 types of options: (1) qualified stock options, which are **incentive stock options (ISOs)** and options granted under an **employee stock purchase plan** (usually used only in large corporations and not discussed any further here), and (2) **nonqualified employee stock options**.

Incentive stock options (ISOs) These are stock options meeting certain statutory requirements and that are granted to employees.

Employee stock purchase plan This is a plan meeting statutory requirements to grant options to employees.

Nonqualified employee stock options These are stock options granted to employees that do not meet statutory requirements.

ISOs. From the employee perspective, income is recognized *not* when the option is granted or exercised, but only when the stock acquired pursuant to the option is sold (provided certain holding periods are met). However, the exercise of an ISO may be an adjustment for purposes of the alternative minimum tax (see Chapter 28).

From the employer perspective, because employees do not have income from the ISO at the time it is granted or exercised, there is no compensation deduction at that time. However, if there is a disqualifying disposition of the stock acquired, the disposition creates compensation income for the employee, which is the difference between the strike price and the stock's fair market value (FMV) at the time of exercise. A disqualifying disposition is a disposition of the stock within either 2 years from the date that the option is granted or one year from the date that the option is exercised.

Nonqualified employee stock options. From the employee perspective, the nonqualified stock option is taxable to the employee at the time it is granted *if* it has a "readily ascertainable fair market value." For closely held corporations, this means the option can be transferred and/or exercised immediately, without restrictions or conditions. If there is no such value, then the employee is taxed when the option is exercised.

The employee can make what is called a Section 83(b) election to report the income when the option is exercised but the stock is not vested (there are restrictions or conditions to transferring the stock), even if he or she is not otherwise required to do so. This election allows an employee to convert what would be ordinary income into capital gain; by reporting some ordinary income now, all future appreciation becomes capital gain. The election must be made within 30 days of receipt of the restricted stock. The election can be on the IRS sample form (Form 7.1) made on the employee's own statement (there is no IRS form for this), which is filed with the IRS service center in which the employee files his or her return; attach a copy to the return for the year in which the election is made.

From the corporation's perspective, a deduction for the value of the nonqualified stock option can be claimed when the option is included in the employee's gross income as compensation. This occurs when the option is granted *if* the option has a readily ascertainable value (something very rare in closely held corporations). If the option does not have a readily ascertainable value, the corporation's deduction is postponed until the employee exercises the option, provided the employee's rights in the stock are vested. If rights in the stock are not vested, then the deduction is further postponed until such rights are vested. The deduction at this time is the amount of income that the employee recognizes (i.e., the value of the stock minus the strike price and any amount paid by the employee, or the net amount received by the employee in exchange for the option).

Section 83(b) Election

The undersigned taxpayer hereby elects, pursuant to § 83(b) of the Internal Revenue Code of 1986, as amended, to include in gross income as compensation for services the excess (if any) of the fair market value of the shares described below over the amount paid for those shares.

1. *The name, taxpayer identification number, address of the undersigned, and the taxable year for which this election is being made are:*

    TAXPAYER'S NAME: _____
    TAXPAYER'S SOCIAL SECURITY NUMBER: _____
    ADDRESS: _____
    TAXABLE YEAR: Calendar Year 20__

2. *The property which is the subject of this election is _____ shares of common stock of _____.*

3. *The property was transferred to the undersigned on **[DATE]**.*

4. *The property is subject to the following restrictions: **[Describe applicable restrictions here.]***

5. *The fair market value of the property at the time of transfer (determined without regard to any restriction other than a nonlapse restriction as defined in § 1.83-3(h) of the Income Tax Regulations) is: $_____ per share x _____ shares = $_____.*

6. *For the property transferred, the undersigned paid $_____ per share x _____ shares = $_____.*

7. *The amount to include in gross income is $_____. **[The result of the amount reported in Item 5 minus the amount reported in Item 6.]***

The undersigned taxpayer will file this election with the Internal Revenue Service office with which taxpayer files his or her annual income tax return not later than 30 days after the date of transfer of the property. A copy of the election also will be furnished to the person for whom the services were performed. Additionally, the undersigned will include a copy of the election with his or her income tax return for the taxable year in which the property is transferred. The undersigned is the person performing the services in connection with which the property was transferred.

Dated: _____   _____

*   Taxpayer*

When an employee exercises the option, you as the employer must report to the employee and the IRS the excess of the fair market value of the stock over the amount that the employee paid for the stock. This reporting is done on the employee's W-2 form.

Deferred Compensation

Owners (and certain employees) may wish to defer the receipt of compensation to a future date. Often deferral is used for bonuses or special payments above a base salary. If the deferred compensation arrangement is done properly, the compensation is not taxed until it is received, postponing the tax on the earnings. Deferred compensation is also used as a way to create retirement income, since receipt is usually postponed until the person retires or leaves the company. The company generally cannot deduct the deferred compensation until it is paid to the employee, although a special rule applies to year-end bonuses paid by accrual-based companies within $2\frac{1}{2}$ months after the close of the year, as explained earlier in this chapter.

Deferred compensation can be created under an agreement, arrangement, or plan set up by the company. Key points to making deferred compensation plans work for maximum tax advantage:

NOTE
Deferred compensation that fails to pass muster results in immediate taxation (even though the employee may not yet be able to touch the funds) as well as a 20% penalty.

- The employee must agree to defer the compensation before it is earned. Once earned, any deferred payments are immediately treated as taxable.
- Receipt of deferred compensation must be postponed to a fixed date, such as separation from service.
- The employer cannot segregate the deferred amounts; they must remain an unfunded promise of payment by the company and subject to the claims of the company's creditors.

Note: Even though compensation is deferred for income tax purposes, it may be subject to payroll taxes when earned (see Chapter 29). There is great uncertainty about tax rates in the future. From a planning perspective, owners may not want to defer compensation at this time if they believe tax rates will be higher when they expect to receive the deferred amounts.

Disallowance Repayment Agreements

If you are an employee of a corporation you own and a portion of your salary is viewed as unreasonable, the corporation loses its deduction for the payment. You are taxed on the payment in any event—either as compensation or as a constructive dividend. However, there is a way you can ensure that the corporation does not lose out if the IRS later characterizes its compensation deduction as partially unreasonable: You can enter into a *disallowance repayment agreement*.

The repayment agreement provides that if certain payments to you by the corporation are disallowed by the IRS, you are required to repay such amounts to your corporation. The agreement must be in writing and enforceable under local law. The agreement should be reflected not only in a separate written agreement between you and your corporation, such as part of your employment contract with the corporation, but also in the corporate minutes as a resolution of the board of directors. The bylaws of the corporation should also reflect the ability of the board to enforce the agreement.

Effect of the Repayment Agreement

The repayment agreement is a way for you to offset dividend income you are required to report if the IRS considers payments to you to be constructive dividends. By virtue of the repayment agreement, you are entitled to deduct the amounts you are contractually required to repay to your corporation as a miscellaneous itemized deduction on your personal return in the year repayment is made. However, some tax experts do not think that a repayment agreement is a good idea. Having one could be viewed as an admission that the corporation expects to pay an unreasonable salary.

Employee Benefits

In General

Employers are not required by law to offer any specific types of employee benefits. However, in today's job market, employers may want to offer various *fringe benefits* (also called perks or perquisites) as a way of attracting and retaining a good work force. Businesses may also want to provide these benefits because owners want such benefits for themselves as well.

If you pay certain expenses for an employee, you can claim a deduction. This is so even though the benefits may be excluded from the employee's gross income. If you are a sole proprietor, partner, or LLC member, you are not an employee and cannot receive these benefits on a tax-free basis. For purposes of this rule, employees who are more than 2% shareholders in their S corporations are treated the same as partners and cannot get these benefits on a tax-free basis. Limits on benefits for sole proprietors, partners, LLC members, and more-than-2% S corporation shareholders are discussed later in this chapter.

The benefits provided to an employee must be ordinary and necessary business expenses. The cost of the benefits must be reasonable in amount. And, in most cases, the benefits must be provided on a nondiscriminatory basis; they cannot be extended only to owner-employees and highly paid workers.

There are 2 main categories of employee benefits. The first is called *statutory employee benefits*. These benefits, specifically detailed in the Internal Revenue Code, include health and accident plans, group term life insurance, dependent care assistance, adoption assistance, medical savings accounts, and cafeteria plans.

The other broad category of benefits is called *nonstatutory fringe benefits*. These refer to specific subcategories into which various miscellaneous benefits can fall. For example, if you provide your employees with a turkey at Christmas, this minimal benefit is classified as a *de minimis fringe*. It is not included in the employee's gross income even though you can claim a deduction for your cost of providing the benefit. Nonstatutory fringe benefits are discussed in greater detail later in this chapter.

Statutory Benefits

Certain types of plans or arrangements are treated as statutory benefits. The law details what constitutes a plan, which employees must be covered, the limits, if any, on the excludability of benefits, and other details.

MEDICAL INSURANCE AND BENEFITS

In general, medical insurance coverage, along with any reimbursements of medical expenses, is excluded from an employee's gross income. You deduct the cost of the medical insurance premiums. If you are *self-insured* (you reimburse employees for medical costs out of your operating expenses under a written medical reimbursement plan), you deduct reimbursements to the employees when and to the extent made. Medical coverage, including health savings accounts (HSAs), long-term care coverage, and medical reimbursement plans, is discussed more fully in Chapter 19.

CELLULAR PHONES

If you give cell phones or smartphones to employees, they are no longer treated as listed property subject to special reporting rules. You can deduct the cost of the phone and monthly service charges without employees reporting their business usage to you.

Personal usage of employer-provided phones to employees is not taxed to the employees if there is a noncompensatory reason for providing the phones. Examples of noncompensatory reasons:

- The employer needs to contact the employee at all times for work-related emergencies.
- The employer requires that the employee be available to speak with customers or clients at times when the employee is away from the office.
- The employee needs to speak with customers or clients located in other time zones at times outside of the employee's normal workday.

Providing a phone to promote the morale or goodwill of an employee, to attract a prospective employee, or as a means of furnishing additional compensation to an employee is *not* providing the phone primarily for noncompensatory business purposes.

DEPENDENT CARE ASSISTANCE

Up to $5,000 may be excluded from an employee's gross income; your outlays are fully deductible. You must set up a program to provide this benefit—a plan that makes clear to your employees what they may be entitled to. You do not have to fund the plan (set money aside); instead you can pay as you go. However, as a practical matter, this benefit may not make sense for a small business since nondiscrimination rules intended to make sure that the plan does not favor owners prevents more than 25% of the amounts paid by the plan from benefiting owners (their spouses or dependents) who own more than 5% of the business.

You may allow your employees to pay for their own dependent care on a pretax basis by setting up a flexible spending arrangement (FSA) discussed later in this section.

For information about building child care facilities or offering child care referral services, see Chapter 23.

GROUP TERM LIFE INSURANCE

You deduct the cost of providing this benefit, which is the cost of the premiums. Typical coverage runs 2 times or more of the annual salary of the employee. The cost for up to $50,000 of coverage is excludable from an employee's gross income. If coverage over $50,000 is provided, an *imputed income* amount for excess coverage is includible in the employee's gross income. The imputed income is calculated according to an age-based IRS table; it is not based on the actual cost of premiums. While you deduct the actual cost of providing this benefit, your employees will be pleased to learn that the income from excess coverage may be modest. Table 7.1 can be used to figure employee income from excess

TABLE 7.1 Employee Income from Excess Coverage

Age	Imputed Income ($)
Under age 25	0.05
25–29	0.06
30–34	0.08
35–39	0.09
40–44	0.10
45–49	0.15
50–54	0.23
55–59	0.43
60–64	0.66
65–69	1.27
70 and older	2.06

coverage that is reported on the employee's Form W-2. The amount shown is the cost per $1,000 of excess coverage *each month*.

The cost for up to $2,000 of coverage for spouses and dependents is also excludable from an employee's gross income as a de minimis fringe benefit. However, if this coverage exceeds $2,000, then *all* of the coverage (not just the amount above $2,000) is taxable to the employee.

If a group insurance plan is considered to be discriminatory, key employees (owners and top executives) will have income from the coverage and will not be able to exclude the cost for the first $50,000 of coverage. In this instance, income to them is the greater of the actual cost of the coverage, or the imputed amount calculated according to the age-based IRS tables. Special insurance coverage arranged on an individual basis (for example, split-dollar life insurance) is discussed later in this chapter.

EDUCATIONAL EXPENSES

If the courses are job related, your payments are deductible as noncompensatory business expenses. If the courses are not job related, your expenses are deductible as wages. If you lay off workers and pay for their retraining, you may also deduct your payments.

There is a special exclusion of up to $5,250 for employer-financed education assistance, including graduate-level courses, under a qualifying plan.

Amounts you pay for an employee under the plan can be excluded from the employee's income even if the courses are not job related. In that case, your payments under the plan would be deductible as noncompensatory business expenses.

As a practical matter, it is generally not advisable for owners of small businesses to set up educational assistance plans for the same reason that dependent care assistance programs may not make sense—no more than 5% of benefits can go to owner-employees or their spouses or dependents.

ADOPTION ASSISTANCE

You may deduct the cost of adoption assistance you provide to your employees. If you set up a special assistance program (a separate written plan to provide adoption assistance), your employees can exclude up to $13,190 per child in 2014. However, in 2014 the exclusion is phased out for those with adjusted gross income (AGI) between $197,880 and $237,880 (regardless of your filing status as married or single).

As in the case of educational assistance plans, adoption assistance plans do not make sense for small employers, since no more than 5% of benefits can go to owner-employees.

RETIREMENT PLANNING ADVICE

If you maintain a qualified retirement plan, you can pay for expert advice for your employees and their spouses with respect to retirement planning, and they are not taxed on this benefit. There is no dollar limit to the exclusion. However, it does *not* apply to tax preparation, accounting, legal, or brokerage services. If you pay for these services on behalf of your employees, they are taxed on this amount, although you can deduct your payments.

HEALTH SAVINGS ACCOUNTS

If you maintain a high-deductible health insurance plan and contribute to a Health Savings Account (HSA) for an employee, you can deduct your contributions. Contribution limits and other rules for Health Savings Accounts are discussed in Chapter 19. Contributions are not taxed to employees and are exempt from payroll taxes. You must complete contributions by April 15, 2015, in order to deduct them on your 2014 return (even if you obtain a filing extension).

Note: If you are a small business or a self-employed individual, you can contribute to an Archer Medical Savings Account (MSA), assuming the account was set up prior to 2008.

HSAs and MSAs are discussed more fully in Chapter 19.

HEALTH REIMBURSEMENT ACCOUNTS (HRAs)

You can contribute a dollar amount to an account for each employee that can be used to pay for unreimbursed medical expenses. HRAs, which typically supplement a high-deductible health plan, are discussed more fully in Chapter 19.

CAFETERIA PLANS AND FLEXIBLE SPENDING ACCOUNTS

If you make contributions to cafeteria plans, you can claim a deduction as an employee benefit expense. Cafeteria plans are designed to offer employees choices among benefits on a nondiscriminatory basis. Simple cafeteria plans for small employers are explained later in this chapter.

Flexible spending accounts (FSAs) are also nondiscriminatory plans but are funded primarily with employee contributions. Flexible spending accounts are intended to cover medical costs or dependent care costs on a pretax basis. Employees agree to salary reductions (within limits set by law) that are then contributed to the FSA to be used for medical costs or dependent care costs. The dollar limit in 2014 on elective deferrals is $2,500 to medical FSAs and $5,000 for dependent care FSAs.

Generally, employee elective deferrals to FSAs are done on a use-it-or-lose-it basis. If qualified expenses for the year do not equal these amounts, contributions are lost. However, *medical* FSAs can add either of these features (but not both):

- *Carryover up to $500*. The plan can allow unused amounts to be carried over to the following year. The carryforward is not cumulative, so that no more than $500 can ever be added to the basic elective deferral for the following year.

- *Grace period*. The plan can allow unused amounts to be used within a period of up to 2½ months after the close of the year (March 15th).

From your perspective, however, you may be on the hook for payments if the plan pays out more than the employee has paid in and the employee then terminates employment. The reason: The plan must pay out benefits equal to the employees' annual commitment for salary reduction contributions, even if they have not been fully paid.

> **Example**
>
> An employee agrees to contribute $100 at the end of each month to an FSA. In January 2014, the employee submits a claim of $1,200 for dependent care payable to an agency to cover the next 6 months. The employee quits the job in the first week of February 2014. The business is out $1,100.

NOTE
You may incur costs to administer these employee benefit plans. If you handle them internally (e.g., with your company bookkeeper), there is no additional cost; it is part of wages you already pay. If you use outside companies to administer these plans, you can separately deduct the costs.

Other Employee Benefits

In addition to the various employee benefit plans just discussed, there are other types of benefits you may provide for employees for which you can claim a deduction for your expenses.

SUPPLEMENTAL UNEMPLOYMENT BENEFITS

If you make contributions to a welfare benefit fund to provide supplemental unemployment benefits for your employees, you may deduct your contributions as ordinary and necessary business expenses. The deduction is claimed as an employee benefit expense, not as a compensation cost. Your deduction cannot exceed the fund's qualified cost for the year. *Qualified cost* is the amount you could have claimed had you provided the benefits directly and been on the cash basis, plus the amount estimated to be actually necessary to build the fund to cover claims incurred but not yet paid and administrative costs for such claims.

MEALS AND LODGING

In general, the costs of providing meals and lodging to your employees are deductible as an expense of operating your business. The costs may or may not be taxable to your employees. The tax treatment of this benefit to your employees affects the amount and how you claim a deduction. Generally, you may deduct only 50% of the cost of providing meals.

The 50% limit on deducting meals does not apply if your employees must include the benefit in income. In this case, you may deduct 100% of the cost as compensation.

The 50% limit on deducting meals does not apply if you operate a restaurant or catering business and provide meals to your employees at your restaurant or work site. However, in this case, the full cost of the meals is not deductible as compensation; instead, it is treated as part of the cost of goods sold.

Example

You pay your employee's meal costs when your employee is out of town on a sales call. (Assume proper substantiation and reimbursement arrangements, as explained in Chapter 8.) The meal costs are not included in your employee's gross income. You deduct 50% of the meal costs.

Example

You give your employee a $200 meal allowance because of seniority. The $200 is included in your employee's gross income. You deduct 100% of the $200 meal allowance.

The 50% limit on meals does not apply if you provide the meals as part of the expense of providing recreational or social activities. For example, the cost of a company picnic is fully deductible.

You may deduct the full amount of meal costs if your employees are able to exclude this amount from their gross income. They do this if the meals are furnished on your premises and for your convenience, or if the meals qualify as a de minimis fringe benefit.

Special rules apply for valuing the meals provided at an employer-operated eating facility. An *employer-operated eating facility* is a lunchroom or other facility that you own or lease and operate directly or by a contract to provide meals on or near your business premises during or immediately before or after your employees' workday. Meals provided at an eating facility on or near your business premises are treated as a de minimis fringe benefit. As such, they are excluded from your employee's income and you can claim a full deduction (you do not have to apply the 50% limit).

If you provide your employees with lodging on your premises (for example, if you run a motel, nursing home, or rental property and the employee must

NOTE

Under a safe harbor rule, meals provided to all your employees are treated as furnished for your convenience (and fully deductible) if more than half of the employees to whom such meals are provided are treated as having been furnished meals for your convenience.

live on the premises in order to manage it), you may deduct your full expenses according to the particular expense involved. For example, you deduct the cost of heating and lighting as part of your utilities, the cost of bedding as part of your linen expenses, and the use of the room as a depreciation item.

However, if you are a self-employed individual, you cannot make your living costs tax deductible. You may not exclude them even if you live at your business (e.g., you own a motel and live in it) since you are *not* an employee of your business.

HOUSING RELOCATION COSTS

While this may be rare, a small business may provide relocation assistance to an employee by helping with the sale of the employee's home. The business may deduct as "compensation" the payment of expenses related to the home where the employee retains the right to negotiate for a final sale price.

TRAVEL AND ENTERTAINMENT COSTS

If you pay for travel and entertainment costs, you may deduct your outlays, subject to certain limits. These expenses are explained in Chapter 6.

EMPLOYEE USE OF A COMPANY CAR

If you allow an employee to use a company car for personal purposes, you must value this personal use and include it in the employee's gross income. It is a noncash fringe benefit. There are several valuation methods for calculating personal use of a company car. The method to use depends on your particular circumstances.

One method is based on the actual fair market value (FMV) of the personal use. This is determined by looking at the cost of leasing a comparable car at a comparable price for a comparable period of time. The cost of the vehicle can be its FMV if the car was purchased in an arm's-length transaction. Under a safe harbor rule, you can use the manufacturer's invoice price (including the price for all options), plus 4%. Under another safe harbor rule, you can use the manufacturer's suggested retail price, minus 8%. Then find out what it would cost to lease a car of this value.

Another method is based on the car's annual lease value (ALV). The ALV is set by the IRS and depends on the FMV of the car on the date the car is first used for personal purposes (see Table 7.2).

Example

During all of 2014 your employee uses a company car 50% of the time for personal purposes and 50% for business purposes. The fair market value of the car as of January 1, 2014, is $15,000. The ALV is $4,350. The amount included in the employee's gross income is $2,175 ($4,350 × .50).

TABLE 7.2 Annual Lease Value (ALV) Table for Cars

FMV	ALV
$0 to 999	$ 600
1,000 to 1,999	850
2,000 to 2,999	1,100
3,000 to 3,999	1,350
4,000 to 4,999	1,600
5,000 to 5,999	1,850
6,000 to 6,999	2,100
7,000 to 7,999	2,350
8,000 to 8,999	2,600
9,000 to 9,999	2,850
10,000 to 10,999	3,100
11,000 to 11,999	3,350
12,000 to 12,999	3,600
13,000 to 13,999	3,850
14,000 to 14,999	4,100
15,000 to 15,999	4,350
16,000 to 16,999	4,600
17,000 to 17,999	4,850
18,000 to 18,999	5,100
19,000 to 19,999	5,350
20,000 to 20,999	5,600
21,000 to 21,999	5,850
22,000 to 22,999	6,100
23,000 to 23,999	6,350
24,000 to 24,999	6,600
25,000 to 25,999	6,850
26,000 to 27,999	7,250
28,000 to 29,999	7,750
30,000 to 31,999	8,250
32,000 to 33,999	8,750
34,000 to 35,999	9,250
36,000 to 37,999	9,750
38,000 to 39,999	10,250

(Continued)

TABLE 7.2 *(Continued)*

FMV	ALV
40,000 to 41,999	10,750
42,000 to 43,999	11,250
44,000 to 45,999	11,750
46,000 to 47,999	12,250
48,000 to 49,999	12,750
50,000 to 51,999	13,250
52,000 to 53,999	13,750
54,000 to 55,999	14,250
56,000 to 57,999	14,750
58,000 to 59,999	15,250

For cars over $59,999, calculate the ALV as follows: Multiply the fair market value of the car by 25% and add $500. The ALV figures apply for a 4-year period starting with the year of the ALV election. Thereafter, the ALV for each subsequent 4-year period is based on the car's then fair market value.

If the car is used continuously for personal purposes for at least 30 days but less than the entire year, you must prorate the value of personal use.

Example

Using the company car example, except that the employee uses the car from May 1 through September 30. The $2,175 is prorated for the 153 days of personal use. The amount included in the employee's gross income is $911.71 ($2,175 × [153 ÷ 365]).

The ALV method already takes into account maintenance and insurance costs. Fuel provided by an employer is not included in the ALV. Fuel provided in kind can be valued at FMV or 5.5¢ per mile for purposes of including it in the employee's gross income. If fuel is paid by a company credit card, the actual charges are used to compute personal use included in the employee's gross income.

An employer may choose to treat all use by an employee of a company-owned car as personal use and include an appropriate amount in the employee's gross income. In this case, it is up to the employee to maintain records substantiating business use and then deduct such business use on his or her individual income tax return. If personal use of a company car is de minimis, then nothing need be included in the employee's gross income. As a practical matter, when the employee is an owner, the decision on how to value personal use of a company car is a mutual decision. Both the employer and employee in this case agree on which method is preferable. Keep in mind that when valuing personal use for an owner, only the fair market value or ALV methods can be used.

Another valuation method for personal use of a company car is the cents-per-mile special rule. This rule can be used only if a car is valued in 2014 at no more than $16,000 ($17,300 for a truck or van) and the car is regularly used in the business (at least 50% of total annual mileage is for the business, or the car is used each workday to drive at least 3 employees to and from work in a carpool) or for a car driven by employees at least 10,000 miles during a calendar year. And the employee cannot be a control employee (see below). If the car is owned or leased for less than a full year, the 10,000 miles are prorated accordingly. The value of personal use is based on the standard mileage rate. The standard mileage rate for 2014 is 56 ¢ per mile.

There is another method for valuing personal use of company vehicles called the fleet valuation method. This applies to companies with a fleet of 20 or more vehicles, something that small businesses do not have; this method is not explained further in this book.

If you want to use the ALV method or the cents-per-mile method, you must elect to do so. This election must be made no later than the first pay period in which the company car is used for personal purposes. You need not inform the IRS of your election.

Another method for figuring income to the employee for using a company car is the fixed and variable rate (FAVR) allowance. This is a reimbursement amount that includes a combination of payments covering fixed and variable costs, such as the cents-per-mile rate for variable operating costs (e.g., oil and gasoline) and a flat amount for fixed costs (e.g., depreciation or lease payments). The FAVR allowance is based on a standard automobile cost that cannot exceed $28,200 in 2014 ($30,400 for trucks and vans).

COMMUTING VEHICLES

If you allow your employees to use company cars to commute to and from work, a special valuation rule is used to determine the amount includable in the employee's gross income. The car must be owned or leased by the employer for use in the business, and the employer must have genuine noncompensatory business reasons for requiring an employee to commute in the vehicle. Also, the employer must have a written policy preventing use of the vehicle for personal purposes other than commuting (or de minimis personal use). The employee cannot be a *control employee* (an employee who is a board-appointed, shareholder-appointed, confirmed, or elected officer with compensation of at least $50,000, a director, a 1% or greater owner, or someone who receives compensation of $100,000 or more). If the special commuting vehicle rule is met, then the value of commuting is $1.50 each way ($3.00 round trip), regardless of the length of the commute. The same flat rate applies to each employee even if more than one employee commutes in the vehicle. While the commuting vehicle rule is optional at the employer's election, it must be used for valuing all commuting if it is used for valuing any commuting.

The deduction for car expenses—depreciation, insurance, gas, oil, and repairs—is explained in Chapter 9. This chapter covers only business use of a company car.

COUNTRY CLUB DUES

If you pay the cost of membership at a golf or other country club, the dues are not deductible. However, an employee who uses the club for business can exclude the benefit from income (it is viewed as a working condition fringe benefit, explained, later even though country club dues are otherwise not deductible). However, you can convert this nondeductible cost of the business into a deductible expense by electing to treat the benefit as additional compensation to the employee—deducting the cost as compensation and not as an entertainment cost. This option is discussed more fully in Chapter 8.

Flights on Employer-Provided Aircraft

Special rules are used to determine the value of personal use of flights provided on employer aircraft. A discussion of these rules is beyond the scope of this book.

Life Insurance Provided on an Individual Basis

Businesses may provide owners and other top employees with coverage on an individual basis. This coverage may be term insurance or permanent insurance (e.g., a whole life policy). This coverage is taxable to the individual and does not have to be provided on a nondiscriminatory basis.

SPLIT-DOLLAR LIFE INSURANCE

Under a split-dollar life insurance plan, the cost of coverage is shared between the business and the insured. Here is how the plan usually works.

A cash value life insurance policy is used for a split-dollar arrangement, with the business paying some or all of the premiums. At the death of the employee, the business recoups its outlay, and the balance of the proceeds is payable to the insured's beneficiary (typically his or her spouse or child). Under final regulations, how the employee is taxed on this benefit depends on who owns the policy:

- *If the employee owns the policy*, premiums paid by the business are treated as loans, with imputed interest taxed to the employee.

- *If the business owns the policy*, the employee is taxed on the value of the life insurance protection (which is the 1-year term cost of this protection).

In view of income tax being imposed on split-dollar life insurance arrangements, they are no longer favored as wealth builders for business owners.

Nonstatutory Fringe Benefits

There is a special category of fringe benefits that you may provide to your employees on a tax-deductible basis but which your employees need not include in their income. These are referred to as *nonstatutory fringe benefits* because there is no separate section in the Internal Revenue Code for each particular benefit—they are all covered in the same section. Nonstatutory fringe benefits are not only excludable from the employee's gross income; they are also not subject to employment taxes. In general, these benefits must be provided on a nondiscriminatory basis. Benefits cannot be provided solely to owners and highly paid employees and not to rank-and-file employees. Nonstatutory fringe benefits include:

- *No-additional-cost service*. You need not include in your employee's gross income the value of a service you offer to customers in the ordinary course of the business in which your employee works (e.g., if you run a ferry line and allow employees to ride for free on scheduled runs). In the case of no-additional-cost service, you generally do not have any expense to deduct by virtue of providing the benefit to the employee. You have already deducted costs related to providing the service.

- *Qualified employee discount*. You need not include in your employee's gross income a price reduction you give on certain property or services you offer to customers in the ordinary course of your business in which the employee performs services (e.g., if you own a clothing boutique and give your salespersons a 15% discount on your merchandise). A qualified employee discount cannot exceed the price at which the item is ordinarily sold to customers multiplied by your *gross profit percent* (total sales price of property less cost of property, divided by total sales price of property) or 20% in the case of services.

  A qualified employee discount does not include any discount on real property. A deduction for the goods or services provided as a qualified employee discount is not taken into account as a compensation expense but rather as some other item. Goods provided to employees at a discount are part of the cost of goods sold.

- *Working condition fringe benefit*. You need not include in your employee's gross income a benefit provided to your employee if the employee could have claimed his or her own deduction had he or she paid for the benefit. For example, if you paid for a job-related course that would have been deductible by your employee had the employee paid for it, the course is a working condition fringe benefit. Other examples of working condition fringe benefits include employer-provided vehicles and outplacement services.

- *De minimis (minimal) fringe.* You need not include in your employee's gross income the value of any small or inconsequential benefits, such as the typing of a personal letter by a company secretary or the occasional use of the company copying machine for personal matters. Holiday gifts of nominal value, such as turkeys and hams, are considered de minimis fringes. However, cash of any amount is not a de minimis fringe and must be included in the employee's gross income. Other examples of de minimis fringes include group term life insurance for spouses and dependents up to $2,000 (discussed earlier in this chapter), meals furnished at an eating facility on or near your premises, coffee or soft drinks furnished to employees, flowers or fruit baskets for special occasions, occasional tickets to sporting or entertainment events, occasional meal money or transportation fare for employees working overtime, and company events (such as parties or picnics) for employees and their guests.

NOTE

As an employer, you can shift the cost of parking or transit passes to employees while still providing them with a tax advantage by permitting them to pay for these benefits on a pretax basis—through a salary reduction agreement. All that is required is for employees to agree to use their salary for payment for the parking or transit pass. The portion of their salary used for this purpose (up to the dollar limits mentioned previously) is not taxed to them. The arrangement must be made before the end of the month for which the salary reduction is to be effective.

- *Qualified transportation fringe benefit.* If you provide your employee with a transit pass for mass transit, transportation in a commuter highway vehicle, or qualified parking, you need not include the benefit in your employee's gross income. The 2014 limit on the exclusion for free parking is $250 per month. The limit for monthly transit passes and vanpooling is $130 per month unless Congress restores parity for 2014 for these benefits with free parking. Check the Supplement for details. The value of parking is based on what a person would have to pay for space in an arm's-length transaction. If you provide parking space to employees that is primarily available to customers, then the parking has no value. If you give employees who carpool preferential parking, the value of the space must be taken into consideration. Employer-paid parking at a temporary job assignment—one expected to last one year or less that does in fact last that period—is fully excludable as paid under an accountable plan (explained in Chapter 8); there is no dollar limit in this situation. If the dollar limits are exceeded, only the excess is includible in gross income. However, in the case of partners, LLC members, and more-than-2% S corporation shareholders who are given public transit passes, the exclusion is limited to $21 per month. If the value of this exceeds the $21 per month limit, then the entire cost of the ticket is includible in the owner's gross income. The entire value of parking provided to partners and more-than-2% S corporation shareholders is taxable to them, even if it is less than $250 per month. There is another transportation fringe benefit for bicycle commuting of $20 per month to cover the cost of buying, maintaining, and storing a bicycle used to get to and from work. You can shift the cost of monthly transit passes to employees—they pay for the passes by means of salary reductions (i.e., pretax dollars); all you pay for is the administrative cost of handling the benefit. A bike-sharing program does not qualify as a transportation fringe benefit. The fact that you offer an employee a choice between a qualified transportation fringe benefit and cash does not make the benefit taxable if the employee chooses the benefit. The employee is, of course, taxed on cash received in lieu of the transportation fringe benefit.

- *Moving expenses.* Payments to an employee (directly to the mover or as an allowance) for nondeductible moving expenses are deductible as wages and subject to employment taxes. Payments or reimbursements that would be deductible by the employee had the employee paid them are not treated as wages and are not subject to employment taxes. They are still deductible by you as noncompensatory business expenses. Moving expenses are explained further in Chapter 22.

- *Certain athletic facilities.* You need not include in your employee's gross income the value of an on-site gym or other athletic facilities for use by employees, their spouses, and children. However, if you pay for a membership to an outside health club or athletic facility open to the general public, you must include the benefit in the employee's gross income. No deduction can be claimed for club dues (see Chapter 8).

Some companies allow employees to use business-generated frequent flyer mileage for personal purposes. This benefit defies classification and, to date, the IRS has not figured out a way to tax it without causing an administrative nightmare. However, in 2014 the IRS said it was going to take another look at taxing frequent flyer miles.

Limits on fringe benefits paid for the benefit of sole proprietors, partners, LLC members, and more-than-2% S corporation shareholders that are otherwise excludable by rank-and-file employees are taxable to sole proprietors, partners, LLC members, and more-than-2% S corporation shareholders. For example, if the business pays their health insurance (which may include long-term care insurance), the coverage is taxable to them. The business can deduct the costs as guaranteed payments to partners or as compensation to S corporation shareholders. Owners can then deduct the amount directly from gross income on page 1 of Form 1040.

The balance can be treated as a deductible medical expense, which is taken as an itemized deduction subject to the applicable adjusted-gross-income floor. Medical coverage for these owners is discussed in Chapter 19.

Cafeteria Plans

A cafeteria plan is a written plan that allows your employees to choose to receive cash or taxable benefits instead of certain tax-free benefits. If an employee chooses to receive a tax-free benefit under the plan, the fact that the employee could have received cash or a taxable benefit instead will not make the tax-free benefit taxable. The plan must be set up and operated on a nondiscriminatory basis; complicated testing rules apply.

Benefits allowed to be offered under a cafeteria plan:

- Health and accident insurance
- Adoption assistance
- Dependent care assistance
- Group-term life insurance
- Health savings accounts

Benefits *not* allowed to be offered under a cafeteria plan:

- Educational assistance
- Meals and lodging
- Moving expense reimbursements
- Transportation (commuting) benefits

Simple Cafeteria Plans

Small employers can offer cafeteria plans without any complicated testing rules to ensure that the plans are nondiscriminatory. A small employer is one with 100 or fewer employees. However, once a plan is established, it can continue as a simple cafeteria plan until there are 200 employees.

What distinguishes the simple cafeteria plan from a regular cafeteria plan is mandatory employer contributions. These must be made regardless of whether employees make salary reduction contributions to the plan.

There are 2 contribution formulas that an employer can choose to use:

1. A uniform percentage (not less than 2%) of the employee's compensation, or

2. An amount not less than 6% of the employee's compensation or twice the employee's salary reduction contribution.

The plan must cover all employees (other than certain S corporation shareholder-employees). The plan *cannot* include sole proprietors, partners, members of LLCs (in most cases), or more-than-2% S corporation shareholder-employees. The plan *can* exclude those under age 21, those with less than one year of service, those covered by a collective bargaining agreement, and non-resident aliens working outside the United States whose income did not come from U.S. sources.

> **NOTE**
> As yet, the IRS has not issued any guidance on simple cafeteria plans beyond information in Publication 15-B.

Small business owners need to decide whether the benefits of offering a cafeteria plan for employees make sense when the owners cannot participate.

Employment Tax Credits

Tax credits are even better than tax deductions. A tax deduction is worth only as much as the tax bracket you are in. For example, if you are in the top federal income tax bracket for individuals, 39.6% in 2014, a $100 deduction saves $39.60 in taxes. Tax credits reduce your taxes dollar-for-dollar. A $100 tax credit saves $100 in taxes.

Employer's Employment-Related Tax Credits

There are a number of tax credits related to the employment of workers. These tax credits reduce your deduction for compensation dollar-for-dollar. For example, if your deduction for compensation is $40,000 and you are entitled to claim a $2,000 employment tax credit, you may deduct only $38,000.

Employment-related tax credits reduce your deduction for wages paid to your employees.

WORK OPPORTUNITY CREDIT

The work opportunity credit expired at the end of 2013, but could be extended retroactively by Congress. The following is included in case there is an extension. Check the Supplement for details.

To encourage employers to hire certain individuals from specially targeted groups, there is a tax credit called the work opportunity credit. A top credit of up to $9,600 applies to certain veterans, but smaller credits are allowed for hiring other individuals.

The credit applies to such targeted groups as Aid to Families with Dependent Children (AFDC) recipients, food stamp recipients, ex-felons, high-risk youth, and those in areas that suffered certain population decline. The credit is 25% of the first $6,000 of wages ($3,000 of wages for summer youth) for those who work between 120 and 400 hours. The top credit is $2,400 ($1,200 for summer youth). The credit is 40% of the first $6,000 of wages ($3,000 of wages for summer youth) for those who work at least 400 hours. The top credit is $2,100 ($1,050 for summer youth). For veterans with service-connected disabilities who have been unemployed for any 6 months or more during a 1-year period ending on the date of hire, qualified wages taken into account in figuring the credit are $12,000.

If you employ an eligible worker, be sure to obtain the necessary certification from your state employment security agency. This is done by having the employee sign IRS Form 8850, *Pre-Screening Notice and Certification Request for the Work Opportunity Credit,* on the first day of work and submitting it to your state workforce agency within 28 days of the new employee's starting work. Without having submitted this form, you cannot claim the credit, but if you make a timely submission, you claim the credit even if the state agency fails to respond to you.

EMPLOYER CREDIT FOR FICA ON TIPS

Owners of restaurants and beverage establishments can claim a credit for the employer portion of FICA paid on tips related to the furnishing of food and beverages on or off the premises. This is 7.65% of tips in excess of those treated as wages for purposes of satisfying the minimum wage provisions of the Fair Labor Standards Act (FLSA).

EMPOWERMENT ZONE EMPLOYMENT CREDIT

The empowerment zone employment credit expired at the end of 2013, but could be extended retroactively by Congress. The following is included in case there is an extension. Check the Supplement for details.

The Departments of Housing and Urban Development and Agriculture initially named 6 cities and 3 rural economically distressed areas across the country as *empowerment zones* (Round I zones) and in 1998 named 22 more (Round II). In addition, the District of Columbia is an enterprise zone—another type of economically distressed area—and employers in the zone are eligible for the empowerment zone employment credit. Eight additional employment zones have been designated (Round III). If you do business in one of these economically depressed zones and hire part-time or full-time employees who perform substantially all of their employment services within the zone, you may claim a credit based on their wages. The credit is 20% of the first $15,000 of qualified wages. The top credit is $3,000 per employee per year. There is no limit on the number of employees for which you may claim the credit. *Wages* for purposes of calculating the credit include not only salary and wages but also training and educational benefits. To determine whether a particular area has received designation, go to www.hud.gov/crlocator.

INDIAN EMPLOYMENT CREDIT

The Indian employment credit expired at the end of 2013, but could be extended retroactively by Congress. The following is included in case there is an extension. Check the Supplement for details.

You can claim a credit if you employ part-time or full-time workers who receive more than 50% of their wages from services performed on an Indian reservation. The employee must be an enrolled member of an Indian tribe or a spouse of an enrolled member. The employee must also live on or near the reservation on which the services are performed. The credit is 20% of the first $20,000 of excess wages and the cost of health insurance. Excess wages and health insurance costs are such costs over amounts paid or incurred during 1993. However, wages paid to any employee earning more than $30,000 are not taken into account; such employee is not a qualified employee.

EMPLOYER WAGE CREDIT FOR ACTIVATED RESERVISTS

The employer wage credit for activated reservists expired at the end of 2013, but could be extended retroactively by Congress. The following is included in case there is an extension. Check the Supplement for details.

If you continue some or all of the wages of employees called to active duty (called a differential wage payment), you can take a tax credit of 20% of the differential that does not exceed $20,000 (a top credit of $4,000).

This credit applies only to small employers (on average fewer than 50 employees) that have a written plan to provide the wage differential. No deduction for compensation can be claimed if the compensation is a differential wage payment used to determine this credit.

GENERAL BUSINESS CREDIT

Some employment tax credits are part of the general business credit. As such, they not only reduce your deduction for wages but are also subject to special limitations. The general business credit is the sum of employment tax credits and certain other business-related credits. The general business credit cannot exceed your net tax liability (tax liability reduced by certain personal and other credits), reduced by the greater of:

- Tentative minimum tax (the alternative minimum tax before the foreign tax credit), or
- 25% of regular tax liability (without regard to personal credits) over $25,000.

The amount of the general business credit in excess of this limit can be carried back for one year. Any additional excess amount can then be carried forward for up to 20 years. You cannot elect to forgo the carryback. (For credits arising in tax years before 1998, the carryback period was 3 years, and the carryforward period was 15 years. For credits arising in 2010 of small businesses with average annual gross receipts not exceeding $50 million, there was a 5-year carryback and a 20-year carryforward.)

Example

Your 2014 tax liability (without regard to personal credits) is $15,000, and you have no alternative minimum tax liability. Your general business credit from eligible small business credits is $17,000. In 2014, you can claim a general business credit of $15,000 (your net tax liability reduced by your tentative minimum tax liability of zero). The $2,000 unused credit can be carried back 1 year. If it cannot be fully used on amended returns, it can be carried forward for up to 20 years starting on your 2015 return.

Employee's Employment-Related Tax Credits

An employee may be entitled to claim certain credits by virtue of working. These include the earned income credit and the dependent care credit. They are personal tax credits, not business credits. They are in addition to any child tax credit to which a person may be entitled ($1,000 for each child under age 17 if income is below a threshold amount).

EARNED INCOME CREDIT

If you employ an individual whose income is below threshold amounts, the employee may be eligible to claim an earned income credit. This is a special type of credit because it can exceed tax liability. It is called a refundable credit, since it can be paid to a worker even though it more than offsets tax liability.

Note: Self-employed individuals who had a bad year in business may be eligible for the earned income credit. Find more details about this personal refundable tax credit in IRS Publication 596, *Earned Income Credit (EIC)*.

DEPENDENT CARE CREDIT

Whether you are an employee or a business owner, if you hire someone to look after your children under age 13 or a disabled spouse or child of any age so that you can go to work, you may claim a tax credit. This is a personal tax credit, not a business tax credit. You claim the credit on your individual tax return.

The credit is a sliding percentage based on your adjusted gross income (AGI). The top percentage is 35%; it scales back to 20% for AGI over $43,000. This is the AGI on a joint return if you are married and do not live apart from your spouse for the entire year.

The percentage is applied to certain employment-related expenses up to $3,000 per year for one dependent, or $6,000 per year if you have 2 or more qualifying dependents. Employment-related expenses include household expenses to care for your dependent—housekeeper, babysitter, or nanny—and out-of-the-house expenses for the care of dependents, such as day-care centers, preschools, and day camps. Not treated as qualifying expenses are the costs of food; travel to and from day care, preschool, or day camp; education; and clothing. Also, the cost of sleep-away camp does not qualify as an eligible expense.

If you are eligible for a credit, be sure to get the tax identification number of anyone who works for you and the day-care center or other organization to which you pay qualified expenses. The tax identification number of an individual is his or her Social Security number. You must include this information if you want to claim the credit.

If you hire someone to work in your home, be sure to pay the nanny tax. This is the employment taxes (Social Security, Medicare, and FUTA taxes) on compensation you pay to your housekeeper, babysitter, or other in-home worker. You must pay Social Security and Medicare taxes if annual payments to a household worker in 2014 exceed $1,900. If you paid cash wages of $1,000 or more in any calendar quarter to a household employee during the current tax year or the previous year, you also must pay federal unemployment tax (FUTA) on the first $7,000 of wages. You do not pay these taxes separately but instead can report them on Schedule H and include them on your Form 1040. You should increase your withholding or estimated tax to cover your liability for them to avoid estimated tax penalties. You cannot deduct employment taxes on household workers as a business expense. However, the tax itself is treated as a qualifying expense for the dependent care credit.

Where to Deduct Compensation Costs

Self-Employed (Including Independent Contractors and Statutory Employees)

Compensation paid to employees and employee benefits paid or provided to/for them are deductible on the appropriate lines of Schedule C. The deduction for wages must be reduced by any employment credits paid. Self-employed farmers deduct compensation costs on Schedule F. If you maintain a cafeteria plan for employees, you must file an information return, Form 5500, annually. If you personally incur dependent care costs for which a credit can be claimed, you must file Form 2441, *Child and Dependent Care Expenses*. The credit is then entered on Form 1040.

Partnerships and LLCs

Compensation paid to employees and employee benefits paid or provided to them are a trade or business expense taken into account in determining the profit or loss of the partnership or LLC on Form 1065, *U.S. Return of Partnership Income*. Report these items on the specific lines provided on Form 1065. Be sure to offset them by employment tax credits. Salaries and wages paid to employees and employee benefits are not separately stated items passed through to partners and members. Partners and members in LLCs report their net income or loss from the business on Schedule E of Form 1040; they do not deduct compensation and employee benefit costs on their individual tax returns.

Guaranteed payments to partners are also taken into account in determining trade or business profit or loss. There is a specific line on Form 1065 for reporting guaranteed payments to partners. They are also reported on Schedule K-1 as a separately stated item passed through to partners and LLC members as net earnings from self-employment. This will allow the partners and LLC members to calculate their self-employment tax on the guaranteed payments. If the partnership or LLC maintains a cafeteria plan for employees, the business must file an information return, Form 5500, annually. Partners and LLC members who personally incur dependent care costs for which a credit can be claimed must file Form 2441 with their Form 1040.

S Corporations

Compensation paid to employees and employee benefits paid or provided to them are trade or business expenses that are taken into account in determining the profit or loss of the S corporation on Form 1120S, *U.S. Income Tax Return for an S Corporation*. They are not separately stated items passed through to shareholders. This applies as well to compensation paid to owners employed by the corporation. Note that compensation to officers is reported on a separate line on the return from salary and wages paid to nonofficers. Be sure to reduce salary and wages by employment tax credits.

Shareholders report their net income or loss from the business on Schedule E of Form 1040; they do not deduct compensation and employee benefit costs on their individual tax returns. If the corporation maintains a cafeteria plan for employees, it must file an information return, Form 5500, annually. Shareholders who personally incur dependent care costs for which a credit can be claimed must file Form 2441 with their Form 1040.

C Corporations

Compensation and employee benefits paid to employees are trade or business expenses taken into account in determining the profit or loss of the C corporation on Form 1120, *U.S. Corporation Income Tax Return*. Compensation paid to officers is segregated from salaries and wages paid to employees. Be sure to reduce salary and wages by employment tax credits. Total compensation exceeding $500,000 paid to officers of the corporation is explained in greater detail on Form 1025-E, which accompanies Form 1120. Remember that the corporation then pays tax on its net profit or loss. Shareholders do not report any income (or loss) from the corporation. If the corporation maintains a cafeteria plan for employees, it must file an information return, Form 5500, annually.

Employment Tax Credits for All Businesses

Employment taxes are figured on separate forms, with the results in most cases entered on Form 3800, *General Business Credit*. Form 3800 need not be completed if you are claiming only 1 business credit, you have no carryback or carryover, and the credit is not from a passive activity.

The separate forms for employment taxes are the following:

- Employer wage credit for activated reservists: Form 8932*
- Empowerment zone credit: Form 8844*
- Indian employment credit: Form 8845*
- Social Security tax credit on certain tips: Form 8846
- Work opportunity credit: Form 5884*

*These credits expired at the end of 2013, but could be extended; see the Supplement for details.

Travel and Entertainment Expenses

Alert

At the time this book was printed, Congress had not extended numerous breaks for 2014 that had expired at the end of 2013. Check the online supplement in February 2015 at www.jklasser.com or www.barbaraweltman.com to see whether these breaks apply for 2014 returns.

Technology has enabled small business owners to market their goods and services in a manner similar to that of larger companies. For example, local radio advertising may expand the market for a small business beyond the general area in which its office is located. To service these expanding markets, you may have to travel to see clients, customers, vendors, suppliers, and others who are part of your business operations. If you travel on business or entertain clients, customers, or employees, you may be able to deduct a number of expenses, provided you follow special substantiation rules.

For further information about travel and entertainment costs, see IRS Publication 463, *Travel, Entertainment, Gift, and Car Expenses*. For a listing of per diem rates, see IRS Publication 1542, *Per Diem Rates*. Business use of your car for travel and entertainment purposes is discussed in Chapter 9.

Local Transportation Costs

Do you travel from your office to see clients or customers? Do you have more than one business location? Do you have an office in your home but go into the field to transact business? If the answer to any of these questions is yes, you may be able to deduct local transportation costs. More specifically, local transportation costs include the cost of work-related travel within the area of your **tax home**.

Tax home   In general, your tax home is the entire city or general area of your regular place of business. If you have more than 1 business interest, then it is the location of your main business interest based on the comparative time spent in each location and the income derived from each business interest. If you do not have a regular place of business, you are considered an itinerant without any tax home.

Deductible Costs

Local transportation costs include the cost of driving and maintaining your car (including tolls and parking) or the cost of taxis, bus fare, train fare, or airfare. Computing the cost of driving and maintaining your car is discussed in Chapter 9.

Commuting Costs

As a general rule, the costs of commuting between your home and workplace are not deductible. Thus, your bus or train fare, gas for your car, bridge and highway tolls, and parking fees are nondeductible. This rule does not change

Example

You have a medical practice with an office across the street from the hospital in which you practice. You sometimes stop to see patients in their homes before going to the office or the hospital. You can deduct the cost of travel from your home to the patients' homes, as well as the cost of travel from their homes to your office or the hospital.

NOTE

NOTE

If you do not have a regular place of business but work at temporary work sites in the metropolitan area of your home, you cannot deduct your transportation costs. Thus, according to the IRS, a lumberjack who worked at a number of temporary cutting sites was not allowed to deduct the cost of transportation to those sites. The entire area of the cutting sites was considered his regular place of business. However, the Tax Court has allowed a deduction for transportation costs in this instance, so the issue is not yet settled.

merely because the commute is unusually long or you do work on the way (e.g., reading reports on the train, talking to clients on your car phone, or displaying advertising on your car). Commuting costs are considered nondeductible personal expenses. This is so despite the distance or time it takes to commute. Even if there is no public transportation to the worksite or any lodging nearby, commuting costs remain nondeductible personal expenses.

However, there are a few exceptions that make certain commuting expenses deductible:

1. If you have one or more regular places of business but work at different locations on a temporary basis (as defined under the following exception), you can deduct the daily cost of travel between your home and the other work site.

2. If you travel from your home to a temporary work site outside the metropolitan area where you live and normally work, you can deduct the daily cost of travel between your home and the temporary work site, regardless of the distance. *Temporary* means that work is realistically expected to last for one year or less. If it turns out to last longer, the period up until the realistic expectation change is treated as temporary.

Example

You have an office downtown but work on a 2-month project at a client's facilities in the next city. You can deduct the cost of travel from your home (which is in the same metropolitan area as your office) to the client's facilities (and back) each day.

If you travel outside your **metropolitan area**, both the IRS and courts agree that the costs of traveling between your home and a temporary work site outside your area are deductible.

Metropolitan area   The area within a city and its surrounding suburbs.

3. If you have a home office that is the principal place of business for the activity conducted there (see Chapter 18), the cost of traveling from your

home to your clients or customers or to other business locations is deductible.

> ### Example
>
> You run a tax return preparation business from your home and generally meet clients in your home office. Occasionally you go to clients' homes to do your work. You may deduct the cost of traveling between your home and the clients' homes and back again.

4. If you must haul tools or equipment to your job site and you use a trailer or have to make other special arrangements, the additional cost of commuting with the tools is deductible. The basic transportation costs are still treated as nondeductible commuting expenses.

> ### Example
>
> You rent a trailer to haul tools to and from home and business. You may not deduct the expenses of using your car; however, you can deduct the cost of renting the trailer that you haul with your car.

Local Overnight Stays

The IRS has liberalized the rules for deducting the cost of local overnight stays. As long as this is not a compensatory benefit, but done for a business purpose, the employee is not taxed on the overnight stay(s), and the employer can deduct the cost. For example, an employer may require its employees to stay at a local hotel for the bona fide purpose of facilitating training or team building directly connected with the employer's trade or business.

Travel within the United States

If you travel on business away from home, you can deduct not only the cost of transportation but also personal costs, such as your food, lodging, and incidentals. You must be away from your tax home (defined earlier) for more than the day. You usually must be required, because of the distance or the length of the business day, to get sleep or rest away from home in order to meet the demands of your work. This is called the *sleep or rest* rule. The *away from home* rule is being eased in certain cases. The IRS has said that the *sleep or rest* rule will not apply to an employee if the lodging is necessary to participate in or be available for a bona fide business meeting or function of the employer and the expense would otherwise be deductible by the employee if he or she had paid it (being away from home is not mandatory). And the Tax Court has allowed a fer-ryboat captain who had layovers of between one and 6 hours to deduct meals and incidental expenses even though he docked at his home port (it was im-practical to go home during layovers, and sleep or rest on the company cot was necessary for him to do his job).

And your travel away from home must be considered **temporary** (discussed later in this chapter).

Temporary   Travel that is expected to last for no more than one year and does in fact last no more than one year. Travel expected to last for more than a year or that actually lasts for more than a year is considered to be indefinite, not temporary.

Example

You fly from New York to San Francisco to meet with a business client. You stay for 5 days, after which time you return to New York. In this case, your travel expenses are deductible.

Deductible Costs

Travel costs include transportation costs, lodging, meals, and other related ex-penses.

TRANSPORTATION COSTS

The cost of a ticket to travel by air, train, or bus between your home and a busi-ness destination is deductible. However, if you receive the fare for free because of frequent flyer miles or otherwise, the cost is not deductible. The cost of travel by ship may not be fully deductible (see the section on Conventions later in this chapter).

Transportation costs also include local costs once you arrive at your busi-ness destination. Thus, the cost of taxi fare between the airport and your hotel is deductible. Local transportation costs at the business location, such as taxi fare from your hotel to the location of clients or customers, are also deductible. Other deductible local transportation costs include bus fare and limousine fare. Transportation costs for personal travel—sightseeing, visiting relatives, shop-ping, and other nonbusiness activities—are not deductible.

If you use your car for travel, see Chapter 9. If you rent a car for travel to or at your business destination, the rental charges, as well as gas, parking, and tolls, are deductible. However, if the rental exceeds 30 days and the value of the car exceeds a dollar limit, there may be income to include, called *inclusion amount*. This concept is also explained in Chapter 9.

LODGING COSTS

The cost of hotel, motel, or other accommodations is deductible if the nature of the business trip requires an overnight stay in order for you to sleep or properly perform your job. If you are self-employed you must keep track of all costs and deduct these actual costs. You cannot use a per diem rate as explained below.

For other businesses, you have a choice when deducting lodging costs: (1) keep track of all costs and deduct these actual costs, or (2) use a standard allowance set by the IRS that covers lodging, meals, and incidental expenses. There are 2 standard allowances—the per diem rates for the continental U.S. or 2 rates under a high-low method (a high rate applies to high-cost areas and the other rate applies to all other areas in the continental United States). The rates for the high-low method are listed later in this chapter. Other per diem rates may be found at www.gsa.gov.

The daily dollar amount of the standard allowance is fixed by the government and can be adjusted for inflation.

Each year, the General Services Administration (GSA) sets the per diem rates for the 48 continental United States (CONUS), which are the maximum allowances that federal employees are reimbursed for expenses incurred while on official travel. Employees in private companies can use these rates as well to substantiate their travel costs.

> **NOTE**
> Using the standard allowance does not eliminate the need for other recordkeeping, as explained later in this chapter.

Most of the CONUS (about 2,600 counties) are covered by the standard CONUS per diem rate in the government's 2014 fiscal year ending September 30, 2014, of $129 ($83 lodging and $46 meals and incidental expenses). There are about 400 nonstandard areas that have per diem rates higher than the standard CONUS rate. For example, the rate for travel to Manhattan can be as high as $303 (it depends on the time of year for the travel). Rates for fiscal year 2015 will be posted in the Supplement to this book.

In addition to the federal per diem rates, the IRS has a simplified high-low substantiation method that is similar. Under this method, there are only 2 basic rates: those for high-cost areas (as defined by the IRS) and those for all other areas within CONUS. The rate for high-cost areas starting October 1, 2013, and running until new rates are posted is $251 (of which $65 is for meals and incidental expenses); the rate for all other areas in CONUS is $170 (of which $52 is for meals and incidental expenses). Again, any changes to these rates can be found in the Supplement to this book.

MEALS

The cost of your meals on a trip away from home is deductible (subject to a percent limit, explained later). The cost of meals includes food, beverages, taxes, and tips. However, if the meals are considered to be lavish or extravagant, the deductible portion is limited to the amount that is reasonable. What is considered reasonable is based on the facts and circumstances of the situation. Lavish or extravagant is not automatically the conclusion when the cost of meals exceeds the standard meal allowance rate or when meals are eaten in deluxe hotels, restaurants, nightclubs, or resorts.

<table>
<tr><td>

NOTE

Using the standard meal allowance does not eliminate the need for other recordkeeping, as explained later in this chapter.

</td><td>

You have a choice when deducting meal costs: (1) keep track of all costs and deduct these actual costs, or (2) use a standard meal allowance (after the federal rate on the IRS' high-low rate). The Tax Court has said that even self-employed individuals can use a standard meal allowance even though they cannot use the per diem rates for lodging.

The daily dollar amount of the standard meal allowance is fixed by the government and is adjusted each year for inflation. The adjustment is made on the govern-

</td></tr>
</table>

ment's fiscal year beginning October 1 of each year. For your calendar year, you may use the rates in effect on January 1 (that became effective the previous October 1) throughout the year. Or you may use the actual rates in effect from January 1 through September 30 and the new rates that commence on October 1.

The dollar amount you can deduct using a standard meal allowance depends on where your business takes you. In most of the United States, the daily amount is $46 (for October 1, 2013, through September 30, 2014). (For rates effective October 1, 2013, through September 30, 2014, see the Supplement to this book.) In certain areas designated by the IRS, the daily amount is slightly higher ($51, $56, $61, $66, or $71). The IRS' high-low substantiation rates for meals and incidental expenses are listed earlier.

There is a percentage limit applied to the deduction for meal costs. Generally, the deduction is limited to 50% of meal costs. (There is an exception for those who are subject to the hours of service limitations under the Department of Transportation (DOT), as explained later in this chapter.) Thus, if you spend $100 on meals while traveling away from home (and you are not subject to DOT hours of service limits), only $50 is deductible. The 50% limit also applies to the standard meal allowance. You will see that this limit is taken into account on the forms that you use for deducting meal costs. For example, self-employed individuals filing Schedule C will note that the total cost of meals is entered, and *then* the 50% limit is applied so that only one-half of meal costs are deductible.

OTHER DEDUCTIBLE TRAVEL COSTS

While you are away from home on business, you may incur a number of miscellaneous or incidental travel expenses. These expenses are deductible in full. They include, for example, the reasonable cost of cleaning and laundering your clothes and tips you pay for services rendered in connection with any deductible expenses (such as a meal, a taxi ride, or a bellhop). However, if you use a per diem travel rate covering lodging, meals, and incidental expenses, then these items are not separately deductible. Or you can use a per diem rate solely for incidental expenses, which is $5 per day. You may also incur any number of miscellaneous expenses that are deductible—telephone charges to talk to your office, fees to send or receive a business fax, computer or cell phone rental fees, or public stenographer's fees. These costs are not considered part of incidental expenses for purposes of per diem allowances, explained later in this chapter.

Travel with Another Person

If you take your spouse, child, or another person on a business trip, the costs related to that person generally are not deductible. The only way in which the costs are deductible is if that person works for you, there is a bona fide business reason for the travel, and the costs would have been deductible had they been incurred by someone who was not accompanying you. If the person provides only incidental services (such as typing notes or acting as assistant), his or her travel expenses are not deductible.

How do you distinguish between expenses that are yours (and deductible) from those of your companion (not deductible)? Clearly, the full cost of the other person's travel fare and meals is not deductible. In the case of lodging costs, if you are sharing a room, you must determine what you would have paid for a single, rather than a double, accommodation. For the most part, this is not simply half the cost. You may be able to deduct two-thirds or more of the cost of lodging.

There is a way for a business to turn nondeductible spousal travel costs into deductible costs. If your corporation treats spousal travel costs as additional compensation to you as an employee, then the corporation can claim a deduction for the costs as compensation rather than as travel and entertainment costs. In most cases, this alternative does not make much sense from your perspective, since it only shifts the tax burden from your corporation to you. However, if your personal tax picture is such that additional compensation will not result in additional tax, consider this alternative.

Major and Minor Job Locations

Some individuals work in more than one location. They may, for example, have a major job in one city and conduct some minor business in another. The cost of travel between the two jobs is deductible.

Part Business—Part Pleasure

If you combine business with pleasure, only part of your costs may be deductible. If your trip was primarily for business, then the portion of the travel costs related to business are deductible. This means that the full amount of airfare may be deductible. Meals and lodging for the days spent on business are also deductible.

> **Example**
>
> An airline pilot based in Minneapolis also flew for the National Guard out of Sioux Falls, South Dakota. His family lived in Sioux Falls. The IRS disallowed his travel expenses from Minneapolis to Sioux Falls, but a district court allowed the deduction. The fact that he derived some pleasure from the trip to Sioux Falls was secondary to the business nature of the trip. He deducted travel costs to that city only when he was required to fly there for Guard Duty.

Whether the time spent is primarily for business is determined by the facts and circumstances. There is no hard-and-fast rule.

> **Example**
>
> You travel from New York to San Diego for 5 days of business. You spend 2 more days sightseeing at the zoo and other attractions before returning to New York. All of your airfare is deductible. Five-sevenths of your lodging and food costs are also deductible. Any incidental expenses related to business are deductible. The cost of sightseeing and other personal expenses is not deductible.

If you stay over on a Saturday at a business location in order to obtain a reduced airfare, the stay is treated as business, and the cost of lodging for that stay is fully deductible. This is so even though you spend the time on personal matters. If the trip is primarily for personal reasons but you do conduct some business, you can deduct the direct costs of the business activities but no part of the travel costs.

> **Example**
>
> You spend a week at a resort location. One afternoon you make a business appointment and take a client out to lunch. None of your airfare to the resort or your lodging costs is deductible. You may, however, deduct the cost of the business lunch (assuming it meets general deductibility requirements).

Foreign Travel

Entirely for Business

If you travel abroad entirely on business, all of your travel costs are deductible. (Meal and entertainment costs are still subject to the 50% limit.) If your trip is considered to be entirely business, then even if some time is spent sightseeing or on other personal activities, all of your transportation expenses are still deductible. There are special rules for determining whether your trip is considered to be *entirely* for business. You are treated as having spent your entire trip on business if you meet any of the following 4 rules.

1. You do not have substantial control over arranging your trip; travel is presumed to be entirely for business. You do not have control if you are an employee who is reimbursed for travel and are not related to your employer nor a managing executive (someone whose actions are not subject to veto by another). As a small business owner, it is virtually impossible to satisfy this rule. However, you can still fall within one of the other rules.

2. You are outside the United States for a week or less (7 or fewer consecutive days). In counting days, do not count the day you leave the United States, but do count the day of your return.

Example

You fly from Washington, D.C., to Tokyo on Sunday, arriving at Narita Airport on Monday morning. You work until Friday morning, then spend Friday and Saturday sightseeing and shopping. You fly out on Saturday night, arriving back in Washington on Sunday morning. You are considered to have been abroad for 7 days (Monday through Sunday). All of your airfare is deductible. The cost of lodging, meals, and incidentals for the business days is also deductible, but meals are subject to the 50% limit.

---

3. You spend less than 25% of the time outside the United States on personal activities, regardless of the length of the stay abroad. In counting days for this rule, count both the day you leave and the day you return.

Example

You fly on Sunday from Chicago to Paris, where you spend 14 days on business and 5 days on personal matters. You spend 1 day flying in each direction. Your total time abroad is 21 days (14 days for business, 5 days for personal activities, and 2 days for travel). Since the time spent on nonbusiness activities is less than 25% of the total travel time abroad (5 days personal/21 days total), you may treat the trip as entirely business. Thus, the entire cost of the airfare is deductible. You may treat the days of travel as business days so that 16/21 of the lodging and meal costs (subject to the 50% limit on meals) are deductible.

4. You can show that a personal vacation or another personal reason was not the major consideration in arranging the trip. You can use this rule even though you do have substantial control over arranging the trip.

Primarily for Business

If your travel abroad is not treated as entirely business (because you do not meet any of the 4 rules), you may still deduct some business expenses if the trip is *primarily* business. There is no mechanical rule to establish that the trip is primarily business. However, if you can show a valid business reason for the trip, you can deduct the portion of business expenses allocable to the business part of the trip, including the allocable portion of transportation costs.

Example

You fly from Boston to Rome, where you spend 10 days on business and 5 days on personal matters. You spend 1 day flying in each direction. Your total time abroad is 17 days (10 days for business, 5 days for personal activities, and 2 days in travel time). You had substantial control over arranging your trip, spent more than a week abroad, more than 25% of your time on personal activities, and cannot establish that a personal vacation was not a major consideration. Thus, you cannot show the trip was entirely for business. However, you can show the trip was primarily for business. You spent the greater part of the time on business and arranged the trip accordingly. In this instance, 12/17 of the costs of the airfare and other expenses are deductible business costs; the balance is treated as nondeductible personal expenses.

COUNTING BUSINESS DAYS

In counting days for business when travel is primarily for that purpose, travel days are treated as business days. However, extra days of travel for personal activities, such as side trips, are not counted. You can also treat any day your presence is required at a business meeting or activity as a business day even if you spend the greater part of the day on personal activities. You can also treat as business days any days you wanted to spend on business but were prevented from doing so by circumstances beyond your control (such as weather, strikes, or civil unrest). Saturday, Sunday, and holidays are treated as business days if they fall between two business days. Thus, if you work on Friday and Monday, you count the weekend days as business days. Weekends following the close of your business activities are not treated as business days if you choose to stay on for personal purposes. However, overnight Saturday stays to obtain a reduced airfare are treated as business even when the time is spent on personal activities.

Primarily for Vacation

If you travel abroad primarily for vacation but attend some business or professional seminar, you may not deduct any portion of the trip as a business expense. You may, however, deduct the cost of the seminar (registration fees and other related expenses) as a business expense.

> **Example**
>
> Your professional association sponsors a 2-week trip abroad. It holds two 3-hour seminars during the trip and awards a Certificate in Continuing Education to those who attend the seminars. The entire cost of the trip is a nondeductible personal expense, as it is viewed as primarily for vacation. However, the registration fees for the seminars are deductible.

Conventions

Travel expenses to conventions held within the United States are deductible if you can show that your attendance benefits your business. The fact that you are appointed or elected to be a delegate to the convention does not, by itself, mean you can deduct expenses; you must show that attendance is connected to your business. You can do this by showing that the convention agenda is related to the active conduct of your business. The same rule applies to both employees and self-employed persons.

Foreign Conventions

The expenses of attending a convention outside the North American area (see Table 8.1) are not deductible unless the meeting is directly related to your business and it is reasonable to hold it outside the North American area.

A number of facts and circumstances are taken into account in showing that it is reasonable to hold the convention outside the North American area. They are:

- The purpose of the meeting and the activities taking place at the meeting
- The purposes and activities of the sponsoring organizations or groups

TABLE 8.1 North American Area

American Samoa	Jarvis Island
Antigua and Barbuda	Johnston Island
Aruba	Kingman Reef
Bahamas	Marshall Islands
Baker Island	Mexico
Barbados	Micronesia
Bermuda	Midway Islands
Canada	Netherlands Antilles
Costa Rica	Northern Mariana Islands
Dominica	Palau
Dominican Republic	Palmyra
Grenada	Panama
Guam	Puerto Rico
Guyana	Trinidad and Tobago
Honduras	United States
Howland Island	U.S. Virgin Islands
Jamaica	Wake Island

- The residences of the active members of the sponsoring organization and the places at which the meetings of the sponsoring organizations or groups have been held or will be held
- Other relevant factors

Cruise Ships

The cost of business conventions or meetings held on a cruise ship is limited. The maximum deduction per year is $2,000 per employee for each individual attending the convention on the cruise ship. In order to get this deduction, a number of requirements must be met:

1. The meeting must be directly related to your business.
2. The cruise ship must be a vessel registered in the United States. (All ships that sail are considered cruise ships.)
3. All of the ship's ports of call must be located in the United States or in U.S. possessions.
4. You must attach a written statement to your return showing the days of the cruise, the number of hours devoted to business, and a program of scheduled business activities.

5. You must also attach a written statement to your return signed by an officer of the organization or group sponsoring the meeting that shows the schedule of the business activities of each day of the meeting and the number of hours you attended.

Living Away from Home on Temporary Assignments

If you work in a location other than your regular place of business and are forced to live away from your home (because the distance is too great to reasonably expect that you would travel back and forth each day), then not only the cost of your transportation to the **temporary assignment** but also living expenses are deductible.

Temporary assignment   An assignment away from the area of your tax home that is realistically expected to last for no more than a year and does, in fact, end at that time.

An assignment that is expected to last for more than a year, or one that does in fact last for more than a year, is considered indefinite. Also, a series of short jobs in the same location that, taken together, last more than a year are considered an indefinite assignment. Probationary work is also treated as indefinite. Thus, for example, if you relocate with the understanding that your job will be permanent if your work is satisfactory, the job is considered indefinite. Transportation to the location of the indefinite assignment from your general area of your tax home is deductible; personal living expenses are not.

Change in Job Assignments

Suppose your assignment gets extended or shortened. How does this affect whether the assignment is treated as temporary or indefinite?

SITUATION 1

You are sent out of town on a job assignment expected to last for 10 months but it is extended and, in fact, lasts for 14 months. As long as the initial expectation of 10 months was reasonable, your living expenses are deductible until the time that the expectation changed. Thus, if at the end of 10 months the assignment projection changed, expenses for the first 10 months are deductible. If, however, at the end of 6 months the assignment projection changed, only expenses for the first 6 months are deductible.

SITUATION 2

You are sent out of town on a job assignment expected to last 14 months, but in fact it is shortened and lasts only 10 months. Since the original expectation of the job length exceeded one year, no part of the living expenses is deductible.

The entire assignment is treated as indefinite even though it did in fact end within a year.

Remember, you must have a tax home to be away from when deducting living expenses on temporary assignments. If all of your assignments are away and you have no tax home, no living expenses will be allowed.

Example

An engineering consultant in Florida took temporary engineering assignments for a period of 3 years in 5 states as well as in his home state. During this time he maintained a home office in his apartment, where he returned after each assignment for periods of 4 to 6 months at a time, and he continued to seek permanent employment there. The IRS argued that he was an itinerant, so his expenses were not deductible. The Tax Court disagreed and found his Florida home to be his tax home. He needed to maintain a permanent address and business number to obtain consulting jobs. He always returned there between assignments and never stopped seeking permanent employment there.

What Expenses Are Deductible?

If a job assignment is temporary, then personal living expenses—rent, utilities, food, and other expenses—are deductible. The reason for this rule: Congress recognized that if you are required to be away from home on a temporary basis, you will have to incur duplicative living expenses, since it would be unreasonable to expect you to relocate for that short period of time.

However, if the job assignment is indefinite, it would be reasonable to expect you to relocate, and there would be no need for duplicative living expenses. If you do move to a new location, the cost of moving expenses may be deductible (see Chapter 22).

If you are on a temporary assignment and return home on weekends, holidays, or visits, the time at home is not treated as away from home, and the cost of your lodging at home is not deductible. The cost of your lodging at the temporary work site, however, continues to be deductible. Thus, for example, if you are living away from home in a motel and return home on a weekend but must pay for the motel room anyway, that cost is deductible. The cost of meals on a return trip home is deductible only to the extent that the cost of meals away would have been deductible. The cost of travel from the temporary assignment home and the return trip is also deductible.

Meal and Entertainment Expenses

If you entertain your client, customer, or employee, the cost of your expenses is deductible, subject to the 50% limit discussed later. (Meal costs for day-care providers are discussed in Chapter 22.) Entertainment may be an important way for you to generate business, create goodwill, and thank employees for a job well done. You may spend a considerable amount of time and expense wining and dining. Be sure to understand the rules to make your costs deductible to the fullest extent possible. Keep in mind that the area of meals and entertainment expenses attracts particular attention from the IRS, but if you meet the requirements for deductibility, your deductions will withstand IRS scrutiny.

General Rules on Deducting Meal and Entertainment Expenses

In order to be deductible as a meal and entertainment expense, an expense must be:

1. An **ordinary and necessary business expense**, and
2. Able to qualify under a directly related test or an associated test.

Ordinary and necessary business expense An *ordinary expense* is one that is common and accepted in your business. *A necessary expense* is one that is helpful and appropriate to your business. To be necessary, an expense need not be indispensable.

The Directly Related Test

You satisfy the *directly related test* if you can show that the main purpose of the entertainment activity was the active conduct of business and that you did, in fact, engage in business during the entertainment period. Entertainment in a clear business setting is presumed to meet the directly related test. You must have more than a general expectation of deriving income or some other business benefit from the activity at some future time. You need not devote more time to business than entertainment in order to satisfy this test. You simply have to demonstrate that all the facts, including the nature of the business transacted and the reasons for conducting business during an entertainment, support a business purpose. Nor do you need to show that business income or some other business benefit actually resulted from a specific entertainment event.

You will be presumed to have failed the directly related test if you are on a hunting, skiing, or fishing trip or on yachts or other pleasure boats unless you can show otherwise. Other locations that are presumed to have failed the directly related test include nightclubs, golf courses, theaters, and sporting events.

You bear a heavy burden of proof when the entertainment is held in a place where there are substantial distractions that prevent the possibility of actively conducting any business. This kind of entertainment is presumed to fail the directly related test. Substantial distractions are present at nightclubs, theaters, sporting events, and social gatherings (cocktail parties or meetings that include persons other than business associates). You can, however, overcome the presumption by showing that you engaged in a substantial business discussion during the entertainment despite the distractions.

> **Example**
>
> Entertainment in a hospitality room or suite at a convention where your business products are on display is in a clear business setting. Goodwill is presumed to be created through this entertainment in a clear business setting.

> **Example**
>
> A price rebate on the sale of your products can be entertainment provided in a clear business setting. Thus, if you own a restaurant and offer a free meal to a customer or supplier, this entertainment in a clear business setting is directly related to your business and is deductible.

> **Example**
>
> Where the entertainment itself is of a clear business nature but there is no personal or social relationship between you and the person or persons entertained, the costs are treated as directly related to your business. For example, if you entertain business leaders at the opening of a shopping mall in order to gain publicity, the cost is treated as a deductible entertainment expense.

Associated Test

If you cannot meet the higher standard of directly related, you may still be able to show that the entertainment is *associated* with the conduct of your business. This test requires showing that the expense is associated with your business and directly precedes or follows a substantial business discussion. You must have a clear business purpose for having the entertainment expense. This includes entertainment to get new business or encourage continued business with existing clients or customers.

How do you know if a business discussion is *substantial*? There is no quantitative way to show this. There is no prescribed amount of time you must spend meeting or discussing business, and you do not have to devote more time to business than to entertainment. You do not even have to discuss business during the entertainment itself. Whether the entertainment meets the associated test depends on the facts and circumstances of the situation. You must be able to show that you actually held a business discussion to get income or other business benefit. Goodwill entertainment satisfies the associated test.

If the entertainment is held on the same day as a business discussion, it is treated as held preceding or following a substantial business discussion.

Example

During working hours, a customer visits your offices and you discuss business for some time. That evening after your office is closed, you take your customer to the theater. This satisfies the associated test, since you held a substantial business discussion preceding the entertainment.

Where the business discussion is not held on the same day as the entertainment, all the facts are taken into account in determining whether the associated test is met. Factors considered are the place, the date, and the duration of the business discussion. For example, if you or your customers are out of town, the dates of arrival and departure may affect entertainment expenses.

Example

A customer flies in from out of town on Tuesday afternoon. You take her to the theater that evening and meet with her in your office on the following morning, at which time you hold a substantial business discussion. The associated test is met in this instance.

Other Requirements

In addition to meeting the directly related or associated test, you must show that the cost of the entertainment was not *lavish or extravagant*. There are no dollar figures used in making this determination; rather, it is based on the facts and circumstances. However, no deduction is allowed for fees paid to scalpers, ticket agents, or ticket brokers for tickets to theater, sporting, or other events. Only the face value of the ticket is deductible. Also, the cost of skyboxes and other private luxury boxes at a sports arena is limited. These boxes generally are rented for a season or a series of events, such as playoff games or a World Series. Where the cost covers more than one event, you cannot deduct more than the total of the face values of nonluxury box seats times the number of seats in the box. Then the 50% limit applies.

Example

You pay $1,200 for a skybox for 2 playoff games. The skybox seats 10 people. The cost of a 10-seat nonluxury box for each game is $200. Your deductible amount is limited to $400 ($200 × 2 events). Then it is subject to the 50% limit. (Had the box been rented for only 1 event at a cost of $600, then the full cost of the skybox, subject to the 50% limit, would have been deductible.)

Food, beverages, and other separately stated charges related to the skyboxes are separately deductible (subject to the 50% limit).

Home Entertainment

If you entertain business associates, customers, or employees at your home, can you deduct your expenses? The answer depends on whether you discuss specific business during the course of the dinner or other entertainment event. Business dinners may be conducive to business discussions. Other types of social gatherings, such as pool parties, may not be as conducive to business discussions and may raise questions with the IRS. It may be helpful to keep the guest list to a minimum (no more than 12) in order to be able to hold discussions with all guests. If you have a larger group, it may be difficult to show that you had business discussions with each guest.

If you do entertain at home, do not combine business with pleasure. The presence of nonbusiness guests may support the conclusion that the gathering was not for business reasons and that business was not discussed. Taxpayers have not fared well in proving that parties for personal events, such as a child's wedding, birthday, or bar mitzvah, were held for business even though business guests attended.

Limit

There is no dollar limit on what you can spend for meal and entertainment expenses. (Remember, though, that there is a lavish or extravagant limit.) However, only a portion of your costs is deductible. Meals and entertainment expenses generally are deductible only to the extent of 50% of cost. The 50% limit applies to meals eaten while traveling away from home even if they are paid with a per diem reimbursement rate.

The 50% limit does not necessarily apply to all business meals or entertainment. There are some important exceptions:

- Promotional activities.
- Meals paid for recreational, social, or similar activities primarily for the benefit of employees. This exception would apply, for example, to your cost of providing food at a company picnic.

Example

A real estate broker selling vacation property gave potential investors a free meal if they agreed to sit through a sales presentation. The IRS allowed the broker to deduct the full cost of the meals in this case, since they were made available to the general public as part of promotional activities.

- Food and beverages provided to employees as a tax-free de minimis fringe benefit. This exception would apply to your expenses of providing an employee cafeteria on your premises.
- Employees (in the transportation industry) who are subject to DOT hours of service limitations are subject to an increased meal deduction for food and beverages consumed while away from home. They can deduct 80% of their meal costs.

Impact of the 50% Limit on Employees

The fact that the company cannot deduct 50% of its costs for meals and entertainment does not affect employees. Employees are not taxed on the nondeductible portion of meal and entertainment costs even though they receive a full reimbursement or an advance for these expenses.

Club Dues

You cannot deduct the cost of dues, including initiation fees, to clubs organized for pleasure, recreation, or other social purposes. For example, the cost of airline clubs is not deductible. However, dues to certain business, professional, and civic organizations continue to be deductible. These include:

- *Business organizations*—business leagues, trade associations, chambers of commerce, boards of trade and real estate boards, business lunch clubs
- *Professional organizations*—bar associations, medical associations
- *Civic organizations*—Kiwanis, Lions, Rotary, Civitan

If you pay club dues for an employee, you can turn what would otherwise be a nondeductible expense into a deductible one. You can treat the payment of club dues on behalf of an employee as additional compensation. In this way the business can claim a deduction for club dues as compensation, not as travel and entertainment costs.

This option applies only to club dues that would otherwise be deductible but for the ban on deductibility. Thus, it applies only if the club is used for business. For example, suppose a corporation pays the country club dues of an employee.

The employee uses the club 100% for entertaining clients for business purposes. The corporation can elect to treat these dues as additional compensation to the employee. Of course, the employee cannot claim any offsetting deduction on his or her individual income tax return. If the country club is used solely for personal purposes, then the cost of dues is not subject to this election rule.

The election to treat club dues as additional compensation can be made on an employee-by-employee basis. Thus, if you own a corporation that pays club dues on behalf of yourself and other employees, the corporation can elect to treat the club dues as additional compensation to your other employees but not to yourself. If the corporation pays your club dues and elects to treat this as compensation to you, all you are really doing is shifting the tax burden from the corporation to you, something that may not have any net advantage. The corporation should weigh this election carefully before making it.

Spouse's Expenses

If you take your spouse or a friend with you on business entertainment or take a client's or customer's spouse along, are the spouse's expenses deductible? In general, the answer is no. However, if you can show that the purpose for including the spouse was clearly for business and not some social or personal purpose, the spouse's costs are deductible.

Example

You entertain a business customer. Assume that the costs of entertaining the customer are clearly deductible. The customer's spouse joins you because it would be impractical to entertain the customer without the spouse. In this case, the cost of the spouse's entertainment is an ordinary and necessary business expense. If your spouse were to join the entertainment because the customer's spouse is along, your spouse's costs would also be deductible.

Business Gifts

In the course of your business, you may give gifts to your dealers, distributors, customers, clients, and employees. The cost of business gifts is deductible, within limits. You may deduct only up to $25 per person per year (the dollar limit that was set back in 1962). This rule applies to both *direct* and *indirect* gifts. An indirect gift includes a gift to a company that is intended for the eventual personal use of a particular person or a gift to a spouse or child of a business customer or client.

In using the $25 limit, do not count incidental costs, such as wrapping, insuring, or shipping the gifts. Also, do not count engraving on jewelry.

Example

You give a $30 gift to client A. You may deduct $25. You give a $20 gift to client B. You may deduct $20.

Exceptions

Certain gifts are not subject to the $25 limit. These include gifts of nominal value ($4 or less) with your company name imprinted on them that you distribute to a number of clients or customers. These gifts would include, for example, pens, plastic bags, kitchen magnets, and calendars. Thus, if you give a customer a $25 gift and also send a calendar, the value of the calendar (assuming it is below $4) is not taken into account. Both gifts are deductible. Another exception to the $25 rule includes signs, display racks, or other promotional material used on business premises. Thus, if you give a dealer a display rack to hold your items, the gift is a deductible business expense, regardless of cost.

In one case the Tax Court recognized another exception to the $25 limit for gifts to employees—gifts designated as an *employee relations expense* rather than as a gift or compensation. The court allowed a deduction in this case of almost $1,500 (the cost of a set of golf clubs) given as incentive for continued good performance by a top salesperson.

> **NOTE**
> Expect the IRS to continue to challenge any gifts in excess of the $25 limit so, if you want to make larger gifts, be sure to have a business rationale for doing so.

When Is an Item an Entertainment Expense?

If you give an item that could be treated as either an entertainment expense or a business gift, how do you know how to classify it? The choice is yours. In making it, take into consideration the fact that an entertainment expense is subject to a 50% limit, while a business gift is subject to the $25 limit. Thus, if you give tickets to the theater or a ball game and you do not go with the client or customer to the performance or event, you can choose to treat the cost as either an entertainment expense or a business gift.

Example

You give your client 2 tickets to the ball game. The tickets cost $20 each. If you treat them as a business gift, you can deduct $25 ($40 business gift up to the $25 limit). However, if you treat the tickets as an entertainment expense, only $20 is deductible ($40 expense subject to the 50% limit).

If you treat an item as a business gift but want to change the treatment, you may do so within 3 years of the filing of your return by filing an amended return.

If you go with the client to the theater or sporting event, you must treat the cost of the tickets as an entertainment expense; you cannot treat it as a business gift. However, if the gift is one of food or beverage intended to be consumed by the client or customer at a later time, you must treat it as a business gift. Thus, if you give bottles of wine or liquor, they constitute business gifts.

Reimbursement Arrangements

If an employer reimburses an employee for travel and entertainment expenses, how you arrange the reimbursement affects what the employer and employee can deduct.

No Reimbursement Arrangement

If an employee on salary has no reimbursement arrangement and is expected or required to pay for travel and entertainment costs by himself or herself, the employee can deduct the expenses on his or her individual income tax return. The business expenses are deductible as miscellaneous itemized deductions. This means that after applying all the limits discussed above, such as the 50% limit on meals and entertainment, costs are deductible only to the extent they exceed 2% of the employee's adjusted gross income. In this instance, the employee is responsible for recordkeeping of business expenses.

Accountable Plans

If an employer maintains an *accountable plan*, the employee does not deduct any expenses. Instead, the employer pays for and deducts all costs. No reimbursements are reported as income to the employee, and the reimbursements are not subject to payroll taxes. Thus, an accountable plan is a tax saver for both the employer and employee.

A reimbursement arrangement is treated as an accountable plan if:

- *The expenses have a business connection.* This means the expenses must have been incurred while performing services as an employee for an employer.

- *The employee must adequately account to the employer for expenses within a reasonable time.* Accounting within 60 days after paying or incurring the expenses is considered a reasonable time. The employee must supply the employer with documentary evidence (canceled checks, receipts, or bills) of mileage, travel, and other business expenses unless reimbursement is made at a per diem rate. All employees must provide the employer with a statement of expense, an account book or diary, or a similar record (including computer logs) in which expenses are entered at or near the time at which they were incurred. All amounts received from an employer must be documented. This includes not only cash advances but also amounts charged to an employer by credit card or other method.

- *The employee must return to the employer within a reasonable period of time any excess reimbursements.* Thus, for example, if an employer advances an employee $400 for a business trip and expenses totaled only $350, the employee must return the excess $50 within a reasonable period of time. A reasonable period of time depends on the facts and circumstances. However, it is automatically treated as reasonable if an advance is made within 30 days of the expense, adequate accounting of the expense is made to the employer within 60 days after it was paid or incurred, and any excess reimbursement is refunded to the employer within 120 days after the expense was paid or incurred. It is also automatically treated as reasonable if an employer furnishes an employee with a periodic (at least quarterly) statement requesting reimbursement of excess amounts and reimbursement is in fact made within 120 days after receipt of the statement.

If the employer maintains an accountable plan but an employee does not meet all the rules (for example, the employee fails to return excess amounts or is reimbursed for nonbusiness expenses), then those expenses are treated as paid under a nonaccountable plan. The remaining expenses are treated as paid under an accountable plan.

Example

An employer maintains an accountable plan. During the year, an employee is reimbursed for business travel expenses and also receives reimbursement for meals eaten while working late for the employer. The meals are nonbusiness expenses. The employer is treated as having 2 plans in this instance: an accountable plan for the travel expenses and a nonaccountable plan for the personal meal expenses.

It is advisable for the company to formally adopt an accountable plan by putting the action into corporate minutes (see Appendix B) or in other written form.

Nonaccountable Plans

If an employer maintains a reimbursement arrangement but it does not qualify as an accountable plan (for example, excess reimbursements need not be returned, or reimbursements cover nondeductible personal expenses), the plan is considered a nonaccountable plan. In this case, the employer must report the reimbursements on an employee's Form W-2. The employee then deducts the expenses on his or her individual income tax return, subject to the 2%-of-adjusted-gross-income floor.

Reimbursement at Per Diem Rates

Reimbursing employees for travel and related expenses at a per diem rate simplifies things for all concerned; employees need not keep track of every expense and retain receipts for all of them, and employers can make reimbursements at a flat rate, easing accounting procedures. If an employer pays for business expenses using a per diem rate, special rules apply. If the rate used by the employer is the same as or lower than the federal per diem rate for the area of travel, reimbursements are not reported on an employee's Form W-2. If an employee's actual expenses exceeded the reimbursement at or below the federal rate, the employee can deduct the excess expenses on his or her individual income tax return. However, if the rate used by the employer is higher than the federal rate, the amounts are reported on Form W-2. The amount of the federal rate is not included in an employee's gross income, though excess reimbursements are included in the employee's gross income. The employee can, however, claim business deductions for these excess amounts (subject to the 2% floor).

There are several acceptable federal rates that an employer can use to make reimbursements, including the federal per diem rate, high-low method, standard meal allowance, and the incidental rate.

Note: Self-employed individuals cannot use the standard rates covering lodging, meals, and incidental expenses to substantiate their travel costs. They can, however, use the standard meal allowance to substantiate meal costs during business travel.

There are several types of per diem or standard rates that can be used for substantiating travel costs. The rules and amounts for each of these rates have been discussed previously in this chapter. These rates include:

- Federal per diem rate
- High-low substantiation rate
- Standard meal allowance

You cannot use the standard meal allowance if you are related to your employer. You are considered related if your employer is your brother, sister (half or whole), spouse, parent, grandparent, child, or grandchild. You are also considered related if you own, directly or indirectly, more than 10% of the value of your employer's stock. Indirect ownership arises when you have an interest in a corporation, partnership, trust, or estate that owns stock in your employer's corporation or if family members own stock in your employer's corporation. However, you can use the standard meal allowance if you are self-employed.

INCIDENTAL RATE

There is a $5 per day rate for incidental expenses, such as tips and transportation between the hotel and place of business. This modest rate can be used to cover incidental expenses only if no meal costs are incurred on such a day (for example, it is a day of personal travel).

PARTIAL DAYS OF TRAVEL

If the federal per diem rate or high-low method is used for any day of travel that does not include a full 24-hour period, the per diem amount must be prorated. The full rate is allocated on a quarterly basis for each 6-hour period in the day (midnight to 6 a.m.; 6 a.m. to noon; noon to 6 p.m.; 6 p.m. to midnight).

Recordkeeping Requirements

Business expenses can be disallowed unless there is adequate substantiation for the expenses claimed. For travel and entertainment expenses, there are 2 main ways to prove costs: actual substantiation or reliance on a per diem rate. First look at actual substantiation; then consider how recordkeeping can be simplified with the use of per diem rates.

There are a number of elements to substantiate for each business expense. In general, to substantiate each item you must show the amount, the time, the place, the business purpose for the travel or the business relationship with the persons you entertain or provide gifts to, and, in some cases, a description of the item. The exact type of substantiation required depends on the item of business expense.

Travel

You must show the amount of each separate expense for travel, lodging, meals, and incidental expenses. You can total these items in any reasonable category. For example, you can simply keep track of meals in a category called daily meals. You must also note the dates you left for the trip and returned, as well as the days spent on the trip for business purposes. You must list the name of the city or other designation of the place of the travel, along with the reason for the travel or the business benefit gained or expected to be gained from it.

While this may sound like a great deal of recordkeeping, as a practical matter hotel receipts may provide you with much of the information necessary. For example, a hotel receipt typically shows the dates you arrived and departed; the name and location of the hotel; and separate charges for lodging, meals, telephone calls, and other items. The IRS says that a charge slip for hotel costs is no substitute for the hotel receipt itself. You must have documentary evidence for the cost of lodging. You do not need documentary evidence if the item (other than lodging) is less than $75 or, in the case of transportation costs, if a receipt is not readily available. Thus, if a cab ride is $9 and the driver does not provide you with a receipt, you are not required to show documentary evidence of this expense.

Meals and Entertainment

List expenses separately. Incidental expenses, such as taxis and telephone, may be totaled on a daily basis. List each date of the meal or entertainment. For meals or entertainment directly before or after a business discussion, list the date and duration of the business discussion. Include the name and address or location of the place for the entertainment and the type of entertainment if not apparent from the name of the place. Also list the place where a business discussion was held if entertainment was directly before or after the discussion. State the business reason or the business benefit gained or expected to be gained and the nature of the business discussion. Include the names of the persons entertained, including their occupations or other identifying information, and indicate who took part in the business discussion.

If the deduction is for a business meal, you must note that you or your employer was present at the meal. Again, a restaurant receipt typically will supply much of the information required. It will show the name and location of the restaurant, the number of people served, and the date and amount of the expense. Be sure to jot down the business aspect of the meal or entertainment, such as asking a client for a referral or trying to sell your services.

Gifts

Show the cost of the gift, the date given, and a description. Also show the business reason for the gift or the business benefit gained or expected to be gained from providing it. Indicate the name of the person receiving the gift, his or her occupation or other identifying information, and his or her business relationship to you.

A canceled check, along with a bill, generally establishes the cost of a business item. A canceled check alone does not prove a business expense without other evidence to show its business purpose.

Using a Diary or Log

Enter your expenses in a diary (see Table 8.2) or log (e.g., in writing or with an app) at or near the time of the event giving rise to the expenses. Computer-generated records are acceptable. Be sure to include all the elements required for the expense (especially the business reason for it).

It is a good idea to total expenses on a monthly basis and then use a recap form to put annual figures together.

TABLE 8.2 Sample Expense Diary

Date	Description	Fares	Lodging	Meals	Entertainment	Other
1/10	Breakfast with Sue Smith, CEO, X Corp., discussed sales.			$21.50		
1/11	Sales trip Buyers in NYC.	$408.00	$455.00	$105.00		$28.00
1/14	Lunch with Mark Hess after sales call.			$38.75		
1/15	Gift for John Jones (boss).					$22.00

Other Substantiation Methods

The IRS has recognized we are in the computer age and has endorsed various computer-based substantiation methods. For example, if each employee has a company credit card, electronic reports from the credit card company can be used to substantiate charged expenses (paper receipts of expenses in excess of $75 are still required).

Missing, Lost, or Inadequate Records

If you do not have adequate records, you may still be able to deduct an item if you can prove by your own statement or other supporting evidence an element of substantiation. A court may even allow an estimation of expenses under the "Cohan rule," under certain circumstances (the Cohan rule is named after entertainer George M. Cohan's case in the last century). Where receipts have been destroyed, you may be able to reconstruct your expenses. You must, of course, show how the records were destroyed (fire, storm, flood). The IRS may require additional information to prove the accuracy or reliability of the information contained in your records. Recordkeeping alternatives are discussed in more detail in Chapter 3.

Per Diem Rates

If you receive reimbursement using one of the per diem rates discussed earlier, you need not retain documentary evidence of the amount of an expense. The per diem rate is deemed to satisfy the proof of the amount of the expense. However, use of the per diem rate does not prove any of the other elements of substantiation. For example, if an employee is reimbursed for business travel using the high-low method, he or she still must show the time, the place, and the business purpose for business travel.

Where to Deduct Travel and Entertainment Expenses

Employees

You calculate your travel and entertainment expenses on Form 2106, *Employee Business Expenses*, or Form 2106-EZ, *Unreimbursed Employee Business Expenses*. You can use the EZ form, which is a simplified version of Form 2106, if you do not get reimbursed by your employer for any expenses and, if you are claiming expenses for a car, you own the car, and are using the standard mileage rate (as explained in Chapter 9). You enter your total from Form 2106 or 2106-EZ on Schedule A, Itemized Deductions, as a miscellaneous itemized expense. These deductions are then limited to the amount they exceed; 2% of adjusted gross income and are subject to an overall reduction in itemized deductions if you are a high-income taxpayer.

DISABLED EMPLOYEES

If you have a physical or mental disability, your impairment-related work expenses are deductible as an itemized deduction, but the 2%-of-AGI floor does not apply. Impairment-related work expenses include expenses for attendant care at your place of work as well as other expenses that are necessary to enable you to work. General medical expenses, however, are not impairment-related work expenses; they are simply personal medical expenses and are deductible as such.

SPECIAL RULE FOR PERFORMING ARTISTS

If you meet certain requirements, you can deduct all of your car expenses as an adjustment to gross income on page 1 of Form 1040 instead of claiming them as miscellaneous itemized deductions on Schedule A. You are treated as a qualified performing artist (QPA) if you meet all of the following tests:

1. You perform services in the performing arts for at least 2 employers in the year.
2. You receive at least $200 each from any 2 of these employers.
3. Your related performing arts business expenses are more than 10% of your adjusted gross income from the performance of such services.
4. Your adjusted gross income from *all* sources does not exceed $16,000 (before deducting business expenses from your performing arts). The $16,000 limit is fixed by law and has not changed since 1987.

5. If you are married and you file a joint return (unless you lived apart from your spouse for the entire year).

You figure tests 1, 2, and 3 based on your separate experience. However, the adjusted gross income in test 4 is based on the combined adjusted gross income of you and your spouse.

If you meet these criteria, you deduct your performing arts business expenses as an adjustment to gross income on page 1 of Form 1040. Enter these expenses on the line used for totaling adjustments to gross income. Write "QPA" next to your expenses.

Self-Employed (Including Independent Contractor and Statutory Employee)

You enter your travel, meals, and entertainment expenses on Schedule C, *Profit and Loss from Business*, or Schedule C-EZ, *Net Profit from Business*. On Schedule C there are separate lines for travel, for meals and entertainment, and for determining the 50% limit on meals and entertainment. Business gifts are reported as other expenses, which are explained on page 2 of Schedule C. Schedule C-EZ can be used only if total business expenses are no more than $5,000. You simply add your travel and entertainment expenses to your other deductible business expenses and enter the total on the appropriate line of Schedule C-EZ. You need not attach an itemized statement explaining the deduction. Be sure that when you total your expenses, you apply the 50% limit on meals and entertainment.

Self-employed farmers deduct travel, meals, and entertainment expenses on Schedule F.

Partnerships and LLCs

Travel, meals, and entertainment expenses are reported on Form 1065 and are taken into account in arriving at the business's ordinary income (or loss). They are entered in the category of Other Deductions on the form. A schedule is attached to the return explaining the deductions claimed in this category. Be sure to apply the 50% limit to meals and entertainment. Travel, meals, and entertainment expenses are not separately stated items. An owner's share of these expenses is reported on Schedule K-1.

S Corporations

Travel, meals, and entertainment expenses are reported on Form 1120S and are taken into account in arriving at the corporation's ordinary income (or loss). They are entered in the category of Other Deductions on the form. A schedule is attached to the return explaining the deductions claimed in this category. Be sure to apply the 50% limit to meals and entertainment. Travel, meals, and entertainment expenses are not separately stated items. A shareholder's share of these expenses is reported on Schedule K-1.

C Corporations

Travel, meals, and entertainment expenses are reported on Form 1120 and are taken into account in arriving at the corporation's taxable income (or loss). They are entered in the category of Other Deductions on the form. A schedule is attached to the return explaining the deductions claimed in this category. Be sure to apply the 50% limit on meals and entertainment.

Car and Truck Expenses

Alert

At the time this book was printed, Congress had not extended numerous breaks for 2014 that had expired at the end of 2013. Check the online supplement in February 2015 at www.jklasser.com or www.barbaraweltman.com to see whether these breaks apply for 2014 returns.

Americans are highly mobile, and the car is the method of choice for transportation. If you use your car for business, you may write off various costs. The IRS reported that on 2011 returns (the most recent year for statistics), car and truck expenses were the second largest category of deductions for sole proprietors (second only to cost of goods sold, which is not relevant to service businesses). In order to nail down deductions for these expenses, you must carefully observe certain recordkeeping rules. There are 2 methods for deducting costs: the actual expense method and the standard mileage allowance. In order to use either method, you must maintain proper records for business driving.

For further information about deductions with respect to business use of your car, see IRS Publication 463, *Travel, Entertainment, Gift, and Car Expenses*.

Deducting Car Expenses in General

The discussion in this chapter applies to **cars** used partly or entirely for business.

Car Any 4-wheel vehicle made primarily for use on public streets, roads, and highways that has an unloaded gross vehicle weight of 6,000 pounds or less (the manufacturer can provide this information). A truck or van is a "light" truck or van if its unloaded gross weight is 6,000 pounds or less and is subject to rules similar to those for passenger cars. Excluded from the definition is an ambulance, hearse, or combination thereof used in business and any vehicle used in business for transporting people or for compensation or hire.

The law allows you to choose between two methods for deducting business-related expenses of a car: the actual expense method or the standard mileage allowance fixed by the IRS, both of which are detailed in this chapter.

Choosing Between the Actual Expense Method and the Standard Mileage Allowance

Read over the rules on the *actual expense method* and the *standard mileage allowance*. For the most part, the choice of method is yours. The choice applies whether you own or lease the car. In some cases, however, you may not be able to use the standard mileage rate. Where you are not barred from using the standard mileage rate and can choose between the methods, which is better? Obviously, it is the one that produces the greater deduction. However, there is no easy way to determine which method will produce the greater deduction. Many factors will affect your decision, including the number of miles you drive each year and the extent of your actual expenses. See the example's comparison.

Example

You buy a car in January 2014 for $15,000 and use it 100% for business. In 2014, the first year the car is in service, you drive 1,500 miles per month. If you use the standard mileage allowance, your car deduction for 2014 is $10,080

(18,000 × 0.56). If your actual costs exceed this amount, it may be advisable to use the actual expense method. If they are less than $10,080, the standard mileage allowance may be better.

In making your decision, bear in mind that the standard mileage allowance simplifies recordkeeping for business use of the car.

You should make the decision in the first year you own the car. This is because a choice of the actual expense method for the first year will forever bar the use of the standard mileage allowance in subsequent years. If you use the standard mileage rate, you can still use the actual expense method in later years. However, if the car has not yet been fully depreciated (using the deemed depreciation rates discussed later), then, for depreciation purposes, you must use the straight-line method over what you estimate to be the car's remaining useful life.

Actual Expense Method

The *actual expense method* allows you to deduct all of your out-of-pocket costs for operating your car for business, plus an allowance for depreciation if you own the car. Actual expenses include:

Depreciation	Licenses	Tires
Garage rent	Loan interest	Tolls
Gas	Oil	Towing
Insurance	Parking fees	Vehicle registration fees
Lease fees	Repairs	

For individuals, whether interest on a car loan is deductible depends on employment status. If you are an employee who uses a car for business, you cannot deduct interest on a car loan; the interest is treated as nondeductible personal interest. However, if you are self-employed, the interest may be treated as business interest. For corporations, interest on a car loan is fully deductible.

If you pay personal property tax on a car used for business, the tax is deductible by an employee only as an itemized deduction. Personal property tax is not grouped with other car expenses. Instead, it is listed on an individual's Schedule A as a personal property tax.

If your car is damaged, destroyed, or stolen, the part of the loss not covered by insurance may be deductible. If the car was used entirely for business, the loss is treated as a fully deductible casualty or theft loss. If it was used partly for personal purposes, the loss may be treated as a casualty or theft loss, but the portion of the loss allocated to personal purposes is subject to certain limitations. See Chapter 17 for a discussion of casualty and theft losses.

Not all car-related expenses are deductible. Luxury and sales taxes cannot be separately deducted even if a car is used entirely for business; these taxes are treated as part of the cost of the car and are added to the basis of the car for purposes of calculating depreciation, as well as gain or loss on the future sale of the car.

Fines for traffic violations, including parking violations, are not deductible, even when they were incurred in the course of business-related travel.

Depreciation

If you own your car and use it for business, you may recoup part of the cost of the car through a deduction called *depreciation*. The amount of depreciation depends on a great many factors. First, it depends on whether you use the depreciation allowance or claim a Section 179 deduction (discussed later in the chapter). It also varies according to the year in which you begin to use your car for business, the cost of the car, and the amount of business mileage for the year as compared with the total mileage for the year. Depreciation is covered in Chapter 14 as well.

Business Use versus Personal or Investment Use

Whether you claim a depreciation allowance or a Section 179 deduction, you can do so only with respect to the portion of the car used for business. For example, if you use your car 75% for business and 25% for personal purposes, you must allocate the cost of the car for purposes of calculating depreciation. The allocation is based on the number of miles driven for business compared to the total number of miles driven for the year.

Example

In 2014, you buy a car for $16,000 and drive it 20,000 miles. Of this mileage, 15,000 miles were for business; 5,000 miles were personal. For purposes of depreciation, you must allocate $12,000 for business use. It is this amount on which you figure depreciation.

If you use a car for investment purposes, you can add the miles driven for investment purposes when making an allocation for depreciation.

Depreciation Allowance

A depreciation allowance is simply a deduction calculated by applying a percentage to the **basis** of the car. Cars are treated as 5-year property under the Modified Accelerated Cost Recovery System (MACRS), the depreciation system currently in effect, as discussed in Chapter 14. As such, you would think that the cost of the car could be recovered through depreciation deductions over a

TABLE 9.1 Straight-Line Half-Year Convention*

Year	Rate (Percent)
1	10
2	20
3	20
4	20
5	20
6	10

*Depreciation may not exceed a dollar limit (see page 217).

period of 5 years. However, this is generally not the case because of a number of different rules that exist. These rules all operate to limit the amount of depreciation that can be claimed in any one year and to extend the number of years for claiming depreciation.

> *Basis*   Generally, this is the original cost of the car. If a car is bought in part with the trade-in of an old car, the basis of the new car is the adjusted basis of the old car plus any cash payment you make. Basis is reduced by any first-year expense deduction and any qualified electric vehicle tax credit. It is also adjusted downward for any depreciation deductions.

Depreciation can take several forms. There is *accelerated depreciation* under MACRS, which results in greater deductions in the early years of ownership and smaller deductions in the later years. There is *straight-line depreciation*, which spreads depreciation deductions evenly over the years the car is expected to last (the fixed number of years may, in fact, have no relation to the actual number of years the car is in operation). Tables 9.1 and 9.2 provide the percentage for depreciation under both methods. There is the *first-year expense*

TABLE 9.2 MACRS Half-Year Convention*

Year	Rate (Percent)
1	20.00
2	32.00
3	19.20
4	11.52
5	11.52
6	5.76

*Depreciation may not exceed a dollar limit (see page 217).

deduction, discussed later in this chapter, which is in lieu of depreciation. It takes the place of depreciation for the first year. Any part of the car not recovered through the first-year expense deduction can then be recovered through depreciation deductions in subsequent years.

Business Use

In order for you to claim an accelerated depreciation deduction or a first-year expense, the car must be used more than 50% for business. Compare the miles driven during the year for business with the total miles driven. If more than 50% of the mileage represents business use, accelerated depreciation (or the first-year expense deduction below) can be claimed.

If you satisfy the 50% test, you may also add to business mileage any miles driven for investment purposes when calculating the depreciation deduction. You may not add investment mileage in order to determine whether you meet the 50% test. If you fail the 50% test (you use the car 50% or less for business), you can deduct depreciation using only the straight-line method. Your deduction is limited to the rates listed in the section on "Conventions."

What if the percentage of business use changes from year to year? You may use your car 75% for business in 1 year but only 40% the next. Where business use in the year the car is placed in service is more than 50% but drops below 50% in a subsequent year, you must also change depreciation rates. Once business use drops to 50% or below, you can use only the straight-line method thereafter. The depreciation rate is taken from the table for the straight-line method (Table 9.1) as if the car had not qualified for accelerated depreciation in a prior year.

Where business use drops to 50% or less, you may have to include in income an amount called *excess depreciation*. This is the amount of depreciation (including the first-year expense deduction) claimed when the car was used more than 50% for business over the amount of depreciation that would have been allowable had the car not been used more than 50% in the year it was placed in service. In addition to including excess depreciation in income, you must increase the basis of your car by the same amount.

Conventions

There are special rules that operate to limit write-offs for depreciation, called *conventions*. Two conventions apply to depreciation for cars: the half-year convention and the mid-quarter convention.

Example

In 2012 you placed in service a car costing $17,000. (Assume the car was used 100% for business, you did not elect first-year expensing or bonus depreciation if applicable, and the half-year convention applied.) In 2014, business use drops to 40%. The depreciation claimed for 2012 and 2013 totaled $8,260 using MACRS (subject to dollar limits). Had the straight-line method been used, depreciation would have been $5,100. Thus, the excess of $3,160 ($8,260 − $5,100) must be included in income. Your new adjusted basis for the car is $11,900 ($17,000 − $8,260 + $3,160). When calculating the 2012 depreciation deduction, you use the old basis, $17,000, and take the percentage of business use (40%). Your basis for depreciation in 2014 is $6,800 ($17,000 × .40). The depreciation percentage for 2014 is 20%. The dollar limit must also be reduced to reflect the percentage of business use.

The *half-year convention*, in effect, assumes that the car was placed in service in the second half of the year. Thus, in the first year you are allowed to claim only one-half the normal rate of depreciation, regardless of when in the year the car was placed in service. Thus, even if the car was placed in service on January 1, the half-year convention must still be used.

You can see in Table 9.1 how the half-year convention operates to limit depreciation in the first year. By the same token, the amount of depreciation denied in the first year will ultimately be allowed in the sixth year. Still, the half-year convention means that even though the car is classified as 5-year property, its cost will be recovered only over a period of 6 years. If the half-year convention applies to property used 50% or less for business, the depreciation rate is in Table 9.1. If the half-year convention applies to property used more than 50% for business, the depreciation rate is in Table 9.2.

The other convention, the *mid-quarter convention*, applies if more than 40% of all the depreciable property you place in service during the year is placed in service in the last quarter of the year.

If the mid-quarter convention applies to property used 50% or less for business, the rate is in Table 9.3.

TABLE 9.3 Straight-Line Mid-Quarter Convention*

Year Placed in Service	1st Quarter	2nd Quarter	3rd Quarter	4th Quarter
1	17.5%	12.5%	7.5%	2.5%
2	20.0	20.0	20.0	20.0
3	20.0	20.0	20.0	20.0
4	20.0	20.0	20.0	20.0
5	20.0	20.0	20.0	20.0
6	2.5	7.5	12.5	17.5

*Depreciation may not exceed a dollar limit (see page 217).

Example

In 2014 you place in service a computer costing $5,000 in January and a used car costing $15,000 in December. The mid-quarter convention applies because more than 40% of the depreciable property you placed in service during the year was placed in service during the last quarter of the year ($15,000 is 75% of the total of $20,000 of depreciable property placed in service in 2014).

Example

The circumstances are the same, except the car was placed in service in January and the computer was placed in service in December. The mid-quarter convention does not apply because only 25% of the depreciable property was placed in service in the last quarter of the year ($5,000 is 25% of the total of $20,000 of depreciable property placed in service in 2014).

If the mid-quarter convention applies to property used more than 50% for business, the rate is in Table 9.4.

Example

In December 2014, you place in service a used car costing $14,000. You use the car 40% for business and 60% for personal purposes. Assume that this is the only depreciable property you place in service in 2014, so the mid-quarter convention applies. Your depreciation deduction for the first year is $140 (2.5% of $5,600 [40% of $14,000]).

TABLE 9.4 MACRS Mid-Quarter Convention*

Year Placed in Service	1st Quarter	2nd Quarter	3rd Quarter	4th Quarter
1	35.00%	25.00%	15.00%	5.00%
2	26.00	30.00	34.00	38.00
3	15.60	18.00	20.40	22.80
4	11.01	11.37	12.24	13.68
5	11.01	11.37	11.30	10.94
6	1.38	4.26	7.06	9.58

*Depreciation may not exceed a dollar limit (see page 217).

> **Example**
>
> In December 2014, you place in service a used car costing $14,000. You use the car 100% for business. Assume that this is the only depreciable property you place in service in 2014, so the mid-quarter convention applies. Your depreciation deduction for the first year is $700 (5% of $14,000).

Section 179 Deduction

The *Section 179 deduction*, also called the first-year expense allowance, is a one-time write-off for the cost of the car. If you use the first-year expense deduction for the year in which you buy the car and place it in service, you cannot then use depreciation in subsequent years. The annual limit for 2014 on the first-year expense deduction is $500,000 if the 2013 limit is extended or $25,000 if not; $25,000 applies for heavy SUVs whether the basic limit is extended. However, because of the dollar limits discussed later, the actual limit on the first-year expense deduction for vehicles other than heavy SUVs is the dollar limit.

So, should you use the first-year expense deduction or depreciation? As a general rule, it is not advisable to use the first-year expense deduction because of the dollar limit. For example, say you buy a car for $15,000 that you use 100% for business. Ordinarily, under the rules for the first-year expense deduction, you would deduct the full $15,000. However, because of the dollar limit, you may be able to deduct only a few thousand dollars. What is more, if you buy other depreciable equipment—a computer, machinery, or other equipment—you may well use up your expensing limit on the other equipment.

Dollar Limit on Depreciation Deduction

The law sets a *dollar limit* on the amount of depreciation that can be claimed on a car used for business (see Table 9.5). The dollar limit is intended to limit

TABLE 9.5 Dollar Limit on Depreciation of Passenger Cars

Date Car Placed in Service	1st Year	2nd Year	3rd Year	4th and Later Years
2014	3,160†	5,100	3,050	1,875
2012 and 2013	11,160*	5,100	3,050	1,875
2010 and 2011	11,060**	4,900	2,950	1,775
2008 and 2009	10,960***	4,800	2,850	1,775

*$3,160 if the car did not qualify for bonus depreciation (i.e., it was a used car).
**$3,060 if the car did not qualify for bonus depreciation (i.e., it was a used car).
***$2,960 if the car did not qualify for bonus depreciation (i.e., it was a used car).
†The limit could be higher if bonus depreciation is extended for 2014; check the Supplement.

depreciation that could be claimed on a nonluxury car. In essence, the government does not want to underwrite the cost of buying high-priced cars. However, in reality the dollar limits do not really correlate with luxury cars, since the average cost of a new American car was more than $32,086 in the first quarter of 2014, according to Interest.com. Still, the dollar limits are a factor you must reckon with in calculating your deduction limit.

Example

In March 2014, you place in service a used car costing $20,000 that is used 100% for business and weighs 3,500 pounds. The dollar limit on depreciation for 2014 is $3,160. For 2015 it will be $5,100; for 2016 it will be $3,050, and for each year thereafter it will be $1,875 as long as you use the car for business, until the car is fully depreciated.

Example

In 2010, you placed in service a car costing $20,000. For 2014 and all later years, your dollar limit is $1,775.

The dollar limits in Table 9.5 do not apply to light trucks and vans (those weighing less than 6,000 pounds). Special (higher) limits apply as explained later in this chapter.

The dollar limit applies only to cars with a gross vehicle weight (the manufacturer's maximum weight rating when loaded to capacity) of 6,000 pounds or less. Most cars fall into this category. However, some sport utility vehicles (SUVs) are heavier. If you use an SUV as your business car, check the manufacturer's specifications to see if the weight exceeds 6,000 pounds (but not 14,000 pounds). If so, the dollar limits in Table 9.5 do not apply and the vehicle's cost can be expensed up to $25,000. In addition, depreciation can be claimed on the portion of the car that is not expensed.

Example

In 2014, you buy a used SUV weighing more than 6,000 pounds that costs $55,000 and use it entirely for business. You elect to expense the purchase up to the $25,000 limit and use MACRS half-year convention (Table 9.2) for the balance of the purchase price. Your expensing and depreciation deductions in

2014 total $31,000 ($25,000 expensing, plus depreciation of 20% of [$55,000 — $25,000]). Your depreciation deductions in future years are:

2015	$9,600
2016	5,760
2017	3,456
2018	3,456
2019	1,728

If the dollar limit applies to your business car, the amount depends on the year in which the car was placed in service and how long you have owned it. Over the years, the dollar limits have been modified by law changes. For a number of years they have been adjusted for changes in the cost-of-living index. For 2014, the first-year dollar limit is $3,160 for vehicles (plus an additional amount if bonus depreciation is extended; see the Supplement). For light trucks and vans placed in service in 2014, the first-year dollar limit is $3,460 (plus an additional amount if bonus depreciation is extended; see the Supplement).

As a practical matter, most individuals will not get to fully depreciate their cars. They will have sold or traded them in long before the cost has been fully written off. This is because of the dollar limit. In the example on page 217, where a $20,000 car was placed in service in 2014, the car will not be fully depreciated until its ninth year (depending upon whether MACRS or the straight-line method was used).

These dollar amounts apply to cars used 100% for business. If you use your car for personal purposes as well as for business, you must allocate the dollar limit. The method for allocating this limit is the same method used for allocating the cost of the car for purposes of depreciation, as described earlier.

Example

In July 2014, you place in service a used car costing $30,000 that is used 75% for business and 25% for personal purposes. The full dollar limit of $3,160 is allocated 75% for business. Thus the 2014 dollar limit for this car is $2,370 (75% of $3,160).

Increase Your Dollar Limit

The dollar limit applies on a per-car basis. If you own 2 cars and use each for business, you may be able to increase your total dollar limit. Be sure to apply the percentage of business use for each car to the applicable dollar limit.

In June 2014 you buy a used car costing $25,000. Assume you drive 24,000 miles during the year, 90% of which (21,600 miles) is for business. Your dollar limit on depreciation is $2,844 (90% of $3,160).

Now, instead assume you own 2 cars, each costing $25,000, which you use for business. You drive car A 22,200 miles, of which 20,000 miles is for business, or 90%. You drive car B 4,400 miles, of which 2,200 is for business, or 50%. Your dollar limit for car A is $2,844 ($3,160 × .90). Your dollar limit for car B is $1,580 ($3,160 × .50). Your total depreciation deduction is $4,424 ($2,844 + 1,580). By using 2 cars instead of 1, your depreciation limit is $1,264 greater than it would be if you used 1 car exclusively for business and the other for only personal driving.

Dispositions of a Car

When you sell your car, trade it in for a new one, or lose it as the result of a casualty or theft, you have to calculate your tax consequences.

SALE

If you sell your car, your gain or loss is the difference between what you receive for the car and your adjusted basis. Your adjusted basis is your original basis reduced by any first-year expensing or depreciation (up to the dollar limit each year). If the car has been fully depreciated, anything you receive for the car is all gain.

If you used the standard mileage allowance, you are considered to have claimed depreciation even though you did not have to figure a separate depreciation deduction. The standard mileage allowance automatically takes into account a deduction for depreciation. You figure your *deemed depreciation* according to the number of miles you drove the car for business each year and the years in which it was used (see Table 9.6).

You bought a car and placed it in service at the beginning of 2011. You drove the car 20,000 miles each year for business. You sell it at the end of 2014. You must adjust the basis of the car for purposes of determining gain or loss on the sale by deemed depreciation of $18,000 (40,000 miles × 23¢/mile + 40,000 miles × 22¢/mile). You reduce your original basis by the total of deemed depreciation but do not reduce the basis below zero.

TABLE 9.6 Deemed Depreciation

Year	Rate per Mile
2014	22¢
2012–2013	23
2011	22
2010	23
2008–2009	21

If you use the actual expense method and sell the car before the end of its recovery period, you can claim a reduced depreciation deduction in the year of disposition. Calculate what the depreciation deduction would have been had you held the car for the full year. Then, if you originally placed your car in service in the first three-quarters of the year (January 1 through September 30), you can deduct 50% of the amount that would have been allowed. If you originally placed your car in service in the last quarter of the year (October 1 through December 31), you can deduct an amount calculated by applying the percentage in Table 9.7 to what would have been allowed.

TRADE-IN

Generally, no gain or loss is recognized if you trade in your car to buy another car for business. Such a trade is treated as a like-kind exchange if you opt for this treatment. This nonrecognition rule applies even if you pay cash in addition to your trade-in or if you finance the purchase. However, if the dealer gives you money back (because the new car costs less than the trade-in), you may have gain to recognize. The gain recognized will not exceed the amount of cash you receive.

If you buy a car by trading in another car, your basis for purposes of determining first-year expensing is only the amount of consideration paid; it does not

TABLE 9.7 Depreciation in Year of Sale*

Month Car Sold**	Percentage
January, February, March	12.5
April, May, June	37.5
July, August, September	62.5
October, November, December	87.5

*Table is not for fiscal-year taxpayers.
**Car placed in service October 1–December 31.

include the basis of the trade-in. But for purposes of depreciation, the basis of the trade-in is included in the basis of the new car.

> **Example**
>
> You buy a new car that costs $15,000 by paying $9,000 cash and receiving $6,000 for the trade-in of your old car that was used 100% for business. The adjusted basis of the old car is $5,000. Your basis for purposes of calculating depreciation is $14,000 ($5,000 adjusted basis of the old car, + $9,000).

A special basis adjustment rule applies when you trade in a car used partially for business (see vehicle trade-in later in this chapter).

CASUALTY OR THEFT

If your car is damaged or stolen and insurance or other reimbursements exceed the adjusted basis of the car, you have a tax gain. However, if you use the reimbursements to buy another car for business or to repair the old car within 2 years of the end of the year of the casualty or theft, then no gain is recognized. The basis of the new car for purposes of depreciation is its cost less any gain that is not recognized.

Standard Mileage Allowance

Instead of keeping a record of all your expenses and having to calculate depreciation, you can use a *standard mileage allowance* fixed by the IRS to determine your deduction for business use of your car. You can use the standard mileage allowance in 2014 whether you own or lease the car. The standard mileage allowance takes the place of a deduction for gasoline, oil, insurance, maintenance and repairs, vehicle registration fees, and depreciation (if you own the car) or lease payments (if you lease the car). Towing charges for the car are separately deductible in addition to the standard mileage allowance. Parking fees and tolls, interest to purchase the vehicle, and personal property tax to register are also allowed in addition to the standard mileage allowance. Deductible parking fees include those incurred when visiting clients and customers or while traveling away from home on business. Fees to park your car at home or at your place of work are nondeductible personal expenses.

The standard mileage allowance for business use of a car in 2014 is 56¢ per mile. Rural letter carriers who use their cars to deliver mail can deduct the amount paid to them by the U.S. Postal Service as an equipment maintenance

TABLE 9.8 Sample Deductions Under the Standard Mileage Allowance for 2014*

Miles Driven	Deduction	Miles Driven	Deduction
5,000	$ 2,800	30,000	$16,800
10,000	5,600	35,000	19,600
15,000	8,400	40,000	22,400
20,000	11,200	45,000	25,200
25,000	14,000	50,000	28,000

*Assuming mileage is ratable each month.

allowance. The IRS standard mileage rate is adjusted annually for inflation. See Table 9.8 for mileage allowances based on the amount of driving.

Standard Mileage Rate Barred

You cannot use the standard mileage rate when:

- You operate more than 4 cars at the same time (such as in a fleet operation). This limit does not apply to the use of more than 4 cars on an alternate basis. For example, if you own cars and vans and alternate the use of these vehicles for business use, then you are not barred from using the standard mileage rate to account for the expenses of the business use for the vehicles.

- You have already claimed MACRS or a first-year expense deduction on the car.

Standard Mileage Rate or Actual Expense Method?

As discussed earlier in this chapter, which method is preferable for you depends on a number of variables. The most important is the number of business miles you drive each year. As a rule of thumb, those who drive a great number of miles each year frequently find the standard mileage rate offers the greater deduction. However, the rate may not adequately reflect your actual driving costs. It is also important to note that the standard mileage rate is not dependent on the price of the car. Less expensive cars can claim the same deduction as more expensive cars, assuming each is driven the same number of business miles. Certainly, those with heavy SUVs can claim a greater deduction with the actual expense method.

Leasing a Car for Business

Leasing a business car is a popular alternative to buying one. If you use the car entirely for business, the cost of leasing is fully deductible. If you make advance payments, you must spread these payments over the entire lease period and deduct them accordingly. You cannot depreciate a car you lease, because depreciation applies only to property that is owned. However, you can choose to deduct the standard mileage rate in lieu of actual expenses (including lease payments).

Lease with an Option to Buy

When you have this arrangement, are you leasing or buying the car? The answer depends on:

- The intent of the parties to the transaction.
- If any equity results from the arrangement.
- If any interest is paid.
- If the fair market value of the car is less than the lease payment or option payment when the option to buy is exercised.

When the factors support a lease arrangement, the payments are deductible. If, however, the factors support a purchase agreement, the payments are not deductible.

Inclusion Amount

If the car price exceeds a certain amount and you deduct your actual costs (you do not use the standard mileage rate), you may have to include in income an *inclusion amount*. This is because the law seeks to equate buying with leasing. Since there is a dollar limit on the amount of depreciation that can be claimed on a luxury car that is owned, the law also requires an amount to be included in income as an offset to high lease payments on a car that is leased. In essence, the inclusion amount seeks to limit your deduction for lease payments to what it would be if you owned the car and claimed depreciation. The inclusion amount, which is simply an amount that you add to your other income, applies if a car is leased for more than 30 days and its value exceeds a certain amount. Amounts are adjusted annually for inflation. The inclusion amount is added to income only so long as you lease the car. It is based on the value of the car as of the first day of the lease term. If the capitalized cost of the car is specified in the lease agreement, that amount is considered to be the fair market value of the car. At the start of the lease, you can see what your inclusion amount will be for that year and for all subsequent years. The inclusion amount is based on a percentage of the **fair market value** of the car at the time the lease begins. Different inclusion amounts apply to gas-driven cars and to electric cars.

> *Fair market value* The price that would be paid for the property when there is a willing buyer and seller (neither being required to buy or sell) and both have reasonable knowledge of all the necessary facts. Evidence of fair market value includes the price paid for similar property on or about the same date.

The inclusion amount applies only if the fair market value of the car when the lease began was more than $16,700 in 2010, $18,500 in 2011 and 2012, $19,000 in 2013, and $18,500 in 2014. Different thresholds for inclusion amounts are applied for cars leased prior to 2010.

Inclusion amounts in Table 9.9 are taken from IRS tables, which can be found in the appendix to IRS Publication 463, *Travel, Entertainment, Gift, and Car Expenses*. Those rates apply to cars first leased in 2014. The full amount in the table applies if the car is leased for the full year and used entirely for business. If the car is leased for less than the full year, or if it is used partly for personal purposes, the inclusion amount must be allocated to business use for the period of the year during which it was used. The allocation for part-year use is made on a day-by-day basis.

Example

The inclusion amount for your car is $500. You used your car only 6 months of the year. You must include $250 in income (183/365 of $500).

Remember that if you use your car for commuting or other nonbusiness purposes, you cannot deduct that allocable part of the lease; there is no inclusion amount for this portion.

There are separate inclusion amount tables for trucks and vans first leased in 2014. This information can be found in IRS Rev. Proc. 2014–21 (Table 6).

Should You Lease or Buy?

The decision to lease or buy a car used for business is not an easy one. There are many financial advantages to leasing. Most important is that you need not put forth more than a small amount of up-front cash to lease, whereas a purchase generally requires a significant down payment. So leasing can enable you to drive a more expensive car than you could afford to buy. However, as a practical matter, if a car is driven extensively (more than 15,000 miles per year), leasing may not make sense because of the annual mileage limit and the charge for excess mileage. In such cases, owning may be preferable. Take into consideration that at the end of the lease term you own nothing, whereas at the end of

TABLE 9.9 Dollar Amounts for Passenger Automobiles (That Are Not Trucks or Vans) with a Lease Term Beginning in Calendar Year 2014

Fair Market Value of Passenger Automobile		Tax Year During Lease				
Over	Not Over	1st	2nd	3rd	4th	5th & Later
$ 18,500	$ 19,000	3	5	8	10	11
19,000	19,500	3	6	10	11	13
19,500	20,000	3	8	11	13	14
20,000	20,500	4	8	13	14	17
20,500	21,000	4	9	14	17	18
21,000	21,500	5	10	15	18	21
21,500	22,000	5	11	17	20	22
22,000	23,000	6	13	18	23	25
23,000	24,000	7	14	22	26	29
24,000	25,000	8	16	25	29	33
25,000	26,000	8	19	27	32	38
26,000	27,000	9	20	31	35	42
27,000	28,000	10	22	33	40	45
28,000	29,000	11	24	36	43	49
29,000	30,000	12	26	39	46	53
30,000	31,000	13	28	41	50	57
31,000	32,000	14	30	44	53	61
32,000	33,000	14	32	47	56	65
33,000	34,000	15	34	50	59	69
34,000	35,000	16	36	52	64	72
35,000	36,000	17	38	55	67	76
36,000	37,000	18	39	59	70	80
37,000	38,000	19	41	61	74	84
38,000	39,000	20	43	64	77	88
39,000	40,000	21	45	67	80	92
40,000	41,000	21	47	70	84	96
41,000	42,000	22	49	73	87	100
42,000	43,000	23	51	75	91	104
43,000	44,000	24	53	78	94	108
44,000	45,000	25	55	81	97	112
45,000	46,000	26	56	84	101	116

TABLE 9.9 *(Continued)*

Fair Market Value of Passenger Automobile		Tax Year During Lease				
Over	Not Over	1st	2nd	3rd	4th	5th & Later
$ 46,000	$ 47,000	27	58	87	104	120
47,000	48,000	28	60	90	107	124
48,000	49,000	28	62	93	111	127
49,000	50,000	29	64	96	114	131
50,000	51,000	30	66	98	118	135
51,000	52,000	31	68	101	121	139
52,000	53,000	32	70	104	124	143
53,000	54,000	33	72	106	128	147
54,000	55,000	34	74	109	131	151
55,000	56,000	34	76	112	135	155
56,000	57,000	35	78	115	138	159
57,000	58,000	36	80	118	141	163
58,000	59,000	37	81	121	145	167
59,000	60,000	38	83	124	148	171
60,000	62,000	39	86	128	153	177
62,000	64,000	41	90	134	159	185
64,000	66,000	43	94	139	167	192
66,000	68,000	44	98	145	173	201
68,000	70,000	46	102	150	180	209
70,000	72,000	48	105	156	188	216
72,000	74,000	50	109	162	194	224
74,000	76,000	51	113	168	200	232
76,000	78,000	53	117	173	208	239
78,000	80,000	55	120	179	215	247
80,000	85,000	58	127	189	226	261
85,000	90,000	62	137	203	243	281
90,000	95,000	67	146	217	260	301
95,000	100,000	71	156	231	277	320
100,000	110,000	77	170	253	303	349
110,000	120,000	86	189	281	337	389
120,000	130,000	95	208	310	370	428

(Continued)

TABLE 9.9 *(Continued)*

Fair Market Value of Passenger Automobile		Tax Year During Lease				
Over	Not Over	1st	2nd	3rd	4th	5th & Later
$130,000	$140,000	103	228	337	405	467
140,000	150,000	112	247	366	438	507
150,000	160,000	121	266	394	473	545
160,000	170,000	130	284	423	507	585
170,000	180,000	138	304	451	541	624
180,000	190,000	147	323	479	575	663
190,000	200,000	156	342	507	609	703
200,000	210,000	164	361	536	643	742
210,000	220,000	173	380	565	676	781
220,000	230,000	182	399	593	710	821
230,000	240,000	190	418	622	744	860
240,000	and over	199	437	650	778	899

the same period of time with a purchased car you own an asset that can be sold or traded in for a newer model. And, if you want to get out of the lease before the end of the lease term, there may be substantial penalties and fees (although there may be ways to avoid them).

Whether there are any tax advantages is difficult to say. With leasing, you deduct the entire lease charge; with a purchase, you generally deduct depreciation, although you may be able to fully expense up to $25,000 for a car weighing more than 6,000 pounds. Given the current dollar limits on depreciation, this may not be as great as the lease charge. While the inclusion amount is designed to offset this differential, it may not be sufficient to make leasing and depreciation equate.

The only way to know whether leasing or buying is more advantageous tax-wise is to run the numbers. Project your deductible costs of leasing versus your costs of purchasing the car.

Arranging Car Ownership

If you have a corporation, should you or your corporation own the car you will use for business? From a tax standpoint, it is generally wise to have the corporation own the car because the corporation can fully deduct the expenses of the car (subject, of course, to the dollar limit on depreciation). If you own the car, your deductions are limited to those relating to business use and can be claimed only as itemized deductions subject to a floor of 2% of your adjusted gross income and an additional reduction if you are a high-income taxpayer.

For insurance purposes, coverage for business-owned cars can be more expensive than personal coverage. However, in some cases it may still be more advantageous to have the corporation own the car. If the corporation owns several vehicles, it can command better insurance rates than an individual who owns only one car. Also, if the car is involved in an accident, the corporation's insurance rates are not affected. If you own the car and it is in an accident, your personal insurance rates will usually be increased.

Finally, if there is a lawsuit involving the car, it is generally preferable to have the corporation sued rather than you personally, since a recovery against the corporation is limited to corporate assets.

Employee Use of an Employer-Provided Car

If your employer gives you a car to use for business, you may be able to deduct certain expenses. Your deduction is limited to the actual expenses of operating the car that were not reimbursed by your employer. The amount of the deduction depends on the amount your employer includes in your income and the number of business and personal miles driven. Your personal use is reported annually on your Form W-2 (see Chapter 7). If your employer owns the car you use, you cannot use the standard mileage allowance for car expenses.

What Is Included on Your W-2?

The employer has a choice of what to report. The employer can either report the actual value of your personal use or assume that you used the car entirely for personal purposes and include 100% of the benefit in your income. This 100% amount is based on the annual lease value for the car (explained in Chapter 7). The full amount reported on your W-2 is income to you. Your W-2 will note whether the 100% annual lease value or actual personal use was reported. Even though you must include the full amount reported on your W-2, whatever it might be, you may be able to reduce your income tax. You can offset this income to the extent that what was reported as personal use was actually business use and you deduct your business expenses. Where to claim these business deductions is detailed at the end of this chapter.

If your employer reported 100% of personal use even though you used the car in part for business, you can deduct your actual expenses for business use that were not reimbursed by your employer. If your employer included only a portion of the use of the car designed to reflect your personal use, then you can deduct any actual expenses for business use that were not reimbursed by your employer.

Vehicle Trade-In

When you are ready to dispose of your old car and find a replacement, what is the best way to handle the arrangements from a tax perspective? Trade it in? Sell it?

- If you trade in the old car to buy a new one, the arrangement can be considered a tax-free exchange if you elect this treatment. The result: The basis of the new car is the remaining basis of the old car, if any, plus any cash paid toward the new car. And if the car that is traded in was used only partially for business, a special adjustment is required for purposes of figuring depreciation on the newly acquired car. In this case you figure basis of the old car as if it were used entirely for business (i.e., you must reduce basis as if you had depreciated 100% of the car's basis). This severely limits your ability to claim write-offs for the new car.

- If you sell the old car to buy a new one, gain or loss results from the difference between the basis of the old car and the amount you receive for it. If the basis is less than what you receive, you have a taxable gain; if the basis is more than what you receive, you have a taxable loss.

Before deciding on which alternative to use, consider the tax results in your situation. If, for example, you are disposing of a large SUV or truck, you may have a taxable gain since you may have already reduced the basis of the car substantially (remember that vehicles that weigh more than 6,000 pounds are not subject to the depreciation dollar limits). In this case, a trade-in postpones gain recognition. However, if you are disposing of another type of vehicle, one with a tax basis that is higher than its fair market value, a sale can produce a taxable loss so a trade-in is ill-advised.

Trucks and Vans

Trucks (including SUVs) and vans that are configured in such a way as to be used for personal purposes only minimally are not subject to the dollar limits on depreciation that apply to passenger cars weighing no more than 6,000 pounds. These trucks and vans are referred to as qualified nonpersonal use vehicles.

Modifications likely to render a truck or van a qualified nonpersonal use vehicle include having a front jump seat, permanent shelving that fills the cargo area, and advertising or a company name printed on the side.

Trucks and vans that are not qualified nonpersonal use vehicles are subject to the following rules:

- For vehicles with a gross vehicle weight rating in excess of 6,000 pounds but not more than 14,000 pounds, the dollar limits on depreciation do not apply (see the treatment of heavy SUVs earlier in this chapter). Their cost

TABLE 9.10 Dollar Limits for Light Trucks and Vans

Tax Year	Dollar Limit
First year (2014)	$3,460*
Second year (2015)	5,500
Third year (2016)	3,350
Each succeeding year	1,975

*If bonus depreciation is extended, a higher dollar limit applies; see the Supplement.

can be expensed up to $25,000 or depreciated as 5-year property without any dollar limit on the annual deduction.

- For lighter vehicles, special dollar limits apply. These dollar limits are slightly higher than for passenger cars. Table 9.10 shows the dollar limits for light trucks and vans first placed in service in 2014.

Credit for Plug-In Electric Vehicles

There is a credit for plug-in highway-ready electric vehicles purchased and placed in service after February 17, 2009 and before 2015. The credit is up to $7,500, regardless of the weight of the vehicle. There was also a credit for low-speed vehicles, motorcycles, and 3-wheeled vehicles of 10% of cost up to $2,500 which expired at the end of 2013; check the Supplement to see if the credit has been extended for 2014.

The full $7,500 credit for such vehicles as the Chevy Volt, Ford Focus Electric, Tesla Model S, and Nissan Leaf applies only to 200,000 cars per manufacturer; there is a partial credit for up to a year after this limit is reached.

If the vehicle is purchased for business, it is part of the general business credit (see Chapter 23).

The credit can be claimed for both regular tax and alternative minimum tax purposes (see Chapter 28).

Reimbursement Arrangements

If your employer reimburses you for the business use of your car, you may or may not need to claim deductions. The answer depends on the reimbursement arrangement with your employer.

Accountable Plan

If your employer maintains an arrangement that reimburses you for business-related use of the car, requires you to adequately account to the employer for these expenses, and also requires you to return within a reasonable time any advances or reimbursements in excess of these expenses, then the plan is treated as an *accountable plan*. (For details on adequate accounting under accountable plans and returning excess amounts within a reasonable time, see Chapter 8.) If your employer maintains an accountable plan for reimbursement of business expenses and the amount of reimbursement does not exceed the standard mileage allowance, the reimbursements are not reported on your W-2, and you do not deduct any expenses. If the reimbursements exceed the standard mileage allowance, only the excess over the standard mileage allowance is included on your W-2. You may then deduct your actual expenses that exceed the standard mileage rate.

Nonaccountable Plan

Your employer must include on your W-2 form all reimbursements made under a nonaccountable plan.

Recordkeeping for Car Expenses

Regardless of whether you use the actual expense method or the standard mileage allowance for your car (or a car that your employer provides you with), certain recordkeeping requirements apply. You must keep track of the number of miles you drive each year for business, as well as the total miles driven each year. You must also record the date of the business mileage, the destination of the business travel, and the business reason for the car expense. It is advisable to maintain a daily travel log or diary in which you record the date, the destination, the business purpose of the trip, and the number of miles driven (use the odometer readings at the start and end of the trip, and then total the miles for each trip). Be sure to note the odometer reading on January 1 each year (Table 9.11).

If you use the actual expense method, you must also keep a record of the costs of operating the car. These include the cost of gasoline and oil, car insurance, interest on a car loan (if you are self-employed), licenses and taxes, and repairs and maintenance. Record these amounts in your expense log or diary.

If you lease a car, you must keep track of the amount of the lease payments, in addition to the number of miles driven (and the number of business miles), the dates of travel, the destinations, and the purpose for the travel.

Use a diary or log to keep track of your business mileage and other related costs. You can buy a car expense log in stationery and business supply stores or reproduce the blank log in Table 9.11. Table 9.12 is a model of an IRS sample daily business mileage and expense log.

You can also use your iPhone, BlackBerry, Android, or other smartphone app, such as ProOnGo, Trip Cubby, or Mile Bug, to keep mileage records. You can then send them to your accounting tool, such as QuickBooks Online edition.

TABLE 9.11 Business Mileage Log

Date	Destination	Business Purpose	Odometer Readings			Expenses	
			Start	Stop	Miles This Trip	Type	Amount

TABLE 9.12 Sample Log

| Date | Destination | Business Purpose | Odometer Readings | | Miles This Trip | Expenses | |
			Start	Stop		Type	Amount
5/4/14	Local—St. Louis	Sales calls	8,097	8,188	91	Gas	$ 38.00
5/5/14	Indianapolis	Sales calls	8,211	8,486	275	Parking	5.00
5/6/14	Louisville	Bob Smith (potential client)	8,486	8,599	113	Gas	37.80
						Repair Flat tire	10.00
5/7/14	Return to St. Louis		8,599	8,875	276	Gas	38.25
5/8/14	Local—St. Louis	Sales calls	8,914	9,005	91		
Weekly total			8,097	9,005	846		129.05
Year-to-date total					5,883		$1,074.75

It is essential that you keep a written record of the business use of your car. You must note on your tax return whether you have such a record. Remember that your return is signed under penalty of perjury.

Example

An interior designer who runs her business from home visits clients using her personal car for this business driving. She records her mileage for the first 3 months of the year, which shows that the car is used 75% for business and 25% for personal driving. Invoices from her business show that business activity was nearly constant throughout the year, indicating that her driving pattern remained the same. Under these facts, she can extrapolate that 75% of her car expenses for the year are business-related.

Example

The same interior designer instead records her mileage for the first week of every month, showing 75% business use. Invoices show that business continued at the same rate throughout the month so that the first week's record was representative of the full month. Under these facts, she can extrapolate that 75% of her car expenses for the balance of the month (and throughout the year) are business-related.

Proving Expenses with a Mileage Allowance

Generally, required recordkeeping includes tracking the odometer at the start and end of each business trip (as well as the date, destination, and purpose of the trip). However, the IRS permits "sampling" in some situations. You are treated as having adequate substantiation if you keep records for a representative portion of the year and can demonstrate that the period for which records are kept is representative of use for the entire year.

Sampling may not be used if you cannot show a consistent pattern of car use. Also, not all substantiation shortcuts are acceptable. For instance, 1 taxpayer used mileage figured by a computer atlas to substantiate his car expenses. Unfortunately, the Tax Court rejected this method, observing that he failed to keep track of his odometer readings at the time the expenses were incurred.

If your employer pays for car expenses with a mileage allowance, it generally is considered to be proof of the amount of expenses. The amount of expenses that can be proven by use of this allowance is limited to the standard mileage allowance or the amount of a fixed and variable rate (FAVR) allowance that is not included on your W-2. The FAVR allowance includes a combination of fixed and variable costs, such as a cents-per-mile rate to cover variable operating costs (e.g., gas, oil, routine maintenance, and repairs) and a flat amount to cover fixed costs (e.g., depreciation, insurance, registration and license fees, and personal property taxes). The FAVR allowance applies only if the car is used for certain employees. Thus, use of this allowance is the employer's choice, not the employee's.

Where to Deduct Car Expenses

Employees

You compute your car expenses on Form 2106, *Employee Business Expenses*, or Form 2106-EZ, *Unreimbursed Employee Business Expenses*. Form 2106-EZ can be used only if:

1. You were not reimbursed by your employer for expenses or, if you were reimbursed, the reimbursements were included in your income on your W-2, and
2. You use the standard mileage rate for deducting your car expenses. If you use the actual expense method to deduct your car expenses, you must use Form 2106.

Enter your total expenses on Schedule A, *Itemized Deductions*, as a miscellaneous itemized expense. These deductions are then limited to the amount they exceed 2% of adjusted gross income; the amount may be further reduced if you are a high-income taxpayer.

Disabled Employees

If you have a physical or mental disability, your impairment-related work expenses are deductible as an itemized deduction, but the 2% floor does not apply. Impairment-related work expenses include costs of attendant care at your place of work and those that are necessary to enable you to work (such as the cost of a driver to bring you to business locations). General medical expenses, however, are not impairment-related work expenses; they are simply personal medical expenses and are deductible as such.

Special Rule for Performing Artists

If you meet certain requirements, you can deduct all of your car expenses as an adjustment to gross income on page 1 of Form 1040 instead of claiming them as miscellaneous itemized deductions on Schedule A. You are treated as a performing artist if you meet *all* of the following 5 tests:

1. You perform services in the performing arts for at least 2 employers during the year.

2. You receive at least $200 each from any 2 of these employers.

3. Your related performing arts business expenses are more than 10% of your adjusted gross income from the performance of such services.

4. Your adjusted gross income (and not merely performing arts income) does not exceed $16,000 (before deducting business expenses from your performing arts).

5. If you are married, you file a joint return (unless you lived apart from your spouse for the entire year).

You perform tests 1, 2, and 3 based on your individual experience. However, the adjusted gross income in test 4 is the combined adjusted gross income of you and your spouse. If you meet these tests, you deduct your performing arts business expenses as an adjustment to gross income on page 1 of Form 1040.

Self-Employed

You enter your car expenses on Schedule C, *Profit and Loss from Business*, or Schedule C-EZ, *Net Profit from Business*. If you are not required to complete Form 4562, *Depreciation and Amortization*, because you did not place any depreciable or amortizable property in service in 2014, then use Part IV of Schedule C and Part III of Schedule C-EZ to report information on your car. You need to know and provide when the car was placed in service and the number of miles driven for business, commuting, or other purposes; whether there is another car available for personal use and whether your business car was available during off-duty hours; evidence to support your deductions and whether this evidence is written. If you are otherwise required to complete Form 4562, then report the information about your car on this form and not on Schedule C or Schedule C-EZ.

Farmers who are self-employed deduct their car expenses on Schedule F. Also complete Part IV of Form 4562, to provide information about car use.

Partnerships and LLCs

Expenses of business-owned cars are reported on the business's Form 1065 as part of the business's ordinary income (or loss). They are entered in the category of Other Deductions. A schedule is attached to the return explaining the deductions claimed in this category. Car expenses are not separately stated items. The owner's share of ordinary income (or loss) is reported on Schedule K-1.

S Corporations

Car expenses of business-owned cars are reported on the corporation's Form 1120S as part of the S corporation's ordinary income (or loss). They are entered in the category of Other Deductions. A schedule is attached to the return explaining the deductions claimed in this category. Car expenses are not separately stated items. The shareholder's share of ordinary income (or loss) is reported on Schedule K-1.

C Corporations

Car expenses are reported on the corporation's Form 1120 as part of its taxable income (or loss). They are entered in the category of Other Deductions. A schedule is attached to the return explaining the deductions claimed in this category.

All Businesses

If you claim depreciation for a car used in business, you must complete Form 4562, *Depreciation and Amortization*. Generally, this form must be filed every year in which the standard deduction or actual vehicle expenses (including depreciation) are claimed to provide certain requested information. However, employees who use their vehicle for business and file Form 2106 or 2106-EZ, or self-employed individuals filing Schedule C-EZ can provide this information on those forms (and do not have to file Form 4565). Those filing Schedule C can include this information on Part IV of the schedule; they do not have to file Form 4562 unless they are otherwise required to do so (e.g., have placed depreciable property in service this year).

The credit for purchasing a plug-in electric vehicle or converting a conventional-fuel vehicle to electric power is computed on Form 8834, *Qualified Plug-in Electric and Electric Vehicle Credit*. For business-owned vehicles, the credit is part of the general business credit, figured on Form 3800, *General Business Credit*.

Repairs, Maintenance, and Energy Improvements

Alert

At the time this book was printed, Congress had not extended numerous breaks for 2014 that had expired at the end of 2013. Check the online supplement in February 2015 at www.jklasser.com or www.barbaraweltman.com to see whether these breaks apply for 2014 returns.

Property and equipment generally need constant repairs to keep them in working order. Preventative maintenance—regular servicing of equipment—can cut down on replacement costs by allowing you to keep your current equipment longer. When your computer goes down, a service person is required to make repairs. When the air-conditioning system in your office building stops working, again, servicing is necessary. If you have property or equipment to which you make repairs, you can deduct these expenses. The only hitch is making sure that the expenses are not *capital expenditures*. The cost of capital expenditures cannot be currently deducted but instead are added to the basis of property and recovered through depreciation or upon the disposition of the property.

For further information about deducting repairs, see IRS Publication 535, *Business Expenses*.

Ordinary Repairs

Deducting Incidental Repairs in General

The cost of repairing property and equipment used in your business is a deductible business expense. In contrast, expenditures that materially add to the value of the property, prolong its life, or adapt the property to a new or different use must be capitalized (added to the basis of the property and recovered through depreciation). In most cases, the distinction is clear. If you pay a repair person to service your copying machine because paper keeps getting jammed, the cost of the service call is a repair expense and is currently deductible. If you put a new roof on your office building, you usually must capitalize the expenditure and recover the cost through depreciation. Sometimes, however, the classification of an expense as a repair or a capital expenditure is not clear. For example, in one case the cost of a new roof was currently deductible where it was installed merely to repair a leak and did not change the structure of the building or add to its value.

Guidelines on Distinguishing Between a Repair and a Capital Item

Repairs are expenses designed to keep property in good working condition. This includes the replacement of short-lived parts. Typically, the cost of repairs is small compared with the cost of the property itself.

Capital items, on the other hand, are akin to original construction. Costs are usually substantial. Final regulations issued in 2013 are designed to clarify when costs can be immediately deducted rather than capitalized. The regulations are effective on January 1, 2014, but businesses can opt to apply them after December 31, 2011. These regulations contain many favorable safe harbors and de minimis rules. Table 10.1 includes some common examples of repairs and capital improvements.

Even though repairs add to the length of a property's useful life, this does not automatically make them capital improvements. It can be argued that *all* repairs produce this result. For example, one business owner with a fleet of tug boats made substantial engine repairs each year. The IRS said that the repairs should be capitalized because they added to the life of the boats, but the Tax Court said no. Despite the cost of the repairs—over $100,000 per tug—and the fact that the repairs kept the tugs afloat longer—they were still ordinary repairs that were currently deductible.

TABLE 10.1 Examples of Repairs versus Capital Items

Repairs	Capital Items
Painting the outside of office building	Vinyl siding the outside of office building
Replacing missing shingles on roof	Replacing entire roof unless strictly for repair purposes
Replacing compressor for air conditioner	Adding air-conditioning system
Cleaning canopy over restaurant entrance	Adding canopy over restaurant entrance
Resurfacing office floor	Replacing office floor

To distinguish repairs from capital improvements, there are no bright line tests; the determination is based on facts and circumstances. Capital improvements include a betterment to or restoration of the unit of property, or an adaptation of the unit of property to a new or different use. A "unit of property" is functionally interdependent components such as a machine or a building. However, certain major building systems (e.g., HAVC, plumbing, and electrical) are treated as separate units of property. The cost (no matter how minor) of restoring property after a casualty loss is not a deductible repair cost if a casualty loss deduction is taken.

The cost of routine maintenance is currently deductible if it is for recurring activities that are expected to be performed more than once a year to keep a unit of property in its ordinarily efficient operating condition. This maintenance safe harbor rule applies to buildings as long as the owner expects to perform the maintenance more than once over a 10-year period. However, you can elect to capitalize repair and maintenance costs for tangible personal property (not realty) if you treat the costs as such on your books and records. The election is made on your tax return (not on an amended return) and, once made, the costs become depreciable. For partnerships and S corporations, the election is made by the entity and not by the individual owners.

Building improvements usually are capitalized. However, under a safe harbor for small taxpayers (those with average annual gross receipts in the three prior years not exceeding $10 million), repairs, maintenance, and improvements during the year do not have to be capitalized if they do not exceed the *lesser* of $10,000 or 2% of the unadjusted basis of the building. This safe harbor applies only to a building with an unadjusted basis no greater than $1 million. The safe harbor applies separately to each such building owned by a small taxpayer. The IRS has the authority to adjust the $10,000, 2%, and $1 million amounts in the future. Again, the election is made on an original tax return. For pass-through entities, the election is made by the entity; not the owners.

The fact that certain repairs are necessitated by governmental directives does not change the character of the expense. If it is a required repair, it is currently deductible; if it substantially improves the property, it is a capital expenditure. For example, in one case, rewiring ordered by local fire prevention inspectors was a capital expenditure. The same is true for capital expenditures ordered by the U.S. Public Health Service and state sanitary or health laws.

Example

Various assets of a business are damaged by a storm; some are nearly destroyed while others suffer less damage. If the business claims a casualty loss deduction, the cost of repairs to any assets in this case must be capitalized.

Environmental Cleanup Costs

If you are forced to take certain actions to comply with Environmental Protection Agency (EPA) requirements, such as encapsulating or removing asbestos, understand which expenses are currently deductible and which expenses must be capitalized. Environmental remediation costs can be currently deducted. For instance, the cost of replacing mold-contaminated drywall in a nursing home was a deductible remediation cost that merely restored the building to its precontamination condition. The costs of cleanups to comply with environmental laws that effectively restore property to its original (precontamination) condition may be deductible. But the cost of capital improvements, even though required to comply with environmental laws, must be capitalized.

Example

The cost of encapsulating asbestos in a warehouse is currently deductible. The cost of removing asbestos from a boiler room must be capitalized. (The removal makes the property substantially more attractive to potential buyers.)

Small business refiners (those with no more than 1,500 individuals engaged in refinery activities on any day during the year and the average daily domestic refinery run for the one-year period ending on December 31, 2002, did not exceed 205,000 barrels) can elect to deduct 75% of costs paid or incurred to comply with the Highway Diesel Fuel Sulfur Control Requirements of the EPA.

Rehabilitation Plans

If you make repairs as part of a general plan to recondition or improve property—typically, office buildings, stores, and factories—then the expenses must be capitalized. This is so even though the expenses would have been deductible if made outside a general plan of repair. This rule is called the *rehabilitation doctrine*. For example, painting generally is treated as a currently deductible repair expense. However, if you add an extension to your office building, the cost of painting the extension upon completion is a capital item under the rehabilitation doctrine.

Protecting the Deduction for Repairs

With proper planning, you can make sure that repair costs are currently deductible even though you also undertake capital expenditures. Schedule repairs separately from capital improvements so they will not be treated as one rehabilitation plan, and get separate bills for the repairs.

Tax Credits for Rehabilitation

While rehabilitation costs generally must be capitalized, in special instances you can claim a tax credit for your expenditures. If you rehabilitate a nonresidential building that was placed in service before 1936, you can claim a credit for 10% of your expenditures. If you rehabilitate a certified historic structure (a building that is listed in the National Register or located in a registered historic district), the credit is 20% of costs. The credit is claimed in the year the property is placed in service, not the year in which the expenditures are made.

Example

If you undertake a 2-year project beginning in 2013 and do not place the building in service until 2014, the credit is taken in 2014.

Rehabilitation requires that you make substantial improvements to the building but leave a substantial portion of it intact. A *substantial portion* means that within any 2-year period you select, the rehabilitation expenditures exceed the adjusted basis of the building or $5,000, whichever is greater. In the case of a pre-1936 building, at least 75% of the external walls must be left intact and at least 50% of external walls must remain as external walls. The Secretary of the Interior must certify that the rehabilitation of certified historic structures will be in keeping with the building's historic status.

The credit is claimed on Form 3468, *Investment Credit*. For individuals and C corporations, it is part of the general business credit computed on Form 3800, *General Business Credit*. The credit may be limited by the passive loss rules explained in Chapter 4. The general business credit limitations are explained in Chapter 23.

Demolition and Removal Expenses

As a general rule, the costs of demolishing a building are not deductible. Instead, they are added to the basis of the new building (that is, the building put up in the place of the demolished building). However, the costs of demolishing only a part of a building may be currently deductible. According to the IRS, if 75% or more of the existing external walls and 75% or more of the existing internal framework are both retained, the costs of demolition need not be capitalized (added to basis) but instead can be currently deducted.

Removal costs for tangible personal property (not realty) being disposed of are currently deductible if you do not realize gain or loss on the disposition.

Special Rules for Improvements for the Elderly and Handicapped

The Americans with Disabilities Act (ADA) may require you to make certain modifications to your office, store, or factory if you have not done so already. You may have to install ramps, widen doorways and lavatories to accommodate wheelchairs, add elevators, or make other similar changes to your facilities to render them more accessible to the elderly and handicapped.

These modifications may be more in the nature of capital improvements than repairs. Still, the law provides two special tax incentives to which you may be entitled. One is a tax credit; the other is a special deduction. These incentives allow for a current benefit rather than requiring capitalization of expenditures that will be recovered over long periods of time.

Disabled Access Credit

Small business owners can claim a tax credit for expenditures to remove barriers on business property that impede the access of handicapped individuals and to supply special materials or assistance to visually or hearing-impaired persons.

Small business Businesses with gross receipts of no more than $1 million (after returns and allowances) or no more than 30 full-time employees for the tax year before the year of the credit. Full-time employees are those who work more than 30 hours per week for 20 or more calendar weeks in the year.

The credit cannot exceed 50% of expenditures between $250 and $10,250. The maximum credit is $5,000.

Example

You, as a small business owner, spend $4,000 to install ramps in your mall. You may take a tax credit of $1,875 ($4,000 − $250 = $3,750 × .50).

The dollar limit applies at both the partner and partnership levels. The same rule applies to shareholders and S corporations, as well as to members and LLCs.

Qualifying Expenditures

Qualifying expenditures are designed to meet the requirements of the ADA. For example, the cost of putting in handicapped parking spaces as required by federal law is a qualified expenditure. Many of these requirements are set forth in connection with the expense deduction for the removal of architectural and transportation barriers. However, eligible expenditures do not include those in connection with new construction. Thus, if you are in the process of building an office complex and you install special bathroom facilities to accommodate a wheelchair,

NOTE
There have been a number of businesses claiming this credit even though they are not entitled to it. The IRS is on the lookout for bogus claims, so make sure that you qualify before claiming this credit.

you cannot claim the credit because this is new construction. If you claim the credit, you cannot also claim a deduction for the same expenditures. Businesses already in compliance with the ADA cannot claim the credit for equipment that may add some benefit for handicapped customers. Also, the IRS has ruled that Web-based businesses using software to enable handicapped customers to shop cannot claim the credit; it is limited to bricks-and-mortar businesses. However, a company with a physical place of business that uses a software service to communicate on-site with hearing-impaired customers qualifies for the credit.

Deduction for Removal of Architectural or Transportation Barriers

As you have seen throughout this chapter, expenditures that improve or prolong the life of property generally must be capitalized and the cost recovered through depreciation. You have already seen two special credits that can be claimed for expenditures that would otherwise have to be capitalized. There is 1 more important exception to this capitalization rule: You can elect to deduct the expenses of removing architectural or transportation barriers to the handicapped and elderly. The election is made simply by claiming the deduction on a timely filed tax return.

The maximum deduction in any one year is $15,000. If your expenditures for a removal project exceed this limit, you can deduct the first $15,000 of costs and capitalize (and then depreciate) the balance.

The dollar limit applies at both the partner and partnership levels. A partner must combine his or her distributive share of these expenditures from one partnership with any distributive share of such expenditures from any other partnerships. The partner may allocate the $15,000 limit among his or her own expenditures and the partner's distributive share of partnership expenditures in any manner. If the allocation results in all or a portion of the partner's distributive share of partnership's expenditures not being an allocable deduction, then the partnership can capitalize the unallowable portion.

While the regulations on applying the dollar limits at both the partner and partnership levels do not specify other pass-through entities, presumably the same rules that apply to partners and partnerships apply as well to shareholders and S corporations.

If the election is made to expense these expenditures, then no disabled access credit can be claimed for the same expenses.

Example

A partner's distributive share of partnership expenditures (after application of the $15,000 limit at the partnership level) is $7,500. The partner also has a sole proprietorship that made $10,000 of expenditures. The partner can choose to allocate the $15,000 limitation as follows: $5,000 to his or her distributive share of the partnership's expenditures and $10,000 to individual expenditures. If the partner provides written proof of this allocation to the partnership, the partnership can then capitalize $2,500, the unused portion of the partner's distributive share of expenditures ($7,500 distributive share less $5,000 allocated as a deduction).

Qualifying Expenditures

These are expenses that conform a facility or public transportation vehicle to certain standards that make them accessible to persons over the age of 65 or those with physical or mental disability or impairment (see Table 10.2). It does not include any expense for the construction or comprehensive renovation of a facility or public transportation vehicle or the normal replacement of depreciable property.

Recordkeeping

If you elect to deduct these expenditures, you must maintain records and documentation, including architectural plans and blueprints, contracts, and building permits to support your claims. How long these records should be kept is discussed in Chapter 3.

Lists of Deductible Repairs and Capital Improvements

Over the years, various expenditures have come under review by the IRS and the courts. The following lists, one of deductible repairs and the other of improvements that must be capitalized, are based on actual cases and rulings.

TABLE 10.2 Guidance on Acceptable Standards for the Elderly and Handicapped

Type of Expense	Requirements
Grading	The ground should be graded to attain a level with a normal entrance to make the facility accessible to individuals with physical disabilities.
Walks	A public walk should be at least 48″ wide and have a gradient of no more than 5%.
	A walkway should have a continuing common surface (not interrupted by steps or abrupt changes in level).
	A walkway or driveway should have a nonslip surface.
Parking lots	At least 1 space that is accessible and proximate to the facility must be set aside and designated for the handicapped.
	The space must be open to 1 side to allow wheelchair access.
	For head-on parking, the space must be at least 12′ wide.
Ramps	A ramp should not have a slope greater than a 1″ rise in 12″.
	There must be a handrail 32″ in height.
	A ramp should have a nonslip surface.
	A ramp should have a level surface at the top and bottom (if a door swings into the platform, the platform should be at least 5′ by 5′).
	A ramp should have level platforms at least every 30′.
	A curb ramp should be provided at every intersection (the ramp should be 4′ wide, with transition between 2 surfaces and a nonslip surface).
Entrances	A building should have at least 1 primary entrance wheelchair accessible and on a level accessible to an elevator.
Doors and doorways	A door should have an opening of at least 32″.
	The floor inside and outside the doorway should be level for at least 51″.
	The threshold should be level with the floor.
	The door closer should not impair the use of the door by someone who is handicapped.
Stairs	Stairs should have handrails at least 32″ from the tread at the face of the riser.
	Steps should not have risers exceeding 7″.
Floors	Floors should have a nonslip surface.
Toilet rooms	The rooms should provide wheelchair access. At least 1 stall should be 66″ wide by 60″ deep, with 32″ door space and handrails.

(Continued)

TABLE 10.2 *(Continued)*

Type of Expense	Requirements
Water fountains	A water fountain or cooler should have up-front spouts and hand and foot controls.
	A water fountain should not be in an alcove unless there is 36″ of space.
Public telephones	Each phone should be placed so the dial and headset can be reached by someone in a wheelchair.
	Coin slots should not be more than 48″ from the floor.
	Public phones should be equipped for those with hearing impairments.
Elevators	An elevator should be on entry levels of buildings and in all areas normally used.
	Cab size should allow a wheelchair to turn.
	The door opening should be at least 32″.
Controls	Switches and controls for all essential uses (light, heat, ventilation, windows, draperies, and fire alarms) should be within reach of a person in a wheelchair (no higher than 48″ from the floor).
Identification	Raised letters or numbers should be used to identify rooms (letters or numbers placed on the left or right of the door at a height of 54″ to 66″).
Warning signals	A visual beaming signal should be accompanied by an audible sound for the benefit of the blind.
Hazards	Hanging signs, ceiling lights, and similar objects and fixtures should be placed at a minimum height of 7′ (measured from the floor).
International	Wheelchair-accessible entrances should be identified with the accessibility symbol.

DEDUCTIBLE REPAIRS

- Altering building for street-widening program
- Caulking seams
- Replacing compressor for air conditioner
- Replacing copper sheeting for cornice (blown off by wind)
- Relining basement walls and floors with cement
- Cleaning a restaurant canopy
- Cutting and filling cracks in storage tanks
- Tuck pointing and cleaning exterior brick walls
- Adding timbers to support walkway over basement

- Mending plaster walls and ceilings
- Painting walls and ceiling over basement
- Papering walls
- Patching a leaking roof
- Relocating steam pipes and radiators
- Resurfacing floors
- Repairing sidewalks
- Shoring up building foundation
- Replacing retaining walls
- Repairing gutters

CAPITAL IMPROVEMENTS

- Installing new doors
- Installing new windows
- Replacing a coal burner with an oil burner heating system
- Installing skylights
- Installing fire escapes
- Replacing a roof
- Adding new floor supports
- Replacing iron piping with brass piping in hot water system
- Raising, lowering, or building new floors
- Erecting permanent partitions
- Installing fire sprinklers
- Bricking up windows
- Installing an air-conditioning system
- Installing a ventilation system
- Rewiring or upgrading electrical service
- Replacing windows and doors
- Expanding a building (building an addition)
- Installing a burglar alarm system
- Blacktopping a driveway
- Improving a storefront
- Adding new plumbing fixtures
- Constructing a drainage system

Energy Improvements

The deduction for energy-efficient buildings expired at the end of 2013, but could be extended retroactively by Congress. The following is included in case there is an extension. Check the Supplement for details.

Usually, capital improvements to a building must be recovered through depreciation, as explained earlier in this chapter. However, certain energy improvements to commercial realty can be immediately deducted. For example, some of the cost of adding insulation to the walls and attic of a commercial building may be deductible.

The deduction applies to property installed in a building as part of the interior lighting system; heating, cooling, ventilation, and hot water systems; or the building envelope as part of a plan to reduce annual energy and power costs by 50% or more in comparison with a reference building meeting Standard 90.1-2001. Standard 90.1-2001 refers to standards of the American Society of Heating, Refrigerating, and Air Conditioning Engineers and the Illuminating Engineering Society of North America (in effect on April 2, 2003).

The deduction is $1.80 per square foot for a 50% energy savings target or 60 ¢ per square foot for a $16\frac{2}{3}$% energy savings target. A reduced deduction can be claimed in certain situations. The basis of the building must be reduced by the amount of any such deduction.

To claim the deduction, you must obtain certification for your improvements from a field inspection conducted by a licensed engineer or contractor.

Other Business Energy Improvements

There is an energy tax credit for a specified percentage of the basis of each qualified energy property placed in service. Qualified energy property includes solar property, geothermal property, qualified fuel cell property or stationary microturbine property, combined health and power system property, qualified small wind energy property, and geothermal heat pumps. For example, the credit is 30% of the basis (generally cost) of qualified small wind energy property used to generate electricity.

The basis of the property for purposes of depreciation must be reduced by the credit. The basis of the property is *not* reduced for energy property financed by subsidized energy financing or industrial development bonds.

Where to Take Deductions

Employees

An employee can deduct repair costs as an itemized employee business expense on Schedule A, subject to the 2%-of-AGI rule discussed in Chapter 1.

Self-Employed

Repair costs are deductible on Schedule C. This schedule contains a line specifically for repairs and maintenance. Repair costs can also be deducted on Schedule C-EZ if total business expenses do not exceed $5,000. Farmers who are self-employed deduct repair costs on Schedule F.

Partnerships and LLCs

Repair costs are trade or business expenses that are taken into account in determining the profit (or loss) of the partnership or LLC on Form 1065. There is a specific line for deducting repair and maintenance costs. They are not separately stated items passed through to partners and members. Therefore partners and members in LLCs report their net income or loss from the business on Schedule E; they do not deduct repair costs on their individual tax returns.

An exception applies to expenditures for the removal of architectural and transportation barriers to the elderly and handicapped that are elected to be expensed. These items must be separately stated, since dollar limits apply at both the owner and entity levels.

S Corporations

Repair costs are trade or business expenses that are taken into account in determining the profit (or loss) of the S corporation on Form 1120S. There is a specific line for deducting repair and maintenance costs. They are not separately stated items passed through to shareholders. Therefore shareholders report their net income or loss from the business on Schedule E; they do not deduct repair costs on their individual tax returns.

An exception applies to expenditures for the removal of architectural and transportation barriers to the elderly and handicapped that are elected to be expensed. These items must be separately stated, since dollar limits apply at both the owner and entity levels.

C Corporations

Repair costs are trade or business expenses that are taken into account in determining the profit (or loss) of the C corporation on Form 1120. This form contains a separate line for deducting repairs and maintenance costs. Shareholders do not report any income (or loss) from the corporation.

Rehabilitation Credit for All Taxpayers

This credit is computed on Form 3468, *Investment Tax Credit*. It is part of the general business credit and is subject to the limitations on the general business credit (explained in Chapter 23), which is computed on Form 3800, *General Business Credit*, filed with Form 1040 and Form 1120. (Partners and S corporation shareholders figure the general business credit limitation on their individual returns.)

Disabled Access Tax Credit for All Taxpayers

This credit is computed on Form 8826, *Disabled Access Credit*. It is part of the general business credit and is subject to the limitations on the general business credit, which is computed on Form 3800, *General Business Credit*, filed with Forms 1040 and 1120. (Partners and S corporation shareholders figure the general business credit limitation on their individual returns.)

Energy Credit for All Taxpayers

The energy credit, which is part of the investment credit, is claimed in Part II of Form 3468, *Investment Credit*. It is part of the general business credit, which is computed on Form 3800, *General Business Credit*, filed with Forms 1040 and 1120. (Partner and S corporation shareholders figure the general business credit limitation on their individual returns.)

Bad Debts

Alert

At the time this book was printed, Congress had not extended numerous breaks for 2014 that had expired at the end of 2013. Check the online supplement in February 2015 at www.jklasser.com or www.barbaraweltman.com to see whether these breaks apply for 2014 returns.

No one thinks that the loans they make to others will go unpaid; otherwise, such loans would not be made in the first place. You never expect that the check you've accepted as payment for the goods or services you've provided will bounce or that you'll have a chargeback for a credit card payment, but unfortunately these are common occurrences (especially in tough economic times). No matter how careful you are, you may get stiffed! If, in the course of your business, you lend money or extend credit for your goods and services but fail to receive payment, you can take some comfort in the tax treatment for these transactions gone sour. You may be able to deduct your loss as a bad debt.

For further information about deducting bad debts, see IRS Publication 535, *Business Expenses*.

Bad Debts in General

If you cannot collect money that is owed to you in your business, your loss may be deductible. You must prove 3 factors to establish a bad debt:

1. The debtor-creditor relationship
2. Worthlessness
3. Loss

The Debtor-Creditor Relationship

You must prove that there is a *debtor-creditor relationship*. This means that there is a legal obligation on the part of the debtor to pay to the creditor (you) a fixed or determinable sum of money. The legal obligation can arise from making a loan or selling goods and services.

If you lend money to a friend or relative, the relationship between you and the borrower is not always clear. You may, for example, lend the money with the expectation of receiving repayment but later forgive some or all of the payments. This forgiveness with a friend or relative transforms what might have been a bad debt into a gift. The law does not bar loans between relatives or friends, but be aware that the IRS gives special scrutiny to loans involving related parties.

The simplest way to prove a debtor-creditor relationship is to have a written note evidencing the loan. The note should state the following terms:

- The amount of the loan
- A stated rate of interest
- A fixed maturity date
- A repayment schedule

If you have a corporation to which you lend money, establishing the debtor-creditor relationship is crucial. Unless you can show that an advance to the corporation is intended to be a loan, it will be treated as a contribution to the capital of the corporation (which is not deductible). Make sure that not only do you have a written note stating the terms of the loan (rate of interest, repayment schedule, etc.), but also that the corporation carries the advance as a loan on its books.

If your corporation lends money to others, it is advisable to include this arrangement in the corporate minutes (e.g., a corporate resolution authorizing the loan and spelling out the loan terms) as well as to carry the loan on the corporation's books.

Worthlessness

You must also show that the debt has become *worthless* and will remain that way. You must be able to show that you took reasonable steps to collect the debt. It is not necessary that you actually go to court to collect the debt if you can show that a judgment would remain uncollectible. If the borrower is in bankruptcy, this is a very good indication that the debt is worthless, at least in part.

Generally, the debt is considered to be worthless as of the settlement date of the bankruptcy action, but facts can show that it was worthless before this time. If you use a collection agency to attempt collection of outstanding accounts receivable or other amounts owed to you and you agree to pay the agency a percentage of what is collected, you can immediately deduct that percentage of the outstanding amount as a bad debt; your agreement establishes that that percentage will never be collected by you.

Example

You have an open accounts receivable of $1,000. After 120 days, you turn it over to a collection agency that charges 30% of what it collects. At the point of your agreement with the agency, you are certain you will never recoup at least $300 of the outstanding amount (the fee that would be paid to the agency if it collects 100% of the debt) and can now deduct that amount.

You may, in fact, deduct more if the agency collects less than the full amount of the debt. For example, if it collects $500 of the $1,000 outstanding, it is entitled to a $150 fee, so you recoup only $350 of the $1,000. Result: You deduct a total of $650 ($300 of which you deducted when the agreement with the agency was made).

Whether a loan is fully or only partially worthless affects whether you can claim a deduction for the loss. Business bad debts are deductible whether they are fully or partially worthless. If the loss is a nonbusiness bad debt, it is deductible only if the debt is fully worthless. No partial deduction is allowed for nonbusiness bad debts. The distinction between business and nonbusiness bad debts is explained later in this chapter.

Loss

You must show that you sustained a *loss* because of the debt. A loss results when an amount has been included in income but the income is never received. This might happen, for example, where an accrual method taxpayer accrues income but later fails to collect it. If you sell goods on credit and fail to receive payment, you sustain an economic loss whether you are on the accrual method or the cash method of accounting.

If you are on the cash basis and extend services but fail to collect, you *cannot* claim a bad debt deduction. You are not considered to have an economic loss even though you might argue that you put in your time and effort and were not justly compensated.

Example

A cash basis accountant prepares an individual's tax return. The bill comes to $400. The accountant never receives payment. She cannot deduct the $400. The accountant never reported the $400 as income, so she is not considered to have suffered an economic loss, even though she extended services and invested her time and energy.

If you make payments to a supplier for future shipments and the supplier fails to deliver because of insolvency, you have a business bad debt, regardless of your method of accounting. Again, you have an economic loss (the money you advanced to the supplier) that gives rise to the bad debt deduction.

Collection of Bad Debts

Suppose you fully investigated a debt, made every effort to collect it, and finally concluded it was worthless. You claim a deduction; then, lo and behold, the debtor repays you a year or two later. You need not go back and amend your return to remove the bad debt deduction. Instead, include the recovery of the bad debt in income in the year you receive payment.

Business versus Nonbusiness Bad Debts

Business bad debts, as the term implies, arise in connection with a business. *Nonbusiness bad debts* are all other debts; they can arise in either a personal or investment context.

Business bad debts are deductible as ordinary losses. A C corporation's debts are always business bad debts. Nonbusiness bad debts are deductible by an individual only as short-term capital losses. As such, they are deductible only to offset your capital gains, and then up to $3,000 of ordinary income.

Business bad debts are deductible if partially or wholly worthless. Nonbusiness bad debts must be wholly worthless to be deductible.

Business Bad Debts

Business bad debts are treated as ordinary losses that offset ordinary business income. To be treated as a business bad debt, the debt must be closely related to the activity of the business. There must have been a business reason for entering into the debtor-creditor relationship.

Business bad debts typically arise from credit sales to customers. They can also be the result of loans to suppliers, customers, employees, or distributors. Credit sales are generally reported on the books of the business as accounts receivable. Loans to suppliers, customers, employees, or distributors generally are reported on the books of the business as notes receivable. When accounts receivable or notes receivable become uncollectible, this results in a business bad debt.

Valuing a Bad Debt

Accounts receivable and notes receivable generally are carried on the books at fair market value (FMV). Thus, when they go bad, they are deductible at FMV. This is so even where that value is less than the face value of the obligations.

Impact of Loans with Your Business or Associates

If you lend money to your corporation and the corporation later defaults, you cannot claim a bad debt deduction unless it was a true loan. If, as explained earlier, the advance to the corporation was in fact a contribution to its capital, then you cannot claim a bad debt deduction.

If you have a partnership that breaks up and there is money owing from the partnership, you may be forced to make payments if your partner or partners do not. This payment may be more than your share of the partnership's debts. In this case, you can claim a bad debt deduction if your partner or partners were insolvent and you were required to pay their share.

If you go out of business but still try to collect outstanding amounts owed to you, potential bad debt deductions are not lost. You can still claim them as business bad debts if the debts become worthless after you go out of business.

Example

An attorney lent money to a friend and is later unable to collect despite a number of attempts. Since the loan had nothing to do with the attorney's business, the failure to collect results in a nonbusiness bad debt if it is wholly worthless.

Nonbusiness Bad Debts

Loans made to protect investments or for personal reasons give rise to nonbusiness bad debts when they go bad.

Loans by Shareholder-Employees

When a shareholder who is also an employee of a corporation lends the corporation money but fails to receive repayment, or guarantees corporate debt and is called upon to make good on the guarantee, it is not always clear whether the resulting debt is a business bad debt or a nonbusiness bad debt.

A business bad debt must arise in the context of a business. A shareholder who lends money to the corporation is doing so to protect his or her investment. An employee who lends money to his or her corporation is doing so to protect his or her business of being an employee. In this instance, employment is treated as a business. When an individual is both a shareholder and an employee, which status governs?

According to the U.S. Supreme Court, the *dominant motive* for making the loan to the corporation is what makes a debt a business or nonbusiness bad debt. Where the dominant motive is to protect one's investment, then the bad debt is treated as a nonbusiness bad debt. Where the dominant motive is to protect one's employment status to ensure continued receipt of salary, then the bad debt is treated as a business bad debt. In making this assessment, several factors are taken into account:

THE SIZE OF YOUR INVESTMENT IN THE CORPORATION

If your investment is substantial, it indicates that a bad debt might be the result of a desire to protect this investment.

THE SIZE OF YOUR AFTER-TAX SALARY FROM THE CORPORATION

If your salary is minimal, this indicates that your real interest may be protecting your investment rather than your salary.

OTHER SOURCES OF INCOME AVAILABLE TO YOU

If the salary is an important source of income to you, then the debt may have been incurred to protect the income. Where the investment is large compared to the salary received and there are other sources of income available, this tends to support the view that the dominant motive was the protection of investment. On the other hand, where the investment is small compared with the salary received and there are no or only insubstantial other sources of income, then the dominant motive may be viewed as protection of salary.

A person's subjective intention in making a loan or guarantee is a factor to be considered, but it is not controlling. Rather, motive is deduced from all the facts and circumstances surrounding the making of the loan or guarantee.

Example

A retired engineer formed a company of which he was the principal shareholder and chief executive officer (CEO). When the company experienced cash flow problems, he lent it money and gave personal guarantees for third-party loans to the company. When the company went under, he lost $450,000 (in addition to his investment in the company). This $450,000 comprised the loans to the company and the guarantees he had to make good on when the company could not. He claimed a business bad debt deduction, which an appellate court allowed. He was a retiree who wanted to continue to work. In view of his age and background, forming his own company was the way to optimal employment. His guarantees in this case far exceeded his initial investment, which was minimal. Therefore his dominant motive in making the loans and guarantees was to protect his employment.

Example

After being terminated from her job as president of a company and spending a year looking for another job, she formed her own company. She did not take salary for the first year; her salary thereafter was between $30,000 and $50,000. Her outside income was substantially more (over $1 million in the year she drew no salary). She guaranteed more than $1 million of loans to the company, which she was called on to repay. But here her bad debt was treated as a nonbusiness bad debt. Her dominant motive was protection of her investment. She could not prove that her dominant motive was protection of salary, since it is not reasonable to believe someone would guarantee over $1 million in loans to protect a salary of $30,000.

WHICH IS BETTER?

Which position should an owner-employee argue in favor of? Naturally, it depends on the person's overall tax position. But generally, nonbusiness bad debt treatment is the better choice. The reason: Losses are treated as short-term capital losses, a deduction for which may be limited in the current year, but unused amounts can be carried forward indefinitely. In contrast, business bad debts of an owner-employee are deductible only as miscellaneous itemized deductions (subject to the 2%-of-AGI floor and the additional reduction in the deduction for high-income taxpayers). And such amounts are *not* deductible for alternative minimum tax (AMT) purposes, so that claiming this write-off can trigger or increase AMT liability.

Guarantees That Result in Bad Debts

Banks and other lending institutions are well aware of the limitation on personal liability of owners in corporations. If corporations are in their infancy and do not have significant assets to use as collateral for loans, shareholders usually are asked to extend their personal guarantees to induce the banks or other lending institutions to advance funds to the corporations. An owner with a 20% or greater ownership interest in the business must give a personal guarantee when applying for an SBA loan (which is a loan guaranteed by the Small Business Administration).

Initially, you do not lend money directly to your business. However, you guarantee, endorse, or indemnify someone else's loan made to your business and are then called on to make good on your guarantee, endorsement, or indemnity. How do you treat this payment?

If the dominant motive for making the guarantee was proximately related to your business (e.g., you guaranteed a loan to the corporation for which you work), then you claim a business bad debt. If the dominant motive for making the guarantee was to protect an investment, you claim a nonbusiness bad debt.

If the guarantee was made for a friend or relative without the receipt of consideration, no bad debt deduction can be claimed. The reason: You did not enter into the arrangement for profit or to protect an investment.

If there is more than one guarantor but only one co-guarantor pays the debt, the co-guarantor who pays the debt can claim only his or her proportional share of the obligation unless it can be proved that the other guarantors were unable to pay.

Example

Three equal shareholders of Corporation X guarantee a bank loan made to the corporation. X defaults, and one of the shareholders pays off the entire loan. That shareholder can deduct only one-third of the debt unless he can prove that the other two shareholders were unable to make any payment.

If you, as guarantor, give your own note to substitute or replace the note of the party for whom you became the guarantor, you cannot claim a bad debt deduction at that time. The deduction arises only when and to the extent you make payments on the notes.

When to Claim the Deduction

In general, a bad debt deduction in the case of a guarantee is claimed for the year in which payment is made by the guarantor. Suppose you guarantee a debt but have the right of subrogation or other right against the debtor to recoup your outlays. In this case, you claim your bad debt deduction only when the right against the debtor becomes worthless.

Special Rules for Accrual Taxpayers

All taxpayers (other than certain financial institutions) use the *specific charge-off method* to account for bad debts. Under this method, business bad debts are deducted when and to the extent that they arise.

Nonaccrual-Experience Method

Taxpayers on the accrual basis have an alternative way to account for bad debts. Income that is not expected to be collected need not be accrued. If, based on prior experience, it is determined that certain receivables will not be collected, then they need not be included in gross income for the year. Since income is not taken into account, there is no need to then claim a bad debt deduction.

The *nonaccrual-experience method* applies only to accounts receivable for performing services in the fields of health, law, engineering, architecture, accounting, actuarial science, performing arts, or consulting. In addition, the business's average annual gross receipts for the 3 prior years cannot be more than $5 million. It cannot be used for amounts owed from activities such as lending money, selling goods, or acquiring receivables or the right to receive payments. Nor can this method be used if interest or penalties are charged on late payments. However, merely offering a discount for early payment is not treated as charging interest or a late penalty if the full amount is accrued as gross income at the time the services are provided and the discount for early payment is treated as an adjustment to gross income in the year of payment.

This method can be used under either a separate receivable system or a periodic system. The separate receivable system applies the nonaccrual-experience method separately to each account receivable; the periodic system applies it to the total of the qualified accounts receivable at the end of the year. This is a highly technical accounting rule that should be discussed with an experienced accountant. The nonaccrual-experience method is explained more fully in IRS Publication 535, *Business Expenses*.

Reporting Bad Debts on the Tax Return

If you want to claim a bad debt deduction on your return, you must do more than simply enter your loss. You also must attach a statement to your return explaining each element of the bad debt. (There is no special IRS form required for making this statement.) These elements include:

- A description of the debt
- The name of the debtor
- Your family or business relationship to the debtor
- The due date of the loan
- Your efforts to collect the debt
- How you decided the debt became worthless

This reporting requirement applies only to individuals who claim bad debts on Schedule A, C, E, or F. Partnerships, LLCs, S corporations, and C corporations need not attach a statement to their returns explaining their bad debt deductions.

The loss is claimed on the return for the year in which the debt becomes worthless (or partially worthless where applicable). Often this is not known by the end of that particular year. Fortunately, there is a 7-year period in which to amend an old return to claim a bad debt.

Example

In 2009, Corporation X (on the accrual basis) provided goods and services to Corporation Y. Partial payment was made in 2009, but the balance due in 2010 was never paid. Due to poor bookkeeping, X failed to claim a bad debt deduction for this nonpayment. X has until March 15, 2017, 7 years from the due date of its 2009 return, to file an amended return and claim the bad debt deduction.

Collection Strategies

Although the tax law may provide some help in alleviating the financial loss of bad debts, a better approach is to avoid or limit the loss by taking action.

Review Credit Policies

To avoid bad debts, consider whether to eliminate or modify your credit policy. For example, instead of billing customers when work is completed or goods are shipped, have customers charge the payments to a credit card that you accept.

If, because of industry policy or personal preference, you want to continue to extend credit to customers, consider:

- *Doing credit checks on customers.* When extending credit for B2C, check a consumer's credit through the business services at one of the 3 major credit bureaus: Equifax (www.equifax.com), Experian (www.experian.com), and TransUnion (www.transunion.com). For B2B, check a business's credit at D&B (www.dnb.com) and Experian (www.experian.com/small-business/services.jsp).
- *Limiting credit to customers.* You do not have to extend the same terms to all customers.
- *Billing wisely.* Instead of billing at the completion of a job, bill at completion points along the way. Bill promptly (don't wait until the end of the month to send invoices). Send bills electronically to make sure they arrive promptly.

Review Collections Policies

The longer an account receivable goes unpaid, the less likely it becomes that you will receive full, or even *any,* payment. Make sure to stay on top of collections by monitoring receivables on a regular basis. Contact delinquent accounts to press for collections (work out payment terms where applicable). Observe debt collection practice rules under the Fair Debt Collection Practices Act (go to www.ftc.gov for more information).

If you are having difficulty collecting what is owed to you, consider:

- *Working with a collection agency.* The agency receives a fee, usually equal to a percentage of what is collected; you receive the balance. You can deduct the fee you pay to the agency.
- *Engaging an attorney.* The attorney can seek to collect on your behalf. Determine in advance what payment the attorney will receive (hourly, a percentage of collection, etc.). You can deduct the attorney's fee.
- *Taking customers to small claims court.* Determine your legal rights and whether you can bring your claim to small claims court. You can deduct any court costs you pay; you cannot deduct any amount for your time and effort.

Strategies When Customers Go Bankrupt

If a customer files for bankruptcy, understand your options. Bankruptcy means you can't continue collection activities. Depending on the amount of money owed to you, you may want to file a proof of claim with the bankruptcy court (you'll get the details when you receive a bankruptcy notice) and pursue collection; expect in most cases to collect only pennies on the dollars you're owed.

Where to Deduct Bad Debts

Employees

Nonbusiness bad debts are deducted on Form 8949 and then on Schedule D as a short-term capital loss. On this schedule, enter the amount of the bad debt and Statement Attached. Then include on an accompanying statement more information about the bad debt, as explained earlier.

Nonbusiness bad debts are deductible only to the extent of an individual's capital gains, plus up to $3,000 of ordinary income. These capital loss limits are taken into account when completing Schedule D. Remember that unused capital losses can be carried forward indefinitely and used against future capital gains and up to $3,000 of ordinary income each year.

Business bad debts are deducted as ordinary losses on Schedule A as a miscellaneous itemized deduction subject to the 2%-of-AGI rule and itemized deduction reduction for high-income taxpayers explained in Chapter 1.

Self-Employed

Business bad debts are deducted from business income on Schedule C as "Other Expenses" (or Schedule F in the case of farming operations). Schedule C does not contain a specific line for claiming bad debts from sales or services. Be sure to attach a statement to the return explaining the bad debts.

Nonbusiness bad debts are reported as short-term capital losses on Schedule D. Self-employed persons report nonbusiness bad debts in the same way as employees.

Partnerships and LLCs

Partnerships and LLCs can deduct business bad debts on their return. Form 1065 contains a specific line for claiming bad debts. These bad debts reduce the partnerships' or LLCs' trade or business income. They are not passed through as separate items to partners or LLC members. Partnerships and LLCs need not attach a statement to the return explaining the bad debts.

To date there have been no cases or rulings in which bad debts of partnerships or LLCs have been treated as nonbusiness bad debts. However, should such debts occur, see the treatment of nonbusiness bad debts for S corporations in the section that follows.

S Corporations

Bad debts are usually business bad debts. Business bad debts are not separately stated items passed through separately to shareholders. Instead, they serve to reduce the amount of business income or loss that passes through to shareholders. They are entered on Form 1120S on the line specifically for bad debts. S corporations need not attach a statement to the return explaining the bad debts.

It should be noted that where the loss is considered a nonbusiness bad debt, it must be separately stated on Schedule K-1 and passed through to shareholders. In this way the short-term capital loss for the shareholder is subject to that shareholder's capital loss limits.

C Corporations

Bad debts are always business bad debts in the case of C corporations. They are reported on Form 1120 on the specific line provided for bad debts. Corporations need not attach a statement to the return explaining the bad debts.

Rents

Alert

At the time this book was printed, Congress had not extended numerous breaks for 2014 that had expired at the end of 2013. Check the online supplement in February 2015 at www.jklasser.com or www.barbaraweltman.com to see whether these breaks apply for 2014 returns.

From a financial standpoint, it might make more sense to rent than to buy property and equipment. Renting may require a smaller cash outlay than buying. Also, the business may not as yet have established sufficient credit to make large purchases but can still gain the use of the property or equipment through renting. If you pay rent to use office space, a store, or other property for your business, or you pay to lease business equipment, you generally can deduct your outlays.

Deducting Rent Payments in General

If you pay to use property for business that you do not own, the payments are *rent*. Leases may take various forms. For example, with a net lease, the tenant pays for the use of the space as well as costs associated with operating the property, such as taxes, property insurance, utilities, sewer and water, and trash collection. Regardless of the form of the lease, the payments are all considered rents (even if they may cover taxes). They may also be called *lease payments*. Rents paid for property used in a business are deductible business expenses. These include obligations you pay on behalf of your landlord. For example, if you are required by the terms of your lease to pay real estate taxes on the property, you can deduct these taxes as part of your rent payments.

The rents must be reasonable in amount. The issue of reasonableness generally does not arise where you and the landlord are at arm's length. However, the issue does come up when you and the landlord are related parties, such as family members or related companies. Rent paid to a related party is treated as reasonable if it is the same rent that would be paid to an unrelated party. A percentage rental is also considered reasonable if the rental paid is reasonable.

If the rent payments entitle you to receive equity in or title to the property at the end of some term, the payments are not rent. They may, however, be deductible in part as depreciation (see Chapter 14).

Rent to Your Corporation

If you rent property to your corporation, the corporation can claim a rental expense deduction, assuming the rents are reasonable. However, you cannot treat the rents as passive income that you could use to offset your losses from other passive activities. A self-rental rule under the passive activity loss rules specifically prohibits you from arranging this type of rental for tax benefit.

If you rent a portion of your home to your employer, see the discussion on Rental of a Portion of Your Home for Business later in this chapter.

Rent with an Option to Buy

Sometimes it is not clear whether payments are to lease or purchase property. There are a number of factors used to make such a determination.

NATURE OF THE DOCUMENT

If you have a lease, payments made pursuant to the lease generally are treated as rents. If you have a conditional sales contract, payments made pursuant to the lease are nondeductible purchase payments. A document is treated as a conditional sales contract if it provides that you will acquire title to or equity in the property upon completing a certain number or amount of payments.

INTENT OF THE PARTIES

How the parties view the transaction affects whether it is a lease or a conditional sales contract. *Intent* can be inferred from certain objective factors. A conditional sales contract exists if any of the following are found:

- The agreement applies part of each payment toward an equity interest.
- The agreement provides for the transfer of title after payment of a stated amount.
- The amount of the payment to use the property for a short time is a large part of the amount paid to get title to the property.
- The payments exceed the current fair rental value of the property (based on comparisons with other similar properties).
- There is an option to buy the property at a nominal price as compared with the property's value at the time the option can be exercised.
- There is an option to buy the property at a nominal price as compared with the total amount required to be paid under the agreement.
- The agreement designates a part of the payments as interest or in some way makes part of the payments easily recognizable as interest.

Example

You lease an office building for a period of 2 years. The lease agreement provides that at the end of that term you have the option of buying the property and all of the payments made to date will be applied toward the purchase price. In this case, your payments probably would be viewed as payments to purchase rather than payments to lease the property.

Advance Rents

Generally, rents are deductible in the year in which they are paid or accrued. What happens if you pay rent in advance? The answer depends on your method of accounting. If you are on the accrual basis, prepaid rent must be capitalized (it cannot be deducted at the time of payment).

Example

X corporation, an accrual basis taxpayer, leases office space from Y corporation at a monthly rental rate of $2,000. On August 1, 2014, X prepays its office rent expense for the first 6 months of 2015 in the amount of $12,000. Because economic performance with respect to X's prepayment of rent does not occur until 2015, X's prepaid rent is not incurred in 2014 and therefore is not properly taken into account in 2014.

If you are on the cash basis, prepaid rent can be immediately deducted provided that prepayments do not extend beyond 12 months.

Example

X corporation uses the cash method of accounting and pays Y corporation $12,000 on August 1, 2014, to cover rent for the first 6 months of 2015. With the 12-month rule, the $12,000 payment is deductible in 2014 because the rights or benefits attributable to X's prepayment of its rent do not extend beyond December 31, 2015.

Security deposits generally are not deductible when paid because the landlord is usually obligated to refund them if the terms of the lease are met. However, if the landlord keeps some or all of the deposit (e.g., because you failed to live up to the terms of the lease), you can then deduct such amount as rent.

Gift-Leasebacks

If you own property that you have already depreciated, you may want to create a tax deduction for your business by entering into a *gift-leaseback* transaction. Typically, the property is gifted to your spouse or children, to whom you then pay rent. In the past, this type of arrangement was more popular, but the passive loss rules put a damper on deducting losses created by these arrangements. If you still want to shift income to your children (who presumably are in a lower tax bracket than you) while getting a tax deduction for your business, be sure that you meet these 3 requirements:

1. You do not retain control over the property after the gift is given.
2. The leaseback is in writing, and the rent charged is reasonable.
3. There must be a business purpose for the leaseback. (For example, where a doctor transferred the property in which his practice was located to his children in fear of malpractice suits, this was a valid business reason for leasing rather than owning the property.)

There are other factors to consider before entering into a gift-leaseback. Consider the impact of the kiddie tax if your children are subject to it. It is strongly suggested that you consult with a tax adviser before giving business property to your children and then leasing it back for use in your business.

Miscellaneous Rentals

Some payments for the use of property that you may not otherwise think of as rentals but that may be required by your business include safety deposit box rental fees and post office box rental fees.

The Cost of Acquiring, Modifying, or Canceling a Lease

The Cost of Acquiring a Lease

When you pay a premium to obtain immediate possession under a lease that does not extend beyond the tax year, the premium is deductible in full for the current year. Where the premium relates to a long-term lease, the cost of the premium is deductible over the term of the lease. The same amortization rule applies to commissions, bonuses, and other fees paid to obtain a lease on property you use in your business.

What is the term of the lease for purposes of deducting lease acquisition premiums when the lease contains renewal options? The tax law provides a complicated method for making this determination. The term of the lease for amortization purposes includes all renewal option periods if less than 75% of the cost is attributable to the term of the lease remaining on the purchase date. Do not include any period for which the lease may be renewed, extended, or continued under an option exercisable by you, the lessee, in determining the term of the lease remaining on the purchase date.

> **Example**
>
> You pay $10,000 to acquire a lease with 20 years remaining on it. The lease has 2 options to renew, for 5 years each. Of the $10,000, $7,000 is paid for the original lease and $3,000 for the renewal options. Since $7,000 is less than 75% of the total cost, you must amortize $10,000 over 30 years (the lease term plus the 2 renewal option periods).

> **Example**
>
> The circumstances are the same as in the previous example, except that $8,000 is allocable to the original lease. Since this is not less than 75% of the total cost, the entire $10,000 can be amortized over the original lease term of 20 years.

The Cost of Modifying a Lease

If you pay an additional rent to change a lease provision, you amortize this additional payment over the remaining term of the lease.

The Cost of Canceling a Lease

If you pay to get out of your lease before the end of its term, the cost generally is deductible in full in the year of payment. However, where a new lease is obtained, the cost of canceling the lease must be capitalized if the cancellation and new lease are viewed as part of the same transaction.

Example

A company leased a computer system for 5 years. To upgrade its system, the company canceled the original lease and entered into a new one with the same lessor. Because the termination of the old lease was conditioned on obtaining a new lease, the cost of termination had to be capitalized (i.e., added to the cost of the new lease and deducted ratably over the term of the new lease).

Improvements You Make to Leased Property

If you add a building or make other permanent improvements to leased property, you can depreciate the cost of the improvements using Modified Accelerated Cost Recovery System (MACRS) depreciation. (For a further discussion of depreciation, see Chapter 14.) Generally, the improvements are depreciated over their recovery period, a time fixed by law. They are not depreciated over the remaining term of the lease.

Example

You construct a building on land you lease. The recovery period of the building is 39 years. When the building construction is completed, there are 35 years remaining on the lease. You depreciate the building over its recovery period of 39 years, not over the 35 years remaining on the lease.

If you acquire a lease through an assignment and the lessee has made improvements to the property, the amount you pay for the assignment is a capital investment. Where the rental value of the leased land has increased since the beginning of the lease, part of the capital investment is for the increase in that value; the balance is for your investment in the permanent improvements. You amortize the part of the increased rental value of the leased land; you depreciate the part of the investment related to the improvements.

Special Rules for Qualified Leasehold, Restaurant, and Retail Improvements

The 15-year period for writing off qualified expenses, as well as bonus depreciation and special first-year expensing, expired at the end of 2013, but could be extended retroactively by Congress. If it is not extended, then such costs are recovered over the usual 39-year period for realty (see Chapter 14). The following is included in case there is an extension of some or all of the special rules for certain qualified realty improvements. Check the Supplement for details.

Improvements to leaseholds (by the landlord or tenant pursuant to the terms of the lease), restaurants, and retail establishments can be deducted over 15 years rather than having to be depreciated along with the building itself over 39 years. Here is what qualifies if the rule is extended:

- *Leasehold improvements.* These are improvements to the interior of a building made more than 3 years after the building was placed in service. Qualified improvements do not include enlargement of the building, elevators or escalators, structural components benefiting common areas, or any internal framework to the building.

- *Restaurant improvements.* These are improvements to a building of which more than 50% is devoted to the preparation of and seating for on-premises consumption of prepared meals.

- *Retail improvements.* These are improvements to the interior of a building open to the general public for the retail trade as long as the improvements are made more than 3 years after the building was placed in service. The improvements must also not involve enlargement, elevators or escalators, or internal framework.

If you enter into a lease after August 5, 1997, for retail space for 15 years or less and you receive a construction allowance from the landlord to make additions or improvements to the space, you are not taxed on these payments provided they are fully used for the purpose intended.

Leasehold improvements qualify for bonus depreciation at the rate of 50% for improvements made before January 1, 2014; this rule may be extended for 2014, so see the Supplement. Qualified restaurant and retail improvements do not qualify for this bonus depreciation unless they also qualify as leasehold improvements.

Qualified leasehold, restaurant, and retail improvements through December 31, 2013, qualify for $250,000 first-year expensing; this rule may be extended for 2014 so see the Supplement. The expensing option permits an immediate deduction if there was sufficient taxable income.

Rental of a Portion of Your Home for Business

If you rent your home and use part of it for business, you may be able to deduct part of your rent as a business expense. This part of the rent is treated as a home office deduction if you meet certain requirements. See Chapter 18 for details on the home office deduction.

Leasing a Car

If you lease a car for business use, the treatment of the rental costs depends upon the term of the lease. If the term is less than 30 days, the entire cost of the rental is deductible. Thus, if you go out of town on business and rent a car for a week, your rental costs are deductible.

If the lease term exceeds 30 days, the lease payments are still deductible if you use the car entirely for business. If you use it for both business and personal purposes, you must allocate the lease payments and deduct only the business portion of the costs. However, depending on the value of the car at the time it is leased, you may be required to include an amount in gross income called an inclusion amount (explained later).

If you make advance payments, you must spread these payments over the entire lease period and deduct them accordingly. You cannot depreciate a car you lease, because depreciation applies only to property that is owned.

Lease with an Option to Buy

When you have this arrangement, are you leasing or buying the car? The answer depends on a number of factors:

1. Intent of the parties to the transaction.
2. Whether any equity results from the arrangement.
3. Whether any interest is paid.
4. Whether the fair market value (FMV) of the car is less than the lease payment or option payment when the option to buy is exercised.

If the factors support a finding that the arrangement is a lease, the payments are deductible. If, however, the factors support a finding that the arrangement is a purchase agreement, the payments are not deductible.

Inclusion Amount

If the car price exceeds a certain amount (which is adjusted periodically for inflation) and you do not use the standard mileage rate to account for expenses, you may have to include in income an amount called an *inclusion amount*. The law seeks to equate buying with leasing. Since there is a dollar limit on the amount of depreciation that can be claimed on a luxury car that is owned, the law also requires an amount to be included in income as an offset to high lease payments on a car that is leased. In essence, the inclusion amount seeks to limit your deduction for lease payments to what it would be if you owned the car and claimed depreciation.

The inclusion amount, which is simply an amount that you add to your other income, applies if a car is leased for more than 30 days and its value exceeds a certain amount. The inclusion amount is added to income only so long as you lease the car. Inclusion amounts are based on the value of the car as of the first day of the lease term. If the capitalized cost of the car is specified in the lease agreement, that amount is considered to be the car's **fair market value**. At the start of the lease, you can see what your inclusion amount would be for that year and for all subsequent years. The inclusion amount is based on a percentage of the FMV of the car at the time the lease begins. Different inclusion amounts apply to gas-driven cars and to electric cars.

Fair market value The price that would be paid for the property when there is a willing buyer and seller (neither being required to buy or sell) and both have reasonable knowledge of all the necessary facts. Evidence of fair market value includes the price paid for similar property on or about the same date.

The inclusion amount applies only if the FMV of the car when the lease began was more than $16,700 for 2010, $18,500 in 2011 and 2012, $19,000 in 2013, and $18,500 in 2014. Different thresholds applied to cars leased in previous years.

Example

The inclusion amount for your car is $500. You used the car only 6 months of the year. You must include in income $250 (183 ÷ 365 of $500).

The inclusion amounts are taken from IRS tables. (See Chapter 9 for inclusion amounts.) The full amount applies if the car is leased for the full year and used entirely for business. If the car is leased for less than the full year, or if it is used only partly for personal purposes, then the inclusion amount must be allocated to business use for the period of the year in which it was used. The allocation for part-year use is made on a day-by-day basis.

Remember that if you use your car for commuting or other nonbusiness purposes, you cannot deduct that allocable part of the lease.

Car leasing, including the advisability of leasing versus buying a business car, is discussed more fully in Chapter 9.

Leveraged Leases

If you are the lessee in a transaction referred to as a **leveraged lease**, you generally can deduct your lease payments.

Leveraged lease A 3-party transaction in which the landlord (lessor) obtains financing from a third party and in which lease payments are sufficient to cover the cost of repaying the financing. Also, the lease term generally covers the useful life of the property.

It is important that the lessor, and not the lessee, be treated as the owner of the property if lease payments are to be deductible. The lessor is treated as the owner if he or she has a minimum amount at risk (at least 20%) during the entire term of the lease and the lessee does not have a contractual right to buy the property at its FMV at the end of the lease term. Other factors that are necessary to show that the lessor and not the lessee is the owner of the property are that the lessor has a profit motive (apart from tax benefits), the lessee does not lend money to the lessor, and the lessee does not invest in the property.

If you are about to become the lessee of a leveraged lease and want to be sure that you will not be treated as the owner (which means your rental expenses would not be deductible), you can ask the IRS for an advance ruling on the issue. (However, the IRS will not issue an advance ruling on leveraged leases of so-called **limited use property**.) There is a user fee for this service. It may be advisable to seek the assistance of a tax professional in obtaining the ruling.

Limited use property **Property not expected to be either useful to or usable by a lessor at the end of the lease term except for continued leasing or transfer to the lessee or a member of a lessee group.**

Special rules apply to leases of tangible personal property over $250,000.

Where to Deduct Rent Payments

Employees

Rent expenses are deductible as itemized expenses on Schedule A. If you lease a car for more than 30 days, you must complete Form 2106, *Employee Business Expenses*, to report the lease payments. (You cannot use the simplified form, 2106-EZ, if you lease rather than own your car.) The results of Form 2106 are then entered on Schedule A and are subject to the 2%-of-AGI rule and itemized deduction reduction for high-income taxpayers discussed in Chapter 1.

If you rent your home and use part of it for business for the convenience of your employer, you can claim a home office deduction for that part of the rent. There is no special form that an employee is required to use for calculating his or her home office deduction. However, you may figure the deduction on a special worksheet for this purpose in IRS Publication 587. The deductible portion of your rent (along with other home office expenses) is entered on Schedule A as an itemized expense, which, again, is subject to the 2%-of-AGI rule.

Self-Employed

Rents are deductible on Schedule C. This schedule provides two separate lines for reporting rents and leases so that rents and leases for vehicles, machinery, and equipment are reported separately from those of other business property. If you lease a car for more than 30 days, you must complete Part IV of Schedule C if you are not otherwise required to file Form 4562, *Depreciation and Amortization*, or directly on this form if you placed in service any property in 2014 that is subject to depreciation or amortization. Farmers who are self-employed deduct rents on Schedule F. Information about leased cars must be entered on Form 4562, *Depreciation and Amortization*.

If you rent your home and use part of it for business and file Schedule C, you can claim a home office deduction for that part of the rent. Home office expenses, including rent, are computed on Form 8829, *Expenses for Business Use of Your Home*, if you use the actual expense method (or on a worksheet in the instructions to Schedule C of Form 1040 if you use the optional method). The deductible portion is entered on Schedule C. If you are a farmer who files Schedule F, figure your home office deduction on the worksheet found in IRS Publication 587. Then enter the deductible portion on Schedule F.

Partnerships and LLCs

Rent and lease payments are deducted by partnerships and LLCs on their returns as part of the entity's ordinary trade or business income, on Form 1065. The return contains a separate line for reporting rents. Rent and lease payments are not passed through to partners or LLC members as separate items.

If you rent your home and use part of it for the business of the partnership, you can claim a home office deduction for that part of the rent. There is no special form that a partner must use for calculating his or her home office deduction. However, you may figure the deduction on a special worksheet for this purpose in IRS Publication 587. The deductible portion of your rent (along with other home office expenses) is entered on Schedule E as part of your share of partnership income and expenses.

S Corporations

Rents and lease payments are deducted by the S corporation as part of its ordinary trade or business income on Form 1120S. The return contains a separate line for reporting rents. Rents and lease payments are not passed through to shareholders as separately stated items.

C Corporations

C corporations deduct rent and lease payments on Form 1120. The return contains a separate line for reporting rents.

Taxes and Interest

Alert

At the time this book was printed, Congress had not extended numerous breaks for 2014 that had expired at the end of 2013. Check the online supplement in February 2015 at www.jklasser.com or www.barbaraweltman.com to see whether these breaks apply for 2014 returns.

Taxes and interest are two types of expenses that are hard to avoid. In the course of your business activities, you may pay various taxes and interest charges. Most taxes and interest payments are deductible; some are not.

For further information about deducting taxes and interest, see IRS Publication 535, *Business Expenses*.

Deductible Taxes

General Rules

In order to deduct taxes, they must be imposed on you. The tax must be owed by the party who pays it. If your corporation owns an office building, it is the party that owes the real property taxes. If, as part of your lease, you are obligated to pay your landlord's taxes, you can deduct your payment as an additional part of your rent; you do not claim a deduction for taxes, since you are not the owner of the property.

Taxes must be paid during the year if you are on a cash basis. If you pay taxes at year end by means of a check or even a credit card charge, the tax is deductible in the year the check is sent or delivered or the credit charge is made. This is so even though the check is not cashed until the following year or you do not pay the credit card bill until the following year. If you pay any tax by phone or through your computer, the tax is deductible on the date of payment reported on the statement issued by the financial institution through which the payment is made. If you contest a liability and do not pay it until the issue is settled, you cannot deduct the tax until it is actually paid. It may be advisable to settle a disputed liability in order to fix the amount and claim a deduction. If you pay tax after the end of the year for a liability that relates to the prior year, you deduct the tax in the year of payment.

If you receive a state or local location tax incentive in the form of an abatement, a credit, a deduction, a rate reduction, or an exemption in order to attract your company to a particular area, the incentive is not deductible. Only the amount of tax you are liable for, after reduction by any location tax incentive(s), is deductible.

Example

An S corporation on a calendar year, using the cash basis method, pays its state franchise fee for 2014 in March 2015. The payment is deductible on the S corporation's 2015 income tax return, not on its 2014 return.

Real Estate Taxes

In general, real property taxes are deductible. Assessments made to real property for the repair or maintenance of some local benefit (such as streets, sidewalks, or sewers) are treated as deductible taxes.

If you acquire real property for resale to customers, you may be required under uniform capitalization rules to capitalize these taxes. The uniform capitalization rules are discussed in Chapter 2.

Special rules apply when real estate is sold during the year. Real property taxes must be allocated between the buyer and seller according to the number of days in the real property tax year. The seller can deduct the taxes up to, but not including, the date of sale. The buyer can deduct the taxes from the date of sale onward.

Accrual basis taxpayers can deduct only taxes accruing on the date of sale. An accrual basis taxpayer can elect to accrue ratably real property taxes related to a definite period of time over that period of time.

> **Example**
>
> X Corporation, a calendar-year taxpayer on the accrual basis, owns an office building on which annual taxes are $1,200 for the fiscal year beginning July 1, 2014, through June 30, 2015. If X elects to ratably accrue taxes, $600 of the taxes is deductible in 2014, the balance in 2015.

The election to accrue taxes ratably applies for each separate business. If one business owns two properties, an election covers both properties. The election is binding and can be revoked only with the consent of the IRS. You make the election by attaching a statement to your return for the first year that real property taxes are due on property that includes the businesses for which the election is being made, the period of time to which the taxes relate, and a computation of the real property tax deduction for the first year of the election. The election must be filed on time with your income tax return (including extensions).

If you have already owned property for some time but want to switch to the ratable accrual method, you must obtain the consent of the IRS. To do so, file Form 3115, *Change in Accounting Method*, within the year for which the change is to be effective.

State and Local Income Taxes

A corporation that pays state and local income taxes can deduct the taxes on its return. Taxes may include state corporate income taxes and any franchise tax (which is a tax for operating as a corporation and has nothing to do with being a franchise business).

A self-employed individual who pays state and local taxes with respect to business income reported on Schedule C can deduct them only as an itemized deduction on Schedule A. Similarly, an employee who pays state and local taxes with respect to compensation from employment usually deducts these taxes on Schedule A.

Self-Employment Tax

Businesses do not pay self-employment tax; individuals do. Sole proprietors, general partners (whether active or inactive), and certain LLC members pay self-employment tax on their net earnings from self-employment (amounts reported on Schedule C or as self-employment income on Schedule K-1). Limited partners do not pay self-employment tax on their share of income from the business. However, limited partners are subject to self-employment tax if they perform any services for the business or receive any guaranteed payments. LLC members who are like general partners pay self-employment tax; those who are like limited partners do not. The IRS was precluded from issuing regulations defining a limited partner before July 1,1998. To date, the IRS has still not issued any regulations nor given any indication when it would.

The tax rate for the Social Security portion of self-employment tax is 12.4% and, in 2014, applies to net earnings from self-employment up to $117,000. The Medicare tax rate is 2.9%, and it applies to *all* net earnings from self-employment (there is no limit for the Medicare portion of self-employment tax).

Those who pay self-employment tax are entitled to deduct one-half of the self-employment tax as an adjustment to gross income on their personal income tax returns. The deduction on page 1 of Form 1040 reduces your gross income and serves to lower the threshold for certain itemized deductions.

In figuring self-employment tax, net earnings from self-employment cannot be reduced by any net operating loss carryback or carryover.

While S corporations are pass-through entities similar to partnerships and LLCs, owners of S corporations who work for their businesses are not treated the same as partners and LLC members for purposes of self-employment tax. Owners of S corporations who are also employees of their businesses do not pay self-employment tax on their compensation—they are employees of the corporation for purposes of employment tax. Their compensation is subject to FICA, not to self-employment tax. Individuals who both are self-employed and have an interest in an S corporation cannot use losses from the S corporation to reduce net earnings from self-employment.

For more on self-employment tax, see Chapter 29.

Additional Medicare Taxes

The additional 0.9% Medicare tax on earnings (wages, other taxable compensation, and self-employment income) over a threshold amount and the 3.8% Medicare tax on net investment income (which includes, for example, income from an S corporation in which you do not materially participate) are *not* deductible. They are viewed as personal taxes even though they relate to business income.

Personal Property Tax

Personal property tax on any property used in a business is deductible. Personal property tax is an *ad valorem tax*—a tax on the value of personal property. For example, a *floor tax* is a property tax levied on inventory that is sitting on the floor (or shelves) of your business. Registration fees for the right to use property within the state in your trade or business are deductible. If the fees are based on the value of the property, they are considered a personal property tax.

Sales and Use Taxes

Sales tax to acquire a depreciable asset used in a trade or business is added to the basis of the asset and is recovered through depreciation. If sales tax is paid to acquire a nondepreciable asset, it is still treated as part of the cost of the asset and is deducted as part of the asset's expense. For example, sales tax on business stationery is part of the cost of the stationery and is deducted as part of that cost (not as a separate sales tax deduction). Sales tax paid on property acquired for resale is also treated as part of the cost of that property.

Sales tax you collect as a merchant or other business owner and turn over to the state is deductible only if you include it in your gross receipts. If the sales tax is not included, it is not deductible.

When sales tax is imposed on the seller or retailer and the seller or retailer can separately state the tax or pass it on to the consumer, then the consumer, rather than the seller or retailer, gets to deduct the tax. When the consumer is in business the tax is treated differently depending on how the asset is acquired. (See the aforementioned details for depreciable property, nondepreciable property, and property held for sale or resale.)

A compensating use tax is treated as a sales tax. This type of tax is imposed on the use, storage, or consumption of an item brought in from another taxing jurisdiction. Typically, it is imposed at the same percentage as a sale tax.

To learn about obtaining a resale number needed for the collection of sales taxes and your sales tax obligations, contact your state tax department (you can find it at www.taxadmin.org).

Luxury Tax

Like sales tax, a luxury tax that is paid to acquire a depreciable asset is added to the basis of the asset; it is not separately deductible. For example, if you pay a luxury tax to acquire a high-priced car to use for business, the amount of the tax becomes part of the car's basis for purposes of depreciation.

Employment Taxes

Employment taxes, also called payroll taxes, are a conglomerate of a number of different taxes:

- The employer share of Federal Insurance Contribution Act (FICA) tax covering Social Security and Medicare taxes
- Federal Unemployment Tax Act (FUTA) tax
- State unemployment tax

Employment taxes are fully deductible by an employer.

The employer portion of the Social Security tax is 6.2%. This tax is applied to a current wage base of up to $117,000 in 2014, which is adjusted annually for inflation. The employer portion of the Medicare tax is 1.45%. This is applied to all wages paid to an employee; there is no wage base limit. If you, as an employer, pay both the employer and employee portion of the tax, you may claim a deduction for your full payments.

TABLE 13.1 Credit Reduction States for 2013 FUTA

Arkansas (0.9%)	Indiana (1.2%)	North Carolina (0.9%)
California (0.9%)	Kentucky (0.9%)	Ohio (0.9%)
Connecticut (0.9%)	Missouri (0.9%)	Rhode Island (0.9%)
Delaware (0.6%)	New York (0.9%)	Wisconsin (0.9%)
Georgia (0.9%)		

If you are in a dispute over employment taxes with the IRS and you lose, requiring you to pay back taxes and you pay the employee share to avoid adverse employee reaction, you may deduct the employee share as well. The IRS views your payment in this instance as having a valid business reason even though you are not legally obligated to pay the employee share of FICA.

You may also be liable for federal unemployment tax (FUTA) for your employees. The gross federal unemployment tax rate is 6%. This is applied to employee wages up to $7,000, for a maximum FUTA tax of $434 per employee. However, you may claim a credit of up to 5.4% for state unemployment tax that you pay, bringing the maximum FUTA tax to $56 per employee. If your state unemployment tax rate is 5.4% or more, then the net FUTA rate is 0.6%. Even if your state unemployment rate is less than 5.4%, you are permitted to claim a full reduction of 5.4%.

However, if your state has failed to repay funds borrowed from the federal government to cover state unemployment tax benefits, the federal credit for FUTA is reduced. For 2013, employers in 13 states were subject to FUTA tax increases when the Department of Labor named the "credit reduction states." Employers in these states (see Table 13.1) had a reduced credit for state unemployment taxes. Affected employers paid an additional FUTA amount as indicated in Table 13.1. The 0.3% additional FUTA amount translates into $21 per employee earning $7,000 or more. The FUTA tax is fully deductible.

The credit reduction states for 2014 FUTA, which is announced by the Department of Labor in November 2014, will be listed in the Supplement to this book and in the instructions to the 2014 Form 940.

These tax payments are deductible by you as an employer. A complete discussion of employment taxes can be found in Chapter 29.

State Benefit Funds

An employer who pays into a state disability or unemployment insurance fund may deduct the payments as taxes. An employee who must contribute to the following state benefit funds can deduct the payments as state income taxes on Schedule A:

- *Alaska*—State Unemployment Fund
- *California*—Nonoccupational Disability Benefit Fund

- *New Jersey*—Nonoccupational Disability Benefit Fund and State Unemployment Fund
- *New York*—Nonoccupational Disability Benefit Fund
- *Pennsylvania*—State Unemployment Fund
- *Rhode Island*—Temporary Disability Benefit Fund
- *Washington*—Supplemental Workmen's Compensation Trust Fund

The deduction for these taxes is not subject to a 2%-of-adjusted-gross-income floor (see Chapter 1), as is the case with other employee business expenses.

Franchise Taxes

Corporate franchise taxes (which is another term that may be used for state corporate income taxes and has nothing to do with whether the corporation is a franchise) are a deductible business expense. Your state may or may not impose franchise taxes on S corporations, so check with your state corporate tax department.

Excise Taxes

Excise taxes paid or incurred in a trade or business are deductible as operating expenses. For example, indoor tanning salons can deduct the 10% excise tax that they pay on their services. A credit for federal excise tax on certain fuels may be claimed as explained in the following section.

Fuel Taxes

Taxes on gas, diesel fuel, and other motor fuels used in your business are deductible. As a practical matter, they are included in the cost of the fuel and are not separately stated. Thus, they are deducted as a fuel cost rather than as a tax.

However, in certain instances, you may be eligible for a credit for the federal excise tax on certain fuels. The credit applies to fuel used in machinery and off-highway vehicles (such as tractors), and kerosene used for heating, lighting, and cooking on a farm.

You have a choice: claim a tax credit for the federal excise tax or claim a refund of this tax. You can claim a quarterly refund for the first 3 quarters of the year if the refund is $750 or more. If you do not exceed $750 in a quarter, then you can carry over this refund amount to the following quarter and add it to the refund due at that time. But if, after carrying the refund forward to the fourth quarter you do not exceed $750, then you must recoup the excise tax through a tax credit.

Alternatively, if you have pesticides or fertilizers applied aerially, you may waive your right to the credit or refund, allowing the applicator to claim it (something that would reduce your application charges). If you want to waive the credit or refund, you must sign an irrevocable waiver and give a copy of it to the applicator. For further information on this credit, see Chapter 29 and IRS Publication 510, *Excise Taxes*.

Foreign Taxes

Income taxes paid to a foreign country or U.S. possession may be claimed as a deduction or a tax credit. To claim foreign income taxes as a tax credit, you must file Form 1116, *Foreign Tax Credit* (unless as an individual you have foreign tax of $300 or less, or $600 or less on a joint return). Corporations claim the foreign tax credit on Form 1118. The same rules apply for foreign real property taxes paid with respect to real property owned in a foreign country or U.S. possession.

Built-In Gains Tax

If an S corporation pays a built-in gains tax on the sale of certain property (see Chapter 4), the tax it pays is deductible. If the tax is attributable to ordinary gain, then it is deductible as a tax (on page 1 of Form 1120S). If it is attributable to short-term or long-term capital gain, then it is claimed as a short-term or long-term capital loss on Schedule D of Form 1120S.

Other Rules

If a corporation pays a tax imposed on a shareholder and the shareholder does not reimburse the corporation, then the corporation, and not the shareholder, is entitled to claim the deduction for the payment of the tax.

Nondeductible Taxes

You may not deduct federal income taxes, even the amount paid with respect to your business income. These are nondeductible taxes.

Other nondeductible taxes include:

- Assessments on real property for local benefits that tend to add to the value of the property. Such assessments may be made, for example, to build sidewalks, streets, sewers, or parks. These assessments are added to the basis of the property. But assessments for maintenance purposes (such as for repairs to sidewalks, streets, and sewers) are deductible. Water bills, sewage, and other service charges are not treated as taxes. They are, however, deductible as business expenses.
- Employee contributions to private or voluntary disability plans.
- Fines imposed by a governmental authority. These are not deductible as a tax even if incurred in a trade or business. For example, if while traveling away from home on business you receive a fine for a speeding ticket, the fine is not deductible.

- Penalties imposed by the federal government on taxes or for failing to file returns. These are not deductible even though they may be computed with regard to the length of time the taxpayer has failed to comply with a tax law requirement.
- Occupational taxes.

Deductible Interest

General Rules

Interest paid or incurred on debts related to your business generally is fully deductible as business interest. Business interest is deductible without limitation, except when such interest is required to be capitalized. (Remember, for example, that construction period interest and taxes must be capitalized, as explained earlier in this chapter.) There is one main exception to the general deductibility rule for business interest: interest on life insurance policies. (The limits on deducting interest with respect to life insurance policies are discussed in Chapter 22.)

Interest is characterized by how and for what the proceeds of the loan that generated the interest are used. *Personal interest* is nondeductible (except to the extent of qualified home mortgage interest and a limited amount of student loan interest). *Investment interest* is deductible only to the extent of net investment income. Interest characterized as incurred in a passive activity is subject to the passive loss rules. The characterization is not dependent on what type of property—business or personal—was used as collateral for the loan. For example, if you borrow against your personal life insurance policy and use the proceeds to buy equipment for your business, you can deduct the interest as business interest. On the other hand, if you take a bank loan using your corporate stock as collateral, and use the proceeds to invest in the stock market, the interest is characterized as investment interest. Interest on a tax deficiency relating to Schedules C, E, or F is nondeductible personal interest. While the Tax Court had allowed a deduction for this interest, several appellate courts have sided with the IRS in denying a deduction for this interest.

If the proceeds are used for more than one purpose, you must make an allocation based on the use of the loan's proceeds. When you repay a part of the loan, the repayments are treated as repaying the loan in this order:

- Amounts allocated to personal use
- Amounts allocated to investments and passive activities
- Amounts allocated to passive activities in connection with rental real estate in which you actively participate
- Amounts allocated to business use

The interest obligation must be yours in order for you to claim an interest deduction. If you pay off someone else's loan, you cannot deduct the interest you pay. If you are contractually obligated to make the payment, you may be able to deduct your payment as some other expense item, but not as interest.

Note: A current deduction for self-charged interest (interest you effectively charge yourself through multiple business activities) is limited under the passive activity loss rules (see Chapter 4).

Debt Incurred to Buy an Interest in a Business

If you use loan proceeds to buy an interest in a partnership, LLC, or S corporation or to make a contribution to capital, this is treated as a *debt-financed acquisition*. In this case, you must allocate the interest on the loan based on the assets of the pass-through business. The allocation can be based on book value, market value, or the adjusted bases of the assets.

> **Example**
>
> You borrow $25,000 to buy an interest in an S corporation. The S corporation owns $90,000 of equipment and $10,000 of stocks (based on fair market value (FMV)). In this case, 9/10 of the interest on the loan is treated as business interest ($90,000 ÷ $100,000); 1/10 of the interest is treated as investment interest ($10,000 ÷ $100,000).

If you, as an S corporation shareholder, LLC member, or partner, receive proceeds from a debt, you must also allocate the debt proceeds. These are called *debt-financed distributions*. Under a general allocation rule, debt proceeds distributed to an owner of a pass-through entity are allocated to the owner's use of the proceeds. Thus, if the owner uses the proceeds for personal purposes, the pass-through entity must treat the interest as nondeductible personal interest. Under an optional allocation rule, the pass-through entity may allocate the proceeds (and related interest) to one or more of the entity's expenditures other than distributions. The expenditures to which the debt is allocated are those made in the same year as the allocation is made (see IRS Notice 89-35 for allocations in pass-through entities).

If you borrow money to buy stock in a closely held C corporation, the Tax Court considers the interest to be investment interest. The reason: C corporation stock, like any publicly traded stock, is held for investment. This is so even if the corporation never pays out investment income *(dividends)* or the purchase of the stock is made to protect one's employment with the corporation.

Loans between Shareholders and Their Corporations

Special care must be taken when shareholders lend money to their corporation, and vice versa, or when shareholders guarantee third-party loans made to their corporation.

CORPORATION'S INDEBTEDNESS TO SHAREHOLDERS

If a corporation borrows from its shareholders, the corporation can deduct the interest it pays on the loan. The issue sometimes raised by the IRS in these types of loans is whether there is any real indebtedness. Sometimes loans are used in place of dividends to transform nondeductible dividend payments into deductible interest. In order for a loan to withstand IRS scrutiny, be prepared to show a written instrument bearing a fixed maturity date for the repayment of the loan. The instrument should also state a fixed rate of interest. There should be a valid business reason for this borrowing arrangement (such as evidence that the corporation could not borrow from a commercial source at a reasonable rate of interest). If the loan is subordinated to the claims of corporate creditors, this tends to show that it is not a true debt, but other factors may prove otherwise. Also, when a corporation is heavily indebted to shareholders, the debt-to-equity ratio may indicate that the loans are not true loans but are merely disguised equity.

When a corporation fails to repay a loan to a shareholder, this may give rise to a bad debt deduction for the shareholder. Bad debts are discussed in Chapter 11.

SHAREHOLDER GUARANTEES OF CORPORATE DEBT

Often for small businesses, banks or other lenders usually require personal guarantees by the corporation's principal shareholders as a condition for making loans to the corporation. This arrangement raises one of the basic rules for deducting interest discussed earlier: The obligation must be yours in order for you to deduct the interest.

Example

A sole shareholder paid interest on a loan made by a third party to his corporation. He agreed that he would pay any outstanding debt if the corporation failed to do so. He was not entitled to claim an interest deduction because it was the corporation, not he, who was primarily liable on the obligation. The shareholder was only a guarantor.

Below-Market and Above-Market Loans

When shareholders and their corporations arrange loans between themselves, they may set interest rates at less than or more than the going market rate of interest. This may be done for a number of reasons, including to ease the financial burden on a party to the loan or to create tax advantage. Whatever the reason, it is important to understand the consequences of the arrangement.

BELOW-MARKET LOANS

If you receive an interest-free or below-market-interest loan, you may still be able to claim an interest deduction. You can claim an interest deduction equal to the sum of the interest you actually pay, plus the amount of interest that the lender is required to report as income under the below-market loan rules. The amount that the lender is required to report as income is fixed according to interest rates set monthly by the IRS. Different rates apply according to the term of the loan.

- *Short-term* loans run 3 years or less.
- *Mid-term* loans run more than 3 but less than 9 years.
- *Long-term* loans run more than 9 years.

Rates required to be charged in order to avoid imputed interest are called the *applicable federal rates* (AFRs). You can find an index of AFRs by entering "applicable federal rates" in the search box at www.irs.gov. If a loan is payable on demand, the short-term rate applies. However, if the loan is outstanding for an entire year, you can use a blended annual rate (0.28% for 2014) provided by the IRS to simplify the computation of the taxable imputed interest.

Example

On January 1, 2014, you borrowed $40,000 from your corporation for investments. You were not charged any interest by your corporation, and the loan was payable on demand. The AFR for determining interest that the lender must report for 2014 is the blended rate of 0.28% for demand loans outstanding for the entire year. Thus, your interest deduction is $112 (subject to the limitation on deducting investment interest).

Whether you are required to report this amount as income (which would, in effect, offset the interest deduction) depends on the amount of the loan and the context in which it was made. If it was treated as compensation or a dividend, you have to include it in income; if it was considered a gift loan, you do not have additional income. Gift loans are loans up to $10,000 (as long as the loan is not made for tax avoidance purposes). The corporation (lender) must report the interest as income. If the loan is to an employee, an offsetting deduction can be taken for compensation. But if the loan is to a nonemployee, such as a shareholder who does not work for the corporation, no offsetting deduction can be taken.

ABOVE-MARKET LOANS

Instead of borrowing from a bank, your corporation may be able to borrow from a relative of yours, such as your child or parent, to whom you want to make gifts. You can turn the arrangement into a profitable one for both your corporation and your relative (the lender). Set the interest rate at more than what would be charged by the bank. Provided that the interest is still considered "reasonable" and the loan is an arm's-length transaction, your corporation deducts the interest, and the lender receives it. If an unreasonably high rate of interest is charged and the arrangement is not at arm's length, however, the IRS will attack the arrangement and may disallow the interest as being a disguised dividend payment to you.

Home Mortgage Interest and Home Offices

If you are self-employed, use a portion of your home for business, and claim a home office deduction under the actual expense method (explained in Chapter 18), you must allocate the home mortgage interest. The portion of the interest on the mortgage allocated to the business use is deducted on Form 8829, *Expenses for Business Use of Your Home*. The balance is treated as personal mortgage interest deductible as an itemized expense on Schedule A.

Nondeductible Interest and Other Limitations on Deductibility

If you borrow additional funds from the same lender to pay off a first loan for business, you cannot claim an interest deduction. Once you begin paying off the new loan, you can deduct interest on both the old and new loans. Payments are treated as being applied to the old loan first and then to the new loan. All interest payments are then deductible.

As in the case of taxes, if interest is paid to acquire a capital asset for resale, you must capitalize the interest expense. The interest is recovered when the asset is sold.

Commitment Fees

Fees paid to have business funds available for drawing on a standby basis are not treated as deductible interest payments. They may, however, be deductible as business expenses. Fees paid to obtain a loan may be treated as deductible interest. However, the fees are not immediately deductible; rather, they are deductible only over the term of the loan. If the loan falls through, the fees can be deducted as a loss.

Similarly, points paid to acquire a loan on business property are treated as prepaid interest. They are not currently deductible as such. Instead, they are deductible over the term of the loan.

Example

Your business pays a $200 commitment fee for a $10,000 loan with a 10-year term. Each year the business may deduct $20 ($200 divided by 10 years).

If you pay off the loan before the end of the term (before you have fully deducted the prepaid interest), you can deduct the remaining balance of prepaid interest in the final year of payment.

Interest Paid on Income Tax Deficiencies

If you pay interest on a tax deficiency arising from business income from your sole proprietorship, S corporation, partnership, or LLC, you cannot deduct the interest on your individual return. This interest is treated as nondeductible personal interest even though business income generated the deficiency.

While a C corporation can deduct interest it pays on any tax deficiency, it cannot deduct tax penalties. This rule applies to both civil and criminal penalties. Amounts assessed for the delay of filing a return are considered penalties. Thus, estimated tax penalties, which are imposed because of a delay in payment, are not deductible even though they are calculated by application of an interest rate. Similarly, amounts owing because of the failure to deposit employment taxes are treated as penalties. Additions to tax contained in sections 6651 through 6658 of the Internal Revenue Code are considered penalties.

Interest Related to Tax-Exempt Income

No deduction is allowed for interest paid or incurred to buy or carry tax-exempt securities.

Where to Deduct Taxes and Interest

Employees

Taxes and interest are deductible only as miscellaneous business expenses reported on Schedule A and subject to the 2%-of-AGI rule and the itemized deduction reduction for high-income taxpayers explained in Chapter 1. However, employees can elect to claim a credit on foreign taxes.

Self-Employed

Taxes and interest are deducted on Schedule C (or Schedule F in the case of farming operations). This form provides separate space for claiming deductions for mortgage interest and for other interest. It also provides a specific line for claiming a deduction for taxes and licenses.

Instead of deducting foreign taxes on Schedule C (or Schedule F), a sole proprietor may choose to claim a foreign tax credit. If foreign taxes are $300 or less (or $600 or less if the self-employed person files a joint return) and result from passive income, an election can be made to claim the credit directly on Form 1040. Otherwise, the credit must be figured on Form 1116, *Foreign Tax Credit*.

Partnerships and LLCs

In general, partnerships and LLCs deduct taxes and interest on Form 1065. Separate lines are provided for deducting interest, taxes, and licenses. These items are part of the business's operating expenses and figure into its income or loss passed through to partners or LLC members on Schedule K-1 and then reported on the owner's Schedule E. These items are not separately reported to partners or LLC members on Schedule K-1 for special treatment on an owner's individual income tax return.

However, interest that may be classified as investment interest is separately stated in Schedule K-1, since it is subject to an investment interest limitation on the partner's or member's individual income tax return.

Also, foreign taxes are separately stated items on Schedule K-1 to allow the owner to decide whether to take a deduction or credit on his or her individual return. Partners and LLC members treat foreign taxes in the same manner as self-employed individuals.

S Corporations

In general, the S corporation deducts taxes and interest on Form 1120S. Separate lines are provided for deducting interest, taxes, and licenses. These items are part of the business's operating expenses and figure into its income or loss passed through to shareholders on Schedule K-1 and then reported on the owner's Schedule E. These items are not separately reported to shareholders on Schedule K-1 for special treatment on an owner's individual income tax return.

However, interest that may be classified as investment interest is separately stated in Schedule K-1, since it is subject to an investment interest limitation on the shareholder's individual income tax return.

Also, foreign taxes are separately stated items on Schedule K-1 to allow the shareholder to decide whether to take a deduction or credit on his or her individual return. S corporation shareholders treat foreign taxes in the same manner as self-employed individuals.

C Corporations

C corporations deduct taxes and interest on Form 1120. Separate lines are provided for deducting interest, taxes, and licenses.

The foreign tax credit is figured on Form 1118, *Foreign Tax Credit—Corporations*.

CHAPTER 14

First-Year Expensing, Depreciation, Amortization, and Depletion

Alert

At the time this book was printed, Congress had not extended numerous breaks for 2014 that had expired at the end of 2013. Check the online supplement in February 2015 at www.jklasser.com or www.barbaraweltman.com to see whether these breaks apply for 2014 returns.

*F*irst-year expensing, which is also called the Section 179 deduction after the section in the Tax Code that creates it, is a write-off allowed for the purchase of equipment used in your business. This deduction takes the place of depreciation—the amount expensed is not depreciated. For example, if you buy a used computer for your business for $2,500, you can opt to deduct its cost in full in the year you place the computer into service. If you don't make this election, you must write off the cost over a number of years fixed by law.

Depreciation is an allowance for a portion of the cost of equipment or other property owned by you and used in your business. Depreciation is claimed over the life of the property, although it may be accelerated, with a greater amount claimed in the early years of ownership. The thinking behind depreciation is that equipment wears out. In theory, if you were to put into a separate fund the amount you claim each year as a depreciation allowance, when your equipment reaches the end of its usefulness, you will have sufficient funds to buy a replacement (of course, the replacement may not cost the same as the old equipment). To claim a depreciation deduction, you do not necessarily have to spend any money. If you have already bought equipment, future depreciation deductions do not require any additional out-of-pocket expenditures. For 2013, there was a special depreciation allowance called *bonus depreciation*; it could be extended for 2014 (see the Supplement).

Amortization is conceptually similar to depreciation. It is an allowance for the cost of certain capital expenditures, such as goodwill and trademarks, acquired in the purchase of a business. Amortization can be claimed only if it is specifically allowed by the tax law. It is always deducted ratably over the life of the property. As you will see, amortization is also allowed as an election for some types of expenditures that would otherwise not be deductible.

Depletion is a deduction allowed for certain natural resources. The tax law carefully controls the limits of this deduction.

For a further discussion of depreciation, amortization, and depletion, see IRS Publication 946, *How to Depreciate Property*.

First-Year Expensing

Instead of depreciating the cost of tangible personal property over a number of years, you may be able to write off the entire cost in the first year. This is *first-year expensing* or a *Section 179 deduction* (named after the section in the Internal Revenue Code that governs the deduction). A first-year expense deduction may be claimed whether you pay for the item with cash or credit. If you buy the item on credit, the first-year expense deduction can be used to enhance your cash flow position (you claim an immediate tax deduction but pay for the item over time).

> **NOTE**
> The rules covered in this chapter are exclusively federal income tax rules. States may have very different rules for expensing, depreciation, amortization, and depletion, so check with the applicable state tax department for state income tax rules.

You can elect to deduct up to a set dollar amount of the cost of tangible personal property used in your business. In 2014, you can deduct up to $500,000 (and more in certain economically distressed communities) if the 2013 limit is extended for 2014. Otherwise, the limit is $25,000; see the Supplement for details.

The property must be acquired by purchase. If you inherit property, for example, and use it in your business, you cannot claim a first-year expense deduction.

If you acquire property in whole or in part by means of a trade, you cannot claim a first-year expense deduction for the portion of the property acquired by trade.

Example

You buy a new car that is used 100% for business. You pay cash and trade in your old car. You cannot compute the first-year expense deduction for the portion of the new car's basis that includes the adjusted basis of the car you traded in.

First-year expensing may be claimed for property that has been pre-owned (i.e., used property), as long as the property is new to you (and you acquire it by purchase).

If you buy property on credit, you can still use the first-year expense deduction even though you are not yet out of pocket for the purchase price. A purchase on credit that entitles you to a first-year expense deduction is a strategy for aiding your cash flow (i.e., you gain a tax deduction even though you have not expended the cash).

The property must have been acquired for business. If you buy property for personal purposes and later convert it to business use, you cannot claim a first-year expense deduction. If you are an employee, be prepared to show the property you expense was acquired for business (not personal) purposes. In one case, a sales manager was allowed to expense the cost of a home computer where she convinced the Tax Court that its use was entirely for her job. She had a heavy workload, she could access company information via her modem, and she was not allowed entry to her office after business hours.

Off-the-shelf computer software is eligible for expensing. (In the past its cost had to be amortized over a period of up to 36 months.) It also applies within limits to certain leasehold improvements (see Chapter 12).

Generally, the first-year expense deduction does not apply to property you buy and then lease to others. (There is no restriction on leased property by corporations.) However, a first-year expense deduction is allowed for leased property you manufactured and leased if the term of the lease is less than half of the property's class life and, for the first 12 months the property is transferred to the lessee, and the total business deductions for the property are more than 15% of the rental income for the property.

Limits on First-Year Expensing

Three limits apply for first-year expensing: a *dollar limit*, an *investment limit*, and a *taxable income limit*.

DOLLAR LIMIT

You cannot deduct more than the applicable dollar amount in any one year. The dollar limit for 2014 is $500,000 if the 2013 limit is extended, or $25,000 if it is not extended (see the Supplement for details). A higher limit may apply in certain designated areas if the special rules for empowerment zones are also extended.

If an individual owns more than one business, he or she must aggregate first-year expense deductions from all businesses and deduct no more than a total of $500,000 if the 2013 limit is extended to 2014, or $25,000 if it is not extended. Married persons are treated as one taxpayer and are allowed a single dollar limit. However, if they file separate returns, each can claim only one half of the dollar limit.

> **NOTE**
> A special dollar limit for cars used in business supersedes the first-year expense deduction limit. (See Chapters 7 and 9 for more details on deducting the costs of business cars.) No first-year expense deduction can be claimed for listed property unless it is used more than 50% for business.

INVESTMENT LIMIT

The first-year expense deduction is really designed for small businesses. This is because every dollar of investments in equipment over $2 million if the 2013 limit is extended to 2014, or $200,000 if it is not extended, reduces the dollar limit.

> **Example**
>
> Assuming that the 2013 limit is extended to 2014, then if in 2014 you buy equipment costing $2,300,000. Your first-year expense deduction is limited to $200,000 ($500,000 − [$2,300,000 − $2,000,000]).

If a business buys equipment costing $2.5 million if the 2013 limit is extended to 2014, or $225,000 if it is not extended, the deduction limit is fully phased out, so no first-year expense deduction is allowed.

TAXABLE INCOME LIMIT

The total first-year expense deduction cannot exceed taxable income from the active conduct of a business. You are treated as actively conducting a business if you participate in a meaningful way in the management or operations of a business.

Taxable income for purposes of this limit has a special meaning. Start with your net income (or loss) from all businesses that you actively conduct. If you are married and file jointly, add your spouse's net income (or loss). This includes certain gains and losses, called Section 1231 gains and losses (see Chapter 6), and interest from working capital in your business. It also includes salary, wages, and other compensation earned as an employee, so even though a moonlighting business that bought the equipment has little or no income, you may still be eligible for a full first-year expense deduction if your salary from your day job is sufficient. Figure taxable income without regard to the expensing deduction, the deduction for the employer portion of self-employment tax, any net operating loss carryback or carryforward, and any unreimbursed employee business expenses. This, then, is your taxable income for purposes of the taxable income limitation. If your taxable income limits your deduction, any unused deduction can be carried forward and used in a future year.

Example

Your taxable income in 2014 (without regard to a first-year expense deduction) is $12,000. You place in service in 2014 a machine costing $14,000. Your first-year expense deduction is limited to $12,000. You can carry forward the additional $2,000 to 2015.

Carryforwards of unused first-year expense deductions can be used if there is sufficient taxable income in the next year. You can choose the properties for which the costs will be carried forward. You can allocate the portion of the costs to these properties as long as the allocation is reflected on your books and records.

Special Rules for Pass-Through Entities

The dollar limit, investment limit, and taxable income limit apply at both the entity and owner levels. This means that partnerships, as well as their partners, and S corporations, as well as their shareholders, must apply all the limits. The same is true for LLCs and members.

Example

Assume that the 2013 limit is extended to 2014 and that you are a 50% shareholder in an S corporation that claims a first-year expense deduction in 2014 of $500,000. Your allocable share as reported on your Schedule K-1 is $250,000. You also own a business that you run as a sole proprietor. You place in service a machine costing $340,000. (Assume sufficient taxable income by the S corporation and for your sole proprietorship.) Your first-year expense deduction for this machine is limited to $250,000. The balance of the cost of the machine, $90,000, cannot be expensed in the current year because of the dollar limit.

For fiscal-year entities, the dollar limit in effect at the start of their fiscal year applies. For owners of fiscal-year pass-through entities, the dollar limit at the owner level applies at the start of the owner's tax year.

Should the First-Year Expensing Election Be Made?

You don't automatically claim this deduction; you must elect it on Form 4562. While first-year expensing provides a great opportunity for matching your tax write-off with your cash outlay, it is not always advisable to take advantage of this opportunity. Consider forgoing the election in the following situations:

- You receive the write-off through a pass-through entity but could claim it for purchases made through a sole proprietorship (see the preceding example).

- You are in a low tax bracket this year but expect to be more profitable in the coming years so that depreciation deductions in those years will be more valuable.

- You want to report income to obtain credits for Social Security benefits.

- You are not profitable this year. The first-year expensing deduction cannot be used to create or increase a net operating loss. **Note:** The first-year expensing election on a federal income tax return does not automatically provide the same tax break for state income tax purposes. Some states restrict this deduction.

Making or Revoking an Expensing Election

Usually a first-year expensing election must be made on an original tax return for the year to which the election applies. Revocation can be made only with IRS consent, which will be granted only in extraordinary circumstances. However, for 2003 through 2013 or later if the rule is extended, you can make or revoke an election to use expensing without obtaining IRS permission. The change is made on an amended return that must specify the item and portion of its cost for which an election is being made or revoked. You have until the time limit for filing an amended return (e.g., April 15, 2018, for a 2014 return filed on April 15, 2015, if this rule is extended for 2014).

Dispositions of First-Year Expense Property

If you sell or otherwise dispose of property for which a first-year expense deduction was claimed, or cease using the property for business, there may be recapture of your deduction. This means that you must include in your income a portion of the deduction you previously claimed. The amount you must recapture depends on when you dispose of the property. The longer you hold it, the less recapture you have. If you sell property at a gain, recapture is not additional income; it is merely a reclassification of income. If you realize gain on the sale of first-year expense property, instead of treating the gain as capital gain, the recapture amount is characterized as ordinary income.

Example

In 2011, you placed in service office furniture (7-year property) costing $10,000, which you fully expensed. In 2014, you used the property only 40% for business (and 60% for personal purposes). You calculate your recapture as shown in Table 14.1.

Recapture is calculated by comparing your first-year expense deduction with the deduction you would have claimed had you instead taken ordinary depreciation.

If you transfer first-year expense property in a transaction that does not require recognition of gain or loss (e.g., if you make a tax-free exchange or contribute the property to a corporation in a tax-free incorporation), an adjustment is made in the basis of the property. The adjusted basis of the property is increased before the disposition by the amount of the first-year expense deduction that is disallowed. The new owner cannot claim a first-year expense deduction with respect to this disallowed portion.

Other Expensing Opportunities

In addition to first-year expensing, the tax law is peppered with provisions that let businesses expense certain types of expenditures instead of amortizing them or treating them simply as a capital cost. Some of these provisions have broad application, while many of them are limited to specific industries.

Film or Television Productions

Small production companies were able to take an immediate write-off of their costs in 2013; this rule may be extended for 2014, so the information is provided accordingly. You can elect to deduct up to $15 million in production costs of a qualified film or television production. A qualified production is one in which total costs do not exceed $15 million. However, under an exception, the dollar limit increases to $20 million for production costs incurred in certain economically depressed areas.

TABLE 14.1 Calculating Recapture

First-Year Expense Deduction		$10,000
Allowable Depreciation		
$10,000 × 14.29%*	$1,429	
10,000 × 24.49	2,449	
10,000 × 17.49	1,749	
10,000 × 12.49 × 40%	500	$6,127
Recapture amount		3,873

*MACRS percentages from Table 14.2.

OTHER EXPENSING OPPORTUNITIES

- Acquired intangibles (later in this chapter)
- Business start-up costs (later in this chapter)
- Corporate organizational expenses (later in this chapter)
- EPA sulfur regulation costs (Chapter 10)
- Expenditures to remove architectural barriers to the elderly and the handicapped (Chapter 10)
- Fertilizer used by farmers (Chapter 20)
- Partnership organizational expenses (later in this chapter)
- Qualified disaster costs (later in this chapter)
- Reforestation expenses (Chapter 20)

General Rules for Depreciation

Depreciable Property

Depreciation is a deduction allowed for certain property used in your business. It is designed to offset the cost of acquiring it, so you cannot depreciate leased property. To be depreciable, the property must be the kind that wears out, decays, gets used up, becomes obsolete, or loses value from natural causes. The property must have a determinable useful life that is longer than one year.

As a practical matter, computations for depreciation are made by computer once the necessary information, such as basis, date of acquisition, and the applicability of any special depreciation rules, are entered in the tax preparation program. However, because depreciation is deduction that extends beyond the current tax year, it is necessary to keep track of depreciation deductions each year (again, something that is done automatically by tax preparation programs).

If you convert personal property to business use (explained later in this chapter), the basis for purposes of depreciation is the lower of its adjusted basis (generally cost) or fair market value at the time of the conversion to business use. If you acquire replacement property in a like-kind exchange or an involuntary conversion, special rules govern basis for purposes of depreciation (see IRS Publication 946, *How to Depreciate Property*).

Example

In 2014, you begin to use a personal computer for a business you have just started up. You paid $2,500 for it in 2012, and it is now worth $1,200. Your basis for depreciation is $1,200. At the same time, you begin to use one room in your home as a home office. You bought your home in 2006 for $200,000, and it is now worth $300,000 (exclusive of land). Assuming that the home office allocation is 12.5% of the home, your basis for depreciation (if you use the actual expense method to figure the home office deduction) is $25,000 (12.5% of $200,000, which is lower than 12.5% of $300,000, or $37,500).

Property that can be expected to last for one year or less is simply deducted in full as some other type of deduction. For example, if you buy stationery that will be used up within the year, you simply deduct the cost of the stationery as supplies. In order to claim depreciation, you must be the owner of the property. If you lease property, like an office, you cannot depreciate it; only the owner can, since it is the owner who suffers the wear and tear on his or her investment.

Depreciable property may be tangible or intangible. *Tangible property* is property you can touch—office furniture, a machine, or a telephone. Tangible property may be personal property (a machine) or real property (a factory). *Intangible property* is property you cannot touch, such as copyrights, patents, and franchises. *Personal property* does not mean you use the property for personal purposes; it is a legal term for tangible property that is not real property.

If you use property for both business and personal purposes, you must make an allocation. You can claim depreciation only on the business portion of the property. For example, if you use your car 75% for business and 25% for personal purposes (including commuting), you can claim depreciation on only 75% of the property. However, special rules apply to a building that is used partly for residential rental and partly for commercial purposes (see later in this chapter).

Certain Property Can Never Be Depreciated

- *Antiques* generally cannot be depreciated because they do not have a determinable useful life; they can be expected to last indefinitely. The same is true for goodwill you build up in your business (though if you buy a business and pay for its goodwill, you may be able to amortize the cost, as explained later in this chapter).

- *Inventory* is property held primarily for sale to customers in the ordinary course of your business. Sometimes you may question whether an asset is really part of your inventory or if it is a separate asset that can be depreciated. For example, containers generally are treated as part of the cost of your inventory and cannot be separately depreciated. However, containers used to ship products can be depreciated if your invoice treats them as separate items, whether your sales contract shows that you retain title to the containers and whether your records properly state your basis in the containers.

- *Land* is not depreciable because it, too, can be expected to last indefinitely. Land includes not only the cost of the acreage but also the cost of clearing, grading, planting, and landscaping. However, some land preparation costs can be depreciated if they are closely associated with a building on the land rather than the land itself. For example, shrubs around the entry to a building may be depreciated; trees planted on the perimeter of the property are nondepreciable land costs. Also, the cost of the minerals on the land may not be depreciated but may be subject to depletion.

When you own a building, you must allocate the *basis* of the property between the building and the land, since only the building portion is depreciable.

There is no special rule for making an allocation of basis. Obviously you would prefer to allocate as much as possible to the building and as little as possible to the land. However, the allocation must have some logical basis. It should be based on the relative value of each portion. What is the land worth? What is the building worth? You may want to use the services of an appraiser to help you derive a fair yet favorable allocation that will withstand IRS scrutiny.

Basis   Generally, basis is the amount you pay for property. It does not matter whether you finance your purchase or pay cash. You add to basis sales taxes and other related expenses (such as nondeductible closing costs if you get a mortgage, or attorney's fees). But you cannot include the value of trade-ins in your basis. You need records to prove basis and cannot merely estimate it.

When to Claim Depreciation

You claim depreciation beginning with the year in which the property is *placed in service*. You continue to claim depreciation throughout the life of the asset. The life of the asset is also called its *recovery period*. Different types of assets have different recovery periods. The length of the recovery period has nothing to do with how durable a particular item may be. You simply check the classifications of property to find the recovery period for a particular item.

Placed in service   When an item is ready and available for a specific use, whether or not the item is actually used.

You stop claiming depreciation on the item when the property's cost has been fully depreciated or when the property is retired from service. Property is retired from service when it is permanently withdrawn from use, by disposing of it (selling or exchanging it, abandoning it, or destroying it).

Example

A machine with a 5-year recovery period is no longer needed after 3 years for the task for which it was purchased. The machine is sold to another company that still has a use for it. Once the machine is sold, it has been permanently removed from your service. You cannot claim depreciation after this occurs.

When you replace a roof or other building component, this is not viewed as a disposition. Thus, you continue to take the same depreciation allowance as you had prior to the replacement.

The amount of depreciation you can claim in the year in which property is placed in service or retired from service is limited and is discussed later in this chapter.

Even if you do not actually claim depreciation, you are treated as having done so for purposes of figuring the basis of property when you dispose of it.

If you failed to claim depreciation in the past, file an amended return to fix the error if the tax year is still open (the statute of limitations on amending the return has not expired). Alternatively, you can correct the underdepreciation (even for a closed tax year) by filing for a change in accounting method on Form 3115 (follow filing instructions to Form 3115). Under a special IRS procedure, you simply adjust your income in the current year. Be sure to write on Form 3115 "Automatic Method Change under Rev. Proc. 98-60."

Example

You place a piece of machinery in service in 2013 and claim a depreciation deduction on your 2012 return. In 2013, your revenues are low, and you forget to report your depreciation deduction on your 2013 return. In 2014, you sell the machine. In calculating gain or loss on the sale, you must adjust basis for the depreciation you actually claimed in 2012 and the depreciation you should have claimed in 2013.

If you abandon property before it has been fully depreciated, you can deduct the balance of your depreciation deductions in the year of abandonment. For instance, if you have a machine with a 7-year recovery period that you abandon in the fifth year because it is obsolete, you can claim the depreciation that you would have claimed in the sixth, seventh, and eighth years in the fifth year along with depreciation allowable for that year.

Modified Accelerated Cost Recovery System

Modified Accelerated Cost Recovery System (MACRS) is a depreciation system that went into effect for tangible property placed in service after 1986. It is composed of 2 systems: a basic system, called the *General Depreciation System* (GDS), and an alternate system, called the *Alternative Depreciation System* (ADS). The difference between the 2 systems is the recovery period over which you claim depreciation and the method for calculating depreciation. You use the basic system unless the alternative system is required or you make a special election to use the alternative system. You cannot use either system for certain property: intangible property (patents, copyrights, etc.), motion picture films or videotapes, sound recordings, and property you elect to exclude from MACRS so that you can use a depreciation method based on some other measuring rod than a term of years (these other methods are not discussed in this book).

Basic System

You can use the basic system (GDS) to depreciate any tangible property unless you are required to use the alternative system, elect to use the alternate system, or are required to use some other depreciation method. To calculate your depreciation deduction, you need to know:

- *The property's basis.* If you purchase property, basis is your cost. If you acquire property in some other way (get it by gift, inheritance, or in a tax-free exchange), basis is figured in another way. For example, if your corporation acquires property from you upon its formation in a tax-free incorporation, then the corporation steps into your shoes for purposes of basis.

Example

You form a corporation (C or S) and contribute cash and a computer. In exchange, you receive all of the stock of the corporation. Your basis for the computer was $4,000. The corporation assumes your basis—$4,000.

A similar rule applies to property you contribute to a partnership or LLC upon its formation. If you are a sole proprietor or an employee and convert property from personal use to business use, your basis for depreciation is the lesser of the fair market value (FMV) on the date of conversion to business use or the adjusted basis of the property on that date.

The cost of property includes sales taxes. If you hire an architect to design a building, the fees are added to the basis of the property and recovered through depreciation. The following are more items to consider when calculating your depreciation deduction.

- *The property's recovery period.* Recovery periods are fixed according to the claim in which a property falls. In the past, recovery period was referred to as the useful life of the property, and you may occasionally see this old phrase still in use.
- *The date the property is placed in service.* Remember, this is the date the property is ready and available for its specific use.
- *The applicable convention.* These are special rules that govern the timing of deductions (explained later in this chapter).
- *The depreciation method.* MACRS has 5 different depreciation methods.

Recovery Periods

The class assigned to a property is designed to match the period over which the basis of property is recovered (e.g., cost is deducted). Five-year property allows the cost of certain equipment to be deducted over 5 years (subject to adjustment for conventions discussed later).

3-YEAR PROPERTY

This property includes taxis, tractor units for use over the road, racehorses more than 2 years old when placed in service (any age after 2008 and before 2014 or later if the 2013 rule is extended), any other horse over 12 years old when placed in service, breeding hogs, certain handling devices for manufacturing food and beverages, and special tools for manufacturing rubber products. Special rules for computer software are discussed under "Amortization" later in this chapter.

5-YEAR PROPERTY

This property includes cars, buses, trucks, airplanes, trailers and trailer containers, computers and peripheral equipment, some office machinery (calculators, copiers, typewriters), assets used in construction, logging equipment, assets used to manufacture organic and inorganic chemicals, and property used in research and experimentation. It also includes breeding and dairy cattle and breeding and dairy goats.

7-YEAR PROPERTY

This property includes office fixtures and furniture (chairs, desks, files); communications equipment (fax machines); breeding and workhorses; assets used in printing; recreational assets (miniature golf courses, billiard establishments, concert halls); assets used to produce jewelry; musical instruments; toys; sporting goods; motorsports entertainment complexes; and motion picture and television films and tapes. This class is also the catchall for other property. It includes any property not assigned to another class.

10-YEAR PROPERTY

This property includes barges, tugs, vessels, and similar water transportation equipment; single-purpose agricultural or horticultural structures placed in service after 1988; and trees or vines bearing fruits or nuts.

15-YEAR PROPERTY

This property includes certain depreciable improvements made to land (bridges, fences, roads, shrubbery).

20-YEAR PROPERTY

This property includes farm buildings (other than single-purpose agricultural or horticultural structures) and any municipal sewers.

RESIDENTIAL RENTAL REALTY

Rental buildings qualify if 80% or more of the gross rental is from dwelling units. The recovery period is 27.5 years.

Some buildings are used partly for residential rentals and partly for commercial activities, such as retail stores. The IRS has ruled privately that if at least 80% of the gross rental income from a mixed-use building is from residential rentals, then the entire building is treated as residential realty depreciated over 27.5 years. The residential rental space includes income from a parking garage. The IRS ruled privately that a house used to operate an adult home care business is treated as residential realty depreciable over 27.5 years.

NONRESIDENTIAL REALTY

This class applies to factories, office buildings, and any other realty other than residential rental realty. The recovery period is 39 years (31.5 years for property placed in service before May 13, 1993). If you begin to use a portion of your home for business (e.g., a home office), use the recovery period applicable on the date of conversion. For example, if you begin to use a home office in your single-family house in 2014 (and use the actual expense method to figure the home office deduction), depreciate that portion of your home using a 39-year recovery period (assuming you use the actual expense method for the home office deduction), even if you bought your home in 1993.

COMPONENTS OF REALTY

Structural components of a building are part and parcel of the realty and generally must be depreciated as such (e.g., over 39 years). However, certain components, such as electrical systems and wiring, carpeting, floor covering, plumbing connections, exhaust systems, handrails, room partitions, tile ceilings, and steam boilers, can be treated as tangible personal property instead of realty. As such, they can be depreciated over shorter recovery periods rather than being treated as part of realty subject to longer recovery periods.

Example

You install a fake floor to cover wiring needed for your computers. The IRS originally said that the floor can be depreciated as personal property over 5 years rather than as part of the realty depreciated over 39 years. However, it later said it would take another look at this conclusion, so beware.

IMPROVEMENTS OR ADDITIONS

In general, improvements or additions to property are treated as separate property and are depreciated separately from the property itself. The recovery period for improvements begins on the later of the date the improvements are placed in service or the date the property to which the improvements are made is placed in service. Use the same recovery period for the improvements that you would for the underlying property (unless an improvement is a component of realty that can be depreciated according to its own recovery period).

COST SEGREGATION

Obtain a cost segregation (or component of cost) study when buying, building, or improving realty. This analysis can be the basis for allocating costs to components that will be separately depreciated over shorter recovery periods for greater upfront deductions. Cost segregation does not apply to components that are part of the operation and maintenance of the building. The analysis should be performed by an engineer, architect, or realty appraiser and not by you or your accountant (unless skilled in cost segregation).

The IRS has created a cost segregation audit technique guide at www.irs.gov (search for "cost segregation audit technique guide"), which details the requirements for an acceptable study.

PROPERTY ACQUIRED IN A LIKE-KIND EXCHANGE

The property acquired in a like-kind exchange is depreciated over the remaining recovery period of the *old* property. Thus, the new property, which has the basis of the old property, also has the old property's remaining recovery period. This enables you to write off the newly acquired asset more rapidly than if the recovery period of the new asset were used.

Conventions

There are 3 conventions that affect the timing of depreciation deductions. Two apply to property other than residential or nonresidential real property (essentially personal property such as equipment); the other applies to residential or nonresidential real property (rental units, offices, and factories).

HALF-YEAR CONVENTION

The *half-year convention* applies to all property (other than residential or nonresidential real property) unless superseded by the mid-quarter convention (explained next). Under the half-year convention, property is treated as if you placed it in service in the middle of the year. You are allowed to deduct only one-half of the depreciation allowance for the first year. This is so even if you place the property in service on the first day of the year. Under this convention, property is treated as disposed of in the middle of the year, regardless of the actual date of disposition.

The half-year convention means that property held for its entire recovery period will have an additional year for claiming depreciation deductions. Only one-half of the first year's depreciation deduction is claimed in the first year;

the balance of depreciation is claimed in the year following the last year of the recovery period.

Example

A desk (7-year property) is placed in service on January 1, 2014. Without regard to expensing, 1/2 of the depreciation deduction that would otherwise be claimed in the first year is allowed. Normal depreciation is claimed in years 2 through 7. The remaining depreciation is claimed in the eighth year.

MID-QUARTER CONVENTION

Under the *mid-quarter convention*, all property placed in service during the year (or disposed of during the year) is treated as placed in service (or disposed of) in the middle of the applicable quarter. The mid-quarter convention applies (and the half-year convention does not) if the total bases of all property placed in service during the last 3 months of the year (the final quarter) exceed 40% of the total bases of property placed in service during the entire year. In making this determination, do not take into consideration residential or nonresidential real property or property placed in service and then disposed of in the same year.

Example

You are on a calendar year. In January 2014, you place in service machine A, costing $3,000. In November 2014, you place in service another machine, machine B, costing $10,000. (Assume neither machine qualifies for bonus depreciation.) You must use the mid-quarter convention to calculate depreciation for both machines. This is because more than 40% of all property placed in service during the year ($13,000) was placed in service in the final quarter of the year ($10,000). (Actually, 77% of all property placed in service in the year was placed in service in the final quarter of the year.)

Example

Continue with the same machine situation, except that machine B is placed in service in January and machine A is placed in service in November. In this instance, the mid-quarter convention does not apply because only 23% of all property placed in service in 2014 was placed in service in the final quarter of the year.

MID-MONTH CONVENTION

This convention applies to real property. You must treat all real property as if it were placed in service or disposed of in the middle of the month. The mid-month convention is taken into account in the depreciation tables from which you can take your deduction. Simply look at the table for the type of realty (residential or nonresidential) you own, and then look in the table for the month in which the property is placed in service.

Depreciation Methods

There are 5 ways to depreciate property: the 200% declining balance rate, the 150% declining balance rate, the straight-line election, the 150% election, and the ADS method. Both 200% and 150% declining balance rates are referred to as accelerated rates.

You may use the 200% rate for 3-, 5-, 7-, and 10-year property over the GDS recovery period. The half-year or mid-quarter convention must be applied. The 200% declining balance method is calculated by dividing 100 by the recovery period and then doubling it. However, as a practical matter, you do not have to compute the rates. They are provided for you in Tables 14.2 and 14.3, which take into account the half-year or mid-quarter conventions.

If the 200% declining balance rate is used, you can switch to the straight line in the year when it provides a deduction of value equal to or greater than the accelerated rate. Of course, total depreciation can never be more than 100% of the property's basis. The switch to straight line merely accelerates the timing of depreciation (the total depreciation is, of course, limited to the basis of the property). Table 14.4 shows you when it becomes advantageous to switch to the straight-line rate.

You use the 150% rate for 15- and 20-year property over the GDS recovery period. Again, you must also apply the half-year or mid-quarter convention. You

TABLE 14.2 MACRS Rates—Half-Year Convention

Year	3-Year Property	5-Year Property	7-Year Property
1	33.33%	20.00%	14.29%
2	44.45	32.00	24.49
3	14.81	19.20	17.49
4	7.81	11.52	12.49
5		11.52	8.93
6		5.76	8.92
7			8.93
8			4.46

TABLE 14.3 MACRS Rates—Mid-Quarter Convention (200% Rate)

Year	First Quarter	Second Quarter	Third Quarter	Fourth Quarter
3-Year Property				
1	58.33%	41.67%	25.00%	8.33%
2	27.78	38.89	50.00	61.11
3	12.35	14.14	16.677	20.37
4	1.54	5.30	8.33	10.19
5-Year Property				
1	35.00	25.00	15.00	5.00
2	26.00	30.00	34.00	38.00
3	15.60	18.00	20.40	22.80
4	11.01	11.37	12.24	13.68
5	11.01	11.37	11.30	10.94
6	1.38	4.26	7.06	9.58
7-Year Property				
1	25.00	17.85	10.71	3.57
2	21.43	23.47	25.51	27.55
3	15.31	16.76	18.22	19.68
4	10.93	11.97	13.02	14.06
5	8.75	8.87	9.30	10.04
6	8.74	8.87	8.85	8.73
7	8.75	8.87	8.86	8.73
8	1.09	3.33	5.53	7.64

TABLE 14.4 When to Change to Straight-Line Method

Class	Changeover Year
3-year property	3rd
5-year property	4th
7-year property	5th
10-year property	7th
15-year property	7th
20-year property	9th

TABLE 14.5 Rates for Residential Realty Years (27 Years), Straight-Line, Mid-Month Convention

	Month in the First Recovery Year the Property Is Placed in Service					
Year	1	2	3	4	5	6
1	3.485%	3.182%	2.879%	2.576%	2.273%	1.970%
2–9	3.636	3.636	3.636	3.636	3.636	3.636
Year	7	8	9	10	11	12
1	1.677%	1.364%	1.061%	0.758%	0.455%	0.152%
2–9	3.636	3.636	3.636	3.636	3.636	3.636

change over to the straight-line method when it provides a greater deduction. Tables for this rate may be found in IRS Publication 946, *How to Depreciate Property*.

Residential and nonresidential realty must use the straight-line rate (see Tables 14.5 to 14.7). *Straight line* is simply the cost of the property divided by the life of the property. However, you begin depreciation with the month in which the property is placed in service. This makes the rate vary slightly over the years. The tables can be used to calculate depreciation for residential and nonresidential real property using basic depreciation (GDS). If you place nonresidential realty in service in 2014, be sure to use the 39-year table. For all tables, find your annual depreciation rate by looking in the column for the month in which the property was placed in service (for example, for calendar-year businesses, March is 3; August is 8). Then look at the year of ownership you are in (e.g., the year in which you place property in service, look at year number 1).

TABLE 14.6 Rates for Nonresidential Realty Years (31.5 Years), Straight-Line, Mid-Month Convention

	Month in the First Recovery Year the Property Is Placed in Service					
Year	1	2	3	4	5	6
1	3.042%	2.778%	2.513%	2.249%	1.984%	1.720%
2–7	3.175	3.175	3.175	3.175	3.175	3.175
8	3.175	3.174	3.175	3.174	3.175	3.174
9	3.174	3.175	3.174	3.175	3.174	3.175
Year	7	8	9	10	11	12
1	1.455%	1.190%	0.926%	0.661%	0.397%	0.132%
2–7	3.175	3.175	3.175	3.175	3.175	3.175
8	3.175	3.175	3.175	3.175	3.175	3.175
9	3.174	3.175	3.174	3.175	3.174	3.175

TABLE 14.7 Rates for Nonresidential Realty Years (39 Years), Straight-Line, Mid-Month Convention

Year	Month in the First Recovery Year the Property Is Placed in Service					
	1	2	3	4	5	6
1	2.461%	2.247%	2.033%	1.819%	1.605%	1.391%
2–39	2.564	2.564	2.564	2.564	2.564	2.564
Year	7	8	9	10	11	12
1	1.177%	0.963%	0.749%	0.535%	0.321%	0.107%
2–39	2.564	2.564	2.564	2.564	2.564	2.564

Example

You are on a calendar year and placed in service a factory in April 2011. In 2014, your depreciation rate is 2.564%. You find this rate by looking at the table for 39-year nonresidential property under month 4, year 4.

Usually, when the actual expense method is used for the home office deduction, a home office is depreciated over 39 years. The 27.5-year recovery period can be used only for a home office in a multifamily residence where more than 80% of the space is leased to third parties.

Tables for depreciation of residential and nonresidential real property using ADS as well as years after year 9 for residential and pre–May 13, 1993, nonresidential realty may be found in Appendix A of IRS Publication 946, *How to Depreciate Property*.

You can elect to use the 150% rate for properties eligible for the 200% rate. If the election is made, the 150% rate is used over the ADS recovery period. Again, a half-year or mid-quarter convention is applied, and there is a changeover to the straight-line method when it provides a greater deduction. The election may be advisable if you do not think you will have sufficient income to offset larger depreciation deductions. It may also be advisable to lessen or avoid the alternative minimum tax.

NOTE
Once you make the election to use the 150% rate over the ADS recovery period, you cannot change your mind.

Alternative Depreciation System

You must use the alternative system (ADS) (and not the basic system, GDS) for the following property (see Table 14.8):

- Listed property not used more than 50% for business. Listed property includes cars and other transportation vehicles, and computers and peripherals (unless used only at a regular business establishment).

TABLE 14.8 Recovery Periods under Alternative Depreciation System

Property	Years
Cars, computers, light-duty trucks	5
Furniture and fixtures	10
Personal property with no class life	12
Nonresidential/residential real estate	40

- Tangible property used predominantly outside the United States.
- Tax-exempt use property.
- Tax-exempt bond-financed property.
- Imported property covered by an executive order of the president of the United States.
- Property used predominantly in farming and placed in service during any year in which you elect not to apply the uniform capitalization rules to certain farming costs.

The ADS requires depreciation to be calculated using the straight-line method. This is done by dividing the cost of the property by the alternative recovery period. In some cases, the recovery period is the same as for the basic system; in others, it is longer.

You can elect to use ADS for other property in order to claim more gradual depreciation. The election applies to all property within the same class placed in service during the year (other than real estate). For residential rental and nonresidential real property, you can make the election to use ADS on a property-by-property basis.

An election to use ADS may be helpful, for example, if you are first starting out and do not have sufficient income to offset large depreciation deductions. Use of ADS can help to avoid alternative minimum tax and the special depreciation computations required for alternative minimum tax.

You can calculate depreciation for regular tax purposes using the same recovery periods as required for alternative minimum tax purposes. This eliminates the need to make any adjustments for alternative minimum tax and to keep separate records of depreciation taken for regular and alternative minimum tax purposes.

Recapture of Depreciation

If you sell or otherwise dispose of depreciable or amortizable property at a gain, you may have to report all or some of your gain as ordinary income. The treatment of what would otherwise have been capital gain as ordinary income is called *recapture*. In effect, some of the tax benefit you enjoy from depreciation deductions may be offset later on by recapture.

Also, if you sell or otherwise dispose of real property (e.g., residence containing a home office) on which straight-line depreciation was claimed after May 6, 1997, all such depreciation is taxed as capital gain up to 25%. This taxable portion is referred to as *unrecaptured depreciation*. The treatment of income from depreciation recapture is explained in Chapter 6.

Recordkeeping for Depreciation

Since depreciation deductions go on for a number of years, it is important to keep good records of prior deductions. It is also necessary to maintain records since depreciation deductions may differ for regular income tax purposes and the alternative minimum tax. Recordkeeping is explained in Chapter 3.

Bonus Depreciation

Bonus depreciation expired at the end of 2013, but could be extended retroactively by Congress or even made permanent. The following is included in case there is an extension. Check the Supplement for details. There is a special first-year depreciation allowance that can be claimed for eligible property placed in service in 2014 if the 2013 rule is extended. The allowance does not change the amount of depreciation over the property's life; it merely accelerates it so you get the greatest benefit up front. The bonus depreciation allowance is 50% of the adjusted basis of the property.

While bonus depreciation is automatic (you don't have to elect it), you can choose *not* to use it. Instead, you can waive it for any or all classes of assets (for example, you can waive it for all 5-year property). However, you cannot use it for some assets within the class but not for others within the same class. Also, state income tax rules on bonus depreciation vary. Even if you claim it for federal income tax purposes, you may not enjoy a similar break at the state income tax level.

No adjustment is required for alternative minimum tax purposes (see Chapter 28). C corporations (but not other businesses) can elect *not* to claim bonus depreciation in order to accelerate pre-2006 alternative minimum tax credits.

Eligible Property

Generally, eligible property means tangible personal property with a recovery period of 20 years or less.

Computer software acquired separately from hardware also qualifies for bonus depreciation. However, software that is Section 197 property does not qualify for bonus depreciation.

A leasehold, restaurant, or retail improvement also qualifies for bonus depreciation as long as it is an improvement to the interior portion of nonresidential realty (i.e., commercial realty) made pursuant to the lease by the lessee, it is placed in service more than 3 years after the building is first placed in service, and the interior of the building is occupied exclusively by the lessee or sublessee.

To qualify for bonus depreciation, you must meet 3 conditions:

1. The original use of the property must commence with you (i.e., bonus depreciation cannot be claimed for used property). There is a limited exception for sale-leaseback arrangements.

2. The acquisition must be made in 2014 if the 2013 rule is extended (i.e., after December 31, 2013, and before January 1, 2015). If you manufacture, construct, or produce property for your own use, the manufacturing, construction, or production must have begun in this same period.

3. The property must be placed in service before January 1, 2014. However, property considered to have a "longer production period," such as property with a recovery period of at least 10 years, has until January 1, 2015, to be placed in service. These dates may be extended, so check the Supplement.

Limitations on Listed Property

Certain property is called *listed property* and is subject to special depreciation limits. Listed property includes:

- Cars
- Other transportation vehicles (including boats)
- Property generally used for entertainment, recreation, or amusement
- Computers and peripherals, unless used only at a regular business establishment owned or leased by the person operating the establishment. (A home office is treated as a business establishment.)

These are the only items considered listed property because they have been specified as such in the tax law. For example, fax machines and noncellular telephones are not treated as listed property.

NOTE

Cellular phones are no longer treated as listed property.

It is advisable to keep a log or other record for the use of listed property. This will help you show that business use is more than 50%. However, if you use listed property, such as a computer, in a home office whose expenses are deductible, the Tax Court says you do not need records. The reason: Recordkeeping for business use does not apply to computers used at a place of business (which includes a home office that is the principal place of business and that is used regularly and exclusively for that business).

If business use of listed property is not more than 50% during the year, the basic depreciation system cannot be used. In this case, you must use the ADS. Under this system, depreciation can be calculated only with the straight-line method. Divide the cost of the property by the alternative recovery period. For cars, computers, and other listed property, the alternative recovery period happens to be the same as the basic recovery period—5 years.

Use of the ADS means that instead of accelerating depreciation deductions to the earlier years of ownership, depreciation deductions will be spread evenly over the recovery period of the property.

NOTE

Weigh carefully an election to use ADS. If you make the election to use ADS, you cannot later change your mind.

Rebuilding Incentives for Certain Disaster Victims

When there are certain extreme federal disasters, such as Hurricanes Katrina, Rita, and Wilma, Congress may create special tax breaks for businesses affected in the disaster areas. Check the supplement for any new breaks.

Putting Personal Property to Business Use

You may already own some items that can be useful to your business, such as a home computer, office furniture, and a cell phone. You don't have to go out and buy new items for the business; you can convert what you already own from personal to business use.

For depreciation purposes, the basis of each item is the lower of its adjusted basis (usually its cost) or its value at the time of conversion. For most items that decline in value over time, this means that depreciation is usually based on value. But for other property, such as realty that typically increases in value, depreciation is usually based on adjusted basis.

Example

In 2013, you purchased a computer for home use at a cost of $3,000. In 2014, you start a business and begin to use the computer for business activities. Its value in 2014 is $1,000. For depreciation purposes, you are limited to $1,000; in this case the computer's value is lower than its adjusted basis.

Example

In 2012, you bought your home for $200,000. In 2014, you start a business from home and use 10% of the space exclusively for this purpose. The house is now worth $240,000. For depreciation purposes, you are limited to $20,000 (10% of $200,000); in this case the adjusted basis is lower than the home's current value.

You cannot use first-year expensing for property you convert from personal to business use in a year that is after the year you acquired the property. The law limits expensing to the year in which property is initially placed in service (and that is usually prior to the year it is first used in business).

Amortization

Certain capital expenditures can be deducted over a term of years. This is called *amortization*. This deduction is taken evenly over a prescribed period of time. Amortization generally applies to the following expenditures:

- Intangibles acquired on the purchase of a business
- Business start-up costs and organizational expenses
- Construction period interest and taxes
- Research and experimentation costs
- Bond premiums
- Reforestation costs
- Pollution control facilities
- Costs of acquiring a lease
- Certain leasehold and qualified restaurant improvements

Intangibles Acquired on the Purchase of a Business

If you buy a business, a portion of your cost may be allocated to certain intangible items:

- Goodwill
- Going concern value
- Workforce in place
- Patents, copyrights, formulas, processes, designs, patterns, and know-how
- Customer-based intangibles
- Supplier-based intangibles
- Licenses, permits, and other rights granted by a governmental unit or agency
- Covenants not to compete
- Trademarks or trade names
- Franchises (including sports franchises) (but ongoing franchise fees are currently deductible)

These items are called *Section 197 intangibles*, named after a section in the Internal Revenue Code. You may deduct the portion of the cost allocated to these items ratably over a period of 15 years.

> ### Example
>
> You buy out the accounting practice of someone else. As part of the sale, the other accountant signs a covenant not to compete with you for 2 years within your same location. You may amortize the portion of the cost of the practice relating to the covenant over 15 years.

Section 197 intangibles do not include interests in a corporation, partnership, trust or estate, interests in land, certain computer software, and certain other excluded items. Also, you cannot amortize the cost of self-created items. Thus, if you generate your own customer list, you cannot claim an amortization deduction.

ANTICHURNING RULES

If you already own a business with goodwill and other intangibles, you cannot convert these into Section 197 intangibles, for which an amortization deduction would be allowed, by engaging in a transaction solely for this purpose. Special antichurning rules prevent amortization for intangibles acquired in transactions designed to create an acquisition date after August 10, 1993 (the date on which Section 197 intangibles came into being), for assets that were previously owned as of that date.

DISPOSITIONS

If you sell a Section 197 asset that you held for more than 1 year, gain is ordinary income up to the amount of amortization allowed; the balance, if any, is Section 1231 gain. If the asset was only held for 1 year or less, all of the gain is ordinary income.

If you sell multiple Section 197 assets in a single transaction or a series of related transactions, ordinary recapture is figured as if all such intangibles were a single asset.

If a Section 197 intangible is sold at a loss but other such intangibles are still owned, no loss can be taken on the sale. Instead the bases of the remaining Section 197 intangibles are reduced by the unclaimed loss. The same rule applies if a Section 197 intangible becomes worthless or is abandoned. No loss is recognized on the worthlessness or abandonment. Instead, the bases of remaining Section 197 intangibles are increased by the unrecognized loss.

Self-Created Intangibles

If you create an intangible, such as a trademark, you cannot amortize the costs you incur (e.g., registration fees to the U.S. Patent and Trademark Office and attorney's fees). These costs are capitalized (carried on the company's books as an asset).

Business Start-Up Costs and Organizational Expenses

When you start up a business, you may incur a variety of expenses. Ordinarily these are capital expenditures that are not currently deductible. They are expenses incurred to acquire a capital asset, namely, your business. However, the tax law allows you to write off start-up costs. The timing of your deduction depends on when you started your business.

- For start-up costs paid or incurred after October 22, 2004, and before January 1, 2010, and after December 31, 2010—you can elect to deduct $5,000 in the first year, with the balance of start-up costs amortized over 180 months. However, if costs exceed $50,000, the $5,000 immediate deduction is reduced dollar-for-dollar, so that no immediate deduction can be claimed when start-up costs exceed $55,000. In this case, *all* start-up costs must be amortized over 180 months.

- For start-up costs paid or incurred in 2010 only—you can elect to deduct $10,000 in the first year, with the balance of start-up costs amortized over 180 months. However, if costs exceed $60,000, the $10,000 immediate deduction is reduced dollar-for-dollar, so that no immediate deduction can be claimed when start-up costs exceed $70,000. In this case, *all* start-up costs must be amortized over 180 months.

Note: Congress is considering changes in the tax treatment of start-up costs. See the Supplement for details.

If you sell your business before the end of the amortization period or the business folds before that time, you can deduct the unamortized amount in your final year.

BUSINESS START-UP COSTS

Generally, you think of start-up costs as expenses you pay during the first few years of your business. But for tax purposes, the term "start-up costs" has a very specific meaning. These include amounts paid to investigate *whether* to start or purchase a business and *which* business to start or purchase (this is called the *whether and which* test for determining amortization of start-up costs). Expenses related to these activities are treated as start-up expenses. Examples of start-up costs include:

- A survey of potential markets
- An analysis of available facilities, labor, and supplies
- Advertisements for the opening of the business
- Travel and other expenses incurred to get prospective distributors, suppliers, or customers
- Salaries and fees for consultants and executives, and fees for professional services

Other similar expenses are amortizable if they would have been deductible if paid or incurred to operate a going business and were actually paid or incurred prior to the commencement of business operations. Otherwise such expenses must be treated as part of the cost of acquiring a capital asset—the business. For example, legal fees to prepare contracts for the purchase of a business are no longer start-up fees but, rather, are expenses that must be added to the cost of the business. You cannot deduct the value of your time spent in exploring a prospective business.

Once you have passed the start-up phase and identified a target business you want to acquire, you can no longer amortize related expenses under this rule.

Example

You are looking for a business to buy and have your accountant review the financial data from several prospects. You then zero in on a business and examine its financial data in detail. The accountant's fee related to the general search is amortizable, but the fee related to the detailed examination of the target business is not.

ORGANIZATIONAL COSTS FOR A CORPORATION

If you set up a corporation (C or S), certain expenses unique to this form of business can be written off under the same rules that apply to business start-up costs. These expenses include the cost of:

- Temporary directors
- Organizational meetings
- State incorporation fees
- Accounting services for setting up the corporate books
- Legal services to draft the charter, bylaws, terms of the original stock certificates, and minutes of organizational meetings

You can deduct any other organizational costs if they are incident to the creation of a corporation, they are chargeable to the capital account, and the cost could have been amortized over the life of the corporation if the corporation had a fixed life.

You cannot amortize expenses related to selling stock, such as commissions, professional fees, and printing costs.

ORGANIZATIONAL COSTS OF A PARTNERSHIP

If you set up a partnership, certain expenses unique to this form of business can be written off under the same rules that apply to business start-up costs. As in the case of corporate organizational costs, partnership organizational costs include those that are incident to the creation of a partnership, are chargeable to the capital account, and would have been amortizable over the life of the partnership if the partnership had a fixed life.

Syndication costs to sell partnership interests are not treated as amortizable organizational costs. These nonamortizable costs include commissions, professional fees, and printing costs related to the issuing and marketing of partnership interests.

Computer Software

There are several different rules for treating the cost of software:

- If it is purchased separately from the purchase of a computer (i.e., it is not bundled with the hardware), the cost can be expensed. Alternatively, if expensing is not elected, the cost can be amortized over 36 months. However, if the useful life of the software is less than 36 months, amortize it over its useful life. If it has a useful life of less than 1 year (e.g., an annual tax preparation program), deduct it in full in the year of purchase (in effect, the same write-off as expensing, but there is no taxable income limitation in this instance as there is for expensing).

- If it is bundled with hardware, depreciate as part of the hardware (generally over 5 years as explained earlier in this chapter).

- If it is purchased as part of the acquisition of a business, it is amortized as a Section 197 asset over 15 years.

- If it is developed by you for use in your business, treat it as a research and development cost (explained later).

- If it is leased, deduct the lease payments over the term of the lease as you would any other rental expense.

Research and Experimentation Costs

If you have research and experimentation costs, you have a choice of ways to deduct them. You can claim a current deduction for amounts paid or incurred in the year.

Alternatively, you can elect to amortize them over a period of not less than 60 months. Where you do not have current income to offset the deduction, it may be advisable to elect amortization.

You may be able to claim a tax credit for increasing your research and experimentation program if the credit is extended or made permanent for 2014. For further information on this credit, see instructions for Form 6765, *Credit for Increasing Research Activities*. The research is further explained in Chapter 23.

Bond Premiums

If you pay a premium to buy bonds (a cost above the face amount of the bonds), you may be required to—or can elect to—amortize the premium. For taxable bonds, there is an election. You can amortize the bond premium or instead treat the unamortized premium as part of the basis of the bond. The bond premium is calculated with the amount that the bond issuer will pay at maturity or the earlier call date if it results in a smaller amortizable bond premium attributable to the period ending on the call date. Do not take into account any premium paid for a conversion feature. (Dealers in taxable bonds cannot deduct the amortizable bond premium.)

For tax-exempt bonds you must amortize the premium. However, you do not deduct the amortizable premium in calculating taxable income.

If you are required or elect to amortize the bond premium, decrease the basis of the bond by the amortizable premium.

Reforestation Costs

If you spend money on forestation or reforestation—planting and seeding, site preparation, and the costs of seeds, tools, and labor—you can elect to deduct up to $10,000 ($5,000 for married persons filing separate returns) in the year paid or incurred.

Costs in excess of the amount deducted are amortized over 84 months. The 84-month period begins on the first day of the first month of the second half of the tax year in which the amortizable basis is acquired.

Example

On January 1, 2014, you incur reforestation expenses of $20,000. You can deduct $10,000 on your 2014 return and charge the remaining $10,000 to the capital account, amortizing the expenses over 84 months. The monthly amortization is $119.50 ($10,000 ÷ 84). The amortization deduction on your 2014 return is $1,434 ($119.50 × 12 months).

Pollution Control Facilities

If you set up a pollution control facility for a plant or other property in operation before 1976, you can elect to amortize your costs over a period of 60 months. A certified pollution control facility is depreciable property that is a new identifiable treatment facility used to abate or control water or atmospheric pollution or contamination by removing, altering, disposing of, storing, or preventing the creation or emission of pollutants, contaminants, wastes, or heat. It must be certified by state and federal certifying authorities. The amortizable cost cannot include amounts recovered through its operation, such as through sales of recovered wastes. The certifying authorities will note this fact and limit the amortizable costs accordingly.

Costs of Acquiring a Lease

If you pay a fee to obtain a lease, you can amortize the cost over the term of the lease. The lease term includes all renewal options if less than 75% of the cost is attributable to the term of the lease remaining on the acquisition date. The remaining term of the lease on the acquisition date does not include any period for which the lease may be subsequently renewed, extended, or continued under an option exercisable by the lessee.

Qualified Leasehold, Restaurant, and Retail Improvements

In some cases, these improvements have a 15-year recovery period over which eligible costs can be amortized if not written off using bonus depreciation or the Section 179 deduction, assuming the 15-year recovery period and bonus depreciation are extended for 2014. For details, see Chapter 10 and the Supplement.

Depletion

Depletion is a deduction allowed for certain mineral properties or timber to compensate the owner for the use of these resources. *Mineral properties* include oil and gas wells, mines, other natural deposits, and standing timber. In order to claim depletion, you must be an owner or operator with an economic interest in the mineral deposits or standing timber. This means that you are adversely affected economically when mineral properties or standing timber is mined or cut. Depletion is claimed separately for each mineral property, which is each mineral deposit in each separate tract or parcel of land. Timber property is each tract or block representing a separate timber account.

NOTE
Claiming depletion may result in alternative minimum tax (AMT) both for individuals and C corporations (not otherwise exempt from AMT).

Methods of Depletion

There are 2 ways to calculate depletion: *cost depletion* and *percentage depletion*.

COST DEPLETION

Cost depletion is determined by dividing the adjusted basis of the mineral property by the total number of recoverable units in the property's natural deposit (as determined by engineering reports). This figure is multiplied by the number of units sold if you use the accrual method of accounting, or the number of units sold and paid for if you use the cash method. Cost depletion is the only method

TABLE 14.9 Percentage for Mineral Properties

Type of Property	Percentage
Oil and gas—small producers	15.0%
Sulfur, uranium, and U.S. asbestos, lead, zinc, nickel, mica, and certain other ores and minerals	22.0
Gold, silver, copper, and iron ore, and certain U.S. oil shale	15.0
Coal, lignite, sodium chloride	10.0
Clay and shale used for sewer pipe	7.5
Clay used for flowerpots and so on, gravel, sand, stone	5.0
Most other minerals and metallic ores	14.0

allowed for standing timber. The depletion deduction is calculated when the quantity of cut timber is first accurately measured in the process of exploitation. Special rules are used to determine depletion for timber, and the deduction is taken when standing timber is cut.

PERCENTAGE DEPLETION

Percentage depletion is determined by applying a percentage, fixed by tax law according to each type of mineral, to your gross income from the property during the tax year (see Table 14.9).

The deduction for percentage depletion is limited to no more than 50% (100% for oil and gas properties allowed to use percentage depletion) of taxable income from the property calculated without the depletion deduction and certain other adjustments. However, percentage depletion on the marginal production of oil or natural gas by independent producers and royalty owners is *not* limited to taxable income from the property (figured without the depletion deduction).

Only small producers are allowed to use percentage depletion for oil and gas properties. If you use percentage depletion for mineral properties but it is less than cost depletion for the year, you must use cost depletion.

Partnership Oil and Gas Properties

The depletion allowance, whether cost depletion or percentage depletion, must be calculated separately for each partner and not by the partnership. Each partner can decide on the depletion method. The partnership simply allocates to the partner his or her proportionate share of the adjusted basis of each oil and gas property. Each partner must keep this information separately.

In separate records the partner must reduce the share of the adjusted basis of each property by the depletion taken on the property each year by that partner. The partner will use this reduced adjusted basis to figure gain or loss if the partnership later disposes of the property. (This partnership rule also applies to members in LLCs.)

S Corporation Oil and Gas Properties

The depletion allowance, whether by cost or by percentage, must be computed separately by each shareholder and not by the S corporation. The same rules apply to S corporations that apply to partnerships, with some modifications. To enable a shareholder to calculate cost depletion, the S corporation must allocate to each shareholder his or her adjusted basis of each oil and gas property held by the S corporation. This allocation is made on the date the corporation acquires the property. The shareholder's share of the adjusted basis of each oil and gas property is adjusted by the S corporation for any capital expenditures made for each property. Again, each shareholder must separately keep records of his or her pro rata share of the adjusted basis of each property and must reduce that share by depletion taken on the property. The reduced adjusted basis is used by the shareholder to determine gain or loss on the disposition of the property by the S corporation.

Where to Claim Depreciation, Amortization, and Depletion

All Taxpayers

In general, depreciation, including any first-year expense deduction, is computed on Form 4562, *Depreciation and Amortization*, regardless of your form of business organization. If you qualify for a higher dollar limit, simply cross out the preprinted dollar limit on Form 4562 and write your applicable dollar limit in the margin. However, special rules apply to different entities.

If an election is made to use the 150% rate for property that could have used the 200% rate, you make the election by entering "150DB" in column (f) of Part III of Form 4562.

An election to use ADS is made by completing line 20a, b, or c of Part III of Form 4562.

If depletion is taken for timber, you must attach Form T to your return.

In general, recapture of the depreciation and the first-year expense deduction is computed on Form 4797, *Sales of Business Property*, regardless of your form of business organization (explained in Chapter 6).

See Figure 14.1 for a worksheet to show depreciation and a completed Form 4562 for a florist shop business that placed equipment in service in both the current year and in prior years (Table 14.10).

Employees

You complete Form 4562 only if you place depreciable property in service in the current year or have amortization costs that begin in the current year. For example, if you buy a laptop computer this year for your work and you want to claim a first-year expense deduction, you must file Form 4562. You do not have

Form **4562**	**Depreciation and Amortization**	OMB No. 1545-0172
	(Including Information on Listed Property)	20**14**
Department of the Treasury Internal Revenue Service (99)	▶ Attach to your tax return. ▶ Information about Form 4562 and its separate instructions is at *www.irs.gov/form4562*.	Attachment Sequence No. **179**

Name(s) shown on return	Business or activity to which this form relates	Identifying number

Part I Election To Expense Certain Property Under Section 179
Note: *If you have any listed property, complete Part V before you complete Part I.*

1	Maximum amount (see instructions)	**1**	
2	Total cost of section 179 property placed in service (see instructions)	**2**	
3	Threshold cost of section 179 property before reduction in limitation (see instructions)	**3**	
4	Reduction in limitation. Subtract line 3 from line 2. If zero or less, enter -0-	**4**	
5	Dollar limitation for tax year. Subtract line 4 from line 1. If zero or less, enter -0-. If married filing separately, see instructions	**5**	

6	(a) Description of property	(b) Cost (business use only)	(c) Elected cost

7	Listed property. Enter the amount from line 29	**7**	
8	Total elected cost of section 179 property. Add amounts in column (c), lines 6 and 7	**8**	
9	Tentative deduction. Enter the **smaller** of line 5 or line 8	**9**	
10	Carryover of disallowed deduction from line 13 of your 2013 Form 4562	**10**	
11	Business income limitation. Enter the smaller of business income (not less than zero) or line 5 (see instructions)	**11**	
12	Section 179 expense deduction. Add lines 9 and 10, but do not enter more than line 11	**12**	
13	Carryover of disallowed deduction to 2015. Add lines 9 and 10, less line 12 ▶	**13**	

Note: *Do not use Part II or Part III below for listed property. Instead, use Part V.*

Part II Special Depreciation Allowance and Other Depreciation (Do not include listed property.) (See instructions.)

14	Special depreciation allowance for qualified property (other than listed property) placed in service during the tax year (see instructions)	**14**	
15	Property subject to section 168(f)(1) election	**15**	
16	Other depreciation (including ACRS)	**16**	

Part III MACRS Depreciation (Do not include listed property.) (See instructions.)

Section A

17	MACRS deductions for assets placed in service in tax years beginning before 2014	**17**	
18	If you are electing to group any assets placed in service during the tax year into one or more general asset accounts, check here . . . . ▶ ☐		

Section B—Assets Placed in Service During 2014 Tax Year Using the General Depreciation System

(a) Classification of property	(b) Month and year placed in service	(c) Basis for depreciation (business/investment use only—see instructions)	(d) Recovery period	(e) Convention	(f) Method	(g) Depreciation deduction
19a 3-year property						
b 5-year property						
c 7-year property						
d 10-year property						
e 15-year property						
f 20-year property						
g 25-year property			25 yrs.		S/L	
h Residential rental property			27.5 yrs.	MM	S/L	
			27.5 yrs.	MM	S/L	
i Nonresidential real property			39 yrs.	MM	S/L	
				MM	S/L	

Section C—Assets Placed in Service During 2014 Tax Year Using the Alternative Depreciation System

20a Class life					S/L	
b 12-year			12 yrs.		S/L	
c 40-year			40 yrs.	MM	S/L	

Part IV Summary (See instructions.)

21	Listed property. Enter amount from line 28	**21**	
22	**Total.** Add amounts from line 12, lines 14 through 17, lines 19 and 20 in column (g), and line 21. Enter here and on the appropriate lines of your return. Partnerships and S corporations—see instructions .	**22**	
23	For assets shown above and placed in service during the current year, enter the portion of the basis attributable to section 263A costs	**23**	

For Paperwork Reduction Act Notice, see separate instructions.	Cat. No. 12906N	Form **4562** (2014)

FIGURE 14.1 Form 4562, Depreciation and Amortization

Form 4562 (2014)   Page **2**

Part V **Listed Property** (Include automobiles, certain other vehicles, certain aircraft, certain computers, and property used for entertainment, recreation, or amusement.)

Note: *For any vehicle for which you are using the standard mileage rate or deducting lease expense, complete **only** 24a, 24b, columns (a) through (c) of Section A, all of Section B, and Section C if applicable.*

Section A—Depreciation and Other Information (Caution: *See the instructions for limits for passenger automobiles.***)**

24a Do you have evidence to support the business/investment use claimed? ☐ Yes ☐ No   24b If "Yes," is the evidence written? ☐ Yes ☐ No

(a) Type of property (list vehicles first)	(b) Date placed in service	(c) Business/ investment use percentage	(d) Cost or other basis	(e) Basis for depreciation (business/investment use only)	(f) Recovery period	(g) Method/ Convention	(h) Depreciation deduction	(i) Elected section 179 cost
25 Special depreciation allowance for qualified listed property placed in service during the tax year and used more than 50% in a qualified business use (see instructions) .					25			
26 Property used more than 50% in a qualified business use:								
		%						
		%						
		%						
27 Property used 50% or less in a qualified business use:								
		%				S/L –		
		%				S/L –		
		%				S/L –		
28 Add amounts in column (h), lines 25 through 27. Enter here and on line 21, page 1 .					28			
29 Add amounts in column (i), line 26. Enter here and on line 7, page 1							29	

Section B—Information on Use of Vehicles

Complete this section for vehicles used by a sole proprietor, partner, or other "more than 5% owner," or related person. If you provided vehicles to your employees, first answer the questions in Section C to see if you meet an exception to completing this section for those vehicles.

	(a) Vehicle 1		(b) Vehicle 2		(c) Vehicle 3		(d) Vehicle 4		(e) Vehicle 5		(f) Vehicle 6	
30 Total business/investment miles driven during the year (**do not** include commuting miles) .												
31 Total commuting miles driven during the year												
32 Total other personal (noncommuting) miles driven												
33 Total miles driven during the year. Add lines 30 through 32												
34 Was the vehicle available for personal use during off-duty hours?	Yes	No	Yes	No	Yes	No	Yes	No	Yes	No	Yes	No
35 Was the vehicle used primarily by a more than 5% owner or related person? . .												
36 Is another vehicle available for personal use?												

Section C—Questions for Employers Who Provide Vehicles for Use by Their Employees

Answer these questions to determine if you meet an exception to completing Section B for vehicles used by employees who **are not** more than 5% owners or related persons (see instructions).

	Yes	No
37 Do you maintain a written policy statement that prohibits all personal use of vehicles, including commuting, by your employees?		
38 Do you maintain a written policy statement that prohibits personal use of vehicles, except commuting, by your employees? See the instructions for vehicles used by corporate officers, directors, or 1% or more owners . .		
39 Do you treat all use of vehicles by employees as personal use?		
40 Do you provide more than five vehicles to your employees, obtain information from your employees about the use of the vehicles, and retain the information received?		
41 Do you meet the requirements concerning qualified automobile demonstration use? (See instructions.) . . .		

Note: *If your answer to 37, 38, 39, 40, or 41 is "Yes," do not complete Section B for the covered vehicles.*

Part VI **Amortization**

(a) Description of costs	(b) Date amortization begins	(c) Amortizable amount	(d) Code section	(e) Amortization period or percentage	(f) Amortization for this year
42 Amortization of costs that begins during your 2014 tax year (see instructions):					
43 Amortization of costs that began before your 2014 tax year			43		
44 **Total.** Add amounts in column (f). See the instructions for where to report			44		

Form **4562** (2014)

FIGURE 14.1 *(Continued)*

TABLE 14.10 Depreciation Worksheet

Description of Property	Date Placed in Service	Cost or Other Basis	Business/ Investment/ Use %	Section 179 Deduction	Depreciation Prior Years	Basis for Depreciation	Method/ Convention	Recovery Period	Rate or Table %	Depreciation Deduction
Building	2-2-12	$65,000	100%		$4,793.75	$65,000	SL/MM	GDS 39	2.564%	$1,666.60
Desk and chair	2-2-12	600	100%	$600	-0-	-0-				-0-
Refrigeration equipment	2-2-12	4,500	100%		3,204.00	4,500	200DB/HY	GDS/5	11.52%	518.40
Work tables	2-2-12	1,200	100%		854.40	1,200	200DB/HY	GDS/5	11.52%	138.24
Cash register	2-2-12	270	100%		192.24	270	200DB/HY	GDS/5	11.52%	31.10
Subtotal— 2012 Property										2,354.34
Delivery truck*	4-16-13	31,500	100%	31,500	-0-	-0-				-0-
Fax machine	7-3-13	300	100%		103.14	300	150BD/HY	ADS/6	16.41%	49.23
Subtotal— 2013 Property										49.23
Computer	6-21-14	3,000	100%	3,000	-0-	-0-				-0-
File cabinets	9-9-14	475	100%	475	-0-	-0-				-0-
Store counters	11-1-14	1,870	100%	1,870	-0-	-0-				-0-
Van*	11-16-14	32,500	100%	32,500	-0-	-0-				-0-
Subtotal— 2014 Property				37,845						
GrandTotal—2014				$37,845						$2,354.34

*Nonpersonal vehicles.

to complete Form 4562 if you are deducting job-related car expenses using either the standard mileage rate or actual mileage rate; you need only complete Form 2106, *Employee Business Expenses*, or Form 2106-EZ, *Unreimbursed Employee Business Expenses*. Your deductions are then entered on Schedule A as miscellaneous itemized deductions subject to the 2%-of-AGI rule and the itemized deduction reduction for high-income taxpayers explained in Chapter 1.

Self-Employed

You complete Form 4562 only if you place depreciable property in service in the current year or have amortization costs that begin in the current year. Your deductions are then entered on Part II of Schedule C or Schedule C-EZ (or Schedule F). Depreciation and first-year expensing not included in Part II of Schedule C (for cost of goods sold) are entered on a specific line in Part I of Schedule C or as part of total expenses on Schedule C-EZ. You do not have to file Form 4562 if you only need to provide information on vehicle use. You can enter this information on Schedule C (Part IV) or Schedule C-EZ.

Partnerships and LLCs

You complete Form 4562 only if you place depreciable property in service in the current year, are claiming depreciation on a car (regardless of when it was placed in service), or have amortization costs that begin in the current year. The partnership or LLC decides on the depreciation method and whether to claim a first-year expense deduction. Ordinary depreciation is then entered on Form 1065 and is taken into account in calculating a partnership's or LLC's ordinary income or loss. Depreciation is reported on a specific line on Form 1065 and is reduced by depreciation included in the cost of goods sold. Similarly, depletion (other than on oil and gas properties) is part of a partnership's or LLC's ordinary income or loss and is reported on the specific line provided for depletion.

Amortization items, such as a deduction for organizational expenses, are part of other deductions. An explanation for these items is included in a separate statement attached to the return.

First-year expense deduction is a separately stated item reported on Schedule K, and the allocable portion is passed through separately to partners or members on Schedule K-1.

Depletion of oil and gas properties is also a separately stated item reported on Schedule K. The allocable portion is passed through separately to partners and/or members on Schedule K-1.

S Corporations

You complete Form 4562 only if the corporation placed depreciable property in service in the current year, is claiming depreciation on a car (regardless of when it was placed in service), or has amortization costs that begin in the current year. The S corporation decides on the depreciation method and whether to claim a first-year expense deduction. Ordinary depreciation is then entered on Form 1120S and is taken into account in calculating an S corporation's ordinary income or loss. Depreciation is reported on a specific line on Form 1120S and is reduced by depreciation included in the cost of goods sold. Similarly, depletion (other than of oil and gas properties) is part of an S corporation's ordinary income or loss and is reported on the specific line provided for depletion.

Amortization items, such as a deduction for organizational expenses, are part of other deductions. An explanation for these items is included in a separate statement attached to the return.

The first-year expense deduction is a separately stated item reported on Schedule K, and the allocable portion is passed through separately to shareholders on Schedule K-1.

Depletion of oil and gas properties is also a separately stated item reported on Schedule K. The allocable portion is passed through separately to shareholders on Schedule K-1.

C Corporations

Form 4562 must be completed if any depreciation is claimed (regardless of the year in which the property is placed in service) or if amortization of costs begins in the current year. The depreciation deduction is then entered on Form 1120 on the specific line provided for depreciation. This deduction must be reduced by depreciation claimed in the cost of goods sold or elsewhere on the return. Depletion is entered on the specific line provided for depletion. Amortization is part of other deductions, an explanation of which must be attached to the return.

Advertising Expenses

Alert

At the time this book was printed, Congress had not extended numerous breaks for 2014 that had expired at the end of 2013. Check the online supplement in February 2015 at www.jklasser.com or www.barbaraweltman.com to see whether these breaks apply for 2014 returns.

You may run advertisements in newspapers, on the radio or television, or in magazines or trade journals to sell your products or services. You can deduct these costs, as well as the costs of other promotional activities. At the same time, you will discover that some costs cannot be deducted or that certain costs need to be deducted as another type of business expense.

Ordinary Advertising Expenses

Like all other business expenses, advertising costs must be ordinary and necessary business expenses in order to be deductible. They must have a reasonable relationship to your business activities, and they must be reasonable in amount. However, there are no guidelines on what is "reasonable" in amount.

Deductible advertising expenses include the costs of:

- Business cards
- Ads in print or the media (such as newspaper or magazine advertisements, charitable organization publications, radio or television spots, or online and mobile messages)
- Ads in telephone directories (such as Yellow Pages listings)
- Package design costs that are part of an advertising campaign
- Billboards (rental fees are an advertising expense)
- Signs with a useful life of not more than one year. (Signs expected to last longer than a year can be depreciated, as explained in Chapter 14.)

In the case of signs placed on the sides of cars or trucks, only the cost of the sign is deductible as advertising. The cost of the driving is not an advertising expense (although business use of the car may be otherwise deductible as explained in Chapter 9).

Example

The cost of metal or plastic signs with a life of more than 1 year has to be capitalized. The cost of restaurant menu folders is currently deductible, since the folders have a life of not more than 1 year.

The cost of public relations can be deducted as an ordinary advertising cost. PR expenses can include fees to PR professionals and agencies, costs associated with PR events (e.g., press conferences), and costs for developing, printing, and distributing press kits.

Some businesses treat the cost of maintaining their websites as an advertising expense. The IRS has not yet ruled on whether this treatment is correct (see "Websites" later in this chapter). However, if a business uses the site only for advertising (e.g., a law firm that posts its areas of specialty and personnel) and not for selling (e.g, a bricks-and-mortar store that posts its online catalog and accepts purchases through the Internet), it seems reasonable to handle the cost in this manner.

Promotion of Goodwill

Expenses designed to create goodwill in the public's eye rather than to obtain immediate sales are also deductible. In fact, the advertising program can be of a long-term nature and still result in an immediate deduction. The IRS has ruled that the ordinary costs of advertising are currently deductible despite the fact that they produce a long-term benefit.

In some instances, design costs may be considered deductible advertising expenses. In one case, the Tax Court said that graphic design costs could be currently deductible as advertising expenses even though they may produce future patronage or goodwill. The IRS has announced its disagreement with this decision, so if you claim a deduction for package design costs, you may face an IRS challenge.

Example

The costs of installing window treatments in model homes as part of an advertising campaign are currently deductible. The costs are incurred to promote the name of the business.

The cost of distributing a company's samples can be deducted as an advertising expense where the distribution is designed to engender goodwill.

Another type of advertising involves sponsorships of teams. Your business may, for example, sponsor a bowling team or a Little League team. In return for the sponsorship, your company's name is displayed on the team uniform and may also be a part of the team's name. These costs of sponsorship are deductible as advertising expenses.

Free services provided to generate goodwill cannot be deducted as an advertising expense. For example, in one case a doctor provided free medical services and deducted the value of his uncompensated services as an advertising expense. The Tax Court disallowed the deduction because the doctor's labor was not an expense (it was not an amount paid or incurred).

Personal versus Business Expenses

Expenses that smack of a personal nature may still constitute deductible advertising costs when it can be shown that the expenses were incurred primarily for business purposes. The following examples demonstrate when expenses may be considered primarily for business and when they may not—the distinction is not always clear.

Example

A restaurant chain owner who maintained show horses for the purpose of advertising the company's name was allowed a current deduction. But an owner who bought a horse, named it after himself, and entered it in shows was not allowed a deduction when he failed to show there was any connection between the horse and his business.

Example

A business owner who invited customers to his child's wedding reception could not deduct the cost for these guests as advertising. The nature of the expense was just too personal and the business aspect of the expense just too attenuated to make the cost a deductible advertising expense or an entertainment expense.

Example

An attorney was not allowed to deduct the cost of new suits as an advertising expense. He claimed he needed to look good to attract new clients. Again, the expense was personal in nature and so was not deductible.

Example

Costs of car racing by an officer of a computer research and design corporation were not deductible. Again, the expenses were personal in nature. In comparison, a meat processor that sponsored a race car could deduct expenses. The sponsorship allowed the company to display its logo on the car, and track announcers mentioned the car's sponsor during the race. Deductibility turns on the facts and circumstances of a particular situation.

Lobbying Expenses

In general, the costs of advertising to influence legislation at the federal, state, or even local level are not deductible. Nondeductible expenses include:

- The costs of participating or intervening in any political campaign for or against any candidate in public office.
- The costs of attempting to influence the general public or segments of the public about elections, legislative matters, or referendums.
- The costs of communicating directly with certain executive branch officials in any attempt to influence the official actions or positions of such officials. These executives include the president, vice president, any officer or employee of the Executive Office of the President and the 2 most

senior officers of each of the other agencies in the Executive Office, and certain other individuals.

- The costs of research, preparation, planning, or coordinating any of the activities already mentioned.

Not all lobbying expenses are nondeductible. You can still claim a deduction for de minimis in-house lobbying expenses. These are expenses that do not exceed $2,000 per year to influence legislation or communicate directly with a specified executive branch official. There is also an exception for expenses to influence local legislation, such as decisions by a local council. And, of course, professional lobbyists are entitled to deduct their own business expenses even though payments to them are not deductible.

Some types of goodwill activities may constitute deductible entertainment expenses (see Chapter 8).

Prizes, Contests, and Other Promotional Activities

Amounts paid for prizes, contests, and other promotional activities may be deducted as advertising expenses if you can show that the expenses have a relationship to your business. The amounts expended must be reasonable; they must not be out of proportion to the amount of business expected to be obtained as a result of the prize, contest, or other promotional activity.

Example

A restaurant owner gives away a car to the holder of a lucky-number ticket. These tickets had been distributed to patrons. The cost of the car was a deductible business expense.

Sponsorships of teams and other events can be deducted as advertising expenses (e.g., sponsorship of a tennis match or golf tournament).

Prizes and other awards given to employees are not treated as advertising costs. They are part of compensation (see Chapter 7).

Help-Wanted Ads

Most advertising is designed to sell products or services. However, you may also advertise when trying to fill a position in your company. The cost of running help-wanted ads in newspapers, trade magazines, and online is deductible as an ordinary and necessary business expense. It is not an advertising cost.

If you are out of work and take out an ad in a newspaper to seek a position, again, the cost may be deductible, but not as an advertising expense. Instead, it may be deducted as a cost of finding a job. For a further discussion on deducting job-hunting costs, see Chapter 22.

Websites

Today, websites are an integral part of advertising and promoting a business. Some companies use websites for e-commerce and to transact business online; others use their sites as online brochures to highlight the features of their businesses and establish credibility. Mobile versions of websites are also a growing part of advertising and promotion, enabling businesses to offer coupons or direct readers to their websites.

Costs of Creation

Creating a website and a mobile version of it is an important way to brand your business and keep your name before the public. Yet it has been reported by Google in March 2013 that 58% of small businesses do not have a website, and Hibu reported in 2014 that only 6% of small businesses have mobile sites. Website creation includes domain registration fees, site design, and, in some cases, professional copy, photography, and artwork used to populate the site. While there have not yet been any cases or rulings on the extent to which website-related expenses are deductible, it can certainly be argued that these expenses relate to the promotion of goodwill for the company and should be treated as fully deductible ordinary advertising costs.

The cost of adapting a website for mobile viewing may be treated similarly to website creation costs. They may qualify as fully deductible ordinary advertising costs.

Maintenance Costs

Web hosting is an ongoing cost for maintaining a website. So, too, is the cost of keeping your website up to date, which can entail fees to outside webmasters. These maintenance fees are fully deductible, as is the cost of search engine optimization (SEO) services.

Social Media

Increasingly, small businesses are relying on social media, such as LinkedIn, Facebook, Pinterest, and Twitter, to market their products and services. Many are using blogs and e-newsletters to reach customers and prospects. Much of social media is free (other than the cost of your own or your staff's time spent working on these sites). However, some social media-related services can cost money, and they are fully tax deductible. **Examples:**

- E-mail distribution costs (such as Constant Contact)
- Google Adwords
- LinkedIn Pro, which is a premium service

- Paid blogging platforms (such as Typepad monthly charges or Blogspot add-ons)
- Surveys (using sites such as Survey Money or Constant Contact)

Note: Deducting the cost of software related to social media, such as offline blogging software, may not necessarily be fully deductible in the year you buy it. How to deduct the cost of software is discussed in Chapter 14.

Where to Deduct Expenses

Employees

An employee generally will not have any advertising expenses. He or she is only in the business of being an employee and need not promote that activity. When an employee takes out an ad in a newspaper or trade journal expressing availability for a new position, this expense may be deductible as a job-hunting expense, which is treated as a miscellaneous itemized deduction subject to the 2%-of-AGI rule and the itemized deduction reduction for high-income taxpayers explained in Chapter 1.

Self-Employed

Advertising costs are deductible on Schedule C. There is a specific line for this type of expense. If you are eligible to file Schedule C-EZ, you claim advertising costs along with other deductible expenses.

Partnerships and LLCs

Advertising costs are trade or business expenses that are taken into account in determining the profit or loss of the partnership or LLC on Form 1065. They are entered in the category of Other Deductions on Form 1065. A schedule is attached to the return explaining the deductions claimed in this category. They are not separately stated items passed through to partners and members. Therefore, partners and members in LLCs report their net income or loss from the business on Schedule E; they do not deduct advertising costs on their individual tax returns.

S Corporations

Advertising costs are trade or business expenses that are taken into account in determining the profit or loss of the S corporation. They are reported on the specific line provided for advertising on Form 1120S. They are not separately stated items passed through to shareholders. Therefore, shareholders report their net income or loss from the business on Schedule E; they do not deduct advertising costs on their individual tax returns.

C Corporations

Advertising costs are trade or business expenses that are taken into account in determining the profit or loss of the C corporation. They are reported on the specific line provided for advertising on Form 1120. The corporation then pays tax on its net profit or loss. Shareholders do not report any income (or loss) from the corporation.

Retirement Plans

Alert

At the time this book was printed, Congress had not extended numerous breaks for 2014 that had expired at the end of 2013. Check the online supplement in February 2015 at www.jklasser.com or www.barbaraweltman.com to see whether these breaks apply for 2014 returns.

The Social Security benefits you may expect to receive will make up only a portion of your retirement income. And income from your business—through a sale, consulting agreement, or otherwise—may not be as much as you expected.

In order to help you save for your own retirement and to encourage employers to provide retirement benefits to employees, the tax laws contain special incentives for retirement savings. Broadly speaking, if a retirement plan conforms to special requirements, then contributions are deductible while earnings are not currently taxable and forever escape employment taxes that would apply if wages had been paid instead of contributions. What is more, employees covered by such plans are not immediately charged with income. If you have employees, setting up retirement plans to benefit them not only gives you a current deduction for contributions you make to the plan but also provides your staff with benefits. This helps to foster employee goodwill and may aid in recruiting new employees and retaining valued talent. For owners, having a retirement plan can be a handy source of funding (see Chapter 25). Funds in retirement plans can provide a secure financial future (see Chapter 31).

Currently, the law does not require you to set up a qualified retirement plan. Federal law encourages you to do so by tax incentives. A number of states are considering some mandates (see State-Sponsored Plans for the Private Sector later in this chapter) as a way to increase retirement savings. The type of plan you set up governs both the amount you can deduct and the time when you claim the deduction. Certain plans offer special tax incentives designed to encourage employers to help with employee retirement benefits. Even though you may be an employer, if you are self-employed (a sole proprietor, partner, or LLC member), you are treated as an employee for purposes of participating in these plans.

For further information about retirement plans, see IRS Publication 560, *Retirement Plans for Small Business*, IRS Publication 590, *Individual Retirement Arrangements*, IRS Publication 3998, *Choosing a Retirement Solution for Your Small Business*, IRS Publication 4222, *401(k) Plans for Small Businesses*, IRS Publication 4333, *SEP Retirement Plans for Small Business*, and IRS Publication 4674, *Automatic Enrollment 401(k) Plans*.

Qualified Retirement Plans

Qualified retirement plans provide retirement benefits and meet stringent requirements under federal law. Some of these laws fall under the jurisdiction of the Treasury Department and the IRS; others fall under the Department of Labor. Qualified plans allow employees to defer reporting income from benefits until retirement while at the same time allowing employers to claim a current deduction for contributions to the plans.

Income earned by the plan is not currently taxed. Eventually it is taxed to employees when distributed to them as part of their benefits.

Types of Retirement Plans

There are 2 main categories of plans: *defined benefit plans* and *defined contribution plans*.

DEFINED BENEFIT PLANS

Defined benefit plans predict what an employee will receive in benefits upon retirement. This prediction is based on the employee's compensation, age, and anticipated age of retirement. It is also based on an estimation of what the plan can earn over the years. Then an actuary determines the amount that an employer must contribute each year in order to be sure that funds will be there when the employee retires. The employer takes a deduction for the actuarially determined contribution.

There are, however, variations of defined benefit plans. For example, in a cash balance defined benefit plan, benefits payable upon retirement depend in part on plan performance.

DEFINED CONTRIBUTION PLANS

Defined contribution plans are more like savings accounts. The employer contributes to an account for each employee. The contribution is based on a defined formula, such as a percentage of the employee's compensation. The account may not really be a separate account. In corporate plans, it is a bookkeeping notation of the benefits that belong to each employee. The benefits that are ultimately paid to an employee are based on what the contributions actually earn over the years.

There are a variety of plans under the umbrella of defined contribution plans. The most common is the *profit-sharing plan*. Under this plan, the employer agrees to contribute a percentage of employee compensation to the plan. The allocation is usually based purely on an employee's relative compensation (other factors, such as age, can be taken into account).

Another common plan is a *money purchase plan*. Under this plan, the employer also agrees to contribute a fixed percentage of compensation each year. Perhaps the most popular type of defined contribution plan today is the 401(k) plan (also called a cash and deferred compensation arrangement). The reason for its popularity: Contributions are made by employees through salary reduction arrangements that let them fund their retirement plan with pretax dollars. These employee contributions are called *elective deferrals*. Employers often match to some extent employee elective deferrals as a way of encouraging participation, something desirable so that owners, executives, and other highly-paid employees can benefit.

Regardless of the plan selected, all plans have the same requirements designed to ensure that they do not benefit only owners and top executives but also ordinary workers. Many of these requirements are highly technical. They are explained here so that you will recognize how complicated the use of qualified plans can become. It may be helpful to discuss your retirement plans or anticipated plans with a retirement plan expert.

Businesses that do not want to become involved with the complexities of qualified plans can use simplified employee pensions (SEPs) or savings incentive match plans for employees (SIMPLEs), discussed later in this chapter in connection with plans for self-employed persons.

Covering Employees

A plan will be treated as qualified only if it allows employees who meet certain requirements to participate and receive benefits under it. In general, the plan must satisfy one of 3 tests. The first test stipulates that the plan must cover at least 70% of all **nonhighly compensated employees**. This is called the *percentage test*.

Nonhighly compensated employees   All employees who are not treated as highly compensated employees and do not have an ownership interest in the business. These essentially are rank-and-file employees.

Highly compensated employees (HCEs)   These include owners and highly paid employees earning specified amounts ($115,000 in 2014). These amounts are adjusted annually for inflation. Thus, the coverage test needs to be checked annually.

Alternatively, the plan must cover a percentage of nonhighly compensated employees that is at least 70% of the percentage of **highly compensated employees**. This second test is called the *ratio test*. The third alternative is called the *average benefit percentage test* (ABP test). This test also looks at the percentage of nonhighly compensated employees to be sure that there is no discrimination against them.

Participation

Participation is the right of an employee to be covered by a plan after meeting certain participation requirements. In order to be qualified, the plan must not only meet a coverage test but also meet a participation test. The plan must benefit the lesser of 50 employees or 40% or more of all employees. If an employer maintains more than one plan, participation must be satisfied by each plan individually. The plans cannot be grouped together (aggregated) for this purpose.

There are also age and service requirements. The plan can defer participation until the later of the employee attaining the age of 21 or completing one year of service. A 2-year service requirement can be used if there is immediate and full vesting (vesting is discussed later in the chapter).

AUTOMATIC ENROLLMENT

Employers can adopt an automatic enrollment feature for 401(k)s to increase employee participation and eliminate the need for testing whether the plan is nondiscriminatory. To use this automatic enrollment feature, (1) employees must be given an opportunity to opt out of contributions, (2) contributions must be fixed at certain percentages, (3) employees' contributions must be invested in a certain way, and (4) the employer must make certain contributions.

Employers must give eligible employees notice at least 30 days before the automatic enrollment date (no more than 90 days before the date and less for plans with a short waiting period for new employees) and each year thereafter of the right to participate, the automatic contribution amount (explained next), how to opt out or elect a different percentage, the enrollment procedures, the 90-day withdrawal rules (which allow those who don't opt out to withdraw their contributions within this period), and how contributions will be invested.

Employee contributions, which are pretax (elective deferrals), must be at least 3% (but no more than 10%) for the initial period. Contributions increase to 4% in year 2, 5% in year 3, and 6% in year 4 and beyond.

Example

An employee is hired on June 1, 2014, and begins participating on July 1, 2014. He's automatically enrolled at 3% on that date; this rate continues through December 31, 2014 (the end of the initial period). On January 1, 2015, his contribution rate becomes 4%; it's 5% in 2016, and 6% in 2017 and thereafter.

NOTE
Under a safe harbor rule for small employers (those with fewer than 100 employees), employees' contributions to the plan are deemed timely if made within 7 business days following receipt or withholding by the employer.

Employers gain fiduciary protection (employees can't object to investment performance) if they use qualified default investment alternatives (QDIAs). The Department of Labor has specified only 4 types of investments that are QDIAs:

1. A product with a mix of investments that takes into account the individual's age or retirement date (for example, a life cycle or targeted retirement date fund).

2. An investment service that allocates contributions among existing plan options to provide an asset mix that takes into account the individual's age or retirement date (for example, a professionally managed account).

3. A product with a mix of investments that takes into account the characteristics of the group of employees as a whole, rather than each individual (for example, a balanced fund).

4. A capital preservation product for only the first 120 days of participation (for example, a money market fund). This option enables plan sponsors to simplify administration if workers opt out of participation before incurring an additional tax.

TABLE 16.1 Safe Harbor Contributions by Employer (You) for Employees in 401(k) Plan

Employee	Compensation	Elective Deferral	Alternative 1	Alternative 2
You	$90,000	$15,500	$2,700	$3,600
#1	75,000	15,500	2,250	3,000
#2	60,000	0	1,800	0
#3	50,000	1,000	1,500	2,000
#4	40,000	0	1,200	0
#5	30,000	3,000	900	1,200
#6	25,000	2,500	750	1,000
#7	20,000	1,000	600	1,000
#8	20,000	0	600	0
			$12,300	$11,800

There is a choice (but you must use the same choice for all participants). You can either:

- Contribute 3% of compensation (whether or not employees contribute to the plan) ("Alternative 1" in Table 16.1).
- Make a matching contribution of 100% of employee elective deferrals, up to 3% of compensation, plus 50% of the deferral in excess of 3%, up to 5% of compensation ("Alternative 2" in Table 16.1). This translates into the following match contribution percentage:

Employee's Elective Deferral (%)	Your Match
0%	0%
1	1
2	2
3	3
4	3.5
5 or more	4

Example

You have a 401(k) plan in which you and your 8 employees participate. Table 16.1 shows what you have to contribute if you use automatic contributions by employees.

Under a regulation that is generally effective November 15, 2013, distressed employers operating at an economic loss that have safe harbor plans can opt to reduce or suspend their safe harbor nonelective contributions to their 401(k) retirement plans midyear. No IRS request for relief in this case is necessary, but you must give notice to employees about the reduction or suspension in employer contributions and allow employees to change their salary deferral amounts. However, for plan years beginning after 2014, not only must you be operating at an economic loss but you have to meet certain procedural requirements. These include adopting a plan amendment before the end of the year in which the suspension applies and giving certain notice to employees. More details about suspending plan contributions mid-year can be found in Treasury Decision 9641.

Vesting

While the plan must permit certain employees to participate and have contributions made on their behalf, employers can, if they choose, require a certain number of years in the plan before benefits will belong absolutely to the participants. This delay in absolute ownership of benefits is called *vesting*. In order for plans to be qualified, employers cannot defer vesting beyond set limits.

For employer contributions, a plan can provide for *cliff vesting*. Under this type of vesting, there is no ownership of benefits before the completion of 3 years in the plan. At the end of 3 years, all benefits are fully owned by the employee.

The other vesting schedule is called *6-year graded vesting*. This permits vesting of 20% of benefits each year after the first year of service. Under this vesting schedule, there is full vesting after 6 years of participation in the plan.

Permitted Disparity

An employer can reduce the cost of covering employees by integrating the plan with Social Security. This means that the employer can take into account the employer contribution to Social Security for each participant. In effect, the employer's contribution to Social Security is treated as the plan contribution so the employer saves the cost of having to make this contribution a second time to a qualified plan. The employer payment of Social Security tax for each participant is deducted as taxes, not as a pension plan contribution.

Ordinarily the disparity in contributions to employees is viewed as discriminatory. But integrating Social Security contributions with plan contributions is viewed as permitted disparity (i.e., is not discriminatory). The rules for permitted disparity are highly complex, and different rules apply to defined benefit plans and defined contribution plans.

Obtaining and Maintaining Plan Approval

Your plan must be qualified, and only the IRS can tell you if your plan falls within this category. You can use a master or prototype plan for setting up your retirement plan. Plans following these prototypes generally meet IRS requirements, although they are not deemed to have automatic IRS approval. If you design your own plan (or have a professional design one for you), in order to be qualified, the plan must obtain IRS approval. This approval is granted on the basis of how the plan is written and how it will operate. There is no requirement that you obtain approval prior to operating a plan, but it is a good idea to get it. The process is complicated, and the use of a tax or pension professional is advisable.

After initial qualification, your plan may be amended from time to time. For example, you may wish to make changes in how the plan operates—for example, increasing the percentage of compensation upon which your contributions are based. You must amend your plan to reflect law changes that are continually being made.

Compensation Limit

Benefits and contributions are based on a participant's taxable compensation reported on an employee's W-2 form. It does not include tax-free fringe benefits or other excludable wages.

The law limits the amount of compensation that can be taken into account. For 2014, there is a $260,000 limit. If an employee earns $275,000, only the first $260,000 is used to compute benefits and contributions.

> **NOTE**
>
> Frequently you have an extended period of time to amend your plan documents to reflect law changes. But you must operate your plan in accordance with new laws as soon as they become effective.

For the Future

The compensation limit may be adjusted for inflation annually in increments of $5,000.

When both spouses work for the same employer, each can receive a contribution based on his or her respective compensation (up to the compensation limit). In the past, spouses working for the same employer were treated as 1 unit.

Contribution Limit

The contribution limit depends on the type of plan involved. For defined contribution plans, the 2014 limit is the lesser of 25% of compensation or $52,000. This percentage is the top limit. Plans can adopt lesser percentages for contributions.

For defined benefit plans, there is no specific limit on contributions. Rather, the limit is placed on the benefits that can be provided under the plan. Contributions are then actuarially determined to provide these benefits. For 2014, the plan cannot provide benefits exceeding $210,000 per year, adjusted annually for inflation.

For the Future

The benefits limit may be adjusted annually for inflation in increments of $5,000.

Borrowing from the Plan

Owners may be able to borrow from the plan without adverse tax consequences. The plan must permit loans, limiting them to the lesser of:

- $50,000, or
- The greater of $1/2$ your accrued benefit or $10,000.

The loan must be amortized over a period of no more than 5 years (except for loans that are used to buy personal residences) and charge a reasonable rate of interest. As an owner, you cannot deduct interest on the loan.

The plan must also allow rank-and-file employees the opportunity to borrow from the plan on the same basis as owners and top executives.

Added Costs for Retirement Plans

In addition to the contributions you make to the plan, there may be other costs to consider. The type of plan you have affects the nature and amount of these added costs.

Whether you have a defined contribution or a defined benefit plan, you may be required to maintain a bond for yourself or someone else who acts as a fiduciary in your plan. You also must update your plan documents so that they reflect the latest law changes.

If you are approaching retirement age and want to obtain the maximum retirement benefits for your contributions (the biggest bang for your buck), you may want to adopt a defined benefit plan. Before doing so, it is important to recognize that these types of plans entail additional costs not associated with defined contribution plans.

Investment Advice

Employers can, but are not required to, provide investment advice to participants and beneficiaries. In the past, doing this was a prohibited transaction that was penalized. Now it is a way to help staff increase their retirement savings.

Bonding Requirement

To ensure that you will not run off with the funds in your company retirement plan, leaving participants high and dry, you are required to be bonded if you have any control over the plan or its assets. This includes, for example, authority to transfer funds or make disbursements from the plan. The bond must be at least 10% of the amount over which you have control ("currently handled assets"). The bond cannot be less than $1,000, but it need not exceed $1 million.

No bond is required if the plan covers only you as the owner (a self-employed person or a single shareholder-employee) or only partners and their spouses.

Plan Amendments

You are required to keep your plan up to date and operate it in accordance with law changes that are enacted from time to time. For example, if your calendar-year plan adds the option to permit borrowing by plan participants starting in 2014, then the amendment reflecting this option must be completed by December 31, 2014.

You may incur professional fees for updating plan documents. If your plan is a prototype plan provided by a bank, brokerage firm, mutual fund, or insurance company, however, there may be no charge for required updates.

If you discover errors in your plan (either in how it is written or how it is being operated), you can correct the errors and avoid or minimize penalties. If you do not take the initiative and the IRS discovers the problems, you can be subject to greater penalties, interest, and even plan disqualification. More information is contained later in this chapter under Correcting Plan Defects.

Actuarial Costs for Defined Benefit Plans

If you have a defined benefit plan, you must use the services of an enrolled actuary to determine your annual contributions. You must expect to pay for this service year after year.

Pension Benefit Guaranty Corporation Premiums for Defined Benefit Plans

The Pension Benefit Guaranty Corporation (PBGC) is a quasi-federal agency designed to protect employee pension plans in the event that the employer goes under. In order to provide this protection, the PBGC charges annual premiums for each participant in the plan. First, there is a flat-rate premium, which for 2014 is $49 per participant (a different rate applies to multiemployer plans).

Then, for underfunded plans of a single employer (other than "small employers"), there is an additional variable-rate premium (interest rates change monthly) applied to the plan's underfunding. (*Underfunding* means that the employer has not contributed sufficient amounts to pay all anticipated pensions that have already vested.) In 2014, the variable-rate premium per participant is $14 per $1,000 of unfunded vested benefits, with a cap of $412 per participant. Small employers (those with 25 or fewer employees) have their variable rate premium capped at $5 multiplied by the number of plan participants.

You can find instructions for submitting your 2014 premiums to the PBGC at www.pbgc.gov/documents/2014-Premium-Payment-Instructions.pdf. Any changes for 2015 premium submissions will be noted in the Supplement to this book.

Starting in 2015, PGGC premiums will increase, with the flat rate premium indexed for inflation. The variable rate premium will increase to at least $19 (depending on inflation) per $1,000 in 2015.

There is a termination premium payable when a company transfers its underfunded pension plan to the PBGC. The premium is $1,250 per participant per year, payable for each of the 3 years after plan termination.

There is an online system, called My Plan Administration Account (PAA), for paying premiums and filing returns. Payments may no longer be made by credit card. For information, go to www.pbgc.gov.

Plan Start-Up Costs

If you set up a plan, you may be eligible for a special tax credit designed to encourage small business owners to start retirement plans. A small employer eligible for the credit is one with no more than 100 employees who received at least $5,000 of compensation from the company in the preceding year. However, the plan must cover at least 1 employee who is not a highly compensated employee. Thus, a self-employed individual with no employees who sets up a profit-sharing plan cannot claim a tax credit for any of her start-up costs.

In addition to the employee requirement, to qualify for the credit you must not have had a qualified plan in any of the 3 preceding years.

The credit is 50% of eligible start-up costs, for a maximum credit of $500. The credit can be claimed for 3 years starting with the year in which the plan is effective. However, you can opt to first claim the credit in the year immediately preceding the start-up year based on costs incurred in the preceding year.

Example

Your corporation sets up a 401(k) plan that begins on January 1, 2015, and the business qualifies as a small employer. The corporation can opt to take a credit for start-up expenses incurred in 2014 on its 2014 return.

The credit applies only to qualified start-up costs. These include ordinary and necessary expenses to set up the plan, run it, and educate employees about the plan and participation in it. Qualified expenses in excess of the $1,000 taken into account in figuring the $500 maximum credit can be deducted as ordinary and necessary business expenses.

The credit is part of the general business credit.

Retirement Plans for Self-Employed Individuals

Self-employed individuals have 3 main options in retirement plans. First, they can set up qualified retirement plans, which used to be called Keogh plans. These plans may also be known by other names. They have been called H.R.10 plans, reflecting the number of the bill in Congress under which qualified plans for self-employed individuals were created in 1962. They may also be called Basic Plans or some other name created by a bank, brokerage firm, insurance company, or other financial institution offering plan investments. A second option in retirement plans for self-employed individuals is a simplified employee pension plan (SEP). A third option in retirement plans is a savings incentive match plan for employees (SIMPLE). There is a single reference on the tax return to these plans: Self-employed SEP, SIMPLE, and qualified plans.

Self-Employed Qualified Plans in General

Qualified plans for self-employed individuals are subject to the same requirements as qualified plans for corporations. (Banks, brokerage firms, mutual funds, and insurance companies offering plans for self-employed individuals generally may denominate them as Keoghs, basic plans, or simply by the type of plan established, such as a profit-sharing plan.) Like corporate qualified plans, self-employed qualified plans must cover employees of a self-employed person on a nondiscriminatory basis. Also like corporate plans, they are limited in the amount that can be contributed and deducted.

There is an important distinction between self-employed qualified plans and corporate qualified plans: the way in which contributions are calculated on behalf of owner-employees.

Contributions to Self-Employed Qualified Plans

Contributions to all retirement plans are based on compensation. For qualified plans covering employees of corporations, this is simply W-2 taxable wages. For self-employed individuals under self-employed qualified plans, the basis for contributions is a little more complicated. Essentially, the basis for contributions on behalf of owner-employees is net earnings from self-employment. But this is not merely the net profit from your business on which self-employment tax is paid. Net earnings from self-employment must be further reduced by the deduction for the employer portion of the self-employment tax.

To calculate compensation of the owner-employee, start with the profit from Schedule C or Schedule C-EZ (or Schedule F in the case of farming) or the net earnings from self-employment on Schedule K-1 of Form 1065. For partners, this is essentially your distributive share of partnership income plus any guaranteed payments. Net earnings from self-employment from various activities are totaled on Schedule SE, *Self-Employment Tax*. After you have your compensation amount, subtract from this amount the employer portion of the self-employment tax computed on Schedule SE. This net amount is the figure upon which contributions to qualified retirement plans are based.

In order to make contributions on your own behalf, you must have net earnings from self-employment derived from your personal services. If you merely invest capital in a partnership while your personal services are not a material income-producing factor, you cannot make a plan contribution. If you are a limited partner, you cannot base a plan contribution on your distributive share of partnership income. Similar rules apply to members in LLCs. Income received from property, such as rents, interest, or dividends, is not treated as net earnings from self-employment.

CALCULATING YOUR CONTRIBUTION RATE

For self-employed individuals, the contribution rate must be adjusted for the employer deduction on behalf of yourself. This is a roundabout way of saying that the base percentage rate you use to determine contributions on behalf of employees, if any, must be adjusted for determining contributions on your own behalf. To arrive at this reduced percentage rate, divide the contribution rate, expressed as a decimal number, by 1 plus the contribution rate.

> **Example**
>
> The contribution rate for your profit-sharing plan is 25%. You divide 0.25 by 1.25 to arrive at the contribution rate on your behalf: 20%.

Remember, the maximum deduction for 2014 contributions cannot exceed the lesser of $52,000 or $260,000 times your contribution rate.

> **Example**
>
> You maintain a 25% profit-sharing plan for your sole proprietorship, for which you are the only worker. In 2014 your net profit reported on Schedule C is $275,000. Your net earnings from self-employment for purposes of calculating plan contributions are $264,062 ($275,000 – $10,938 [employer portion of the self-employment tax]). Your contribution is limited to $52,000 (20% of $260,000). You cannot base your contribution on your full net earnings from self-employment because of the $260,000 compensation limit and $52,000 deduction limit.

Simplified Employee Pensions in General

Simplified employee pensions, or SEPs, are another type of retirement plan that self-employed individuals can use to save for retirement on a tax-advantaged

---

Form **5305-SEP** (Rev. December 2004) Department of the Treasury Internal Revenue Service	Simplified Employee Pension—Individual Retirement Accounts Contribution Agreement (Under section 408(k) of the Internal Revenue Code)	OMB No. 1545-0499 **Do not** file with the Internal Revenue Service

_____ makes the following agreement under section 408(k) of the
(Name of employer)   Internal Revenue Code and the instructions to this form.

Article I—Eligibility Requirements (check applicable boxes—see instructions)

The employer agrees to provide discretionary contributions in each calendar year to the individual retirement account or individual retirement annuity (IRA) of all employees who are at least _____ years old (not to exceed 21 years old) and have performed services for the employer in at least _____ years (not to exceed 3 years) of the immediately preceding 5 years. This simplified employee pension (SEP) ☐ includes ☐ **does not** include employees covered under a collective bargaining agreement, ☐ includes ☐ **does not** include certain nonresident aliens, and ☐ includes ☐ **does not** include employees whose total compensation during the year is less than $450*.

Article II—SEP Requirements (see instructions)

The employer agrees that contributions made on behalf of each eligible employee will be:

A. Based only on the first $205,000* of compensation.
B. The same percentage of compensation for every employee.
C. Limited annually to the smaller of $41,000* or 25% of compensation.
D. Paid to the employee's IRA trustee, custodian, or insurance company (for an annuity contract).

_____   _____
Employer's signature and date   Name and title

FIGURE 16.1 Form 5305-SEP Simplified Employee Pension

---

basis. (Corporations can use SEPs as well.) The name is a misnomer because the plan does not provide a pension; it merely allows funds to accumulate and be used in retirement. But, as the name implies, these plans do not entail all the administrative costs and complications associated with other qualified retirement plans. There are no annual reporting requirements, as is the case for qualified plans and qualified corporate retirement plans.

Simplified employee pensions are individual retirement accounts set up by employees to which an employer makes contributions, then deducts them. The contributions are a fixed percentage of each employee's compensation. To set up a SEP, an employer need only sign a form establishing the percentage rate for making contributions and for setting eligibility requirements. This is a 1-page form, Form 5305-SEP, *Simplified Employee Pension-IRA Contribution Agreement* (Figure 16.1).

The form is not filed with the IRS. Instead, it serves merely as an agreement under which the employer makes contributions. The employer then instructs employees where to set up SEP-IRAs to receive employer contributions. Banks, brokerage firms, and insurance companies generally have prototype plans designed for this purpose.

The maximum deduction for a contribution under a SEP is essentially the same as for a deferred contribution plan: 25% of compensation or $52,000, whichever is less. For contributions made on behalf of self-employed individuals (called owner-employees), this percentage works out to 20%. As with other qualified plans, no more than $260,000 of compensation in 2014 can be taken into account in computing contributions.

Covering employees in SEPs. You must cover all employees who meet an age and service test. The SEP must cover employees who are 21 or older, earn over $550 in 2014, and have worked for you at any time in at least 3 out of 5 years. You can provide for more favorable coverage (for example, you can cover employees at age 18). The compensation requirement of $550 is adjusted annually for inflation in $50 increments.

Employees over the age of 70½ can continue to participate in a SEP and receive employer contributions. However, required minimum distributions must also be made to these employees.

Salary reduction arrangements for SEPs. Before 1997, a SEP of a small business (with no more than 25 employees who were eligible to participate in the SEP at any time during the prior year) could be designed so that employees funded all or part of their own retirement plans. Employees agreed to reduce their compensation by a set amount. That amount, called an *elective deferral*, was then contributed to the SEP. Employees were treated as not having received the amount by which their salary was reduced so that they did not pay income taxes on that amount. Salary reduction arrangements in SEPs (SARSEPs), were repealed for 1997 and later years. However, employers that had SARSEPs before 1997 can continue these plans, and employees hired after 1996 may participate in these plans. So, for example, if you had a SARSEP plan in 1996, you can continue to fund it with salary reduction amounts in 2014.

Savings Incentive Match Plans for Employees

Self-employed individuals as well as other small employers have another retirement plan alternative: Savings Incentive Match Plans for Employees (SIMPLE). These plans are open to **small employers** who want to avoid complicated nondiscrimination rules and reporting requirements. These SIMPLE plans can be used by corporations as well as by self-employed business owners.

Small employers Those employers with 100 or fewer employees who received at least $5,000 in compensation in the preceding year.

Savings Incentive Match Plans for Employees may be set up as either IRAs or 401(k) plans. The rules for both types of SIMPLE plans are similar but not identical. Employees can contribute to the plans on a salary reduction basis up to $12,000 in 2014 (plus an additional $2,500 if age 50 or older by the end of the year). Self-employed individuals can make similar contributions based on earned income.

Employers satisfy nondiscrimination rules simply by making required contributions. Employers have a choice of contribution formulas:

- Matching contributions (dollar-for-dollar) up to 3% of employee's compensation for the year. For example, in 2014, if an employee under age 50 earning $35,000 makes the maximum salary reduction contribution of

$12,000, the employer must contribute $1,050 (3% of $35,000). The maximum matching contribution per employee in 2014 to a SIMPLE 401(k) is $7,800 (100% of the matching employee contribution, which is up to 3% of $260,000). However, there is no limit on compensation taken into account for employer matching contributions to a SIMPLE-IRA.

For the Future

The elective deferral of $12,000 will be adjusted annually for inflation in increments of $500. The catch-up contribution for those age 50 or older by year-end may also be adjusted annually for inflation in increments of $500.

- Nonelective contributions of 2% of compensation (regardless of whether the employee makes any contributions) for any employee earning at least $5,000. For example, in 2014, if an employee's compensation is $25,000, the employer's contribution is $500 (2% of $25,000). The maximum contribution per employee in 2014 is $5,200 (2% of $260,000, the maximum compensation that can be used to determine contributions).

Contribution reduction for distressed companies. The 3% matching contribution can be reduced at the employer's election, but not below 1%. The reduction cannot be made for more than 2 years of the 5-year period that ends with the year of the election, and you must give notice of the reduced limit to your employees within a reasonable time *before* the 60-day election period in which employees make their salary reduction agreements.

Self-employed persons can make employer contributions to SIMPLE-IRAs on their own behalf as well as make their own contributions. In effect, they are treated as both employer and employee.

Employee and employer contributions vest immediately. This means that employees can withdraw contributions at any time (although withdrawals prior to age $59\frac{1}{2}$ are subject to a 25% penalty if taken within the first 2 years of beginning participation, and 10% if taken after that period).

Employers who want to let employees choose their own financial institutions can adopt SIMPLE plans merely by completing Form 5304-SIMPLE (Figure 16.2). Employers who want to choose the financial institutions for their employees use Form 5305-SIMPLE. Whichever option is chosen, the form is not filed with the IRS but is kept with the employer's records. This form gives the necessary notification to eligible employees and a model salary reduction agreement that can be used by employees to specify their salary reduction contributions. Employers who use SIMPLE plans cannot maintain any other type of qualified retirement plan.

Form **5304-SIMPLE**	Savings Incentive Match Plan	OMB No. 1545-1502
(Rev. March 2012) Department of the Treasury Internal Revenue Service	for Employees of Small Employers (SIMPLE)—Not for Use With a Designated Financial Institution	**Do not** file with the Internal Revenue Service

_____ establishes the following SIMPLE
  Name of Employer

IRA plan under section 408(p) of the Internal Revenue Code and pursuant to the instructions contained in this form.

Article I—Employee Eligibility Requirements *(complete applicable box(es) and blanks—see instructions)*

1   **General Eligibility Requirements.** The Employer agrees to permit salary reduction contributions to be made in each calendar year to the SIMPLE IRA established by each employee who meets the following requirements (select either 1a or 1b):

a   ☐ **Full Eligibility.** All employees are eligible.

b   ☐ **Limited Eligibility.** Eligibility is limited to employees who are described in both (i) and (ii) below:

    (i)   **Current compensation.** Employees who are reasonably expected to receive at least $ _____ in compensation (not to exceed $5,000) for the calendar year.

    (ii)   **Prior compensation.** Employees who have received at least $ _____ in compensation (not to exceed $5,000) during any _____ calendar year(s) (insert 0, 1, or 2) preceding the calendar year.

2   **Excludable Employees.**

    ☐ The Employer elects to exclude employees covered under a collective bargaining agreement for which retirement benefits were the subject of good faith bargaining. **Note:** *This box is deemed checked if the Employer maintains a qualified plan covering only such employees.*

Article II—Salary Reduction Agreements *(complete the box and blank, if applicable—see instructions)*

1   **Salary Reduction Election.** An eligible employee may make an election to have his or her compensation for each pay period reduced. The total amount of the reduction in the employee's compensation for a calendar year cannot exceed the applicable amount for that year.

2   **Timing of Salary Reduction Elections**

a   For a calendar year, an eligible employee may make or modify a salary reduction election during the 60-day period immediately preceding January 1 of that year. However, for the year in which the employee becomes eligible to make salary reduction contributions, the period during which the employee may make or modify the election is a 60-day period that includes either the date the employee becomes eligible or the day before.

b   In addition to the election periods in 2a, eligible employees may make salary reduction elections or modify prior elections _____ , _____ . If the Employer chooses this option, insert a period or periods (for example, semi-annually, quarterly, monthly, or daily) that will apply uniformly to all eligible employees.

c   No salary reduction election may apply to compensation that an employee received, or had a right to immediately receive, before execution of the salary reduction election.

d   An employee may terminate a salary reduction election at any time during the calendar year. ☐ If this box is checked, an employee who terminates a salary reduction election not in accordance with 2b may not resume salary reduction contributions during the calendar year.

Article III—Contributions *(complete the blank, if applicable—see instructions)*

1   **Salary Reduction Contributions.** The amount by which the employee agrees to reduce his or her compensation will be contributed by the Employer to the employee's SIMPLE IRA.

2a   **Matching Contributions**

    (i)   For each calendar year, the Employer will contribute a matching contribution to each eligible employee's SIMPLE IRA equal to the employee's salary reduction contributions up to a limit of 3% of the employee's compensation for the calendar year.

    (ii)   The Employer may reduce the 3% limit for the calendar year in (i) only if:

      (1) The limit is not reduced below 1%; **(2)** The limit is not reduced for more than 2 calendar years during the 5-year period ending with the calendar year the reduction is effective; and **(3)** Each employee is notified of the reduced limit within a reasonable period of time before the employees' 60-day election period for the calendar year (described in Article II, item 2a).

b   **Nonelective Contributions**

    (i)   For any calendar year, instead of making matching contributions, the Employer may make nonelective contributions equal to 2% of compensation for the calendar year to the SIMPLE IRA of each eligible employee who has at least $ _____ , (not more than $5,000) in compensation for the calendar year. No more than $250,000* in compensation can be taken into account in determining the nonelective contribution for each eligible employee.

    (ii)   For any calendar year, the Employer may make 2% nonelective contributions instead of matching contributions only if:

      (1) Each eligible employee is notified that a 2% nonelective contribution will be made instead of a matching contribution; and

      (2) This notification is provided within a reasonable period of time before the employees' 60-day election period for the calendar year (described in Article II, item 2a).

3   **Time and Manner of Contributions**

a   The Employer will make the salary reduction contributions (described in 1 above) for each eligible employee to the SIMPLE IRA established at the financial institution selected by that employee no later than 30 days after the end of the month in which the money is withheld from the employee's pay. See instructions.

b   The Employer will make the matching or nonelective contributions (described in 2a and 2b above) for each eligible employee to the SIMPLE IRA established at the financial institution selected by that employee no later than the due date for filing the Employer's tax return, including extensions, for the taxable year that includes the last day of the calendar year for which the contributions are made.

* *This is the amount for 2012. For later years, the limit may be increased for cost-of-living adjustments. The IRS announces the increase, if any, in a news release, in the Internal Revenue Bulletin, and on the IRS's internet website at **IRS.gov**.*

For Paperwork Reduction Act Notice, see the instructions.   Cat. No. 23377W   Form **5304-SIMPLE** (Rev. 3-2012)

FIGURE 16.2 Form 5304-SIMPLE Savings Incentive Match Plan for Employees of Small Employers

Individual Retirement Accounts as a Plan Alternative

If the cost of covering employees is prohibitive for a self-employed individual, neither a qualified plan, a SEP, nor a SIMPLE plan may be the answer. Instead, the self-employed individual may want to use an IRA. In this case, the maximum that can be deducted is $5,500 (plus $1,000 if the person is age 50 or older by year-end). However, if a self-employed's spouse is a participant in a qualified plan, the self-employed person may deduct $5,500 only if the couple's combined adjusted gross income in 2014 does not exceed $181,000. The $5,000 deduction phases out as the couple's adjusted gross income (AGI) reaches $191,000. If a self-employed individual contributes $5,500 to a Roth IRA, he or she cannot make deductible contributions to an IRA. Individual retirement accounts are discussed later in this chapter.

Regular 401(k)s, Designated Roth Accounts, and Db(k)s

A 401(k) plan is a qualified retirement plan that is funded primarily through employee contributions via salary reductions (self-employed individuals can make so-called employee contributions). Companies can or must make certain matching contributions, depending on the circumstances. Company (employer) contributions vest for participants in the same manner as contributions to other defined contribution plans explained earlier in this chapter. They were legislatively created in 1978, and by 1981, half of all large corporations had adopted them. Today, use of 401(k)s is not exclusive to large corporations; even a sole proprietor with no employees can use a 401(k).

These 401(k) plans allow employers to offer retirement benefits to employees that are largely funded by the employees themselves. To encourage employees to participate in the plans (employers cannot force employees to make contributions), employers may offer matching contributions. For example, an employer may match each dollar of employee deferral with a dollar of employer contributions or some other ratio. Employers who offer 401(k) plans must be careful that stringent nondiscrimination rules are satisfied.

Essentially, these rules require that a sufficient number of rank-and-file employees participate in the plan and make contributions. If the nondiscrimination rules are not satisfied, the plan will not be treated as a qualified plan, and tax benefits will not be available. Explaining the advantages of participating to rank-and-file employees and offering matching contributions are 2 ways to attract the necessary participation; adopting automatic enrollment (as explained earlier in this chapter in connection with participation) is yet another way.

Employees who take advantage of elective deferral options cannot deduct their contributions to the 401(k) plan. They have already received a tax benefit by virtue of the fact that deferrals are excluded from taxable income for income tax purposes. They are still treated as part of compensation for purposes of FICA and FUTA.

From an employer perspective, using 401(k) plans can shift the investment responsibility to employees. Instead of making all of the investment decisions, the employer simply has to offer a menu of investment options to employees. Then the employees decide how they want their funds invested. Employees can be as conservative or as aggressive as they choose. Treasury and Department of Labor regulations detail the number and types of investment options that must be offered and what must be communicated to employees about these investment options.

There is a dollar limit on the elective deferral. In 2014, the elective deferral cannot exceed $17,500. The catch-up (additional) elective deferral limit for those who attain age 50 by December 31, 2014, is $5,500. Thus, the top elective deferral for a participant age 50 or older in 2014 is $23,000.

Those who work for certain tax-exempt organizations—schools, hospitals, and religious organizations—may be able to make elective deferrals used to buy tax-deferred annuities, called 403(b) annuities. The same elective deferral limit applies here.

For the Future

The limits on the basic elective deferral limit as well as the catch-up amount will be adjusted annually for inflation.

One-Person 401(k) Plans

If you work alone, with no employees, can you have a 401(k) plan? The answer is yes, even if you are self-employed. This type of plan may enable you to maximize contributions because you can make both employee salary reduction contributions (elective deferrals) and employer contributions.

Example

You are self-employed, age 45, and have net earnings from self-employment of $152,500. If you have a profit-sharing plan, your contribution is limited to $28,641 (20% of $152,500, after a reduction of $9,296, which is one half of the self-employment tax). But with a one-person 401(k) plan, the maximum contribution of $52,000 can be attained with these earnings (salary reduction contribution of $17,500, plus employer contribution of $34,500). For those with an incorporated business, the maximum contribution is attained with salary of $133,000.

Designated Roth Accounts

Now, 401(k) plans can offer an option that's like a Roth IRA called a designated Roth account. Contributions to designated Roth accounts are made with after-tax dollars (rather than salary reduction amounts). Thus, there is no tax advantage when the money goes into the plan. However, the benefit to this alternative is that all withdrawals (not merely contributions) can be withdrawn tax free after age 59½ (or on account of disability or death or up to $10,000 for first-time homebuying expenses) as long as they have been in the plan for at least 5 years. The 5-year period starts on January 1 of the year in which designated Roth contributions are first made.

Contribution limits to these accounts are the same as for regular 401(k)s. Contributions can be split between regular and Roth 401(k)s as long as the total does not exceed the annual limit. Plans can permit in-plan rollovers from traditional 401(k)s to designated Roth accounts. There is no 20% mandatory withholding, but those making such a rollover must report the amount as taxable income (it is a conversion from a tax-deferred to a tax-free account). There is no 10% early distribution penalty even if the person making the conversion is under age 59½.

Funds from a designated Roth account can be rolled over tax free to another designated Roth account or to a Roth IRA.

How do designated Roth accounts compare with Roth IRAs? Unlike Roth IRAs, designated Roth accounts cannot be undone once the conversion is made. Also, there are lifetime withdrawal requirements on designated Roth accounts that do not apply to Roth IRAs. But there are no income limits for making contributions to designated Roth accounts as there are for contributing to Roth IRAs.

Db(k) Plans

Small businesses (500 or fewer employees) can opt for a new type of qualified plan that combines a small pension (funded by the employer) with a 401(k)-type option (funded by the employee through salary reduction contributions, along with an employer matching contribution). This new plan option, called a Db(k) plan, was created by a law in 2006.

The pension is a defined benefit equal to 1% of final average pay for each year of the employee's service, up to a maximum of 20 years. The 401(k) portion must automatically enroll employees at 4% of pay (although they can opt out or reduce their contributions). The employer must match at least 50% of the employee contribution, with a maximum match of 2% of pay.

As of yet, there has been no IRS guidance on these plans, so financial institutions have yet to offer them; check the Supplement for any developments.

Loans from 401(k) Plans

The rules governing loans from 401(k) plans are the same as those discussed earlier in connection with loans from corporate plans. However, it should be noted that all participants, not just owners, are prohibited from deducting interest on plan loans. But the interest is really being paid to the participant's own account, so the loss of a deduction is not so important.

Selecting Plan Investments

Generally, a 401(k) plan must offer a menu of investment options to participants. Usually this is done by opting to have the plan with a family of mutual funds, such as Fidelity or Vanguard. In choosing the mutual fund or other company with which to place the plan, consider:

- *Investment choices.* The Department of Labor has regulations governing the minimum number and type of investment choices that must be offered by the plan.
- *Fees.* The Departments of Labor and the Treasury have rules regarding fees and their disclosure. Check on administrative fees (the amount charged for maintaining the plan), asset-based fees (amounts paid for specific types of investments), and service fees (amounts paid for optional services).

Individual Retirement Accounts

Another retirement plan option to consider is an IRA. There are now 3 types of personal IRAs to consider for retirement savings: traditional deductible IRAs, traditional nondeductible IRAs, and Roth IRAs. The maximum amount that can be contributed in 2014 is $5,500 (or taxable earned income if less than $5,500). If you have a nonworking spouse, the contribution limit is $5,500 for each spouse (as long as you have earned income of at least $11,000). (The account for a nonworking spouse is called a Kay Bailey Hutchison IRA.) Therefore the limit is considerably lower than the limit for other retirement plans.

In addition to the basic contribution limit, those who attain age 50 by year-end can make additional catch-up contributions. The limit on catch-up contributions to IRAs in 2014 is $1,000.

If you are self-employed and have more than one business, you must aggregate your business income to determine compensation for purposes of calculating contributions. You cannot base an IRA contribution on a pension or annuity income or income received from property, such as rents, interest, or dividends. (A special rule allows alimony and military combat pay to be treated as compensation for purposes of IRA contributions.)

However, if you are in business and set up an IRA for yourself, you need not cover your employees. For some, this factor alone may dictate in favor of an IRA.

If you are age 70$^1/_2$ and have a business, you cannot make contributions to a deductible or traditional nondeductible IRA. In this instance, you may want to explore other retirement plans, such as the Roth IRAs.

Individual Retirement Accounts and Other Retirement Plans

Whether you can make deductible contributions to both an IRA and another retirement plan depends on your overall income. Individuals who are considered active participants in qualified retirement plans cannot deduct contributions to an IRA if adjusted gross income exceeds a certain amount. More specifically, in

2014 no deduction can be claimed by an active participant when adjusted gross income exceeds $70,000 in the case of single individuals, $116,000 for married persons filing jointly and surviving spouses, or $10,000 for married persons filing separate returns. The deduction is phased out for AGI of up to $10,000 less than the phase-out limit (phase-out starts at $60,000 for singles; $96,000 for married persons filing joint returns). The phase-out limits will be indexed for inflation each year.

You are considered an *active participant* if, at any time during the year, either you or your spouse is covered by an employer retirement plan. An employer retirement plan includes all of the following plans:

- Qualified pension, profit-sharing, or stock bonus plan
- SEP plan
- SIMPLE plan
- Qualified annuity plan
- Tax-sheltered annuity
- A plan established by the federal, state, or political subdivision for its employees (other than a state Section 457 plan)

If you are an active participant (or your spouse is an active participant) and your AGI is over the limit for your filing status, you can make a traditional non-deductible IRA contribution. There is no AGI limit on making this type of IRA contribution.

Alternatively, you may want to make contributions to a Roth IRA. Contributions must be based on compensation (just as they are for traditional IRAs), but there are some important differences between the Roth and a traditional IRA. First, contributions to a Roth can be made regardless of your age. So, for example, if you have a consulting business and you are 75 years old, you can still fund a Roth IRA. Second, there are no required lifetime minimum distributions, as there are from traditional IRAs commencing at age 70½. Third, contributions can be made regardless of whether you (or your spouse) are an active participant in a qualified retirement plan. Fourth, and most significantly, if funds remain in the Roth IRA for at least 5 years, withdrawals after age 59½, or because of disability, or to pay first-time home-buying expenses (up to $10,000 in a lifetime) are completely free from income tax.

The 5-year period starts on the first day of the year in which contributions are made (or to which they relate). So, for example, if you make a 2014 contribution to a Roth IRA on April 15, 2015 (the due date of your 2014 return), the 5-year holding period commences on January 1, 2014, the year to which the first contribution relates. However, you can make full Roth IRA contributions only if your AGI is no more than $114,000, or $181,000 on a joint return. (The contribution limit is reduced if your AGI is between $114,000 and $129,000 if you are single, or $181,000 and $191,000 on a joint return.)

Spousal IRAs. Called Kay Bailey Hutchinson IRAs, these accounts can be opened for a nonworking spouse to enable a couple to double the annual contributions to IRAs and Roth IRAs. If one spouse is age 50 or older, add $1,000 to the contribution limit; if both are age 50 or older, add $2,000 to the contribution limit.

Example

In 2014, you are self-employed (and you don't work for anyone else with a retirement plan), while your spouse does not work outside the home and does not perform services for your business. Assuming you are both under age 50, you can contribute up to $11,000 ($5,500 for your IRA and $5,500 for your spouse's IRA). If your contributions are to a traditional IRA, then you can deduct $11,000 on your joint return as long as your net earnings from self-employment are at least $11,000. (If one spouse was age 50 or older, the deduction would be $12,000; if both were age 50 or older, the deduction would be $13,000. If your contributions are to a Roth IRA, no deduction is allowed, but you still must file jointly to make the Roth IRA contributions.

Converting to a Roth IRA. In planning to maximize your retirement funds, you may want to convert your traditional IRAs to a Roth IRA if you did not do so already. This will allow you to build up a tax-free retirement nest egg (provided the funds remain in the Roth IRA at least 5 years and are not withdrawn unless you meet a withdrawal condition). The price of conversion is that you must report all the income that would have resulted had you simply taken a distribution from your IRAs.

There is no 10% penalty on conversion income even if you are under age 59½, as long as the funds remain in the Roth IRA for at least 5 years. This 5-year period is measured from January 1 of the year in which the conversion is made.

In deciding to use a traditional IRA, be aware of certain restrictions designed to encourage savings and prevent dissipation of the account prior to retirement. First, you generally cannot withdraw IRA contributions, or earnings on those contributions, before age 59½. Doing so may result in a 10% early distribution penalty. There are a number of exceptions to the early distribution penalty:

- Disability
- Withdrawals taken ratably over your life expectancy
- Distributions to pay medical expenses in excess of the applicable percentage of AGI
- Distributions to pay health insurance premiums by those who are unemployed (self-employed can be treated as unemployed for this purpose)
- Distributions to pay qualified higher education costs

- Distributions for first-time home-buying expenses (up to $10,000 in a life-time)
- Involuntary distributions resulting from IRS levies upon IRAs to satisfy back taxes
- Distributions by reservists called to active duty

However, there is no exception to the 10% penalty for economic or financial hardship.

Second, you must begin withdrawals from traditional IRAs no later than April 1 of the year following the year of attaining age 70½. The failure to take certain minimum distributions designed to exhaust the account over your life expectancy results in a 50% penalty tax. The minimum distribution requirement applies as well to qualified retirement plans, SEP-IRAs, and SIMPLE plans.

MyRAs

Created by an executive order in early 2014, MyRAs (pronounced My-R-As) can be offered as a retirement savings option to your employees if your business does not have another qualified retirement plan once government rules are set (they are expected to be announced before the end of 2014 and will be included in the Supplement). Likely MyRAs will begin in 2015, at least for some employers participating in an expected pilot program. This is a modest plan designed to enable low-income employees to begin retirement savings that can be funded with payroll withholding of at least $5. As the employer, you do not make any contributions to their accounts. You do not have to decide on how funds are invested; they automatically earn a rate of interest comparable to the rate earned by the Thrift Savings Plan Government Securities Investment Fund (which is open only to federal employees). The value of employees' accounts can never decline.

Participation in MyRAs is limited to employees with adjusted gross income (AGI) up to Roth IRA limits (above). Thus, the AGI limit is $191,000 for joint filers and $129,000 for singles). Once the account balance reaches $15,000, or after 30 years, the funds must be moved to a Roth IRA.

More details about MyRAs were not available at the time this book was published; see the Supplement for more details.

State-Sponsored Plans for the Private Sector

At present, there is no federal mandate requiring employers to offer qualified retirement plans. However, some states are taking this route. California may become the first state to put a plan into action starting in 2015 or some time thereafter.

Under the California Secure Choice Retirement Savings (CSCRS) Trust Act, employers with 5 or more employees that do not offer a qualified retirement plan will be required to withhold 3% of employees' wages and contribute it to the state's CSCRS Investment Board. Employers with fewer than 5 employees that do not offer a qualified retirement plan can choose to have their employees participate in the state-sponsored plan.

California is not alone. More than a dozen other states, including Connecticut and Maryland, are currently exploring similar options. Check the Supplement for any updates.

When to Take Action

Using a retirement plan for your business means setting one up within set time limits, making timely contributions, and taking other action when required.

Setting Up a Plan

You must complete and sign the paperwork, even if you don't contribute a penny, by a set date dependent on the type of plan you use:

- Qualified retirement plans, such as 401(k) plans—December 31, 2014, for a 2014 plan.
- SEPs—extended due date of your return (e.g., October 15, 2015, for a 2014 plan for a sole proprietor with a filing extension).
- SIMPLEs—October 1, 2014, for a 2014 plan. For a new employer coming into existence after October 1, the deadline is as soon as it is administratively feasible in 2014.
- IRAs and Roth IRAs—April 15, 2015, for 2014 contributions.

Making Contributions

Contributions to defined benefit plans must be made on a quarterly basis. In order to avoid a special interest charge, contributions made in quarterly installments must be at least 90% of contributions for the current year or 100% of contributions for the prior year. If contributions are based on the current year, the balance of the contributions may be made as late as the due date for the employer's return, including extensions.

Contributions for defined contribution plans and SEPs can be made at any time up to the due date of the employer's return, including extensions. In fact, contributions can be made even after the employer's tax return is filed as long as they do not exceed the return's due date. In effect, contributions can be funded through a tax refund.

> ### Example
>
> An employer (C corporation), whose 2014 return is ordinarily due on March 15, 2015, obtains a filing extension to September 15, 2015. The return is filed on June 1, 2015, and a refund is received on August 15, 2015. The employer has

until September 15, 2015, to complete contributions to its profit-sharing plan, a deduction for which was reported on the return. The employer can use the refund for this purpose. However, the refund cannot be directly deposited into the profit-sharing plan as is the case with a direct deposit of a refund in an IRA.

The only way to extend the deadline for making contributions is to obtain a valid filing extension. For example, an owner of a professional corporation on a calendar year who wants to extend the time for making contributions must obtain an extension of time to file Form 1120, the return for that corporation. To do this, Form 7004, *Application for Automatic Extension of Time to File Corporation Income Tax Return*, must be filed no later than March 15, the due date for Form 1120 for calendar-year corporations.

NOTE

Contributions to defined benefit plans subject to minimum funding requirements must be made no later than September 15 (even if there is an extension of time to file the return until October 15).

Filing Form 7004 gives the corporation an automatic 6-month filing extension, to September 15. The corporation then has until September 15 to make its contributions to the plan.

Contributions generally must be made in cash. When cash flow is insufficient to meet contribution requirements (and there are no refunds available for this purpose, as explained earlier), employers may be forced to borrow to make contributions on time. In some instances, contributions can be made by using employer stock.

Watch the timing of making contributions to a SIMPLE plan. While employer contributions can be made up to the extended due date of the employer's return, contributions through elective deferrals must be made no later than 30 days after the end of the month for which the contributions are to be made (e.g., January 30, 2015, for a 2014 plan).

Example

Sally, age 45, has a SIMPLE IRA plan for her consulting business in which she nets $90,000. For 2014, her elective deferral contribution is $12,000, and the business makes a $2,700 contribution (3% of $90,000). The $12,000 must actually be contributed by January 30, 2015. If Sally obtains an automatic filing extension, she has until October 15, 2015, to make the $2,700 contribution.

Contributions for 2014 to IRAs and Roth IRAs must be completed no later than April 15, 2015, even if you obtain a filing extension. Contributions to an IRA or a Roth IRA can be made directly or through direct deposit of a tax refund. The deposit is made by providing account information directly on the return or, if directing the refund to 2 or 3 different accounts, on Form 8888, *Direct Deposit of Refund to More Than One Account*. If you are using a direct deposit to make a 2015 contribution, be sure that the return is filed early enough in 2014 to allow for processing and fund transfer to the IRA before April 15, 2015 (the deadline for 2014 IRA contributions).

Filing Information Returns

Qualified retirement plans (other than some small plans as well as SEPs and SIMPLE IRAs of any size) are required to report their activities annually to the Department of Labor's Employee Benefits Security Administration. For details, see Appendix A.

Actions to Avoid

While qualified retirement plans offer the opportunity for building wealth on a tax-advantaged basis, they are fraught with potential penalties for missteps. Some errors can be easily corrected, as explained later in this chapter. Others can be fatal to the plan, and cost owners and other participants dearly. Here are some actions that should *not* be taken.

Excess Contributions

If you contribute more than the dollar amount permissible, you have made an excess contribution. The excess contribution is subject to an excise tax (essentially a penalty) of 6% per year, each year, for as long as the excess amount remains in the plan.

You can avoid or limit the tax by withdrawing the funds or applying them to future contributions. No penalty applies if the excess contributions are withdrawn by the due date of the return (including extensions) for the year to which the excess contributions relate.

Plan Errors

Because retirement plan rules are complicated, it's easy to make mistakes. The IRS has this list of common errors:

- Not covering the proper employees
- Not giving employees required information
- Not depositing employee deferrals timely
- Not depositing employer contributions timely
- Not following the terms of the plan document
- Not limiting employee deferrals and employer contributions to the proper maximum limits

You can correct mistakes using the IRS' Employee Plans Compliance Resolution System (EPCRS). Some mistakes can be self-corrected without penalty; others require IRS approval and entail a penalty. Always consult a benefits expert if you have questions about your plan and possible errors that may exist.

Prohibited Transactions

The tax law has strict rules about what you can and cannot do when it comes to your qualified retirement plans and IRAs. The funds are designed for retirement savings; the rules prevent you from self-dealing and certain other actions that are thought to run counter to the purpose of these plans.

Paraphrasing the Senate Report from 1974, the purpose of prohibited transactions is to prevent taxpayers from using their qualified retirement plans to engage in transactions that could place plan assets and income at risk of loss before retirement. Prohibited transactions are listed in Section 4975 of the Internal Revenue Code. They include any direct or indirect:

1. Sale, exchange, or leasing of any property between a plan and a disqualified person.
2. Lending of money or other extension of credit between a plan and a disqualified person.
3. Furnishing of goods, services, or facilities between a plan and a disqualified person.
4. Transfer to, or use by or for the benefit of, a disqualified person of the income or assets of a plan.
5. Action by a disqualified person who is a fiduciary whereby he deals with the income or assets of a plan in his own interests or for his own account.
6. Receipt of any consideration for his own personal account by any disqualified person who is a fiduciary from any party dealing with the plan in connection with a transaction involving the income or assets of the plan.

The fact that a transaction would qualify as a prudent investment under the highest fiduciary standards does not change the character of the transaction. Prohibited transactions are subject to excise taxes:

- 15% excise tax. For example, failing to deposit employee contributions into 401(k) plans on time is a prohibited transaction subject to a 15% excise tax. It's a prohibited transaction because the company is holding onto the funds (i.e., a disqualified entity is using funds for its own purposes).
- 100% excise tax if the prohibited transaction is not corrected in time.

In some situations, the prohibited transaction results in the loss of tax-deferred status for the plan or account as of the first day of the year in which the prohibited transaction occurs. This means that all of the funds in the account become immediately taxable to the account owner. And, if the account owner is under age 59¹/₂ at the time, there is a 10% early distribution penalty as well.

The best way to avoid problems is to talk with a knowledgeable tax advisor before making any moves with a qualified plan or IRA that could raise questions about self-dealing.

Comparison of Qualified Retirement Plans

The different choices of qualified retirement plans have been discussed at length. But how do you know which plan is best for you? There are several factors to consider:

- How much money do you have to set aside in a retirement plan? If your business is continually profitable, you may want to commit to a type of plan that requires contributions without regard to profits. If your business is good in some years but bad in others, you may want to use a profit-sharing-type plan that does not require contributions in poor years.

- How much will it cost to cover employees? When there are few or no employees, then the choice of plan is largely a question of what will be the most beneficial to you. When a great number of employees will have to be covered, the cost may be too prohibitive to provide substantial retirement benefits. However, if your competitors offer plans to their employees, you may be forced to offer similar benefits as a means of attracting or retaining employees.

- How soon do you expect to retire? The closer you are to retirement, the more inclined you may be to use a defined benefit plan to sock away as much as possible.

- Also consider the costs of administration, the amount of entanglement with the IRS, and your financial sophistication and comfort level with more exotic arrangements.

Table 16.2 offers a comparison of the retirement plans.

Defined Benefit Plans versus Defined Contribution Plans

Defined benefit plans offer owners the opportunity to slant more contributions to their own benefit, especially if they are older than their employees. However, most small business employers are moving away from defined benefit plans because of the complexities and costs of administration. Defined benefit plans are by far more costly to administer than defined contribution plans. First, there are the costs of plan design. Defined benefit plans may be specially tailored to each employer, whereas defined contribution plans generally use prototypes

TABLE 16.2 Comparison of Retirement Plans in 2014

Type of Plan	Maximum Contribution	Last Date for Contribution
IRA	$5,500 or taxable compensation, whichever is smaller ($6,500 for those 50 or older)	Due date of your return (without extensions)
SIMPLE plan	$12,000 (not to exceed taxable compensation), plus catch-up contributions, plus employer contributions	Due date of employer's return for employer contributions (including extensions); 30 days after end of month for salary reduction contributions
SEP-IRA	$52,000 or 20% of participant's taxable compensation, whichever is smaller	Due date of employer's return (including extensions)
Qualified plan	Defined contribution plan—smaller of $52,000 or 25% of compensation (20% of self-employed's income)	Due date of employer's return (including extensions). Note: Plan must be set up no later than the last day of the employer's tax year.
	Defined benefit plan—amount needed to provide retirement benefit no larger than the lesser of $210,000 or 100% of the participant's average taxable compensation for highest 3 consecutive years	Due date of employer's return (including extensions) but not later than the minimum funding deadline. Note: Plan must be set up no later than the last day of the employer's tax year.

readily available. Second, there is the cost of the actuary to determine contributions necessary to fund the promised benefits. Third, there are annual premiums paid to the Pension Benefit Guaranty Corporation (PBGC), a federal agency designed to provide some measure of protection for employees (somewhat akin to FDIC insurance for bank accounts). These premiums are calculated on a per-participant basis, with an additional premium for underfunded plans (as discussed earlier in this chapter).

Another factor to consider when deciding between defined benefit and defined contribution plans is the timing of making contributions. Contributions to defined contribution plans can be made at any time during the year to which they relate but can also be made as late as the due date for the employer's return, including extensions. In the case of defined benefit plans, contributions must be made more rapidly than those to defined contribution plans. Defined benefit plans have quarterly contribution requirements, and the failure to make sufficient contributions quarterly can result in penalties.

Qualified Plan versus Simplified Employee Pension

If you use a profit-sharing plan, the contribution limit is the same for both self-employed qualified plans and SEPs. However, there are some reasons for using one or the other type of retirement plan.

NOTE
Those who were born before 1936 can continue to use 10-year averaging to report distributions from qualified plans, an option not open to distributions from SEPs, regardless of the participant's age.

A SEP offers a couple of advantages over self-employed qualified plans. A qualified plan must be set up no later than the last day of your tax year, even though contributions can be made up to the due date of the return, including extensions. In contrast, a SEP can be set up as late as the date for making contributions, which is also the due date of your return, including extensions. There is less paperwork involved in a SEP than in a qualified plan. While qualified plans must file information returns with the IRS annually, SEPs have no similar annual reporting requirements.

In the past, qualified plans offered one advantage over SEPs—the ability to use 5-year averaging to reduce the tax cost on distributions. This option no longer applies, and all distributions are taxed the same as distributions from SEP (i.e., ordinary income).

SIMPLE-IRA versus Self-Employed Qualified Plan or SEP

Business owners with modest earnings may be able to put more into a SIMPLE-IRA than a qualified plan. The reason: The employee contribution (which a self-employed individual can also make) to a SIMPLE-IRA is not based on a percentage of income but rather a dollar amount up to $12,000 in 2014 ($14,500 for those age 50 or older). (The 25% annual compensation limit applies to employee contributions to SIMPLE-401(k)s.) For example, assume a 40-year-old self-employed individual's net earnings from self-employment are $25,000. The top contribution to a SIMPLE-IRA is $12,750 ($12,000 salary reduction contribution, plus $750 employer matching contribution). In contrast, the contribution limit to a profit-sharing plan or SEP in this instance is only $5,000, considerably less than that allowed for a SIMPLE-IRA.

The bottom line is that business owners who want to maximize their retirement plan contributions need to run the numbers to determine which plan is preferable.

ESOPs

An employee stock option plan (ESOP) is a type of employee benefit plan that effectively gives workers an ownership interest in your business. Since it is a stock-based plan, it can be used only for corporations (both C and S), although it cannot be used for most professional corporations.

How an ESOP Works

The corporation sets up a trust into which it contributes either shares of its stock or cash to buy shares. Or the corporation can borrow money to buy shares and contribute cash to the trust to repay the loan. Shares are then allocated to plan participants (employees) in a manner similar to a profit-sharing plan; vesting rules apply.

Typically, professional fees and other costs for setting up an ESOP are substantial ($25,000 to $50,000 for even small companies). Thus, such plans are not used for very small companies (e.g., fewer than 50 employees).

Tax Breaks

For the corporation:

- Contributions of cash to buy shares or to repay a loan, or to buy shares of stock are tax deductible. Contribution limits are lower for S corporations than for C corporations.
- In C corporations, once the ESOP owns 30% of all the shares in the company, the seller can reinvest the proceeds of the sale in other securities and defer any tax on the gain.
- In S corporations, the percentage of ownership held by the ESOP is not subject to income tax at the federal level (and usually not the state level, either). This means earnings of the S corporation escape federal income tax; they are not taxed to the corporation because it is an S corporation, and they are not taxed to the ESOP because it is an exempt trust. For example, there is no income tax on 40% of the profits of an S corporation that has an ESOP holding 40% of the stock, and no income tax on the profits of an S corporation wholly owned by its ESOP. However, the ESOP still must get a pro-rata share of any distributions the company makes to owners.
- Dividends used to repay an ESOP loan, passed through to employees, or reinvested by employees in company stock are tax-deductible.

For employees:

- Employees are not taxed on contributions made to the plan on their behalf.
- For stock in C corporations, departing employees can roll over the shares to an IRA or other qualified retirement plan. If they opt to report the income, then any future appreciation on the shares will be taxed at capital gains rates when the shares are eventually sold. No rollover of S corporation stock is allowed.

Uses for ESOPs

ESOPs are a way to shift ownership to employees. This is viewed as an important employee benefit.

ESOPs can also be used to buy out the interest of a departing owner. For example, say an owner wants to retire but has no obvious person, such as a son or daughter, to be the successor-owner; the employees become the owners through the ESOP. From the owner's perspective, a sale of 30% or more of an interest in a closely held business enables the owner to defer tax on the gain from the sale by buying so-called replacement securities; gain is recognized when and to the extent that replacement securities are sold.

ESOPs can borrow money and effectively convert repayments of *both* interest and principal into tax-deductible amounts. The borrowed funds are used to buy company shares or shares from existing owners. The corporation then makes tax-deductible contributions to the ESOP to repay the loan.

Correcting Plan Defects

Running a business and overseeing your company's retirement plan may be a big challenge, and problems in the plan can creep in. Maybe someone who should be allowed to participate has been prevented from doing so; maybe you failed to deposit employees' contributions within the required period; or maybe you did not update your plan documents. The IRS's Employee Plans Corrections Resolution System (EPCRS) can be used to correct defects and problems with little or no penalty. Find details at www.irs.gov and search "correcting plan errors." It is best to work with a tax professional to use the proper correction option.

Nonqualified Retirement Plans

If you have a business and want to provide retirement benefits without the limitations and requirements imposed on qualified plans, you can use nonqualified plans. Nonqualified plans are simply plans you design yourself to provide you and/or your employees with whatever benefits you desire. Benefits under the plan are not taxed to the employees until they receive them and include them in their income. But the plan must restrict distributions to fixed events (e.g., separation from service, a fixed date, a change in company ownership, or an unfortunate emergency), or participants become subject to interest and penalties.

There are no nondiscrimination rules to comply with. You can cover only those employees you want to give additional retirement benefits, and this can be limited to owners or key executives. There are no minimum or maximum contributions to make to the plan. However, because nonqualified plans give you all the flexibility you need to tailor benefits as you see fit, the law prevents you, as the employer, from enjoying certain tax benefits. You cannot deduct amounts now that you will pay in the future to employees under the plan. Your deduction usually cannot be claimed until benefits are actually paid to employees. However, there is a circumstance under which you can deduct these amounts: If you segregate the amounts from the general assets of your business so that they are not available to meet the claims of your general creditors, the amounts become immediately taxable to the employees and thus deductible by you.

How a Nonqualified Plan Works

Suppose you want to allow your key employees the opportunity to defer bonuses or a portion of their compensation until retirement. To do this, you set up a nonqualified plan. These employees can defer specified amounts until termination, retirement, or some other time or event. The employees in the plan must agree to defer the compensation before it is earned. They generally have no guarantee that the funds they agree to defer will, in fact, be there for them upon retirement. If your business goes under, they must stand in line along with all your other creditors. Employees should be made to understand the risk of a deferred compensation arrangement.

Once you set up the terms of the plan, you simply set up a bookkeeping entry to record the amount of deferred compensation. You may also want to credit each employee's deferred compensation account with an amount representing interest. In the past, there had been some controversy on the tax treatment of this interest. One court allowed a current deduction for the interest. The IRS, on the other hand, had maintained that no deduction for the interest could be claimed until it, along with the compensation, was paid out to employees and included in their income. However, that court changed its view and now agrees with the IRS. As long as receipt of the interest is deferred, so, too, is your deduction for the interest.

Rabbi Trusts

This is a special kind of nonqualified deferred compensation that got its name from the original employees covered by the plan—rabbis. The plans provide a measure of security for employees without triggering current taxation on contributions under the plan. Employers are still prevented from claiming a current deduction. These plans have now been standardized, and the IRS even provides model rabbi trust forms to be used in setting them up.

Deferred Compensation Plans

These are explained in Chapter 7.

Glossary of Terms for Retirement Plans

The following terms have been used throughout this chapter in connection with retirement plans.

Catch-up contributions Additional employee contributions that can be made only by those who attain age 50 by the end of the year.

Compensation The amount upon which contributions and benefits are calculated. Compensation for employees is taxable wages reported on Form W-2. Compensation for self-employed individuals is net profit from a sole proprietorship or net self-employment income reported to a partner or limited liability member on Schedule K-1.

Coverage Qualified plans must include a certain percentage of rank-and-file employees.

Db(k) Hybrid qualified retirement plans combining an employer-funded pension with a 401(k).

Defined benefit plans Pension plans in which benefits are fixed according to the employee's compensation, years of participation in the plan, and age upon retirement. Contributions are actuarially determined to provide sufficient funds to cover promised pension amounts.

Defined contribution plans Retirement plans in which benefits are determined by annual contributions on behalf of each participant, the amount these contributions can earn, and the length of time the participant is in the plan.

Designated Roth Accounts An option for a 401(k) plans to permit after-tax contributions that grow tax free.

Elective deferrals A portion of the employee's salary that is contributed to a retirement plan on a pretax basis. Elective deferrals apply in the case of 401(k) plans, 403(b) annuities, SARSEPs (established before 1997), and SIMPLE plans.

Employee plans corrections resolution system (EPCRS) An IRS program that can be used to correct defects and problems in qualified retirement plans with little or no penalty.

Employee stock ownership plans (ESOPs) An employee benefit plan giving ownership interests in a corporation to employees.

Excess contribution penalty A 6% cumulative penalty imposed on an employer for making contributions in excess of contribution limits.

Funding In the case of defined benefit plans, the amount of assets required to be in the plan in order to meet plan liabilities (current and future pension obligations).

Highly compensated employees Owners and employees earning compensation over certain limits that are adjusted annually for inflation.

Keogh plans A term that had been used to designate qualified retirement plans for self-employed individuals (also called H.R.10 plans). This term is no longer in use.

Master and prototype plans Plans typically designed by banks and other institutions to be used for qualified retirement plans.

Money purchase plans Defined contribution plans in which the annual contribution percentage is fixed without regard to whether the business has profits.

MyRAs Modest nondeductible IRA-like savings accounts for workers who are not covered by a qualified retirement plan.

Nondiscrimination Requirements to provide benefits for rank-and-file employees and not simply to favor owners and highly paid employees.

Participation The right of an employee to be a member of the retirement plan and have benefits and contributions made on his or her behalf.

Pension Benefit Guaranty Corporation (PBGC) A federal agency that will pay a minimum pension to participants of defined benefit plans in companies that have not made sufficient contributions to fund their pension liabilities.

Premature distribution penalty A 10% penalty imposed on a participant for receiving benefits before age 59½ or some other qualifying event.

Profit-sharing plan A defined contribution plan with contributions based on a fixed percentage of compensation.

Prohibited transactions Dealings between employers and the plan, such as certain loans, sales, and other transactions between these parties. Prohibited transactions result in penalties and can even result in plan disqualification.

Qualified default investment alternative (QDIA) Permissible 401(k) investments by a plan with automatic enrollment.

Required distributions Plans must begin to distribute benefits to employees at a certain time. Generally, benefits must begin to be paid out no later than April 1 following the year in which a participant attains age 70½. Failure to receive required minimum distributions results in a 50% penalty on the participant.

Roth 401(k)s See Designated Roth accounts.

Roth IRAs Nondeductible IRAs that permit tax-free withdrawals if certain holding period requirements are met.

Salary reduction arrangements Arrangements to make contributions to qualified plans from an employee's compensation on a pretax basis. In general, salary reduction arrangements relate to 401(k) plans, 403(b) annuities, SARSEPs in existence before 1997, and SIMPLE plans.

Savings incentive match plans of employees (SIMPLEs) IRA- or 401(k)-type plans that permit modest employee contributions via salary reduction and require modest employer contributions. SIMPLE plans are easy to set up and administer.

Simplified employee pensions (SEPs) IRAs set up by employees to which an employer makes contributions based on a percentage of income.

Stock bonus plans   Defined contribution plans that give participants shares of stock in the employer rather than cash.

Top-heavy plans   Qualified retirement plans that provide more than a certain amount of benefits or contributions to owners and/or highly paid employees. Top-heavy plans have special vesting schedules.

Vesting   The right of an employee to own his or her pension benefits. Vesting schedules are set by law, although employers can provide for faster vesting.

Where to Claim Deductions for Retirement Plans

Employees

If you contribute to an IRA and are entitled to a deduction, you claim it on page 1 of Form 1040 as an adjustment to gross income. If you contribute to a salary reduction plan (such as a SIMPLE or a 401(k) plan), you cannot deduct your contribution.

All Employers

To claim the credit for plan start-up costs of small employers, file Form 8881, *Credit for Small Employer Pension Plan Startup Costs*. The credit is part of the general business credit and so must be entered on Form 3800, *General Business Credit*, if you have another credit that is part of the general business credit.

Self-Employed

Contributions you make to self-employed qualified retirement plans, SEPs, or SIMPLEs on behalf of your employees are entered on Schedule C (or Schedule F for farming operations) on the specific line provided on the form, called pension and profit-sharing plans. Contributions you make on your own behalf are claimed on page 1 of Form 1040 as an adjustment to gross income. Contributions you make to an IRA are also claimed on page 1 of Form 1040 as an adjustment to gross income.

Partnerships and LLCs

Deductions for contributions to qualified plans on behalf of employees are part of the partnership's or LLC's ordinary trade or business income on Form 1065. The deductions are entered on the line provided for retirement plans.

The entity does not make contributions on behalf of partners or members. Partners and members can set up their own retirement plans based on their self-employment income. Thus, if partners and members set up qualified retirement plans, they claim deductions for their contributions on page 1 of Form 1040.

As a practical matter, small partnerships and LLCs generally do not establish qualified plans for employees, since the partners and members do not get any direct benefit.

S Corporations

Deductions for contributions to qualified plans are taken by the corporation as part of its ordinary trade or business income on Form 1120S. Enter the deduction on the line provided for pension plans, profit-sharing plans, and so on. This line includes contributions to nonqualified plans if the corporation is entitled to claim a current deduction for such contributions.

C Corporations

C corporations deduct contributions to retirement plans on Form 1120. The deduction is entered on the line provided for pension plans, profit-sharing plans, and so on. This line includes contributions to nonqualified plans if the corporation is entitled to claim a current deduction for such contributions.

Other Reporting Requirements for All Taxpayers

Qualified plans entail annual reporting requirements. If you maintain a qualified plan, you must file certain information returns each year to report on the amount of plan assets, contributions, number of employees, and such (unless you are exempt from reporting). (There is no annual reporting for SEPs, regardless of assets or the number of employees.) Information returns in the 5500 series are *not* filed with the IRS. Instead, these rules are filed with the Department of Labor's Pension and Welfare Benefits Administration (PWBA) at www.efast.dol.gov. These returns must be filed electronically in most cases. There are penalties for failure to file these returns on time and for overstating the pension plan deduction.

Plans other than one-person plans must file Form 5500, *Annual Return/Report of Employee Benefit Plan*, each year. The return is due by the last day of the seventh month following the close of the plan year (July 31 of a calendar-year plan).

One-participant plans are automatically exempt from annual reporting if the plan assets at the end of the year are $250,000 or less. (This exemption does not apply to the final plan year.) For plans with fewer than 25 participants, there is voluntary reporting. Details of eligibility for voluntary reporting and what to report are in instructions to Form 5500.

For businesses that have defined benefit plans for which premiums must be paid to the Pension Benefit Guaranty Corporation, the deadline for premium payments is October 15 of the year following the end of the year for calendar-year plans of small employers (fewer than 500 participants) (e.g., October 15, 2015, for the 2014 year of a defined benefit plan on a calendar-year basis). Payment is accompanied by PBGC Form 1 or PBGC Form 1-EZ; for details about which form to use, where to file, and more, see www.pbgc.gov.

Alert

The 2014 form was not available at the time of publication. The 2013 version here is for informational purposes and should not be filed for the 2014 plan year.

Form **5500-EZ**	**Annual Return of One-Participant (Owners and Their Spouses) Retirement Plan**	OMB No. 1545-0956
Department of the Treasury Internal Revenue Service	This form is required to be filed under section 6058(a) of the Internal Revenue Code. *Certain foreign retirement plans are also required to file this form (see instructions).* ▶ Complete all entries in accordance with the instructions to the Form 5500-EZ. ▶ Information about Form 5500-EZ and its instructions is at *www.irs.gov/form5500ez.*	**20̲14** This Form is Open to Public Inspection.

Part I   Annual Return Identification Information

For the calendar plan year 2014 or fiscal plan year beginning (MM/DD/YYYY) _____ and ending _____

A   This return is: (1) ☐ the first return filed for the plan;   (3) ☐ the final return filed for the plan;
                 (2) ☐ an amended return;   (4) ☐ a short plan year return (less than 12 months).

B   If filing under an extension of time, check this box (see instructions) . . . . ▶ ☐
C   If this return is for a foreign plan, check this box (see instructions) . . . . ▶ ☐

Part II   Basic Plan Information — enter all requested information.

1a Name of plan	1b Three-digit plan number (PN) ▶
	1c Date plan first became effective (MM/DD/YYYY)
2a Employer's name	2b Employer Identification Number (EIN) (Do not enter your Social Security Number)
Trade name of business (if different from name of employer)	2c Employer's telephone number
In care of name	2d Business code (see instructions)
Mailing address (room, apt., suite no. and street, or P.O. Box)	
City or town, state or province, country, and ZIP or foreign postal code (if foreign, see instructions)	
3a Plan administrator's name (If same as employer, enter "Same")	3b Administrator's EIN
In care of name	3c Administrator's telephone number
Mailing address (room, apt., suite no. and street, or P.O. Box)	
City or town, state or province, country, and ZIP or foreign postal code (if foreign, see instructions)	
4a Name of trust (optional)	4b Trust's EIN (optional)

5	If the name and/or EIN of the employer has changed since the last return filed for this plan, enter the name, EIN, and plan number for the last return in the appropriate space provided:	5b	EIN
a	Employer's name	5c	PN

6a	Total number of participants at the beginning of the plan year	6a	
b	Total number of participants at the end of the plan year	6b	

Part III   Financial Information

		(1) Beginning of year	(2) End of year
7a Total plan assets	7a		
b Total plan liabilities	7b		
c Net plan assets (subtract line 7b from 7a)	7c		

For Privacy Act and Paperwork Reduction Act Notice, see the instructions for Form 5500-EZ.   Cat. No. 63263R   Form **5500-EZ** (2014)

FIGURE 16.3 Form 5500-EZ Annual Return of One-Participant Retirement Plan

Part III *(Continued)*

8	Contributions received or receivable from:			Amount
a	Employers		8a	
b	Participants		8b	
c	Others (including rollovers)		8c	

Part IV **Plan Characteristics**

9 Enter the applicable two-character feature codes from the List of Plan Characteristics Codes in the instructions:

☐☐ ☐☐ ☐☐ ☐☐ ☐☐ ☐☐ ☐☐ ☐☐ ☐☐ ☐☐

Part V **Compliance and Funding Questions**

		Yes	No	Amount
10	During the plan year, did the plan have any participant loans? If "Yes," enter amount as of year end **10**			
11	Is this a defined benefit plan that is subject to minimum funding requirements? If "Yes," complete Schedule SB (Form 5500) and line 11a below. (See instructions.) . **11**			
a	Enter the unpaid minimum required contribution for current year from Schedule SB (Form 5500), line 39 . . . . **11a**			
12	Is this a defined contribution plan subject to the minimum funding requirements of section 412 of the Code? . . . . **12** If "Yes," complete lines 12a or 12b, 12c, 12d, and 12e below, as applicable:			
a	If a waiver of the minimum funding standard for a prior year is being amortized in this plan year, enter the month, day, and year (MM/DD/YYYY) of the letter ruling granting the waiver (see instructions) **12a**			
b	Enter the minimum required contribution for this plan year **12b**			
c	Enter the amount contributed by the employer to the plan for this plan year **12c**			
d	Subtract the amount in line 12c from the amount in line 12b. Enter the result (enter a minus sign to the left of a negative amount) **12d**			

		Yes	No	N/A	
e	Will the minimum funding amount reported on line 12d be met by the funding deadline? **12e**				

Caution. A penalty for the late or incomplete filing of this return will be assessed unless reasonable cause is established.

Under penalties of perjury, I declare that I have examined this return including, if applicable, any related Schedule MB (Form 5500) or Schedule SB (Form 5500) signed by an enrolled actuary, and to the best of my knowledge and belief, it is true, correct, and complete.

Sign Here ▶

_____   _____   _____
Signature of employer or plan administrator   Date   Type or print name of individual signing as employer or plan administrator

Preparer's name (including firm name, if applicable) and address, including room or suite number (optional)	Preparer's telephone number (optional)

Form **5500-EZ** (2014)

FIGURE 16.3 *(Continued)*

NOTE
There are no special annual reporting requirements for IRA plans, SEPs, or SIMPLE-IRAs.

The return is due by the last day of the seventh month following the close of the plan year. Thus, if the plan is on a calendar year, the return is due no later than July 31 of the following year. Obtaining an extension to file an income tax return generally does *not* extend the time for filing these returns. However, if you are self-employed and obtain a filing extension for your individual return to October 15, you have until the extended due date to file Form 5500-EZ (Figure 16.3). If you do not have a filing extension for your personal return, you can request an extension of time to file Form 5500-EZ by filing Form 5558, *Application for Extension of Time to File Certain Employee Plan Returns*, to obtain an automatic 2½ month extension (to October 15).

Casualty and Theft Losses

Alert

At the time this book was printed, Congress had not extended numerous breaks for 2014 that had expired at the end of 2013. Check the online supplement in February 2015 at www.jklasser.com or www.barbaraweltman.com to see whether these breaks apply for 2014 returns.

Tornadoes in Alabama, Arkansas, and Mississippi, wildfires in Oklahoma, winter storms in the Midwest, mudslides in Washington, and hurricanes in the Gulf Coast—these are just some examples of the types of weather-related events that can do severe damage to your business property. Terrorist attacks are another means of causing damage to business property as are man-made accidents, such as oil spills. If you suffer casualty or theft losses to your business property, you can deduct the losses. You may also suffer a loss through condemnation or a sale under threat of condemnation. Again, the loss is deductible. Certain losses—those from events declared to be federal disasters—may even allow you to recover taxes you have already paid in an earlier year. But if you receive insurance proceeds or other property in return, you may have a gain rather than a loss. The law allows you to postpone reporting of the gain if certain steps are taken.

For further information about deducting casualty and theft losses, see IRS Publication 547, *Casualties, Disasters, and Thefts (Business and Nonbusiness)* and IRS Publication 2194B, *Disaster Losses Kit for Businesses*.

Casualties and Thefts

If you suffer a casualty or theft loss to business property, you can deduct the loss. There are no dollar limitations on these losses, as there are on personal losses. Nor are there adjusted gross income (AGI) limitations on these losses, as there are on casualty and theft losses to personal property.

NOTE
Business losses
are deductible without
having to establish
that the cause of the loss
was a casualty. Thus,
if your equipment rusts
or corrodes over time,
you can deduct your loss
even though it does not
fit into the definition of a
casualty loss (assuming
you can fix the time
of the loss). The reason
for understanding
the definition
of the term "casualty" is
that it determines where
the loss is reported.
It also comes into play in
connection with deferring
tax on gains from
casualties, as discussed
later in this chapter.

Definition of Casualty

If your business property is damaged, destroyed, or lost because of a storm, earthquake, flood, or some other "sudden, unexpected or unusual event," you have experienced a *casualty*. For losses to nonbusiness property (such as your personal residence), the loss must fall squarely within the definition of a casualty loss. Losses to business property need not necessarily satisfy the same definition.

The tax law details what is considered a "sudden, unexpected or unusual event." To be sudden, the event must be one that is swift, not one that is progressive or gradual. To be unexpected, the event must be unanticipated or unintentional on the part of the one who has suffered the loss. To be unusual, the event must be other than a day-to-day occurrence. It cannot be typical of the activity in which you are engaged.

EXAMPLES OF CASUALTIES

Certain events in nature automatically are considered a casualty: earthquake, hurricane, tornado, cyclone, flood, storm, and volcanic eruption. Other events have also come to be known as casualties: sonic booms, mine cave-ins, shipwrecks, and acts of vandalism. The IRS has also recognized as a casualty the destruction of crops due to a farmer's accidental poisoning of his fields. Fires are considered casualties if you are not the one who started them (or did not pay someone to start them). Car or truck accidents are casualties provided they were not caused by willful negligence or a willful act.

Progressive or gradual deterioration, such as rust or corrosion of property, is not considered a casualty.

PROOF OF CASUALTIES

You must show that a specific casualty occurred and the time it occurred. You must also show that the casualty was the direct cause of the damage or destruction to your property. Finally, you must show that you were the owner of the property. If you leased property, you must show that you were contractually liable for damage so that you suffered a loss as a result of the casualty.

Definition of Theft

The taking of property must constitute a theft under the law in your state. Generally, *theft* involves taking or removing property with the intent to deprive the owner of its use. Typically, this includes robbery, larceny, and embezzlement.

If you are forced to pay extortion money or blackmail in the course of your business, the loss may be treated as a theft loss if your state law makes this type of taking illegal.

If you lose or misplace property, you cannot claim a theft loss unless you can show that the disappearance of the property was due to an accidental loss that was sudden, unexpected, or unusual. In other words, if you misplace property and cannot prove a theft loss occurred, you may be able to deduct a loss if you can establish a casualty was responsible for the loss.

PROOF OF THEFT

You must show when you discovered the property was missing. You must also show that a theft (as defined by your state's criminal law) took place. Finally, you must show that you were the owner of the property.

Determining a Casualty or Theft Loss

To calculate your loss, you must know your **adjusted basis** in the property.

Adjusted basis   **This is generally your cost of the property, plus any improvements made to it, less any depreciation claimed. Basis is also reduced by any prior casualty losses claimed with respect to the property.**

You also need to know the fair market value (FMV) of the property. If the property was not completely destroyed, you must know the extent of the damage. This is the difference between the FMV of the property before and after the casualty.

Example

Your business car is in an accident, and you do not have collision insurance. The car's FMV before the accident was $9,000. After the accident, the car is worth only $6,000. The decrease in the FMV is $3,000 ($9,000 value before the loss, less $6,000 value after the loss).

How do you determine the decrease in FMV? This is not based simply on your subjective opinion. In most cases, the decrease in value is based on an appraisal by a competent appraiser. If your property is located near an area affected by a casualty that causes your property value to decline, you cannot take this general decline in value into account. Only a direct loss of value may be considered. Presumably, a competent appraiser will be able to distinguish between a general market decline and a direct decline as a result of a casualty. The IRS looks at a number of factors to determine whether an appraiser is competent and his or her appraisal can be relied upon to establish FMV. These factors include:

- Familiarity with your property both before and after the casualty
- Knowledge of sales of comparable property in your area
- Knowledge of conditions in the area of the casualty
- Method of appraisal

Remember that if the IRS questions the reliability of your appraiser, it may use its own appraiser to determine value. This may lead to legal wrangling and ultimately to litigation on the question of value. In order to avoid this problem and the costs entailed, it is advisable to use a reputable appraiser, even if this may seem costly to you.

Appraisals used to secure a loan or loan guarantee from the government under the Federal Emergency Management Agency (FEMA) are treated as proof of the amount of a disaster loss. Disaster losses are explained later in this chapter.

You may be able to establish value without the help of an appraiser in certain situations.

If your car is damaged, you can use "blue book" value (the car's retail value, which is printed in a book used by car dealers). You can ask your local car dealer for your car's retail value reported in the blue book (or look it up at www.kbb.com). You can modify this value to reflect such things as mileage, options, and the car's condition before the casualty. Book values are not official, but the IRS has come to recognize that they are useful in fixing value. Of course, if your car is not listed in the blue book, you must find other means of establishing value. Value before the casualty can be established by a showing of comparable sales of similar cars in your area. According to the IRS, a dealer's offer for your car as a trade-in on a new car generally does not establish value.

Repairs may be useful in showing the decrease in value. To use repairs as a measure of loss, you must show that the repairs are needed to restore the property to its precasualty condition and apply only to the damage that resulted from the casualty. You must also show that the cost of repairs is not excessive and that the repairs will not restore your property to a value greater than it had prior to the casualty. Making repairs to property damaged in a casualty can result in double deductions: one for the cost of repairs and the other for the casualty loss.

Example

Severe flooding destroys a business owner's property. He is not compensated by insurance. The IRS, in a memorandum to a district counsel, allows him to claim a casualty loss for the damage as well as deducting the cost of repairs to the property where such repairs merely restore it to its precasualty condition.

The last piece of information necessary for determining a casualty or theft loss is the amount of insurance proceeds or other reimbursements, if any, you received or expect to receive as a result of the casualty or theft. While insurance proceeds are the most common reimbursement in the event of a casualty or theft, there are other types of reimbursements that are taken into account in the same way as insurance proceeds. These include:

- Court awards for damages as a result of suits based on casualty or theft. Your reimbursement is the net amount of the award—the award less attorney's fees to obtain the award.

- Payment from a bonding company for a theft loss.

- Forgiveness of a federal disaster loan under the Disaster Relief and Emergency Assistance Act. Typically, these are given under the auspices of the Small Business Administration (SBA) or the Farmers Home Administration (FHA). The part that you do not have to repay is the amount of the reimbursement. Services provided by relief agencies for repairs, restoration, or cleanup are considered reimbursements that must be taken into account.

- Repairs made to your property by your lessee, or repayments in lieu of repairs.

What happens if you have not received an insurance settlement by the time you must file your return? If there is a reasonable expectation that you will receive a settlement, you treat the anticipated settlement as if you had already received it. In other words, you take the expected insurance proceeds into account in calculating your loss. Should it later turn out that you received more or less than you anticipated, adjustments are required in the year you actually receive the insurance proceeds, as explained later in this chapter.

If the amount of insurance proceeds or other reimbursements is greater than the adjusted basis of your property, you do not have a loss. Instead, you have a gain as a result of your casualty or theft loss. How can this be, you might ask? Why should a loss of property turn out to be a gain for tax purposes? Remember that your adjusted basis for business property in many instances reflects deductions for depreciation. This brings your basis down. But your insurance may be based on the value of the property, not its basis to you. Therefore, if your basis has been adjusted downward for depreciation but the value of the property has remained constant or increased, your insurance proceeds may produce a gain for you. Gain and how to postpone it are discussed later in this chapter.

CALCULATING LOSS WHEN PROPERTY IS COMPLETELY DESTROYED OR STOLEN

Reduce your adjusted basis by any insurance proceeds received or expected to be received and any salvage value to the property. The result is your casualty loss deduction. The FMV of the property does not enter into the computation.

If the casualty or theft involves more than one piece of property, you must determine the loss (or gain) for each item separately. If your reimbursement is paid in a lump sum and there is no allocation among the items, you must make an allocation. The allocation is based on the items' FMV before the casualty.

Example

Your machine is completely destroyed by a flood. You have no flood insurance, and the destroyed machine has no salvage value. The adjusted basis of the machine is $6,000. Your casualty loss is $6,000 (adjusted basis of the property [$6,000], less insurance proceeds [zero]).

CALCULATING LOSS WHEN PROPERTY IS PARTIALLY DESTROYED

Calculate the difference between the FMV of the property before and after the casualty. Reduce this by any insurance proceeds. Compare this figure with your adjusted basis in the property, less any insurance proceeds. Your casualty loss is the smaller of these two figures.

Example

Your machine is damaged as a result of a flood. You do not have flood insurance. The machine is valued at $8,000 before the flood and $3,000 after it. Your adjusted basis in the machine is $6,000. Your loss is $5,000, the difference between the FMV of the machine before and after the flood, which is smaller than your adjusted basis.

If you lease property from someone else (e.g., if you lease a car used for business), your loss is limited to the difference between the insurance proceeds you receive, or expect to receive, and the amount you must pay to repair the property.

Inventory and Crops

Typically, a casualty or theft to inventory is not treated as a separate loss. Instead, the amount of opening and closing inventories for cost of goods sold is increased, and any insurance or other recovery for the loss is taxable. You can, however, opt to take the loss separately; the loss deduction must be reduced by any insurance or other reimbursement received. If you deduct the loss, then adjust the opening inventory or purchases to remove the loss items (so they are not counted twice).

In the case of crops, the cost of raising them has already been deducted, so no additional deduction is allowed if they are damaged or destroyed by a casualty.

Recovered Property

What happens if you deduct a loss for stolen property and the property is later recovered? Do you have to go back and amend the earlier return on which the theft loss was taken? The answer is no. Instead, you report the recovered property as income in the year of recovery.

But what if the property is not recovered in good shape or is only partially recovered? In this instance, you must recalculate your loss. You use the smaller of the property's adjusted basis or the decrease in the FMV from the time it was stolen until you recovered it. This smaller amount is your recalculated loss. If your recalculated loss is less than the loss you deducted, you report the difference as income in the year of recovery. The amount of income that you must report is limited to the amount of loss that reduced your tax in the earlier year.

Insurance Received (or Not Received) in a Later Year

If you had anticipated the receipt of insurance proceeds or other property and took that anticipated amount into account when calculating your loss but later receive more (or less) than you anticipated, you must account for this discrepancy. As with recovered stolen property, you do not go back to the year of loss and make an adjustment. Instead, you take the insurance proceeds into account in the year of actual receipt.

If you receive more than you had expected (by way of insurance or otherwise), you report the extra amount as income in the year of receipt. You do not have to recalculate your original loss deduction. The additional amount is reported as ordinary income to the extent that the deduction in the earlier year produced a tax reduction. If the additional insurance or other reimbursement, when combined with what has already been received, exceeds the adjusted basis of your property, you now have a gain as a result of the casualty or theft. The gain is reported in the year you receive the additional reimbursement. However, you may be able to postpone reporting the gain, as discussed later in this chapter.

If you receive less than you had anticipated, you have an additional loss. The additional loss is claimed in the year in which you receive the additional amount.

Example

In 2014, your business car was completely destroyed in an accident. Your adjusted basis in the car was $8,000. The car had a value of $10,000 before the accident and no value after the accident. You expected the driver responsible for the accident to pay for the damage. In fact, a jury awarded you the full extent of your loss. However, in 2015, you learn that the other driver will not pay the judgment and does not have any property against which you can enforce your judgment. In this instance, you have received less than you anticipated. You do not recalculate your 2014 taxes. Instead, you deduct your loss (limited to your adjusted basis of $8,000) in 2015.

Basis

If your property is partially destroyed in a casualty, you must adjust the basis of the property:

- Decrease basis by insurance proceeds or other reimbursements and loss deductions claimed.
- Increase basis by improvements or repairs made to the property to rebuild or restore it.

Year of the Loss

In general, the loss can be claimed only in the year in which the casualty or other event occurs. However, in the case of the theft, the loss is treated as having occurred in the year in which it is discovered.

Coordination with Repairs

You cannot take both a casualty loss deduction and a deduction for repair costs. If you claim a casualty loss deduction, then no deduction can be taken for repair costs, even if the amount of the casualty loss relative to the repair expenditure is small.

Condemnations and Threats of Condemnation

The government can take your property for public use if it compensates you for your loss. The process by which the government exercises its right of eminent domain to take your property for public use is called *condemnation*. In a sense, you are being forced to sell your property at a price essentially fixed by the government. You can usually negotiate a price; sometimes you are forced to seek a court action and have the court fix the price paid to you. Typically, an owner is paid cash or receives other property upon condemnation of property.

Sometimes the probability of a condemnation becomes known through reports in a newspaper or other news medium or proposals at a town council meeting. For example, there may be talk of a new road or the widening of an existing road that will affect your property. If you do not voluntarily sell your property, the government will simply go through the process of condemnation.

Where there is a condemnation, you may also voluntarily sell other property. If the other property has an economic relationship to the condemned property, the voluntary sale can be treated as a condemnation.

Not every condemnation qualifies for special tax treatment. When property is condemned because it is unsafe, this is not a taking of property for public use. It is simply a limitation on the use of the property by you.

For tax purposes, a condemnation or threat of condemnation of your business property is treated as a sale or exchange. You may have a gain or you may have a loss, depending on the condemnation award or the proceeds you receive upon a forced sale. But there is something special in the tax law where condemnations are concerned. If you have a gain, you have an opportunity to avoid immediate tax on the gain. This postponement of reporting the gain is discussed in Chapter 6.

Condemnation Award

The amount of money you receive or the value of property you receive for your condemned property is your *condemnation award*. Similarly, the amount you accept in exchange for your property in a sale motivated by the threat of condemnation is also treated as your condemnation award. The amount of the condemnation award determines your gain or loss for the event.

If you are in a dispute with the city, state, or federal government over the amount that you should be paid and you go to court, the government may deposit an amount with the court. You are not considered to have received the award until you have an unrestricted right to it. This is usually after the court action is resolved and you are permitted to withdraw the funds for your own use.

Your award includes moneys withheld to pay your debts. For example, if the court withholds an amount to pay a lien holder or mortgagee, your condemnation award is the gross amount awarded to you, not the net amount paid to you.

The condemnation award does not include **severance damages** and **special assessments**.

Severance damages Compensation paid to you if part of your property is condemned and the part not condemned suffers a reduction in value as a result of the condemnation. Severance damages may cover the loss in value of your remaining property or compensate you for certain improvements you must make to your remaining property (such as replacing fences, digging new wells or ditches, or planting trees or shrubs to restore the remaining property to its condition prior to the condemnation of your other property).

Special assessments Charges against you for improvements that benefit the remaining property as a result of the condemnation of your other property (such as widening of the streets or installing sewers).

TREATMENT OF SEVERANCE DAMAGES

Severance damages are not reported as income. Instead, they are used to reduce the basis of your remaining property. However, only net severance damages reduce basis. This means that you must first subtract from severance damages any expenses you incurred to obtain them. You also reduce severance damages by any special assessments levied against your remaining property if the special assessments were withheld from the award by the condemning authority. If the severance damages relate only to a specific portion of your remaining property, then you reduce the basis of that portion of the property.

If the net severance damages are greater than your basis in the remaining property, you have a gain. However, you can postpone reporting the gain, as discussed in Chapter 6.

Generally, you and the condemning authority will contractually agree on which portion of an award is for condemnation and which part, if any, is for severance damages or other awards. This allocation should be put in writing. You cannot simply go back after the transaction is completed and try to make an allocation. You may, however, be able to convince the IRS that the parties intended to make a certain allocation if the facts and circumstances support this argument. If there is no written allocation and you cannot convince the IRS otherwise, all of the amounts received will be treated as a condemnation award (and no part will be treated as severance damages).

TREATMENT OF SPECIAL ASSESSMENTS

Special assessments serve to reduce the condemnation award. They must actually be withheld from the award itself; they cannot be levied after the award is made, even if it is in the same year.

If a condemnation award includes severance damages, then the special assessments are first used to reduce the severance damages. Any excess special assessments are then used to reduce the condemnation award.

Disaster Losses

In the past several years, our country has experienced a large number of major disasters, including hurricanes, floods, fires, blizzards, earthquakes, and terrorist attacks. When large areas suffer sizable losses, the president may declare the areas eligible for special federal disaster relief. This disaster assistance comes in the form of disaster relief loans, special grants (money that does not have to be repaid), special unemployment benefits, and other types of assistance. Still, despite all these efforts by the federal government, as well as state, local, and private agencies, you may experience serious disruption to your business and loss to your business property. The tax law provides a special rule for certain disaster losses that will give you up-front cash to help you get back on your feet.

Typically, you deduct your loss in the year in which the disaster occurred. However, you may elect to deduct your loss on a prior year's return, which can result in a tax refund that may provide you with needed cash flow.

Example

In January 2015, you suffer an uninsured disaster loss of $25,000. You may, of course, deduct the loss on your 2015 return, which is filed in 2016 (assuming you are on a calendar-year basis). Alternatively, you may elect to deduct your loss on your 2014 return.

If your loss occurs later in the year, after you have already filed your tax return for the prior year, you can still get a tax refund by filing an amended return for the prior year. For example, if in the Example your loss occurred in December 2015 (after you filed your 2014 return), you can file an amended return for 2014 to claim the disaster loss.

You must make the election to claim the loss on the prior year's return by the later of:

- The due date (including extensions) for filing your income tax return for the year in which the disaster occurred, or
- The due date (including extensions) for the preceding year's return.

From time to time, the IRS may grant more time to make an election. For example, in the case of Hurricane Sandy, which occurred at the end of October 2012, the IRS gave affected taxpayers until October 15, 2013, to make the election.

Not all seeming disasters qualify for this special tax election. To be treated as a disaster, your loss must have resulted from a casualty in an area declared by the president to be eligible for federal disaster assistance.

If you suffer a loss in your inventory due to a disaster, you need not account for your loss simply by a reduction in the cost of goods sold. Instead, you can claim a deduction for your loss. The loss can be claimed on the return for the year of the disaster or on a return (or amended return) for the preceding year. If you choose to deduct your inventory loss, then you must also reduce your opening inventory for the year of the loss so that the loss is not also reflected in the inventory; you cannot get a double benefit for the loss.

If you suffer a net operating loss (NOL) and you are in a federally-declared disaster area, you can carry the NOL back for 3 years (rather than the usual 2 years) to obtain a tax refund (see Chapter 4).

The IRS has a landing page entitled *Disaster Assistance and Emergency Relief for Individuals and Businesses* at http://www.irs.gov/Businesses/ Small-Businesses-&-Self-Employed/Disaster-Assistance-and-Emergency-Relief- for-Individuals-and-Businesses-1. Here you will find helpful links to publications and other disaster-related information.

Deducting Property Insurance and Other Casualty/ Theft-Related Items

It is well and good that you can write off your casualty and theft losses. But as a practical matter, you should carry enough insurance to cover these situations so that you will not suffer any financial loss should these events befall your business. If you carry insurance to cover fire, theft, flood, or any other casualty related to your business, you can deduct your premiums (see Chapter 22).

If you maintain a home office, you must allocate the cost of your homeowner's policy and deduct only the portion allocated to the business use of your home as part of your home office deduction, assuming you use the actual expense method for figuring this deduction (as discussed in Chapter 18). Be sure to check your homeowner's policy to see that it covers your business use. You may have to obtain additional coverage if you use your home for certain types of business activities. For example, if clients or customers come to your home, it may be advisable to increase your liability coverage. The cost of additional coverage for business guests (which may be in the form of a rider to your policy) may be rather modest. Similarly, your homeowner's policy may not cover business equipment in your home office (e.g., computer, fax, or copying machine). Again, a small rider may be necessary to protect you against equipment loss.

If you are a manufacturer who includes business insurance as part of the cost of goods sold, no separate deduction can be taken for these insurance premiums.

If you self-insure to cover casualty or theft by putting funds aside, you cannot deduct the amount of your reserves. In this case, only actual losses are deductible, as explained earlier in this chapter. Self-insurance may be advisable to cover certain casualties that may not be covered by your policy. For example, your policy may not cover damage from civil riots. Self-insurance is also a good idea where you have a high deductible (for example, a state-prescribed deductible for flood insurance in a coastal area). Be sure to review carefully your policy's exclusions (the types of events not covered by your insurance).

Use and Occupancy Insurance

If you carry insurance to cover profits that are lost during a time you are forced to close down due to fire or other cause, you may deduct the premiums. If you then do shut down and collect on the insurance, you report the proceeds as ordinary income.

Car Insurance

The same rule that applies to business property insurance also applies to insurance for your car or other vehicles used in your business. This insurance covers liability, damages, and other losses in accidents involving your business car. However, if you use your car only partly for business, you must allocate your insurance premiums. Only the portion related to business use of your car is deductible. The portion related to personal use of your car is not deductible.

If you use the standard mileage allowance to deduct expenses for business use of a car, you cannot deduct any car insurance premiums. The standard mileage rate already takes into account an allowance for car insurance. Deductions for various types of insurance are discussed in greater detail in Chapter 22.

Appraisals

If your property is damaged by a casualty and you pay a qualified appraiser to establish the FMV of the property in order to prove your damage and the extent of your loss, you claim a separate deduction for appraisal fees. You do not take the appraisal fees into account when calculating your casualty loss deduction.

Certain Disaster Victims

If your business is located in an area affected by certain storms, or other federal disasters, you may be eligible for special tax breaks. These include additional time for filing certain returns and paying certain taxes, increased write-offs for certain property purchases (intended to restore the area following the disaster), and an extended net operating loss carryback. These breaks are discussed in relevant sections throughout this book.

NOTE

For links to disaster assistance and emergency relief for businesses, go to www.irs.gov and search "disaster assistance and emergency relief for individuals and businesses."

Disaster Assistance

Tax rules can certainly ameliorate losses resulting from disasters impacting your business. However, planning to avoid or mitigate a disaster and having monetary assistance, in the form of loans and grants, may be more helpful. Usually, disaster mitigation payments, grants, and other similar payments to businesses are taxable (an exclusion for qualified disaster mitigation payments apply only to individuals). Some resources for disaster help:

- Farm Services Agency (FSA). The Agricultural Act of 2014 indefinitely extended the four disaster programs that were previously authorized by the Food, Conservation, and Energy Act of 2008. Find details at www .fsa.usda.gov/FSA/webapp?area=home&subject=diap&topic=landing.
- FEMA. FEMA has a disaster relief fund, which consists of appropriations that it can direct to states for disaster assistance; it does not provide any direct relief for businesses, but does offer disaster planning continuity planning templates to help you plan for a disaster (go to www.fema .gov/planning-templates).
- SBA loans. Two low-interest loan programs—Disaster Loans and Economic Injury Loans—are available for small businesses impacted by a federal disaster. Find details at www.sba.gov.
- State government. Your state can help to plan and may provide disaster recovery assistance. Find links to your state from www.sba.gov/content/state-government-information.

Find links to many resources through DisasterAssistance.gov at www.disaster assistance.gov.

Where to Deduct Casualty and Theft Losses and Related Items

Employees

Casualty and theft losses to business property are calculated in Section B of Form 4684, *Casualty and Theft Worksheet for Individuals*. Losses are then netted against gains and are entered on Form 4797, *Sales of Business Property*. Your losses are entered directly on page 1 of Form 1040. They are not taken on Schedule A, as are casualty and theft losses to personal property (such as your personal residence). Nor are they limited by the $100 per casualty or 10%-of-adjusted-gross-income limitation that applies to casualty and theft losses to nonbusiness property.

If the casualty or theft happened to property used for both business and personal purposes, you must make an allocation. Only the business portion of the loss is free from the $100/10% limitations. For example, if you use a car 75% for business and 25% for personal purposes and the car is totaled in an accident for which you do not have collision insurance, 75% of your loss (the business portion) is claimed without regard to the $100/10% limits; the other 25% of your loss (the personal portion) is subject to both the $100 and 10% limits.

Self-Employed

Casualty and theft losses to business property are calculated in Section B of Form 4684. Losses are then netted against gains and are entered on Form 4797. The net result is then entered on page 1 of Form 1040; you do not enter the amount on Schedule C.

Losses from involuntary conversions are netted against gains and losses from Section 1231 property. This is essentially depreciable property, used in a trade or business and held for more than one year, that is not held for inventory or for sale to customers in the ordinary course of business. (Certain livestock, crops, timber, coal, and domestic iron ore can also be Section 1231 property.) Thus, even if you have a casualty loss, you may not get the benefit of the loss if you have gains from the sale or exchange of Section 1231 property. However, losses to inventory are taken into account in the cost of goods sold.

Partnerships and LLCs

The partnership or LLC reports income or loss from an involuntary conversion (casualty, theft, or condemnation) on Form 4797. The net gain or loss is taken into account when arriving at the total trade or business income or loss on Form 1065 on the specific line provided for net gain or loss from Form 4797.

Even if you are a silent partner in an activity that is treated as a passive activity, casualty and theft losses are not subject to the passive loss limitations. You may claim these losses as long as they are not a recurrent part of the business.

S Corporations

If the S corporation has income or loss from an involuntary conversion (casualty, theft, or condemnation), it must file Form 4797. The net gain or loss is taken into account in arriving at the S corporation's total trade or business income or loss on Form 1120S. Net gain or loss from Form 4797 is reported on the specific line provided on Form 1120S for this purpose.

Even if you are a silent partner in an activity that is treated as a passive activity (a shareholder who does not materially participate in the business), casualty and theft losses are not subject to the passive loss limitations. You may claim these losses as long as they are not a recurrent part of the business.

C Corporations

C corporations report net gains or losses from involuntary conversions on Form 4797 and then use the net amount to arrive at taxable income on Form 1120. Net gains or losses from Form 4797 are reported on the specific line provided on Form 1120 for this purpose.

Home Office Deductions

Alert

At the time this book was printed, Congress had not extended numerous breaks for 2014 that had expired at the end of 2013. Check the online supplement in February 2015 at www.jklasser.com or www.barbaraweltman.com to see whether these breaks apply for 2014 returns.

Today over 40 million Americans work at home at least some of the time, and the number is growing. Computers, smartphones, and the information highway make it easier and, in some cases, more profitable to operate a home office. The U.S. Small Business Administration reported that 52% of all small businesses are home-based and that they generate $102 billion in annual revenue; the average return on gross revenues for these businesses is 36%, compared with just 21% for non-home-based businesses.

As a general rule, the cost of owning or renting your home is a personal one and, except for certain specific expenses (such as mortgage interest, real estate taxes, and casualty losses), you cannot deduct personal expenses. However, if you use a portion of your home for business, you may be able to deduct a number of expenses, including rent or depreciation, mortgage and real estate taxes, maintenance, and utilities.

The SBA says the average home office deduction is $3,686. On the 23.4 million Schedule C filers in 2011 (the most recent year for statistics), home office deductions totaled over $10 billion (the average write-off by those who claimed home office deductions was not provided).

The deduction may take the form of a write-off of your actual expenses or an allowance according to an IRS-set amount called the simplified method. Whichever type of write-off method you use, the result is a home office deduction.

The deduction is allowed for both self-employed individuals and employees who meet special requirements.

This chapter covers home *office* expenses; however, you need not use your home as an office to claim this deduction. Home office is simply a name assigned to a category of deductible business expenses. For example, you may use your garage to do mechanical repairs, or a greenhouse to grow plants for sale. The expenses related to these uses may be treated as home office expenses.

It has long been thought that claiming a home office deduction is an automatic red flag for an audit. However, there are no statistics to show that this is true. If you meet the tests for claiming a home office deduction as explained in this chapter and you have proof of your expenses, you should have nothing to fear, even if your return is questioned.

For more information about home office deductions see IRS Publication 587, *Business Use of Your Home.*

Home Office Deductions in General

Whether you own your home or rent it, you may be able to deduct a portion of the costs of your home if you use it for business. This is so for both employees and self-employed individuals. However, the law is very strict on what constitutes business use of a home. First, you must use the portion of your home exclusively and regularly for business. Then you must meet one of 3 tests. The home office must be:

1. Your principal place of business,
2. A place to meet or deal with patients, clients, or customers in the normal course of your business, or
3. A separate structure (not attached to your house or residence) that is used in connection with your business.

Exclusively and Regularly

Exclusive use of a home office means that it is used solely for your business activities and not for personal purposes, including investment activities. If you have a spare bedroom or a den that you have equipped with a computer, telephone, and perhaps a fax/modem, you cannot meet the exclusive use test for a home office if you also use that room as a guest room or family den. A kitchen will never qualify even though it is used for a legitimate business purpose because it is also used for personal reasons (although a portion may be used solely for business in some cases).

The exclusive use test does not require you to set aside an entire room for business purposes. You can meet this test if you clearly delineate a portion of a room for business. It must be a separately identifiable space. However, you need not mark off this separate area by a permanent partition to satisfy the separately identifiable space requirement.

The fact that you have some personal papers in your home office, however, won't disqualify you from meeting the exclusive use test.

There have been several cases that help to define *exclusive use*. It appears that if a taxpayer or family member merely walks through a room used as a home office, this nominal use does not prevent the taxpayer from meeting the exclusive use test. However, even occasional use of a space by family, relatives, or other guests prevents a taxpayer from meeting the exclusive use test.

There are two important exceptions to the exclusive use requirement: day-care facilities and storage space. Each of these exceptions is discussed later in this chapter.

The home office must also be used on a regular basis for your business activity. This determination is based on all the facts and circumstances. There is no minimum number of hours to meet. Occasional or incidental use of a home office will not satisfy this requirement, even if such space is used exclusively for business purposes.

Principal Place of Business

Your home office is treated as your principal place of business if it is the place where you conduct your business. It may be your prime activity or a sideline business. As long as it is the main location for the particular activity, it is your principal place of business. Generally this means the location where you earn your money. However, one court has recognized that a musician who spends considerably more time using one room in a home for practice so that she can perform with symphonies and make recordings

NOTE

Because the IRS may question your home office deduction (an IRS agent can even come into your home to view your claimed home office), it is a good idea to photograph your home office and keep it with the copy of your return as proof that you used it exclusively for business. This is especially important if you have stopped using a home office (e.g., moved into outside business space) by the time the IRS examines your return.

can treat that room as the principal place of business. It remains to be seen whether this reasoning will be extended to other types of professionals—for example, an attorney who prepares and rehearses his opening and closing arguments in a home office.

Your home office is also considered to be your principal place of business if it is used for substantial managerial or administrative activities and there is no other fixed location for such activities.

Example

You run an interior design business, seeing clients in their homes and offices. You use your home office to schedule appointments, keep your books and records, and order supplies. You can treat your home office as your principal place of business because you use it for substantial managerial or administrative activities and you do not have a store front or other office for such work.

Examples of substantial administrative or management activities include:

- Billing customers, clients, and patients
- Forwarding orders
- Keeping books and records
- Ordering supplies
- Reading professional or trade journals and papers
- Scheduling appointments
- Writing reports

Even if you perform administrative or management activities at places other than your home office, you can still take the home office deduction if you fall into one of the following categories:

- You do not conduct substantial administrative or management activities at a fixed location other than your home office, even if such activities are performed by other people at other locations. For example, another company handles your billing from its own place of business.
- You carry out administrative or management activities at sites that are not fixed locations of the business in addition to performing the activities at home. For example, you do these tasks in your car or in a motel room while on the road.
- You conduct insubstantial amounts of administrative and management activities at a fixed location other than the home office. For example,

you do minimal paperwork at an office—not your home office—once in a while.

- You conduct substantial nonadministrative and nonmanagement business activities at a fixed location other than a home office. For example, you meet with or provide services to customers, clients, or patients at a fixed location other than your home office.
- You have suitable space to conduct administrative or management activities outside your home but instead choose to use your home office for doing these activities.

Example

Same as the earlier example, but you schedule appointments for your interior design business from your car phone. Because your car is not considered a fixed location, you can still claim a home office deduction.

MORE THAN ONE BUSINESS

If you are an employee and also conduct a sideline business from a home office, such as actively selling on eBay or Amazon, you may deduct your home office expenses for the sideline business. The business activity from the home office need not be your main activity; the home office simply must be the principal place of business for the sideline activity.

However, if you conduct more than one activity from a home office, be sure that each activity meets all home office requirements. Otherwise you may lose out on deductions. For example, if you are an employee and also have a business that you run from your home, if you use the home office for your employment-related activities (and not for the convenience of your employer), then you fail the exclusive use test for the home-based business. You will not be able to deduct any home office expenses even though the home office is the principal place of business for the home-based activity.

Place to Meet or Deal with Patients, Clients, or Customers

If you meet with patients, clients, or customers in a home office, you can deduct home office expenses. The home office need not be your principal place of business. You can conduct business at another location, and your home office can be a satellite office. However, if you use your home office only to make or receive phone calls with patients, clients, and customers, you do not meet this test. While making or receiving phone calls can arguably be viewed as dealing with patients, clients, or customers, the IRS does not view it as such.

This test generally allows professionals—attorneys, doctors, accountants, architects, and others—to deduct home office expenses. Even though they have another office, they can still use a home office and deduct related expenses. Of course, the meeting or dealing with clients and others must be more than occasional; it must be on a regular basis. However, the home office must be used exclusively for business. You cannot use it for personal activities during the time when it is not used for business.

> ## Example
>
> An attorney with an office in the city has a den in her home in the suburbs that she uses to meet with clients on weekends and in the evenings. If the den is also used by her family for recreation, then it cannot be treated as a home office because it fails the exclusive use test. However, if it is used only for regularly meeting with her clients, home office expenses are deductible.

Separate Structure

If you have a separate freestanding structure on your property, you can treat it as a home office if you use it exclusively and regularly for your home office activity. A separate structure may be a garage, a studio, a greenhouse, or even a barn. It need not be an office in order for expenses to be deducted as home office expenses. Nor does the separate structure need be the principal place of your business activity. Further, it need not be a place to meet or deal with patients, clients, or customers in the normal course of your business. It simply must be used in connection with your business. Expenses related to a separate structure are deductible without regard to the gross income limit (explained later).

> ## Example
>
> You own a flower shop in town. You have a greenhouse on your property in which you grow orchids. You can deduct the home office expenses of the greenhouse.

What constitutes a separate structure? The answer is not always clear. An attached garage is not viewed as a separate structure, nor is a freestanding garage 12 feet from the house because of its close relationship to the home. If your local real estate law treats a separate structure as *appurtenant* to the house, then it is not a separate structure for purposes of the home office deduction rules.

Examples of separate structures that may qualify as home offices include an artist's studio, a florist's greenhouse, and a carpenter's workshop.

Special Requirements for Employees

Telecommuters take heart. If you use your home for business, you can deduct home office expenses provided your use is for the convenience of your employer. However, this is not an easy standard to satisfy. There is no hard-and-fast rule for proving that your use of a home office is for the convenience of your employer. Neither the tax law nor regulations provide any guidelines.

Your home office use is not treated as being for the convenience of your employer simply because it is appropriate or helpful to your job; there must be a real need on the part of your employer for you to use an office at home. In this age of computers, if your employer allows you to telecommute from a home office because it suits your schedule, this is not necessarily for your employer's convenience. As long as your employer provides you with an office, there must be some other compelling reason for you to use a home office for business. Simply getting a letter from your employer that the home office use is for the employer's convenience may not be enough to satisfy the IRS if your return is questioned. But if your employer has no office space for you to use so that telecommuting is the only arrangement feasible, then clearly such arrangement is for the convenience of the employer. Of course, there may be situations where it is not clear whether the arrangement is for the convenience of the employer. Then, factors such as office space, arrangements with other workers, and other factors must be considered.

If you employ your spouse, you may be able to deduct home office expenses by requiring your spouse to use the home office for your convenience. There have been no cases or rulings testing this arrangement, but if there is a real need on your part for it, the arrangement just might work.

You cannot claim a home office deduction if you rent a portion of your home to your employer and then perform services in it as an employee. If you do rent space to your employer, the rent is still taxable to you.

Actual Expenses or Safe Harbor Amount

You can choose the way in which to figure your home office deduction. You can deduct the actual expenses for the business use of your home or rely on an amount under a simplified method. You can change your election from year to year.

Why use the actual expense method. You probably can deduct a greater amount if you use the actual expense method, especially if your home office space is greater than 300 square feet or you have unusually high utility costs or other expenses related to the home office. It also makes sense to use the actual expense method if the home office deduction is greater than the gross income limit (explained later in this chapter). The unused home office deduction (the amount in excess of the gross income limit) can be carried forward indefinitely, to save you taxes in future years.

Why use the simplified method. You can eliminate some time-consuming recordkeeping by relying on the IRS-set deduction amount for your home office. You do not have to track and retain records showing what you paid for electricity and other expenses that are part of the home office deduction. Also, tax preparation time is greatly reduced by using this easy method.

Actual Expense Method

If you deduct the actual expenses related to your home office, some expenses are directly related to business use and are fully deductible. For example, if you paint your home office, the entire cost of the paint job is a business expense. Other expenses are indirectly related to business use of your home office; rather, they relate to your entire home. Indirect expenses include:

- Deductible mortgage interest
- Real estate taxes
- Depreciation
- Rent
- Utilities
- Insurance
- Lawn care
- General repairs to the home (such as servicing the heating system)
- Security systems
- Snow removal
- Cleaning

Only the portion of indirect expenses related to the business use of your home is deductible. How do you make an allocation of expenses? If you have 5 rooms and use one for business, can you allocate one-fifth of expenses, or 20%, for business? The answer is yes if the rooms are more or less the same size. This is often not the case. If rooms are of unequal size, you allocate expenses based on the square footage of business use. Determine the size of your home; then determine the size of your home office. Divide the size of your home office by the size of your home to arrive at a percentage of business use.

Example

Your home is 1,800 square feet. Your home office is 12 feet × 15 feet, or 180 square feet. Therefore, your home office use is 10% (180 divided by 1,800).

Once you have determined your business percentage, you apply this percentage against each indirect expense.

Example

Your business percentage is 20%, and your total real estate taxes for the year are $5,000. You may treat $1,000 ($5,000 × 20%) as part of your home office deduction. The balance of your real estate taxes continues to be deductible as an itemized deduction on Schedule A.

Example

Your business percentage is 20%, and instead of owning your home you rent it. If your annual rent is $12,000, you may treat $2,400 ($12,000 × 20%) as part of your home office deduction. The balance of your rent is not deductible, since it is a personal expense.

You apply the business percentage against deductible mortgage interest. You can include a second mortgage and deductible points in this figure. The portion of your mortgage interest not treated as part of your home office deduction continues to be deductible as an itemized deduction on Schedule A.

Casualty losses not covered by insurance may be either an indirect or direct expense, depending upon the property affected by the casualty. If, for example, your home office is damaged in a storm and you are not fully compensated by insurance, you claim your loss as a direct expense. If, however, the damage is to your entire home (such as a roof leak), you treat the loss as an indirect expense. Remember that the limits on deducting casualty losses to nonbusiness property ($100 per incident/10%-of-adjusted-gross-income floor) do not apply to business casualties. See Chapter 17 for more information on deducting casualty losses.

If you rent your home, you can deduct the business portion of rent as an indirect expense. If you own your home, you cannot deduct the fair rental value of your home office. However, you can claim depreciation on your home office. Usually, depreciation is based on a 39-year recovery period, the period that applies for commercial property. However, when a landlord of a multi-unit apartment building uses one room within the unit he lives in as a home office, that room can be depreciated as residential realty using a 27.5 year recovery period; 80% or more of the gross rental income must be from rental income within the dwelling units within the building to qualify as residential property. In a Tax Court case, a couple who ran an adult home care service from their residence was allowed to use a 27-year recovery period. See Chapter 14 for more information on depreciation.

Generally, utility expenses—for electricity, gas, oil, trash removal, and cleaning services—are treated as indirect expenses. The business portion is part of your home office deduction; the nonbusiness portion is not deductible. However, in some instances you may be able to deduct a greater portion of a utility expense. For example, if you can show that electrical use for your home office is greater than the allocable percentage of the whole bill, you can claim that additional amount as a direct expense.

The business portion of a homeowner's insurance policy is part of your home office deduction. It is an indirect expense. If you also pay additional coverage directly related to your home office, treat the additional coverage as a direct expense. You may, for example, carry special coverage for your home office equipment (computer, library, etc.). In fact, if you do not now maintain special coverage for home office equipment, you should check your homeowner's policy to see if damage or loss to your business equipment would be covered. You may think your computer is covered, but some homeowner policies may exclude business equipment or inventory. Also check whether your homeowner's policy covers personal liability for on-premises injury to patients, clients, and customers who visit your home office. Again, you may have to carry additional insurance for this type of liability.

Repairs may be direct or indirect expenses, depending on their nature. A repair to a furnace is an indirect expense; a repair to a window in the home office itself is a direct expense.

A home security system for your entire home can give rise to 2 types of write-offs. First, the business portion of your monthly monitoring fees is an indirect expense. Second, the business portion of the cost of the system itself may be depreciated. This depreciation also becomes part of your indirect expenses.

You cannot deduct expenses for any portion of the year during which there was no business use of the home. If you use your home office for only part of the year for business, you can take into account only expenses for the home related to that portion of the year.

Telephone Expenses

Telephone expenses are not part of your home office deduction. They are separately deductible. However, if you maintain a home office, there is a special rule that limits a deduction for a telephone line: You may not deduct the basic monthly service charge for the first telephone line to your home as a business expense. You can, however, deduct business-related charges, such as long-distance calls for business or call answering, call waiting, and call forwarding. You can also deduct the entire phone bill of a second phone line used exclusively for business. You can deduct any additional lines used for business, such as dedicated fax lines.

Nondeductible Expenses

Not every home-related expense can be treated as a home office deduction. For example, the cost of landscaping cannot be treated as a home office expense because it is a capital expense.

Deduction Limits

The home office deduction cannot exceed your gross income from the home office activity. For those who conduct their primary business from home, this gross income limit poses no problem. Income from the home office activity usually will more than exceed home office expenses. Thus, for example, if a dentist conducts his or her practice from a home office, there should be no problem in deducting all home office expenses. For those who use a home office for a sideline activity, however, the gross income limit may pose a problem.

What Is Gross Income?

For purposes of limiting home office deductions, *gross income* is income from the business activity conducted in the home office.

> **Example**
>
> A teacher who teaches full-time at school conducts a retail business from a home office. For purposes of limiting home office deductions, gross income includes only the income from the retail business.

To calculate gross income, look to your profit reported on Schedule C if you are self-employed, or the portion of your salary earned in the home office if you are an employee. You can adjust your Schedule C profit for certain items. If you sold your home, the portion of the gain related to the home office increases your gross income for purposes of limiting home office deductions. If you suffer a loss on the home office portion, you reduce your gross income.

If your gross income from your home office business activity is less than your total business expenses, your home office deduction is limited. Your deduction for otherwise nondeductible expenses (such as utilities or depreciation) cannot exceed gross income from the business activity, reduced by the business portion of otherwise deductible expenses (such as home mortgage interest or real estate taxes) and business expenses not attributable to business use of the home (such as salaries or supplies). This sounds rather complicated, but Form 8829, *Expenses for Business Use of Your Home*, incorporates this limitation. This rule merely orders the categories of deductions.

If, after applying this ordering of deductions, you still have an unused home office deduction, you can carry forward the unused portion, provided you used the actual expense method; there is no carryforward under the safe harbor method. The carryforward can be deducted in a future year when there is gross income from the same home office activity to offset it. There is no time limit on the carryforward. You can claim it even though you no longer live in the home in which the deduction arose, as long as there is gross income from the same activity to offset the deduction. Be sure to keep adequate records to support your carryforward deduction.

Simplified Method

Instead of deducting the actual costs of the home that relate to the home office, you can rely on an IRS-created simplified method. This method lets you deduct up to $5 per square foot for up to 300 square feet for a home office. Thus, the maximum deduction is $1,500 ($5/sq. ft. x 300 sq. ft.). If the space you use for a home office is smaller than 300 square feet, your deduction will be less than $1,500. Figure the deduction for the simplified method using an IRS worksheet (see Figure 18.1).

Looking Ahead

The IRS may, from time to time, increase the $5 per square foot limit. However, there is no automatic inflation adjustment scheduled.

To use the simplified method, the space must still meet the basic home office deduction rules (e.g., you use the space regularly and exclusively for business and the home office is your principal place of business or meets another home office deduction rule). If two people in the same home, such as spouses, each have a home office, each can use the safe harbor method as long as each office is a different portion of the home.

If the home office is only used for a portion of the year (e.g., the business starts in August or the business is seasonal), then you must make an allocation to determine the average monthly allowable square footage; more than 300 square feet may be taken into account for any one month. You are treated as having a qualified home office in a month only if the office is used as such for at least 15 days in that month.

Example

You begin using 400 square feet of your home for a qualified business use on July 20, and continue that use until the end of the taxable year. The office has an average monthly allowable square footage of 125 sq. ft. (300 sq. ft. for each month from August through December divided by the number of months in the taxable year ([300 + 300 + 300 + 300 + 300]/12]).

The amount of the deduction cannot exceed the gross income limit (explained in connection with the actual expense method).

Depreciation. If the simplified method is used for a home office in a residence owned by you, no depreciation allowance can be claimed; depreciation for the year is deemed to be zero, and no basis adjustment to the home is required.

Simplified Method Worksheet   *Keep for Your Records*

1. Enter the amount of the gross income limitation. See Instructions for the Simplified Method Worksheet . . . .   1. _____

2. Allowable square footage for the qualified business use. Do not enter more than 300 square feet. See Instructions for the
   Simplified Method Worksheet . . . .   2. _____

3. Simplified method amount
   a. Maximum allowable amount 3a. $5
   b. For daycare facilities not used exclusively for business, enter the decimal amount from the Daycare Facility Worksheet;
      otherwise, enter 1.0 . . . .   3b. _____
   c. Multiply line 3a by line 3b and enter result to 2 decimal places . . . .   3c. _____

4. Multiply line 2 by line 3c . . . .   4. _____

5. **Allowable expenses using the simplified method.** Enter the smaller of line 1 or line 4 here and include that amount on
   Schedule C, line 30. If zero or less, enter -0- . . . .   5. _____

6. **Carryover of unallowed expenses from 2013 that are not allowed in 2014.**
   a. Operating expenses. Enter the amount from your 2013 Form 8829, line 42 . . . .   6a. _____
   b. Excess casualty losses and depreciation. Enter the amount from your 2013 Form 8829, line 43 . . . .   6b. _____

Instructions for the Simplified Method Worksheet

Use this worksheet to figure the amount of expenses you may deduct for a qualified business use of a home if you are electing to use the simplified method for that home. If you are not electing to use the simplified method, use Form 8829.

Line 1. If all gross income from your trade or business is from this qualified business use of your home, figure your gross income limitation as follows.

A. Enter the amount from Schedule C, line 29 . . . .   _____
B. Enter any gain derived from the business use of your home and shown on Form 8949 (and included on Schedule D) or Form 4797 . . . . .   _____
C. Add lines A and B . . . .   _____
D. Enter the loss (as a positive number) shown on Form 8949 (and included on Schedule D) or Form 4797 that are allocable to the business,
but not allocable to the use of the home . . . .   _____
E. Gross income limitation. Subtract line D from line C. Enter the result here and on line 1 . . . .   _____

If some of the income is from a place of business other than your home, you must first determine the part of your gross income (Schedule C, line 7, and gains from Form 8949, Schedule D, and Form 4797) from the business use of your home. In making this determination, consider the amount of time you spend at each location as well as other facts. After determining the part of your gross income from the business use of your home, subtract from that amount the total expenses shown on Schedule C, line 28, plus any losses shown on Form 8949 (and included in Schedule D) or Form 4797 that are allocable to the business in which you use your home but that are not allocable to the use of the home. Enter the result on Line 1.

Note. If you had more than one home in which you conducted this business during the year, include only the income earned and the deductions attributable to that income during the period you owned the home for which you elected to use the simplified method.

Line 2. If you used the same area for the entire year, enter the smaller of the square feet you actually used and 300. If you and your spouse conducted the business as a qualified joint venture, split the square feet between you and your spouse in the same manner you split your other tax attributes. If you shared space with someone else, used the home for business for only part of the year, or the area you used changed during the year, see *Figuring your allowable expenses for business use of the home* before entering an amount on this line. Do not enter more than 300 square feet on this line.

Line 3b. If your qualified business use is providing daycare, you may need to account for the time that you used the same part of your home for other purposes. If you used the part of your home exclusively and regularly for providing daycare, enter 1.0 on line 3b. If you did not use the part of your home exclusively for providing daycare, complete the *Daycare Facility Worksheet* to figure what number to enter on line 3b.

Line 6. Since you are using the simplified method this year, you cannot deduct the amounts you entered on lines 6a and 6b this year. If you file Form 8829 next year for your qualified business use of this home, you will be able to include these expenses when you figure your deduction.

FIGURE 18.1 Simplified Method Worksheet for Home Office Deduction

If you use the actual expense method in a subsequent year, figure the depreciation deduction allowable in the subsequent year using the appropriate optional depreciation table applicable for the property, regardless of whether you used an optional depreciation table for the property in its placed-in-service year. Figure the allowable depreciation deduction for a subsequent year by multiplying the remaining adjusted depreciable basis allocable to the home office by the annual depreciation rate for the applicable year specified in the appropriate optional depreciation table. The applicable year is the year that corresponds with the current taxable year based on the placed-in-service year of the property.

Example

In January 2012, you started a business from home (assume you own your home) and claimed a home office deduction in 2012 and 2013. In 2014, you opt to use the safe harbor method. In 2015, you use the actual expense method. In figuring depreciation in 2015, the applicable year is 3 even though you did not take any depreciation allowance in 2014.

Electing the simplified method. The election is made on a year-by-year basis. Making the election in 2014 does not bind you to using the safe harbor method in 2015. However, once you make the election, it is irrevocable and can only be changed with IRS approval.

The simplified method cannot be elected by an employee who is reimbursed for home office use under a reimbursement or other expense allowance arrangement.

Special Business Uses of a Home

There are 2 exceptions to the exclusive use requirement: day-care facilities and storage space. If either of these exceptions apply, you can deduct your home office expenses even though the space is also used for personal purposes.

Day-Care Facilities

If you use all or part of your home on a regular basis as a facility to provide day-care services, you may claim home office deductions if you meet certain tests.

- You must provide day care for children, elderly persons (age 65 and older), or persons who are physically or mentally unable to care for themselves.
- You must have a license, certificate, registration, or other approval as a day-care center or family or group day-care home under your state law. You can claim home office expenses if you have applied for approval and are awaiting it. You cannot claim home office expenses if your application has been rejected or your approval revoked.

Note: Special rules for meal costs of day-care providers are covered in Chapter 22.

CALCULATING YOUR HOME OFFICE DEDUCTION FOR DAY-CARE SERVICES

If you use a portion of your home exclusively for day-care services (e.g., a basement playroom), you can deduct your expenses for any other type of business use of a home. If, however, you use a portion of your home for day-care services but also use it for personal purposes (e.g., your living room), you must follow special allocation rules to determine your home office deduction. You must compare the business use of the space with the total use of the space. There are 2 methods for making this comparison:

1. Compare the number of hours of business use in a week with the number of hours in a week (168 hours).
2. Compare the number of hours of business use in the tax year with the number of hours in a tax year (8,760 in a 365-day year).

Then this percentage is applied to the business percentage of total space.

> **Example**
>
> An individual uses her basement to provide day-care services. The basement represents 50% of her house's total square footage. She uses her basement for 12 hours per day, 5 days per week, 50 weeks per year, for day-care services. Her family uses the basement during the times it is not being used for day-care services. She uses her home for a total of 3,000 hours per year for business, or 34.25% of the total hours in the year (3,000 ÷ 8,760). In calculating the amount of indirect expenses allocable to her business use, she can deduct 17.13% (34.25% × 50%).

If meals are provided as part of the day-care services, the cost of the meals is not included in a home office deduction. It is a separate expense. In calculating the deductible portion of the meal costs, 100% of the costs to day-care recipients is deductible. If you also provide meals to employees, only 50% of the cost of meals for them is deductible. No percentage of the cost of meals consumed by you or your family is deductible. If you receive reimbursements under the Child and Adult Food Care Program under the U.S. Department of Agriculture, you must include in income any reimbursements in excess of your expenses for eligible children.

Storage

If space is used on a regular basis for the storage of your inventory or sample products, you can deduct home office expenses even though you also use the space for personal purposes and thus fail the exclusive use test. The storage space that is deductible is only the actual space used. For example, if a portion of a basement is used for storage, only the expenses related to that portion are deductible even if the rest of the basement is not used for other purposes.

Expenses of storage space are deductible even though the exclusive use test is not satisfied if:

- The home is the fixed location of the business activity (you run the business from home).
- The business activity is selling goods wholesale or retail.
- The space is used as a separately identifiable space suitable for storage.

> **Example**
>
> An individual runs from home a gift basket business and uses her family room to store samples. She may deduct the portion of the family room used to store her samples even though the family room is also used for personal purposes.

Bed and Breakfasts

Typically, owners of a bed and breakfast live at their inn, using a portion of the premises as their personal residence. There is no exception to the exclusive use rule for bed and breakfasts as there is for day care and storage. The Tax Court has determined that no deduction can be taken for the portion of the inn used for both personal and business purposes (e.g., lobby, kitchen, and laundry room). A deduction is limited only to areas used *exclusively* for business (e.g., guest rooms).

Ancillary Benefits of Claiming Home Office Deductions

Claiming home office deductions means more, tax wise, than simply deducting the expenses related to that office. It means additional tax benefits may be available.

Having a home office means that travel to and from the office for business is fully deductible (there is no such thing as commuting from a home office). So travel from your home to a customer's location and back again is a fully deductible business expense. Business use of your car is explained in Chapter 9.

Having a home office also means it is not necessary to keep a log of computer use. A computer used in a regular business establishment is not treated as listed property for which an owner must prove business use exceeds 50% in order to claim first-year expensing or accelerated depreciation. A home office for which a deduction is allowed is treated as a regular business establishment. First-year expensing and depreciation are explained in Chapter 14.

Impact of Home Office Deductions on Home Sales

Claiming a home office deduction does *not* impact your ability to claim the home sale exclusion (up to $250,000 of gain; $500,000 on a joint return) if you otherwise qualify for it. In the past it had been reasoned that gain on the portion of the home used as a home office would have to be reported. However, regulations make it clear that the exclusion can be applied to the home office portion as well, as long as the office is within the dwelling unit.

However, any depreciation taken on a home office after May 6, 1997, must be *recaptured* at the rate of 25% (for taxpayers in tax brackets over this amount). This means you must report your total depreciation deductions related to home office use after this date and must pay tax on the total amount at the rate of 25%. You cannot use the exclusion to offset this tax.

You cannot avoid this recapture by choosing not to report depreciation to which you are entitled when you use the actual expense method to figure the home office deduction. Recapture applies to depreciation both allowed (the amount you actually claimed) *and* allowable (what you were entitled to claim). If you want to avoid depreciation recapture, you must sidestep the home office deduction entirely by disqualifying your home office or use the safe harbor method for the home office deduction. You can do this easily by *not* using the space exclusively for business. By disqualifying your home office, you lose out on depreciation but can still claim many related costs, such as office maintenance and utility costs, as ordinary and necessary business expenses.

Where to Deduct Home Office Expenses

Employees

Employees do not compute their home office deduction for the actual expense method on Form 8829, *Expenses for Business Use of Your Home*. Instead, use the special worksheet in IRS Publication 587, which largely follows Form 8829. You will find this worksheet (Figure 18.2) on the following page.

Your home office deduction is entered on Form 2106, *Employee Business Expenses*, or Form 2106-EZ, *Unreimbursed Employee Business Expenses*, if you are otherwise allowed to use this form. Then the deductions from Form 2106 or 2106-EZ are entered on Schedule A as miscellaneous itemized deductions subject to the 2%-of-AGI rule and reduction for high-income taxpayers discussed in Chapter 1.

Worksheet To Figure the Deduction for Business Use of Your Home

PART 1—Part of Your Home Used for Business:

1)	Area of home used for business	1) _____
2)	Total area of home	2) _____
3)	Percentage of home used for business (divide line 1 by line 2 and show result as percentage)	3) _____ %

PART 2—Figure Your Allowable Deduction

4) Gross income from business (see instructions) . . . . 4) _____

		(a) Direct Expenses	(b) Indirect Expenses
5)	Casualty losses	5) _____	_____
6)	Deductible mortgage interest	6) _____	_____
7)	Real estate taxes	7) _____	_____
8)	Total of lines 5 through 7	8) _____	_____
9)	Multiply line 8, column (b), by line 3		9) _____
10)	Add line 8, column (a), and line 9		10) _____
11)	Business expenses not from business use of home (see instructions)		11) _____
12)	Add lines 10 and 11		12) _____
13)	Deduction limit. Subtract line 12 from line 4		13) _____
14)	Excess mortgage interest	14) _____	_____
15)	Insurance	15) _____	_____
16)	Repairs and maintenance	16) _____	_____
17)	Utilities	17) _____	_____
18)	Other expenses	18) _____	_____
19)	Add lines 14 through 18	19) _____	_____
20)	Multiply line 19, column (b) by line 3		20) _____
21)	Carryover of operating expenses from prior year (see instructions)		21) _____
22)	Add line 19, column (a), line 20, and line 21		22) _____
23)	Allowable operating expenses. Enter the **smaller** of line 13 or line 22		23) _____
24)	Limit on excess casualty losses and depreciation. Subtract line 23 from line 13		24) _____
25)	Excess casualty losses (see instructions)	25) _____	
26)	Depreciation of your home from line 38 below	26) _____	
27)	Carryover of excess casualty losses and depreciation from prior year (see instructions)	27) _____	
28)	Add lines 25 through 27		28) _____
29)	Allowable excess casualty losses and depreciation. Enter the **smaller** of line 24 or line 28		29) _____
30)	Add lines 10, 23, and 29		30) _____
31)	Casualty losses included on lines 10 and 29 (see instructions)		31) _____
32)	Allowable expenses for business use of your home. (Subtract line 31 from line 30.) See instructions for where to enter on your return		32) _____

PART 3—Depreciation of Your Home

33)	Smaller of adjusted basis or fair market value of home (see instructions)	33) _____
34)	Basis of land	34) _____
35)	Basis of building (subtract line 34 from line 33)	35) _____
36)	Business basis of building (multiply line 35 by line 3)	36) _____
37)	Depreciation percentage (from applicable table or method)	37) _____
38)	Depreciation allowable (multiply line 36 by line 37)	38) _____

PART 4—Carryover of Unallowed Expenses to Next Year

39)	Operating expenses. Subtract line 23 from line 22. If less than zero, enter -0-	39) _____
40)	Excess casualty losses and depreciation. Subtract line 29 from line 28. If less than zero, enter -0-	40) _____

FIGURE 18.2 Worksheet to Figure the Deduction for Business Use of Your Home

Remember that if you lease your home to your corporation, you cannot take any home office deductions (other than the mortgage interest, real estate taxes, and casualty and theft losses allowed to all homeowners).

Self-Employed

Self-employed individuals compute home office deductions for the actual expense method on Form 8829, *Expenses for Business Use of Your Home* (Figure 18.3). This form allows you to calculate the portion of your home used for business. This portion, or percentage, is then used to allocate your

Form **8829**	**Expenses for Business Use of Your Home**	OMB No. 1545-0074
Department of the Treasury	▶ File only with Schedule C (Form 1040). Use a separate Form 8829 for each home you used for business during the year.	20**14**
Internal Revenue Service (99)	▶ Information about Form 8829 and its separate instructions is at *www.irs.gov/form8829*.	Attachment Sequence No. **176**
Name(s) of proprietor(s)		Your social security number

Part I   Part of Your Home Used for Business

1	Area used regularly and exclusively for business, regularly for daycare, or for storage of inventory or product samples (see instructions)		1	
2	Total area of home		2	
3	Divide line 1 by line 2. Enter the result as a percentage		3	%
	For daycare facilities not used exclusively for business, go to line 4. All others, go to line 7.			
4	Multiply days used for daycare during year by hours used per day	4		hr.
5	Total hours available for use during the year (365 days x 24 hours) (see instructions)	5	8,760 hr.	
6	Divide line 4 by line 5. Enter the result as a decimal amount	6	.	
7	Business percentage. For daycare facilities not used exclusively for business, multiply line 6 by line 3 (enter the result as a percentage). All others, enter the amount from line 3 . . . . . ▶		7	%

Part II   Figure Your Allowable Deduction

		(a) Direct expenses	(b) Indirect expenses		
8	Enter the amount from Schedule C, line 29, **plus** any gain derived from the business use of your home, **minus** any loss from the trade or business not derived from the business use of your home (see instructions)			8	
	See instructions for columns (a) and (b) before completing lines 9–21.				
9	Casualty losses (see instructions)	9			
10	Deductible mortgage interest (see instructions)	10			
11	Real estate taxes (see instructions)	11			
12	Add lines 9, 10, and 11	12			
13	Multiply line 12, column (b) by line 7		13		
14	Add line 12, column (a) and line 13			14	
15	Subtract line 14 from line 8. If zero or less, enter -0-			15	
16	Excess mortgage interest (see instructions)	16			
17	Insurance	17			
18	Rent	18			
19	Repairs and maintenance	19			
20	Utilities	20			
21	Other expenses (see instructions)	21			
22	Add lines 16 through 21	22			
23	Multiply line 22, column (b) by line 7		23		
24	Carryover of prior year operating expenses (see instructions)		24		
25	Add line 22, column (a), line 23, and line 24			25	
26	Allowable operating expenses. Enter the **smaller** of line 15 or line 25			26	
27	Limit on excess casualty losses and depreciation. Subtract line 26 from line 15			27	
28	Excess casualty losses (see instructions)		28		
29	Depreciation of your home from line 41 below		29		
30	Carryover of prior year excess casualty losses and depreciation (see instructions)		30		
31	Add lines 28 through 30			31	
32	Allowable excess casualty losses and depreciation. Enter the **smaller** of line 27 or line 31			32	
33	Add lines 14, 26, and 32			33	
34	Casualty loss portion, if any, from lines 14 and 32. Carry amount to **Form 4684** (see instructions)			34	
35	**Allowable expenses for business use of your home.** Subtract line 34 from line 33. Enter here and on Schedule C, line 30. If your home was used for more than one business, see instructions ▶			35	

Part III   Depreciation of Your Home

36	Enter the **smaller** of your home's adjusted basis or its fair market value (see instructions)	36	
37	Value of land included on line 36	37	
38	Basis of building. Subtract line 37 from line 36	38	
39	Business basis of building. Multiply line 38 by line 7	39	
40	Depreciation percentage (see instructions)	40	%
41	Depreciation allowable (see instructions). Multiply line 39 by line 40. Enter here and on line 29 above	41	

Part IV   Carryover of Unallowed Expenses to 2015

42	Operating expenses. Subtract line 26 from line 25. If less than zero, enter -0-	42	
43	Excess casualty losses and depreciation. Subtract line 32 from line 31. If less than zero, enter -0-	43	

For Paperwork Reduction Act Notice, see your tax return instructions.   Cat. No. 13232M   Form **8829** (2014)

FIGURE 18.3 Form 8829, Home Office Deduction

home-related expenses. You also use the form to calculate any carryover of unused home office expenses.

If you first begin to use your home office this year and you own your home, you must also complete Form 4562, *Depreciation and Amortization*, to calculate the depreciation deduction entered on Form 8829.

Depreciation is explained in full in Chapter 14. Note that when you begin to use part of your home for business, it is usually depreciated as nonresidential realty over 39 years (31.5 years if you began home office use before May 13, 1993). You must determine the basis of your home office in order to calculate depreciation. Basis on the conversion of property from personal use to business use is the lesser of the FMV of the office on the date you begin business use or the adjusted basis of the property on that date. If you are not sure about the FMV of your home office, get an appraisal. Ask a local real estate agent to assist you in this task.

The home office deduction calculated on Form 8829 is entered on a specific line on Schedule C for expenses for business use of your home. You cannot use Schedule C-EZ, Net Profit From Business, if you claim a home office deduction.

Farmers

Self-employed farmers who file Schedule F instead of Schedule C and want to deduct their actual expenses do not compute home office deductions on Form 8829. Instead, they should calculate these deductions on the Worksheet (see Figure 18.2 on page 412) in the same way as employees. Then the home office deduction is entered on Schedule F.

Partners and LLC Members

If you use a home office for your business, you figure your deduction for the actual expense method in the same way as an employee. Use the worksheet (Figure 18.2) on page 412 (do not use Form 8829 to figure your home office deduction).

Simplified Method

Figure the home office deduction on the worksheet in Figure 18.1 on page 407.

Medical Coverage

Alert

At the time this book was printed, Congress had not extended numerous breaks for 2014 that had expired at the end of 2013. Check the online supplement in February 2015 at www.jklasser.com or www.barbaraweltman.com to see whether these breaks apply for 2014 returns.

Medical coverage is an expensive personal expense for most people. So, for many, a job that provides medical coverage offers an important benefit. For the small business owner there is often a need to obtain personal coverage. It may also be good business practice to offer medical coverage as a benefit to attract and keep good employees. A write-off of all or a portion of the cost of medical coverage is a significant cost-saving feature of providing such coverage.

On March 23, 2010, the historic Patient Protection and Affordable Care Act was signed into law; the following week the Health Care and Education Reconciliation Act became law. Essentially, these acts mandate that every individual in the United States have health coverage, and that certain employers provide affordable coverage or pay a penalty. On June 28, 2012, the U.S. Supreme Court upheld the constitutionality of the individual mandate. The financial impact of this law on small business owners remains to be seen.

For more information about deducting medical coverage, see IRS Publication 535, *Business Expenses,* and IRS Publication 969, *Health Savings Accounts and Other Tax-Favored Health Plans.*

Health Care Mandates

Starting on January 1, 2014, all individuals (other than exempt individuals) are subject to a health care mandate created by the Patient Protection and Affordable Care Act. This requires individuals to have health coverage or pay a tax penalty. The following information is merely an overview of complex rules. Three government agencies: the IRS, the U.S. Department of Labor, and the U.S. Department of Health and Human Services (HHS) are each part of the regulatory mix.

Self-employed individuals. If you are self-employed and do not have health coverage through a spouse's employer, Medicare, Medicaid, or other insurance program providing minimum essential coverage, you must obtain coverage yourself through a private insurer or through a government marketplace for individuals (self-employed individuals cannot use the Small Business Health Insurance Options Program, or SHOPs). You must also carry coverage for your dependents. If you cannot afford the coverage, you may qualify for assistance in the form of a tax credit. The premium tax credit applies to those with household income between 100% and 400% of the poverty line (the 2013 poverty line is used for purposes of 2014 credit eligibility). The credit is payable on an advanced basis, so it can be used monthly to lower premium costs.

If you opt *not* to have coverage and do not qualify for an exemption from the individual mandate, you owe a penalty, which is an additional tax reported on your tax return. In 2014, the penalty is $95 per adult and $47.50 per child (up to age 18), up to a family maximum of $285 or 1% of family income in excess of your filing threshold (e.g., $10,150 if you're single and under age 65), whichever is greater.

Looking Ahead

In 2015, the penalty is $325 per adult and $162.50 per child, up to a family maximum of $975 or 2% of family income in excess of filing status, whichever is greater. In 2016, the penalty is $695 per adult and $347.50 per child, up to a family maximum of $2,085 or 2.5% of family income, whichever is greater.

The IRS is prevented from aggressively collecting the penalty, but could withhold tax refunds where appropriate. Find more at HealthCare.gov.

Employer mandate. The requirement to offer certain health coverage or pay a penalty ("play or pay") applies only to "large employers." Like the individual mandate, it was supposed to start on January 1, 2014, but has been delayed until 2015 for employers with 100 or more employees, or 2016 for employers with 50 to 99 employees. The definition of a large employer is a company with more than 50 full-time and/or full-time equivalent employees employees. Determining whether you meet this threshold is not as simple as doing a body count. This is because part-timers can add up to full-time equivalent employees (FTEs). A combination of employees working 120 hours per month (around 30 hours per week) counts as one employee.

To determine your payroll size, first tally the number of full-time employees (those working 120 hours per month or more). Then figure full-time equivalent employees:

- Step 1: Figure the aggregate number of hours of service (but not more than 120 hours of service for any employee) for all employees who were not employed on average at least 30 hours of service per week for that month (part-timers).
- Step 2: Divide the total hours of service in Step 1 by 120. This is the number of FTEs for the calendar month.

Note: The definition of and the way in which FTEs are figured for the employer mandate differ from the FTE rules for the small employer health insurance credit discussed later in this chapter.

In determining the number of FTEs for each calendar month, fractions are *not* taken into account.

Example

In a calendar month, your company has employees who were not employed on average at least 30 hours of service per week; they have a total of 1,260 hours of service. In this situation there would be 10.5 FTEs for that month

> (1,260 ÷ 120). In addition, there are 12 full-time employees. The company is treated as having 22 FTEs; the fraction is disregarded.

Off-time counts. In figuring the hours worked, take into account paid leave for vacation, sick days, personal days, and maternity leave for your employees. Do not count unpaid days off.

Seasonal businesses. You don't have to be in retail or agriculture to have a seasonal business. As long as you are seasonal, there's a special rule to follow: If your workforce exceeds 50 FTEs for 120 days or fewer during a calendar year, and the employees in excess of 50 who were employed during that period of no more than 120 days were seasonal workers, you are not a large employer subject to the employer mandate.

Annual determination. The determination of payroll size is made year by year, and is based on payroll for the prior year, called the look-back period. For example, your 2014 payroll information is used to determine whether you are subject to the employer mandate in 2015. You must average the number of employees over the months to find your payroll numbers for the employer mandate. The look-back period usually is the full 12 months.

Controlled businesses. Can you avoid the employer mandate by splitting up your business into multiple companies so that each has no more than 50 FTEs? Unfortunately not. Controlled groups of corporations and unincorporated businesses with a certain level of common ownership are treated as a single business for purposes of the employer mandate. Interestingly, the definitions of controlled groups of corporations and businesses under common control are the same tax-law definition used for qualified retirement plans. In addition, affiliated groups in service organizations (e.g., accounting firms; third-party administrators) are also treated as a single entity when there is some common ownership (it seems to be a 10% threshold).

Penalty. The penalty is $2,000 per year for each employee (after subtracting the first 30 employees); the penalty is $3,000 for any full-time employee receiving a premium tax credit (explained under *self-employed individuals*).

Looking Ahead

Starting in 2018, there is an excise tax imposed on so-called Cadillac health plans. These are deluxe health plans; there is no exemption from the tax for small employers. The tax is imposed on the excess benefit, which is the amount by which single coverage exceeds $10,200, or family coverage exceeds $27,500 (higher thresholds apply to high-risk employees and retired workers not yet eligible for Medicare). You have to compute the amount of the excess benefit and report this to the insurance company. The dollar limits will be indexed for inflation after 2018.

Alert

If your business may be or become subject to the employer mandate, tread carefully. For example, cutting employee hours only to be exempt from the mandate may violate federal law protecting employee benefits. Also Congress may change the rules; check the Supplement for further details.

Deducting Medical Insurance for Employees

For 2014, you are not required by federal law to provide medical insurance for employees (there are some state mandates). According to a study from the Kaiser Family Foundation released in September 2013, 45% of all small businesses with 3 to 9 employees offer this benefit to their employees. But 68% of those with 10 to 24 employees, 85% for firms with 25 to 49 employees, and 91% of companies with more than 50 employees offer health coverage. If you choose to provide medical insurance, you can deduct the cost of their group hospitalization and medical insurance. Deductible medical coverage also includes premiums for **long-term care insurance**.

Long-term care insurance An insurance contract that provides coverage for long-term care services necessary for diagnostic, preventive, therapeutic, curing, treating, mitigating, and rehabilitative services, as well as maintenance or personal care services required by a chronically ill person and provided pursuant to a plan of care prescribed by a licensed health care practitioner.

To be deductible, long-term care insurance must:

- Be guaranteed renewable.
- Not provide for a cash surrender value or other money that can be repaid, assigned, pledged, or borrowed.
- Provide that refunds of premiums, other than refunds on the death of the insured or complete surrender or cancellation of the contract, and dividends under the contract may be used to reduce future premiums or increase future benefits.

- Not pay or reimburse expenses incurred for services or items that would be reimbursed under Medicare, except where Medicare is a secondary payer or the contract makes per diem or other periodic payments without regard to expenses.

Medical coverage provided to employees is treated as a tax-free fringe benefit. According to the IRS, medical coverage provided to a domestic partner is taxable to the employee because a domestic partner is not a spouse under state law. However, an employer providing such medical coverage can still deduct it (since the employee is taxed on the cost of coverage for a domestic partner as additional compensation).

The value of long-term care insurance provided through a cafeteria plan or other flexible spending arrangement is not excludable from the employees' income.

You deduct medical premiums according to your method of accounting. If you use the cash method, you generally deduct premiums in the year you pay them. If you are on the accrual method, you generally deduct premiums in the year you incur the liability for them (whether you actually pay the bill at that time). The IRS maintains that premiums covering a period of more than one year cannot be deducted except for the portion of the premium that relates to the current year.

You cannot deduct amounts you set aside or put into reserve funds for self-insuring medical costs (see medical reimbursement plans). However, your actual losses (when you pay for uninsured medical costs) are deductible.

Note: Employers doing $500,000 or more in annual business must provide certain notice to newly-hired employees about health coverage. Find a sample notice form at www.dol.gov/ebsa/pdf/FLSAwithplans.pdf.

COVERAGE FOR RETIREES

You are not required to continue providing medical coverage for employees who retire (beyond COBRA requirements discussed later in this chapter or any contractual obligation). If you choose to pay for such coverage, you may deduct it. You may terminate your obligation for this coverage as long as you retained the right to do so in any plan or agreement you made to provide the coverage (for example, in an employee's early retirement package).

Special Rules for Partnerships and S Corporations

The business may provide coverage not only for rank-and-file employees but for owners as well. Partnerships and S corporations follow special rules for health insurance coverage provided to owners because owners cannot receive this benefit on a tax-free basis.

First, partnerships deduct accident and health insurance for their partners as guaranteed payments made to partners. Alternatively, partnerships can choose to treat the payment of premiums on behalf of their partners as a reduction in distributions. In this alternative, the partnership cannot claim a deduction.

S corporations deduct accident and health insurance for its shareholder-employees in the same way they do for other employees.

Payment of accident and health insurance for a shareholder means the premiums are not treated as wages for purposes of FICA (includes Social Security and Medicare taxes) if the insurance is provided under a plan or system for employees and their dependents. Of course, even where the payment is not treated as wages for FICA, it is still taxable to the shareholder for income tax purposes and reported on the shareholder's Form W-2.

A partnership must report the medical insurance that it provides to owners on the owners' Schedule K-1. This is picked up by the partners as income (unless the partnership does not claim a deduction). Owners may be entitled to deduct a percentage of health insurance, as explained in the next section.

Deducting Health Coverage by Self-Employed Persons and More-Than-2% S Corporation Shareholders

Self-employed persons (sole proprietors, partners, and LLC members), as well as more-than-2% S corporation shareholders, may deduct the cost of health insurance (including long-term care coverage) they receive through their business, but not as a business expense (this rule has not been changed by the Patient Protection and Affordable Care Act). A self-employed person who buys coverage in his or her personal name can deduct the premiums above-the-line (assuming there is sufficient income from the business as explained later). However, a more-than-2% S corporation shareholder can only claim an above-the-line deduction for a policy purchased by the corporation, or the corporation reimburses the shareholder for premiums, and includes this amount on the shareholder's Form W-2. If the policy is purchased by the shareholder, premiums must be treated as an itemized medical expense (subject to the adjusted gross income floor). This is so even if state law bars a one-person S corporation from purchasing a policy.

The deduction is taken from gross income on page 1 of Form 1040 (other than for a one-person S corporation whose shareholder personally buys the policy). This means the deduction is allowed even if the self-employed person does not itemize deductions. The policy can be purchased individually (it need not be purchased by the business).

The deduction cannot exceed the net earnings from the business in which the medical insurance plan is established. You cannot aggregate profits from 2 or more businesses to establish the net earnings ceiling required for deducting health insurance premiums. For S corporation shareholders, the deduction cannot be more than wages from the corporation (if this was the business in which the insurance plan was established).

You cannot take the deduction for any month if you were eligible to participate in any employer subsidized health plan (including your spouse's) at any time during the month. For example, suppose you are a single, self-employed individual and pay for your own health coverage. On July 1, 2014, you begin a job in which your employer provides you with health insurance. You can deduct the applicable percentage of your health insurance from January 1 through June 30, 2014 (the time you did not receive any subsidized health coverage).

You can include "above the line" your Medicare Part B and Part D premiums. You can add your spouse's Medicare premiums if your spouse is covered by Medicare. There has been no IRS guidance on whether COBRA payments by a self-employed person can be deducted as an adjustment to gross income.

In calculating self-employment tax, do not reduce net earnings from self-employment by your allowable medical insurance deduction.

Using Medical Reimbursement Plans

Businesses can set up special plans, called *medical reimbursement plans*, to pay for medical expenses not otherwise covered by insurance. For example, medical reimbursement plans can pay for the cost of eye care or cover co-payments and other out-of-pocket costs. Medical reimbursement plans are self-insured plans; they are not funded by insurance.

Medical reimbursement plans can cover only employees. These include owners of C corporations (but not S corporations). The plans cannot discriminate in favor of highly compensated employees, such as owners and officers.

The IRS has endorsed a way around the ban on deducting medical costs of self-employed owners. If the business has a medical reimbursement plan for employees and your spouse is an employee (nonowner), the medical reimbursement plan can cover the medical expenses of your spouse-employee and your employee's spouse (you) and dependents. In this way, your medical costs are deductible by the business and are not taxable to you.

Disadvantages

While self-insured medical reimbursement plans provide advantages to employers, there is a significant risk of substantial economic exposure (that claims will run higher than anticipated and planned for). This problem can be addressed by setting a dollar limit (such as $2,500) on medical reimbursements for the year.

Another disadvantage to this type of plan is the administration involved (reviewing and processing reimbursement claims). For a very small employer, however, this may not be significant.

Tax Credit for Contributions to Employee Health Coverage

There is a credit to encourage small employers (no more than the equivalent of 25 full-time employees) to help pay for employee health coverage. The credit is *very* complicated; it varies with the number of employees, their average full-time wages, the amount of premiums paid, and the average premiums by state for the small group market.

The tax credit is up to 50% of the employer's contribution to pay for employee health insurance. This credit is limited to small employers; they are defined as having no more than the equivalent of 25 full-time employees (FTEs) with average annual wages of less than $50,800. A full credit is available to those with 10 or fewer FTEs with average wages of less than $25,400.

The amount of the credit is based on a percentage of the lesser of: (1) the amount of nonelective contributions paid by an eligible small employer on behalf of employees, or (2) the amount of nonelective contributions the employer would have paid under the arrangement if each such employee were enrolled in a plan that had a premium equal to the average premium for the small group market in the state (or in an area in the state) in which the employer is offering health insurance coverage. The average premium amounts are fixed by the Department of Health and Human Services. The average premium amounts for 2013 are found in Table 19.2. The amounts for 2014 can be found in the Supplement.

The credit applies only for a maximum of 2 years (2014 and 2015), and only for small employers that purchase health coverage through the Small Business Health Options Program (SHOP) marketplace. The federal marketplace was supposed to open in the fall of 2013 so that employers could find coverage for 2014. Instead, the federal marketplace used in 32 states has been delayed until 2015. States with their own SHOPs (as indicated in Table 19.1) have been granted relief until 2016. However, federal SHOP coverage is available by downloading an application from HealthCare.gov, by calling the SHOP Small Employer Call Center at 800-706-7893, or by purchasing coverage directly through an insurance agent (the IRS has yet to rule on whether use of this option will disqualify a small employer from claiming the credit).

The credit is part of the general business credit. The credit can be used to offset alternative minimum tax liability.

TABLE 19.1 State Marketplaces Delayed until 2016

States		
Alabama	Louisiana	North Carolina
Alaska	Maine	Oklahoma
Arizona	Michigan	Pennsylvania
Delaware	Montana	South Carolina
Illinois	New Hampshire	South Dakota
Kansas	New Jersey	West Virginia

TABLE 19.2 Average Premiums for 2013 by State for the Small Group Market

State	Single (Employee-Only) Coverage	Family Coverage
Alabama	$5,363	$13,185
Alaska	7,961	16,808
Arizona	4,946	12,006
Arkansas	4,546	10,575
California	5,345	12,809
Colorado	5,445	13,937
Connecticut	6,307	16,011
Delaware	6,555	15,144
District of Columbia	6,133	16,079
Florida	5,602	13,261
Georgia	5,605	12,369
Hawaii	5,246	12,782
Idaho	4,901	10,738
Illinois	6,017	14,453
Indiana	5,710	13,029
Iowa	4,963	12,071
Kansas	5,164	12,322
Kentucky	4,936	11,981
Louisiana	5,390	12,691
Maine	5,590	13,064
Maryland	5,610	13,965
Massachusetts	6,323	16,502
Michigan	5,569	13,256
Minnesota	5,588	14,077
Mississippi	5,042	11,964
Missouri	5,268	12,366
Montana	5,433	11,739
Nebraska	5,463	13,270
Nevada	5,417	12,125
New Hampshire	6,153	15,367
New Jersey	6,250	15,225
New Mexico	5,639	13,121
New York	6,242	15,478
North Carolina	5,510	12,541
North Dakota	5,073	12,343
Ohio	5,174	12,710
Oklahoma	5,142	11,995
Oregon	5,413	12,811
Pennsylvania	5,618	13,753
Rhode Island	6,345	15,363
South Carolina	5,351	12,473
South Dakota	5,364	12,750
Tennessee	5,251	11,663
Texas	5,327	13,313
Utah	4,951	12,619
Vermont	5,800	13,409
Virginia	5,449	13,241
Washington	5,292	12,196
West Virginia	5,947	13,734
Wisconsin	5,786	14,623
Wyoming	5,948	14,314

Shifting the Cost of Coverage to Employees

Health insurance is increasingly costly to employers. There are several ways in which business owners can reduce their costs without putting employees out in the cold.

Sharing the Cost of Premiums

Instead of employers paying the entire cost of insurance, employers can shift a portion of the cost to employees. For example, employers may provide free coverage for employees but shift the cost of spousal and dependent care coverage to employees.

Flexible Spending Arrangements

Businesses can set up flexible spending arrangements (FSAs) to allow employees to decide how much they want to pay for medical expenses. The maximum amount that employees can add to a medical FSA in 2014 is $2,500.

> **Looking Ahead**
>
> The maximum amount that employees can add to a medical FSA in 2015 is in the Supplement to this book.

Employees pay for qualified medical expenses (prescription drugs and insulin as well as doctor-prescribed over-the-counter medications) on a pretax basis. At the beginning of the year, they agree to a salary reduction amount that funds their FSA. Contributions to an FSA are not treated as taxable compensation (and are not subject to FICA). Employees then use the amount in their FSA to pay for most types of medical-related costs, such as medical premiums, orthodontia, or other expenses during the year that are not covered by medical insurance (including over-the-counter medications, such as pain relievers and cold remedies, not prescribed by a doctor). This plan cannot be used to pay for cosmetic surgery unless it is required for medical purposes (such as to correct a birth defect).

> **Example**
>
> Your employee agrees to a monthly salary reduction amount of $100. This means that the employee has $1,200 during the year to spend on medical costs.

The downside for employers is that employees can use all of their promised contributions for the year whenever they submit proof of medical expenses. This means that if employees leave employment after taking funds out of their FSA but before they have fully funded them, the employer winds up paying the difference. So, for example, if an employee who promises to contribute $100 per month submits a bill for dental expenses of $1,200 on January 15 and leaves employment shortly thereafter, the employee has contributed only $100; the employer must bear the cost of the additional $1,100 submission.

Of course, the flip side benefits the employer. If employees fail to use up their FSA contributions before the end of the year or the 2½ month grace period (referred to as the "use it or lose it" rule) or the limited carryover rule does not apply, the employer keeps the difference. Nothing is refunded to the employees.

Cafeteria Plans

Employers can set up cafeteria plans to let employees choose from a menu of benefits. This makes sense for some employers, since cafeteria plans allow working couples to get the benefits they need without needless overlap. For example, if one spouse has health insurance coverage from his employer, the other spouse can select dependent care assistance or other benefits offered through a cafeteria plan. Cafeteria plans do not require employees to reduce salary or make contributions to pay for benefits. Benefits are paid by the employer.

Premium-Only Plans

In these plans, employees choose between health coverage or salary. If they select the coverage, it is paid by means of salary reduction. In effect, employees are paying for their own coverage, but with pretax dollars. The employer deducts the compensation (whether the employee chooses the coverage or takes the salary). The only cost to the employer under this type of plan is the cost of administering it. (Many payroll service companies will administer the plan for a modest charge.) Bonus: Both the employer and employee save on FICA if the medical coverage is chosen.

NOTE
Health Savings Accounts (HSAs) cannot be part of cafeteria plans.

Setting Up Health Savings Accounts (HSAs)

The high cost of health insurance is considered by many small-business owners to be their number-one concern. Now there's a way to cut costs by 40% or more by combining a high-deductible (lower-cost) health policy with a special savings account called a Health Savings Account (HSA). With the liberalization of certain HSA rules, combined with an ever-growing range of investment options, these accounts should gain in popularity. According to the Employee Benefits Institute, 24.4 million people were covered by HSAs by the end of 2013. Fidelity Investments reported that their HSAs increased by 48% in 2013. It now administers HSAs for 269,000 account holders at more than 100 companies, with assets increasing 39% to $653 million.

MSAs Alternative

The congressional experiment of combining high-deductible health insurance with savings accounts continues in the form of Archer Medical Savings Accounts (MSAs). (In 2005, the last year for which statistics are available, only about 18,000 individuals claimed deductions for MSA contributions.) These accounts are available only to self-employed individuals and small-business owners who had MSAs set up by December 31, 2007. There are many restrictions on eligibility. If eligible, you can use an MSA instead of an HSA. You can roll over amounts to an HSA. MSAs are discussed later in this chapter.

Eligibility

HSAs are open to anyone who, on the first day of the month, is covered by a high-deductible health insurance plan, is not covered by another type of health insurance plan (other than workers' compensation, long-term care, disability, and vision and eye care), and who is not eligible for Medicare. This means that self-employed individuals, small-business owners, and those who work for small businesses and are under age 65 can use HSAs to obtain necessary health coverage. Each spouse's eligibility is determined separately; the fact that one spouse cannot have an HSA does not taint the other spouse's eligibility.

HIGH-DEDUCTIBLE PLAN

This is defined as a plan with an annual deductible in 2014 of at least $1,250 for self-only coverage or $2,500 for family coverage, and the sum of the annual deductible and other annual out-of-pocket expenses in 2014 is no more than $6,350 for self-only or $12,700 for family coverage (these dollar limits will be adjusted annually for inflation; 2015 limits are in the online Supplement).

Benefits of HSAs

HSAs give you an affordable way to offer health coverage for yourself and your employees. This example from the National Small Business Association shows you how.

Example

A company with 15 employees is currently paying $72,000 for a low-deductible health insurance. It changes to a high-deductible health plan with a $2,500 deductible for participants. The annual cost of the new plan is $40,000. The company also contributes $1,000 to each participant's HSA, so its total cost is $55,000 ($40,000 insurance premiums + $15,000 HSA contributions). This is $17,000 less than the company was paying for low-deductible health coverage.

Contributions to HSAs are *not* subject to payroll taxes, which makes HSAs a better option than paying additional compensation to employees as a way to cover unreimbursed medical expenses.

Contributions

For 2014, contributions are limited to $3,300 for those with self-only coverage or $6,550 for family coverage (any plan other than self-only); these limits will be adjusted annually for inflation. The full contribution limit applies even though eligibility starts sometime during the year. For example, if a business buys a high-deductible health plan starting on July 1, a contribution of $3,300 can be made for someone with self-only coverage (in the past such contribution had to be prorated so that only one-half of this amount was permissible).

> **For the Future**
>
> The contribution limits for 2015 are $3,350 for self-only coverage and $6,650 for family coverage, plus an additional $1,000 if age 55 or older by year-end.

For those age 55 or older by the end of the year, the contribution limit is increased by $1,000. Contributions are fully deductible.

You are not required by law to make contributions for your employees, but if you choose to do so, it must be on a nondiscriminatory basis (you can't simply contribute for owners and not for rank-and-file employees).

Like IRAs, contributions to HSAs can be made up to the due date of the return (e.g., April 15, 2015, for 2014 contributions). Contributions can be made via a direct deposit of a tax refund. For example, if a refund is due on a 2014 return, it can be deposited into an HSA. But the return should be filed early enough to allow the IRS to process it and transfer the funds to the designated account if it is to be credited to the prior year contribution.

Taxation of HSAs

There is no current tax on earnings in HSAs (most but not all states also exempt HSAs from state income tax). Funds withdrawn from HSAs to pay qualified medical costs (prescription drugs and insulin as well as doctor-prescribed over-the-counter medications) are not subject to tax. Money can be taken out for any purpose, but nonmedical withdrawals are taxable, and there is a 20% penalty (the penalty is waived for disability or attainment of age 65).

When taking withdrawals for medical purposes, you are not required to prove this to the financial institution acting as the account's trustee or custodian. If you maintain the accounts for your employees, they are not required to prove the purpose of their withdrawal to you (it is their responsibility). But you should save receipts and other proof to show that the withdrawals should not be subject to a 20% penalty if you are under age 65.

Note: Employees own their HSAs and can take them when they leave the company.

Archer Medical Savings Accounts (MSAs)

Small employers and self-employed individuals can use MSAs in lieu of Health Savings Accounts to combine low-cost high-deductible health coverage with a savings-type account. The opportunity to set up new MSAs expired at the end of 2007. However, existing MSAs can continue to receive contributions.

Eligibility

Archer MSAs are open only to small employers (those with 50 or fewer employees) and self-employed individuals with high-deductible plans. In 2014, they are health insurance plans with an annual deductible between $4,350 and $5,550 for family coverage, or $2,200 and $3,250 for single (self-only) coverage. The health insurance must have an annual limit on out-of-pocket expenses of $8,000 or less for families, or $4,350 or less for singles.

Contributions

As in the case of HSAs, employer contributions to MSAs for employees are not taxable to employees. Contributions are limited to 75% of the annual deductible for family coverage or 65% of the annual deductible for self-only coverage.

If a high-deductible health plan is not in place for the entire year, the contribution is limited to the ratable portion of the annual deductible for the time the plan is in effect.

These same contribution limits apply to self-employed individuals and employees who make contributions on their own behalf. Personal contributions within these limits are deductible. Contributions must be made in cash (they cannot be made in the form of stock or other property). The contribution must be made no later than the due date of the return (without regard to extensions).

Contributions can only be made on behalf of individuals who are under age 65. However, those age 65 and older have the option of selecting Medicare-MSAs, which are a type of coverage alternative to traditional Medicare (called "fee for service"). Medicare-MSAs are not funded by employers, employees, or self-employed individuals; they are funded entirely by contributions from the federal government. Medicare-MSAs will not generate any tax deductions for small businesses for self-employed individuals.

MSAs versus HSAs

While the options are strikingly similar, MSAs have not achieved any significant success in the public eye. This is partly because the plans were temporary.

As discussed earlier, those with existing MSAs might want to continue funding them rather than changing plans. However, there is the option to roll over funds in MSAs to HSAs (see above).

Health Reimbursement Arrangements

If you want to limit your outlays for employee medical costs, consider a relatively new option called a health reimbursement arrangement (HRA). You contribute a fixed amount to an account for each employee that can be tapped to cover unreimbursed medical expenses. You can (but are not required to) complement the HRA by switching medical insurance to a less extensive, less costly plan. Overall you save on your medical costs. And the HRA does not entail any costly and complex design requirements associated with other types of plans such as flexible spending arrangements within cafeteria plans (for details on HRAs see Rev. Rul. 2002-41). It is essentially a bookkeeping entry on the part of the business (no separate funding is required).

The benefit to your employee is that neither contributions to nor qualified reimbursements from the plan are taxable. Qualified disbursements include prescription drugs and insulin as well as doctor-prescribed over-the-counter medications. Funds in the account can be accessed by credit or debit cards that you set up for this purpose. Also, unused amounts in an employee's account can be carried forward and used in future years (there is no use-it-or-lose-it feature). However, when an employee leaves, any balance remaining in the HRA is not portable; it is forfeited.

COBRA Coverage

Employers who normally employ 20 or more employees and who provide coverage for employees must extend continuation coverage (referred to as COBRA—the initials for the law that created continuation coverage). COBRA entitles employees who are terminated (whether voluntarily or otherwise) to pay for continued coverage of what they received while employed. It also covers families of deceased employees and former spouses of divorced employees. COBRA coverage generally applies for 18 months (36 months in some cases).

Employers can charge for COBRA coverage but only up to the cost of the coverage to the employer plus an administrative fee. This limit on the total cost to the individual for COBRA coverage is 102% of the cost of the insurance. Employers who fail to provide COBRA and/or to provide proper notice of COBRA can be subject to a substantial penalty.

A number of states have their own COBRA rules, referred to as *mini-COBRA*. Mini-COBRA rules may require coverage from one month to 18 months for firms with as few as 2 employees. Be sure to check any state law requirements on providing continuation health coverage to terminated employees.

> **NOTE**
> Federal COBRA does not include the cost of long-term care insurance.

Wellness Programs

As a way to reduce health care expenditures, some companies have offered programs designed to encourage good health. These include weight-loss and stop-smoking programs.

A company can pay for wellness programs and deduct the costs as long as the programs adhere to government regulations. Access to a company's program must be nondiscriminatory (i.e., not limited to owners or other key people). Group wellness programs fall into two categories: participatory wellness programs (programs that are not conditioned on a participants health and do not provide a reward that is based on an individual's satisfying a standard that is related to a health factor) and health-contingent wellness programs (programs that require an individual to satisfy a requirement related to a health factor in order to obtain a reward); each has its own rules.

Reporting Health Coverage on W-2s

Employer-paid health coverage continues to be a tax-free fringe benefit (see Chapter 7). However, employers (other than "small employers") must include the value of this coverage on employees' W-2s. The amount reported is the amount paid by the employer, employee, or a combination of both. Small employers are those who issue fewer than 250 Forms W-2 for the previous calendar year. The IRS could end this small-employer exemption from reporting at any time; check the Supplement for any change.

Where to Write-Off Health Insurance Costs

Employees

If you pay for your own health insurance, you can deduct premiums only as an itemized deduction on Schedule A. Premiums, along with other unreimbursed medical expenses, are deductible only to the extent they exceed 10% of adjusted gross income (7.5% of AGI if age 65 or older by year end).

Health Savings Account contributions are treated separately from other medical expenses. If you make contributions to HSAs or MSAs, they are deductible on page 1 of Form 1040 (regardless of whether you itemize your other deductibles).

You must complete Form 8889 to claim a deduction for HSA contributions or Form 8853 to claim a deduction for MSA contributions. The premium tax credit is claimed on Form 8962, *Premium Tax Credit*. Exemption from the individual mandate is claimed on Form 8965, *Health Coverage Exemptions*.

Self-Employed

Coverage provided to employees is fully deductible on Schedule C (or Schedule F for farming operations). The cost coverage for the self-employed person is deducted on page 1 of Form 1040.

Contributions to a Health Savings Account or Archer MSA on your own behalf are also deductible on page 1 of Form 1040. You must complete Form 8889 to claim a deduction for HSA contributions or Form 8853 to claim a deduction for MSA contributions. The premium tax credit is claimed on Form 8962, *Premium Tax Credit*. Exemption from the individual mandate is claimed on Form 8965, *Health Coverage Exemptions*.

Partnerships and LLCs

Insurance paid by the partnership is deducted on Form 1065. Coverage for partners is included in guaranteed payments and reported to them on Schedule K-1. If the partnership chooses to treat the payment of insurance premiums for partners as a reduction in distributions, no deduction can be claimed.

The cost of coverage for partners is deducted on page 1 of their individual returns (Form 1040). You must complete Form 8889 to claim a deduction for HSA contributions or Form 8853 to claim a deduction for MSA contributions.

S Corporations

Insurance paid by the S corporation is deducted on Form 1120S. Coverage for more-than-2% S corporation shareholders is reported to them on Schedule K-1 as well as on their W-2 forms (as wages).

The cost of coverage for more-than-2% S corporation shareholders is deducted on page 1 of their individual returns (Form 1040). You must complete Form 8889 to claim a deduction for HSA contributions or Form 8853 to claim a deduction for MSA contributions.

C Corporations

Insurance paid by the corporation is deducted on Form 1120.

All Employers

If you claim the credit for paying health insurance premiums, file Form 8941, *Credit for Small Employer Health Insurance Premiums*.

Deductions and Tax Credits for Farmers

Alert

At the time this book was printed, Congress had not extended numerous breaks for 2014 that had expired at the end of 2013. Check the online supplement in February 2015 at www.jklasser.com or www.barbaraweltman.com to see whether these breaks apply for 2014 returns.

The U.S. Department of Agriculture reports that there were more than 2.1 million farms in the U.S. in 2012 (the last census for farms) Business owners engaged in farming activities may be entitled to special deductions not claimed by other businesses. These special deductions are in addition to the same types of deductions that other business owners enjoy. A *farm* includes stock, dairy, poultry, fish, fruit, and truck farms. Thus, it encompasses plantations, ranches, ranges, and orchards.

Farmers have been given these special rules in recognition of their unique business arrangements and to make their tax reporting easier. Some of these rules have been highlighted in other parts of this book. For example, farmers (other than farming syndicates) generally are allowed to use the cash method of accounting to report their income and expenses.

For further information about deducting farming expenses, see IRS Publication 225, *Farmer's Tax Guide.*

Farm Expenses

Ordinary and necessary business expenses related to farming generally are deductible. The timing of the deduction is determined by your method of accounting (cash or accrual). However, in addition to the types of expenses claimed by nonfarm businesses, farmers may be able to claim deductions for expenses unique to farming activities and in ways more favorable than general tax rules would allow.

Prepaid Farm Supplies

If you are on the cash method of accounting, expenses generally are deductible when paid. However, if you prepay farm supplies, they must be deducted ratably over the period during which they will be used unless you qualify for an exception to this prepayment rule.

Prepaid farm supplies include:

- Feed, seed, fertilizer, and similar farming supplies not consumed during the year (other than what is on hand at the end of the year but would have been consumed had it not been for fire, storm, flood, drought, disease, or other casualty).

- Poultry bought for use in your farm business that would be deductible in the following year if you had capitalized the cost and deducted it ratably over the lesser of 12 months or the useful life of the poultry.

- Poultry bought for resale and not resold during the year.

Prepaid farm expenses are deductible to the extent they do not exceed 50% of other deductible farm expenses in the year (including depreciation and amortization). Any prepaid expenses in excess of this limit are deductible in the following year.

Example

In 2014, you bought fertilizer ($4,500), feed ($1,500), and seed ($750) for use in the following year for a total of $6,750. Your other farm expenses in 2014 total $12,000. You can deduct prepaid expenses up to $6,000 (50% of $12,000). The excess $750 is deductible in 2015, the year in which such items will be consumed.

If you are *a farm-related taxpayer* (your main home is a farm, your principal business is farming, or a member of your family lives on the farm or has farming as his or her principal business), you are not subject to the 50% limit if:

- Your prepaid farm supplies expense is more than 50% of your other deductible farm expenses because of a change in business operations caused by unusual circumstances, or
- Your total prepaid farm supplies expense for the preceding 3 years is less than 50% of your total other deductible farm expenses for those 3 years.

Livestock Feed

Generally, even though you are on the cash basis, feed must be deducted in the year that your livestock consumes it. However, if you meet all of the following 3 tests for the advance payment of feed, you can deduct in the year of payment the cost of feed your livestock will consume in a later year (subject to the prepaid farm supplies limit):

1. The expense is a payment for the purchase of feed and not a deposit. A binding contract for delivery shows this is not a deposit.
2. The prepayment has a business purpose and is not merely a tax avoidance scheme. A business purpose would include securing more favorable payment terms and prices.
3. The deduction of these costs does not result in a material distortion of income. For example, if this is your customary practice, then the deduction will have roughly the same impact on your income each year and will not produce a material distortion.

This limit on deducting the advance payment of feed does not apply to the purchase of commodity futures contracts.

Labor and Related Costs

You can deduct reasonable wages that you pay for regular farm labor, piecework, contract labor, and other forms of labor hired to work your farm. This includes payments to your spouse or child as long as there is a true employer-employee relationship.

You can also deduct related costs including:

- The cost of maintaining houses and their furnishings for tenants or hired help (e.g., heat, light, insurance, depreciation, and repairs).
- Insurance related to the workers (e.g., health insurance and workers compensation).
- Employer's share of FICA on farm wages.

You must reduce your deduction for wages by any employment tax credits you may be entitled to claim on such wages. These credits are explained in Chapter 7.

Breeding Fees

Cash method farmers may deduct breeding fees as a farm business expense. Accrual method farmers must capitalize such fees and allocate them to the cost basis of the calf, foal, and so on to which they relate.

Fertilizer and Lime

You have a choice of when to deduct the cost of fertilizer and lime used to enrich, neutralize, or enhance farmland.

- You can deduct it in the year you paid or incurred the expense (subject to the prepaid farm supplies rule discussed earlier in this chapter), or
- If the benefit from the material lasts more than 1 year, you can capitalize the cost and deduct a part of it each year in which the benefit lasts.

After you make your choice, you cannot change your reporting method without IRS consent.

Depreciation

Property used in farming generally is subject to the same depreciation rules as property used in nonfarm businesses. The rules for depreciation are discussed in Chapter 14. However, certain farming property has special recovery periods. Table 20.1 shows the recovery periods for property used in farming.

Instead of depreciating certain farm-related property, you may claim a first-year expensing deduction (see Chapter 14). In addition to equipment and machinery used in farming, this deduction can be taken with respect to single-purpose agricultural or horticultural structures, grain bins, and drainage facilities.

Soil and Water Conservation Expenses

Generally, soil and water conservation expenses must be capitalized. However, you can elect to deduct such expenses within limits. The deduction cannot be more than 25% of gross income from farming. Expenses must be consistent with a plan approved by the Natural Resources Conservation Service (NRCS) of the Department of Agriculture or a comparable state agency. Expenses eligible for this special write-off include:

- Treating or moving earth (e.g., leveling, conditioning, grading, terracing, contour furrowing, and restoration of soil fertility)
- Constructing, controlling, and protecting diversion channels, drainage or irrigation ditches, earthen dams, watercourses, outlets, and ponds

- Eradicating brush
- Planting windbreaks

They also include assessments by conservation districts for any of these expenses (but not more than 10% of your deductible share plus $500 and subject to the total limitation).

Endangered species recovery expenditures are included with soil and water conservation expenditures and land erosion expenditures to be currently deductible. Endangered species recovery expenditures are costs incurred for

TABLE 20.1 Recovery Periods for Farm Property

Type of Property	General Depreciation System	Alternative Depreciation System
Agricultural structures (single purpose)	10	15
Automobiles	5	5
Cattle (dairy or breeding)	5	7
Cotton-ginning assets	7	10
Drainage facilities	15	20
Farm buildings (other than single purpose)	20	25
Farm machinery and equipment	7	10
Fences (agricultural)	7	10
Goats and sheep (breeding)	5	5
Grain bins	7	10
Hogs (breeding)	3	3
Horses (age when placed in service)		
Breeding and working (12 years or less)	7	10
Breeding and working (more than 12 years)	3	10
Race horses (2 years or less)*	3	12
Horticultural structures (single purpose)	10	15
Logging equipment and machinery	5	6
Tractor units (over-the-road)	3	4
Trees or vines bearing fruit or nuts	10	20
Trucks		
Unloaded weight		
13,000 pounds or more	5	6
Weight less than 13,000 pounds	5	5
Water wells	15	20

*In 2013, all race horses were 3-year property; this rule could be extended to 2014 so check the Supplement.

the purpose of achieving site-specific management actions recommended in recovery plans approved pursuant to the Endangered Species Act of 1973.

Reforestation Expenses

You can deduct up to $5,000 annually ($10,000 if married filing jointly) in qualified reforestation expenses. Amounts in excess of this dollar limit can be amortized over 84 months. For further details, see Chapter 14.

Miscellaneous Expenses

Ordinary and necessary business expenses common to all businesses (e.g., advertising costs or attorney's fees) are deductible. Other expenses specific to farming activities that may be deductible as ordinary and necessary expenses include:

- Chemicals
- Fuels and oil
- Freight and trucking
- Ginning
- Insect sprays and dusts
- Litter and bedding
- Livestock fees
- Storage and warehousing
- Tying materials and containers
- Veterinary fees and medicine

Farm Losses

If your deductible farm expenses exceed your farm income, you have a loss from the operation of your farm. The amount you can deduct of your farm loss may be limited by a number of rules. However, consider how the following rules may especially impact on farming activities.

PASSIVE ACTIVITY RULES

Losses from an activity in which you do not materially participate and any rental activity cannot exceed your income from passive activities. Thus, if you own the farm but do not work it yourself, you may not be able to deduct your losses.

AT-RISK RULES

These rules, which limit your deduction for losses to your economic investment, apply to farming activities in the same way in which they apply to nonfarming activities.

HOBBY LOSS RULES

If you are not engaged in the farming activity with a realistic profit motive, then your losses are not deductible. They do not carry over to another year; they are gone forever. There is considerable litigation each year involving *gentlemen farmers*, and their success in deducting losses depends on demonstrating a profit motive. For details, see Chapter 26.

FARMING LOSSES

Farming losses cannot be used as a tax shelter. Farming losses by those receiving certain subsidies are limited in how much can be used to offset nonfarm income on Schedule F. The limit is the greater of $300,000 ($150,000 for married persons filing separately) or the net farm income received over the past 5 years.

Losses limited by this rule are not lost forever; they can be carried forward and used in future years to the extent allowed by this rule.

The limit applies to farmers (other than those operating as C corporations) who receive any direct or countercyclical payments under Title I of the Food, Conservation, and Energy Act of 2008, or Commodity Credit loans. For partnerships and S corporations, the limit applies at the partner or shareholder level, based on the year in which the entity's tax year ends.

Net Operating Losses

Farmers are subject to special rules for net operating loss (NOL) carrybacks. Instead of the usual 2-year carryback applicable to most other businesses, farmers can use a 5-year carryback for farming losses. However, there is a 3-year carryback for the part of the NOL attributable to a federal disaster.

You can choose to forgo the carryback and simply carry forward the loss for up to 20 years. There is no special carryforward period for farmers. For farms operated through a partnership or S corporation, the losses pass through to the owners who claim the NOLs on their individual returns.

Net operating losses—figuring them and claiming quick refunds—are discussed in greater detail in Chapter 4.

Farm-Related Tax Credits

Farmers may be entitled to claim the same tax credits available to other businesses (discussed in Chapters 7 and 23). For example, if they pay wages to certain types of workers, they may be eligible to claim employment credits. But, there are also credits unique to farmers.

Credits for Farming Activities

In addition to credits available to nonfarm businesses, certain credits may be unique (or more relevant) to farmers. These include the following.

UNDYED KEROSENE AND UNDYED DIESEL FUEL FOR HOUSEHOLD USE

The credit is the amount of excise tax paid on kerosene used in your home for heating, lighting, and cooking.

FEDERAL TAX PAID ON FUELS

The credit is the amount of excise tax paid on gasoline, special motor fuels, diesel-water fuel emulsion, and compressed natural gas used on a farm for farming purposes. The credit is claimed by the ultimate purchaser, rather than the ultimate vendor—the farmer who bought the fuel and did not resell it.

FUELS USED IN OFF-HIGHWAY BUSINESS USE

The credit is for the amount of excise tax paid on fuels, including alternative fuels, used in running stationary machines (such as generators), for cleaning purposes, or in other vehicles not registered for highway use. However, if undyed diesel fuel or undyed kerosene is used on a farm, the fuel is not considered as being used in an off-highway vehicle.

Claiming a Credit or Refund

You can claim the aforementioned credits for fuel-related excise taxes on your income tax return. The credits are claimed on Form 4136. Alternatively, you can claim a refund of the excise taxes you already paid. The claim for refund can be made for any quarter of your tax year for which you can claim $750 or more.

If for any quarter the excise tax paid on all fuels used for qualifying purposes is less than $750, you carry the amount over to the next quarter of your tax year to determine if you can claim at least $750 for that quarter. If you cannot claim at least $750 at the end of the fourth quarter of your tax year, you must claim a credit on your income tax return.

You can use Form 8849 to file a claim for refund. If you file Form 720, you can use the Schedule C portion of Form 720 for your claims, rather than Form 8849.

You must file a quarterly claim by the last day of the first quarter following the end of the last quarter included in the claim. If you do not file a timely refund claim for the fourth quarter of your tax year, you will have to claim a credit for that amount on your income tax return.

If you claimed taxes as an expense deduction that reduced your income, you must now include any credit or refund of excise taxes on fuels.

> **Example**
>
> A cash basis farmer filed his 2013 Form 1040 return on April 15, 2014, on which he deducted gasoline that included $110 of excise tax. He then claimed a credit of $110 for excise tax paid on fuel. The $110 is reported as additional income in 2014.

Who Claims a Credit or Refund?

If fertilizer or pesticides are applied to your farm aerially or otherwise, the applicator is treated as having used the fuel. For kerosene used in aviation, the registered ultimate vendor is the claimant.

Exemption from Excise Tax on Fuels

As a farmer, you can buy diesel fuel and kerosene excise tax free (and so are not eligible to claim any credit with respect to these fuels). To obtain tax exemption, you must provide the vendor with a signed certificate and keep a copy of it with your other business records. A Sample Exemption Certificate (Table 20.2) is reproduced on page 442.

For more information about these special tax credits, see IRS Publication 510, *Excise Taxes (Including Fuel Tax Credits and Refunds)*.

Nondeductible Farm-Related Expenses

Not every expense of the farm can be written off. Some expenses are personal in nature and are nondeductible. Other expenses may be subject to limitations. Nondeductible expenses include:

- Personal or living expenses that do not produce farm income (e.g., taxes, insurance, and repairs to the home). If you pay expenses (such as electricity) that is used for both personal and farm purposes, you must allocate the expenses accordingly (and deduct only the farm portion). While personal expenses are not deductible, there is one exception. You may claim a tax credit for the excise tax on kerosene used in your home for heating, lighting, and cooking (discussed earlier in this chapter). Also, a portion of the home may qualify for a home office deduction as discussed in Chapter 18.

- Expenses of raising anything consumed by you and your family.

- The value of animals or crops you raised that died. The costs of raising the animals or crops were separately deductible (under the rules discussed throughout this chapter).

- The cost of raising unharvested crops sold with land owned more than one year if you sell both at the same time to the same person. Instead, add these costs to the basis of the land for purposes of determining your gain or loss on the sale. Similarly, the cost of unharvested crops you buy with land is added to the purchase price of the land. This cost is then taken into account to determine your profit (or loss) when you later sell the land.

- Fines and penalties. However, penalties you pay for exceeding marketing quotas are deductible. If such penalties are paid by the purchaser of your crop, you simply report the net amount you receive as income (you do not claim a separate deduction for the penalties).

TABLE 20.2 Sample Exemption Certificate

WAIVER FOR USE BY ULTIMATE PURCHASERS OF KEROSENE FOR USE IN COMMERCIAL AVIATION

(To support vendor's claim for a credit or payment under § 6427 of the Internal Revenue Code.)

Name, address, and employer identification number of ultimate vendor

The undersigned ultimate purchaser ("Buyer") hereby certifies the following under penalties of perjury that the kerosene for use in aviation to which this waiver relates is purchased for use in commercial aviation (other than foreign trade).

This waiver applies to the following (complete as applicable):

_____ This is a single purchase waiver:

1. _____ Invoice for delivery ticket number
2. _____ Number of gallons

_____ This is a waiver covering all purchases under a specified account of order number:

1. Effective date _____
2. Expiration date _____ (period not to exceed 1 year after the effective date)
3. Buyer's account number _____

Buyer will provide a new waiver to the vendor if any information in this waiver changes.

If Buyer uses the kerosene for use in aviation to which this waiver relates for a use other than the use stated above, Buyer will be liable for tax.

Buyer understands that by signing this waiver, Buyer gives up its right to claim any credit or payment for the kerosene for use in aviation used in a nontaxable use.

Buyer acknowledges that it has not and will not claim any credit or payment for the kerosene for use in aviation to which this waiver relates.

Buyer understands that the fraudulent use of this waiver may subject Buyer and all parties making such fraudulent use of this waiver to a fine or imprisonment, or both, together with the costs of prosecution.

Printed or typed name of person signing

Title of person signing

Name of Buyer

Employer identification number

Address of Buyer

Signature and date signed

Where to Claim Farming Expenses

Self-Employed

Farming expenses are deductible in Part II of Schedule F. There are specific lines for various types of farming expenses. There is also a catchall line for reporting other expenses. If there are more than 6 other expenses, attach a statement to the return listing these other deductions.

Partnerships and LLCs

Farming expenses are deductible in Part II of Schedule F. There are specific lines for various types of farming expenses. There is also a catchall line for reporting other expenses. Schedule F is attached to the partnership return, Form 1065.

Most expenses are not separately stated items passed through to partners and members. They are simply part of the entity's ordinary business income or loss. Therefore, partners and members in LLCs report their net income or loss from the farm on Schedule E.

S Corporations

Farms operating as S corporations claim deductions on the corporation's return, Form 1120S. Most expenses are not separately stated items passed through to shareholders. They are simply part of the corporation's ordinary business income or loss. Therefore, shareholders report their net income or loss from the farm on Schedule E.

C Corporations

Farms operating as C corporations report their expenses on the corporation's return, Form 1120. This form contains separate lines for deducting certain costs. Other costs must be reported on the catchall line for "other deductions" with an explanation attached. Shareholders do not report any income (or loss) from the corporation.

All Taxpayers

The credit for federal tax on fuels is figured on Form 4136, *Credit for Federal Tax Paid on Fuels*.

Instead of claiming the credit on the current return, the taxpayer may be entitled to a refund. The refund is claimed on Form 8849, *Claim for Refund of Excise Taxes*.

Domestic Production Activities Deduction

Alert

At the time this book was printed, Congress had not extended numerous breaks for 2014 that had expired at the end of 2013. Check the online supplement in February 2015 at www.jklasser.com or www.barbaraweltman.com to see whether these breaks apply for 2014 returns.

How often does Uncle Sam reward taxpayers for simply doing a good job? There is a special deduction designed to encourage domestic production activities. Also referred to as the "manufacturer's deduction," this write-off effectively slashes the tax rate applied to such activities and does not require any additional cash outlay to qualify.

There have been suggestions to eliminate this deduction entirely, as part of overall tax reform. To date, there have been no formal proposals, but stay alert for possible developments.

Background

In the past, there were 2 special tax regimes designed to assist U.S. companies doing business abroad: the domestic international sales corporation (DISC) and the Extraterritorial Income Exclusion Act. The World Trade Organization viewed these regimes as discriminatory in favor of U.S. companies, and the European Union was authorized to impose sanctions on U.S. goods. In response, these regimes have been replaced by a deduction for domestic production activities. The deduction does *not* require any foreign distribution of goods or services; it is based on producing things within the United States.

Qualified Producers

Only "qualified producers" can claim the deduction. The term is not limited to traditional manufacturers in the United States. It applies to a business that engages in any of the following activities:

- Selling, leasing, or licensing items manufactured, produced, grown, or extracted in the United States in whole or significant part (see safe harbor discussed later). One district court said that creating gift baskets by putting together candy, cheese, wine, crackers, and such made by others was a qualified activity for which sales could be taken into account in figuring the domestic production activities deduction.

- Selling, leasing, or licensing films (other than sexually explicit productions) produced in the United States (50% or more of compensation relating to production relates to services of actors, directors, producers, and service personnel performed in the United States).

- Construction in the United States includes both erection and substantial renovation of residential and commercial buildings. While there is no IRS guidance on what constitutes a substantial renovation, it can be assumed to be any cost that would be required to be capitalized (as opposed to a currently deductible repair).

- Engineering and architectural services relating to a construction project performed in the United States.

- Software developed in the United States, regardless of whether it is purchased off-the-shelf or downloaded from the Internet. The term "software" includes video games. But, with some de minimis exceptions, the term does not include fees for online use of software, fees for customer support, and fees for playing computer games online.

While it could be argued that every business produces something, not every business is treated as a qualified producer. Businesses engaged in the following activities are specifically *not* qualified producers:

- Cosmetic activities related to construction, such as painting.
- Leasing or licensing to a related party.
- The sale of food or beverages prepared at a retail establishment. However, if a business both manufactures food and sells it at a restaurant or take-out store, income and expenses can be allocated so that those related to manufacturing and wholesale distribution qualify for the deduction. Thus, in the so-called Starbucks situation, roasting and packaging coffee beans could qualify, but selling the beans or brewed coffee at stores would not.

Safe Harbor

The deduction is limited to activities that are in whole or "in significant part" in the United States. Under a safe harbor, labor and overhead costs incurred in the United States for the manufacture, production, growth, and extraction of the property are at least 20% of the total cost of goods sold of the property.

Even if you fail to meet this safe harbor, you can still demonstrate that the activity is "in significant part" a U.S. activity based on all the facts and circumstances.

Figuring the Deduction

The deduction is 9% of income from domestic production activities and is figured on Form 8903, *Domestic Production Activities Deduction* (Figure 21.1). This results in an effective top tax rate on corporations of 32% (instead of the maximum 35% rate). "Income" means gross receipts reduced by certain expenses.

Allocable Gross Receipts

Start with gross receipts from qualified domestic production activities, called domestic production gross receipts (DPGR). If your business is entirely domestic, then all gross receipts are taken into account. If you have both domestic and foreign activities, use any reasonable method to allocate gross receipts to qualified domestic activities.

Under a de minimis rule, if less than 5% of total gross receipts are derived from nonqualified domestic production activities, you do not have to make any allocation; all gross receipts are treated as attributable to qualified domestic production activities.

If there is a service element in the activity, allocate gross receipts between the qualified activity and the services. However, no allocation is required if the gross receipts relate to a qualified warranty and other gross receipts from these services are 5% or less of the gross receipts from the property.

Qualified production activity income (QPAI) is determined on an item-by-item basis. An "item" is something offered for sale to customers; it produces

Form **8903**
(Rev. December 2010)
Department of the Treasury
Internal Revenue Service

Domestic Production Activities Deduction

▶ Attach to your tax return. ▶ See separate instructions.

OMB No. 1545-1984

Attachment
Sequence No. **143**

Name(s) as shown on return

Identifying number

		(a) Oil-related production activities		(b) All activities	
1	Domestic production gross receipts (DPGR)	**1**			
2	Allocable cost of goods sold. If you are using the small business simplified overall method, skip lines 2 and 3	**2**			
3	Enter deductions and losses allocable to DPGR (see instructions) .	**3**			
4	If you are using the small business simplified overall method, enter the amount of cost of goods sold and other deductions or losses you ratably apportion to DPGR. All others, skip line 4	**4**			
5	Add lines 2 through 4	**5**			
6	Subtract line 5 from line 1	**6**			
7	Qualified production activities income from estates, trusts, and certain partnerships and S corporations (see instructions) . . .	**7**			
8	Add lines 6 and 7. Estates and trusts, go to line 9, all others, skip line 9 and go to line 10	**8**			
9	Amount allocated to beneficiaries of the estate or trust (see instructions)	**9**			
10a	Oil-related qualified production activities income. Estates and trusts, subtract line 9, column (a), from line 8, column (a), all others, enter amount from line 8, column (a). If zero or less, enter -0- here .	**10a**			
b	Qualified production activities income. Estates and trusts, subtract line 9, column (b), from line 8, column (b), all others, enter amount from line 8, column (b). If zero or less, enter -0- here, skip lines 11 through 21, and enter -0- on line 22	**10b**			
11	Income limitation (see instructions): • Individuals, estates, and trusts. Enter your adjusted gross income figured without the domestic production activities deduction . . . . } • All others. Enter your taxable income figured without the domestic production activities deduction (tax-exempt organizations, see instructions) . . . . }	**11**			
12	Enter the smaller of line 10b or line 11. If zero or less, enter -0- here, skip lines 13 through 21, and enter -0- on line 22	**12**			
13	Enter 9% of line 12	**13**			
14a	Enter the smaller of line 10a or line 12	**14a**			
b	Reduction for oil-related qualified production activities income. Multiply line 14a by 3% . .	**14b**			
15	Subtract line 14b from line 13	**15**			
16	Form W-2 wages (see instructions)	**16**			
17	Form W-2 wages from estates, trusts, and certain partnerships and S corporations (see instructions)	**17**			
18	Add lines 16 and 17. Estates and trusts, go to line 19, all others, skip line 19 and go to line 20	**18**			
19	Amount allocated to beneficiaries of the estate or trust (see instructions)	**19**			
20	Estates and trusts, subtract line 19 from line 18, all others, enter amount from line 18 . . .	**20**			
21	Form W-2 wage limitation. Enter 50% of line 20	**21**			
22	Enter the smaller of line 15 or line 21	**22**			
23	Domestic production activities deduction from cooperatives. Enter deduction from Form 1099-PATR, box 6	**23**			
24	Expanded affiliated group allocation (see instructions)	**24**			
25	Domestic production activities deduction. Combine lines 22 through 24 and enter the result here and on Form 1040, line 35; Form 1120, line 25; or the applicable line of your return . .	**25**			

For Paperwork Reduction Act Notice, see separate instructions.   Cat. No. 37712F   Form **8903** (Rev. 12-2010)

FIGURE 21.1 Form 8903, Domestic Production Activities Deduction income from the lease, rental, license, sale, exchange, or other disposition of property manufactured, produced, grown, or extracted in whole or significant part in the United States. Also qualifying are domestic films, construction, and engineering and architectural services.

QPAI is taken into account for purposes of this computation under your usual method of accounting (e.g., cash or accrual basis).

Allocable Cost of Goods Sold and Related Expenses

Next, reduce these gross receipts by the cost of goods sold and related expenses. Related expenses include direct costs of production, plus a portion of indirect expenses. The allocation is based on your books and records if possible, or if not, on any reasonable method. Small businesses (those with average annual gross receipts of $25 million or less) can use a simplified method to allocate deductions on relative gross receipts.

Design and development costs, including packaging, labeling, and minor assembly operations, are *not* taken into account in determining manufacturing or production activities.

The deduction applies for both regular and alternative minimum tax purposes, so claiming it will not trigger or increase AMT liability.

Limitations on the Deduction

The deduction is subject to 2 limitations:

1. It cannot exceed taxable income (for C corporations) or adjusted gross income for sole proprietors and owners of partnerships, limited liability companies, or S corporations.
2. It cannot exceed 50% of W-2 wages. W-2 wages include both taxable compensation and elective deferrals (e.g., employee contributions to 401(k) plans).

All W-2 wages used to determine the wage limitation on the domestic production activities deduction must be allocated to the business's DPGR. For pass-through entities, allocated W-2 wages are no longer limited to a percentage of the business's allocated QPAI. Thus, the wage limitation is 50% of the wages that the business deducts in figuring its QPAI. There are 3 methods provided for determining W-2 income, called "(e)(1) wages" under Treasury regulations. One method looks to the lesser of Box 1 or Box 5 of Form W-2, while the other alternatives are more complex.

W-2 wages do not include payments to independent contractors, self-employment income, or guaranteed payments to partners.

For exporters, there is another limitation related to the phase-out of the tax rate on extraterritorial income (ETI). But some businesses that are exporters may be able to qualify for both benefits.

This deduction cannot be used to create or increase a net operating loss.

Pass-Through Entities

The deduction is applied at the owner (not entity) level. This means that the business must allocate gross receipts, cost of goods sold, and related expenses from qualified production activities to the owners so they can claim the deduction on their personal returns.

A special allocation rule applies for purposes of the limitation to 50% of W-2 wages. The allocation of this amount is the lower of the owner's allocable share of wages or 2 times 9% of production activities income for 2014.

> **NOTE**
>
> State income tax rules may differ for the domestic production activities deduction. For example, New York, California, and more than a dozen other states do not allow the domestic production activities deduction.

Where to Claim the Deduction

Self-Employed

The domestic production activities deduction is figured on Form 8903, *Domestic Production Activities Deduction*.

The deduction is then entered in the "Adjusted Gross Income" section of Form 1040. It is *not* a business deduction reported on Schedule C.

Partnerships and LLCs

The domestic production activities deduction is figured on Form 8903, *Domestic Production Activities Deduction*. However, the partnership or LLC does not claim the deduction; it is a pass-through item.

The information necessary to enable owners to figure their shares of this deduction is reported to them on line 13 of Schedule K-1 (Code "T," "U," and "V"). Owners then figure the deduction, applying their own adjusted gross income limitation, and enter the deduction in the "Adjusted Gross Income" section of Form 1040.

S Corporations

The domestic production activities deduction is figured on Form 8903, *Domestic Production Activities Deduction*. However, the corporation does not claim the deduction; it is a pass-through item.

The information necessary to enable owners to figure their share of this deduction is reported to them on line 12 of Schedule K-1 (Codes "P," "Q," and "R").

Owners then figure the deduction, applying their own adjusted gross income limitation, and enter the deduction in the "Adjusted Gross Income" section of Form 1040.

C Corporations

The domestic production activities deduction is figured on Form 8903, *Domestic Production Activities Deduction*, and entered on Form 1120.

Miscellaneous Business Deductions

Alert

At the time this book was printed, Congress had not extended numerous breaks for 2014 that had expired at the end of 2013. Check the online supplement in February 2015 at www.jklasser.com or www.barbaraweltman.com to see whether these breaks apply for 2014 returns.

Some miscellaneous business items defy classification. They do necessarily fall into categories for which there is a line on the tax return. Still, you may be able to deduct them.

Some of the deductions in this chapter apply only to individuals; others apply only to corporations. Review all of the categories to see which deductions may apply to you. Checklists of deductible and nondeductible expenses are found in (see Table 22.3, page 478).

For more information on other business expenses, see IRS Publication 535, *Business Expenses.*

Other Business Expenses in General

You generally can deduct any business expense if it is considered ordinary and necessary. It need not fit neatly into a specific category as long as it meets 3 tests:

1. The expense must be related to the business you carry on (be it employ-ment or a business you own).

2. The expense cannot be a capital expenditure. *Capital expenditures* are costs related to the acquisition of a capital asset. For example, you can-not deduct the cost of improvements to property. These costs are capital in nature. However, some capital expenditures can be recovered through deductions for depreciation or amortization (see Chapter 14).

3. The expense must be **ordinary** and **necessary**.

Ordinary   Common and accepted in your business.
Necessary   Helpful or appropriate to your business. To be necessary, an expense need not be indispensable. For example, if you send flowers to your employee in the hospital, you may deduct the cost of the flowers.

Another requirement that applies to all deductions is that the expenses must be reasonable in amount. What is reasonable is a question of fact based on the particular situation. Checklists of various miscellaneous deductions related to your business status can be found toward the end of this chapter.

Job-Seeking Expenses

Being an employee is treated like a trade or business. It is considered to be the business of being an employee. Therefore, certain expenses related to getting a job may be deductible as ordinary and necessary business expenses. These include:

- Cost of resumes
- Postage and telephone charges

- Travel costs for interviews
- Career counseling
- Advertising your availability in a newspaper or magazine

These costs are deductible if you are already in a job and are seeking a new one. If you lost your job because you quit, you were fired, or your company downsized, you can still deduct these expenses as long as you are still in the business of being an employee. You cannot deduct these expenses if you have been out of the job market for many years, because you are no longer considered to be in the business of being an employee. Thus, for example, women who return to the job market after a number of years of staying home to raise children cannot treat their job-hunting costs as deductible business expenses.

You cannot deduct the expenses of obtaining your first job. You are not yet in the business of being an employee.

If you are laid off and receive outplacement services from your former employer (such as office space and resume counseling), you need not include this benefit in income. It is treated as a tax-free fringe benefit. If you pay for these services yourself, they are deductible.

If you receive reimbursement from a prospective employer for the costs of traveling to an interview, you cannot deduct your costs. But the good news is that you are not taxed on the reimbursement.

Employer Reimbursements and Outplacement Services

If you are an employer and reimburse a prospective employee for the costs of traveling to an interview, you can deduct the allowance as a business expense. You do not have to treat the reimbursement as wages or as payments subject to employment taxes.

If you provide outplacement services for discharged employees to help them find new employment, you can deduct your costs as a business expense. Some of your costs may fall into specific deduction categories. For example, if you rent a separate office for use by discharged employees looking for new employment, you treat the cost of the office as a rental deduction. Utilities related to the office are deducted along with other utility costs.

Employer Job Candidate Search Expenses

Employers may incur various costs to attract and hire new employees. These are fully deductible ordinary and necessary business expenses, such as:

- Advertising in newspapers, magazines or online
- Agency job placement fees

Moving Expenses

If you move your business to another location (e.g., you relocate your offices to larger quarters) or you move equipment to another location (e.g., you move machinery from one plant to another), your moving costs are deductible. There is no requirement that your new location be any special distance from the old one.

In general, if you personally move from one home to another, you cannot deduct the cost of moving your furnishings and family because these are personal expenses. However, if you relocate because of a change in jobs or a new business, you may be able to deduct your moving expenses. The tax law allows a personal deduction for moving expenses for certain job-related moves.

To claim deductible moving expenses, you must show 3 things:

1. That your move was of a sufficient distance (distance test).
2. That you worked at your new location for the required length of time—or were prevented from doing so (time test).
3. That, if you are an employee, your expenses are not paid or reimbursed by your employer.

Distance Test

The distance between your new job or business location and your former home must be at least 50 miles more than the distance between your old job or business location and your former home. If you move to another city or state, generally you have no difficulty in satisfying the distance test. Where you simply move across town, be sure that the move is of a sufficient distance to make your expenses deductible.

Example

You take a job in the same metropolitan area, but way across town. You move to an apartment in the part of town in which your new job is located. The distance between your new job location and your former home is 57 miles. The distance between your old job location and your former home is 5 miles. The distance test is met because the difference is at least 50 miles (57 miles − 5 miles = 52 miles).

In calculating the distance test, use the most commonly traveled routes between locations. You need not measure distance "as the crow flies."

What if you have been out of work a long time or you are changing from part-time to full-time employment? In this case, the new job location must be at least 50 miles from your former home.

Usually the distance between your new home and job locations is not considered. However, if the distance between your new home and new job location is more than the distance between your old home and new job location, you may not be able to deduct your moving expenses. The only way to deduct moving expenses in this situation is to show that you are required to live in your new home as a condition of employment or the move results in an actual decrease in commuting time or expense.

Work in Your New Location (Time Test)

If you are an employee, you must remain on the job at your new location for at least 39 weeks during the 12-month period that starts with your arrival at the new location. You need not stay with the same employer for all those weeks. You can get another job in the same location and deduct moving expenses as long as the total employment time is at least 39 weeks. In general, only full-time employment is used to satisfy the 39-week requirement, although there is a special rule for certain seasonal employment.

If you are laid off or fired from your employment without any willful misconduct on your part, the 39-week test is waived. The time test is also waived if you fail to meet the 39-week requirement because of circumstances beyond your control—strikes, temporary absences, illness, natural disasters, and such. The time is waived if you are transferred from your new job to another location for your employer's benefit. According to the IRS, this waiver does not apply if you request a transfer for your benefit. The waiver does not apply if you resign, are fired for willful misconduct, or reach the mandatory retirement age of your new employment where you anticipated this retirement.

If you are self-employed or a partner or an LLC member, there is a 78-week test. You must work full-time in your business for 78 weeks in a 24-month period beginning with the move to the new location. At least 39 weeks must occur within the first 12 months of arrival.

You need not wait out the time requirements before claiming the deduction for moving expenses. You can deduct your costs in the year of the move under the assumption that you will meet the time test. If you do not (e.g., if you move again before the end of the 39 or 78 weeks), then you must report your deduction as income in the subsequent year. Alternatively, you can amend the earlier return to delete the deduction for moving expenses.

If you are not sure whether you will meet the time test, you can file your return for the year of the move without the deduction and then amend it after the time test has been satisfied.

Change in Employment Status

If you change your employment status to that of an employee (e.g., if you shut down your business and find a job in your new location), you need only meet the 39-week test. If you change your employment status from employee to self-employed person before satisfying the 39-week test, you must meet the 78-week test to deduct moving expenses.

Deductible Moving Expenses

Only certain moving expenses are deductible. You may deduct the actual cost of moving your household goods and personal effects. What constitutes a *personal effect* has been rather liberally interpreted. For example, one taxpayer was able to deduct moving costs for a sailboat. The cost of packing, crating, and transporting furniture, the related insurance, and some storage costs are examples of deductible expenses.

You can also deduct the travel costs for you and members of your household. You need not all travel together. For example, you may relocate immediately, and your family may follow when your old home is sold or when the school year ends. Keep track of all transportation expenses for you and members of your household.

Travel costs include transportation and lodging to get from your old home to your new one. If you travel by your car, you can use a standard mileage allowance in 2014 of 23.5¢ per mile, plus tolls and parking. (You cannot deduct your mileage at the business mileage rate even though the move is business-motivated.) Alternatively, you can deduct your actual expenses for gas, oil, and repairs on the trip, plus tolls and parking. You cannot deduct the cost of meals on the trip from your old home to your new home.

If your employer pays your moving expenses or you receive reimbursement from your employer, you cannot deduct your costs. Your employer will not include the reimbursements in your income if the employer believes that you would have been entitled to a deduction had you not received reimbursement.

As an employer, if you pay employee moving expenses, you may deduct the costs even though they are not taxable to the employee.

Educational Expenses

If you take educational courses, you may be able deduct their cost as a business expense (or you may qualify for new tax credits, explained later under personal education incentives). The tax law clearly states what types of educational courses are deductible and what types are not.

You can deduct education courses that are primarily undertaken to:

- *Maintain or improve skills required in your employment or in your business.* If you have been away from the job market for some time, you may no longer be considered in a business (the business of being an employee). In this case, education costs are not deductible.

- *Meet the requirements of an employer or applicable law or regulations imposed as a condition of retaining your salary, status, or employment.* For example, continuing professional education courses are deductible as business expenses.

You cannot deduct education courses designed to:

- *Meet minimum educational requirements.* This precludes you from deducting the cost of obtaining any professional degree in law, accounting, medicine, or dentistry. The fact that you may already be performing service in an employment status within the profession does not necessarily mean that you have met the minimum education requirements. For example, if a second-year law student is hired to do research, the cost of the third year of law school is not a deductible education expense since the student has not yet met the minimum education requirements to practice law (3 years of law school and admission to the bar). If new minimum requirements are imposed after you have met old minimum requirements, however, the cost of taking the additional courses is deductible.

- *Qualify you for a new business.* A mere change in duties is not treated as a new business if it involves the same general type of work. For example, all teaching and related duties are treated as the same general type of work. However, if the education qualifies you for a new business (often denoted by certification or licensing), you cannot deduct courses even though you intend to remain in your old line of work. For example, a certified public accountant (CPA) who attends law school at night cannot deduct the cost of courses, since this leads to a new line of work—law. This is so even if the CPA never plans to practice law. A bookkeeper who takes courses to get a B.A. in accounting cannot deduct education expenses because the courses lead to a new business of being an accountant. However, a practicing attorney who takes courses toward an LL.M. can deduct expenses because the courses do not lead to a new line of work. Similarly, in a Tax Court case a salesperson encouraged by his employer to obtain an M.B.A. was able to deduct education costs because the degree did not qualify him for a new profession and was not required by the employer. The court allowed him a deduction even though the degree helped him advance in the company.

- *Relate to something that does not pertain directly to your business.* For example, an attorney could not deduct the cost of an English course that he argued would help him write better briefs. The courses were not directly related to his business of law even though they were helpful to his work.

Deductible Expenses

If education costs are deductible, the following types of expenses may be deducted:

- Tuition and fees
- Books
- Travel costs to and from school

These travel costs include going to or from home to school, as well as travel between work and school. If you attend a seminar at a resort, see Chapter 8 to determine whether or to what extent you may deduct your education-related travel costs.

NOTE
You cannot deduct your education costs if you claim an education credit for the same expenses, as explained later.

However, you may not deduct the cost of travel as a form of education. Thus, for example, an architect cannot deduct the cost of a trip to Rome to look at ancient Roman architecture as an educational expense. However, if the architect takes education courses in Rome on architecture, then the cost of the trip may become deductible.

Employer-Paid Education

If your employer pays for the cost of your courses, you cannot take a deduction. Employer-provided education may be a tax-free fringe benefit on which you are not taxed. Such benefits are discussed in Chapter 7. If you have a C corporation and the corporation pays your education costs, the corporation can deduct the costs whether or not you are taxed on the benefits.

Personal Education Incentives

There are a number of personal tax incentives designed to encourage higher education, whether or not it is job-related. Here are some to consider:

- *American opportunity tax credit.* There is a credit per student in 2014 of up to $2,500 for the cost of tuition and fees for the first 4 years of college (100% of the first $2,000 of these costs, plus 25% of the next $2,000). The full credit can be claimed for the taxpayer, spouse, or dependents, but only if modified adjusted gross income (MAGI) is not over $80,000 if single, or $160,000 on a joint return. The credit phases out for MAGI between $80,000 and $90,000 if single, or $160,000 to $180,000 on a joint return. No credit can be claimed if MAGI is over $90,000 if single, or $180,000 on a joint return. No credit can be claimed by a married person who files a separate return. The credit is 40% refundable (you can receive a refund for up to this portion even though it exceeds your tax liability for the year).

- *Lifetime learning credit.* There is a credit of up to $2,000 (20% of up to $10,000) per return for the cost of tuition and fees for any college, graduate school, or vocational training. Like the American opportunity scholarship, the lifetime learning credit can be claimed for the taxpayer, spouse, or dependents, but only if modified AGI is below threshold amount (the phase-out range for singles is $54,000 to $64,000; for joint filers it is $108,000 to $128,000). Unlike the American opportunity scholarship, there is no limit on the number of years you can claim this credit. This credit cannot be claimed if the American opportunity credit is elected for any student (but you can claim the credit for any other eligible student). For example, if your child begins college and you take a graduate course, you can elect the American opportunity credit for your child and the lifetime learning credit for yourself if your modified AGI is below the threshold amount.

- *Deduction for tuition and fees.* There is an above-the-line deduction of up to $4,000 ($2,000 for certain higher-income taxpayers) for tuition and related expenses for higher education. However, the deduction can be claimed only if modified AGI is no more than $65,000 for singles and $130,000 on a joint return ($80,000 for singles and $160,000 on joint returns for the $2,000 deduction limit). Even $1 of excess AGI means no deduction can be taken. *This deduction expired at the end of 2013 but could be extended for 2014; see the Supplement.*

- *Interest on student loans.* Interest of up to $2,500 on student loans is deductible as an adjustment to gross income on page 1 of Form 1040. The full deduction can only be claimed if your AGI is below a threshold amount ($65,000 for singles or $130,000 on a joint return). The deduction phases out over the next $15,000 of adjusted gross income for singles or $30,000 for joint filers, so that no deduction can be claimed once adjusted gross income exceeds $80,000 for singles or $160,000 on a joint return.

- *Penalty-free IRA withdrawals.* Withdrawals used to pay qualified higher education costs by those under age 59½ are not subject to the 10% premature distribution penalty. However, using IRA funds for education is still costly since the distribution is subject to regular income tax and you lose the opportunity for tax-free compounding.

Charitable Contributions Made by Your Business

Your business may contribute cash or property to various charities. In general, the amount of your charitable contribution is deductible, but there are certain limits and requirements that must be followed. Donations of your time and effort are not deductible.

Example

An attorney performs services for a charitable organization. She cannot deduct the value of her uncompensated legal services as a charitable contribution.

Charitable giving and other activities can be a business plus even if no deduction is allowed. For example, donating items for which no deduction is allowed (as explained later), such as a fully depreciated computer or cell phone, can still benefit a charity and the people it serves. While you cannot deduct the value of your time spent when serving on a board of a nonprofit organization (you can claim only a personal charitable contribution deduction for your out-of-pocket expenses), you not only serve a cause but also gain visibility and make important connections in your community that can benefit your business in the long run.

Unincorporated Businesses

Individuals can deduct charitable contributions only as itemized deductions. For example, if you are a partner and the partnership makes a charitable contribution, the contribution is passed through to you as a separately stated item and you then deduct it on your Schedule A as an itemized deduction. The same is true for members of LLCs and shareholders in S corporations. Self-employed individuals who file Schedule C do not take business-related charitable contributions as a business expense. Charitable contributions are reported as an itemized deduction on Schedule A. Similarly, an employee who makes a charitable contribution at work (e.g., amounts are withheld from pay as contributions to the United Fund or another charity) deducts the contribution on Schedule A as a charitable contribution (not as an employee business expense). Charitable contributions by individuals are subject to certain AGI limits.

Donations of property by a partnership, limited liability company, or S corporation can affect the owner's basis in his or her business interest.

Example

If a partnership owned equally by two individuals donates a painting worth $80,000 that the partnership bought for $50,000, each partner can deduct $40,000 on his or her individual return (50% of $80,000). Each partner must also reduce the basis in the partnership interest by $25,000 (50% of the property's basis). An S corporation shareholder's stock basis must be reduced by his or her pro rata share of the corporation's adjusted basis of the contributed property.

Sometimes it is not clear whether an expense is a charitable contribution or some other business expense. For example, if you pay to run an ad in a journal of a tax-exempt organization, the expense may be an advertising expense rather than a charitable contribution.

Unincorporated businesses that donate food inventory can claim the same enhanced deduction as C corporations (explained later in this chapter).

Corporations

Corporations may make charitable contributions and deduct them on their returns. The contributions must be made to public charities. The corporation cannot take a deduction if the organization receiving the contribution benefits any private shareholder or individual.

The corporation's accounting method may affect the timing of the deduction for a contribution. Cash method corporations deduct the contribution only in the year it is actually made. Corporations on the accrual method can choose to deduct contributions made within $2^1/_2$ months after the close of its year as having been made in the prior year. To do this, the board of directors of the corporation must authorize the payment of the contribution within $2^1/_2$ months after the close of the year. This authorization should be reflected in the corporate minutes.

A corporation can deduct only charitable contributions that total no more than 10% of its taxable income. Taxable income for purposes of this limitation does not include the deduction for contributions, the deduction for dividends received and dividends paid, net operating loss (NOL) carrybacks, and capital loss carrybacks.

Contributions in excess of the 10% limit can be carried forward for up to 5 years. If the corporation makes contributions in the carryforward years, the current deductions are taken into account before the carryforwards. Carryovers of excess charitable contributions cannot be deducted in a subsequent year if they increase a net operating loss carryover.

Corporations cannot claim a charitable contribution deduction for amounts given to an organization that conducts lobbying activities on matters of direct financial interest to their business.

Inventory

If you donate items from your inventory, the deduction is limited to the fair market value (FMV) of the property on the date of the contribution, reduced by any gain that would have been realized if you had sold the property at its FMV instead of donating it. Be sure to remove from opening inventory any contributions you make (namely, the costs for the donated property included in prior years). These costs are not part of the cost of goods sold for the year in which the contribution is made.

If you have excess or dated inventory that you wish to dispose of but do not know of an organization interested in it, consider working with an organization that can find a place for your inventory, such as:

- Good 360 at www.good360.org
- National Association for the Exchange of Industrial Resources at www.naeir.org
- World Vision's Gifts-in-Kind Program at www.worldvision.org

Donations for the Ill, Needy, or Infants

If a C corporation donates items from inventory to a public charity or an operating foundation where the inventory will be used for the care of the ill, the needy, or infants, add to the deduction 50% of the difference between the basis and the FMV of the inventory (but not more than 200% of the basis of the property). The donations must be for necessities of life, such as food, clothing, and shelter, so donations of cosmetics won't qualify for this special inventory rule. This special inventory rule does not apply to S corporations.

Certain Donations of Scientific Property and Computers

A C corporation can claim a larger deduction than ordinarily allowed if certain scientific property used for research is donated to an institution of higher education. This special rule allows the corporation to increase its deduction by 50% of the difference between its basis and the FMV of the property (but not more than 200% of the basis of the property). This special deduction is not allowed for S corporations, personal holding companies, or service organizations.

Food Inventory Donations

The deduction for donations of food inventory expired at the end of 2013, but could be extended retroactively by Congress. The following is included in case there is an extension. Check the Supplement for details.

Donations of food qualify for the same enhanced deduction applicable to scientific property explained previously. To qualify, food must be apparently wholesome and meet all labeling standards.

Donations of Conservation Easement by Farmers

The enhanced charitable deduction for donations of conservation easements by farmers and ranchers expired at the end of 2013, but could be extended retroactively by Congress. The following is included in case there is an extension. Check the Supplement for details.

Generally, a charitable deduction up to 50% of a contribution base is allowed for donations of conservation easements. A conservation easement is a restriction placed on real property for a public purpose to preserve the land or building for future generations. However, farmers and ranchers can claim a deduction up to 100% of their contribution basis (essentially adjusted gross income).

Appraisal Rules for Corporate Donations

All corporations that donate property valued at more than $5,000 must obtain a qualified appraisal. However, certain property donations are exempt from this requirement: donations of inventory, publicly traded stock, intellectual property, and vehicles for which a written statement is obtained from the charity.

If the deduction for a donation is more than $500,000, the appraisal must be attached to the return.

Contributions of Intellectual Property

All types of businesses may make charitable contributions of their intellectual property. The deduction for such contributions is limited to the lesser of the basis of the property or its fair market value. Intellectual property includes:

- Patents, copyrights, and trademarks
- Trade names, trade secrets, and know-how
- Software
- Other similar property or applications

ADDITIONAL DEDUCTION BASED ON INCOME

You can also deduct an amount based on the income derived by the charity from the intellectual property. The amount of the additional deduction is the applicable percentage found in Table 22.1.

No additional deduction can be claimed after the legal life of the intellectual property ends or after the 10th anniversary of the donation, whichever happens first. Donations to private foundations do not qualify.

How will you know how much income the organization derived from your donated property? At the time you make the donation, inform the organization that you intend to claim the additional deduction. The organization is then

TABLE 22.1 Applicable Percentage for Additional Contribution

Tax Year	Deductible Percentage
1	100%
2	100%
3	90%
4	80%
5	70%
6	60%
7	50%
8	40%
9	30%
10	20%
11	10%
12	10%

required to file Form 8899, *Notice of Income from Donated Intellectual Property*, showing the income it derived from the property.

Special Deduction for Whaling Captains

Those recognized by the Alaska Eskimo Whaling Commission as whaling captains charged with the responsibilities of sanctioned whaling activities can deduct reasonable and necessary whaling expenses as a charitable contribution deduction. The deduction is limited to $10,000 per year.

Licenses and Permits

If you obtain licenses and permits in the course of your business, the cost is usually deductible. However, there are 2 exceptions:

1. Licenses for vehicles cannot be deducted if the deduction for vehicle expenses is based on the IRS standard mileage allowance (you must use the actual expense method to account for vehicle costs if you want to deduct licenses).
2. Permits obtained for the construction of realty are a capital cost added to the basis of the property and recovered through depreciation.

Customs Expenses

If you import or export wares, you may incur special customs-related costs. These include customs fees, duties, and tariffs, as well as charges by customs brokers and international handlers. All of these fees are deductible. However, when they relate to inventory purchases, you may be able to add to inventory costs and recover them as part of the cost of goods sold.

Dues and Subscriptions

Dues

Certain dues are deductible; others are not. Dues paid to unions are deductible. If you pay dues to professional, business, or civic organizations, they, too, are deductible, as are dues to the following:

- American Bar Association, American Institute of CPAs, American Medical Association, and other professional associations
- Chambers of commerce, business leagues, trade associations, boards of trade, real estate boards, and business lunch clubs
- Civitan, Rotary, Lions, and other civic organizations

However, no deduction is allowed for dues to other types of clubs, such as athletic, sporting, airline, hotel, or other recreational clubs, even though membership is for business.

Subscriptions

The cost of subscriptions to business or professional publications is deductible. However, if you are on the cash basis and prepay subscriptions—that is, your subscription covers a period of more than one year—your deduction may be limited to the cost related to one year. You can deduct an allocable portion of the subscription cost in each succeeding year.

> **Example**
>
> In January 2014, you pay for a 3-year subscription to a trade magazine. Your total cost is $150. (Assume you are on a calendar year for reporting your income and deductions.) In 2014, you can deduct $50 (one-third of your total cost). In 2015 and again in 2016, you can deduct $50, the remaining portion of your subscription cost.

Legal and Professional Fees

Legal and professional fees related to your business are deductible. Professional fees may include, for example, not only legal fees but also accounting fees, actuarial fees, systems analyst fees, and appraisal fees.

Legal Fees

Legal fees for business matters generally are deductible as an ordinary and necessary business expense. Examples of deductible legal fees include fees incurred for:

- Assistance in collecting outstanding accounts payable
- Defending against a claim of infringement of intellectual property
- Defending against charges of mismanagement of a retirement plan
- Defending against shareholder allegations of misconduct
- Defending against wrongful discharge actions
- Obtaining an IRS ruling
- Tax advice

Not all legal fees are currently deductible. Examples of nondeductible legal fees include fees incurred for:

- *Acquiring a capital asset.* The fees are added to the basis of the asset. For example, if you pay attorney's fees to handle the closing when you buy your office building, the fees become part of the basis of the office building and are recovered through depreciation.

- *Actions that are personal in nature*, such as legal fees to pursue a personal injury action, even if the injury occurred during a business trip; to prepare a will even if it includes a business; and to settle a divorce even if it relates to reserving your interest in a business. The portion of fees that can be allocated to tax advice, however, is deductible.

- *Incorporating a business or setting up a partnership or LLC.* These costs are treated as incorporation fees or organizational costs for a partnership, and are currently deductible up to a set dollar limit; excess amounts must be amortized, as discussed in Chapter 14.

- *Suing for infringement.* The costs are added to the basis of the intellectual property.

Accounting and Tax Preparation Fees

If you pay an accountant to show you how to set up your books or to keep your books for you, the accounting fees are deductible. Also deductible are fees for accounting advice, such as advice on whether to change your method of accounting or your method of inventory. The same is true for fees for accounting representation at an IRS audit.

Accounting fees incurred in investigating whether to buy a business are not currently deductible but may qualify as start-up expenses. The treatment of start-up costs is discussed in Chapter 14.

If you pay an accountant or other tax professional (paid preparer) to complete your tax return or contest a tax deficiency for your business (Form 1065, Form 1120, or Form 1120S), the cost is fully deductible on the appropriate return. If you are self-employed, the allocable cost of preparing Schedule C or contesting a tax deficiency related to it is a deductible business expense that can be claimed on Schedule C. The balance of tax preparation fees is deductible as a miscellaneous itemized expense on Schedule A, subject to the 2%-of-AGI rule.

Recovering Legal Fees and Other Costs from the Government

If you are involved in a tax dispute with the IRS and you win, you may be able to make the government pay any reasonable costs of your tax contest. You must have exhausted your administrative remedies and have substantially prevailed in your tax dispute. The IRS has the burden of proving that its position in going after you was substantially justified. If the IRS did not follow published regulations, revenue rulings, revenue procedures, information releases, notices or announcements, private letter rulings, determination letters, or technical advice memoranda issued to you, then there is a rebuttable presumption that the IRS's position was not substantially justified. Also, the fact that the IRS has lost in other appellate courts on substantially similar issues must be taken into account in determining whether the IRS's position was not substantially justified. If you succeed, you can recover attorney's fees at the rate of $190 per hour in 2014. In limited circumstances, a higher award may be possible.

If you are successful in your claim to recover costs from the government (e.g., if the IRS fails to prove that it was substantially justified in its position), you cannot also take a deduction for these costs. If you have already taken a deduction for your costs, you must include the government's award in your income.

The opportunity to recover legal fees from the government is limited to an individual with a net worth below $2 million. In the case of businesses, the net worth requirement is below $7 million and fewer than 500 employees.

Lobbying Costs

Fees paid to professional lobbyists to influence legislation on the federal, state, or local level are not deductible. However, in-house lobbying costs up to $2,000 are deductible.

Bank and Merchant Fees

All banking fees for your business bank account are deductible. These include not only monthly account maintenance and check processing fees, but also ATM charges, check printing costs, online banking charges, account closing fees, and other special charges (e.g., returned check fees). These fees can amount to several hundred dollars a month. You can reduce or eliminate these costs by banking with an institution that is pro–small business (e.g., offers free business checking) or by maintaining a minimum monthly balance.

Like banking fees, merchant authorization costs to process credit and debit cards are deductible. These costs include an initial setup cost, processing fees per transaction, monthly account maintenance costs, and other charges.

If you accept PayPal as a payment method for sales, you can deduct PayPal fees as well. While there are no setup or monthly fees, you pay a per-transaction charge of 30 ¢ plus a percentage of the transaction ranging from a high of 2.9% to a low of 1.9%, depending on the size of the transaction, with special charges for international transactions.

NOTE

Financial institutions processing merchant accounts, including PayPal, must report transactions to the IRS; there is a small business exception. For more details, see Appendix A.

Supplies, Materials, and Office Expenses

NOTE

The IRS has noted that overstated deductions for items, including supplies and materials, account for up to $30 billion in unpaid taxes each year, so expect careful scrutiny of a deduction for supplies if a return is examined.

The cost of incidental supplies and materials used in your business is deductible as an ordinary and necessary business expense. This includes copy paper, cleaning supplies, and other miscellaneous costs. However, if you are on the cash basis and order such large quantities that the supplies or materials will last you more than a year, you can deduct only the portion of the cost related to supplies or materials expected to be used within the year.

Supplies used directly or indirectly in manufacturing goods are part of the cost of goods sold (see Chapter 4). The purchase of a capital asset (an item with a useful life greater than one year) cannot be written off merely by calling it a supply (although it, too, may be deducted through expensing, as explained in Chapter 14).

Usually, you need to retain receipts or other proof of any supplies and materials you deduct. However, the Tax Court in one case allowed a deduction for some office supplies based on the *Cohan* rule (explained in Chapter 4). Despite lack of receipts, the Tax Court estimated the amount of deductible expenses in this case.

Postage and Shipping

The costs of postage, delivery charges, courier and messenger charges, and other mailing and shipping costs are deductible. However, freight charges to obtain inventory are part of the cost of goods sold. Similarly, freight charges for business assets, such as furniture or equipment, are added to the basis of these assets and recovered through depreciation.

The IRS has ruled privately that a business can deduct deposited funds for a postal meter as long as they relate to stamps that will be used within $3^{1}/_{2}$ months of the end of the deposit year.

Books, Software, and Equipment

Books, software, and professional equipment that normally have a life of one year or less can be deducted. For example, if you buy a business book that is updated annually (such as this book), you can deduct its cost. By the same token, if you buy tax return preparation software that applies to one tax year, you can deduct its cost. However, if you buy a professional library or other equipment that can be expected to last for more than a year, its cost is subject to depreciation (also, first-year expensing may apply). See Chapter 14 for depreciation rules.

Office Expenses

The cost of miscellaneous office expenses not deducted separately (such as rent and utilities) is deductible as long as the expenses are ordinary and necessary for your business. Examples of deductible office expenses include:

- Aquarium and its maintenance
- CDs for office sound system
- Cleaning and janitorial services
- Decorator fees
- Flowers and plants
- Magazines and newspapers for the waiting room
- Snacks, coffee, tea, water, and other small refreshments

Uniforms and Clothing

The cost of uniforms required by the job generally is deductible. Thus, for example, the cost of nurse's uniforms is deductible. However, clothing that is adaptable to ordinary street use is not deductible even if used solely in business.

Nondeductible clothing costs cannot be transformed into deductible costs by calling the clothing something else. For example, an attorney cannot deduct the cost of business suits by claiming they are an advertising expense, even though a prosperous look is a way of attracting new clients. If the cost of the clothes is deductible as a business expense, then the cost of cleaning and altering the clothes is also deductible.

Example

An actor who buys a tuxedo for a role cannot deduct the cost because the tuxedo is adaptable to street use—in other words, it can be used in other ways than on-the-job uses.

Insurance

The cost of most types of business-related insurance is deductible. (Medical insurance is discussed in Chapter 19.) Examples of other deductible insurance include:

- *Casualty insurance* to cover fire, storm, and other casualty destruction to property. Casualty insurance may include coverage for data recovery necessitated by destruction or damage to a computer system. This may be a separate policy or part of a comprehensive business owner's policy (BOP). Casualty insurance also covers loss of property by theft. Check to make sure your policy covers theft of laptop computers. If the policy does not provide this specific coverage, you can obtain a separate policy for this purpose. You may need separate coverage for certain casualties, such as floods, earthquakes, and wind damage.

- *Liability coverage* protects clients and customers injured on your premises. It may be a separate policy or part of a business owner's policy (BOP).

- *Accident and health insurance* (including long-term care insurance). The business can deduct this coverage for its employees, spouses, and dependents. Employees can exclude this benefit from their income (with a limited exclusion for long-term care insurance). Self-employed individuals (partners, LLC members, and more-than-2% S corporation shareholders) cannot enjoy this tax-free fringe benefit. Instead, self-employed persons and more-than-2% S corporation shareholders can deduct a percentage of their health insurance costs on their individual returns. (Deducting medical coverage is explained more fully in Chapter 19.)

- *Errors and omissions (E&O) insurance* to provide protection for doing or failing to do something in the line of work (similar to professional liability coverage but for nonprofessionals). Self-employed individuals can carry the coverage to protect themselves. Businesses can carry the coverage to protect themselves with respect to the acts of their employees.

- *Employment practices liability (EPL)* protects employers from claims by employees based on sexual harassment, age discrimination, wrongful termination, or other similar work-related claims.

- *Group-term life insurance* for employees. This type of coverage allows employees to name the beneficiaries who will receive the proceeds. What is more, up to $50,000 of coverage is not taxable to employees if the coverage is provided on a nondiscriminatory basis (coverage does not favor owners and top executives at the expense of rank-and-file employees). (This type of coverage is discussed in more detail in Chapter 7.)

- *Key-person life insurance* for employees. This type of coverage protects the business from the loss of a key employee. The proceeds are payable to the business, allowing it to look for replacement help and to cover losses in the interim.

- *Credit insurance* to cover nonpayment of debts owed to the business.

- *Overhead insurance* to cover the costs of rent, salaries, and other overhead expenses during periods of illness by the owner.

- *Business interruption coverage*. Like overhead insurance, this type of coverage provides payment during a period in which a business is forced to close, such as during a natural disaster or a civil riot.

- *Workers' compensation.* Businesses are required to provide coverage for employees.

- *Automobile insurance* on business cars. However, if you use the IRS's standard mileage rate to write off car expenses in lieu of deducting actual costs, you may not separately deduct car insurance. This expense is built into the standard mileage rate.

- *Professional liability coverage* to provide protection from malpractice claims. However, premiums paid to physician-owned carriers may not be deductible unless most of the policyholders are not economically related to one another and none of them owns a controlling interest in the insuring company.

- *Directors and officers (D&O) coverage* provides financial protection for these people in case they are sued in connection with the performance of their duties to the company.

- *Cyber-liability coverage* to provide protection from copyright or trademark infringement or actions arising from misinformation on your web site. This coverage may supplement professional liability or other coverage or act as a stand-alone policy. Why supplement professional liability coverage with cyber coverage? If you do not charge for advice or other information provided on your web site, then your professional liability coverage will not protect you from claims because you do not have an attorney-client or doctor-patient relationship required as a condition of protection under your professional liability policy.

- *Product liability coverage* to provide protection from claims that products you manufacture or sell are defective and have caused injury to the public.

- *Performance bonds* to ensure the faithful performance of employees, and bonds to ensure a company's performance on a contract. These are also called surety bonds.

- *Fidelity bonds* to protect clients and customers against theft or embezzlement by company employees.

- *Pension Benefit Guaranty Corporation (PBGC)* premiums for defined benefit plans to provide a minimum retirement benefit to employees if the plan goes under. (This premium amount is discussed in Chapter 16.)

- *Environmental and pollution liability insurance* for coverage needed because of environmental contaminations, accidents, and compliance with stricter government regulations.

Disability insurance you pay for your employees is deductible. But if you buy insurance coverage for yourself, you cannot deduct your premiums even though the insurance relates to your work. Of course, if you receive benefits under a policy you took for yourself (in which premiums were nondeductible), you are not taxed on the benefits.

In most cases, insurance premiums are currently deductible in full. However, if you are on the cash basis and your premium covers a period of more than 12 months, you may deduct only the portion of the premium related to the current year. The balance of the premium is deductible over the period to which it relates.

> **Example**
>
> Your business reports on a calendar year basis, and you pay your business owner's policy (BOP) effective July 1, 2014, to cover you for a term of 3 years at a premium of $6,000. You can deduct $1,000 in 2014, $2,000 in 2015, $2,000 in 2016, and $1,000 in 2017.

If, however, the premiums cover no more than 12 months or the end of the tax year after the year in which the payment is made, whichever is earlier, you can deduct the full premiums (the 12-month rule).

> **Example**
>
> This example is the same as the preceding example, except you pay $2,000 for 1 year's coverage. Under the 12-month rule, you can deduct all of the $2,000 premium in 2014 because it covers a period of no more than 12 months (which is shorter than a period extending to the end of 2015, the end of the year after the year in which the payment is made).

If you are a business owner and enter into a cross-purchase buy-sell agreement with other owners to acquire the interests of an owner who dies, the agreement may be funded with life insurance. In this instance, the cost of the premiums is not deductible. The reason: No deduction is allowed for premiums paid on life insurance if you are, directly or indirectly, the policy beneficiary.

> **Example**
>
> A and B are partners in the AB Partnership. They have a buy-sell agreement that requires A to buy B's interest in the event of B's death, and vice versa. A takes out life insurance on B and will use the proceeds of the policy to buy out B's interest if B dies before A. Similarly, B takes out life insurance on A. Neither A nor B may deduct the premiums on this life insurance arrangement even though there is a business reason for the purchase.

Interest on Life Insurance Policies

If you take out a loan on a life insurance policy covering the life of anyone in whom you have an insurable interest, you may not deduct the interest on the loan. So, if you borrow on a policy maintained to fund a buy-sell agreement, you may not deduct the interest. Corporations (and other nonnatural persons) generally may not deduct a portion of interest on any of their outstanding loans to the extent of any *unborrowed policy cash value* (cash surrender value of the policy reduced by any loans). This interest deduction rule, however, does not apply if the business owns a policy covering only one individual who owns at least 20% of the business or is an employee, officer, or director of the company.

Commissions

Payments you make to independent parties for services they perform for you are deductible. These payments can include commissions, finders' fees, referral fees, or other similar payments. There is no dollar limit on the amount you can deduct. If these payments are made to independent contractors and they total $600 or more for the year, they must be reported to the IRS (see Appendix A).

For the treatment of commissions paid to employees, see Chapter 7.

Outsourced Workers

Fees paid to temporary agencies for temporary workers (who remain the employees of the agencies and not your employees) are deductible. So, too, are fees paid to professional employer organizations (PEOs) that are co-employers of your workers; they are responsible for taxes and insurance, and you pay the PEOs a fee.

Payments to Directors and Independent Contractors

Payments to directors and independent contractors are not treated as compensation. Rather, they are miscellaneous payments that are deductible as a business expense. Since they are not compensation, they are not subject to employment taxes. However, you must report nonemployee compensation of $600 or more on Form 1099-MISC (see Appendix A).

Individuals who work for their corporations and also serve as directors may receive both salary (as an employee) and self-employment income (as a director). Such individuals may be able to reduce the tax on directors' fees by setting up retirement plans based on this self-employment income. For a discussion of whether a worker is an employee or an independent contractor, see Business Organization, Chapter 1.

Penalties, Fines, and Damages

If you contract to perform work and are subject to penalty for noncompletion or lateness, you can deduct the penalty.

Example

You contract to remodel a kitchen. The contract calls for a penalty if the job is not completed within a month. You do not bring the job in on time and must pay a penalty for each day beyond the month. You can deduct this penalty.

You can also deduct compensatory damages paid to the government. However, you cannot deduct nonconformance penalties imposed by the Environmental Protection Agency for failing to meet certain emission standards.

If you lose a business lawsuit and must pay damages, you deduct your outlays. For example, if you lose a malpractice case and your insurance carrier pays 95% of the damages while you pay 5%, you can deduct your payment.

If you are subject to governmental fines or penalties because you violated the law, no deduction is allowed. Such penalties include:

- Parking tickets
- Amounts paid as penalties to plead no contest or to plead guilty to a criminal offense
- Penalties imposed by federal, state, or local law (e.g., additions to tax imposed by the Internal Revenue Code)
- Payments to settle actual or possible civil or criminal litigation
- Fines for violation of housing codes
- Fines by truckers for violating state highway maximum weight limits or air quality laws
- Civil penalties for violating federal laws on mine safety or discharge into navigable waters

Nongovernment fines or penalties are deductible. For example, one broker who was fined by the Chicago Mercantile Exchange for violating trading limitations was allowed by the Tax Court to deduct his payment.

Treble Damages for Antitrust Violations

One-third of the treble damages—3 times the actual damages—for antitrust violations is deductible; the balance is treated as a nondeductible penalty.

Restitution Payments

These payments generally are regarded as fines and are deductible. They must be compensatory and not punitive in nature. However, if restitution payments are made in lieu of a prison sentence, they are viewed as a nondeductible governmental penalty even though the funds go to a private person rather than to the government.

Related Expenses

Certain expenses related to nondeductible fines or penalties may themselves be deductible. For example, legal fees to defend your business against prosecution or civil action for a violation of a law imposing a fine or civil penalty are deductible.

Meal Costs for Day-Care Providers

If you provide family day-care services and include meals to children you are caring for, you can deduct the cost of the meals. There are 2 ways to figure your deduction:

1. Your actual costs, for which you need records and receipts to support your deduction.
2. Reliance on an IRS per diem amount, for which you need only keep records of the number of children you care for and the meals they consume.

The per diem amounts are based on a per person rate. The rates for 2014 may be found in Table 22.2.

To use the standard rates, you must provide care in your home to minor children, other than children who are full-time or part-time residents in your home. If you opt to use the standard meal rates, you must do so for all food costs provided to eligible children during the year.

TABLE 22.2 Standard Meal and Snack Rates for 2014

Your Location	Breakfast	Lunch and Dinner	Snack
States other than Alaska and Hawaii	$1.28	$2.40	$0.71
Alaska	$2.04	$3.89	$1.16
Hawaii	$1.49	$2.81	$0.83

Source: Redleaf National Institute.

Expenses of Disabled Persons

Individuals with handicaps or disabilities may incur certain expenses to enable them to work. For example, a blind individual may hire a reader. In general, the cost of work-related expenses of disabled persons is deductible.

Sometimes it may be difficult to decide whether the expense is a personal medical expense that is subject to an adjusted-gross-income floor or a business expense. If the expense is required for the individual to perform his or her job and the goods or services are not used primarily for personal purposes, the expense can be treated as a business expense. For example, attendant care services at the office generally are treated as business expenses. You must show a physical or mental handicap that results in a functional limitation to employment, such as blindness or deafness.

Work-related business expenses of handicapped persons are itemized deductions that are not subject to the 2%-of-AGI rule floor. However, they are subject to the reduction in itemized deductions for high-income taxpayers. If the handicapped person is self-employed, the expenses are deductible as any other business expense on Schedule C.

If you, as an employer, incur special costs because of compliance with the Americans with Disabilities Act, you may deduct these costs as ordinary and necessary business expenses. If they are capital in nature, you may be able to claim a special deduction or credit, as explained in Chapter 10.

The Dividends-Received Deduction

Corporations cannot deduct the dividends they pay out to shareholders. But C corporations may be able to claim a special deduction for a percentage of certain stock dividends they receive. This is called a dividends-received deduction. Other taxpayers—individuals, partnerships, LLCs, and S corporations—cannot claim this deduction.

Percentages of the Dividends-Received Deduction

The percentage of the dividend that can be deducted depends on the amount of stock your corporation owns and the type of company paying the dividends. Other factors may operate to further limit the percentage.

FORTY-TWO PERCENT DEDUCTION

If your corporation owns less than 20% of the preferred stock issued before October 1992 of a taxable public utility, your dividends-received deduction is limited to 42% of the dividends received from that public utility. If your corporation owns more than 20% of the utility, the dividends-received deduction increases to 48%.

SEVENTY PERCENT DEDUCTION

If your corporation owns less than 20% of the stock of the dividend-paying corporation, your dividends-received deduction is 70% of the dividends you receive from that corporation.

EIGHTY PERCENT DEDUCTION

If your corporation owns at least 20% of the stock of the dividend-paying corporation, your dividends-received deduction is 80% of the dividends you receive from that corporation.

ONE HUNDRED PERCENT DEDUCTION

If your corporation and the dividend-paying corporation are members of an affiliated group, all of the dividends received are deductible. The full deduction also applies to small business investment companies that receive dividends from domestic corporations.

Other Limits on the Dividends-Received Deduction

In addition to the percentage limitation, other limits may apply to reduce or eliminate entirely the deduction.

LIMIT FOR DEBT-FINANCED PORTFOLIOS

If your corporation borrows to buy or carry a stock portfolio, the 70% and 80% dividends-received deductions must be reduced by the percentage related to the amount of debt.

OVERALL LIMIT

There is an overall limit on the deduction for dividends received. This limit is calculated on Schedule C of Form 1120.

NO DEDUCTION ALLOWED

Certain types of deductions do not qualify for the dividends-received deduction. These include dividends from:

- Foreign corporations (with limited exceptions).
- Real estate investment trusts.

- Corporations whose stock has been held for only 46 days or less during the 90-day period beginning on the date that is 45 days before the date on which the shares become ex-dividend.
- Corporations whose stock has been held for 91 days or less during the 180-day period beginning on the date that is 90 days before the date on which the shares became ex-dividend, if the stock has preference as to dividends and the dividends received on it are attributable to a period of more than 365 days.
- Tax-exempt corporations.
- Corporations to which your corporation is obligated (pursuant to a short sale or otherwise) to make related payments for positions in substantially similar or related property.

See Table 22.3 for a checklist of deductible and nondeductible expenses.

TABLE 22.3 Checklists of Deductible and Nondeductible Expenses

Deductions for Self-Employed Individuals
Abandonment of assets, loss for
Accounting fees
Acquiring a lease, cost of
Actuary fees for defined benefit plans
Advertising
Agreement not to compete
Air transportation taxes
Alarm system monitoring fees
Allowances and returns
Amortization of acquired intangibles
Association dues
Attorney's fees
Automobiles (see Cars)
Bad debts
Bank fees
Black Lung benefit trust contributions
Bond premium
Bonuses to employees
Breach of contract damages
Bribes

TABLE 22.3 *(Continued)*

Deductions for Self-Employed Individuals

Buildings, demolition of
Business conventions
Business interruption insurance
Capital losses
Cars
Casualty insurance
Casualty losses
Cellular and smart phones
Commissions paid to independent contractors
Computers
Conventions
Copyrights
Cruise ship, conventions on
Dependent care
Depreciation
Dues for professionals
Education expenses
Employee compensation
Employment taxes
Entertainment expenses
Equipment
Excise taxes
Experimental costs
Fax machines
Fines
First-year expensing of equipment
Franchise fees (acquisition costs and annual payments)
Franchise taxes
Freight
Fuel taxes
FUTA tax for employees
Gifts
Going concern value

(Continued)

TABLE 22.3 *(Continued)*

Deductions for Self-Employed Individuals
Goodwill
Handicapped, improvements for
Health insurance for employees
Health savings account contributions
Home office expenses
Insurance
business owner's policy
business interruption
car
casualty
cyber-liability
environmental and pollution liability
errors and omissions
health
liability
long-term care
malpractice
overhead
workers' compensation for employees
Intangible drilling costs
Interest
Internet-related fees
Involuntary conversions
Journals
Kickbacks
Labor costs
Lease payments
Legal fees
Liability insurance
Libraries
License fees
Maintenance costs (repairs)
Malpractice insurance
Materials

TABLE 22.3 *(Continued)*

Deductions for Self-Employed Individuals

Meals for business

Medical insurance

Medical reimbursement plans

Merchant fees for credit card processing

Mortgages

Moving expenses

Net operating losses

Office in home

Oil and gas wells

Organizational expenses

Outplacement services for employees

Overhead insurance

Pagers

Patents

PayPal fees

Penalties

Pension plans

Pollution control facilities

Postage

Qualified retirement plan contributions

Real estate taxes

Reforestation expenses

Registration fees

Removal of architectural barriers

Rent

Research costs

Retirement plan contributions

Royalty payments

Sales tax

Section 197 intangibles

Self-employment tax (one half)

SEP-IRAs

Sick pay to employees

(Continued)

TABLE 22.3 *(Continued)*

Deductions for Self-Employed Individuals
SIMPLE plan contributions
Software
Start-up costs
Subscriptions
Supplemental unemployment benefits for employees
Supplies
Tax return preparation fees
Telephone charges and answering service
Thefts
Timber
Tools
Trade names
Trademarks
Transportation expenses
Trucks (see Cars)
Travel expenses
Unemployment payments to state compensation fund for employees
Uniforms
Use tax
Utilities
Vandalism
Wages for employees
Work clothes
Workers' compensation for employees

Deductions for Employees
Advances for travel and entertainment expenses
Association dues
Automobiles (see Cars)
Bad debts
Breach of contract damages
Breakage charges
Business conventions
Cars

TABLE 22.3 *(Continued)*

Deductions for Employees

Cellular and smart phones

Cleaning costs for deductible uniforms

Computers

Conventions

Cruise ships, conventions on

Dependent care

Depreciation

Dues for professional associations/unions

Entertainment expenses

Equipment

Fax machines

First-year expensing of equipment

Gifts

Health savings account contributions

Home office expenses

Impairment-related job expenses

Insurance for business, car

Interview expenses

IRAs

Job-hunting expenses

Journals

Jury fees returned to employer

Lease payments for business property

Legal fees

License fees

Materials and supplies

Meals for business

Moving expenses

Nonbusiness bad debts

Office in home

Performing artist expenses

Resumes

Section 1244 losses

(Continued)

TABLE 22.3 *(Continued)*

Deductions for Employees
Small tools
Subscriptions
Supplies
Tax return preparation fees
Telephone
Tools
Transportation expenses
Travel expenses
Trucks (see Cars)
Uniforms
Union dues
Utilities in a home office
Work clothes

Deductions for Small Corporations
Abandonment of assets, loss for
Accident and health plans, contributions to
Accounting fees
Acquiring a lease, cost of
Actuary fees for defined benefit plans
Advances for travel and entertainment expenses
Advertising agreement not to compete
Air transportation taxes
Alarm system monitoring fees
Allowances and returns
Amortization of acquired intangibles
Amortization of premium on bonds
Appraisal fees
Association dues
Attorney's fees
Automobiles (see Cars)
Awards and prizes to employees
Bad debts
Bank fees

TABLE 22.3 *(Continued)*

Deductions for Small Corporations

Black Lung benefit trust contributions

Bond premiums

Bonuses

Breach of contract damages

Bribes

Buildings, demolition of

Business conventions

Business interruption insurance

Capital losses

Cars

Casualty insurance

Casualty losses

Cellular phones and PDAs

Charitable contributions

Commissions paid to independent contractors

Computers

Conventions

Copyrights

Cruise ships, conventions on

Dependent care

Depreciation

Disability insurance

Dividends-received deduction

Education expenses

Employee benefit plans

Employee compensation

Employment taxes

Entertainment expenses

Equipment

Excise taxes

Experimental costs

Fax machines

FICA

(Continued)

TABLE 22.3 *(Continued)*

Deductions for Small Corporations
Fines
First-year expensing of equipment
Foreign taxes
Franchise fees (acquisition fee and annual fees)
Franchise taxes
Freight
Fringe benefits
Fuel taxes
FUTA tax
Gifts
Going concern value
Goodwill
Group term life insurance
Handicapped, improvements for
Health plans, contributions to
Health savings account contributions
Incorporation fees
Insurance
business interruption
car
casualty
cyber-liability
employment practices liability
environmental and pollution liability
errors and omissions
group term
health
key person life
liability
life
long-term care
malpractice
overhead
workers' compensation

TABLE 22.3 *(Continued)*

Deductions for Small Corporations
Intangible drilling costs
Interest
Internet-related fees
Involuntary conversions
Journals
Kickbacks
Labor costs
Lease payments
Legal fees
Liability insurance
Libraries
License fees
Life insurance
Maintenance costs (repairs)
Malpractice insurance
Materials
Meals for business
Medical insurance
Medical reimbursement plans
Medicare tax
Merchant account fees for credit card processing
Mortgages
Moving expenses
Net operating losses
Oil and gas wells
Organizational expenses
Outplacement services
Overhead insurance
Patents
PayPal fees
Penalties
Pension plans

(Continued)

TABLE 22.3 *(Continued)*

Deductions for Small Corporations
Pollution control facilities
Postage
Prizes to employees
Qualified retirement plan contributions
Real estate taxes
Reforestation expenses
Registration fees
Removal of architectural barriers
Rent
Research costs
Retirement plan contributions
Royalty payments
Salaries
Sales tax
Section 197 intangibles
SEP-IRAs, contributions to
Sick pay
SIMPLE plans, contributions to
Social Security tax
Software
Start-up costs
State income tax
Subscriptions
Supplemental unemployment benefits
Supplies
Tax return preparation fees
Telephone charges and answering service
Thefts
Timber
Tools
Trademarks
Tradenames
Transportation expenses

TABLE 22.3 *(Continued)*

Deductions for Small Corporations
Travel expenses
Trucks (see Cars)
Unemployment payments to state compensation fund
Unemployment tax (FUTA)
Use tax
Utilities
Vacation pay
Vandalism
Wages
Workers' compensation insurance
Workforce in place
Worthless securities

Deductions Not Allowed
Advances to one's corporation (they are loans or contributions to capital)
Anticipated liabilities
Architect's fees (generally capitalized)
At-risk, losses in excess of
Bad debt deduction for income not reported
Bar examination fees
Car used for commuting
Club dues for recreational, social, and athletic clubs
Commuting expenses
Containers treated as part of inventory
Corporation's expenses paid by shareholder under no obligation to pay them
Demolition of entire buildings
Disability insurance for yourself
Dividend payments
Educational costs to meet minimum job requirements
Embezzlement losses of income not yet reported
Estimated tax penalties
Extortion payments
Federal income tax
FICA by employees

(Continued)

TABLE 22.3 *(Continued)*

Deductions Not Allowed
Fines
401(k) contributions by employees
Gifts to business clients or customers over $25
Hobby losses
Interest on life insurance policy loans funding buy-sell agreements
Inventory
IRA contributions by participants in qualified plans with AGI over set limit
IRA rollovers
Job-hunting costs for a first job
Land costs
Loans (principal repayment)
Lobbying expenses (other than de minimis in-house)
Not-for-profit activity losses
Passive activity losses in excess of passive activity limits
Payments to a minister for prayer-based solutions to business problems
Penalties paid to the government
Political contributions
Reimbursed expenses (payments received by employees under accountable plans)
Related parties, losses on sales to
Roth IRA and Roth 401(k) contributions
Salary reduction contributions to retirement plans
Self-insurance reserve funds
Spousal travel costs
State and local income taxes on self-employment income
Tax penalties
Travel costs as a form of education
Treble damage awards—two-thirds

Other Expenses

Not every cost made on behalf of a business fits neatly into a deduction category or, in fact, is even deductible. As long as the cost is ordinary and necessary for your business and is not designated as "nondeductible" by the tax law, you can deduct it in a catchall category called "other expenses." Examples of other expenses include:

- Prizes to customers or suppliers
- Research expenses (other than costs related to the research credit or capitalized and amortized over 60 or more months, as explained in Chapter 14)
- Trade show fees

Where to Deduct Miscellaneous Business Expenses

Employees

In general, employee business expenses are deductible as itemized expenses on Schedule A, subject to the 2%-of-AGI rule and the reduction in itemized deductions for high-income taxpayers discussed in Chapter 1.

SPECIAL RULE FOR PERFORMING ARTISTS.   Expenses are fully deductible from gross income if you meet certain tests:

- You must perform services as a performing artist as an employee for at least 2 employers.
- Your business deductions must exceed 10% of your gross income from the performance of services.
- Your AGI without regard to these business deductions must not exceed $16,000.

If you meet these tests to fully deduct your expenses, they are not claimed as itemized deductions on Schedule A, but rather as an adjustment to gross income on page 1 of Form 1040. Be sure to write "QPA" next to your deduction.

HANDICAPPED PERSONS.   Business-related expenses of disabled or handicapped individuals are itemized deductions that are not subject to the 2%of-AGI rule but are subject to the reduction for high-income taxpayers.

MOVING EXPENSES.   Moving expenses that are not reimbursed by an employer are deductible from gross income on page 1 of Form 1040. They are deductible regardless of whether other deductions are itemized. Complete Form 3903, *Moving Expenses*, to determine your deductible moving expenses.

EDUCATION CREDITS.   The American opportunity and lifetime learning credits are figured on Form 8863, *Education Credits*, the amount of which is then entered on page 2 of Form 1040.

Self-Employed

Certain items discussed in this chapter are itemized on Schedule C. These include commissions and fees, insurance, and legal and professional services. Other miscellaneous business expenses discussed in this chapter are grouped together and deducted as other expenses on Schedule C. Other expenses are separately listed and explained in Part V of Schedule C. You can use Schedule C-EZ only if total business expenses do not exceed $5,000.

For self-employed farmers, certain expenses discussed in this chapter, such as insurance, are itemized on Schedule F. Other miscellaneous business expenses, such as legal and accounting fees, are grouped together and deducted as other expenses on Schedule F. Farming expenses are explained in Chapter 20.

Moving expenses are a personal expense claimed directly on your Form 1040 rather than on Schedule C. You figure your deductible moving costs on Form 3903 and then enter the deduction on page 1 of Form 1040 as an adjustment to gross income.

The American opportunity and lifetime learning credits for higher education are personal credits claimed directly on your Form 1040. You figure your credits on Form 8863, *Education Credits*, and then enter the credit amount on page 2 of Form 1040.

Partnerships and LLCs

All of the miscellaneous business expenses discussed in this chapter to which a partnership or limited liability company is entitled are entered on Form 1065 as other expenses. Attach a schedule to the return, itemizing these expenses.

Charitable contributions made by the partnership or LLC are subject to limitations and are treated differently. Contributions are reported on Schedule K and passed through to partners/members on Schedule K-1. These are separately stated because they are subject to limitation at the owner level. Partners/members report their net income or loss from the business on Schedule E. However, separately stated items are reported on the owner's personal return in the appropriate space. For example, charitable contribution deductions are reported on the owner's Schedule A.

Partners and LLC members who have deductible moving expenses claim them on page 1 of their Form 1040. Partners and LLC members who are eligible for education credits claim them on page 2 of their Form 1040. For details, see Employees.

S Corporations

All of the miscellaneous business expenses discussed in this chapter to which the S corporation is entitled are entered on Form 1120S as other deductions. Attach a statement to the return explaining these deductions.

However, deductions that are subject to special limitations at the shareholder level are separately treated items reported on Schedule K and passed through to shareholders on Schedule K-1. For example, charitable contributions by the S corporation are separately stated items because they are subject to limitation at the shareholder level. Shareholders report their net income or loss from the business on Schedule E. Separately stated items are reported on the shareholder's personal return in the appropriate space. For example, charitable contribution deductions are reported on the owner's Schedule A.

Shareholders who are also employees of their S corporations and who have unreimbursed moving expenses compute them on Form 3903 and then enter the deduction on page 1 of Form 1040 as an adjustment to gross income.

C Corporations

Miscellaneous business expenses are taken into account in determining the profit or loss of the C corporation on Form 1120. The corporation then pays tax on its net profit or loss. Shareholders do not report any income (or loss) from the corporation.

Charitable contributions by the corporation, as well as NOLs and special deductions for dividends received, are listed separately on Form 1120. All other miscellaneous deductions are grouped together and reported as other deductions. Attach a schedule to the return explaining these deductions.

If a corporation claims a dividends-received deduction, it must also complete Schedule C, *Dividends and Special Deductions*, of Form 1120. The net amount of the dividends-received deduction is then entered on page 1 of Form 1120 after any NOL has been taken. The dividends-received deduction is not part of the other deductions reported on this form.

All Businesses

If your business makes payments of more than $600 to independent contractors for services during the year, you may be required to file an annual information return, Form 1099—Miscellaneous Income. Report the payments as nonemployee compensation in the appropriate box on the form. Also use this form to report payments to corporate directors. See Appendix A for details on furnishing and filing Form 1099-MISC.

Roundup of Tax Credits

Alert

At the time this book was printed, Congress had not extended numerous breaks for 2014 that had expired at the end of 2013. Check the online supplement in February 2015 at www.jklasser.com or www.barbaraweltman.com to see whether these breaks apply for 2014 returns.

Just as deductions offset business income, tax credits offset tax liability. In effect, tax credits are considerably more valuable than deductions since they offset taxes on a dollar-for-dollar basis.

Businesses may be entitled to a variety of credits that Congress created to encourage certain activities—hiring special workers, using alternative energy sources, pouring money into research, and so on. Not every business credit applies to small business owners (but all business-related credits are listed within this chapter to alert you to their existence).

Many of these credits have been discussed throughout this book in the chapter to which they relate. However, here you will find a roundup of tax credits, a brief explanation of what they are all about, and where you can find more information on them within this book (see Table 23.1, page 504).

Employment-Related Credits

The tax law encourages you to hire certain workers by permitting you to claim tax credits for certain wages you have paid.

WORK OPPORTUNITY CREDIT

The work opportunity credit expired at the end of 2013, but could be extended retroactively by Congress. The following is included in case there is an extension. Check the Supplement for details.

The work opportunity credit applies for hiring workers from certain economically disadvantaged designated groups:

> **NOTE**
>
> Employment credits reduce both your deduction for wages as well as your tax liability. Employment credits (other than the empowerment zone employment credit) are part of the general business credit.

- Recipient of Temporary Assistance for Needy Families (TANF) (someone who is a member of a family receiving TANF or its predecessor, AFDC, for any 9 months during the past 18 months ending on the hire date).

- Qualified veteran (someone with a service-related disability who has been unemployed for any 6 months or more during a 1-year period ending on the hire date).

- Qualified ex-felon (someone convicted of a felony under any statute of the United States or any state, who received food stamps for at least 3 months during the 12-month period ending on the hiring date, and is hired not more than 1 year after the date of conviction or release from prison).

- Designated community resident (someone at least age 18, but not yet 40, on the hiring date, who resides in an empowerment zone, enterprise community, renewal community, or rural renewal community).

- Summer youth employee (someone 16 or 17 years old who performs services between May 1 and September 15, and who resides in an empowerment zone, enterprise community, renewal community, or rural renewal community).

- Vocational rehabilitation referral (someone certified as having a physical or mental disability that constitutes a substantial hardship to employment, including an individual participating in the Ticket to Work and Self-Sufficiency Program).

- Food stamp recipient (someone at least age 18, but not yet 40, on the hiring date who received food stamps for at least 3 months during the 12-month period ending on the hiring date).

- Supplemental Security Income recipient (someone receiving SSI for any month ending within 60 days of the hiring date).

- Long-term family assistance recipient (a member of a family that received long-term family assistance for at least 18 months ending on the hiring date, or who is no longer eligible for assistance and is hired within 2 years of the expiration of eligibility).

- Returning heroes: 40% of the first $6,000 of wages (top credit of $2,400) for hiring a veteran who has been unemployed at least 4 weeks but less than 6 months in the year preceding the hiring date; 40% of the first $14,000 of wages (top credit of $5,600) for hiring a veteran who has been unemployed at least 6 months in the prior 1-year period.

- Wounded warriors (those with a service-related disability): 40% of the first $12,000 of wages (a top credit of $4,800) for hiring any such veteran within a year of release from active duty; 40% of the first $24,000 of wages (top credit of $9,600) for hiring a veteran with service-connected disabilities who has been unemployed at least 6 months in the year preceding the hiring date.

EMPLOYER CREDIT FOR FICA ON TIPS

If you own a food or beverage business, you may claim a credit for the employer portion of Social Security and Medicare taxes (FICA) on tips in excess of those treated as wages for purposes of satisfying the minimum wage provisions of the Fair Labor Standards Act. The credit applies to tips both on premises as well as off premises (e.g., earned for pizza deliveries). The credit is based on the old federal minimum wage rate of $5.15 per hour (even though the federal minimum wage rate is $7.25 per hour).

EMPOWERMENT ZONE EMPLOYMENT CREDIT

The empowerment zone employment credit expired at the end of 2013, but could be extended retroactively by Congress. The following is included in case there is an extension. Check the Supplement for details.

This credit is 20% of the first $15,000 of wages and may be claimed for workers who reside in and perform services for an employer located within designated empowerment zones. Wages taken into account for the work opportunity credit may not also be used for the empowerment zone employment credit.

INDIAN EMPLOYMENT CREDIT

The Indian employment credit expired at the end of 2013, but could be extended retroactively by Congress. The following is included in case there is an extension. Check the Supplement for details.

This credit is 20% of the first $20,000 in wages and health care costs in excess of amounts paid in 2003 and may be claimed for employing Indian tribe members who live and work on a reservation. The top credit is $4,000 per employee.

EMPLOYER DIFFERENTIAL WAGE PAYMENTS CREDIT

The employer wage differential payment credit expired at the end of 2013, but could be extended retroactively by Congress. The following is included in case there is an extension. Check the Supplement for details.

If you continue some or all of the wages of employees called to active duty (called a differential wage payment), you can take a tax credit of 20% of the differential that does not exceed $20,000. This credit applies only to small employers (on average less than 50 employees) that have a written plan to provide the wage differential. No deduction for compensation can be claimed if the compensation is a differential wage payment used to determine this credit.

WORK-RELATED PERSONAL CREDITS

If you work as an employee or as a self-employed person, you may be eligible for certain personal tax credits.

EARNED INCOME CREDIT

Workers with wages or self-employment income whose income is below threshold amounts may be eligible to claim an earned income credit. This credit is a type of negative income tax—it may be paid even though it exceeds tax liability. The amount of the credit depends on the number of qualifying dependents, if any, and AGI.

DEPENDENT CARE CREDIT

Whether you are an employee or a business owner, if you hire someone to look after your child under age 13 or a disabled spouse or disabled child of any age so that you can go to work, you may claim a personal tax credit. The credit is a sliding percentage based on your AGI. The top percentage is 35%, but scales back to 20% for AGI over $43,000. The percentage applies to eligible expenses up to $3,000 for one dependent and $6,000 for 2 or more dependents.

PREMIUM TAX CREDIT

Whether you are an employee or a self-employed individual, you must have minimum essential health coverage in order to avoid a penalty. If you do not have such coverage through an employer (yours or your spouse's) or a government plan (e.g., Medicare), and you cannot afford coverage, you may be eligible for a tax credit to help pay the premiums. The credit is explained in Chapter 19.

Capital Construction–Related Credits

The tax law encourages certain types of construction.

DISABLED ACCESS CREDIT

If you make capital improvements to make your premises more accessible to the handicapped, you may qualify for a credit of 50% of expenditures over $250, but not over $10,250. Thus, the top credit is $5,000. If you claim this credit, you cannot claim depreciation on these costs.

LOW-INCOME HOUSING CREDIT

If you invest in the construction or rehabilitation of housing for low-income individuals, you may be eligible for a tax credit of 70% of new construction or 30% of federally subsidized buildings. The credit is claimed over a 10-year period.

REHABILITATION CREDIT

If you rehabilitate or reconstruct certain buildings, you may claim a credit of 10% of your costs if the building was originally placed in service before 1936. If the building is a certified historic structure listed on the National Register of Historic Places, the credit is 20% of your expenditures. To qualify, your expenditures must be more than the greater of $5,000 or your adjusted basis in the building and its structural components.

NEW MARKETS CREDIT

The new markets credit expired at the end of 2013, but could be extended retroactively by Congress. The following is included in case there is an extension. Check the Supplement for details.

To encourage investments in certain economically disadvantaged areas, you may claim a credit for purchasing stock in a community development entity (CDE). A CDE is a domestic corporation or partnership that provides investment capital for low-income communities or persons, maintains accountability to the residents of the area, and has been certified as a CDE by the Community Development Financial Institutions (CDFI) Fund of the Department of the Treasury. The credit is claimed over a period of 7 years. The amount of the credit is the equity investment multiplied by 5% in years one through 3 and 6% in years 4 through 7. The credit is subject to recapture if the CDE ceases to be qualified, the proceeds cease to be used to make qualified investments, or the investment is redeemed by the entity (there is no recapture if you merely sell your investment).

ENERGY-EFFICIENT HOME CREDIT

The energy-efficient homes credit expired at the end of 2013, but could be extended retroactively by Congress. The following is included in case there is an extension. Check the Supplement for details.

To encourage the construction of energy-efficient homes, contractors may qualify for a tax credit of up to $2,000 per dwelling unit for site-built homes or $1,000 or $2,000 (depending on energy conservation) for manufactured homes. To qualify for the credit, a home must be certified to provide a level of heating and cooling energy consumption that is at least 30 to 50% in the case of a manufactured home, and 50% for other homes, below that of a comparable home constructed in accordance with the standards of the 2004 Supplement to the 2003 International Energy Conservation Code. It must also have building envelope component improvements providing a level of heating and cooling energy consumption that is at least 10% below that of a comparable home.

Other Tax Credits

Other tax credits in the law are intended to encourage specific things— research, alternative energy improvements, and so on.

SMALL EMPLOYER HEALTH TAX CREDIT

If you pay more than half of your employees' health care costs in 2014 and meet certain payroll limits, you may qualify for a tax credit of up to 50% of your premiums. This credit is explained in Chapter 19.

CREDIT FOR EMPLOYER-PROVIDED CHILD CARE FACILITIES AND SERVICES

You can claim a credit for providing child care facilities and child care referral services. The credit is 25% of qualified facility expenses, plus 10% of referral service costs, for a maximum credit of $150,000. If a company builds a child care facility, the basis of the facility for purposes of depreciation must be reduced by the expenses taken into account in figuring the credit. If the facility ceases to be used for child care within 10 years, the credit is subject to recapture.

RESEARCH CREDIT

The research credit expired at the end of 2013, but could be extended retroactively by Congress or even made permanent. The following is included in case there is an extension. Check the Supplement for details.

If you engage in search and experimentation, you may claim a credit of 20% of increased research activities (increased costs this year compared with a base period). For companies long in existence, the base period is 1984 to 1988 ("existing company rule"). For others, it is three years of a fixed base period ("start-up company rule"); this also applies to older companies that did not previously have research expenses. Alternatively you may claim an alternative simplified credit, which works best for a company that had little or no R&D spending in the previous 3 years. This credit is 14% of the amount of current-year R&D spending that exceeds 50% of the average spent in the previous 3 years.

This alternative is figured without regard to gross receipts. The alternative simplified credit can be elected on an original or amended return.

ALCOHOL FUELS CREDIT

The credit applies to alcohol (ethanol and methanol) you sold or used as fuel in your business.

ENHANCED OIL RECOVERY CREDIT

The credit applies to certain oil recovery costs if you are in the oil and gas business.

FEDERAL EXCISE TAX ON FUELS

The federal excise tax you pay on certain fuels used in your business (particularly farming activities) may be claimed either as a credit or a tax refund. The credit is the amount of this tax paid on fuel used in machinery and off-highway vehicles (such as tractors) and on kerosene used for heating, lighting, and cooking on a farm.

FOREIGN TAX CREDIT

If you pay tax to a foreign country—on business income or investments made abroad—you may be eligible for a tax credit. The purpose of the tax credit is to prevent you from paying tax twice on the same income (once to a foreign country and again on your federal income tax).

ENERGY CREDIT

There is an energy tax credit (which is part of the investment credit) for a specified percentage of the basis of each qualified energy property placed in service.

RENEWABLE ENERGY PRODUCTION CREDIT

The credit is the cost of selling electricity produced from alternative energy sources within 10 years of placing the production facility in service.

CREDIT FOR SMALL EMPLOYER PENSION PLAN START-UP COSTS

Small employers (those with no more than 100 employees who received at least $5,000 of compensation in the preceding year) may claim a tax credit for starting up a qualified retirement plan. The credit is 50% of administrative and employee-education expenses up to $1,000, for a top credit of $500. The credit may be claimed for 3 years, starting with the year in which the plan becomes effective or the prior year. (This credit is explained in Chapter 16.)

ORPHAN DRUG CREDIT

If your business engages in research on diseases and afflictions that are not widespread, you may claim a special credit for your related expenses.

BIODIESEL FUELS CREDIT

This credit is the sum of 2 tax credits: the biodiesel mixture credit and the biodiesel credit. There is a higher credit limit for agribiodiesel.

LOW-SULPHUR DIESEL FUEL PRODUCTION CREDIT

Small business refiners can claim a credit for the production of low-sulfur diesel fuel that complies with the EPA's Highway Diesel Fuel Sulphur Control Requirements. A small refiner is one with an average daily domestic refinery run for a one-year period ending on December 31, 2002, that is 205,000 barrels or less and cannot employ more than 1,500 individuals on any day during the year.

MARGINAL OIL AND GAS WELL PRODUCTION CREDIT

The credit is $3 per barrel of qualified crude oil production and 50 ¢ per 1,000 cubic feet of qualified natural gas production.

MINIMUM TAX CREDIT

If you paid AMT in a prior year, you may be eligible for a tax credit this year. Different rules apply to individuals and C corporations. (This credit is explained in Chapter 28.)

General Business Credit

Most tax credits discussed in this chapter are part of the general business credit. This means that after figuring each separate credit, there is an overall limit to credits under the general business credit. Total credits in excess of these limits can be carried back and/or forward within limits.

The general business credit is comprised of the following:

- Investment credit (rehabilitation credit, renewal energy credit, and the credit from cooperatives)
- Research credit*
- Low-income housing credit
- Distilled spirits credit
- Disabled access credit
- Renewable electricity production credit
- Indian employment credit*
- Nonconventional source fuel credit*
- Orphan drug credit
- Credit for contributions to selected community development corporations

- Credit for employer-provided child care facilities and services
- Credit for small employer retirement plan start-up costs
- New markets credit*
- Biodiesel and renewable diesel fuels credit
- Low-sulfur diesel fuel production credit
- Marginal oil and gas well production credit
- Energy-efficient homes credit*
- Energy-efficient appliance credit*
- Alternative motor vehicle credit
- Alternative fuel vehicle refueling property credit
- Credit for employer differential wage payments
- Plug-in electric drive motor vehicle credit
- Work opportunity credit*
- Small employer health insurance credit

*These credits expired at the end of 2013 but could be extended for 2014.

The empowerment zone employment credit, which expired at the end of 2013 but could be extended for 2014, is not part of the general business credit and is not subject to the general business credit limitations. Excess empowerment zone credits may be carried over in a manner similar to the general business credit.

Credit Limitations

First you figure each separate credit of the general business credit and then total them. The total is then subject to special limits, determined by your regular and alternative minimum tax liability and certain other tax credits. Your limit is your net tax liability (regular tax reduced by certain personal credits, including the foreign tax credit), reduced by the greater of:

- Your tentative AMT liability (figured before comparing it with regular tax).
- 25% of regular tax liability (before personal tax credits) over $25,000.

Example

In 2014, your regular tax liability is $12,000. You are entitled to claim $1,000 in personal tax credits. You have no AMT liability. Your general business credit is limited to $11,000 (net tax liability of $11,000, reduced by zero since you do not have any AMT liability and 25% of your regular tax does not exceed $25,000).

ALTERNATIVE MINIMUM TAX

Small business credits in the general business credit can offset AMT liability of eligible small businesses (gross receipts not exceeding $50 million).

CARRYBACKS AND CARRYFORWARDS

If the credit limitation prevents you from claiming the full general business credit that you are otherwise entitled to, you do not lose the benefit of this excess amount—you simply cannot claim it in the current year. You may be able to use the excess credit to offset your tax liability in prior and/or future years.

You may carry back the excess amount of credits for one year. If there continues to be an excess, you may then carry forward the excess up to 20 years.

EXPIRED CARRYFORWARDS

If you still have unused amounts and the carryforward period expires or the business ceases (or you die), the unused amounts may be deducted in the year after the carryforward expiration or in the year of business cessation (or death). However, to the extent the credit relates to the research credit, it must be cut in half before deducting it.

Where to Claim Tax Credits

Self-Employed Individuals

Employment tax credits are reported on Schedule C as a reduction to wages paid to employees. (Schedule C-EZ cannot be used if you have employees, so no credits are reported on this form.) All other credits—both business and personal—are claimed directly on Form 1040.

Farmers

The credit for federal excise tax on fuels is claimed directly on Form 1040 (it is not reported on Schedule F). All other credits are also claimed directly on Form 1040.

Partnerships and LLCs

All business credits pass through separately to owners and are claimed on their individual returns.

S Corporations

The credit for the federal tax on fuels is claimed by the S corporation on Form 1120S. All other business credits pass through separately to shareholders and are claimed on their individual returns.

TABLE 23.1 Guide to Tax Credits

Business Credits	Tax Form	More Info
Alcohol fuels credit	Form 6478	
Alternative motor vehicle credit	Form 8910	Chapter 9
Credit for FICA tax on tips	Form 8846	Chapter 7
Disabled access credit	Form 8826	Chapter 10
Employer-provided child care facilities and services credit	Form 8882	Chapter 23
Employer differential wage payment credit*	Form 8932	Chapter 7
Empowerment zone employment credit*	Form 8844	Chapter 7
Energy-efficient home credit*	Form 8908	Chapter 23
Energy-efficient appliance credit	Form 8909	
Enhanced oil recovery credit	Form 8830	
Federal excise tax on fuel	Form 4136	Chapter 13
Foreign tax credit		
corporations	Form 1118	Chapter 13
individuals	Form 1116	Chapter 13
General business credit	Form 3800	Chapters 7 and 23
Indian employment credit*	Form 8845	Chapter 7
Investment credit (rehabilitation credit, energy credit, advanced coal project credit, and qualifying gasification project credit)	Form 3468	Chapter 10
Minimum tax credit		
corporations	Form 8827	Chapter 26
individuals	Form 8801	Chapter 26
New markets credit*	Form 8874	Chapter 23
Orphan drug credit	Form 8820	
Plug-in electric drive motor vehicle credit	Form 8834	Chapter 9
Renewal electricity production credit	Form 8835	
Research credit*	Form 6765	Chapter 14
Small employer health insurance credit	Form 8941	Chapter 19
Small employer pension plan startup costs	Form 8881	Chapter 23
Work opportunity credit*	Form 5884	Chapter 7
Personal Work-Related Credits	**Tax Form**	**More Info**
Earned income credit	Form EIC	Chapter 7
Education credits	Form 8863	Chapter 22
Dependent care credit	Form 2441	Chapter 7
Premium tax credit	Form 8962	Chapter 19

*These credits expired at the end of 2013 but could be extended for 2014.

C Corporations

All tax credits are claimed on Form 1120. Some credits are taken into account on Form 1120, Schedule J, *Tax Computation*, in figuring tax liability while other credits are claimed directly on Form 1120 as an offset to tax liability.

All Taxpayers

All taxpayers use the same form, Form 3800, *General Business Credit*, for figuring the general business credit, limitations, and carrybacks/carryforwards. However, if you have only one credit that is part of the general business credit, you need not complete Form 3800. Instead, complete the form for the specific credit and then figure the general business credit limitation on a separate attachment.

When claiming any carrybacks or carryforwards, you must attach your own explanation that includes the following information:

- The year in which the credit originated
- The amount of the credit
- The amount allowed in the year of origination
- The amount allowed in each carryback year
- The amount allowed in each carryforward year

See Table 23.1 for a guide to tax credits.

Tax Planning for Your Small Business

Income and Deduction Strategies

Alert

At the time this book was printed, Congress had not extended numerous breaks for 2014 that had expired at the end of 2013. Check the online supplement in February 2015 at www.jklasser.com or www.barbaraweltman.com to see whether these breaks apply for 2014 returns.

Understanding what income you must report and the various business deductions you may claim is only half the job. You must also know when to report income and when to postpone it, when to claim certain deductions and when not to claim them. You should also be aware of the common traps that business owners often fall into with their income and deductions.

Finally, it is important to recognize that you should not always go at it alone. You may need to get the assistance of tax professionals or additional information from the IRS. You need to know how to obtain referrals to tax professionals. You also need to know some important IRS telephone numbers to call for assistance. This information is included throughout this chapter for your convenience.

Tax-Saving Tips

Tax-Planning Decisions

Some deductions are under your control because you can decide whether to incur the expenditure. Also, sometimes you are permitted to make tax elections on when to report income or when to claim write-offs. Here are some pointers that can help you minimize your income and maximize your deductions. Or, you can follow the reverse strategy if you already have losses for the year and want to accelerate income to offset those losses (and defer deductions).

- *Cash-basis businesses*. If you account for your expenses and income on a cash basis, you can influence when you receive income and claim deductions for year-end items. For example, you can delay billing out for services or merchandise so that payment will be received in the following year. In deferring income for services or goods sold, do not delay billing so that collection may be in jeopardy. Also factor in your tax bracket for this year and the bracket you expect to be in next year. If you will be in a higher tax bracket next year because your income will be greater or because of tax law changes, you may not want to defer income. You may prefer to bill and collect as soon as possible to report the income in the lower-tax year.

  On the flip side, you can accelerate deductions by paying outstanding bills and stocking up on supplies. Again, determine whether accelerating deductions makes sense for you.

  However, in accelerating deductions, do not prepay expenses that relate to items extending beyond one year. For example, if you pay a 3-year subscription to a trade magazine, you can deduct only the portion of the subscription (one-third) that relates to the current year; the balance is deductible in future years as allocated.

- *Accrual method businesses*. The board of directors of an accrual-basis C corporation can authorize a charitable contribution and make note of it in the corporate minutes. A current deduction can be claimed even if the contribution is paid after the end of the year (as long as it is paid no later than $2^{1/2}$ months after the close of the year). Charitable contributions are discussed in Chapter 22.

  Similarly, accrual method businesses can accrue bonuses and other payments to employees in the current year that are paid within $2^{1/2}$ months of the close of the year. However, this rule does not extend to payments to S corporation owner-employees—payments are deductible only when received by the owner-employees.

- *Owner participation*. If you own a business, be sure that your level of participation is sufficient to allow you to deduct all your losses under the passive loss limitation rules. Increase your level of participation, and keep records of how and when you participated in the business. Passive loss rules and the various participation tests under these rules are discussed in Chapter 4.

- *Increase basis to fully utilize losses*. If you are an owner in a pass-through entity, your share of losses generally is deductible only to the extent of your basis in the business. Explore ways in which to increase your basis so that the losses can be fully utilized. For example, if you are an S corporation shareholder, you can increase basis by lending funds to your business. Alternatively, you can work with the corporation's lenders to restructure debt, making you primarily liable for the amount borrowed (which you then lend to the corporation and increase basis). Basis rules and their impact on deducting losses are discussed in Chapter 4.

- *Minimize FICA*. Owners who work for their corporations may be able to extract distributions on a FICA-free basis by arranging loans or rentals to the business and taking payments in the form of interest or rents. Of course, these arrangements must be bona fide. However, S corporation shareholders who perform substantial services for their corporation should not erroneously characterize compensation as dividends.

- *Review qualified plan selection*. If you are self-employed and use an IRA, SEP, SIMPLE, or other qualified plan to save for retirement, review your choice of plan annually to see if it optimizes your benefits while keeping costs down.

  Similarly, corporations should review existing plans to see whether terminations or other courses of action are warranted as cost-cutting measures. If you want to terminate one plan and begin another, do not do so without consulting a pension expert. You must be sure that your old plan is in full compliance with the tax laws—including recent changes—before it is terminated.

- *Carry medical coverage for yourself and employees*. Buy the kind of coverage you can afford, as long as it meets minimum essential coverage requirements. The business picks up the expense for your personal insurance protection. Even if you cannot receive this benefit on a tax-free basis (if, for example, you are a partner or S corporation shareholder who must include business-paid insurance in your income), you can deduct 100% of the coverage on your individual return.

  You can reduce the cost of coverage to the business by buying a high-deductible plan that allows employees to contribute to medical savings accounts on a tax-deductible basis. Alternatively, you can make deductible contributions to Health Savings Accounts (HSAs) on behalf of your employees. You can shift most of the cost of coverage to employees by adopting a premium-only cafeteria plan.

  If you have a C corporation and are a shareholder-employee, you can institute a medical reimbursement plan to cover out-of-pocket medical costs not otherwise covered by insurance (such as dental expenses, eye care, or prescription drugs). Medical coverage strategies are discussed in Chapter 19.

If you pay more than half the premiums for your employees and qualify as a small employer, you can claim a tax credit for a percentage of your payments (Chapter 19).

- *Institute other employee benefit plans.* If you have a C corporation that is profitable and you are a shareholder-employee, you may be able to turn your nondeductible personal expenses into deductible business expenses. For example, you can have the corporation institute a group term life insurance plan for employees and obtain tax-free coverage up to $50,000. Of course, in weighing the advantages and disadvantages of employee benefit plans, be sure to consider the cost of covering rank-and-file employees, since most benefit plans have strict nondiscrimination rules. Also, take into account the fact that employer-paid educational assistance and adoption assistance plans cannot give more than 5% of benefits to shareholders owning more than 5% of the stock, usually making such plans undesirable for such closely held corporations. Employee benefits are discussed in Chapter 7.

- *Reimbursement arrangements.* If your company reimburses you for travel and entertainment costs, be sure that the arrangement is treated as an *accountable plan.* This will ensure that not only does the company save on employment taxes but also that you are not taxed on reimbursements, since your offsetting deductions would be subject to the 2%-of-AGI rule and the reduction in itemized deductions for high-income taxpayers. With an accountable plan, the company deducts the expenses, and no income is reported to you. Reimbursement arrangements are discussed in Chapter 8.

- *Abandonment versus selling of property.* If you have property that simply is of no value to the business, you may want to abandon it rather than sell it for a nominal amount. This will allow the business to take an ordinary loss deduction rather than a capital loss on a sale. A sale of Section 1231 property may result in a capital or ordinary loss, depending on other Section 1231 transactions for the current year and prior Section 1231 losses. Abandonment of property and Section 1231 property are discussed in Chapter 6.

- *Disaster losses.* If you suffer a disaster loss to business property in an area declared by the president to be eligible for federal disaster assistance, consider claiming the deduction on a return for the year preceding the year of the loss if this will give you needed cash flow or result in a greater benefit from the deduction. Disaster losses are discussed in Chapter 17.

- *Review the business structure.* Changes in the business climate, in business goals, tax laws, and state laws may warrant a change in the form of business organization. For example, your business may start as a sole proprietorship;

later you may want to incorporate in order to take advantage of certain employee benefit plans. Review the options that will afford tax reduction and other benefits. Business organization is discussed in Chapter 1.

- *Do year-end planning.* Businesses have an opportunity to save on taxes with year-end planning. Well-timed deductions may prove advantageous. Begin year-end planning well before the end of the year in order to have time to implement your decisions.
- *Stay abreast of tax law changes.* New opportunities are continually being created—through Congressional action, court decisions, and IRS rulings. You need to know what these changes are in order to take advantage of them. Download a free Supplement to this book (available in February 2015) on tax developments affecting small businesses from www.jklasser.com and www.barbaraweltman.com.

Post-Year Tax Elections to Cut Your Tax Bill

Even though the tax year is over, there are still certain decisions that you can make after the year has ended to favorably impact your tax liability. Here are some elections and actions that can be helpful when you file your tax return for the current year:

Take optimum write-offs for business equipment purchase. When the business can benefit from a larger deduction, instead of depreciating the cost of equipment over the life of the property, consider electing first-year expensing. Alternatively, when the business cannot benefit from a current depreciation deduction because it does not have sufficient income to offset the deduction, consider electing alternative depreciation to spread deductions over future years. Time business equipment purchases carefully in view of the mid-quarter convention. Depreciation and expensing are discussed in Chapter 14.

Elect to forgo a net operating loss carryback. If the business has an NOL in 2014, it can generally carry the loss back 2 years (3 years for small business disaster losses; 5 years for farmers and ranchers; 10 years for product liability) and forward for 20 years. Alternatively, it can elect to forgo the carryback and simply carry the loss forward. Where a corporation was in a low tax bracket in prior years but is in a higher tax bracket now (and expects to remain in a high bracket in the future), it may be advisable to elect to forgo the carryback. If the business simply does not have any prior income to offset by an NOL, do not make an election; simply carry the loss forward. By not making the election, you preserve the right to carry back the NOL if the IRS subsequently audits an earlier return and income results. Net operating losses are discussed in Chapter 4.

Installment sale. If you sold property on an installment basis where at least one payment is due after the year of sale, you report the gain over the period in which payments are made. However, you can opt to report *all* of the gain in the year of sale, regardless of when payments are received. This is done simply by reporting the full amount of gain on the 2014 return. Reporting the full gain may be advisable if you have losses in the year of sale or loss carryovers to offset the gains. It may also make sense if you expect to be in a higher tax bracket when additional installment payments will be received.

Real estate professionals. If you own multiple rental properties that produce a net loss, you can escape the passive activity loss limitation imposed on investors by aggregating the properties to qualify as a real estate professional. To do this, you must attach an election to your return. Without the election, a reported net loss may be disallowed. What's more, without qualifying as a real estate professional, income from real estate activities cannot escape the additional Medicare tax on net investment income if you are a high-income taxpayer.

SEP contribution. If 2014 is a profitable year but you don't have a qualified retirement plan for your business, it may not be too late to create and fund one. You have until the extended due date of the return to set up a SEP and add the deductible contribution for 2014.

Track Carryovers

You may have tax write-offs that you are unable to use because of a dollar, a percentage, or some other limit. Be sure to keep track of the carryovers so you can use them in future years to the extent allowed. Here are some common carryovers to keep records on:

Capital losses. Unused capital losses for individuals have an unlimited carryforward. Unused capital losses of C corporations have a 5-year carryover limit.

Charitable contribution carryover. If charitable contributions are limited because of adjusted gross income (AGI) or taxable income, excess amounts can be carried forward for up to 5 years (15 years for contributions of conservation easements).

General business credit carryover. If you have any unused general business credit, it can be carried forward for up to 20 years.

Home office deduction carryover. If your home office deduction in 2014 (figured using the actual expense method) is limited because of your gross income from the home office activity, the excess deduction can be used on the 2015 return to the extent there is sufficient gross income from the home office activity. You do not have to be in the same home office in the carryover year in order to use the carryover. There is no time limit on the use of a home office deduction carryover. There is no carryover if your home office deduction for 2014 is figured using the simplified method.

Investment interest. Unused investment interest by individuals has an unlimited carryover period. Investment interest may arise, for example, on borrowing to purchase stock in your incorporated business.

Net operating loss carryover. If you have a net operating loss (NOL) carryover that has not been used up, carry it forward for up to 20 years. The NOL is reported as a negative figure on the "other income" line on Form 1040.

Audit-Proofing Your Return

It is impossible to completely audit-proof your return. However, you can take steps to minimize your exposure.

Perhaps the number one audit trigger for small business is improper classification of workers. Small business owners may treat workers as independent contractors when they should be treated as employees. If the IRS successfully reclassifies workers as employees, you could owe back employment taxes, interest, and penalties as well as risk loss of qualified status for your retirement plan. In other words, the monetary risks of misclassification are substantial.

You can rely on a safe harbor to avoid misclassification. You need to show that it is an industry practice to treat such workers as independent contractors. All company practices should be consistent.

- Contract terminology in any agreements with these workers should reflect independent contractor status.
- Form 1099-MISC should be issued each year to all your independent contractors.
- Treat all workers on a consistent basis every year (independent contractors should remain independent contractors).
- Treat all workers with similar responsibilities on a consistent basis (all workers who handle a particular job should be treated *either* as employees *or* independent contractors, depending on the circumstances).

Many audit problems arise in connection with deductions. Your goal should be to claim all the deductions to which you are entitled in order to minimize your business income. At the same time, you want to *audit-proof* your return to avoid confrontations with the IRS. The following are some tips you can use to ensure that your write-offs will be allowed.

- *Report business income.* While there is an underground economy operating strictly for cash, do not join these ranks. The failure to report income can result in criminal charges punishable by fines and jail time. The IRS is becoming increasingly sophisticated about discerning unreported income. It has developed audit guides for various industries to enable its auditors to detect unreported income. For example, by examining the amount of flour ordered by a pizzeria, the IRS can determine how many pizzas should have been sold—the failure to fall within reasonable parameters can lead to charges of failing to report income.

- *Keep good records.* You need proof to back up your deductions, such as when the expense was paid or incurred, the amount of the expense, and why you think it is deductible. If you develop good recordkeeping practices, you will automatically be assured of the necessary evidence to support your deductions. For example, if you want to claim deductions for travel and entertainment expenses, you must have certain proof of expenditures. Using a computer to keep your books and records can simplify both recordkeeping requirements and tax return preparation. Recordkeeping is explained in detail in Chapter 3.

- *Formalize agreements between corporations and shareholders.* If loans are made to or from shareholders, be sure that the interest rate, terms of repayment, and other particulars of the loans are written down. Have the note signed by all of the parties. Formal agreements should also be made if property is leased by a shareholder to the corporation. In addition to promissory notes, contracts, or other agreements between the parties, it is a good idea to put any agreements into the minutes of the corporation.

- *Be careful when claiming deductions and credits.* Make sure you meet eligibility requirements before taking write-offs. Be aware that the IRS may flag returns that claim excessive deductions. Some tax professionals advise that you keep deductible expenses under 52% of gross income on Schedule C (50% on Schedule F) and suggest that deductions over 67% of income on Schedule C (or 71% on Schedule F) are likely to attract IRS attention. These numbers are only guidelines, and using them does not guarantee you will be free from being audited. Claim *all* deductions to which you are entitled. Even if the IRS examines your return, you can prove entitlement to your write-offs.

- *Supply all necessary information.* In completing business returns, be sure to fill out all forms and schedules required. Also include all required information for claiming certain deductions. For example, if you have a bad debt, you cannot simply deduct the loss. You must attach a statement to the return detailing the nature and extent of the bad debt.

- *Review the IRS audit guide for your industry* (if such a guide has been released). This guide is used by IRS personnel to review returns of businesses within an industry and thus provides key information about what the IRS is on the lookout for. Currently there are more than 3 dozen "Audit Technique Guides" available free from the IRS at www.irs.gov.

- *Review special information for your industry.* The IRS has created industry-based guidance for farming, automotive, entertainment, fishing, gas retail, manufacturing, online auctions, real estate, restaurants, and some links for other industries and professions at www.irs.gov/ (search: "industries professions").

- *Ask for the IRS's opinion.* If you are planning a novel transaction or want to take a deduction about which you are unsure, you may be able to get the IRS's view on the situation. You may want to request a private letter ruling. If the ruling is favorable, you can be confident of your position. If it is unfavorable, you may be able to modify the situation as the ruling suggests. The IRS charges a user fee for issuing letter rulings (the amounts vary). Before asking for a ruling, though, it may be better to discuss the situation with a tax professional who can research existing precedent and help you prepare a ruling request.

- *File on time.* If you delay filing, you face not only penalties and interest but also the loss of deductions. For example, you must claim a deduction for contributions to a qualified retirement plan no later than the due date of your return. If you cannot meet the filing deadline, be sure to ask for a filing extension in a timely manner. File the correct form for claiming a filing extension appropriate to your business return. (See Table 24.1.) Also, check state income tax rules for filing extensions that may require a separate form.

- *Get good advice.* If you are unsure of whether you need to report certain income or whether you are entitled to claim a particular deduction, ask a tax professional. You may have special questions concerning the new tax law.

    Be sure to understand the protection you receive from attorney-client privilege. This privilege also applies to accountants and other federally authorized tax practitioners with respect to federal civil tax matters. But the

TABLE 24.1 Forms for Filing Extensions

If You File	Ask for an Extension On
Schedule A, Form 1040, for employees	Form 4868
Schedule C, Form 1040, for sole proprietors	Form 4868
Schedule F, Form 1040, for farmers	Form 4868
Form 1065, for partnerships and LLCs	Form 7004
Form 1120, for C corporations	Form 7004
Form 1120S, for S corporations	Form 7004

accountant-client privilege does not apply to mere tax return preparation, state tax matters (unless your state extends similar protection), or other federal nontax matters (such as securities matters).

Make sure your tax advisor is *not* taking erroneous deductions or making other false reporting on your behalf. The IRS is cracking down on unscrupulous tax return preparers, and their clients can get caught in an audit web.

- *Use the right tax return preparer.* The IRS has stepped up its review of tax return preparers, looking for those who take questionable positions on clients' returns. If you use a preparer who falls in the IRS's net, your return may be examined.

Planning Ahead

The ever-changing tax laws make it challenging to devise long-term tax strategies for your business. This is especially true at this time when historic budget deficits may result in new tax hikes and the elimination of some tax breaks; some changes could even be made retroactive. Still, it is important to be able to plan ahead so you can decide in which year it may be more favorable to purchase capital equipment, hire new workers, or take other actions that can affect your after-tax profits.

Many of the tax changes that take place each year are the result of cost-of-living adjustments (COLA). Others are the product of phased-in law changes, while still others are IRS devised. In Appendix C you will find a listing of some common scheduled adjustments and law changes affecting small businesses over the next several years.

Common Errors and How to Avoid Them

The IRS has identified the most common errors that businesses make on their returns. Having one or more of these errors can trigger a closer look by the IRS, which is something you want to avoid. The most common error is failing to sign the return. Here are 25 of the most common errors on income tax, employment tax, and other returns:

1. Illegible or incomplete business name and address (e.g., use of individual name instead of the business name).
2. Missing or multiple tax periods on Form 941 (quarterly employment tax return).
3. Incomplete Schedule B of Form 941 (supplemental record of federal tax liability).

4. Entering the same amount from a previous return (e.g., entering the same amount on line 3, total tax withheld from wages, tips, and sick pay, and line 7d, current year's tax withheld, on Form 941).

5. Not filing Form 941X to correct information.

6. Incomplete line 8 of Form 941 (total taxes after adjustments).

7. Missing or incorrect North American Industry Classification System (NAICS) code or incorrect principal business activity (PBA).

8. Incorrect sequencing of forms according to instructions to Forms 1120 (C corporations), 1120S (S corporations), and 1065 (partnerships and limited liability companies).

9. Unexplained short tax periods.

10. Missing or incomplete balance sheet.

11. Failing to properly apply limitations (e.g., 50% limitation on meals and entertainment).

12. Missing number of partners.

13. Missing, incomplete, or invalid SSN, TIN, or PTIN of the preparer.

14. Improperly showing real estate rental income or expense on Schedule E. This belongs on Form 8825 for partnerships and S corporations.

15. Showing income and expenses from sources other than real estate on Form 8825.

16. Missing or incomplete Schedule K-1.

17. Missing Schedule K (partners' distributive share items) or Schedule L (balance sheet per books) for Form 1065.

18. Missing additional statement detailing line 7 (other income) or line 20 (other deductions) on Form 1065.

19. Late or inaccurate filing of Form 2553 (election by a small business corporation to be treated as an S corporation).

20. Missing number of shares on Schedule L of Form 2553.

21. Missing Form 8869 (qualified subchapter S subsidiary election) when making such an election.

22. Missing or incorrect EIN.

23. Failing to elect association treatment on Form 8832 (entity classification election) when an LLC is electing S corporation status.

24. Missing or invalid effective date on line E of Form 2553.

25. Missing information in Part II of Form 2553 when selecting a tax year other than a calendar year.

Also pay special attention to include the following areas.

Salary of Corporate Officers

Some corporations have been claiming deductions for management or consulting fees paid to the corporation's owners. At the same time, these corporations have not claimed deductions for salary. This leads the IRS to conclude that the corporations are misclassifying payments to corporate officers as fees rather than compensation in order to avoid payroll taxes. Corporations may be liable for penalties for failing to withhold and deposit payroll taxes and for failing to file required payroll tax returns. Of course, sometimes payments to shareholders may very well be management or consulting fees for occasional outside assistance. But if these individuals conduct the actual business of the corporation—perform the services for which the corporation was organized or provide management services on a full-time or consistent basis—the payments look more like compensation.

S corporations especially may also fail to deduct compensation paid to owner-employees and instead call distributions to them *dividends*. The rationale for this strategy is to reduce the corporation's liability for payroll taxes. Again, the IRS has identified this strategy as a common error and has imposed penalties on S corporations that have followed it. If an owner-employee performs substantial services for the S corporation, some reasonable amount of payment for services must be treated as deductible compensation subject to payroll taxes.

Below-Market Loans

Loans from shareholders to their corporations that bear an interest rate lower than the applicable federal rate (a rate set monthly by the IRS, which varies with the term of the loan) result in phantom or *imputed* interest. Shareholders must report this interest; corporations can deduct the imputed interest. Of course, in today's low-interest rate environment, IRS attention to below-market loans may be minimal. Nonetheless, here are the rules to note. If the corporation fails to take an interest deduction, the IRS may conclude that the shareholder has not really made a loan but rather a contribution to the capital of the corporation, and no deduction for the corporation will be allowed.

Loans to shareholders from their corporations may also present tax deduction problems. Shareholders are entitled to deduct imputed interest in this case (as business or investment interest), with the corporation picking up the imputed interest as interest income. Unfortunately, some corporations are failing to report the income, but they are still showing the loan on their balance sheets. This is an unnecessary error for corporations to make. If the shareholders are also employees of the corporation, then the corporation can claim a deduction for compensation to the shareholder-employees to offset the imputed interest income. If, however, the shareholders are not employees of the corporation, the payments to them must be treated as dividends, which are not deductible by the corporation.

Travel and Entertainment Deductions

Some businesses claim a full deduction for business meals and entertainment. They do not correctly apply the 50% limit on these deductions. This problem commonly occurs for meals and entertainment away from home.

Bad Debt Deductions

Some individuals are claiming bad debt deductions as ordinary losses rather than short-term capital losses. In other words, they are classifying the bad debt as a business bad debt when, in fact, it may be a nonbusiness bad debt. For example, if a shareholder has a bad debt for a loan to the corporation, the loan should be treated as a nonbusiness bad debt because it is not incurred in a trade or business; rather, it is made to protect one's investment as a shareholder.

Casualty Losses

Some businesses fail to reduce deductions for casualty losses by any insurance reimbursements received. This results in an overstatement of casualty losses.

Claiming Losses in General

Some taxpayers claim losses in excess of amounts that are otherwise allowed. They fail to observe the passive loss limitation rules that limit loss deductions for activities in which there is no material participation. Just because someone owns stock in an S corporation, for example, does not mean that he or she is a material participant in the business. The shareholder must meet special material participation tests to deduct losses in excess of passive income.

Other taxpayers may be deducting hobby losses in excess of income from this type of activity. While income from a hobby-type activity is fully taxable, losses are deductible only to the extent of income from the activity.

Also, some shareholders in S corporations claim losses in excess of their basis in the corporation. Losses are deductible only to the extent of a shareholder's basis in stock and loans to the corporation. Basis is adjusted annually for various transactions—shareholder's distributive share of S corporation income that is taxable to the shareholder, distributions by the corporation, and losses claimed. Losses in excess of basis are not lost. They can be carried forward and used in a subsequent year when there is sufficient basis to offset them. *Important:* States may have different rules on the treatment of losses.

Tax Assistance

Your primary focus should be on running your business and making it profitable. This may leave you little or no time to attend to tax matters. It may be cost effective to use the services of a tax professional to maintain your books and records, file your returns, and provide needed tax advice.

There are many different types of tax professionals to choose from. The particular type of counsel you seek depends in part on your needs and what you can afford to pay for the services provided. The types of tax professionals you can consult include:

- Certified public accountants (CPAs)
- Enrolled agents
- Tax attorneys
- Tax return preparers who are not attorneys, CPA, or enrolled agents. The IRS will commence an Annual Filing Season Program that will allow unenrolled return preparers to voluntarily complete certain continuing education that will qualify them for limited permission to practice before the IRS. Note: AICPA has challenged this program in court.

Storefront tax return preparation services may provide assistance with filing your returns. They generally are not staffed to provide tax guidance.

Keep in mind that any information you disclose to an attorney is completely confidential under the attorney-client privilege. This privilege has been extended to other federally authorized tax practitioners (such as accountants) in civil tax matters. However, it does not apply to the following situations:

- Tax return preparation
- Criminal tax matters
- State tax matters (unless there is a special state-created accountant-client privilege)
- Matters involving other federal agencies (such as the Securities and Exchange Commission)

If there is anything you absolutely want to remain confidential, then you must use an attorney. The attorney may hire an accountant to perform accounting tasks and, as the attorney's agent, tax information disclosed to the accountant in this situation remains completely confidential.

If you do not know the name of a specific individual to help you, ask business acquaintances for referrals. Other sources of references are the Yellow Pages of your phone book and the Internet. For example, you can search for a tax attorney at www.martindale.com. If you wish to check whether a particular CPA is licensed as claimed, you can contact your state Society of CPAs. Similarly, if you want to check on a particular attorney, call your state Bar Association. Do not hesitate to ask the professional what he or she charges for the services to be provided.

Help from the IRS

The IRS has a web site exclusively for small business and self-employed individuals at www.irs.gov/Businesses/Small-Businesses-&-Self-Employed/Small-

Business-and-Self-Employed-Tax-Center-1. This site contains industry-specific information so, for example, if you are in construction you will find the hot issues relating to the construction industry. You will also find audit guides that tell IRS agents what to look for when examining returns of businesses within your industry. And there is a Self-Employed Individuals Tax Center at www.irs.gov/Businesses/Small-Businesses-&-Self-Employed/Self-Employed with help for Schedule C filers. You will also find links to other tax sites that may be helpful to you.

The IRS provides a number of publications, some of which have been mentioned throughout the book, that can give you important information on income and deductions. Table 24.2 lists some of these publications.

These publications are available directly from the IRS by calling (800) 829-3676 or by visiting your local IRS office, post office, or library. You can also download them from the IRS web site at www.irs.gov. Forms are also available by fax at (703) 368-9694.

The IRS provides a number of resource tools on CD-ROM. These include the Small Business Resource Guide, the Virtual Small Business Workshop, and Introduction to Federal Taxes (all of which are free).

Another valuable source of assistance is the instructions for particular tax returns. For example, if your business is an S corporation, you can obtain guidance on claiming various tax deductions from the instructions for Form 1120S.

You may want to attend a free IRS seminar offered to new business owners. Topics covered in these seminars include recordkeeping, tax filing requirements, employment taxes, and federal tax deposit rules. There are also special seminars for different types of businesses (e.g., S corporations). To find out about a seminar in your area, call the IRS's Taxpayer Education Coordinator (listed in your local phone book and available through the IRS's general number, (800) 829-1040). Or your can learn with your computer using the Virtual Small Business Workshop (mentioned earlier).

If you have questions, you may direct them to the IRS. There is a special telephone number to call for questions about your business return: (800) 829-4933. However, do not simply rely on statements made to you by someone in your local IRS office or over the telephone. If you want to rely on IRS advice, be sure to get it in writing (note the IRS employee's ID number). The IRS is not bound by oral advice, but it is bound by any written advice it may give you.

If you have a thorny tax issue involving substantial dollars and are not sure how the IRS will rule on the subject, you may want to obtain a special ruling. You can ask for a private letter ruling without the assistance of a tax professional, but this may not be the best course of action. You need to frame your question appropriately. Also, you need to supply a great deal of information to the IRS before it will take any action. A tax professional can ensure that your request will receive the attention you desire. The procedure entails the payment of a user fee that must accompany your ruling request.

TABLE 24.2 IRS Publications of Interest

Publication Number	Title
1-EP	Understanding the Employee Plans Examination Process
15	Circular E, Employer's Tax Guide
15-A	Employer's Supplemental Tax Guide
15-B	Employer's Guide to Fringe Benefits
51	Circular A, Agricultural Employer's Tax Guide
225	Farmer's Tax Guide
334	Tax Guide for Small Business
463	Travel, Entertainment, Gift, and Car Expenses
509	Tax Calendars
510	Excise Taxes
521	Moving Expenses
526	Charitable Contributions
535	Business Expenses
536	Net Operating Losses
537	Installment Sales
538	Accounting Periods and Methods
541	Partnerships
542	Corporations
544	Sales and Other Dispositions of Assets
547	Casualties, Disasters, and Thefts (Business and Nonbusiness)
550	Investment Income and Expenses
551	Basis of Assets
560	Retirement Plans for Small Business
583	Starting a Business and Keeping Records
584B	Business Casualty, Disaster, and Theft Loss Workbook
587	Business Use of Your Home (Including Use by Day-Care Providers)
590	Individual Retirement Arrangements (IRAs)
908	Bankruptcy Tax Guide
925	Passive Activity and At-Risk Rules
946	How to Depreciate Property
963	Federal–State Reference Guide
966	Electronic Choices to Pay All Your Federal Taxes
969	Health Savings Accounts and Other Tax-Favored Health Plans

TABLE 24.2 *(Continued)*

Publication Number	Title
1518	IRS Tax Calendar for Small Businesses and Self-Employed
1542	Per Diem Rates (available online only)
1544	Reporting Cash Payments of Over $10,000
1635	Understanding Your EIN
1779	Employee Independent Contractor Brochure
1932	How to Make Correct Federal Tax Deposits
1976	Do You Qualify for Relief under Section 530?
2194	Disaster Resource Guide
3066	Have you had your Checkup this Year for Retirement Plans
3144	Tips on Tips (A Guide to TIP Income Reporting) for Employer
3151-A	The ABC's of Federal Tax Deposits
3402	Taxation of Limited Liability Companies
3780	Tax Information for Small Construction Businesses
3909	Business e-File Talking Points
3998	Choosing a Retirement Solution for Your Small Business
4222	401(k) Plans for Small Businesses
4224	Retirement Plan Correction Programs
4263-E	Small Business Tax Workshops
4275	EFTPS Express Enrollment for New Businesses
4333	SEP Retirement Plans for Small Businesses
4334	SIMPLE IRA Plans for Small Businesses
4460	The Retirement Plan Productions Navigation
4591	Small Business Federal Tax Responsibilities
4674	Automatic Enrollment 401(k) Plans for Small Businesses
4806	Profit-Sharing Plans for Small Business
5022	Fast Track Settlement (for small business/self-employed tax issues)

If you have a problem with the IRS and cannot seem to get a satisfactory answer, you may want to ask the IRS to direct your question to its Problem Resolution section.

If you are having IRS problems that are causing you financial difficulty or significant cost, including the cost of professional representation, contact the National Taxpayer Advocate service (www.irs.gov/advocate) for free and confidential help.

CHAPTER 25

Tax Strategies for Opening or Closing a Business

Alert

At the time this book was printed, Congress had not extended numerous breaks for 2014 that had expired at the end of 2013. Check the online supplement in February 2015 at www.jklasser.com or www.barbaraweltman.com to see whether these breaks apply for 2014 returns.

Two of the most challenging times of running a business are, perhaps, the start-up and close-down phases. Taxwise, there are certain opportunities that should not be overlooked.

For further information, see IRS Publication 583, *Starting a Business and Keeping Records*.

Initial Tax Decisions to Make

When you start a business of any kind, whether a full-time or part-time one, you need to make certain choices. Here is a checklist of the elections, choices, and decisions to make when commencing a business (the chapter in which the item is discussed is also noted):

- *Type of entity* (Chapter 1). Should you incorporate? Form an LLC?
- *Tax year* (Chapter 2). Should you use a calendar year? A fiscal year (and which fiscal year)?
- *Accounting method* (Chapter 3). Should you use the cash method? Accrual method? Some other method?
- *Investing your own resources.* When you add money or property to a start-up, are there any immediate tax results to you? To the business?
- *Financing* (see below). If you need more money beyond what you can add, should you borrow money to start up? Should you take in investors?
- *Equipment* (Chapter 14). Should you start with the things you already own? Buy new equipment? Lease new equipment?
- *Home office* (Chapter 18). Should you start from home? Rent space? Buy a facility?
- *Workers* (Chapter 7). Should you hire employees or use independent contractors to perform the work that the business needs to get done?
- *Professional advisors* (Chapter 22). Who is going to be your company attorney? Accountant? Insurance agent? IT expert? Marketing expert?

None of the decisions you make initially are carved in stone. You can make changes, but often they come with tax consequences. For instance, if you start as a corporation and then want to become a limited liability company, you may incur taxes upon the corporation's liquidation. Similarly, when you change tax years or accounting methods, you may have additional income to report from the changeover.

It is always a good idea to work with knowledgeable professionals to get started on the right foot. The money you pay for this advice can be considerably less than the cost of mistakes for doing things incorrectly on your own.

Investing Your Own Resources

Most small businesses are started with the owner's own resources. When you add cash to your start-up, there are no immediate tax consequences to you or your business. The cash you add becomes part of your tax basis for your interest in the business. The company includes the cash on its balance sheet as an asset as well as owner equity.

However, when you add property to a business, things get a little more complicated. The results can depend on whether the business is incorporated or is a partnership as well as whether there is any outstanding liability on the property (e.g., a mortgage on a building you contribute to your business).

Partnerships and Limited Liability Companies

No gain or loss is recognized when you transfer property to a partnership or limited liability company (LLC) in exchange for an interest in the partnership or LLC. Gain may be recognized if your liabilities are assumed by noncontributing partners and these liabilities exceed your adjusted basis in the property you transfer to the business. Gain can also be recognized when a partnership or LLC interest is given in exchange for services you render.

Business's basis in transferred property. The business's basis in the property received is the same as your basis (increased by any gain you may have had to recognize). The business's holding period in the property it received includes your holding period in the property.

Owner's basis in partnership/LLC interest. Your basis in the interest is the same as your basis in the property transferred to the business, decreased by any liabilities you are relieved of and increased by any liabilities assumed by the business and any gain you recognize on the transfer.

Example

You and your sister form a partnership. You contribute cash of $60,000 for a 60% interest in the capital and profits of the business. Your sister contributes equipment with a fair market value of $110,000 and an adjusted basis of $45,000 and subject to a $70,000 liability for a 40% interest.

Your partnership basis: $60,000 cash + (60% × $70,000) = $102,000

Your sister's basis: $45,000 − $70,000 + (40% × $70,000) = $3,000

Partnership's basis in equipment: $45,000

Corporations

No gain or loss is recognized if property is transferred to a corporation by you and other persons solely in exchange for stock in such corporation, and immediately after the exchange such person or persons are in control of the corporation (at least 80% of the total combined voting power of all classes of stock entitled to vote and at least 80% of the total number of shares of all other classes of stock of the corporation). So if you transfer your computer, office furniture, truck, and $10,000 cash to your corporation in exchange for 100% of its stock, you aren't taxed on the transfer of the property. You cannot recognize any loss on the transfer.

If any loans are transferred as part of the incorporation (e.g., a loan on the truck), there may or may not be immediate tax results to you. You must recognize gain to the extent that the sum of your liabilities assumed by the corporation exceeds your basis in the property transferred.

The corporation does not have any gain or loss when it issues its stock for money or other property received during the incorporation.

Corporation's basis in transferred property. The corporation's basis in the assets you transfer to it is the same as your basis in the transferred property, increased by any gain recognized by you. The corporation's holding period in the property received includes your holding period in the property you transferred.

Shareholder basis in stock. Your basis in the stock received equals the basis of the property you transferred to the corporation. Your holding period in the property transferred carries over to the stock received, so you may immediately have a long-term holding period (depending on when you acquired the property you transferred to the corporation).

Debt versus Equity Financing

More than 80% of start ups require $10,000 or less of capital to get started. As mentioned earlier, most small business owners start with their own money, but some need additional financing. Even in this tight credit environment, you can still find the seed money you need if you know where to look. There are 2 main ways to get the capital you need for starting a business:

1. Debt (borrowing the money)
2. Equity (taking in investors)

You can use one financing method, the other method, or both. There are also alternative financing options. There are practical, legal, and tax considerations to your decision.

Debt Financing

Debt means borrowing money that must be repaid. For instance, you may go to a friend or a bank to raise the $10,000 you need to start up. The $10,000, plus interest, must be repaid to the lender (creditor) over a fixed period.

There are many places to look for loans: your own resources (e.g., using home equity loans), family and friends, and commercial loans (e.g., SBA-backed loans are obtained through commercial lenders and not directly from the SBA).

The positive thing about debt financing is that the relationship is limited in a couple of ways. First, the lender usually has no say in how you run your business. As long as you repay the loan on time, the lender is happy (you may be required to provide financial information on an ongoing basis to keep your loan in good standing). Second, the relationship has a limited duration. Once you've repaid the loan, you do not have to deal with the lender (unless you borrow new money).

The negative thing about debt is that it can be costly to you. Except when borrowing from family or friends in some cases, you must repay not only the amount you borrow ("principal"), but also interest. Typically, you will have to make money payments to the lender and this can be a drain on your cash flow.

Taxwise, you can deduct the interest you pay to the lender as a business expense. Repayment of principal is not deductible. You cannot disguise equity financing as debt in order to create an interest deduction. "Thin capitalization" (too much debt compared with equity) can raise IRS eyebrows and result in the disallowance of interest deductions.

There are a number of online ways to obtain loans for your business. For example, peer-to-peer lending may provide small amounts of needed capital. Sites include Lending Club (www.lendingclub.com), Peer-Lend (www.peer-lend.com), and Prosper.com (www.prosper.com).

Royalty financing. A twist on debt financing is an arrangement called royalty financing. It uses a percentage of company's revenue over a set period of time to repay a loan; there usually is a ceiling on the amount that the lender will be paid.

Equity Financing

Equity means ownership, so equity financing means sharing some ownership with an investor in exchange for money and/or property. For instance, say you need to raise $10,000 and you find an investor willing to provide it; you might give a 1%, 5%, or other interest in your business to the investor to secure this money.

There are a number of ways to find investors: Ask family or friends or look for angel investors (private individuals or groups who want to invest in small businesses). You can find interested angels through Angel Capital Association (www.angelcapitalassociation.org). Venture capital is typically used for startups with rapid, high-growth potential in such fields as biotechnology, information technology, and other emerging technology, that need $500,000 and up to launch; it is usually not suitable for the average small business start-up.

The positive thing about equity financing is that you are not required to make any paybacks to the investor; the investor is gambling on your success and will share in that some time in the future. In other words, with an investor, there is no monthly drain on cash flow as there is with debt servicing.

The negative thing about equity financing is that you have to share your profits. You also have created a long-term relationship with your investor: There is no fixed end to the relationship as there is with debt, which ends when the loan is repaid. Depending on the size of the investor's interest in your business, the investor may have a say in your day-to-day operations.

Taxwise, there is usually no immediate tax impact when an investor joins you in the business. Neither you, nor the company is taxed on the capital contribution (money and/or property) made to the company.

Equity crowdfunding. Small businesses can seek funding from small investors without having to go through extensive and costly government registration. Businesses cannot raise the funds directly from investors; they must use Securities and Exchange Commission (SEC)–approved portals (web sites designed for this purpose).

The SEC proposed a rule that has not yet been finalized to enable equity crowdfunding platforms to begin offerings (check the Supplement for any update). You can follow developments on equity crowdfunding through the Small Business & Entrepreneurship Council at www.sbecouncil.org/resources/crowdfunding.

Some states have created an exemption from the federal rules to allow intrastate equity crowdfunding. This means residents can invest in businesses within their state through crowdfunding platforms in their state. Thus far, Georgia, Indiana, Kansas, Maine, Michigan, Washington, and Wisconsin have created an intrastate exemption. Alabama, New Jersey, North Carolina, and other states may do so soon. If you are interested in raising capital through crowdfunding and are based in a state permitting intrastate equity crowdfunding, look for a platform in your state (a website dedicated to equity crowdfunding).

Other Financing

Debt and equity are not the only financing options for start-ups.

Grants. Business-related grants usually are limited to companies that will create jobs within an economically distressed area or provide some other community benefit; the grant application process is complex, so this financing option is limited. Grants are tax free. But some payments, called grants, may not be tax free (e.g., government assistance following natural disasters).

Contests. Contests, usually sponsored by major corporations, can provide first-prize winnings of $5,000, $25,000, or more. There is no central listing for contests; just stay alert to these opportunities. Prize winnings are fully taxable.

ROBS. In recent years, some businesses are using an owner's 401(k) fund to get started. Rollovers as business start-ups (ROBS), which are being aggressively marketed to would-be entrepreneurs, have been identified by the IRS as *potential* abusive transactions, according to Monika Templeton, director of the Employee Plan Examinations Office. The IRS also has a compliance project for ROBS (go to www.irs.gov and search "rollovers as business start-ups compliance project"). Here's how ROBS work: An entrepreneur uses his/her 401(k) or other plan benefits to finance a new venture without paying taxes on the funds in the plan. The entrepreneur incorporates the business and sets up a qualified retirement plan into which the owner rolls over the 401(k); the funds in the new qualified plan are then used to buy company stock (i.e., put cash into the company). While the IRS hasn't gone so far as to define this arrangement as abusive, it's on the IRS watch list so entrepreneurs should beware!

Other crowdfunding. Raise money in small increments from complete strangers through websites designed for this purpose. These people essentially donate small amounts to help businesses get started. In some cases, there is no return to the contributors; in others there is a nominal benefit to contributors. Crowdfunding websites include 40Billion.com (www.40billion.com/), CoFolio (http://mycofolio.com/), Kickstarter (www.kickstarter.com), Indiegogo (www.indiegogo.com), MicroVentures (www.microventures.com/business_funding), NewJelly (www.newjelly.com), and Startup Addict (www.startupaddict.com).

Find general information about small business loans, grants, and other financing at SBA.gov (www.sba.gov/catergory/navigation-structure/loans-grants).

Tax Identification Numbers

For personal returns, your Social Security number is your tax identification number. But for business you may have several different numbers.

Your tax identification number is a 9-digit number unique to you. You use this number when filing tax returns, making tax deposits, hiring employees, opening a business bank account, applying for a loan, and setting up a qualified retirement plan. Usually you use a federal employer identification number (EIN) obtained from the IRS as your tax identification number (even if you are not an employer because you do not have any employees).

If you are a sole proprietor (or the sole owner of a limited liability company), you can usually use your Social Security number as your tax identification number on your income tax return. But even this type of business must use an EIN for a business bank account, to report payroll taxes, and to start a Keogh, SEP, or SIMPLE plan. And, in this era of identity theft, you may want to use an EIN if you pay an independent contractor $600 or more for the year and are required to report this income to the IRS and the contractor on Form 1099-MISC, so that you do not have to give your Social Security number to the contractor.

Where to Get Your EIN

You can obtain your federal EIN by completing IRS Form SS-4, *Application for Employer Identification Number*, online at www.irs.gov and search "EIN Online" (see Chapter 1).

When you apply online, the IRS automatically enrolls you in the Electronic Federal Tax Payment System (EFTPS) (www.eftps.gov). This electronic system enables you to make tax payments, including estimated taxes, online. After automatic enrollment, you will receive an enrollment confirmation, along with a PIN and instructions within a few days. Without a payroll, you are not required to use EFTPS, but may choose to do so for the convenience. Millions of small businesses have voluntarily signed on to use EFTPS.

State EINs

States may assign their own tax identification numbers (also called business registration numbers) to your business for unemployment insurance reporting for employees and for other purposes, typically at the time you register to do business in your state. For more information about your state EIN, contact your state tax, revenue, or finance department.

If you do business in New York, Massachusetts, and South Carolina, you can register with the IRS and state in one step (go to www.irs.gov, search "state and federal online business registration," and click on the applicable state).

> **NOTE**
>
> Changing the name of your business requires you to notify the IRS. How you do this depends on your entity type:
>
> - Sole proprietors can simply write to the IRS about the change.
> - Partnerships should mark the appropriate box on their return for the year (line G, box 3 of Form 1065).
> - Corporations should mark the appropriate box on their return for the year (line E, box 3 of Form 1120 for C corporations and line H, box 2 of Form 1120S for S corporations).
>
> You may also need a new employer identification number in some cases (check with the IRS).

Resale Number Distinguished

Business owners are responsible not only for income and employment taxes, but also for state and local sales taxes on the goods and services they sell. In order to properly remit sales tax that you collect to your state and to avoid paying sales tax on items you buy for resale, you need a resale number (states without sales tax—Alaska, Delaware, Montana, New Hampshire, and Oregon—do not issue resale numbers). Your state sales tax number (called a resale number, a seller's permit, or sales tax license) is *not* the same as your federal tax identification number.

Once you have your resale number, your state may permit you to continue to use it as long as you are in business; in other states you must renew the resale number periodically. For information on obtaining a resale number, contact your state tax, revenue, or finance department.

Other Numbers

As a business, you may need other identification numbers:

- The DUNS number is one assigned to you by D&B, a business credit rating service. This number is not used for tax purposes, but is required if you do any government contracting. Having this number also enables you to more easily build business credit.

- State unemployment insurance may assign your business a number when you enroll to pay this tax.

Tax Reporting for the First Year

Most businesses do not start on January 1, so the first year of business may be a "short year" (less than a full 12 months). From a tax-reporting standpoint, a return must be filed for the short year. For example, if a business that reports on a calendar-year basis starts to operate on August 10, 2014, it must file a return for 2014. It does *not* have to prorate deductions for the period in which it operates.

Indicate on the appropriate tax return that, being the first year of the business, this is the initial return. This is done as follows:

- Schedule C—Line H
- Form 1065—Line H(1)
- Form 1120S—Line F(1)
- Form 1120—Line E(1)

How to Write Off Start-Up Costs

Once you're in business, most expenses become deductible items (tax rules may affect when you can claim deductions or may place certain limits on the amount you can write off). Before you open your doors, you do not have a business in which to claim the deductions. Therefore, it is important to separate start-up costs from those incurred by an operating business.

Start-up costs may be deductible once you actually start your business, but they are not deductible during your preopening phase.

A complete discussion of items viewed as start-up costs and how to deduct them is found in Chapter 14.

Setting Up a Business Bank Account and Credit Card

Once you have set up your business and obtained your tax identification number, it is highly advisable to set up a separate business bank account. Use this account exclusively to deposit business receipts and to pay business expenses.

Do not commingle the funds in your business bank account with your personal money.

If you are self-employed, it is also advisable to set up another account for your personal estimated taxes. Use this account to set aside the funds needed to pay your quarterly estimated taxes. Often small-business owners who were formerly employees of large corporations that had withheld income taxes on their behalf are unfamiliar with estimated tax requirements on their share of business income and can fall short of the money needed to meet this tax obligation.

It is also a good idea to use a separate credit card solely for business purchases. Having both a separate business bank account and credit card simplifies recordkeeping for your business. Further, it helps to show that you are running your company in a businesslike fashion in case the IRS questions whether losses should be disallowed under the hobby loss rules (see Chapter 26).

Moving a Business

Businesses may relocate. The full cost of moving company property is deductible. Tax rules for deducting moving costs by self-employed individuals are in Chapter 22.

However, if your business receives relocation payments from a state agency under the federal Uniform Relocation Assistance and Real Property Acquisitions Act, you do not have to report the payments as income; you *cannot* deduct your moving costs.

Use Form 8822-B, *Change of Address–Business*, to inform the IRS of a change of address or change of location.

Aborted Business Ventures

What happens if you investigate the purchase of a business or the start of a venture but the deal never goes through? Or if you hire an architect to design a building but never get town approval for the construction? The costs of starting up and organizing a business are not immediately deductible in full (but may be amortized, as explained in Chapter 14). However, the costs of an aborted business venture are immediately deductible.

To deduct your costs, you must have proceeded beyond a general search. Once you focus on a particular business and the deal falls through, you can deduct your expenses. Mere investigatory expenses are not deductible; only those related to a specific business are. Thus, for example, if you travel to look at various business opportunities, you cannot deduct your travel costs. But once you select one particular business and begin drawing up contracts, your legal costs for the contracts are deductible even if they never get signed.

The Tax Court has allowed a deduction for a $25,000 fee paid to acquire a franchise where the purchaser decided to walk away rather than complete the deal after learning that the franchisor had flooded the area with stores, many of which were losing money.

Bankruptcy

Bankruptcy, the "b" word, is a last resort for businesses on the ropes that cannot resolve things with their creditors. That was the action that Hostess Brands (manufacturer of Twinkies and Wonderbread), Dewey & LaBoeuf (a national law firm), and Eastman Kodak took in 2012, and many small businesses have to do the same. Bankruptcy is a legal process that can enable a company to stay in business ("reorganization" where a plan is used to provide partial satisfaction to creditors so the business can emerge after the process with a fresh start) or go out of business in an orderly fashion ("liquidation" where assets are sold and the proceeds used to pay off creditors to the extent possible).

Which Form of Bankruptcy to Use

Your choices for bankruptcy protection depend on how your business is organized (entity type) and whether you want to stay in business if possible.

- *Sole proprietors.* Owners are treated like other individuals. They can get a fresh start under Chapter 7 of the bankruptcy law, but most are forced to use a payment plan under Chapter 13.
- *Family farmers.* Farmers can use a simplified reorganization plan under Chapter 12 of the bankruptcy law if debts fall within a certain limit.
- *Other business entities.* The entities can be liquidated with proceeds distributed to creditors under Chapter 7, or can be reorganized under court supervision to continue operations under Chapter 11. *Caution:* General partners can be sued by the trustee in bankruptcy if partnership assets fall short of partnership debts.

Which type of bankruptcy solution is best for a business? It depends on the facts and circumstances. Sole proprietors may have no choice but to use the repayment plan, whether or not they continue the business operations.

Other entities may prefer to liquidate if they see the business as a failure (they have no heart for continuing the business); if the market is such that even if economic conditions recover, the business wouldn't be viable; or if the debts are so overwhelming that restructuring doesn't make economic sense.

Tax Implications of Bankruptcy

If some or all of your debts are extinguished in bankruptcy, you are not taxed on the discharge (cancellation) of indebtedness.

Bankruptcy can provide some relief from taxes. First, filing for bankruptcy creates an automatic stay on collection activities (the IRS as well as state and local tax authorities must stop hounding you for money). Second, some outstanding taxes can be dischargeable; others cannot. This is a highly complex area, and you are advised to work with a knowledgeable tax advisor if you are considering filing for bankruptcy.

Bankruptcy Alternative

If you want to continue your business, you can work with a credit professional to help restructure the company's debts. This lets you work your way out of debt in a manageable manner and avoid bankruptcy. For example, Corporate Turnaround (www.corporateturnaround.com) negotiates on your behalf with vendors, lessors, credit card companies, and other business creditors to set up a repayment plan that you can handle.

When you are seeking a company to help restructure your debt, look for members of the Turnaround Management Association (www.turnaround.org/ Membership/Browse.aspx), an international nonprofit association dedicated to corporate renewal and turnaround management. Members sign a code of ethics to provide professional, competent assistance.

Tax Implications of Debt Forgiveness

If you don't file for bankruptcy and instead convince creditors to accept partial payment, the amount of debt forgiven is treated as discharge (or cancellation) of indebtedness income. Whether such income is taxable to you depends on whether you are insolvent at the time of the forgiveness (insolvency means your liabilities exceed your assets). If you are insolvent, no tax consequences result from the discharge of indebtedness. If you are not insolvent, the forgiveness is taxable, but you can opt to adjust tax attributes so you'll effectively pay the tax later. See Chapter 5.

Expenses of Winding Up a Small Business

Unfortunately, the cold statistics show that many small businesses fail. Some last longer than others, but a large number of ventures will reach a point where they are so unprofitable that the owners must simply give up. Certain expenses relate to the closing up of a small business. They are deductible business expenses.

Unamortized Costs

If you have been amortizing certain items, such as organizational or incorporation fees, you can deduct the unamortized amounts on a final return for the business. For example, say the business was formed in January 2012 and elected to amortize organizational costs above $5,000 over 180 months, but it goes under after 30 months. You can deduct 150/180 of your organizational costs on the final return, in addition to any of the amortization allowed for the final year of the return.

Other Expenses

You may incur special costs for going out of business. For example, a corporation may have to pay a special fee to the state corporation or franchise department when terminating. There may also be additional legal and accounting fees for winding up a business. Again, these costs are deductible business expenses.

Professionals who wind up their practice but continue to carry professional liability coverage to protect themselves from claims arising from work already performed can deduct the insurance premiums in full as a current deduction in the final year of the practice.

Tax Reporting in the Final Year

As is the case in starting a business, most businesses do not shut their doors on December 31, so the final year of business may be a "short year" (less than a full 12 months). From a tax-reporting standpoint, a return must be filed even though the business did not operate for the entire year. For example, if a business that reports on a calendar year basis ceases operations on August 10, 2014, it must file a return for 2014. It does *not* have to prorate deductions for the period in which it operates. For example, if the business closes 8 months after paying a one-year subscription, it can deduct the full 12 months, even though it enjoyed only 8 months' worth of magazines.

Indicate on the appropriate tax return that this is the final year of the business. This is done as follows:

- Schedule C—no entry required
- Form 1065—Line G(2)
- Form 1120S—Line F(2)
- Form 1120—Line E(2)

Obtain a *tax clearance* or *consent to dissolution* from your state to close your tax account. If you fail to do this, you may continue to be liable for annual filings and be subject to penalty for not doing so.

Special Rules for Corporations

Corporations must notify the IRS of their termination. This is done by filing Form 966, *Corporate Dissolution or Liquidation*, with the IRS within 30 days after the plan or resolution of liquidation is adopted.

The corporation must recognize gain or loss on the distribution of its assets to shareholders in complete liquidation. In determining gain or loss, the assets

TABLE 25.1 Checklist of Actions for Closing a Business

Done	N/A	Action
		Cancel business credit cards
		Cancel business insurance policies; obtain refunds of premiums paid
		Cancel permits, licenses, and registrations
		Close business bank accounts after all business matters have been concluded
		Get out of leases for office/store space, rented equipment, and business vehicles
		Keep records safe (e.g., retain tax returns, employment records, corporate minutes, and other necessary documentation)
		Notify employees, customers, and suppliers
		Notify the state unemployment division
		Resolve outstanding financial obligations (settle debts; pay bills that are owed)

are valued at their fair market value on the date of the distribution. Thus, a C corporation should retain sufficient cash to cover its tax liability resulting from a liquidation.

Shareholders are taxed on the liquidation distribution of money and assets. Their gain (or loss) is the difference between their basis in the stock of the corporation and what they receive. This is the final so-called double tax, because a C corporation pays tax on the liquidation and then the shareholders do, too, on the net amount they receive.

You must also follow state rules for dissolving your corporation. Even if you shut your doors for business, you have to formally terminate the corporation under state law in order to avoid continuing tax and fee obligations to the state. In order to dissolve the corporation, your state tax obligations must be up to date; you cannot dissolve the corporation if you owe the state any money. Check state rules through www.statelocalgov.net.

Other Details

Once the business has been terminated and a final return filed, be sure to wind up all other matters for the company (see the checklist of actions to take in Table 25.1). This includes notifying suppliers, canceling leases and permits, and closing bank accounts and business credit cards.

Be sure to retain business records even after you have closed your doors. Follow basic recordkeeping rules. This means retaining income tax–related records for a minimum of 3 years and employment tax–related records for a minimum of 4 years.

Tax Strategies for a Sideline Business

Alert

At the time this book was printed, Congress had not extended numerous breaks for 2014 that had expired at the end of 2013. Check the online supplement in February 2015 at www.jklasser.com or www.barbaraweltman.com to see whether these breaks apply for 2014 returns.

Millions of Americans today have a sideline business, especially today when many have only part-time jobs are are underemployed. Having a sideline business has become easy with the advent of eBay and other online marketplaces. But sideline businesses, such as dog breeding and gentleman farming, have been around for years.

Starting and running a sideline business can be a savvy move, especially in tough economic times. It can be a way to supplement your current income. It can be a safety net in case of a job dislocation. And it can be a way to test the waters for a full-time business in the future, say, on retirement.

For a further discussion of business expenses, see IRS Publication 535, *Business Expenses*.

Reporting Sideline Business Income

There's a basic rule when it comes to income from a sideline business: You must report it. There is no minimum revenue or number of sales you must make before income becomes reportable. You must report income, whether or not it is reported to the IRS (such as on Form 1099 for payments to independent contractors).

Of course, all of the revenue you take in may not necessarily be profit. You can deduct expenses (subject to the limits explained throughout this book as well as the hobby loss limit next), which may mean that there is no income subject to tax.

Hobby Losses

If your unincorporated business sustains losses year after year, you may not be able to deduct the losses in excess of your business income unless you can show that you have undertaken the business in order to make a profit. This limitation on losses is called the *hobby loss rule*, because it is designed to prevent individuals who collect coins and stamps, breed dogs or cats, or carry on other hobby activities from deducting what the tax law views as personal expenses. Any activity you do mainly for recreation, sport, or personal enjoyment is particularly suspect.

But the hobby loss rule is not limited to these types of activities. It can apply to any activity—even investment activities intended to produce only tax losses for investors. In fact, the IRS even tried to apply the hobby loss rule to a young attorney just starting her practice. The IRS argued that the losses she sustained were not deductible because of the hobby loss rule. The attorney was able to show a profit motive (proof of a profit motive is explained later), and she was allowed to deduct her losses.

The hobby loss rule applies to individuals (including partners and LLC members) and S corporations. It does not apply to C corporations. For partnerships, LLCs, and S corporations whose business losses pass through to owners, the determination of whether there is a profit motive is made at the business level rather than at the owner level. In other words, the business itself must have a reasonable expectation of making a profit. The fact that an individual owner has a profit motive does not transform a hobby loss into a deductible loss if the business does not reasonably have a profit motive. A business may be able to establish a profit motive in one year even if this cannot be done for another year.

Impact of Hobby Classification

If your business is classified as a hobby, then any year in which you make a profit you must pay taxes on your entire profit. Any year you have losses (expenses exceeding income), you cannot deduct them. What is more, you cannot carry over the unused losses to claim them in another year. You lose the deduction for your losses forever.

Proving a Profit Motive

There is no hard and fast way for proving that you have *profit motive*. Rather, a profit motive is something that is inferred on the basis of various factors. The burden of proof is on you, the taxpayer. No single factor is determinative. Some or all of the factors used to determine profit motive include:

- *Whether you carry on the activity in a businesslike manner.* This means that you keep good books and records separate and apart from your personal records, and have a business bank account, telephone, stationery, and other indices of a business. Having a written business plan and marketing plan is also helpful. Some tax experts also believe that taking the formal steps to create a limited liability company or an S corporation helps to prove a profit motive.
- *Whether the time and effort you put into the activity shows that you intend to make a profit.* If you spend only a small amount of time on it, this may show that there is no realistic way in which you can make a profit.
- *Whether you depend on the income from the activity for your livelihood.* If you do, then obviously you hope to make a profit to live on.
- *Whether you change methods of operation to improve profitability.* If you get the advice of experts, this shows you want to make a profit.
- *Whether the activity is profitable in some years, and how much profit is realized in those years.* Certainly an activity may not always be profitable, but if there has already been a profit in some years and that profit is substantial, this shows an expectation of continued profit.
- *Whether you or your advisers have the know-how needed to carry on your business at a profit.* If you undertake some activity that you enjoy but know nothing about, this may indicate a lack of profit motive.
- *Whether you can expect to see a profit from the appreciation of the assets used in the activity.* You may not necessarily realize profit from the operations of the business, but its assets may prove to be profitable. A realistic expectation of this profit from the appreciation of business assets shows profit motive.

The Court of Federal Claims has allowed a taxpayer with multiple activities to aggregate them in order to establish a profit motive. In other words, if one activity has a loss but is part of an overall plan to make a profit, the loss may be allowed.

Presumption of a Profit Motive

Your business may not be profitable, particularly in the early or start-up years. The tax law gives you a special presumption on which you can rely to show a profit motive (and delay an IRS inquiry into your activity). An activity is presumed to be engaged in for profit if you have a profit in at least 3 out of 5 years. If the activity is breeding, training, showing, or racing horses, the presumption period is 2 out of 7 years. If you meet this presumption, then the hobby loss rules do not apply, and your losses in the off years can be claimed in excess of your income from the activity.

You can rely on this presumption and avoid having the IRS question your losses by filing Form 5213, *Election to Postpone Determination as to Whether the Presumption Applies that an Activity Is Engaged in for Profit*. In effect, the form asks the IRS to delay a determination of your profit motive until the end of the 5-year (or 7-year) period.

Generally, you must file Form 5213 within 3 years of the due date of the return for the year in which you first carry on the activity. You should know within this time whether you can reasonably expect to be profitable and avoid the hobby loss rules or whether you need to rely on the presumption to gain additional time for the business to make a profit.

The downside to filing this form is that it extends the statute of limitations (the period in which the IRS can question your return and assess additional taxes). In this case, the statute of limitations is extended to 2 years after the due date of the return for the last year of the presumption period. However, it is extended only for deductions from the activity and any related deductions. Other items on your return, such as your personal itemized deductions, are not affected by this extension of the statute of limitations.

Is it a good idea to file Form 5213 and raise the presumption? Doing so is almost a guarantee that the IRS will look closely at your return. Should you not show a profit in the required number of years during the presumption period, you will be forced to argue that you have a profit motive despite recurrent losses. Thus, you are probably no better off than if you had not filed the form.

Business Expenses

Any type of expense you could deduct for a full-time business applies to a sideline activity as well. The only question is whether the hobby loss rule limits your annual write-off.

Home Office Deduction

If you run a sideline activity from your home, you can claim a home office deduction as long as you meet the home office rules (see Chapter 18). The office need not be used for a full-time activity. As long as it is your principal place of business for a sideline activity, you can deduct related expenses.

Other Business Expenses

From start-up to shut-down and in between, expenses incurred in a sideline activity are viewed as deductible costs just as if it were a full-time business. There are *no* deductions barred to you merely because you do not work full-time at this activity.

Where to Report Hobby Income and Expenses

Unless the activity is a business, hobby income is reported as "Other Income" on Form 1040. There is no additional form or schedule to complete, although you can attach your own statement explaining the income.

Deductions from a hobby activity are reported as miscellaneous itemized deductions on Schedule A subject to the 2%-of-AGI rule and the reduction in itemized deductions for high-income taxpayers.

Tax Strategies for Multiple Businesses

Alert

At the time this book was printed, Congress had not extended numerous breaks for 2014 that had expired at the end of 2013. Check the online supplement in February 2015 at www.jklasser.com or www.barbaraweltman.com to see whether these breaks apply for 2014 returns.

"Multiple businesses" connotes multinational corporations with intertwining ownership of many entities. But small business owners may conduct different activities through various entities. These entrepreneurs simultaneously own and usually run 2 or more businesses.

There may be sound legal, business, and tax reasons for using multiple businesses rather than funneling all activities through a single entity. Liability issues, for example, are one good reason for operating separately activities through more than one business. This chapter focuses primarily on the tax implications of running multiple businesses.

Advantages and Disadvantages of Multiple Entities

Some activities can naturally and logically exist within a single entity. For example, a beauty salon can provide grooming services and sell beauty products using a single business. This makes sense. This can be done, for example, using a single entity or a holding company, with different activities run by different divisions, each with its own name.

For other situations, however, conducting different activities through separate entities makes more sense. Here are some pros and cons to using multiple entities.

Legal Reasons

There are usually no legal bars under state law to operating different activities within a single business. But separate entities are a way to create the utmost liability protection. Typically, building owners form separate LLCs or corporations for each property. In this case, it is not the owner's personal liability that is being protected in case of lawsuits, but rather the assets of the properties on which the liability did *not* arise. For instance, say an individual owns 2 small motels. If there is a legal action against one motel, the other can be at risk unless each is a separate legal entity.

Business Reasons

Administratively it may be easier and less costly to run a single entity, but the activities may not be suitable to be joined in a single business. For example, say a computer consultant operating as a single-member LLC also has an active eBay business. From a marketing perspective, it does not make good business sense to conduct the eBay activities through the LLC; they can be run as a sole proprietorship or other entity formed exclusively for online selling.

Tax Reasons

There may be tax reasons for separating businesses into different entities. Depending on the nature of each activity, one might be better operated on a calendar year, while it makes better sense to use a fiscal year for another.

It is usually wise to use a separate entity to own real estate that will be used by the business. This allows the owner to make decisions regarding the real estate without involving the business. For example, a single owner of a dental practice run as a professional corporation may buy a professional building, using an LLC. The practice can lease space from the LLC, but the owner can decide when or if to sell the building. For instance, for estate planning reasons, the owner may decide to gift interests in the LLC to family members and cede ownership and/or control to younger relatives. As long as the terms of the lease are fair (i.e., a reasonable rent is charged), the practice can deduct its lease payments even though it is the dentist who is ultimately receiving the rents as owner of the LLC.

In deciding between a single entity or multiple entities, factor in the passive activity loss rules. If you are a silent partner in one activity and active in the other, losses from the silent (passive) activity cannot be used to offset income from the active business; if these separate activities were run within a single entity, income could be offset by losses, and it might be possible that no activity would be viewed as a passive activity because of your level of participation in the overall business.

In deciding between a single entity or multiple entities, take state taxes into account. The added cost of additional state taxes for multiple entities may make using a single entity preferable.

When to Run Multiple Activities within One Business

It is not always better to use multiple businesses. Sometimes a single entity can meet business needs, with no tax disadvantages. Here are some reasons to opt for a single entity:

- *Savings on legal and accounting costs*. A single entity cuts down on the cost for entity formation as well as ongoing costs for accounting and tax return preparation. Series LLC (also referred to as cell LLCs), which is a group of individual LLCs, can be formed in Delaware, Illinois, Iowa, Kansas, Missouri, Montana, Nevada, Oklahoma, Tennessee, Texas, Utah, (to a lesser extent) Wisconsin, and the District of Columbia. In this type of organization, the debts and liabilities of each LLC remain separate from those of the other LLCs. But using a master LLC makes things administratively easier and less costly.

- *State tax savings*. Where state law imposes a tax, a single entity reduces franchise or other annual tax costs. For example, California charges an annual fee for LLCs (in addition to the annual fee on their revenues), so using separate entities can get pricey.

Treatment of Multiple Corporations

C corporations that have certain intertwining ownership are called "controlled corporations" and are subject to special tax treatment. There are 2 types of controlled corporations:

1. *Parent-subsidiary controlled group*. One corporation owns (directly or indirectly) at least 80% of the stock of one or more other corporations.

2. *Brother-sister controlled group*. Two or more corporations are owned by 5 or fewer persons (persons include not only individuals, but also estates

and trusts), who together possess at least 50% of the total voting power or value of the corporation and more than 50% of the combined voting power or value of all stock.

Example

An individual owns all the stock of Corporation A and 75% of the stock of Corporation B. A and B are a brother-sister controlled group.

The status of a group can change from year to year. For instance, in the brother-sister situation, a sixth shareholder can enter the picture so that the group of corporations is no longer a controlled group.

Advantages and Disadvantages

There are both advantages and disadvantages of a controlled group.
Advantages include:

- Minimizing payroll taxes when an employee works for more than one related corporation. Under the "common paymaster rule," one corporation is designated as the paymaster responsible for payroll taxes so that each corporation does not pay payroll taxes that could have been avoided. For instance, in 2014 if a shareholder works for his 2 controlled corporations, earning $125,000 from each, one is designated as a paymaster and pays the employer's Social Security portion of FICA on wages up to $117,000, a tax of $7,254. Without a common paymaster, each corporation would owe this tax.
- Flexibility to sell off property or business units without selling the entire business. But if a member of a brother-sister group sells property at a loss to another member of the group, the loss is not deductible in the year of sale but is postponed until the property is sold outside the group.
- State tax simplification (filing a single return for the group).
- Ability to attract investors or obtain financing.
- Different tax elections (accounting method and tax year) are still allowed.

Disadvantages include:

- Graduated corporate tax brackets must be allocated (to prevent each corporation from enjoying the benefit of the lower brackets).
- Allocation required for other tax breaks, including first-year expensing (Sec. 179 deduction), the AMT exemption, the accumulated earnings tax exemption, the disabled access credit, and certain other tax breaks.
- Postponement of loss recognition on intergroup sales.

- Employees of each corporation are treated as a group for purposes of employee benefits and retirement plans (e.g., testing for nondiscrimination of a plan must take employees of all group members into account).

The losses of one corporation cannot be used to offset the profits of another unless the group files a consolidated corporate income tax return.

Tax Rules for Owners of Multiple Businesses

The tax impact of multiple businesses is not limited to controlled corporations. There may be special rules or limitations on owners of multiple businesses.

Tax Returns

Each entity is required to file separate federal income tax returns. For example, a sole proprietorship for consulting and another for a gift basket business must each complete a separate Schedule C.

Separate returns are also due at the state level in states that impose an income tax or annual filing requirement.

Entities that own or are owned by other entities may have to disclose this information on their tax returns. For example, corporations must include detailed information about ownership in Schedule K of Form 1120 if any foreign or domestic corporation, disregarded entity, partnership, or trust owns (directly or indirectly) 20% or more of the total voting power of all classes of the corporation's stock entitled to vote. Such information includes the name of the entity, its employer identification number, type of entity, country of organization, and percentage owned of the voting stock.

First-Year Expensing

The Section 179 deduction applies at the owner level for pass-through entities. Thus, individuals who own more than one such business must use care to optimize this write-off.

Example

An individual has a sole proprietorship and is a 50% member of a limited liability company. In 2014, the sole proprietorship buys equipment exceeding $500,000 (assuming that the 2013 limit is extended for 2014; see the Supplement) and elects to take the full first-year expensing. The LLC also buys equipment and elects the full expensing amount. As a result, the individual's Schedule K-1 from the LLC allocates $250,000 to her (50% of the $500,000 deduction). Even though her total expensing amount is $750,000 ($500,000 + $250,000), on her personal return she can only claim a maximum deduction of

$500,000; $500,000 is wasted. It cannot be carried forward. Instead of this result, her sole proprietorship could have elected to expense only $500,000 of equipment purposes and depreciate the balance, allowing her both the full expensing amount and some depreciation as well.

Retirement Plans

Having separate entities can help owners boost their retirement savings.

Example

B has a sole proprietorship and an LLC. Each is highly profitable. Each business can set up a simplified employee pension (SEP) plan and add for 2014 up to $52,000 on behalf of B, so that the owner's retirement savings for the year is $104,000.

But owners of multiple businesses are subject to an overall limitation on salary reductions, the so-called employee share of contributions, to 401(k) plans and SIMPLE plans. In 2014, for example, the maximum employee contribution to a 401(k) plan is $17,500 ($23,000 for those 50 and older by year-end). If an owner's multiple businesses each maintains 401(k) plans, the most he or she can add in 2014 is this dollar limit.

Example

C, age 45, has a sole proprietorship with a solo 401(k) and is a 50% owner of an S corporation that maintains a 401(k) plan. If he contributes $17,500 to his sole proprietorship's plan, he cannot make any salary reduction contributions to the S corporation's plan. In this situation, the salary reduction should be made to the plan that provides the greater employer contribution.

Multiple businesses with common ownership are treated as a single business for qualified retirement plan rules (see Chapter 16).

Employer Mandate

Whether you are required to provide minimum essential health coverage depends on the number of your full-time and full-time equivalent employees (see Chapter 19). All employees of your multiple businesses are taken into account using the same rules that apply to retirement plans (see above).

Alternative Minimum Tax

Alert

At the time this book was printed, Congress had not extended numerous breaks for 2014 that had expired at the end of 2013. Check the online supplement in February 2015 at www.jklasser.com or www.barbaraweltman.com to see whether these breaks apply for 2014 returns.

Reducing regular tax is only part of the battle that a small business owner wages to increase after-tax returns. Minimizing or avoiding alternative minimum tax (AMT) where applicable is another important front that must be addressed. Some business owners may find themselves subject to AMT if they have certain substantial deductions and/or credits.

Alternative Minimum Tax Basics

Alternative minimum tax is designed to ensure that all taxpayers pay at least some tax. Years ago, with tax shelters and other loopholes, wealthy individuals and corporations often paid little or no tax. In an effort to make all taxpayers share the tax burden, an AMT was imposed.

The AMT is a separate tax system, with its own deductions and tax rates. A taxpayer computes the regular income tax as well as a tentative AMT. The extent to which the tentative AMT exceeds regular tax liability is reported as AMT.

Alternative minimum tax liability for individuals can be reduced by certain personal tax credits, including a limited foreign tax credit (corporations can reduce their AMT liability only by a limited foreign tax credit). There are 2 different AMT structures: one for C corporations and another for individuals.

C corporations pay AMT at the rate of 20%. This rate is applied to *alternative minimum taxable income* (AMTI) reduced by an exemption amount of $40,000 (reduced by 25% of the amount by which AMTI exceeds $150,000). Alternative minimum taxable income includes an *adjusted current earnings* (ACE) adjustment. This adjustment is designed to measure income tax on as broad a basis as it is for financial reporting purposes.

Individuals have a two-tier AMT rate structure of 26% on the first $182,500 of income subject to AMT in 2014 (called alternative minimum taxable income or AMTI), plus 28% on any excess amount. For married persons filing separately, the 26% rate applies to AMTI up to $91,250. The amount subject to these tax rates is reduced by an exemption amount. This exemption amount is phased out for high-income taxpayers.

The AMT exemption amounts for 2014 are:

- $52,800 for single (unmarried) individuals
- $82,100 for married persons filing jointly and surviving spouses
- $41,050 for married persons filing separately

The exemption for individuals phases out when AMTI exceeds a threshold amount that depends on your filing status. For 2014, the thresholds are:

- $117,300 for single (unmarried)
- $156,500 for married persons filing jointly and surviving spouses
- $78,250 for married persons filing separately

Fortunately, AMT liability can be offset by nonrefundable personal credits.

Who is subject to the AMT? Potentially all businesses are subject to AMT. However, small C corporations may be exempt, as explained later in this chapter. Owners of pass-through entities (partnerships, LLCs, and S corporations) figure AMT on their individual returns. They include business items passed through to them and identified as AMT items on their Schedule K-1.

Exemption for Small Corporations

Small corporations are entirely exempt from AMT.

Small corporation A C corporation with average gross receipts of $7.5 million or less for the prior 3 tax years ($5 million for the first 3 years, or portion of time in business).

Example

X, Inc., a C corporation, had average gross receipts of $275,000 for the 3-year period that included 2011, 2012, and 2013. For 2014, X is a small corporation and therefore is exempt from AMT.

New C corporations (those with the first tax year being 2014), other than those aggregated with other corporations, are exempt from AMT in 2014 without regard to gross receipts. The tax law simply assumes that start-ups are small corporations.

Once your business is established as a small corporation, it retains that status (and is exempt from AMT) as long as its average gross receipts for the prior 3-year period do not exceed $7.5 million. The first year of small corporation status is ignored for purposes of this 3-year period.

LOSS OF SMALL CORPORATION STATUS

If your business succeeds to the extent that it loses its small corporation status, special AMT rules continue to apply *to formerly small corporations*. These rules simplify AMT for such corporations. In general, these corporations start fresh for certain AMT items and never have to make certain AMT adjustments.

NOTE

While a C corporation generally can claim a tax credit with respect to AMT liability incurred in a prior year, a small corporation can claim only a limited AMT credit.

Deduction Limits for Alternative Minimum Tax

Certain deductions that were allowed for regular tax purposes may be disallowed or modified for AMT. The following deductions that were claimed on individual returns may not be deducted for AMT purposes:

- Personal exemptions
- Any addition to the standard deduction
- Itemized deduction for taxes
- Itemized deduction for miscellaneous expenses

The following deductions that were claimed on individual returns must be modified for AMT purposes:

- Investment interest.
- Itemized deduction for medical expenses (only expenses in excess of 10% of adjusted gross income are deductible for AMT purposes, while those in excess of 7.5% of AGI are deductible by those age 65 and older for regular tax purposes).
- Itemized deduction for home mortgage interest (only interest to buy, build, or substantially improve a principal residence or second home is deductible for AMT purposes, while interest on home equity loans used for other purposes may be deductible for regular tax purposes).
- Depreciation.
- Net operating losses (NOLs).
- Mining exploration and development costs (the regular tax deduction must be amortized over 10 years).
- Research and experimentation expenditures (costs must be amortized over 10 years if you are not a material participant in the business).
- Passive activity losses from nonfarming activities (losses are adjusted for items not deductible for AMT purposes).

ADJUSTMENTS FOR DEPRECIATION

The depreciation method that you use for regular tax purposes may require that an adjustment be made for AMT purposes. For AMT purposes you are allowed only a limited depreciation deduction. If you claimed more for regular tax purposes, you must adjust your AMT income accordingly.

For property (other than real property) acquired after 1986, your AMT depreciation is limited to the 150% declining balance method, switching to straight line when a larger depreciation deduction results. For real property acquired after 1986, your AMT depreciation is limited to straight line over 40 years.

NOTE

Different adjustments apply to property placed in service before 1987. Follow the instructions to Form 6251.

For real property placed in service after December 31, 1998, an AMT adjustment is no longer required. For personal property placed in service after this date, a depreciation election can be made to use the same depreciation method for regular and AMT purposes so that an AMT adjustment is avoided. By making this election, depreciation is figured using the 150% declining balance method over the regular tax recovery period (instead of the 200% declining balance method). For an explanation of these depreciation methods, see Chapter 14.

PREFERENCE ITEMS

Certain items that may have escaped the regular tax are subject to AMT. These include:

- Tax-exempt interest on private activity bonds issued after August 7, 1986.
- Exclusion of 50% of the gain on the sale of small business stock (see Chapter 5).
- Oil and gas preferences.
- Accelerated depreciation on real property acquired before 1987.

NET OPERATING LOSSES

The NOL deduction for regular tax purposes must be adjusted for AMT. This is because only a limited NOL deduction is allowed for AMT purposes. The NOL for AMT purposes is the regular tax NOL except that the nonbusiness deduction adjustment includes only AMT itemized deductions (i.e., state and local taxes and certain other deductions cannot be used to figure the NOL deduction).

You may be able to eliminate your AMT liability because of your NOL deduction. However, the NOL deduction cannot be more than 90% of AMT income (without regard to the NOL deduction). If you cannot use all of your NOL because of the 90% limit, you may carry it back and forward under the applicable carryback/carryforward periods (explained in Chapter 4). However, the carryback and carryforward NOLs are also subject to the 90% limit.

OTHER ADJUSTMENTS AND PREFERENCES

In figuring AMT income on which AMT tax is imposed, certain income items are also given special treatment. These include incentive stock options, long-term contracts, tax-exempt interest on private activity bonds, and basis adjustments for AMT gain or loss.

For C corporations other than small C corporations, the key adjustment that can trigger AMT is the ACE adjustment. However, since small corporations are exempt from AMT, this adjustment is not explained further.

Credit Offsets

Only certain tax credits can be used to offset AMT liability. Components of the general business credit *cannot* be used to offset this tax. In 2014, the only credits that can offset AMT liability include:

- *Foreign tax credit*.
- *Certain personal tax credits*. Nonrefundable personal credits can be used to offset the AMT.

Minimum Tax Credit

If you paid AMT last year, you may be eligible for a tax credit this year. Different minimum tax credits apply for individuals and corporations.

Individuals

You qualify for a minimum tax credit if you meet any of the following 3 conditions:

1. You paid any AMT in 2013.
2. You had an unused minimum tax credit that you carried forward from 2013 to 2014.
3. You had certain unallowed business-related credits in 2013.

The credit is the amount of AMT paid in 2013 reduced by the part of the tax related to exclusion items (standard deduction, medical expenses, taxes, miscellaneous itemized deductions, gains on small business stock, tax-exempt interest from private activity bonds, and depletion). The credit may be increased by minimum tax credit carryforwards, and unallowed credits for nonconventional-source fuel, and orphan drugs.

Compute the credit on Form 8801. If the credit exceeds your AMT liability for 2014, the excess amount may be carried forward and used to offset AMT liability in a future year. There is no limit on the carryforward period.

Corporations

Unlike an individual's minimum tax credit which is limited to exclusion items, corporations that paid AMT in a prior year may claim a tax credit in 2014 if they have no AMT liability this year. Compute the credit on Form 8827, *Credit for Prior Year Minimum Tax—Corporations*.

Of course, since small corporations are exempt from AMT, only large corporations can have a minimum tax credit.

Where to Figure Alternative Minimum Tax

Self-Employed

If you have any adjustments or preference items, you must complete Form 6251, *Alternative Minimum Tax—Individuals*. You may or may not have any AMT liability. You can use a special AMT Assistant from the IRS at http://www.irs.gov/Businesses/Small-Businesses-&-Self-Employed/Alternative-Minimum-Tax-(AMT)-Assistant-for-Individuals to see immediately whether you will owe any AMT. The entries are anonymous and the results instantaneous.

Partnerships and LLCs

The business reports an owner's share of AMT items on Schedule K-1. As an owner, you must complete Form 6251 to see if you owe any AMT.

S Corporations

The business reports an owner's share of AMT items on Schedule K-1. As an owner, you must complete Form 6251 to see if you owe any AMT.

C Corporations

Small C corporations exempt from AMT are not required to complete any special forms. Other C corporations figure their AMT liability on Form 4626, *Alternative Minimum Tax—Corporations*.

Other Taxes

Alert

At the time this book was printed, Congress had not extended numerous breaks for 2014 that had expired at the end of 2013. Check the online supplement in February 2015 at www.jklasser.com or www.barbaraweltman.com to see whether these breaks apply for 2014 returns.

Federal income taxes may be your primary concern and your greatest tax liability, but as a business owner you may have other tax obligations as well. You may owe state income and franchise taxes, employment taxes, sales and use taxes, and excise taxes.

Estimated taxes, which are not a separate tax but rather a way in which to pay taxes, are discussed in Chapter 30.

For more information about various other taxes, see IRS Publication 15, *Circular E, Employer's Tax Guide*; IRS Publication 15-A, *Employer's Supplemental Tax Guide*; IRS Publication 15-B, *Employer's Guide to Fringe Benefits*; and IRS Publication 510, *Excise Taxes*.

State Income Taxes

You may owe state income taxes on your business profits in each state in which you do business. Your obligation does *not* depend on where the business is set up. For example, if you incorporate your business in Nevada but operate in California, you owe income taxes to California, the state in which you do business. (And you may owe a tax or fee to Nevada as well.)

Generally, state income taxes usually depend on having a nexus (connection) to the state. This is based on having a physical presence there, which may be evidenced by maintaining an office or sending a sales force into the state; merely shipping goods into the state without some additional connection is not enough to establish a business presence within the state. You may have a nexus to more than one state, no matter how small your business is.

If there is a business connection to more than one state, the business income is apportioned among those states. Apportionment is based on a sales factor, a payroll factor, and a property factor (each state has different apportionment formulas). The apportionment rules are highly complex, but there is some flexibility that permits you to shift income into the state with the lower taxes within certain limits.

Some states are moving toward commercial or financial nexus as a basis for imposing state income tax. Doing business with consumers and companies in other states may expose you to taxes that you never dreamed of. States are reaching out across their borders to grab revenue from out-of-state businesses in any way they can.

- *Sourcing of services revenue.* This is a tax on services performed out of state that benefit businesses within the state that imposes the tax. For example, an advertising firm based in Connecticut provides services for a business in California. The State of California imposes a tax, to be paid by the Connecticut firm, on the services that benefit the California business. Believe it or not, a business can be subject to double taxation—income tax on revenue earned in its state plus the sourcing of services tax on the benefits received in another state. There is no credit that can be claimed for the out-of-state taxes; they are, however, deductible. So far, this type of income tax applies in California, Georgia, Illinois, Iowa, Maine, Maryland, Michigan, Minnesota, Ohio, Oklahoma, Utah, Washington, and Wisconsin.

- *Gross receipts tax.* This is a tax on all business-to-business transactions within the state. Unlike an income tax, there are no deductions or other write-offs to reduce the tax exposure. Currently, this tax is imposed in Arizona (called a transaction privilege tax), Delaware, Hawaii (general excise tax), New Mexico, Ohio (commercial activity tax), Oregon (business and occupation tax), Pennsylvania, Texas (margin tax), Washington (business and occupation tax), and West Virginia (to a very limited extent).

If you are a sole proprietor or an owner of a pass-through entity, you must file a state income tax return in every state in which your company does business (if such state has a personal income tax). For example, if an LLC does business in 12 states, all of which impose an income tax, each member of the LLC must file a personal income tax return in those 12 states.

Of course, even if you do business within a state, there may be no tax liability. For example, Wyoming does not have a personal or corporate income tax so there is no tax even if you do business in this state.

The filing deadlines for state business returns are not the same as the federal deadlines in all cases, so check with your state tax authority for the forms to file and when to file them. You may also need to obtain a state tax identification number for your business.

Corporations

Corporations may owe state corporate income tax. In some states this is called a **franchise tax**.

Franchise tax   State tax imposed on a state-chartered corporation for the right to do business under the corporate name within the state (it has nothing to do with whether the business is a franchise).

S corporations in most states are taxed in the same way as they are taxed for federal income tax purposes (i.e., income, losses, etc., pass through to shareholders to be reported on their personal income tax returns). However, if the S corporation has shareholders who are not residents of the state, special rules may apply (for example, the corporation may be required to make tax payments on behalf of these shareholders).

In most taxes, the S election for state tax purposes is automatic if a federal election is filed. However, in about half a dozen states you must file a separate state tax election for S corporation status (merely filing the federal election is not sufficient for state tax purposes).

Some states, such as New York and Rhode Island, allow S status but also impose an annual corporate-level tax for the privilege of being an S corporation. The corporate-level tax applies even though the income and deductions of the corporation pass through to shareholders and are taxed on their personal returns.

Some states that recognize S status still tax some of the S corporation's income (e.g., S corporations in Indiana pay tax on their capital gains and excess passive income).

Some localities, such as the District of Columbia, do not recognize S corporation status. They tax the entity as a regular C corporation.

For more information about the state income taxes, contact the tax or revenue departments of each state in which you do business. You can find contact information in Table 29.1 or through www.statelocalgov.net.

TABLE 29.1 State Tax Authorities

State/Agency	Telephone	Website
Alabama—Department of Revenue	(334) 242-1170	www.ador.alabama.gov
Alaska—Department of Revenue	(907) 465-2320	www.revenue.state.ak.us
Arizona—Department of Revenue	(602) 255-3381	www.azdor.gov
Arkansas—Department of Finance and Administration	(501) 682-7089	www.dfa.arkansas.gov
California—Franchise Tax Board	(800) 852-5711	www.ftb.ca.gov
Colorado—Department of Revenue	(303) 238-7378	www.colorado.gov/revenue
Connecticut—Department of Revenue Services	(800) 382-9463 (860) 297-5962 (out of state)	www.ct.gov/drs
Delaware—Division of Revenue	(800) 577-8205	http://revenue.delaware.gov
District of Columbia—Office of Chief Financial Officer	(202) 727-2476	http://cfo.dc.gov
Florida—Department of Revenue	(800) 352-3671	http://dor.myflorida.com/dor
Georgia—Department of Revenue	(877) 423-6711	https://etax.dor.ga.gov
Hawaii—Department of Taxation	(808) 587-4242	http://tax.hawaii.gov
Idaho—State Tax Commission	(208) 334-7660	http://tax.idaho.gov/
Illinois—Department of Revenue	(217) 782-3336	www.revenue.state.il.us/
Indiana—Department of Revenue	(800) 457-8283	www.ai.org/dor
Iowa—Department of Revenue	(515) 281-3114	www.iowa.gov/tax
Kansas—Department of Revenue	(785) 368-8222	www.ksrevenue.org
Kentucky—Department of Revenue	(502) 564-4581	http://revenue.ky.gov
Louisiana—Department of Revenue	(225) 219-7462	www.rev.state.la.us/
Maine—Maine Revenue Services	(207) 626-8475	www.state.me.us/revenue/

(Continued)

TABLE 29.1 *(Continued)*

State/Agency	Telephone	Website
Maryland—Comptroller of Maryland	(410) 260-7980	www.comp.state.md.us
Massachusetts—Department of Revenue	(617) 887-6367	www.mass.gov/dor
Michigan—Department of Treasury	(517) 373-3200	www.michigan.gov/treasury
Minnesota—Department of Revenue	(651) 556-3075	www.revenue.state.mn.us
Mississippi—Department of Revenue	(601) 923-7000	www.dor.ms.gov
Missouri—Department of Revenue	(573) 751-4541	http://dor.mo.gov
Montana—Department of Revenue	(406) 444-6900	http://revenue.mt.gov
Nebraska—Department of Revenue	(402) 471-5729	www.revenue.nebraska.gov
Nevada—Department of Taxation	(775) 684-2000	http://tax.state.nv.us/
New Hampshire—Department of Revenue Administration	(603) 271-2191	www.revenue.nh.gov
New Jersey—Division of Revenue	(609) 826-4400	www.state.nj.us/treasury/taxation
New Mexico—Taxation and Revenue Department	(505) 827-0700	www.tax.newmexico.gov
New York—Department of Taxation and Finance	(800) 338-0054	www.tax.ny.us
North Carolina—Department of Revenue	(877) 252-3052	www.dor.state.nc.us
North Dakota—Tax Commissioner	(701) 328-7088	www.nd.gov/tax
Ohio—Department of Taxation	(800) 282-1780 (individuals) (888) 405-4039 (businesses)	www.tax.ohio.gov
Oklahoma—Tax Commission	(405) 522-8165	www.tax.ok.gov
Oregon—Department of Revenue	(503) 378-4988	www.oregon.gov/DOR
Pennsylvania—Department of Revenue	(717) 787-1064	www.revenue.state.pa.us
Rhode Island—Division of Taxation	(401) 574-8829	www.tax.ri.gov

TABLE 29.1 *(Continued)*

State/Agency	Telephone	Website
South Carolina—Department of Revenue	(803) 898-5709 (401) 574-8829	www.sctax.org
South Dakota—Department of Revenue	(605) 773-3311	http://dor.sd.gov
Tennessee—Department of Revenue	(615) 253-0600	www.tennessee.gov/revenue
Texas—Comptroller of Public Accounts	(800) 252-1381	www.window.state.tx.us/taxes
Utah—Tax Commission	(801) 297-2200	http://tax.utah.gov
Vermont—Department of Taxes	(802) 828-5723	www.state.vt.us/tax
Virginia—Department of Taxation	(804) 367-8031	www.tax.virginia.gov
Washington—Department of Revenue	(800) 647-7706	http://dor.wa.gov
West Virginia—Department of Revenue	(304) 558-3333	www.revenue.wv.gov
Wisconsin—Department of Revenue	(608) 266-2776	www.revenue.wi.gov
Wyoming—Department of Revenue	(307) 777-7961	http://revenue.wyo.gov

Other Income-Based State Taxes

States seem to be able to dream up new taxes when there is a need for revenue. For example, in New York, there is a Metropolitan Commuter Transportation Mobility tax imposed on self-employed individuals and business owners in New York City and the 7 counties that surround it. For self-employed individuals, the tax is 0.0034 of net earnings from self-employment, even if they do not venture into New York City. The tax is payable 4 times a year, but is not included with income taxes or payroll taxes. Find information about this tax at www.tax.state.ny.us/mctmt/default.htm.

Employment Taxes

You may be liable for the payment of certain taxes with respect to the compensation you paid to your employees. If you own a corporation, these obligations apply even if you are its *only* employee. If you are a single member limited liability company, you are treated as a separate entity for employment taxes, even though you are a "disregarded entity" for reporting and paying your own income taxes; you must report employment taxes on wages paid to employees, under your entity name and using an employer identification number (not your Social

Security number). As a small business owner, you need to know what taxes you are responsible for, where and when to deposit the taxes, and what returns you must file for employment taxes. The returns you must file are discussed later in this chapter. In this section you will learn about employment taxes and where to deposit them. The deductibility of these taxes is discussed in Chapter 13.

Employment taxes (also called *payroll taxes*) is a term that collectively refers to an employer's tax obligations with respect to employee compensation. Employment taxes include income tax withholding (both federal and, where applicable, state), FICA (the employer and employee share, as explained later), FUTA (federal unemployment tax, as explained later), and state unemployment tax. There may also be state disability taxes.

You may find assistance on employment tax obligations for small businesses at www.irs.gov and search "small business and self-employed tax center." You should also contact your state tax department to learn about your state employment tax obligations.

Employment Tax Obligations

The Federal Insurance Contribution Act (FICA) set up a (Social Security and Medicare) system to provide for old age, survivors, disability, and hospital insurance of workers. Both you, the employer, and your employees contribute to this system. The Federal Unemployment Tax Act (FUTA), together with state unemployment systems, provides payment to workers in the event of unemployment. Only employers pay this tax.

NOTE
The U.S. Justice Department's Tax Division has indicated it will aggressively pursue unpaid employment taxes, which can include paying employees in cash so that wages are unreported. A willful failure to collect or pay employment taxes is punishable by fines up to $250,000 for individuals and/or jail time up to 5 years.

You must withhold from your employees' wages income tax and the employee portion of Social Security and Medicare tax. These taxes are referred to as *trust fund* amounts because you, as employer, are holding the funds in trust for your employees. You must pay over these amounts to the IRS. You must also pay the IRS the employer portion of Social Security and Medicare tax, which is the same amount that the employee paid, plus FUTA.

Are severance payments paid to terminated workers treated as wages for purposes of employment taxes? It depends on which court you ask. In a *Quality Stores* case in 2010, a U.S. district court ruled that severance payments are not wages for purposes of FICA; the Sixth Circuit agreed with the lower court. However, in an earlier case called *CSX Corporation Inc.*, a federal appeals court said just the opposite. Now the U.S. Supreme Court has settled the matter in favor of the government, ruling that severance payments to terminated workers are wages for employment tax purposes.

Employment taxes must be figured to the penny. You cannot round off employment taxes to the nearest dollar (as you can with income taxes).

FICA

The tax rate for the Social Security portion of FICA is 6.2% of the first $117,000 of wages in 2014. This wage base is adjusted annually for inflation. Both the employer and employee pay this tax rate on the taxable compensation up to the wage base limit. The tax rate for the Medicare portion of FICA is 1.45% on all compensation. There is no wage base ceiling for purposes of computing this tax. You must withhold this amount from the employee's compensation and pay a similar amount as the employer. Usually, FICA is paid on deferred compensation when it is earned, not when it is paid.

FUTA

The tax rate for FUTA is 6.0% of the first $7,000 of each employee's wages. However, you may claim a credit for payments to state unemployment funds of up to 5.4% of taxable wages if all state payments were made in a timely fashion. Thus, the effective FUTA rate in most cases is 0.8% of the first $7,000 of each employee's wages.

States that owe the federal government money borrowed to pay unemployment benefits give employers a reduced credit. Information about credit reduction states for 2014 can be found in Chapter 13.

INCOME TAX WITHHOLDING

In addition to FICA and FUTA tax you may owe, you may also be required to withhold income taxes from employee compensation. Your withholding is based on each employee's withholding allowances and marital status as reported to you on Form W-4, *Employee's Withholding Allowance Certificate.* These forms should be completed when employment commences and need not be updated each year (unless the employee chooses to do so). If an employee fails to complete Form W-4, then withhold as if the employee were single with no withholding allowances. Employers must retain these forms and make them available to the IRS if requested.

It is important to note that the definition of compensation is, in some instances, different for purposes of income taxes and employment taxes. For example, a salary reduction that is contributed to an employee's 401(k) plan or Savings Incentive Match Plan for Employees (SIMPLE) plan is not treated as compensation subject to income tax. However, the salary reduction is still subject to FICA and FUTA.

Wage differential payments made to employees while they are on active duty for more than 30 days are subject to income tax withholding but not to FICA and FUTA. Withholding on wage differential payments can be made

NOTE

The IRS looks closely at family hiring. Make sure that the wages are reasonable for the work performed. Keep timesheets as proof of work performed by your relatives.

by using withholding tables, or ordinary pay can be aggregated with wage differential payments and subjected to a flat 25% withholding, as long as this compensation is less than $1 million.

Table 29.2 can be used to determine your employment tax obligations for various fringe benefits you may provide to employees in 2014.

EMPLOYING FAMILY MEMBERS

If you are self-employed and employ your child who is under age 18, his or her wages are not subject to FICA. If you employ your spouse in your business, his or her wages are fully subject to FICA. If you have a corporation that employs a child under age 18, his or her wages are still subject to FICA. Your child's wages are exempt from FUTA until he or she reaches age 21.

LEASED EMPLOYEES

If you lease employees from a corporation that supplies workers for your business, the employees may be treated as in the employ of the corporation that does the leasing rather than as your employees. The leasing corporation, and not you, is responsible for the payment of employment taxes.

Special Rules for Tips

Tips that employees receive are taxable wages for purposes of employment taxes. Employees are *supposed* to report their tips to employers so that employment taxes can be applied. However, as a practical matter, this is not always the case.

The U.S. Supreme Court has said that the IRS can use an estimated aggregation of unreported tips to assess FICA tax on employers; the IRS does not have to audit each employee to determine actual unreported tips for purposes of determining the employer share of FICA.

To avoid this forced rate upon employers, the IRS has developed voluntary compliance agreements for industries, such as the restaurant industry, where tipping is customary. These agreements are designed to enhance tax compliance among tipped employees through education and avoid employer examination during the period that the agreements are in place. They include:

- Tip reporting alternative commitment (TRAC)—avoids the establishment of a tip rate, requires all employers to educate employees on tip reporting requirements, requires employees to report monthly to employers, and provides for audits of those employees who underreport.
- Tip rate determination agreement (TRDA)—sets a tip rate through employers cooperating with the IRS; requires employees to sign a Tipped Employee Participation Agreement with the employer (75% of whom must sign).

TABLE 29.2 Your Employment Tax Obligation on Common Fringe Benefits

Fringe Benefit	Withhold Income Tax	Pay Social Security and Medicare Taxes	Pay Federal Unemployment Tax (FUTA)
Achievement awards (within limits)	No	No	No
Adoption assistance up to $13,190	No	No	No
Athletic facilities	No	No	No
Company car personal use	Yes	Yes	Yes
De minimis benefits	No	No	No
Dependent care assistance up to $5,000			
Rank-and-file employees	No	No	No
HCEs* (if plan discriminates)	Yes	Yes	Yes
Education assistance up to $5,250—not job related	No	No	No
Any job related	No	No	No
Elective deferrals to 401(k), SEP, or SIMPLE plans	No	Yes	Yes
Employee discounts			
Rank-and-file employees	No	No	No
HCEs* (if plan discriminates)	Yes	Yes	Yes
Flexible spending arrangement salary contribution	No	No	No
Group term life insurance	No	No up to cost of $50,000 of coverage	No
Health insurance			
Rank-and-file employees	No	No	No
More-than-2% S corporation shareholders	Yes	Yes	Yes
Health savings account contributions	No	No	No
Lodging on the premises	No	No	No
Meals on the premises	No	No	No
Medical care reimbursements under a self-insured plan	No	No	No

*HCEs are highly compensated employees—owners and employees earning over a set dollar limit that adjusts annually for inflation.

TABLE 29.2 *(Continued)*

Fringe Benefit	Withhold Income Tax	Pay Social Security and Medicare Taxes	Pay Federal Unemployment Tax (FUTA)
Moving expenses	No	No	No
No-additional cost services	No	No	No
Stock options ISOs	No	No when granted; yes when exercised	No when granted; yes when exercised
Employee stock purchase plans	No	No when granted; Yes when exercised	No when granted; Yes when exercised
Nonqualified stock options	Yes when exercised	Yes when exercised	Yes when exercised
Supplemental unemployment compensation plan benefits	Yes	No	No

Transportation benefits
   Rank-and-file employees
   More-than-2%
   S corporation shareholders
	
	No
	Yes
		
		No
		Yes
			
			No
			Yes

Vacation pay	Yes	Yes	Yes
Working condition benefit	No	No	No

- Employer-designed tip reporting alternative commitment (EmTRAC)—solely for those in the food and beverage industry whose employees receive both cash and charged tips, this program generally follows the TRAC program.
- Gaming Industry Tip Compliance Agreement (GITCA)—solely for the gaming (casino) industry.

SERVICE CHARGES

As of January 1, 2014, restaurants that have an 18% service charge for large groups (e.g., 8 or more people) or other similar charge cannot treat the charge as a tip. Instead, service charges are considered wages subject to the usual income tax and FICA withholding. This means that the service charges are not taken into account by employers when figuring the credit for FICA on tips (see Chapter 23).

Sometimes it's not easy to distinguish between a tip and a service charge. A customer's payment can be treated as a tip only if *all* of the following conditions are met:

1. The payment is made free from compulsion
2. The customer has the unrestricted right to determine the amount

3. The payment is not the subject of negotiation or dictated by the employer's policy

4. The customer has the right to determine who receives the payment

If you show computations of various percentages as tips possibilities, this does not create a service charge

---

Examples

The customer's bill comes to $68.43. The printed bill presented to the customer shows a calculation for a 10% tip of $6.43, a 15% tip of $10.26, and an 18% tip of $12.31. It's up to the customer what, if anything, to add to the bill for the server. Whatever is added is a tip.

The customer's bill comes to $142.58 for a party of 6. As is the practice in the restaurant, 18% is automatically added to the bill, bringing the total to $167.80 ($142.58 + $25.22). The 18% addition to the bill is a service charge representing wages for the server.

Paying Employment Taxes

When employment taxes must be paid to the IRS is determined in part by the size of the tax liability. The largest employers (more than $50,000 in employment taxes in the previous calendar quarter) pay ("deposit") their employment taxes semiweekly (every 2 weeks); those that are not quite as large ($50,000 or less in employment taxes) do so every month. Employers of very small businesses (less than $2,500 in employment taxes in the calendar quarter or previous calendar quarter) can submit their employment taxes along with their quarterly employer tax returns. The smallest employers ($1,000 or less for income tax withholding and FICA or a FUTA payment under $500) can pay annually. For FUTA, this means employers with 8 or fewer employees qualify for making one annual payment.

In the past, most employers deposited their taxes with a bank using a paper deposit coupon issued by the IRS. Now all employers, other than those that pay their taxes with returns, must deposit taxes electronically using the Electronic Federal Tax Payment System (EFTPS) (www.eftps.gov). With EFTPS, funds are transferred from your bank directly to the U.S. Treasury.

Very small employers that are not required to use EFTPS can voluntarily do so. One benefit of doing so is the ability to schedule payments in advance. Note that using EFTPS does not give the IRS access to your bank account. If you wish to voluntarily enroll, you can do so online at www.eftps.gov or call 1-800-945-8400 or 1-800-555-4477.

TABLE 29.3 Deposit Schedule

Type of Deposit Schedule	Due
Monthly	15th day of the following month
Semiweekly	
Payment on Wednesday, Thursday, and/or Friday	Following Wednesday
Payment on Saturday, Sunday, Monday, and/or Tuesday	Following Friday

DEPOSIT DATES

Depending on the size of your payroll, you are put on one of 2 deposit schedules, *monthly* or *semiweekly*. (See Table 29.3.) The IRS notifies all employers each November of their schedule for the coming calendar year. The determination of your deposit schedule is based on your employment taxes during a lookback period (2 years prior to the upcoming year). If your employment taxes were $50,000 or less in the lookback period, you are on a monthly deposit schedule. If your employment taxes exceeded $50,000 in the lookback period, you are on a semiweekly deposit schedule. It is important to note that even if you are put on a monthly deposit schedule, you need not file the quarterly employment tax return monthly or more frequently unless the IRS instructs you to file Form 941-M, *Employer's Monthly Federal Tax Return*. Remember, the amount of your employment taxes, not the time you pay your employees (i.e., weekly, semimonthly, monthly), determines your depositor status.

If the bank is closed on the required deposit date, the deposit is made on the next banking day.

PAYMENT WITH RETURNS

Instead of depositing employment taxes, you can pay them directly to the IRS along with your return if your net tax liability for the quarterly return is less than $2,500. Thus, for example, if you have 1 employee who earned only $10,000 for the quarter, employment taxes will be under $2,500, so you can pay them directly to the IRS when you file your return, Form 941. If you are not sure whether your quarterly employment taxes will cross the $2,500 threshold, it is advisable to deposit the taxes monthly in order to avoid a penalty.

For FUTA taxes, the deposit threshold is $500. This means that companies with 8 or fewer employees can pay this tax annually when the annual FUTA return is filed.

You can pay employment taxes by credit card to cover any balance due on the return. There is a convenience fee charged by the credit card service provider: Official Payments at www.officialpayments.com, LINK2GOV Corporation at https://www.pay1040.com/, and PayUSAtax at www.payUSAtax.com.

Penalty for Failure to Pay Employment Taxes

As an employer, you are required to deduct and withhold income taxes and FICA from your employee's compensation. If you fail to do so, or if you withhold an insufficient amount, you are still liable for the correct amount.

There is a 100% penalty imposed on persons who are responsible for paying employment taxes but fail to do so. This penalty, called the *trust fund recovery penalty* (because an employer pays income tax withholding and the employee's share of Social Security and Medicare taxes into a trust fund maintained by the government for the employee's benefit), is a personal one against an owner, officer, or other responsible person. Thus, for example, a shareholder in a corporation who serves as company president may be personally liable for this penalty even though a shareholder generally is not liable for corporate debts.

Even if there is more than one responsible person, the IRS can collect the entire tax and penalty from one person. It is up to that one person to try to recover a portion of the payment from other responsible persons. If you make a written request, the IRS must notify you of the name of the person that it has determined to be responsible and whether it has attempted to collect the penalty from other responsible persons. There is *federal right of contribution* (to collect a share of the penalty by someone who has paid it from someone else who is also responsible) where there are multiple responsible persons.

Penalty for Delinquent Deposits

Unless you can show reasonable cause for failing to deposit required amounts or paying deposits directly to the IRS instead of depositing the employment taxes, you will be subject to a penalty. The penalty schedule is designed to encourage employers to comply with deposit requirements as quickly as possible. The penalty is 2% if deposits are made from one to 5 days late; it increases to 5% for deposits 6 to 15 days late. The penalty jumps to 10% for deposits more than 15 days late, deposits made at unauthorized financial institutions or directly to the IRS, and amounts paid to the IRS within 10 days of a first notice asking for tax due. A 15% penalty applies to amounts outstanding more than 10 days after a first notice from the IRS of amounts due or the day on which you receive a notice and demand for immediate payment, whichever is earlier. However, you can designate the period for which payment is made to avoid cascading penalties.

> **CAUTION**
> In view of this substantial penalty, it is essential that employment taxes be paid. If you are experiencing a cash crunch, see that these taxes are paid before satisfying other creditors.

State Employment Tax Obligations

As mentioned earlier in this chapter, as an employer, you should check out your obligation, if any, for state employment taxes.

Self-Employment Tax

Self-employed individuals—sole proprietors, general partners, and LLC members who are not treated as limited partners—are not employees of their businesses even though they may be compensated for their services. Thus, they are not subject to FICA. However, self-employed individuals bear the same tax burden as owners who work for their corporations; they pay self-employment tax.

As a general rule, self-employed individuals pay self-employment tax on net earnings from self-employment. This includes a sole proprietor's net profit reported on Schedule C (or C-EZ) or Schedule F, and a general partner's self-employment earnings reported on Schedule K-1 of Form 1065, plus any guaranteed loans to them. This means self-employed individuals pay self-employment tax on more than just what might be viewed as compensation for their services; they pay the tax on a full share of their net profits (even if they don't actually receive this as payment). This is so even if they do no work at all for their business and hire someone else to run it.

Net earnings from self-employment tax include earnings abroad, even if they qualify for the foreign earned income exclusion.

Net earnings not subject to self-employment tax are investment income (dividends, interest, and capital gains); rentals from real estate by someone who is not a real estate dealer; income received as a retired partner; and Conservation Reserve Program (CRP) payments to a retired or disabled farmer.

Self-employed individuals pay both the employee and employer portion of FICA, called self-employment tax (SECA). The rate for self-employment tax is 12.4% on net earnings from self-employment up to $117,000 in 2014 and 2.9% on all net earnings from self-employment tax. To more closely equate self-employed individuals with corporations, self-employed individuals may claim a deduction for one-half of self-employment tax (what amounts to the employer portion of FICA). Farmers who have low net earnings or even losses from farming activities can opt to create Social Security credits by using a farm optional method to report self-employment earnings. The tax is figured on Schedule SE, *Self-Employment Tax*, of Form 1040 (see Figure 29.1). There is a short schedule (Section A), which can be used by most self-employed individuals.

Those with a loss or minimal earnings who want to contribute more to the Social Security system in order to build up retirement income can use the optional methods in Part II of the schedule to figure net earnings on which the self-employment tax is based.

- *Optional farm method.* You can use this method to figure your net earnings from farm self-employment if your gross farm income was $7,200 or less or your net farm profits were less than $5,198. Under this method, report two-thirds of your gross farm income, up to $4,800, as your net earnings

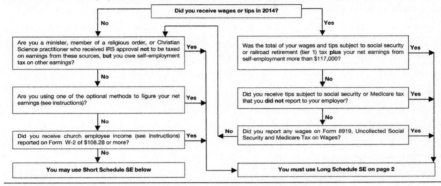

FIGURE 29.1 Schedule SE

for figuring self-employment tax. There is no limit on the number of years that you can use this method.

- *Optional nonfarm method.* You can use this method to figure your net earnings from nonfarm self-employment if your net nonfarm profits were less than $5,198 and also less than 72.189% of your gross nonfarm income. To use this method, you also must be regularly self-employed. You meet this requirement if your actual net earnings from self-employment were $400 or more in 2 of the 3 years preceding the year you use the nonfarm optional method. Under this method, report two-thirds of your gross nonfarm

Schedule SE (Form 1040) 2014	Attachment Sequence No. **17**	Page **2**

Name of person with **self-employment** income (as shown on Form 1040 or Form 1040NR)	Social security number of person with **self-employment** income ▶

Section B—Long Schedule SE

Part I Self-Employment Tax

Note. If your only income subject to self-employment tax is **church employee income**, see instructions. Also see instructions for the definition of church employee income.

A	If you are a minister, member of a religious order, or Christian Science practitioner **and** you filed Form 4361, but you had $400 or more of **other** net earnings from self-employment, check here and continue with Part I . . . . . . ▶ ☐			
1a	Net farm profit or (loss) from Schedule F, line 34, and farm partnerships, Schedule K-1 (Form 1065), box 14, code A. **Note.** Skip lines 1a and 1b if you use the farm optional method (see instructions)	**1a**		
b	If you received social security retirement or disability benefits, enter the amount of Conservation Reserve Program payments included on Schedule F, line 4b, or listed on Schedule K-1 (Form 1065), box 20, code Z	**1b**	(	)
2	Net profit or (loss) from Schedule C, line 31; Schedule C-EZ, line 3; Schedule K-1 (Form 1065), box 14, code A (other than farming); and Schedule K-1 (Form 1065-B), box 9, code J1. Ministers and members of religious orders, see instructions for types of income to report on this line. See instructions for other income to report. **Note.** Skip this line if you use the nonfarm optional method (see instructions)	**2**		
3	Combine lines 1a, 1b, and 2	**3**		
4a	If line 3 is more than zero, multiply line 3 by 92.35% (.9235). Otherwise, enter amount from line 3	**4a**		
	Note. If line 4a is less than $400 due to Conservation Reserve Program payments on line 1b, see instructions.			
b	If you elect one or both of the optional methods, enter the total of lines 15 and 17 here . .	**4b**		
c	Combine lines 4a and 4b. If less than $400, **stop;** you do not owe self-employment tax. **Exception.** If less than $400 and you had **church employee income,** enter -0- and continue ▶	**4c**		
5a	Enter your **church employee income** from Form W-2. See instructions for definition of church employee income . . .	**5a**			
b	Multiply line 5a by 92.35% (.9235). If less than $100, enter -0- . .	**5b**		
6	Add lines 4c and 5b	**6**		
7	Maximum amount of combined wages and self-employment earnings subject to social security tax or the 6.2% portion of the 7.65% railroad retirement (tier 1) tax for 2014	**7**	117,000	00
8a	Total social security wages and tips (total of boxes 3 and 7 on Form(s) W-2) and railroad retirement (tier 1) compensation. If $117,000 or more, skip lines 8b through 10, and go to line 11	**8a**		
b	Unreported tips subject to social security tax (from Form 4137, line 10)	**8b**		
c	Wages subject to social security tax (from Form 8919, line 10)	**8c**		
d	Add lines 8a, 8b, and 8c	**8d**		
9	Subtract line 8d from line 7. If zero or less, enter -0- here and on line 10 and go to line 11 . ▶	**9**		
10	Multiply the **smaller** of line 6 or line 9 by 12.4% (.124)	**10**		
11	Multiply line 6 by 2.9% (.029)	**11**		
12	**Self-employment tax.** Add lines 10 and 11. Enter here and on **Form 1040, line 57,** or **Form 1040NR, line 55**	**12**		
13	**Deduction for one-half of self-employment tax.** Multiply line 12 by 50% (.50). Enter the result here and on **Form 1040, line 27,** or **Form 1040NR, line 27**	**13**		

Part II Optional Methods To Figure Net Earnings (see instructions)

Farm Optional Method. You may use this method **only** if **(a)** your gross farm income[1] was not more than $7,200, **or (b)** your net farm profits[2] were less than $5,198.

14	Maximum income for optional methods	**14**	4,800	00
15	Enter the **smaller** of: two-thirds (²/₃) of gross farm income[1] (not less than zero) **or** $4,800. Also include this amount on line 4b above	**15**		

Nonfarm Optional Method. You may use this method **only** if **(a)** your net nonfarm profits[3] were less than $5,198 and also less than 72.189% of your gross nonfarm income,[4] **and (b)** you had net earnings from self-employment of at least $400 in 2 of the prior 3 years. **Caution.** You may use this method no more than five times.

16	Subtract line 15 from line 14	**16**	
17	Enter the **smaller** of: two-thirds (²/₃) of gross nonfarm income[4] (not less than zero) **or** the amount on line 16. Also include this amount on line 4b above	**17**	

[1] From Sch. F, line 9, and Sch. K-1 (Form 1065), box 14, code B.
[2] From Sch. F, line 34, and Sch. K-1 (Form 1065), box 14, code A—minus the amount you would have entered on line 1b had you not used the optional method.
[3] From Sch. C, line 31; Sch. C-EZ, line 3; Sch. K-1 (Form 1065), box 14, code A; and Sch. K-1 (Form 1065-B), box 9, code J1.
[4] From Sch. C, line 7; Sch. C-EZ, line 1; Sch. K-1 (Form 1065), box 14, code C; and Sch. K-1 (Form 1065-B), box 9, code J2.

Schedule SE (Form 1040) 2014

FIGURE 29.1 *(Continued)*

income as your net earnings, but not less than your actual net earnings from nonfarm self-employment. Use of the nonfarm optional method from nonfarm self-employment is limited to 5 years, but the 5 years do not have to be consecutive.

Limited partners (and LLC members treated as limited partners) are not subject to self-employment tax on their distributive share of partnership income.

They are viewed as mere investors. At the present time, there is no guidance on how to treat LLC members for purposes of self-employment tax. The IRS was prevented, by law, from issuing regulations on this issue before July 1, 1998. The IRS has still not given any indication of forthcoming regulations on this issue.

Unlike FICA, self-employment tax is not deposited with a Federal Reserve Bank or other authorized financial institution. Instead, it is paid along with income taxes. This means that self-employed individuals must ensure that quarterly estimated taxes cover not only their income tax obligations but also their self-employment tax for the year (see later in this chapter).

Self-employed individuals are not subject to FUTA. They cannot cover themselves for periods of no work because, by definition, self-employed persons are never employed.

State Income Tax Withholding

If your business is located in a state that imposes a personal income tax, you are required to withhold state income tax from your employees' compensation. You can obtain information about state withholding rates by contacting your state tax authority (see Table 29.1).

If you have employees who live in another state, you are only required to withhold tax for the state in which your business is located. (The employees may be entitled to a credit for taxes paid to another state.) However, you *may* withhold state income tax for the state in which the employees reside so that they do not have to grapple with state estimated taxes. If you make such an accommodation, you must still withhold state taxes for the state in which your business is located. If you do business in more than one state and have employees who work in more than one location, you must withhold state income tax in each state in which they work. In one case, for example, withholding was required for a professional baseball player for each state in which he played ball, not just in the home state. Withholding in this case was based on the number of days he played in each of these other states.

Employment Tax Filing for All Businesses

If you have employees (even if you are your corporation's only employee) and your annual taxes exceed $1,000, you must report quarterly to the IRS. Use Form 941, *Employer's Quarterly Federal Tax Return*, to report any income tax withholding and FICA withholding and payments made during the quarter.

If your annual employment taxes are anticipated to be no more than $1,000 (total compensation is about $4,000), you may qualify to file annually, rather than quarterly. The IRS notifies eligible employers that they do not have to file quarterly on Form 941 but instead can file Form 944, *Employer's Annual Federal Tax Return*. Once you have been notified by the IRS to file Form 944, you continue to do so until you are notified that you are no longer eligible for this form. If you think you qualify for annual filing but have not received notification from the IRS, you should contact the IRS and say you want to file annually. Even if you qualify to file annually, you can opt out of using Form 944 and instead file quarterly if you follow simple IRS guidelines. If you are a farmer required to file Form 943, you cannot use Form 944 in any event, even if you meet the definition of a small employer.

You must also file an annual return to report the payment of federal unemployment insurance. Use Form 940, *Employer's Annual Federal Unemployment (FUTA) Tax Return*.

Employment tax forms can be signed by facsimile, including alternative signature methods such as computer software programs or mechanical devices.

Note: Reporting for employment tax obligations is separate from income tax reporting.

If you discover an error in a previously filed Form 941 or 944, correct the error using Form 941-X, *Adjusted Employer's QUARTERLY Federal Tax Return or Claim for Refund*, or Form 944-X, *Adjusted Employer's ANNUAL Federal Tax Return or Claim for Refund*. There is no "X" form for amending Form 940; simply use Form 940 and check the "amended return" box at the top of the return.

SPECIAL REPORTING FOR EMPLOYING A WORKER IN YOUR HOME

If you are a sole proprietor and have a nanny or other household employees, as well as regular business employees, you can report the FICA and FUTA taxes for your household employee on Schedule H and pay the taxes with your Form 1040. Alternatively, you can report and pay the FICA taxes for your household employee with the quarterly reports for your regular business employees on Form 941, and you can pay the FUTA taxes on Form 940.

Sales and Use Taxes

There is no federal sales or use tax. But there are nearly 10,000 states, counties, cities, and towns with their own sales taxes, in many cases generating the greatest revenue for these jurisdictions. Many also impose a **use tax**.

Use tax   Tax imposed on the purchaser of certain goods from out-of-state vendors.

The rules for these taxes vary considerably from one locality to another. For example, the sale of one type of product may be subject to sales tax in one state but exempt in another. Because these taxes produce significant revenue in some places, taxing authorities may be aggressive in their collection activities, so you should understand your responsibilities.

Sales Taxes

If you sell goods or provide certain services within a state that has a sales tax, as the vendor you are required to collect the tax from the purchaser and remit the tax to the state agency. Generally, the same test used for state income tax purposes to determine whether you do business within a state applies for sales tax purposes as well. If you do not do business within a state, you are not required to collect sales tax on goods shipped within that state. If you sell online, you may or may not have a presence in another state (for example, maintaining a server in another state may establish a nexus there).

Currently, it is not well established precisely when Internet sales to a customer in another state are subject to sales tax. The federal moratorium on state sales tax, titled the Internet Tax Freedom Act Amendments Act of 2007 applies only to the tax on Internet access, not to Internet sales. The moratorium is set to expire on November 3, 2014. The House voted in July 2014 to make the moratorium permanent; check the Supplement for further details on Congressional actions.

The Streamlined Sales and Use Tax Agreement, which took effect in some states on October 1, 2005, attempts to simplify and standardize some sales tax rules to make it easier for businesses to collect this important revenue. For information about states participating in the agreement, go to www.streamlinedsalestax.org. Pending legislation, called the Marketplace Fairness Act, which is supported by many small business groups but opposed by others, would require most online sellers to collect sales tax.

Familiarize yourself with how the sales tax works. For example, some states impose an origin-based sales tax while others have a destination-based tax. If goods are returned and you refund the purchaser's money, you may be entitled to a deduction or credit for the sales tax you originally collected.

When you must remit sales tax to the state depends on how much you collect. You must also file certain returns reporting your collection activities.

Contact your state tax authority (see Table 29.1) to request a sales tax package. This will explain whether you must collect tax (and how much) and when to pay it to the state and file sales tax returns. You can simplify your sales tax obligations by using a Certified Service Provider (CSP), a company approved by the Streamlined Sales Tax governing board:

- Avalara (www.avalara.com)
- Accurate Tax (www.accuratetax.com)
- CCH (www.cchgroup.com)
- Exactor (www.exactor.com)
- FedTax (https://taxcloud.net)
- Taxware (www.taxware.com)

The CSP will provide technology assistance to ensure proper collection and remittance of the tax to the CSP for payment to the appropriate state or states. There is no cost to you for using a CSP (it is paid by the states), and you are insulated from a state audit on sales tax (the state can only audit the CSP with respect to your collections).

Use Taxes

If you buy goods out-of-state, you may be liable for a use tax on the purchase. (In effect, your state is collecting the sales tax you would have paid had you made the purchase in-state.) Generally, the tax is imposed on the purchaser (though some states may collect the tax from the seller).

Before you pay any use tax, check to see if the sale is exempt from the tax. Exemptions often exist for items that will be resold (including components of products for resale), used for capital improvements, or used in research and development.

Even if the vendor does not charge a use tax because it has no responsibility to pay the tax to your state, you may still be liable for it. In effect, you may be required to "self-assess" the tax.

Excise Taxes

An excise tax is a tax imposed on the manufacture and distribution of certain nonessential consumer goods, such as spirits and tobacco, although it now applies to many essential goods and services as well (such as gasoline and telephone service). Until the advent of the income tax in 1913, the federal government ran entirely on excise taxes. Today, excise taxes are only a small part of the government's revenue, but may still be an obligation for you. In 2003 (the last year for which statistics are available), more than half a million taxpayers filed returns for heavy highway vehicle use tax and nearly 200,000 for federal excise tax on certain fuels. Excise taxes include:

- Environmental taxes on the sale or use of ozone-depleting chemicals
- Communications and air transportation taxes
- Fuel taxes
- Manufacturers' taxes on various items (including sport fishing equipment, bow and arrow components, etc.)
- Retail tax on the sale of heavy trucks, trailers, and tractors (imposed on the seller)
- 10% excise tax on indoor tanning salon services. Salon owners must collect this tax from patrons and pay the tax to the IRS in quarterly installments, along with Form 720, *Quarterly Federal Excise Tax Return*.

Many small companies have no liability for excise taxes because of the nature of their business. However, there are no specific exemptions from these taxes because a business is a small one. For example, small farmers are subject to certain fuel taxes, although they may be entitled to a credit or refund, and an owner of a heavy truck (one with a gross taxable weight of 55,000 pounds or more) is subject to a use tax for the vehicle. Disregarded entities (e.g., one-member LLCs) must pay the tax under the entities' tax identification numbers; the entities and not their owners are liable for excise taxes.

Businesses with 25 or more trucks, tractors, or other heavy vehicles used on highways are now required to make their excise tax filings electronically. Form 2290, *Heavy Highway Vehicle Use Tax Return*, is used for this purpose and generally is due by August 31.

The deduction for excise taxes is discussed in Chapter 13. Tax credits for certain farm-related excise taxes are discussed in Chapter 20.

Filing Income Tax Returns and Paying Taxes

Alert

At the time this book was printed, Congress had not extended numerous breaks for 2014 that had expired at the end of 2013. Check the online supplement in February 2015 at www.jklasser.com or www.barbaraweltman.com to see whether these breaks apply for 2014 returns.

It's one of the facts of a business owner's life to file returns and pay taxes. The filing deadlines and tax payment rules for businesses and their owners may be different from those for individuals. Making sure you comply with filing and payment requirements is essential for avoiding unnecessary penalties and interest.

For more information about the electronic federal tax payment system, see IRS Publication 966, *Electronic Federal Tax Payment System*.

TABLE 30.1 Filing Deadlines

Type of Entity	Income Tax Return	Return Due Date
Sole proprietorship	Schedule C (or C-EZ) of Form 1040	April 15
Partnership	Form 1065	April 15
Limited liability company	Form 1065	April 15
S corporation	Form 1120S	March 15
C corporation	Form 1120	March 15

Filing Deadlines and Extensions

The date by which your business return must be filed depends on your type of entity and tax year. The information in Table 30.1 applies to businesses reporting on a calendar-year basis.

Partnerships, limited liability companies, and S corporations must also furnish owners with a Schedule K-1 by the due date.

For corporations on a fiscal year, the due date is $2^1/_2$ months after the close of their fiscal year. For example, a C corporation on a fiscal year ending on June 30 has a filing deadline of September 15.

For all other entities on a fiscal year, the due date is $3^1/_2$ months after the close of their fiscal year. For example, a limited liability company reporting on a fiscal year ending September 30 has a filing deadline of January 15 of the following year.

If any due date falls on a Saturday, Sunday, or legal holiday, the due date becomes the next business day. For example, the deadline for furnishing W-2s to employees for 2015 will be February 1, 2016, because January 31 is on a Sunday. W-2s for 2014 must be furnished by February 2, 2015 (January 31 is on a Saturday).

Filing Methods

Small business owners can choose to file paper returns or file electronically; certain large entities must file electronically (explained later in this chapter). The filing method does not affect the filing deadline.

Filing Extensions

If, for any reason, you are unable to file on time, you can avoid penalties by requesting an automatic 6-month filing extension (5 months for partnership returns). The request must be made no later than the due date of the return (see Table 30.1). The form used to request the extension and the extended due date depends on your type of entity, as shown in Table 30.2.

TABLE 30.2 Filing Extensions

Type of Entity	Form to Request Filing Extension	Extended Due Date
Sole proprietorship	Form 4868	October 15
Partnership	Form 7004	September 15
Limited liability company	Form 7004	September 15
S corporation	Form 7004	September 15
C corporation	Form 7004	September 15

There are no extensions available beyond the extended due date, regardless of the reasons involved; returns filed after the extended due date are usually subject to penalty. The only exception to the rule against having more time to file is a blanket extension granted by the IRS to taxpayers located in certain areas affected by extreme disasters. Find news about this on an IRS landing page entitled "Tax Relief in Disaster Situations" at www.irs.gov/uac/Tax-Relief-in-Disaster-Situations.

Late Filing Penalties

If you fail to file your return on time—by the due date or the extended due date if you obtain a filing extension—you will be subject to a late filing penalty. A penalty can apply in some cases even if you have deposited your taxes on time and owe no additional tax with your return.

The late filing penalty is usually 0.5% of the amount due for each month or part of a month that the return is late, up to a maximum of 25% of the tax due. However, the penalty increases to 15% of the amount due for each month or part of a month that the return is late, up to a maximum of 75% of the tax due, if the failure to file is fraudulent. If the return is more than 60 days late, the minimum penalty is $100 or the amount of any tax due, whichever is smaller.

For partnerships, there is a late filing penalty of $195 per owner per month for up to 12 months. Similarly, for S corporations, the penalty is $195 per owner per month up to 12 months. All owners for any part of the year are taken into account in figuring this penalty.

PENALTY ABATEMENT

You can ask to have penalties waived if you have reasonable cause for not filing on time. This penalty abatement must be requested by you; it is not granted automatically by the IRS. To request abatement of penalties, send the IRS your own written statement explaining the reasons why you were unable to file on time. You must sign the statement under penalty of perjury.

For small partnerships and S corporations (those with 10 or fewer owners), reasonable cause is met *automatically* if all owners are natural persons (and not nonresident aliens), all owners receive equal allocations of each entity item, and all owners have reported these items on their personal returns.

Online Filing of Business Income Tax Returns

Today the vast majority of tax returns for individual business owners as well as their business entities are filed e-filed with the IRS and with state tax or revenue departments. While e-filing is not mandatory (other than for large corporations), there are compelling reasons to submit returns in this way:

- *Faster refunds*. Those who are owed a refund can expect to receive it in about half the time that it would take had the return been filed the traditional way in paper form. With electronic filing of returns and direct deposit of refunds, you can receive a refund in as little as 7 days.
- *Accuracy*. There is a less than 1% error rate with electronically filed returns (compared with a more-than-20% error rate for paper returns). This is because the IRS reviews the return before accepting it. The IRS acknowledges acceptance of a return within 48 hours of submission. This acknowledgment is your proof of filing and assurance that the IRS has your return information.
- *Convenience*. You can use your personal computer to file your return 7 days a week, 24 hours a day. If you lack the software to *e-file*, you can use an authorized IRS *e-file* provider (for a modest fee). In 37 states, you can file your federal and state returns simultaneously. If you owe taxes, you can file early and postpone payment until the return's due date. (Payment can be made by authorizing an automatic withdrawal [direct debit] from a savings or checking account through IRS Direct Pay, an electronic transfer through EFTPS.gov, payment by credit or debit card [American Express, Discover, MasterCard or Visa], or by mailing a check payable to the United States Treasury along with Form 1040-V, *Payment Voucher*, to your service center.)
- *Preparers required to e-file*. Paid tax return preparers are required to e-file client returns if they expect to file 11 or more Forms 1040, 1040A, 1040EZ, and 1041, so if you use a paid preparer, your return likely will be e-filed.

If you *e-file*, then you do not have to attach any information returns that would otherwise be required. For example, if you are a sole proprietor but your spouse is an employee with a W-2 form, that form need not be sent to the IRS if you file your return electronically.

State income taxes. Check whether you can file any required state income tax returns electronically. For individuals, e-filing both federal and state returns for many states can be done with a single click.

ELECTRONIC SIGNATURES

To e-file, the signature of an electronically-filed return is handled through a *self-select personal identification number* (PIN). This is a self-created 5-number code that is used in conjunction with your prior year's adjusted gross income, total tax, and date of birth to verify that the return being filed is your own. You do not have to register your PIN number, nor even notify the IRS. But if you are a sole proprietor filing a joint return, both you and your spouse need a PIN.

DEEMED FILING DATE

An electronically filed return is deemed timely if it is transmitted on or before the due date *and* an acknowledgment of processing by the IRS is issued.

Sole Proprietorships

You can *e-file* your income tax return if you are a sole proprietor filing a Schedule C, C-EZ, or F. Virtually all the forms and schedules you need can be filed electronically.

Partnerships and LLCs

Form 1065 may be filed electronically. Other than large partnerships (those with 100 or more partners), there is no requirement to use *e-file*. But the same benefits of *e-filing* for individuals applies to partnership returns.

S Corporations

S corporations with total assets over $10 million and 250 or more returns filed annually (including income tax, excise tax, information—W-2 and otherwise—and employment tax returns) *must* file Form 1120S electronically. Smaller S corporations can opt to e-file. Whether *e-file* is used, if the corporation owes any income tax, it must deposit it electronically if it is otherwise required to use EFTPS as explained later in this chapter.

S corporation shareholders can, however, file their personal tax returns electronically, even if the corporation files by mail (and vice versa). Thus, they can obtain the benefit of *e-filing* on their share of business items.

C Corporations

The return can be filed under the 1120/1120S *e-file* program. C corporations with total assets over $10 million and 250 or more returns filed annually (including income tax, excise tax, information—W-2 and otherwise—and employment tax returns) *must* file Form 1120 electronically. Whether *e-file* is used, you must still deposit corporate income taxes electronically if you are required to use EFTPS as explained later in this chapter.

Estimated Taxes

Estimated taxes are not separate tax obligations; they are a method of paying throughout the year what you expect to owe when you ultimately file your return. Estimated taxes are paid by individuals (including owners of partnerships, limited liability companies, and S corporations on their share of business income) and C corporations. If you do not pay enough estimated taxes (plus withholding taxes on wages and certain other payments), you may be subject to penalties.

INDIVIDUALS

Estimated taxes cover:

- Regular income tax (including income taxes on your share of business income)
- Alternative minimum tax for high-income taxpayers (see Chapter 28)
- Self-employment tax (discussed earlier in this chapter)
- Additional Medicare taxes on earned income and net investment income

You must pay estimated taxes if you expect tax liability for the year to be at least $1,000 and you do not meet a safe harbor test (or file your return and pay the tax in full by January 31). The safe harbor test means that your withholdings and tax credits (e.g., applying an excess payment from last year toward this year's taxes) are less than the smaller of:

- 90% of the tax shown to be on this year's return ($66^2/_3$% for farmers and commercial fishermen), or
- 100% of the tax shown on last year's return (110% if your adjusted gross income last year is more than $150,000, or $75,000 if married filing separately).

There is a special estimated tax rule for farmers and commercial fishermen. No estimated tax penalties are owed if the income tax return is filed and any taxes paid by February 28. If you don't file by this date, then any estimated tax penalties will be figured only from 1 payment date—January 15.

Use the Estimated Tax Worksheet (Figure 30.1) to figure what you must pay in order to avoid penalties. An updated version should be used for 2015 estimated taxes.

Estimated taxes are due on April 15, June 15, September 15, and January 15 of the following year (the due date is extended to the next business day if any payment date falls on a Saturday, Sunday, or legal holiday).

1	Adjusted gross income you expect in 2014 (see instructions)	**1**		
2	• If you plan to itemize deductions, enter the estimated total of your itemized deductions. **Caution:** *If line 1 is over $152,525, your deduction may be reduced. See Worksheet 2-5.* • If you do not plan to itemize deductions, enter your standard deduction.	**2**		
3	Subtract line 2 from line 1	**3**		
4	Exemptions. Multiply $3,950 by the number of personal exemptions. **Caution:** *If line 1 is over $152,525, the amount of your personal exemptions may be limited. See Worksheet 2-6.*	**4**		
5	Subtract line 4 from line 3	**5**		
6	**Tax.** Figure your tax on the amount on line 5 by using the **2014 Tax Rate Schedules Caution:** *If you will have qualified dividends or a net capital gain, or expect to exclude or deduct foreign earned income or housing, see Worksheets 2-7 and 2-8 to figure the tax*	**6**		
7	Alternative minimum tax from **Form 6251** or included on **Form 1040A, line 28**	**7**		
8	Add lines 6 and 7. Add to this amount any other taxes you expect to include in the total on Form 1040, line 44	**8**		
9	Credits (see instructions). **Do not** include any income tax withholding on this line	**9**		
10	Subtract line 9 from line 8. If zero or less, enter -0-.	**10**		
11	Self-employment tax (see instructions)	**11**		
12	Other taxes including, if applicable, Additional Medicare Tax and/or NIIT (see instructions)	**12**		
13a	Add lines 10 through 12	**13a**		
b	Earned income credit, additional child tax credit, fuel tax credit, and refundable American opportunity credit	**13b**		
c	**Total 2014 estimated tax.** Subtract line 13b from line 13a. If zero or less, enter -0- . . . . ▶	**13c**		
14a	Multiply line 13c by 90% ($66\frac{2}{3}$% for farmers and fishermen)	**14a**		
b	Required annual payment based on prior year's tax (see instructions)	**14b**		
c	**Required annual payment to avoid a penalty.** Enter the **smaller** of line 14a or 14b . . . . ▶	**14c**		
	Caution: *Generally, if you do not prepay (through income tax withholding and estimated tax payments) at least the amount on line 14c, you may owe a penalty for not paying enough estimated tax. To avoid a penalty, make sure your estimate on line 13c is as accurate as possible. Even if you pay the required annual payment, you may still owe tax when you file your return. If you prefer, you can pay the amount shown on line 13c.*			
15	Income tax withheld and estimated to be withheld during 2014 (including income tax withholding on pensions, annuities, certain deferred income, etc.)	**15**		
16a	Subtract line 15 from line 14c	**16a**		
	Is the result zero or less? ☐ **Yes.** Stop here. You are not required to make estimated tax payments. ☐ **No.** Go to line 16b.			
b	Subtract line 15 from line 13c	**16b**		
	Is the result less than $1,000? ☐ **Yes.** Stop here. You are not required to make estimated tax payments. ☐ **No.** Go to line 17 to figure your required payment.			
17	If the first payment you are required to make is due April 15, 2014, enter ¼ of line 16a (minus any 2013 overpayment that you are applying to this installment) here, and on your estimated tax payment voucher(s) if you are paying by check or money order	**17**		

FIGURE 30.1 Estimated Tax Worksheet

Estimated taxes can be paid in several ways: by check made payable to the U.S. Treasury, along with Form 1040-ES, by charging the payment to a major credit card, or by transferring funds using EFTPS.gov.

If you do not pay enough through estimated taxes, figure your penalty on Form 2210 (Form 2210-F for farmers and commercial fishermen).

CORPORATIONS

S corporations usually are not separate taxpayers and therefore need not be concerned with estimated taxes (shareholders pay estimated taxes). C corporations are separate taxpayers and must meet estimated tax payment obligations to avoid penalties.

Corporations are required to prepay current tax liability by making estimated tax payments during the year if the tax liability is $500 or more. Estimated tax for corporations covers the regular corporate income tax, alternative minimum tax, and the tax on gross transportation income of foreign corporations from U.S. sources.

Estimated tax is figured on Form 1120-W, *Corporation Estimated Tax*. This form is not filed with the IRS. Instead, payments are made through deposits at federal depositories or through electronic transfers (whichever method is required or selected). The payment slip accompanying the deposit or transfer can be checked off to indicate that it is for estimated tax purposes.

Corporations must pay 25% of the "required annual payment" in each of 4 installments. For a corporation other than a "large corporation," the required payment is either 100% of the tax shown on the current year's return or 100% of the tax on the preceding year's return. However, there are other methods that can be used to satisfy payment requirements while avoiding penalties. For calendar-year corporations, these are due April 15, June 15, September 15, and December 15.

ESTIMATED TAX STRATEGIES

It can be challenging for individuals and businesses to have the funds on hand to pay estimated taxes on time. It is advisable to set aside funds on a regular basis for this purpose. For example, say a sole proprietor with fee income is in the 25% tax bracket. It might make sense to deposit 10% to 20% of fee income (taking into account the fact that deductions reduce the income that's taxable) into a separate bank account for estimated taxes so that it is available for making timely estimated tax payments.

However, when figuring estimated taxes, it is not advisable to overpay so that you are making an interest-free loan to the government. In the current low-interest environment, it is probably better to err on the side of underpaying so that you have the use of your money now and do not have to wait until you file a return to recoup an overpayment.

If you find that you have overpaid estimated taxes, you can recover the money by:

- Filing your tax return as quickly as possible to receive a refund.

- Applying your overpayment to next year's taxes, thus reducing your out-of-pocket payments for estimated taxes for next year. Just indicate this choice on your tax return to apply some or all of the overpayment to next year's taxes. Usually, this will allow you to skip one or two estimated tax payments (depending on the size of your overpayment and your projections for next year's taxes).

Making Tax Payments

There are several ways to pay taxes: By check, by transferring payment using the Electronic Federal Tax Payment System (EFTPS), by charging payment to a major credit card, and by using IRS Direct Pay.

Paying by Check

Most small business owners can pay their tax bill via check made payable to the United States Treasury. Remember that the bulk of the taxes should have been paid through estimated taxes; the check that accompanies the return should be modest.

Corporations cannot pay their income taxes by writing a check to accompany their tax return. They must pay amounts owed by depositing them with an authorized depository (explained below) or by transferring funds through EFTPS.

Paying Taxes Online

Some businesses *must* deposit their taxes through the Electronic Federal Tax Payment System (EFTPS) while others may choose to do so. EFTPS processes over 100 million transactions per year, totaling nearly $2 trillion, with an error rate of 0.18%. Under this payment method you authorize the transfer of funds from your bank account by using your telephone or personal computer. This payment method can be used whether or not returns are filed electronically and enables you to designate up to 120 days in advance the amount of payment to be made and the time of payment. As long as the transfer is initiated at least one business day before the due date of the deposit, the electronic fund transfer is considered timely.

Required Use of EFTPS

More than 97.5% of all federal tax deposits are now made electronically. The use of federal tax coupons allowing deposits to certain banks can no longer be used; all deposits (with some exceptions) must be made using EFTPS.

Payment can be made with the tax return and is not required to be deposited electronically if employment taxes are less than $2,500 per pay period.

You can enroll online at www.eftps.gov. If you prefer to submit a paper application, file Form 9779, *EFTPS Business Enrollment Form*, with the EFTPS Enrollment Processing Center (it can take several weeks to process a paper application).

Voluntary Use of EFTPS

Even if you are *not* required to use EFTPS, you may wish to do so—for convenience. You initiate payment so you remain in control of your funds until you want them disbursed to the government. You receive an acknowledgment number as a record of your payment.

You may voluntarily participate in EFTPS. To obtain more information on EFTPS or to enroll in the system, call (800) 555-4477 or (800) 945-8400. If you enroll, you can use the Internet or receive free Windows-based software for use on your PC. You also receive a PIN to use when making payments.

You can update existing passwords (to make them *more* secure) at "My Profile" at www.eftps.gov.

Electronic Transfer Payment Methods

There are different ways you can make an electronic transfer of funds to the government:

- Through EFTPS-OnLine at www.eftps.gov. This is a secured web site that individuals and businesses can use to pay taxes through the Internet. After enrolling online, you'll receive a confirmation kit by mail, including instructions for obtaining your password (a PIN number is mailed separately). Payments can be scheduled in advance and even canceled, with instant acknowledgments to confirm transactions.

- Directly to EFTPS through your personal computer or telephone. You choose the automated clearing house (ACH) debit method when you enroll. Then, when you want to make a payment, you instruct EFTPS to transfer funds from your account to the U.S. Treasury.

- Using the IRS' Direct Pay option. Individuals can use this secure service through the IRS website to transfer funds from a checking or savings account with no IRS charge and no registration; it takes only 5 easy steps.

- Through your bank or other financial institution through its payment service. You choose the ACH credit method when you enroll and follow the bank's instructions on how to direct payment. Before designating a particular financial institution, check whether they can accommodate this payment method. Also ask about any fees or other charges for using this payment method.

If you use a payroll company to process your payroll, you may also authorize them to pay your employment taxes. Special enrollment rules for EFTPS apply in this case. You can also enroll separately so you keep the flexibility of making your own electronic payments.

Credit Card Charges

Businesses can pay taxes via credit card (American Express, Discover, Master-Card, or Visa) in some, but not all, instances. Balances owed with respect to employment tax returns (Forms 940, 941, and 944) can be charged to a credit card. However, federal tax deposits cannot be made by credit card.

Taxes owed on income tax returns of sole proprietors and owners of pass-through entities on Form 1040 can also be charged to a credit card.

As of now, taxes owed on Form 1120 or Form 1120S (in those limited situations where an S corporation owes tax) cannot be charged to a credit card. This could change in the future.

There are only 3 credit card processors authorized by the IRS to process tax payments:

1. Official Payments Corporation: www.officialpayments.com or 800-2PAYTAX.

2. LINK2GOV Corporation: https://www.pay1040.com/ or 888-PAY1040.

3. RBS WorldPay, Inc.: www.payUSAtax.com or 888-877-0450.

These companies charge a convenience fee (currently up to 2.35% of the amount charged); the IRS does not impose any additional cost for charging taxes.

IRS Direct Pay

You can transfer funds from your checking or savings account using this online payment method. There is no registration or fees required. Go to www.irs.gov/Payments/Direct-Pay for details.

Late Payment Penalties

If you fail to pay the taxes due on time, you can be subject to late payment penalties and interest on the outstanding amount. Taxes must be paid in full by the due date of the return to avoid penalties and interest. Obtaining an extension of time to file the return does not give you more time to pay your taxes.

The penalty is 0.5% of the tax due, per month, with a maximum of 25%. In addition, interest is charged at the IRS interest rate, which adjusts quarterly. For news releases of IRS quarterly interest rates, go to www.irs.gov and search "news releases", and fact sheet archives.

The penalty may be waived if you can show that lateness was due to reasonable cause and not to willful neglect.

Online Filing of Other Business Returns

At present, employment tax returns and employee benefit returns are not required to be filed online. Certain information returns *must* be filed online by certain taxpayers—others who are not required to do so may choose to file online.

Employment Tax Returns

Employment tax returns may be filed electronically. These include:

- Form 940, *Employer's Annual Federal Unemployment (FUTA) Tax Return*
- Form 941, *Employer's Quarterly Federal Tax Return*
- Form 944, *Employer's Annual Federal Tax Return*

You can e-file employment tax returns through a third-party transmitter using the 940, 941, and 944 On-Line Filing Program. Or you can authorize a reporting agent to prepare, sign, and e-file for you. Find out more about your e-file options for employment tax returns from the IRS at http://www.irs.gov/uac/Employment-Taxes—Electronic-Filing-and-Payment-Options.

Looking for a company to transmit your employment tax returns for your company? You can find a list of IRS-approved e-file Business Providers at http://www.irs.gov/Tax-Professionals/e-File-Providers-&-Partners/Approved-IRS-e-file-for-Business-Providers.

Information Returns

You may choose to submit certain information returns to the IRS electronically even though you must provide paper returns to your employees or others. You *must* file electronically if you file 250 or more information returns (Form 1042-S, 1098, 1099, 5498, 8027, or W-G).

You do not have to be concerned about the security of the information you submit in this manner. The IRS has set up FIRE (Filing Information Returns Electronically) to protect the confidentiality of the data you submit. To learn more about FIRE, see www.irs.gov and search "filing information returns electronically (FIRE)" or call the Martinsburg Computer Center at (304) 263-8700.

You can provide information returns to payment recipients electronically *if* they consent to receive them in this manner. So, for example, if you paid an independent contractor $1,200 in 2014 and want to send the Form 1099-MISC to her electronically, you must obtain her consent to do so.

EMPLOYEE BENEFIT RETURNS

Forms in the 5500 series must now be filed electronically with the Department of Labor (not with the IRS). (There is an exception for small plans.) For information about EFAST (ERISA Filing Acceptance System) and EFAST *e-filing* employee benefit returns, see http://www.efast.dol.gov/welcome.html.

DUE DATE OF ELECTRONICALLY FILED INFORMATION RETURNS

Filing electronically extends the due date of Forms 1098, 1099, and W-2G from February 28 to March 31. For example, for 2014 information returns, you have until March 31, 2015, to *e-file* the returns with the IRS. For Form 1042-S, the due date remains March 15, the same date for paper returns. Similarly, the due date for furnishing information returns to payment recipients (January 31) remains the same (use of electronic filing does not extend this date). Of course, if the due date falls on Saturday, Sunday, or a legal holiday, the due date of an electronically filed return is extended to the next business day.

Excise Tax Returns

Under the ExSTARS (Excise Summary Terminal Activity Reporting System), terminal operators and bulk fuel carriers can file their monthly information returns (Fuel Transaction Reports) electronically instead of using paper returns.

Retirement and Succession Planning

Alert

At the time this book was printed, Congress had not extended numerous breaks for 2014 that had expired at the end of 2013. Check the online supplement in February 2015 at www.jklasser.com or www.barbaraweltman.com to see whether these breaks apply for 2014 returns.

What happens to your business when you retire or die? Have you made any decisions about whether to sell your interest, pass it on to children, or make other arrangements? If you are planning to retire, will the sale of your business provide you with sufficient funds for a comfortable retirement? The plans you make will have practical and tax implications for you, your family, and your business.

Succession planning is a complex and ongoing process involving both practical (business) and legal concerns. This chapter is designed to acquaint you with some of the issues you'll need to address in succession planning; it does not address every issue that may apply to you. Work with a knowledgeable advisor to help you structure, monitor, and modify your succession plans.

Retirement Planning

Looking ahead to the day when you can stop working and retire may be a pleasurable notion, and something to keep you going when you're working round the clock, dealing with business crises, and worrying about how you'll meet the next payroll. Many business owners expect that the sale of their business will provide them with the funds to have a financially secure retirement. Unfortunately, this doesn't always happen, especially if they sell during an economic downturn or their industry falls out of favor.

The best way to make sure you have the money to provide you with a comfortable retirement is to optimize your retirement savings. Chapter 16 discusses your retirement plan options, the rules for making annual contributions, and annual reporting requirements. Now let's focus on ways to optimize the returns from your retirement plans.

Rollovers

You can change investments solely within your discretion in order to make the most of your retirement plan contributions. One way to do this is to change financial institutions. The best way from a tax perspective is to make a trustee-to-trustee transfer of the funds from one retirement plan account to another. (There is no need to transfer assets; you can liquidate one account and, if desirable, reacquire the same investments in the new account, because gains and losses within retirement plans are not taxed.) With a direct transfer, you never get your hands on the money; it goes from one financial institution directly to another. This is called a *direct rollover*, and you can do it as often as you deem advantageous. There are no tax consequences to a direct rollover. However, check with the financial institution from which you're taking the funds for any fees or penalties that may apply.

Alternatively, you can take a distribution from one account and roll it over to another. As long as you deposit the withdrawn funds into a new rollover account within 60 days, the distribution is not taxable to you (with the exception of a rollover to a Roth IRA or designated Roth account, which is taxable). If you fail to replace the funds within 60 days, you are taxed on the distribution. And if you're under age $59^{1}/_{2}$, you'll also owe a 10% early distribution penalty.

You can shift funds from your qualified retirement plan to an IRA or other types of plans. Table 31.1 shows the rollover options for various types of qualified retirement plans (the chart omits 403(b) plans for tax-exempt organizations and 457 government plans). The term "in-plan rollover" means a rollover from a 401(k) plan to a designated Roth account of the same plan.

TABLE 31.1 Rollover Options

Roll From	Roll To					
	Traditional IRA	Roth IRA	SIMPLE-IRA	SEP	401(k) or other qualified plan	Designated Roth Account
Traditional IRA	Yes	Yes	No	Yes	Yes	No
Roth IRA	Yes	No	No	No	No	No
SIMPLE-IRA	Yes (after 2 years)	Yes (after 2 years)	Yes	Yes (after 2 years)	Yes (after 2 years)	No
SEP	Yes	Yes	No	Yes	Yes	No
401(k) or other qualified plan	Yes	Yes	No	Yes	Yes	Yes, if it's an in-plan rollover
Designated Roth Account	No	Yes	No	No	No	Yes, if made via direct trustee to trustee transfer

Plan Loans

A qualified retirement plan can allow you to take a loan. You can use the funds for any business or personal purpose, such as paying for business expansion plans. The plan document must permit you (and other plan participants) to take a loan. And the tax law limits the amount of the loan you can take. The loan cannot be greater than 50% of your vested account balance or $50,000, whichever is less. The loan must contain a reasonable rate of interest, and repayment must be made ratably over 5 years (with an exception for loan proceeds used to buy a principal residence).

Loans are only permissible from qualified retirement plans. You cannot take a loan from IRAs and IRA-like plans, such as SEPs and SIMPLE-IRAs. However, you can make use of funds in your plan for a limited time without adverse tax consequences. If you take a distribution and replace the funds within 60 days, you effectively have made a short-term loan to yourself, and the distribution is not taxable. But use extreme caution here: As mentioned earlier in connection with rollovers, if you fail to replace the funds within 60 days, you are taxed on the distribution. And if you're under age 59 1/2, you'll also owe a 10% early distribution penalty.

Work with Professionals

Discuss your current retirement plan holdings and your plans for retiring with a financial planner or other expert. This person can help you craft retirement planning strategies so you can achieve your goals.

Exit Strategies

There may be a variety of reasons why you leave your company. They include retirement, disability, being a serial entrepreneur (selling this company to start another one), or death. Whatever the reason, there are several exit strategies.

Before you make any plans, it is a good idea to determine what the business is worth now (the value may change in the future, but plans can be adapted to accommodate valuation shifts). This is done by obtaining a business appraisal. There are various formulas used to determine the value of a business:

- Asset and earnings valuations (factoring in intangibles such as goodwill)
- Asset-based formulas (based on book value or liquidation value)
- Comparable sales of similar businesses
- Earnings (revenue) formulas (multiples of revenue or capitalization of earnings)

Resources to help you find a qualified appraiser (someone with the requisite professional experience who meets certain standards) include the following:

- American Institute of CPAs—Accreditation in Business Valuation (http://apps.aicpa.org/credentialsrefweb/ABVCredentialSearchPage.aspx)
- American Society of Appraisers (www.appraisers.org/BVhome.aspx)
- Institute of Business Appraisers (www.go-iba.org)

You can use free online tools to learn the approximate valuation of your business. These tools are no substitute for an actual valuation by a qualified appraiser. Free tools are available from:

1. BizEquity (https://www.bizequity.com)
2. BizEx (http://www.bizex.net/business-valuation-tool)

Financing Options to Fund Buyouts

Buying out the interest of a departing owner can be paid for in a variety of ways. Most common are:

- ***Company buyouts.*** The interest of the departing owner is acquired by the business, leaving the remaining owners with greater ownership interests. The company may set aside money for this purpose (e.g., a corporation may use retained earnings to buy out a retiring owner). Alternatively, the company may pay for the departing owner's interest through profits over time.
- ***Life insurance.*** Usually, insurance is used to buy out a deceased owner's interest. However, insurance can also be used to pay for a retiring owner. Work with a knowledgeable insurance agent to structure insurance financing for a buyout.
- ***Installment sales.*** A departing owner may sell an interest under an installment payment agreement.

In the past, private annuities were often used in family situations to transfer ownership to the younger generation at favorable transfer tax costs. However, changes in the tax treatment of private annuities mean this method is no longer used.

Consulting Agreements

If you retire but want to continue your association with the company, negotiate a consulting agreement. Being a consultant means you are a self-employed individual who is paid a fixed amount for consulting services over a set period (typically 2 to 5 years following a buyout).

From the company's perspective, consulting fees it pays to you are fully tax deductible. There are no payroll taxes with respect to consulting fees.

Estate Taxes

If your net worth (the value of your personal assets, including your business interests) are more than the federal estate tax exemption amount ($5.34 million in 2014), then succession planning must include estate tax concerns. Your state may have a death tax imposed on estates valued at less than the federal exemption amount (e.g., $675,000 in New Jersey; $921,655 in Rhode Island for 2014), making tax planning important even for more modest estates. If you fail to address estate taxes, your family may be forced to sell your business (or your ownership interest) at a fire sale price in order to raise the cash needed to pay the estate tax bill.

Estate Planning Concerns

When you die, if you have not made any special plans, your business interest passes to your heirs according to the terms of your will or state law governing intestacy when there is no will. However, you are free to make whatever plans you want when it comes to your business interest.

Factors in estate planning decisions. Is there a relative (e.g., spouse or child) who already works in the business and is your natural successor to run the business when you die? Or does your family want nothing to do with your business after your death? Do co-owners prefer to take over your ownership interest? Answering these questions can help direct you toward the best way to decide now what will happen to your interest when you die.

Buy-sell agreements. These are contracts among co-owners of a business to fix the actions that will be taken when 1 owner dies. There are 2 basic types of buy-sell agreements:

1. *Redemption-type agreements (also called the entity plan).* Here the business buys back the deceased owner's interest, leaving the remaining owner or owners with greater interests. For example, say there are 2 co-owners who each own half of a limited liability company. When one owner dies, assets of the company are used to buy back the deceased owner's interest, leaving the remaining owner with 100% control. If the business is incorporated, the buy-back is done through a redemption of the deceased owner's stock.

2. *Cross-purchase agreements.* Here each remaining owner buys out the deceased owner's interest. Say there are 3 equal co-owners in a corporation. When one owner dies, the remaining 2 buy half of the deceased owner's stock, leaving each remaining owner with a 50% ownership interest.

There are also hybrid agreements that use elements of each type of basic agreement to accomplish their goals.

From a tax perspective, as long as the buy-back is fixed and there is a mechanism for setting the buyout price, the IRS usually will respect the agreement. This means that the price paid under the agreement can be used to set the value of the ownership interest for estate tax purposes.

Funding buy-sell agreements. In most cases, life insurance is used to pay for the buyout at death. If the corporation receives the life insurance, use care to avoid unwarranted income tax effects. If a C corporation is involved, the alternative minimum tax (AMT) may be imposed, depending on the corporation's pretax profits and preference items for income tax purposes.

Example

If a $150,000 AMT will be paid on $1 million of life insurance proceeds, this creates an additional tax that may create a hardship for the corporation, as the after-tax proceeds available for the buyout will be only $850,000 ($1 million – $150,000 AMT).

From your perspective, consulting fees are earned income for purposes of the 0.9% additional Medicare tax. You may want to set the consulting fees below your threshold amount ($200,000 if single; $250,000 if married filing jointly; $125,000 if married filing separately), factoring in any other earned income you may receive.

Special estate tax rules. If a business owner's estate is sizable, meaning more than the applicable estate tax exemption amount ($5.34 million in 2014), there may be federal estate tax as well as state death taxes. These taxes typically must be paid within 9 months after the date of death. However, estates of business owners enjoy certain special tax breaks:

- ***Special valuation for closely held business real property.*** Instead of valuing the realty at its highest and best use, it can be valued according to its actual use. This can considerably reduce the value of the property included in the owner's estate.

- ***Tax deferral.*** If the decedent's interest in a closely held business exceeds 35% of the adjusted gross estate, the estate can elect to defer the payment of estate taxes. Deferral means that only interest is due during the first 4 years; taxes plus interest are then paid over the following 10 years (for a total deferral period of 14 years). A 2% interest rate applies to the tax attributable to the first $1.45 million of the taxable estate for owners dying in 2014 (this dollar amount may be adjusted in the future).

- *Stock redemption to pay estate tax.* If the closely held business interest exceeds 35% of the gross estate (minus certain deductions) and the business interests remain with the family, then the estate can elect to have the stock redeemed in order to pay estate taxes. This can be done without incurring income tax liability on a partial redemption of the stock.

Information Returns

Alert

At the time this book was printed, Congress had not extended numerous breaks for 2014 that had expired at the end of 2013. Check the online supplement in February 2015 at www.jklasser.com or www.barbaraweltman.com to see whether these breaks apply for 2014 returns.

Businesses are in a unique position to monitor certain activities with which they are involved, and the federal government has harnessed this power by requiring certain reporting for tax and financial purposes. Reporting enables the government, where possible, to make sure that income is reported as it should be and to keep tabs on certain monetary activities.

Reporting requirements vary from return to return. However, filing deadlines are completely independent of your tax year (when you file your income tax return). If a filing deadline falls on a Saturday, Sunday, or legal holiday, then the deadline becomes the next business day that is not a Saturday, Sunday, or legal holiday.

The following is a review of the most common business-reporting requirements, some or all of which may apply to you. (Some of these responsibilities are explained in greater detail within the book as indicated.)

Dividends

WHO MUST REPORT

If your corporation pays out dividends or distributions to shareholders (including yourself), payments of $10 or more ($600 or more for liquidations) must be reported to the IRS and to the recipient.

File Form 1099-DIV, *Dividends and Distributions*. Request a copy from the IRS at (800) 829-FORM or purchase it from an office supply company (the form is a triplicate form that cannot be downloaded from the IRS web site). The IRS copy of Form 1099-DIV must be accompanied by Form 1096, *Annual Summary and Transmittal of U.S. Information Returns*.

WHEN TO REPORT

Furnish the recipient with a copy of the form no later than January 31 of the year following the year in which dividends or distributions were paid.

File the form with the IRS no later than February 28 of the year following the year in which the dividends or distributions were paid. But if you file the form electronically, you have an additional month (to March 31) to file with the IRS.

WHERE TO REPORT

The filing location you use depends on where your corporation is located—there are 4 IRS service centers in which this information return is filed.

PENALTIES FOR NONFILING

The amount of the penalty for late filing depends on how late you are—the quicker you correct the nonfiling, the smaller your penalty will be. For example, the penalty is $15 per information return if you miss the due date but then file correctly within 30 days (up to a maximum penalty of $25,000 for small businesses). You are a small business if your average annual gross receipts for the 3 most recent tax years (or the period for which you are in existence, if shorter) are $5 million or less.

Large Cash Transactions

WHO MUST REPORT

If you receive more than $10,000 in cash in one or more related transactions in the course of your business, you must report the transaction to the IRS. You must also report your reporting to the party that paid you. "Cash" for reporting purposes does not mean only currency; it includes cashier's checks, money orders, bank drafts, and traveler's checks having a face amount of $10,000 or less received in a transaction used to avoid this reporting requirement.

File Form 8300, *Report of Cash Payments Over $10,000 Received in a Trade or Business*.

WHEN TO REPORT

The form must be filed with the IRS by the 15th day after the date the cash was received. For example, if you receive a payment of $12,000 on February 2, 2015, you must report it by February 16, 2015. If the deadline falls on a Saturday, Sunday, or legal holiday, file by the next business day.

You must give a written statement to the party who paid you, but you have until January 31 of the year following the year in which the cash was received to do so. For example, on that February 1, 2015, cash payment, your written statement must be furnished by February 1, 2016 (January 31 is on a Sunday).

WHERE TO REPORT

File Form 8300 with the IRS, Detroit Computing Center, P.O. Box 32621, Detroit, MI 48232 (regardless of where you file your business return).

PENALTIES FOR NONFILING

Unless you can show your failure to timely report the transaction to the IRS and to the payer was due to reasonable cause, you may be subject to penalties. A minimum penalty is imposed if you intentionally or willfully fail to report the transaction. Criminal penalties (fines and imprisonment) can result if you cause or attempt to cause a business to fail to file a required report or file a report containing a material omission or misstatement of fact or for structuring a transaction to avoid reporting requirements.

Payments to Independent Contractors

WHO MUST REPORT

If you use independent contractors, freelancers, or subcontractors in your business and pay them $600 or more within the year, you must report these payments to the IRS as well as the contractors. In most cases, payments to corporations are not subject to this reporting requirement. However, you are required to report payments in the course of your business to incorporated attorneys and law firms.

File Form 1099-MISC, *Miscellaneous Income*. Request a copy of the form from the IRS at (800) 829-FORM or purchase it from an office supply company (the form is a triplicate form that cannot be downloaded from the IRS web site). The IRS copy of Form 1099-MISC must be accompanied by Form 1096, *Annual Summary and Transmittal of U.S. Information Returns*.

WHEN TO REPORT

You must furnish a copy of the form to the independent contractor no later than January 31 of the year following the year in which the payments were made.

You must provide the IRS with its copy no later than February 28 of the year following the year of payment (reporting for 2014 must be made by March 2 because February 28, 2015, is on a Saturday). But if you file the form electronically, you have an additional month (to March 31) to file with the IRS.

If you need additional time to file, request a filing extension on Form 8809, *Request for Extension of Time to File Information Returns*.

WHERE TO REPORT

The filing location you use depends on where your business is located—there are 4 IRS service centers in which this information return is filed.

PENALTIES FOR NONFILING

The amount of the penalty for late filing depends on how late you are—the quicker you correct the nonfiling, the smaller your penalty will be. For example, the penalty is $15 per information return if you miss the due date but then file correctly within 30 days (up to a maximum penalty of $25,000 for small businesses). You are a small business if your average annual gross receipts for the 3 most recent tax years (or the period for which you are in existence, if shorter) are $5 million or less.

Pension and Retirement Plan Distributions

WHO MUST REPORT

You must report any distributions from qualified retirement plans to the recipient of the distributions as well as to the IRS.

Furnish Form 1099-R, *Distributions from Pensions, Annuities, Retirement or Profit-Sharing Plans, IRAs, Insurance Contracts, Etc.*, and file Copy A of this form with the IRS. Submit the copy with Form 1096, *Annual Summary and Transmittal of U.S. Information Returns*.

WHEN TO REPORT

You must furnish a copy of the form to the distribution recipient no later than January 31 of the year following the year in which the payments were made.

You must provide the IRS with its copy no later than February 28 of the year following the year of payment. But if you file the form electronically, you have an additional month (to March 31) to file with the IRS.

If you need additional time to file, request a filing extension on Form 8809, *Request for Extension of Time to File Information Returns.*

WHERE TO REPORT

The filing location you use depends on where your business is located—there are 4 IRS service centers in which this information return is filed.

PENALTIES FOR NONFILING

The penalty is $25 per day for late filing, up to a maximum of $15,000.

Retirement and Employee Benefit Plans

WHO MUST REPORT

If you have a qualified retirement plan, such as a profit-sharing plan, or an employee benefit plan, such as a funded deferred compensation plan, you must report annually on the plan's activities. Reporting includes information on annual contributions, distributions, and the number of participants.

File Form 5500, *Annual Return/Report of Employee Benefit Plan.* For plans with 25 or fewer participants, there is simplified reporting (you can choose not to file Schedules D and R, and to provide limited information on Schedule A of Form 5500).

If you are self-employed and the only participant is you (or you and your spouse, or you and your partners and spouses), you can file Form 5500-EZ, *Annual Return of One Participant (Owners and Their Spouses)*, a simplified form. You do not have to file *any* form if you qualify to file Form 5500-EZ and plan assets did not exceed $250,000 at the end of the plan year. And you must file this form, regardless of the amount of plan assets, for the final year of the plan.

WHEN TO REPORT

The form is due on the last day of the seventh month following the close of the plan year (for example, for the 2014 plan year that was on a calendar year, July 31, 2015).

If you need additional time to file, obtain an automatic $2^{1}/_{2}$-month filing extension on Form 5558, *Application for Extension of Time to File Certain Employee Plan Returns.* If you obtained an automatic 6-month filing extension for your personal income tax return, you automatically have until October 15, 2015, to file Form 5500 or 5500-EZ for 2014 (attach a copy of your personal extension when you file the form).

WHERE TO REPORT

File the form with the Pension and Welfare Benefits Administration (not with the IRS), which is now called the Employee Benefits Security Administration (the addresses for paper filing, filing by disc, CD-ROM, or tape; or by private delivery service are listed in the instructions to the form). For plans with 25 or fewer participants, there is simplified reporting.

The form can be *e-filed* through a filing professional. For more information, click on www.efast.dol.gov.

PENALTIES FOR NONFILING

The late filing penalty is $25 per day (up to $15,000). Various other penalties may also be imposed.

Small Cash Transactions

WHO MUST REPORT

If you are in a business that sells or redeems money orders or traveler's checks in excess of $1,000 per customer per day or issues your own value cards, you are asked by the government to report suspicious transactions that exceed $2,000. Such businesses include convenience stores, groceries, liquor stores, travel agencies, courier services, and gas stations (the government estimates that there are about 158,000 business within these categories and that they provide financial services of $200 billion each year).

Suspicious activities include a customer who:

- Attempts to bribe or threaten you or your employee
- Buys multiple money orders in even hundred-dollar denominations or in unusual quantities
- Provides false or expired identification
- Refuses to proceed with a transaction once you notify him/her that a form will be completed
- Tries to keep the transaction from being reported or asks you how to avoid reporting requirements
- Works with one or more other individuals who split up to conduct separate transactions that combine for more than $3,000

All reporting is done electronically. First, you must submit Registration of Money Services Business (RMSB) form through the BSA e-filing system (http://bsaefiling.fincen.treas.gov/main.html). Then you must renew this registration every two years. When reporting suspicious activity, file FinCEN Form 109, *Suspicious Activity Report by Money Services Businesses*. Filing the form does not give you any financial exposure; you have complete protection from civil liability (the person you report cannot sue you for damages). Find more details at www.fincen.gov/financial_institutions/msb/msbsar.html.

WHEN TO REPORT

File the form within 30 days of the suspicious activity.

WHERE TO REPORT

File the form with the U.S. Treasury Department's Money Services Businesses Division, through the BSA e-filing system at http://bsaefiling.fincen.treas.gov/main.html.

PENALTIES FOR NONFILING

None since filing is voluntary.

Wages

WHO MUST REPORT

If you have any employee (including yourself if your business is incorporated), you must report annual compensation and benefits to the employee and to the Social Security Administration.

File Form W-2, *Wage and Tax Statement*, with the Social Security Administration and furnish a copy to the employee. Also file Form W-3, *Transmittal of Income and Tax Statement*, with the Social Security Administration. Large employers (those filing 250 or more W-2 forms) must file electronically. Smaller employers can continue to file paper forms, but are encouraged to file electronically through an extended filing deadline.

NOTE

Large employers must include on employee W-2 forms the value of health insurance benefits, whether paid for by the employer, the employee, or a combination of both. Small employers are exempt at this time.

WHEN TO REPORT

Different deadlines apply to different parties:

- *Employees*. Furnish the form to them by January 31 of the year following the year in which the wages were paid (whether you furnish the Form W-2 by paper or electronically).
- *Social Security Administration*. File the forms by February 28 (March 31 if filing electronically).

You can request additional time to file with the Social Security Administration by sending Form 8809, *Request for Extension of Time to File Information Returns*, to gain an additional 30 days to file. But you must still furnish the form to employees by the regular deadline; there is no extension in this case.

WHERE TO REPORT

File forms electronically using the Social Security Administration's Business Services Online at http://ssa.gov/employer. File paper forms (copy A of W-2 and the entire page of W-3) with the Social Security Administration, Data Operations Center, Wilkes-Barre, PA 18769-0001. If you use certified mail, change the ZIP code to 18769-0002. If you use an IRS-approved private delivery service, add "Attn.: W-2 Process, 1150 E. Mountain Drive" to the address and change the ZIP code to 18702-7997.

PENALTIES FOR NONFILING

The amount of the penalty for late filing depends on how late you are—the quicker you correct the nonfiling, the smaller your penalty will be. For example, the penalty is $15 per information return if you miss the due date but then file correctly within 30 days (up to a maximum penalty of $25,000 for small businesses). You are a small business if your average annual gross receipts for the 3 most recent tax years (or the period for which you are in existence, if shorter) are $5 million or less.

For more information about wage reporting, see Chapter 7.

Merchant Transactions

Payment settlement companies that process credit cards, debit cards, and electronic payments (such as PayPal) must report the gross amount of these transactions, broken down monthly, to the IRS and merchants. Form 1099-K, *Merchant Card and Third-Party Payments*, is used for this purpose.

Gross amounts do not take into account any adjustments for credits, cash equivalents, discount amounts, fees, chargebacks, refunded amounts, or any other amounts. It will be up to you as a seller to report your income accurately on your return, but you do not have to reconcile it with amounts reported on Form 1099-K.

Small merchant exception. Reporting is not required for merchants with annual gross sales on merchant cards of no more than $20,000 or 200 or fewer transactions; reporting is required only if gross amounts for the year exceed $20,000 *and* there are more than 200 transactions.

Checklist of Tax-Related Corporate Resolutions

If you own a corporation (whether it is a C or S corporation), it is important to keep good records on actions taken by shareholders and/or your board of directors at their meetings. The reason: If your corporation fails to act like a corporation, creditors can "pierce the corporate veil" and hold you personally liable. Retain these records in the corporate minutes book.

The following is a listing of key votes that should be taken for tax actions. Some apply only to C corporations, while others apply to both C and S corporations.

- Adopting a fiscal year.
- Adopting any of the following employee benefit plans:
  - Accountable plan.
  - Adoption assistance plan.

- Deferred compensation plan.
- Cafeteria plan.
- Educational assistance plan.
- Employee stock ownership plan (ESOP).
- Group legal services plan.
- Medical reimbursement plan.
- Qualified retirement plan.
- Stock option plan.

- Authorizing a sale/leaseback transaction.
- Authorizing compensation and bonuses to employees (including share-holder-employees) and payments to corporate directors. To justify larger compensation to C corporation shareholder-employees, note in the minutes why the payment is reasonable under the circumstances (e.g., the payment reflects a catch-up for years in which little or no compensation was paid). Also, if desired, include a resolution requiring officers to repay excess compensation (amounts determined to be nondeductible because they are unreasonable).
- Authorizing a reimbursement arrangement for officers' expenses.
- Declaring dividends.
- Making or terminating an S corporation election.
- Retaining earnings. C corporations that want to amass funds for future projects rather than distribute earnings currently to shareholders should use corporate minutes to reflect the reason for accumulating earnings to avoid a penalty on excess accumulations. These are earnings over a set limit ($250,000, or $150,000 for personal service corporations). However, to the extent earnings are retained for *specific* reasons spelled out clearly in corporate minutes, the penalty can be avoided if the accumulations are reasonable. For example, if funds are being accumulated to purchase property, to build a factory, or to buy out the interest of an owner who dies or is about to retire, the penalty will not be imposed as long as there is a record of this purpose and the amount of the set-aside is appropriate to the reason.
- Authorizing the purchase of the assets of another company.
- Transactions between the corporation and shareholder (e.g., a lease of property by the shareholder to the corporation; an interest-free loan from the corporation to the shareholder).

Other corporate resolutions that you might consider include:

- Acquiring assets or shares of stock in another business.
- Adopting a trade name.

- Assigning a lease, terminating a lease, or subletting space.
- Authorizing banking activities, including setting up a bank account, obtaining a corporate credit card, and establishing a line of credit.
- Borrowing money from outside parties, including individuals related to owners.
- Commencing litigation.
- Factoring accounts receivable.
- Filing for bankruptcy protection and approving a reorganization plan under Chapter 11 of the Bankruptcy Code.
- Issuing a guarantee or indemnification.
- Leasing equipment (including vehicles).
- Purchasing large equipment and realty.
- Retaining an outside professional (accountant, attorney, business broker, consultant).
- Selling corporate assets or shares.
- Terminating contracts, leases, and certain employees.

List of Dollar Limits and Amounts Adjusted for Inflation

| Items Adjusted Annually for | | Items Fixed by the Tax Code | 612 |
| Inflation | 611 | Items Set by the IRS | 613 |

Alert

At the time this book was printed, Congress had not extended numerous breaks for 2014 that had expired at the end of 2013. Check the online supplement in February 2015 at www.jklasser.com or www.barbaraweltman.com to see whether these breaks apply for 2014 returns.

Taxes are a moving target because many dollar limits and percentages change annually due to increases in inflation. However, some limits and amounts are fixed in the Tax Code and cannot be changed without an act of Congress. Still others are set by the IRS for administrative convenience and are not adjusted annually but could change at the IRS' whim. To help you plan ahead, here are lists of items that may or may not change for the next tax year.

Items Adjusted Annually for Inflation

401(k) plans—the annual contribution limit through salary reductions as well as the additional contribution limit for those age 50 and older by year end.

Adoption assistance—excludable employer-provided adoption assistance for employees ($12,970 for 2013; $13,190 for 2014).

Archer medical savings accounts (MSAs)—the dollar limit on contributions for plans established before 2008.

Health savings accounts (HSAs)—the dollar limit on contributions as well as the definition of a high-deductible health plan (HDHP).

IRAs and Roth IRAs—the contribution limits as well as the income limits on making contributions in certain situations.

Medical flexible spending accounts (FSAs)—the most that employees can add annually on a pre-tax basis is capped at $2,500 for 2013; because of low inflation there was no increase for 2014. This cap may increase after 2014.

Retirement plan contributions and benefits—the limits on making tax-advantaged contributions to qualified retirement plans.

Shared responsibility payment—there is no penalty if the cost of employer health coverage is deemed to be unaffordable, which in 2014 is more than 9.5% of household income; for 2015, it's 9.56% of household income.

Small employer health insurance credit—the amount of average compensation, originally fixed at $25,000, is $25,400 for 2014; it may be increased for 2015.

Social Security wage base—the amount that is used to figure the Social Security portion of FICA and self-employment tax ($113,700 for 2013; $117,000 for 2014).

Tax brackets for individuals—the amount of taxable income within each bracket may be increased annually; this impacts sole proprietors and owners of pass-through entities.

Items Fixed by the Tax Code

Additional Medicare tax on earned income—the threshold above which earned income is subject to this 0.9% tax is fixed according to filing status; the threshold does not change annually.

Corporate tax rates—the amount of taxable income subject to corporate tax brackets are not increased for inflation.

Cruise ship travel—the cost of business meetings held on cruise ships is deductible up to $2,000 if certain requirements are met.

Dependent care assistance—employer-paid dependent care assistance is excludable up to $5,000 annually.

Disabled access credit—the maximum amount of expenses that can be taken into account in figuring the credit is between $250 and $10,250.

Education assistance—employer-paid education assistance for employees is capped at $5,250.

Gifts—the deduction for business gifts is limited to $25 (exclusive of shipping)

Net investment income tax—the additional 3.8% Medicare tax depends on modified adjusted gross income over a threshold amount that varies with filing status but the threshold does not change annually.

Prizes and awards to employees—the maximum deduction for nonqualified award to any one employee is capped at $400 per year. Total awards (qualified and nonqualified) to any one employee is limited to $1,600 per year.

Reforestation expenses—up to $5,000 ($10,000 if married filing jointly) can be expensed.

Start-up costs—up to $5,000 can be deducted in the first year of business.

Items Set by the IRS

Annual reporting by retirement plans—one-participant plans are exempt from reporting if plan assets at the end of the year do not exceed $250,000 (and this is not the final year of the plan).

Below market loans—low- and no-interest loans can trigger taxable income to the lender; the interest rate for determining whether a loan is below the market rate is fixed by the IRS. An annual blended rate applies for below market loans outstanding for the full year (e.g., 0.28% for 2014).

Building improvements—under a safe harbor method for small taxpayers, they can be capitalized if they do not exceed the lesser of $10,000 or 2% of the unadjusted basis of the building as long as the building's unadjusted basis is no more than $1 million.

Dollar limits on depreciating vehicles under 6,000 pounds—the amount of depreciation each year that the vehicle is owned is capped (the year in which the vehicle is placed in service affects the applicable cap for the remainder of the period of ownership).

Deemed depreciation for business vehicles—if expenses for business use of a personal vehicle owned by the taxpayer is figured using the IRS's standard mileage allowance, then the basis of the vehicle is reduced by a set amount per mile (e.g., 23¢ per mile in 2013; 22¢ per mile in 2014).

Group-term life insurance—the value of coverage over $50,000 that is taxable to employees.

Home office deduction—under the simplified method, the deduction is figured at $5 per square foot up to 300 square feet of space.

Inclusion amount—the amount of income taken into account for business use of a personal vehicle that is leased.

Mileage allowance—the rate per mile used to determine the deduction for business use of a personal vehicle instead of deducting the actual costs.

Per diem travel rates—the IRS sets the rate for a daily deduction covering lodging, meals, and incidental expenses for travel to high-cost areas and all other areas within the continental U.S. The General Services Administration also has per diem rates.

Simplified Schedule C—it can only be filed if business expenses are $5,000 or less.

Travel and entertainment costs—no receipt is required for the cost of travel and entertainment expenses under $75. However, a receipt is required for lodging costs, regardless of amount.

Index

Flights on employer-provided aircraft, 166
Floor taxes, 280
FLSA. *See* Fair Labor Standards Act (FLSA)
FMV. *See* Fair market value (FMV)
Food inventory donations, 462
Foreclosure on or repossession of property,
 132–134
 equipment and other personal property,
 134
 lender's perspective, 133–134
 real property, 134
Foreign tax credit, 500
Foreign taxes, 284
Foreign travel, 187–189
Forest health protection payments, 80
Form of business organization. *See* Business
 organization, factors in choosing form of
Forms, IRS. *See* IRS Forms
401(k) retirement plans. *See also* Rollovers
 as business start-ups (ROBS)
 income tax withholding and, 565
 multiple businesses and, 550
 "in-plan rollover," 593
Franchise taxes, 283, 560
Fringe benefits. *See also* Medical coverage
 adoption assistance, 158
 business organization and, 30–31
 cafeteria plans, 170–171
 commuting vehicles, 165–166
 country club dues, 166
 educational expenses (*see* Educational
 expenses)
 employee use of company car, 162–165
 employment tax obligations on, 567–568
 flights on employer-provided aircraft, 166
 generally, 30–31, 155–156
 group term life insurance, 157–158, 470
 health reimbursement accounts, 156
 Health Savings Accounts (*see* Health
 Savings Accounts (HSAs))
 housing relocation costs, 162
 life insurance on individual basis, 166
 limits on, 169
 meals and lodging, 160–162
 nonstatutory, 167–170
 split-dollar life insurance, 166–167
 statutory (*see* Statutory employee
 benefits)
 supplemental unemployment benefits, 160
 travel and entertainment costs, 162

FSA. *See* Farm Services Agency (FSA)
FSAs. *See* Flexible spending accounts (FSAs);
 Flexible spending arrangements (FSAs)
FTEs. *See* Full-time equivalent employees
 (FTEs)
Fuels:
 exemption from excise tax on, 441, 442
 tax credits on, 440, 443, 501
 taxes on, 283–284, 440
Full-time equivalent employees (FTEs),
 417–418, 423
FUTA. *See* Federal Unemployment Tax Act
 (FUTA); Federal Unemployment Taxes
 (FUTA)

Gains and losses on business property. *See
 also* Capital gains and losses
 abandonment, 132–133
 built-in gains, 19, 86–87
 generally, 125–126
 installment sales, 128
 involuntary conversions, 129–132
 recapture, 128–129
 sale of all assets, 134–135
 Section 1231 gains and losses, 126–127
 short-term gains, 112
General business credit, 501–503
 alternative minimum tax, 503
 carrybacks and carryforwards, 503
 carryovers and, 514
 generally, 173–174, 501–502
 limitations on, 502–503
General Depreciation (basic) System, 302,
 303
General partnerships, 11
Gentlemen farmers, 439
Gift cards, 49–50
Gift-leasebacks, 269
Gift loans, 288
Gifts:
 generally, 198–200
 recordkeeping requirements, 204
Goodwill, promotion of, 331–334
Grants, 531
Gross income, 405–406
Gross profit percent, 167
Gross profits, 79
Gross receipts:
 cash method of accounting and, 47
 domestic production activities, 446, 448

Perquisites. *See* Fringe benefits

Personal education initiatives, 458–459

Personal effect, 456

Personal holding company penalty, 27

Personal holding corporation (PHC), 27

Personal identification number (PIN), 584, 589

Personal interest, 285

Personal liability and business organization, 29–30

Personal property:
    business use of, 315–316
    defined, 300
    repossession of, 134
    taxes on, 280

Personal service corporations (PSCs), 20–21, 42, 47–48, 90

Phantom interest, 520

PHC. *See* Personal holding corporation (PHC)

PIN. *See* Personal identification number (PIN)

Placed in service, defined, 301

Plug-in electric vehicles, 231, 238

Pollution control facilities, amortization of, 321–322

Pollution liability insurance, 471

Postage costs, 452, 468

Post-year tax elections to cut bills, 513–514

PR (public relations) expenses, 331

Premium assistance credit, 497

Premium-only medical plans, 426

Prepaid expenses:
    cash method of accounting and, 46
    deduction of, 46–47
    farm supplies, 434–435
    rent, 83

Prepaid interest, cash basis and prepayment, 67

Prepaid rent, 83

Prepayments (advances), 75–77

Principal business activity (PBA), 519

Principal place of business, 397–399

Private letter rulings, 69, 517

Prizes:
    as advertising expenses, 334
    for employees, 148–149

Product liability coverage, 471

Professional employer organizations (PEOs), 144

Professional fees, 465–467

Professional liability coverage, 471

Profitability, lack of, and business organization, 30

Profit motive and sideline businesses, 541, 542–543

Profit(s), gross, 79

Promotional activities, 334

Promotion of goodwill, 331–334

Property. *See also* Casualty and theft losses; Depreciation; First-year expensing; Improvements to property; Property, gains and losses from sale of; Repairs and maintenance
    abandonment of, 132–133, 302, 512
    deduction of rents, 275–276
    depreciable, 436
    donations of (*see* Charitable contributions)
    incidental, 110
    limited use, 275
    listed property, limitations on, 314–315
    oil and gas, 323, 324
    personal (*see* Personal property)
    personal property taxes, 280
    placed in service, 301
    replacement, 131
    tangible and intangible, 300, 316–317
    transfer of, 528, 529

Property, gains and losses from sale of. *See* Gains and losses on business property

Property insurance, 390–391

PSCs. *See* Personal service corporations (PSCs)

PWBA. *See* Pension and Welfare Benefits Administration (PWBA)

QPAI. *See* Qualified production activity income (QPAI)

QPAs. *See* Qualified performing artists (QPAs)

Qualified achievement awards, 149

Qualified cost, defined, 160

Qualified default investment alternatives, 373

Qualified employee discounts, 167

Qualified intermediaries, 110

Qualified leasehold, restaurant, and retail improvements:
    amortization of, 322
    leases, 271–272